NEW ENGLAND

Maine Tourism Office

| **Executive Editorial Director** | David Brabis |
| **Chief Editor** | Cynthia Clayton Ochterbeck |

THE GREEN GUIDE NEW ENGLAND

Editor	Gwen Cannon
Contributing Writers	Diane Bair and Pamela Wright (Bair-Wright Associates)
Production Coordinator	Allison Michelle Simpson
Cartography	Peter Wrenn
Photo Editors	Brigitta L. House, Lydia Strong
Proofreader	Gaven R. Watkins
Layout & Design	Tim Schulz
Cover Design	Laurent Muller, Ute Weber
Production	Pierre Ballochard, Renaud Leblanc

Contact Us:

The Green Guide
Michelin Maps and Guides
One Parkway South
Greenville, SC 29615, USA
☎ 1-800-423-0485
www.michelintravel.com
michelin.guides@us.michelin.com

Michelin Maps and Guides
Hannay House
39 Clarendon Road
Watford, Herts WD17 1JA, UK
☎ (01923) 205 240
www.ViaMichelin.com
Travelpubsales@uk.michelin.com

Special Sales:

For information regarding bulk sales,
customized editions and premium sales,
please contact our Customer Service
Departments:
USA   1-800-423-0485
UK   (01923) 205 240
Canada 1-800-361-8236

Note to the reader
While every effort is made to ensure that all information printed in this guide is correct and up-to-date, Michelin Maps and Guides (Michelin Tyre PLC; Michelin North America, Inc.) accepts no liability for any direct, indirect or consequential losses howsoever caused so far as such can be excluded by law.

One Team …
A Commitment to Quality

There's just one reason our team is dedicated to producing quality travel publications—you, our reader. We want you to get the maximum benefit from your trip—and from your money. In today's multiple-choice world of travel, the options are many, perhaps overwhelming.

In our guidebooks, we try to minimize the guesswork involved with travel. We scout out the attractions, prioritize them with star ratings, and describe what you'll discover when you visit them.

To help you orient yourself, we provide colorful and detailed, but easy-to-follow maps. Floor plans of some of the cathedrals and museums help you plan your tour.

Throughout the guides, we offer practical information, touring tips and suggestions for finding the best views, good places for a break and the most interesting shops.

Lodging and dining are always a big part of travel, so we compile a selection of hotels and restaurants that we think convey the feel of the destination, and organize them by geographic area and price. We also highlight shopping, recreational and entertainment venues, especially the popular spots.

If you're short on time, driving tours are included so you can hit the highlights and quickly absorb the best of the region.

For those who love to experience a destination on foot, we add walking tours, often with a map. And we list other companies who offer boat, bus or guided walking tours of the area, some with culinary, historical or other themes.

In short, we test and retest, check and recheck to make sure that our guidebooks are truly just that: a personalized guide to help you make the most of your visit. After all, we want you to enjoy traveling as much as we do.

The Michelin Green Guide Team

PLANNING YOUR TRIP

INTRODUCTION TO NEW ENGLAND

SYMBOLS

- 🐾 **Tips to help improve your experience**
- 🐾 **Details to consider**
- 🐾 **Entry Fees**
- 🐾 **Walking tours**
- ⚷ **Closed to the public**
- 🕐 **Hours of operation**
- 🕐 **Periods of closure**

CONTENTS

DISCOVERING NEW ENGLAND

HOW TO USE THIS GUIDE

Orientation

To help you grasp the "lay of the land" quickly and easily, so you'll feel confident and comfortable finding your way around the region, we offer the following tools in this guide:

- Detailed table of contents for an overview of what you'll find in the guide, and how it is organized.
- Map of Principal Sights showing the starred places of interest at a glance.
- Detailed maps for major cities and villages, including driving tour maps and larger-scale maps for walking tours.
- Map of Regional Driving Tours, each one color coded.
- Principal Sights ordered by states, alphabetically.

Practicalities

At the front of the guide, you'll see a section called "Planning Your Trip" that contains information about planning your trip, the best time to go, different ways of getting to the region and getting around, basic facts and tips for making the most of your visit. You'll find suggestions for outdoor fun and a calendar of popular annual events. Information on shopping, sightseeing, kids' activities and sports and recreational opportunities is also included.

LODGINGS

We've made a selection of hotels, arranged them within the cities and categorized them by price to fit all budgets (*see the Legend on the cover flap for an explanation of the price categories*). For the most part, we selected accommodations based on their unique regional quality, their New England feel, as it were. So, unless the individual hotel embodies local ambience, it's rare that we include chain properties, which typically have their own imprint.

RESTAURANTS

We thought you'd like to know the popular eating spots, so we selected restaurants that capture the New England experience—those that have a unique regional flavor and local atmosphere. We're not rating the quality of the food per se. As we did with the hotels, we selected restaurants for many towns and villages and categorized by price to appeal to all wallets (*see the Legend on the cover flap for an explanation of the price categories*).

Attractions

Principal Sights are arranged alphabetically within each state. Within the Principal Sights, attractions for each town, village, or geographical area are divided into local Sights or Walking Tours, nearby Excursions to sights outside the town, or detailed Driving Tours—suggested itineraries for seeing several attractions around a major town. Contact information, admission charges and hours of operation are given for the majority of attractions. Unless otherwise noted, admission prices shown are for a single adult only. Discounts for seniors, students, teachers and others may be available; be sure to ask. If no admission charge is shown, entrance to the attraction is free. If you're pressed for time, we recommend you visit the three- and two-star sights first: the stars are your guide.

STAR RATINGS

Michelin has used stars as a rating tool for more than 100 years:

★★★	Highly recommended
★★	Recommended
★	Interesting

SYMBOLS IN THE TEXT

Besides the stars, other symbols in the text indicate tourist information 🖪; wheelchair access ♿; on-site eating facilities ✗; camping facilities △; on-site parking 🅿; sights of interest to children 🇰🇮🇩🇸; and beaches ⌂.

See the box appearing on the Contents page for other symbols used in the text.

See the Maps explanation below for symbols appearing on the maps.

Throughout the guide you will find peach-colored text boxes, or sidebars, containing anecdotal or background information. Green-colored boxes contain information to help you save time or money.

Maps

All maps in this guide are oriented north, unless otherwise indicated by a directional arrow. See the map Legend at the back of the guide for an explanation of other map symbols. A complete list of the maps found in the guide appears at the back of this book.

Addresses, phone numbers, opening hours and prices published in this guide are accurate at press time. We welcome corrections and suggestions that may assist us in preparing the next edition. Please send your comments to:

Michelin Travel Publications
Editorial Department
P.O. Box 19001
Greenville, SC   29602-9001
Email: michelin.guides@us.michelin.com
Web site: www.michelintravel.com

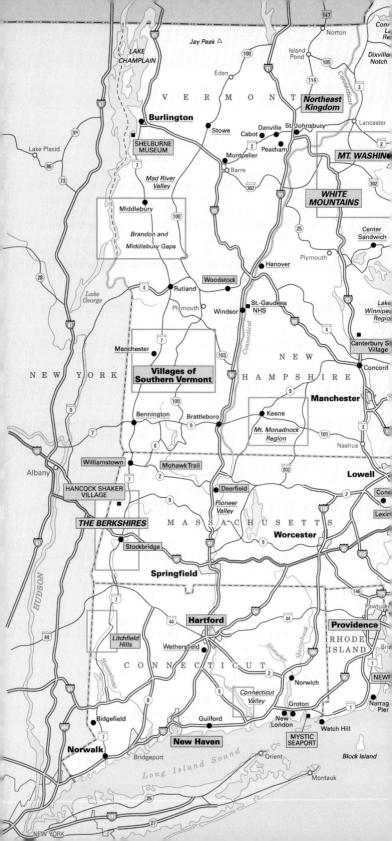

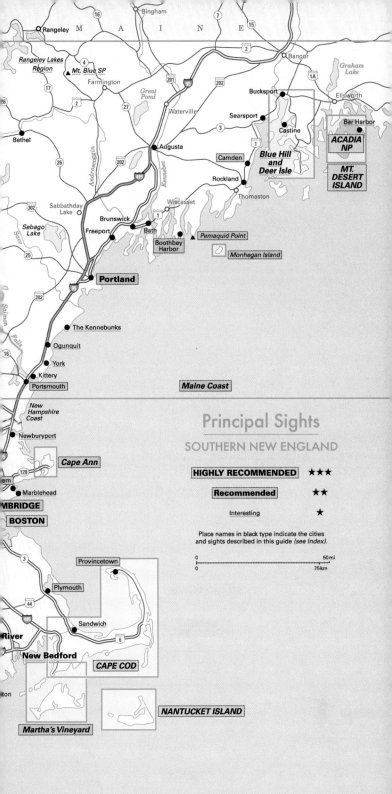

Principal Sights

SOUTHERN NEW ENGLAND

HIGHLY RECOMMENDED	★★★
Recommended	★★
Interesting	★

Place names in black type indicate the cities and sights described in this guide *(see Index)*.

0 — 50mi
0 — 75km

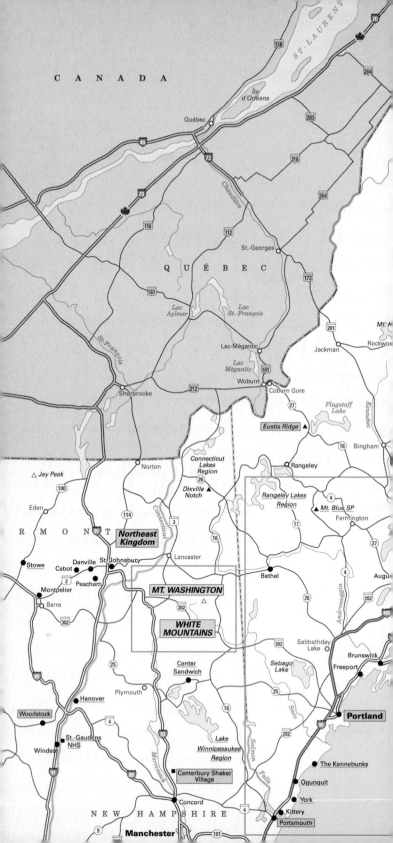

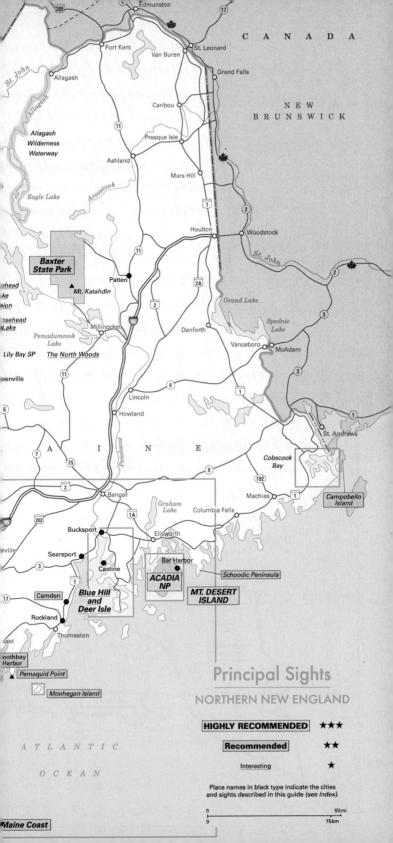

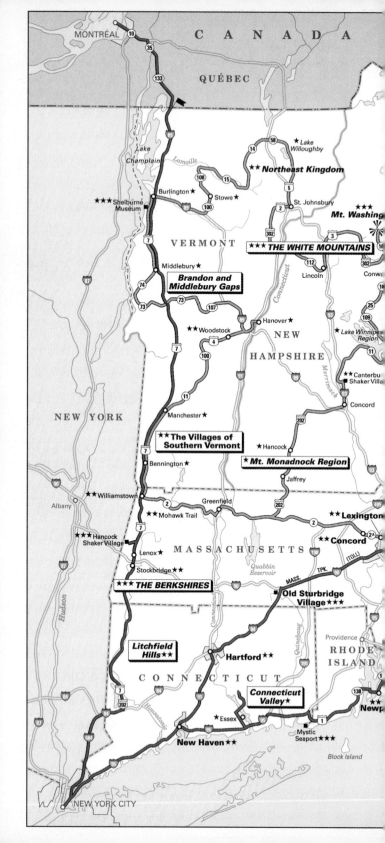

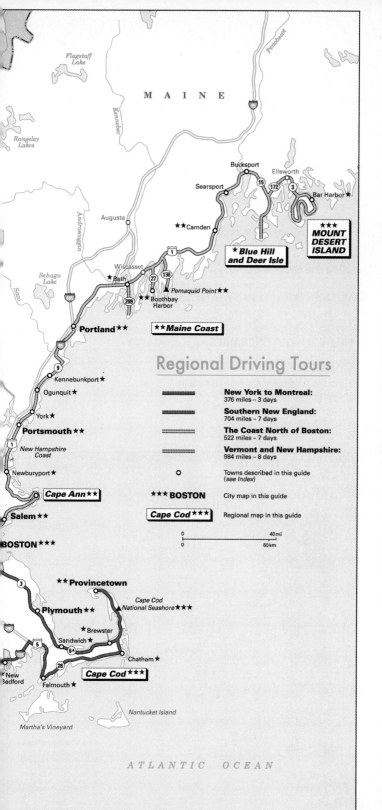

MAINE

Flagstaff Lake

Rangeley Lakes

Kennebec

Androscoggin

Augusta

Bucksport
Searsport
15
Ellsworth
172 **3**
Bar Harbor ★

★★ Camden

★ **Blue Hill and Deer Isle**

★★★
MOUNT DESERT ISLAND

Wiscasset
★ Bath
27 **130**
▲ Pemaquid Point ★★
★★ Boothbay Harbor

Sebago Lake

Saco

208

495

95

Portland ★★   **★★ Maine Coast**

9

Kennebunkport ★

Ogunquit ★

York ★

Portsmouth ★★

1 *New Hampshire Coast*

Newburyport ★

Cape Ann ★★

Salem ★★

BOSTON ★★★

Regional Driving Tours

▬▬▬	**New York to Montreal:** 376 miles – 3 days
▬▬▬	**Southern New England:** 704 miles – 7 days
▬▬▬	**The Coast North of Boston:** 522 miles – 7 days
▬▬▬	**Vermont and New Hampshire:** 984 miles – 8 days
○	Towns described in this guide (*see Index*)
★★★ BOSTON	City map in this guide
Cape Cod ★★★	Regional map in this guide

0 ———— 40mi
0 ———— 60km

3

★★ **Provincetown**

Plymouth ★★

Cape Cod National Seashore ★★★

★ Brewster

495

6

Sandwich ★

6A

Chatham ★

28

New Bedford

Falmouth ★   **Cape Cod** ★★★

Nantucket Island

Martha's Vineyard

ATLANTIC   OCEAN

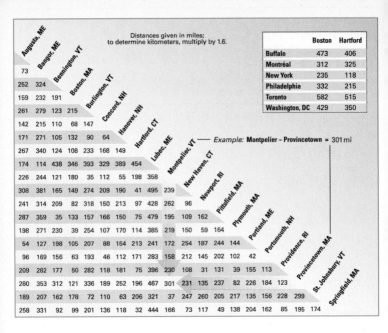

Distances given in miles;
to determine kilometers, multiply by 1.6.

	Boston	Hartford
Buffalo	473	406
Montréal	312	325
New York	235	118
Philadelphia	332	215
Toronto	582	515
Washington, DC	429	350

Augusta, ME
Bangor, ME — 73
Bennington, VT — 252 324
Boston, MA — 159 232 191
Burlington, VT — 261 279 123 215
Concord, NH — 142 215 110 68 147
Hartford, CT — 171 271 105 132 90 64
Lubec, ME — 267 340 124 108 233 168 149
Montpelier, VT — 174 114 438 346 393 329 389 454
New Haven, CT — 226 244 121 180 35 112 55 198 358
Newport RI — 308 381 165 149 274 209 190 41 495 239
Pittsfield, MA — 241 314 209 82 318 150 213 97 428 262 96
Plymouth, MA — 287 359 35 133 157 166 150 75 479 195 109 162
Portland, ME — 198 271 230 39 254 107 170 114 385 219 150 59 164
Portsmouth, NH — 54 127 198 105 207 88 154 213 241 172 254 187 244 144
Providence, RI — 96 169 156 63 193 46 112 171 283 158 212 145 202 102 42
Provincetown, MA — 209 282 177 50 282 118 181 75 396 230 108 31 131 39 155 113
St. Johnsbury, VT — 280 353 312 121 336 189 252 196 467 301 231 135 237 82 226 184 123
Springfield, MA — 189 207 162 178 72 110 63 206 321 37 247 260 205 217 135 156 228 299
258 331 92 99 201 136 118 32 444 166 73 117 49 138 204 162 85 195 174

Example: Montpelier – Provincetown = 301 mi

FALL FOLIAGE ITINERARIES *(see maps pp 16-19)*

1 Outside Boston
2 Northern Vermont and New Hampshire
3 Central Connecticut
4 The Berkshires and Southern Vermont
5 Central Maine
6 Coastal Maine

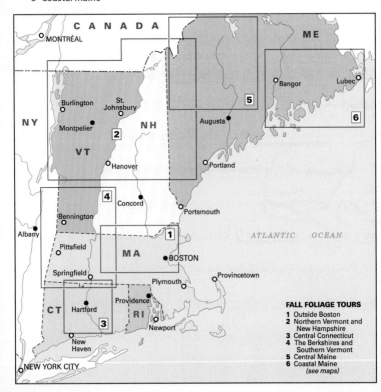

FALL FOLIAGE TOURS
1 Outside Boston
2 Northern Vermont and
New Hampshire
3 Central Connecticut
4 The Berkshires and
Southern Vermont
5 Central Maine
6 Coastal Maine
(see maps)

Sampling New England's Cities and Museums

The villages and cities that developed along the coast looked out toward the sea and the rest of the world. This expansive point of view contributed to the richness of local architecture and home decoration, enhanced by treasures brought back by sailors and whalers who traveled to faraway ports. The region's most beautiful seaports include:

Nantucket★★★ (Massachusetts)
Newburyport★ (Massachusetts)
Newport★★★ (Rhode Island)
Plymouth★★ (Massachusetts)
Portsmouth★★ (New Hampshire)
Salem★★ (Massachusetts)

A growing appreciation for the strength and beauty of Colonial design, and renewed interest in renovation and restoration, have resulted in new life for old districts. Arts and crafts stalls, shops and restaurants eventually appeared, and today visitors can enjoy a leisurely stroll or meal in the following colorful districts:

Bowen's Wharf★ (Newport)
Market Square District★ (Newburyport)
Old Port Exchange★★ (Portland)
Quincy Market★★ (Boston)

The museums of New England vary widely in their conception and in their collections. A listing of must-see art and marine museums follows:

Clark Art Institute★★★ (Williamstown)
Isabella Stewart Gardner Museum★★★ (Boston)
Museum of Art, Rhode Island School of Design★★ (Providence)
Museum of Fine Arts★★★ (Boston)
Maine Maritime Museum★★ (Bath)
Mystic Seaport★★★ (Mystic)
Peabody Essex Museum★★★ (Salem)
Penobscot Marine Museum★ (Searsport)
Wadsworth Atheneum Museum of Art★★ (Hartford)
Whaling Museum★★ (Nantucket)
Whaling Museum★★ (New Bedford)
Worcester Art Museum★★ (Worcester)
Yale University Art Gallery★★ (New Haven)

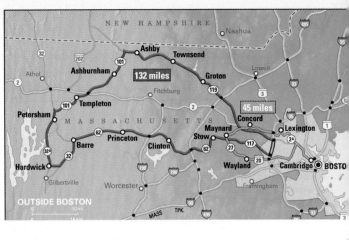

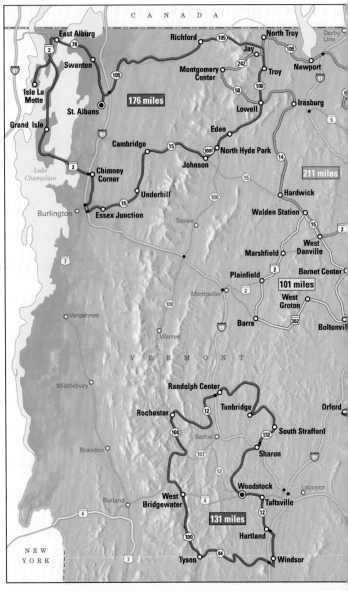

Fall Foliage Tours

ITINERARIES

--- Suggested routes

○ Town/village along tour

211 miles   Tour distance

◉ Starting point of tour

NORTHERN VERMONT AND NEW HAMPSHIRE

0 — 10mi
0 — 15km

C A N A D A

MAINE

NEW HAMPSHIRE

Pittsburg

66 miles

Colebrook

Dixville Notch

Errol

Oquossoc

119 miles

Island Pond

Bloomfield

East Haven

West Milan

97 miles

Upton

Mexico

Guildhall

Groveton

Newry

Lancaster

69 miles

Berlin

Bethel

St. Johnsbury

Jefferson Highlands

Gorham

Littleton

Twin Mountain

Mt. Washington
6288/1917

163 miles

Glen

odsville

76 miles

North Woodstock

Lincoln

Conway

Waterville Valley

Campton

North Sandwich

entworth

Center Sandwich

Moultonboro

Center Ossipee

Plymouth

109

59 miles

Wolfeboro

Laconia

Franklin

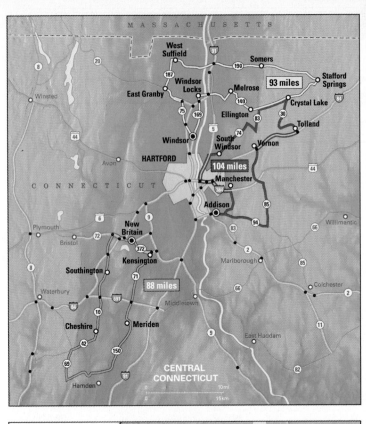

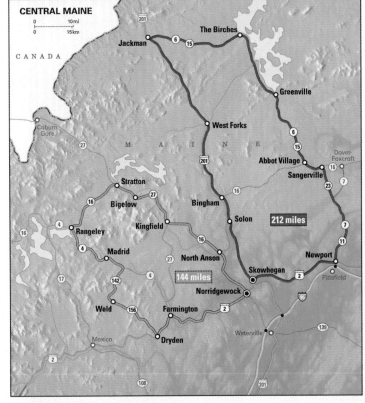

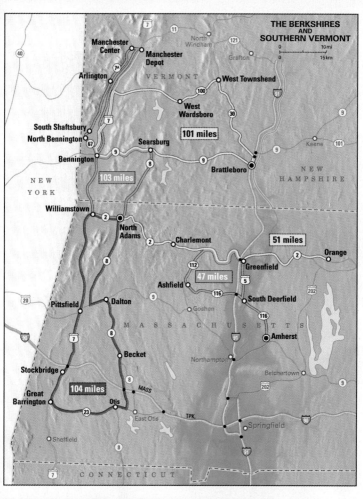

VERMONT

NEW HAMPSHIRE

NEW YORK

Manchester Center
Manchester Depot
Arlington
South Shaftsbury
North Bennington
Bennington
Williamstown
North Adams
Pittsfield
Dalton
Becket
Stockbridge
Great Barrington
Otis
Sheffield

North Windham
West Townshend
West Wardsboro
Searsburg
Brattleboro
Charlemont
Greenfield
Ashfield
South Deerfield
Amherst
Goshen
Northampton
Belchertown
East Otis
Springfield
Grafton
Keene
Orange

MASSACHUSETTS

CONNECTICUT

101 miles
103 miles
51 miles
47 miles
104 miles

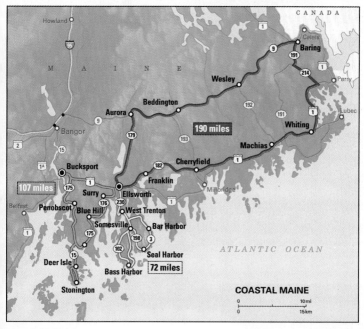

COASTAL MAINE

CANADA

MAINE

Howland
Bangor
Belfast
Bucksport
Penobscot
Blue Hill
Surry
Ellsworth
West Trenton
Somesville
Bar Harbor
Deer Isle
Bass Harbor
Seal Harbor
Stonington
Franklin
Cherryfield
Machias
Whiting
Aurora
Beddington
Wesley
Baring
Calais
Perry
Lubec
Millbridge

ATLANTIC OCEAN

190 miles
107 miles
72 miles

Lobster Buoys
©Photo Disc, Inc.

PLANNING YOUR TRIP

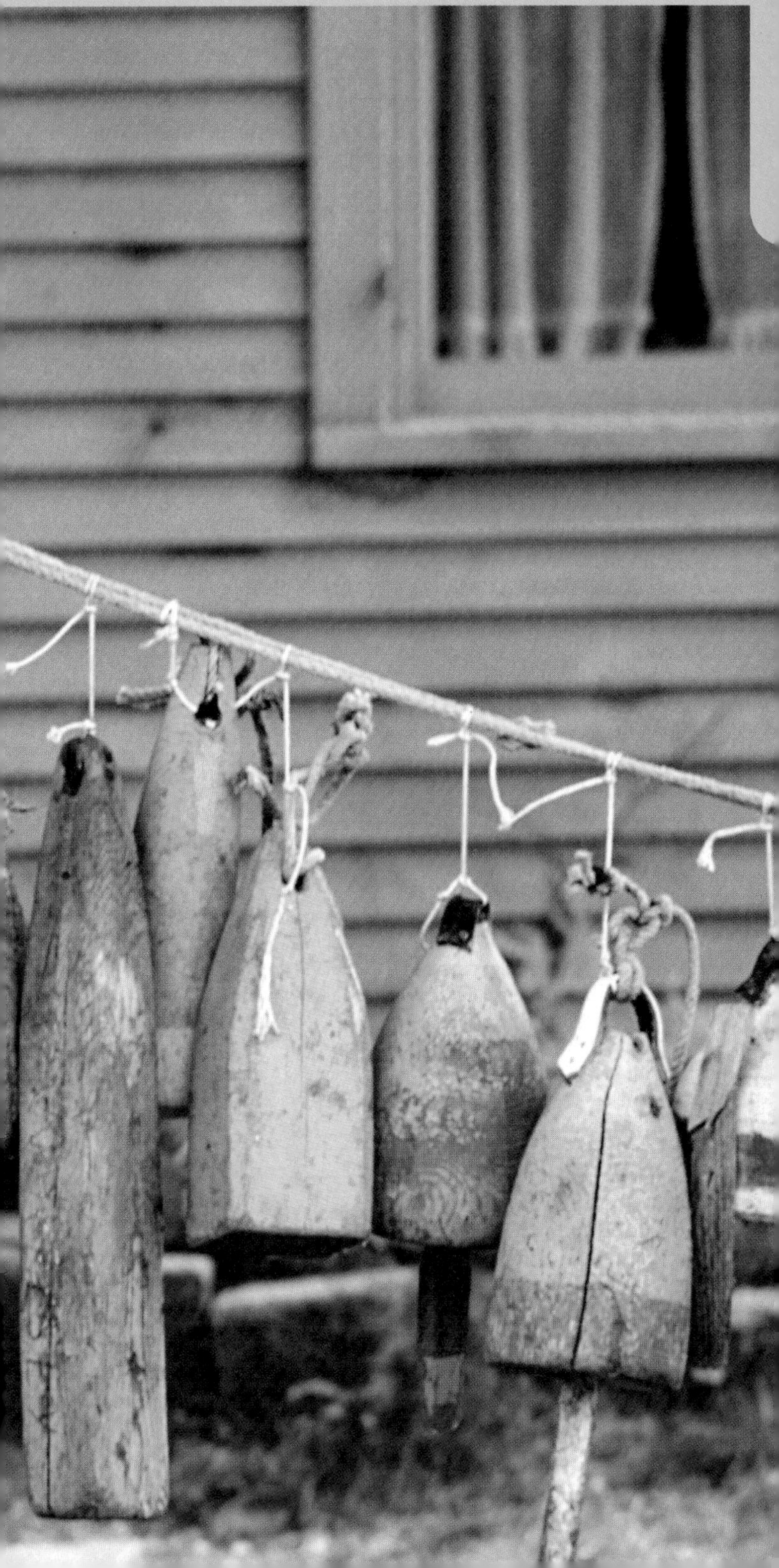

Explanation of Symbols

The following symbols are used throughout this section:

- New England
- Connecticut
- Maine
- Massachusetts
- Rhode Island
- New Hampshire
- Vermont

See individual entry headings (listed in the Index) for detailed practical information about the following regions and cities:

- Mystic Seaport
- Acadia National Park, Maine Coast, Monhegan Island, The North Woods, Portland
- The Berkshires, Boston, Cape Cod, Martha's Vineyard, Nantucket Island
- Newport
- The White Mountains

WHEN AND WHERE TO GO

Driving Tours

See the Regional Driving Tours Map on pages 12–13.

Seasons

A resort area for more than a century, New England continues to attract vacationers to its mountains and shores in every season. **Summer** months are generally mild. Daytime temperatures along the coast and in the north average 70 to 80°F (21 to 27°C); in the central region temperatures rarely climb above 90°F (32°C)—July being the warmest month. Summer nights tend to be cool and comfortable.

In the north, long summer days begin to fade into the clear, crisp days of autumn by late August. Considered the glory of New England, **Indian summer** (a period of warm, mild weather in late autumn or early winter) is often accompanied by the spectacle of blazing autumn color. In autumn the countryside teems with activity, including country fairs, auctions and flea markets. *For fall foliage hotlines, see p 33.*

Skiers and other snow enthusiasts await the long New England **winter**, typically lasting from late November through April. Daytime temperatures in the south and along the coast average 20° to 30°F (–7° to –1°C). In the north and at higher elevations, temperatures may stay below 0°F (–18°C) for 60 days annually. Snowfall is heavier in the higher elevations, with an annual average of 60in/154cm; the greatest snowfall occurs in January. There are more than 100 ski areas in the region, and opportunities abound for ice-skating, snowmobiling and snowboarding as well. New England's infamous **"nor'easter"** storms, typically lasting two to three days, can dump 10 or more inches (25cm) of snow in a single day.

The **spring** thaw, a mixture of warm days and cold nights, brings forth budding flowers—often peeking through an unexpected layer of snow—and is the perfect weather for the cultivation of maple syrup.

Many New England attractions are open only from Memorial Day to mid-October (except in large cities); some sights extend their season from mid-April through late October. *Also see Climate in the Introduction.*

Average Daily Temperatures		
State	**January**	**July**
Connecticut	27°F (–2.5°C)	73°F (23°C)
Maine	16°F (–9°C)	67°F (19°C)
Massachusetts	26°F (–3°C)	70°F (21°C)
New Hampshire	13°F (–10°C)	60°F (15°C)
Rhode Island	30°F (–1°C)	71°F (21.5°C)
Vermont	16°F (–9°C)	70°F (21°C)

KNOW BEFORE YOU GO

Useful Web Sites

www.bostonusa.com
Greater Boston Convention & Visitors Bureau site offers a comprehensive guide to attractions, accommodations, restaurants and events.

www.yankeemagazine.com
Regional guide to fall foliage tours, New England travel and other highlights from the magazine.

www.vermontmagazine.com
Good for arts calendar listings, including theater, music, craft events and festivals.

www.boston.com
Features up-to-date museum and gallery exhibits, music, theater and dance listings, restaurant reviews, local weather and traffic reports.

www.explorenewengland.com
A travel site compiled by the *Boston Globe* and Boston.com.

www.newenglandtimes.com
This site features getaways, vacations, events, real estate, history, folklore, news and lifestyles.

www.bostonmagazine.com
News, lifestyles stories and trends, covering Boston and beyond. Especially good for sleuthing out their annual "Best of Boston" award winners (restaurants, nightlife, hair salons and more). For content culled from *Boston Magazine*'s annual travel publication, *New England Travel & Life*, also see www.bostonmagazine.com/travel.

www.downeast.com
On-line version of the "magazine of Maine" is a great source for up-to-date events listings.

Tourist Offices

State tourism offices provide information and brochures on points of interest, seasonal events and accommodations, as well as road and city maps. In this guide, contact information for local tourism offices (if available) is indicated by the 🄸 symbol. On maps, Information centers are indicated by the 🄸 symbol.

Dept of Economic & Community Development
505 Hudson St., Hartford, CT 06106
☎ 860-270-8080, 800-282-6863
www.ctbound.org

Maine Tourism Association
P.O. Box 369, Kittery, ME 03904
☎ 207-623-0363, 888-624-6345
www.visitmaine.com

Office of Travel & Tourism
10 Park Plaza, Suite 4510
Boston, MA 02116
☎ 617-973-8500, 800-227-6277
www.mass-vacation.com

Office of Travel & Tourism Development
172 Pembroke Road, P.O. Box 1856
Concord, NH 03302-1856
☎ 603-271-2665, 800-386-4664
www.visitnh.gov

State Tourism Division
1 W. Exchange St.
Providence, RI 02903
☎ 401-222-2601, 800-556-2484
www.visitrhodeisland.com

Department of Tourism & Marketing
6 Baldwin St., Drawer 33
Montpelier, VT 05633-1301
☎ 802-828-3676, 800-837-6668
www.travel-vermont.com

International Visitors

EMBASSIES AND CONSULATES

Visitors from outside the US can obtain information from the tourism agencies listed on the previous page; from the nearest US embassy or consulate in their country of residence; or on the Internet *(www.travel.state.gov)*.

Australia
Moonah Place,
Yarralumla ACT 2600
☎ (02) 6-214-5600
http://usembassy-australia.state.gov

Canada
490 Sussex Drive.
Ottawa ON K1N 1G8
☎ 613-238-5335
www.usembassycanada.gov

France
2, avenue Gabriel, 75008 Paris
☎ (33) 1-43-12-22-22
www.amb-usa.fr

Germany
Neustädtische Kirchstr. 4-5
10117 Berlin
☎ (49) 030-8305-0
www.usembassy.de

Italy
Via V. Veneto 119/A, 00187 Rome
☎ (39) 06-46741
www.usembassy.it

Japan
1-10-5, Akasaka, Minato-ku
Tokyo 107-8420,
☎ (81) 3-3224-5000
http://japan.usembassy.gov

Mexico
Paseo de la Reforma 305,
Colonia Cuauhtemoc, 06500
☎ (52) 55-5080-2000
www.usembassy-mexico.gov

Spain
Calle Serrano 75, 28006 Madrid
☎ (34) 91587-2200
www.embusa.es

United Kingdom
24 Grosvenor Square,
London W1A 1AE
☎ (44) 0-20-7894-0925
www.usembassy.org.uk

DOCUMENTS

Citizens of countries participating in the Visa Waiver Pilot Program (VWPP) are not required to obtain a visa to enter the US for visits of fewer than 90 days if they have a machine-readable passport. Citizens of nonparticipating countries must have a visitor's visa. Upon entry, nonresident foreign visitors must present a valid passport and round-trip transportation ticket. Canadian citizens should note that the exemption allowing them to enter the US without a passport is being phased out. Naturalized Canadian citizens should carry their citizenship papers. Inoculations are generally not required, but check with the US embassy or consulate before departing. For details, see www.travel.state.gov.

CUSTOMS

All articles brought into the US must be declared at the time of entry. The following items are **exempt** from customs regulations: personal effects; one liter of alcoholic beverage (providing visitor is at least 21 years old); either 200 cigarettes, 50 cigars or 2 kilograms of smoking tobacco; and gifts (to persons in the US) that do not exceed $100 in value. **Prohibited items** include plant material, firearms and ammunition (if not intended for sporting purposes), and meat and poultry products. For further information regarding US Customs *(www.customs.gov)*, contact the US embassy or consulate before you depart. Foreign visitors should contact the customs service in their country of residence to determine reentry regulations.

HEALTH

The US does not have a national health program. Before departing, visitors from abroad should check with

Waits River, Vermont

their health-care insurance agency to determine if it covers doctor's visits, medication and hospitalization in the US. Prescription drugs need to be properly identified and accompanied by a copy of the prescription.

Accessibility

Federal law requires that businesses (including hotels and restaurants) provide access for the disabled, devices for the hearing impaired, and designated parking spaces. Many public buses are equipped with wheelchair lifts; numerous hotels have rooms designed for visitors with special needs. For further information, contact the state access offices: ☏ 800-842-7303 ☏ 800-452-1948 ☏ 800-322-2020 ☏ 800-852-3405 ☏ 401-462-0100 ☏ 802-241-2400.

NATIONAL PARKS

All national parks have restrooms and other facilities for the disabled (such as wheelchair-accessible nature trails or tour buses). Disabled persons are eligible for the Golden Access Passport *(free)*, which entitles the bearer to free admission to all national parks and a 50% discount on user fees (campsites, boat launches). For information, con-

tact the National Park Service: Office of Public Inquiry, ☏ 202-208-4747; www.nps.gov.

STATE PARKS

Some state parks offer permanently disabled persons a discount on campsites and day-use fees. Carry proof of identification and disability.

TRANSPORTATION

Train travel: Amtrak publishes a handy book, entitled *Access Amtrak*. Passengers who will need assistance should give 24hr-advance notice *(☏ 800-872-7245 or 800-523-6590/TDD www.amtrak.com).* **Bus travel:** Disabled riders are encouraged to notify **Greyhound** 48hrs in advance *(☏ 800-752-4841 (US only) or 800-345-3109/TDD www.greyhound.com).* For general information contact the Society for Accessible Travel & Hospitality ☏ 212-447-7284; www.sath.org.

Vertical text on photo: Vermont Department of Tourism & Marketing/ Andre Jenny

GETTING THERE

By Air

Most flights to New England stop at La Guardia or John F. Kennedy international airports in New York, or Logan International Airport in Boston before making connecting flights to the principal New England airports.

Logan International Airport (BOS)
3mi northeast of downtown Boston, MA
☎ 800-235-6426
www.massport.com

John F. Kennedy International Airport (JFK)
15mi southeast of Midtown, Manhattan, NY
☎ 718-244-4444
www.jfkinternationalairport.org

La Guardia Airport (LGA)
8mi northeast of Midtown, Manhattan, NY
☎ 718-533-3400
www.panynj.gov

Bangor International Airport (BGR)
2mi north of Bangor, ME
☎ 207-947-0381
www.flybangor.com

Bradley International Airport (BDL)
12mi north of Hartford, CT
☎ 860-292-2000
www.bradleyairport.com

Burlington International Airport (BTV)
3mi east of Burlington, VT
☎ 802-863-3626
www.vermontairports.com

Manchester Airport (MHT)
4mi south of Manchester, NH
☎ 603-624-6539
www.flymanchester.com

Portland International Jetport (PWM)
3mi south of Portland, ME
☎ 207-874-8877
www.portlandjetport.org

T.F. Green Airport (PVD) Warwick, RI
10mi south of Providence, RI
☎ 401-737-8222
www.pvdairport.com

By Train

With access to over 50 communities in New England, the **Amtrak** rail network offers a relaxing alternative for the traveler with time to spare. Advance reservations are recommended. First class, coach and sleeping accommodations are available; fares are comparable to air travel. The high-speed rail travels daily from New York City to Boston in just over five hours. For schedules and routes, call ☎ 800-872-7245 *(toll-free in North America only; outside North America, contact your local travel agent)* or visit www.amtrak.com.

By Bus

Greyhound, the largest bus company in the US, offers access to most communities in New England at a leisurely pace. Overall, fares are lower than other forms of public transportation. The **Discovery Pass** allows unlimited travel for anywhere from 4 to 60 days. Advance reservations are suggested. For fares, schedules and routes, call ☎ 800-231-2222 or visit www.greyhound.com.

Driving in New England

New England has an extensive system of well-maintained major roads. In remote areas, minor roads tend to be unmarked, and many small rural routes are unpaved.

DOCUMENTS

Visitors bearing valid driver's licenses issued by their country of residence are not required to obtain an International Driver's License to drive in the US. Drivers must carry vehicle registration and/or rental contract and proof of automobile insurance at all times.

ROAD REGULATIONS

Road regulations in the US require that vehicles be driven on the right side of the road. Distances are posted in miles *(1 mile = 1.6 kilometers)*. Travelers are advised to obey posted speed limit signs.

The maximum speed limit on major freeways is 65mph (105km/h) in rural areas and 55mph (90km/h) in and around cities (in Rhode Island, maximum speed limits are 55mph). Speed limits range from 30 to 40mph (45-65km/h) within cities, and average 25mph (30km/h) in residential areas. Use of **seat belts** is mandatory for all persons in the car in all states except New Hampshire (required only for passengers under 18 years of age) and Connecticut. In Connecticut, seat-belt use is mandatory for all persons 16 or under; for persons over 16, seat-belt use is mandatory only in the front seat. In Rhode Island children aged 4 to 5 years must ride in the back seat with a seat belt fastened.

Child safety seats are required in Vermont, Connecticut and Massachusetts for children under 5 years; they are required in Connecticut, Maine, Rhode Island and New Hampshire for children under 4 years (or 40lbs and below). **School bus** law in effect for the six-state area requires motorists to bring vehicles to a full stop when red lights on a school bus are activated. Unless otherwise posted, it is permissible to turn right at a red traffic light after coming to a complete stop. Parking spaces identified with ♿ are reserved only for disabled persons. Anyone parking in these spaces without proper identification is subject to a ticket with a hefty fine attached.

In Case of Accident

If you are involved in an accident resulting in personal or property damage, you must notify the local police and remain at the scene until dismissed. If blocking traffic, vehicles should be moved if possible.

CAR RENTAL

Most large rental-car agencies have offices at major airports and in the larger cities in New England. A major credit card and valid driver's license are required for rental (some agencies also require proof of insurance). Drop-off charges may apply if a vehicle is returned to a location other than where it was rented.

Rental Company	☎ Reservations
Alamo	800-462-5266 www.alamo.com
Enterprise	800-736-8222 www.enterprise.com
Avis	800-230-4898 www.avis.com
Hertz	800-654-3131 www.hertz.com
Budget	800-527-0700 www.budget.com
National	800-227-7368 www.nationalcar.com
Dollar	800-800-3665 www.dollar.com
Thrifty	800-847-4389 www.thrifty.com

(Toll-free numbers may not be accessible outside North America.)

GASOLINE

Gasoline is sold by the gallon *(1 US gallon = 3.8 liters)*. Many self-service gas stations do not offer car repair, although many do sell standard maintenance items. Some also sell maps and snacks.

WHERE TO STAY AND EAT

Where to Stay

Hotels and Restaurants are described in the Address Books within the *Discovering New England* section.

Luxury **hotels** are generally found in major cities, **motels** in clusters on the edge of town, or where two or more highways intersect. In rural areas, motels are found on roads frequently traveled by tourists. **Bed and breakfasts** (B&Bs) are normally located in residential areas of cities and villages. Local tourist offices (telephone numbers are listed under entry headings in the *Discovering New England* section) provide detailed information about accommodations. In season and during weekends, advance reservations are recommended. Always advise reservations clerk of late arrival; rooms, even though reserved, might not always be held after 6pm otherwise. Off-season and weekday rates are usually lower than seasonal and weekend rates, although many city hotels offer discount packages on weekends. Some New England accommodations offer either the American Plan (three meals included) or the Modified American Plan (breakfast and dinner included).

For a copy of Maine's statewide lodging guide, call ☎ 207-865-6100 or visit www.maineinns.com.

Hotel/Motel	☎ / Web Site
Best Western	800-780-7234 www.bestwestern.com
Hyatt	800-233-1234 www.hyatt.com
Comfort Inn	877-424-6423 www.comfortinn.com
Marriott	888-236-2427 www.marriott.com
Days Inn	800-329-7466 www.daysinn.com
Radisson	888-201-1718 www.radisson.com
Hilton	800-774-1500 www.hilton.com
Ramada	800-272-6232 www.ramada.com
Holiday Inn	800-465-4329 www.holiday-inn.com
Ritz-Carlton	800-241-3333 www.ritzcarlton.com
Howard Johnson	800-446-4656 www.hojo.com
Westin	800-228-3000 www.westin.com

(toll-free numbers may not be accessible outside of North America)

HOTELS/MOTELS

Accommodations range from luxury hotels to budget motels. Rates vary with season and location; rates tend to be higher in cities and in coastal and vacation areas. Many hotels and motels offer packages (including meals, passes to local sights and access to facility-sponsored events) and weekend specials. Amenities may include television, restaurant, swimming pool, and smoking/non-smoking rooms. More elegant hotels also offer in-room dining and valet service. Above is a list of major hotel chains with locations throughout New England.

BED AND BREAKFASTS/ COUNTRY INNS

Many B&Bs are privately owned and located in historic homes. Breakfast, and in some cases, afternoon tea, is included in the rates; private baths are not always available. Smoking indoors may not be allowed.

Some inns have been in operation since colonial times. Inns often include a restaurant that serves three meals a day. The price of breakfast may not be included in the lodging fee, as it is with B&Bs.

Many inns and B&Bs participate in one-day and weekend inn-to-inn tours for bikers, hikers and cross-country skiers.

Some establishments may charge a 10-15% gratuity (inquire when reserving). ◉ Maine: for a free copy of *Lodging and Dining Guide,* contact the Maine Innkeepers Assn: 304 US Route 1, Freeport, ME 04032; ☎ 207-865-6100; www.maineinns.com.

Reservations services

◉ Nutmeg B&B Agency, P.O. Box 271117, West Hartford, CT 06127; ☎ 860-236-6698 or 800-727-7592; www.bnb-link.com. ◉ Bed & Breakfast of Maine, 377 Gray Rd., Falmouth, ME 04105; ☎ 207-797-5540. ◉ Bed & Breakfast Rhode Island, P.O. Box 3291, Newport, RI 02840; ☎ 401-849-1298 or 800-828-0000; www.visitnewport.com/bedandbreakfast. ◉ Destinnations, 16 East Pond Rd., Nobleboro, ME 04555; ☎ 800-333-4667; www.destinnations.com.

HOSTELS

A simple, low-cost alternative to hotels and inns, hostels average $12–$17/night; amenities may include community living room, showers, laundry facilities, full-service kitchen and dining room, and dormitory-style rooms (blankets and pillows are provided, but guests are required to bring their own linens). Membership cards are recommended. **Hostelling International USA**, 8401 Coleville Rd., Suite 600, Silver Spring, MD 20910; ☎ 301-495-1240; www.hiayh.org.

CAMPING

Campsites are located in national and state parks, national forests and in private campgrounds. Amenities range from full RV hook-ups to rustic backcountry sites. Most camping areas provide recreational and sporting amenities. Advance reservations are recommended from mid-May through mid-October. **Wilderness camping** is available on most public lands. Topographic maps of most wilderness areas and other information are available from specific parks or state tourism offices.

FARM VACATIONS

Host farms allow paying visitors the opportunity to participate in the daily activities of a working farm. Rates vary from $45 to $135/night. For more information, contact the following organizations: ◉ Dept. of Agriculture, 765 Asylum Ave., Hartford, CT 06105; ☎ 800-861-9939; www.state.ct.us. ◉ Maine Farm Vacation B&B Assn.; www.mainefarmvacation.com. ◉ Dept. of Food & Agriculture, 251 Causeway St., Boston, MA 02114; ☎ 617-626-1700; www.massgrown.org. ◉ NH Dept. of Agriculture, Markets, and Food, P.O. Box 2042, Concord, NH 03302; ☎ 603-271-3551; www.nhfarms.com. ◉ Vermont Farm Vacations, 617 Comstock Rd., Berlin, VT 05602; ☎ 802-223-0929 or 888-892-6748; www.vermontfarms.org.

Where to Eat

From meatloaf and mashed potatoes to Malaysian cuisine, dining in New England is an adventure in itself. Fresh seafood plays a starring role on local menus, especially along the coast. The **clam shack** is quintessentially "New England," with a certain rustic charm. If the place uses the phrase "eat in the rough," expect picnic tables, paper plates, and plastic lobster bibs. Decor, such as it is, runs to old lobster traps and giant plastic crustaceans. Dine on boiled lobster and fried clams, served with heaping piles of French fries and onion rings, and a side of slaw—a grand, greasy indulgence that often comes with an ocean view.

The **diner** is another classic New England eating spot. In fact, the region is credited as the birthplace of the diner. The first "night lunch wagon'" appeared in Providence, Rhode Island in 1858, serving late-shift workers at the *Providence Journal.* Those handsome dining cars still dot the landscape of New England's small towns and rural countryside. The diner experience hasn't changed a bit, and the pie is just as good as ever.

New England's big cities offer the full spectrum of fine-dining options, as well as an exotic array of ethnic eateries. But here's a great secret: some of the region's finest dining happens in **country inns**, where innkeepers entice visitors off the beaten path with dazzling, creative cookery and award-winning wine lists.

Wherever you go, keep in mind that many New Englanders are "early to bed" Yankees, so you probably won't be seated for a meal after 9 pm.

WHAT TO DO AND SEE

Outdoor Fun

SELECTED STATE PARKS

Connecticut
State Parks Division
79 Elm St., Hartford, CT 06106;
☎ 860-424-3200
www.dep.state.ct.us

- **Gillette Castle SP**
- **Housatonic Meadows SP**
- **Kent Falls SP**
- **Macedonia Brook SP**
- **Sleeping Giant SP**
- **Talcott Mountain SP**

Maine
Bureau of Parks and Land
286 Water St., Key Bank Plaza,
Augusta, ME 04333;
☎ 207-287-3821
www.state.me.us/doc/parks

- **Baxter SP**
- **Camden Hills SP**
- **Cobscook Bay SP**
- **Crescent Beach SP**
- **Grafton Notch SP**
- **Mt. Blue SP**
- **Popham Beach SP**
- **Quoddy Head SP**
- **Rangeley Lake SP**
- **Sebago Lake SP**
- **Two Lights SP**
- **Wolfe's Neck Woods SP**

Massachusetts
Division of Forests and Parks
251 Causeway St., Suite 600
Boston, MA 02114;
☎ 617-626-1250
www.massparks.org

- **Halibut Point SP**
- **Natural Bridge SP**
- **Nickerson SP**
- **Skinner SP**
- **Western Gateway Heritage SP**

New Hampshire
Division of Parks & Recreation
P.O. Box 1856
172 Pembroke Rd.
Concord, NH 03302;
☎ 603-271-3556
www.nhparks.state.nh.us

- **Lake Francis SP**
- **Monadnock SP**
- **Mt. Sunapee SP**
- **Rhododendron SP**
- **Rye Harbor SP**
- **Wallis Sands SP**
- **Wellington SP**
- **White Lake SP**

Rhode Island
Department of Parks and Recreation
2321 Hartford Ave.
Johnston, RI 02919;
☎ 401-222-2632; *www.riparks.com*

- **Brenton Point SP**
- **Colt SP**
- **Fort Adams SP**

Vermont
Department of Forests, Parks & Recreation
103 S. Main St.
Waterbury, VT 05671;
☎ 802-241-3655
www.vtstateparks.com

- **Branbury SP**

- **Button Bay SP** ⛺ 🥾 🏊 🎣
- **Lake St. Catherine SP** ⛺🥾🏊🎣
- **Silver Lake SP** ⛺ 🏊 🎣
- **Woodford SP** ⛺ 🥾 🏊

⛺ *camping;* 🥾 *hiking;* 🏊 *swimming;* 🎣 *fishing*

HIKING AND BIKING

Many trail systems lace the region. State and local parks provide opportunities for hiking and biking. The **Long Trail** 🥾 *(265mi)* in Vermont runs north to south along the Green Mountains from the Canadian to the Massachusetts border; in New England, the **Appalachian Trail** 🥾 extends from Mt. Katahdin in Maine to the Connecticut/New York border. **Acadia National Park** offers 165 acres of moderately easy hiking trails. The 175mi of wilderness trails in **Baxter State Park** and 1,200mi of trails **White Mountain National Forest** are more challenging. When hiking in the backcountry, stay on marked trails. ☺ Taking shortcuts is dangerous and causes erosion. If hiking alone, notify someone of your destination and proposed return time. In addition, 1,003mi of former railroad tracks throughout New England have been converted into paved and dirt paths for bikers and pedestrians *(for maps and information, contact: Rails-to-Trails Conservancy, 1100 17th St. NW, Washington, DC 20036; ☎ 202-331-9696; www. railtrails.org).*

Bicycles are prohibited on most unpaved trails. Riders should stay on paved paths and roads (on public roads, stay to the right and ride in single file). Bicyclists are encouraged to wear helmets and other protective gear.

☺ Both hikers and bicyclists are cautioned to be well equipped (including detailed maps of the areas to be explored) and alert to weather conditions, particularly in higher elevations. For more information on trails and on local mountain biking regulations, contact local tourism offices.

Llama hikes provide a novel way to enjoy the terrain while allowing these gentle creatures to carry the meals and gear. Several outfitters sponsor llama treks: Northern Vermont Llama Company, Rt. 1, Box 544, Waterville, VT 05492 (☎ 802-644-2257;www. northernvermontllamaco.com); Telemark Inn's Llama Treks, 591 Kings Hwy, Bethel, ME 04217 (☎ 207-836-2703; www.telemarkinn.com); and Berkshire Mountain Llama Hike, 322 Lander Rd., Lee, MA 01238 (☎ 413-243-2224; www. hawkmeadowllamas.com).

Courtesy New England Hiking Holidays

Hiking in Barr Hill Nature Preserve, Vermont

The following organizations provide information about hiking and cycling trails in New England:

- **New England Hiking Holidays**, P.O. Box 1648, North Conway, NH 03860; ☎ 800-869-0949 or 603-356-9696; www.nehikingholidays.com.
- **Bike Riders Tours,** P.O. Box 130254, Boston, MA 02113; ☎ 800-473-7040 or 617-723-2354; www.bikeriderstours.com.
- **Appalachian Mountain Club**, 5 Joy St., Boston, MA 02108; ☎ 617-523-0636; www.outdoors.org.
- **Appalachian Trail Conference,** P.O. Box 807, Harpers Ferry, WV 25425; ☎ 304-535-6331; www.atconf.org.
- **Back Country Excursions**, 42 Woodward Rd., Parsonsfield, ME 04047; ☎ 207-625-8189; www.bikebackcountry.com.
- **Bike Vermont Inc.,** Box 207, Woodstock VT 05091; ☎ 800-257-2226 or 802-457-3553; www.bikevermont.com.
- **Vermont Bicycle Touring**, 614 Monkton Rd., Bristol, VT 05443; ☎ 800-245-3868; www.vbt.com.
- **Vermont Department of Forests, Parks & Recreation**, 103 S. Main St., Waterbury, VT 05671; ☎ 802-241-3655; www.vtstateparks.com.
- **Green Mountain National Forest**, Supervisor, 231 N. Main St., Rutland, VT 05701; ☎ 802-747-6700; www.fs.fed.us/r9/gmfl.
- **The Green Mountain Club**, 4711 Waterbury-Stowe Rd., Waterbury Center, VT 05677; ☎ 802-244-7037; www.greenmountainclub.org.

HUNTING AND FISHING

With an abundance of game and fish (including deer, moose and trout), New England is a hunting and angling paradise. Licenses are required to hunt and fish in all six states. Nonresident fishing licenses are available in fishing-supply stores (some offer rental equipment). Nonresident hunting licenses tend to be considerably more expensive than resident licenses. Many fish are in season year-round, whereas most game can only be hunted seasonally. If being transported, a rifle or shotgun must be unloaded (no permit required; some states require it to be in a secure case).

Contact the following agencies for additional information (including regulations on transporting game out of state):

- **Department of Environmental Protection**, Wildlife Division, 79 Elm St., Hartford, CT 06106; ☎ 860-424-3000; http://dep.state.ct.us.
- **Department of Inland Fisheries and Wildlife**, 284 State St., 41 State House Station, Augusta, ME 04333, ☎ 207-287-8000; www.maine.gov/ifw; the *Maine Guide to Hunting and Fishing* is available from the Maine Tourism Association.
- **Division of Fisheries and Wildlife**, Field Headquarters, One Rabbit Hill Rd., Westboro, MA 01581; ☎ 508-792-7270; www.state.ma.us/dfwele/dfw/dfw_toc.htm.

Vermont Department of Tourism & Marketing/ Dennis Curran

- ⊚ **Fish & Game Department**,
  11 Hazen Dr., Concord, NH 03301;
  ☏ 603-271-3211; www.wildlife.
  state.nh.us.
- ⊚ **Division of Fish & Wildlife**,
  Government Center,
  4808 Tower Hill Rd.,
  Wakefield, RI 02879;
  ☏ 401-789-3094;
  www.dem.ri.gov/topics.
- ⊚ **Department of Fish and Wildlife**,
  103 S. Main St., Building 10 South,
  Waterbury, VT 05671;
  ☏ 802-241-3700;
  www.vtfishandwildlife.com.

WATER SPORTS

New England's coastal waters, lakes and rivers offer ample opportunities for canoeing, kayaking, sailing (especially in Newport, RI), and whitewater rafting. Contact the individual state tourism offices for listings of outfitters. Kayakers will want to check out the 325mi-long **Maine Island Trail**, which links 100 public and private islands between Casco Bay and the Canadian border *(for information, contact the Maine Island Trail Association in Portland, ME; ☏ 207-761-8225; www.mita. org)*. For canoers, Maine's **Allagash Wilderness Waterway** traverses ponds and rivers through the North Woods. To canoe the entire 92mi length of the waterway takes from 7 to 10 days *(for information, contact the Maine Dept. of Conservation, Bureau of Parks & Lands, 22 State House St., Augusta, ME 04333; ☏ 207-287-3821; www.maine.gov/doc)*.
Whitewater rafting is popular on Maine's Kennebec, Penobscot and Dead rivers from May to mid-October. **Raft Maine** is an association of whitewater outfitters conducting raft trips on all three rivers *(PO Box 3, Bethel, ME 04217; ☏ 800-723-8633; www. raftmaine.com)*. In New Hampshire **Saco Bound, Inc.** and the **Rapid River Rafting Co**. in Conway *(☏ 603-447-2177; www.sacobound.com)* offer paddling and kayaking classes, as well as raft trips on Maine's Androscoggin River—a popular whitewater passage

best suited to experienced paddlers—and canoe treks on Maine's Saco River.

Ocean Swimming – Beaches along the coast of New England are generally clean and sandy; several are rocky, the beaches a mixture of sand with pebbles (walking barefoot may be uncomfortable). Summer water temperatures vary: Connecticut and Rhode Island waters range from 65° to 75°F (18°–24°C); in southern Massachusetts (including Cape Cod), water temperatures average 65° to 75°F (18°–24°C); northern Massachusetts, New Hampshire and Maine waters average a brisk 50° to 65°F (10°–18°C). Excellent surfing can be found along the coastlines of Rhode Island, Massachusetts and Maine. Swimmers should be aware of the occasional riptide or undertow (strong underlying currents that pull swimmers away from shore). Many New England communities employ lifeguards seasonally. Care should be taken when swimming at an unguarded beach. Children should be supervised at all times.

Activities for Children

Throughout this guide, sights of particular interest to children are indicated with a 🧒 symbol. Many museums and other attractions have special children's programs and resource centers. Most attractions throughout New England offer discounted admission to visitors under 18 years of age. In addition, various hotels make family discount packages available, and many restaurants provide a children's menu.

Family Fun

FALL FOLIAGE TOURS

Maps pp 16-19. New England's grand foliage season traditionally begins in early September along the Canadian border and higher elevations, and moves progressively southward until the end of October. Advance reservations (two to three months) are recommended during this time period.

Local Color
Call the **fall foliage hotlines** or access the Web sites below for up-to-date information on fall color (mid-Sept–Oct):
☎ 800-282-6863, www.ctbound.org
☎ 888-624-6345 www. mainefoliage.com
☎ 800-227-6277 www.mass-vacation.com
☎ 800-556-2484 www.visitrhodeisland.com
☎ 800-386-4664, www.visitnh.gov
☎ 800-837-6668 www.travel-vermont.com
www.visitnewengland.com; www.yankeefoliage.com

HISTORIC TOURS

The following organizations offer their members free admission to their historic properties in New England:
Society for the Preservation of New England Antiquities, 141 Cambridge St., Boston, MA 02114, ☎ 617-227-3956, www.spnea. org (annual dues $35);
Antiquarian and Landmarks Society, 255 Main St., Hartford, CT 06106, ☎ 860-247-8996, www.hart-net.org/als (annual dues $35).
The **National Trust for Historic Preservation** maintains sights located nationwide: 1785 Massachusetts Ave. NW, Washington, DC 20036, ☎ 202-588-6000, www.nthp.org (annual dues $20).

WHALE-WATCHING

Because of the abundance of plankton, whales can be seen in large numbers on their migration route from the Caribbean to Greenland and Newfoundland from early spring to mid-October, primarily along the Stellwagen Bank (27mi east of Boston) in the Gulf of Maine.

Selected Cruise Companies

Massachusetts:
◆ **Boston Harbor Cruises,** Boston, www.bostonharborcruises.com, ☎ 617-227-4321, May–mid-Oct
◆ **New England Aquarium** Boston, www.neaq.org, ☎ 617-973-5200, Apr–Oct
◆ **Cape Ann Whale Watch** Gloucester, www.caww.com, ☎ 800-877-5110, May–mid-Oct
◆ **Captain Bill's Whale Watch** Gloucester, www.captainbillandsons.com, ☎ 800-339-4253, May–Oct
◆ **Seven Seas Whale Watching** Gloucester, www.7seaswhalewatch.com, ☎ 888-283-1776, or 800-520-0017, May–mid-Oct
◆ **Yankee Whale Watch** Gloucester, www.yankee-fleet.com, ☎ 800-942-5464, Apr–Oct
◆ **Captain John Boats** Plymouth, www. captjohn.com, ☎ 800-242-2469, Apr–Oct
◆ **Provincetown's Portuguese Princess Whale Watch** Provincetown, www. princesswhalewatch.com, ☎ 800-442-3188, Apr–Oct
◆ **Newburyport Whale Watch** Newburyport, ☎ 800-848-1111, May–Oct
◆ **Hyannis Whale Watcher Cruises** Hyannis, www. whales.net, ☎ 508-362-6088, Apr–Oct

Maine
◆ **Bar Harbor Whale Watch Co.** Bar Harbor, www. barharborwhales.com, ☎ 888-533-WALE, May–Oct
◆ **Cap'n Fish's Boat Cruises** Boothbay Harbor, www.mainewhales.com, ☎ 207-633-3244, May-Oct

PUFFINS

Between June and early August (prime viewing time: July) you can spot puffins in their summer colonies in the Gulf of Maine on Easter Egg Rock, Matinicus Rock and Machias Seal Island. On-land viewing *(bring binoculars)* is allowed only on Machias Seal Island by the following companies: **Cap'n Fish's Boat Cruises**, Boothbay Harbor, ME *(☎ 207-633-3244; www.mainewhales.com)*; **Norton of Jonesport**, Jonesport, ME *(☎ 207-497-5933, www.machiassealisland.com)*.

Winter Activities

SKIING

The primary ski areas in New England are the Green Mountains of Vermont and the White Mountains of New Hampshire; there are also excellent ski resorts in northwestern Maine, western Connecticut and the Berkshires of Massachusetts. Many ski area communities offer a variety of accommodations including major hotel chains, B&Bs and alpine lodges. Discount packages for stays of 3 or more days, which may include lift tickets, equipment rental, meals and transportation to the slopes, are often available. Radio stations throughout the northeast report local ski conditions. Most ski resorts have snow-making equipment.

Ski New England: On-line Resources

- *www.snocountry.com*
- *www.skinh.com*
- *www.skivermont.com*

CROSS-COUNTRY SKIING

Many local parks and recreation departments maintain trail systems through recreation areas and forests. Always ask permission before skiing on private land. Some of the trail systems have warming huts, while others offer cabins with sleeping accommodations. Most backcountry trails are ungroomed.

Trail Conditions & Information

- **Maine**
  ☎ 888-624-6345,
  800-754-9263 (XC);
  *www.visitmaine.com,
  www.mnsc.com*
- **New Hampshire**
  ☎ 800-887-5454 (downhill & XC);
  www.skinh.com, www.xcskinh.com
- **Vermont**
  ☎ 802-223-2439;
  www.skivermont.com

SNOWMOBILING

New England offers enthusiasts miles of maintained trails on both public and private lands. The organizations listed below provide guided tours, rental equipment and trail information, as well as details about regional snowmobile licensing requirements, registration, fees and restrictions.

Skiing near Stowe, Vermont

©Chuck Waskuch/ Courtesy Stowe Mountain Resort

Office of State Parks & Recreation
☎ 860-424-3200,
www.dep.state.ct.us

Snowmobile Association
☎ 413-369-8092,
www. sledmass.com

Snowmobile Associates
☎ 207-622-6983;
www. mesnow.com

The Maine Way – Recreation
www. mainerec.com

Snowmobile Association
☎ 603-224-8906, www. nhsa.com

Association of Snow Travelers
☎ 802-229-0005, www. vtvast.org

Snowmobile Vermont
☎ 802-422-2121,
www.snowmobilevermont.com

Trails Bureau, NH State Parks
☎ 603-271-3254,
www.nhparks.state.nh.us.

DOGSLEDDING

This ancient mode of transportation offers a unique way to view the beauty of Maine's winter wilderness. Trips vary from one-hour excursions to day and overnight trips. **Mahoosuc Guide Service** (Bear River Rd., Newry, ME 04261; ☎ 207-824-2073; www.mahoosuc.com) offers day and overnight trips throughout Maine, New Hampshire and Canada. **Moose Country Safaris** (191 North Dexter Rd., Sangerville, ME 04479; ☎ 207-876-4907; www.moosecountrysafaris.com) offers one-hour to full day trips in the Moosehead Lake region.

Calendar of Events

Below is a selection of New England's most popular annual events; some dates may vary from year to year. For detailed information, contact local tourism offices (☎ telephone numbers are given the in *Discovering New England* section) or state tourism offices (listed in the section **Planning Your Trip**).

FESTIVALS AND SPORTING EVENTS

JANUARY

late Jan: **Stowe Winter Carnival**
www.stowewintercarnival.com
☎ 802-253-7321, Stowe (VT)
late Jan–Feb: **Chinese New Year Parade**
www.bostonusa.com
☎ 888-733-2786, Boston (MA)

FEBRUARY

Dartmouth Winter Carnival
www.dartmouth.edu
☎ 603-646-1110, Hanover (NH)
Late Feb: **Newport Winter Festival**
www.newportwinterfestival.com
☎ 401-847-7666, Newport (RI)
Mount Washington Ice Festival
www.ime-usa.com
☎ 603-356-7064, North Conway (NH)

MARCH

early Mar: **Jackson Ski Festival**
www.jacksonnh.com
☎ 800-866-3334, Jackson (NH)
☎ 888-733-2786, Boston (MA)
mid–late Mar: **New England Spring Flower Show**
www.masshort.org
☎ 617-933-4970, Boston (MA)

APRIL

mid-Apr: **Boston Marathon**
www.bostonmarathon.com
☎ 617-236-1652, Boston (MA)
Apr 1–30: **Daffodil Days**
www.blithewold.org
☎ 401-253-2707, Bristol (RI)

Apr–Oct: **Waterfire**
  www.waterfire.org
  ☎ 401-272-3111, Providence (RI)

late Apr: **Fishermen's Festival**
  www.boothbayharbor.com
  ☎ 207-633-2353,
  Boothbay Harbor (ME)

Vermont Maple Festival
  www.vermontmaple.org
  ☎ 802-763-7435; St. Albans (VT)

MAY

mid-May: **Dogwood Festival**
  www.fairfieldct.org
  ☎ 203-256-3000; Fairfield (CT)

late May: **New Hampshire Annual Lilac Festival**
  www.visitnh.gov
  ☎ 800-386-4664; Lisbon (NH)

May–Jun: **MooseMainea**
  www.mooseheadlake.org
  ☎ 207-695-2702;
  Moosehead Lake Region (ME)

JUNE

early Jun: **Yale-Harvard Regatta**
  www.yale.edu
  ☎ 203-432-4771; New London (CT)

Old Port Festival
  http://portlandme.about.com/library/
  ☎ 207-772-6828; Portland (ME)

Jun–late Aug: **Jacob's Pillow Dance Festival**
  www.jacobspillow.org
  ☎ 413-243-0745; Becket (MA)

mid-Jun: **Market Square Days Celebration**
  www.seacoastnh.com
  ☎ 603-427-2020; Portsmouth (NH)

mid-Jun: **International Festival of Arts and Ideas**
  www.artidea.org;
  ☎ 203-624-1825; New Haven (CT)

mid-Jun–Aug: **Williamstown Theater Festival**
  www.wtfestival.org
  ☎ 413-597-3400;
  Williamstown (MA)

late Jun: **Block Island Race Week**
  www.blockislandraceweek.com
  ☎ 203-458-3295; Block Island (RI))

late Jun–late Aug: **Berkshire Theatre Festival**
  www.berkshiretheatre.org
  ☎ 866-811-4111; Stockbridge (MA)

late Jun: **Windjammer Days**
  www.boothbayharbor.com
  ☎ 207-633-2353;
  Boothbay Harbor (ME)

JULY

early Jul: **Riverfest**
  www.riverfront.org; Hartford (CT)

Harborfest
  www.bostonharborfest.com
  ☎ 617-227-1528; Boston (MA)

Vermont Quilt Festival
  www.vqf.org
  ☎ 802-485-7092; Northfield (VT)

Seacoast Jazz Festival
  www.artfest.org
  ☎ 603-436-2848; Portsmouth (NH)

Wickford Art Festival
  www.wickfordart.org
  ☎ 401-294-6840; Wickford (RI)

Jul 4: **Bristol Fourth of July Parade**
  www.onlinebristol.com
  ☎ 401-253-7000; Bristol (RI)

mid-Jul: **Litchfield Open House Tour**
  www.litchfieldct.com
  ☎ 860-567-4045; Litchfield (CT)

Newport Music Festival
  www.newportmusic.org
  ☎ 401-849-0700; Newport (RI)

late Jul: **Lowell Folk Festival**
  www.lowellfolkfestival.com
  ☎ 617-973-8500; Lowell (MA)

Great Connecticut Jazz Festival
  www.ctjazz.org
  ☎ 800-468-3836; Guilford (CT)

late Jul–early Aug: **Yankee Homecoming Days**
  www.yankeehomecoming.com
  ☎ 978-462-4760;
  Newburyport (MA);

AUGUST

early Aug: **Lobster Festival**
  www.mainelobsterfestival.com
  ☎ 207-596-0376; Rockland (ME)

League of New Hampshire Craftsmen's Fair
  www.leagueofnhcraftsmen.com
  ☎ 603-224-3375;
  Mt. Sunapee Resort, Newbury (NH)

Southern Vermont Art and Fine Craft Fair
www.craftproducers.com
☏ *802-425-3399; Manchester (VT)*

2nd weekend in Aug: **Newport JVC Jazz Festival**
www.gonewport.com
☏ *800-976-5122; Newport (RI)*

mid-Aug: **Fall River Celebrates America**
www.fallrivercelebrates.com
☏ *508-676-8226; Fall River (MA)*

Portland Chamber Music Festival
www.pcmf.org
☏ *800-320-0257; Portland (ME)*

late Aug: **National Folk Festival**
www.nationalfolkfestival.com
☏ *207-992-2630; Bangor (ME)*

International Quahog Festival
www.quahog.com
☏ *401-885-4118; Wickford (RI)*

Mt. Washington Hillclimb (bicycle race)
www.visitwhitemountains.com
☏ *603-745-8720; Gorham (NH)*

late Aug–early Sept: **Champlain Valley Fair**
www.cvfair.com; ☏ *802-878-5545; Essex Junction (VT)*

SEPTEMBER

early Sept: **Vermont State Fair**
www.rutlandherald.com/vermontstatefair; ☏ *802-775-5200; Rutland (VT)*

Norwalk Oyster Festival
www.seaport.org
☏ *203-838-9444; Norwalk (CT)*

mid-Sept: **Eastern States Exposition**
www.thebige.com; West Springfield (MA)

Highland Games at Loon Mountain
www.nhscot.org; Lincoln (NH)

late Sept–early Oct:

Northeast Kingdom Fall Foliage Festival
www.travelthekingdom.com
☏ *802-525-4386; Northeast Kingdom (VT)*

Annual Sheep and Wool Festival
www.vermontsheep.org
☏ *802-434-5646; Essex Junction (VT)*

late Sept–mid-Oct: **Fall Foliage Festival**
www.nberkshirechamber.com; Northern Berkshires (MA)

OCTOBER

early Oct: **Pumpkin Festival**
www.pumpkinfestival.com
Keene (NH)

late Oct: **Haunted Happenings**
www.salemhauntedhappenings.org
☏ *978-744-3663; Salem (MA)*

early Nov: **Maine Brewer's Festival**
www.mainebrew.com;
Portland (ME)

Thanksgiving Day: **Plimoth Plantation: Thanksgiving Celebration**
www.plimoth.org
☏ *508-746-1622; Plymouth (MA)*

NOVEMBER

Nov–mid-Mar: **Vermont Mozart Festival**
www.vtmozart.com
☏ *802-862-7352; Burlington (VT)*

late Nov–Dec: **Nantucket Noel**
www.nantucketchamber.org
☏ *508-228-1700; Nantucket (MA)*

DECEMBER

early Dec: **Woodstock Wassail Celebration**
www.woodstockvt.com
☏ *802-295-7900; Woodstock (VT)*

Festival of Trees & Traditions
www.wadsworthfestival.com
☏ *860-278-2670; Hartford (CT)*

Dec 31: **First Night Boston**
www.firstnight.org
☏ *617-542-1399; Boston (MA)*

Shopping

Business Hours

Businesses generally operate Monday–Friday 9am or 10am to 5pm; some retail shops may stay open until 9pm on Thursday. Shopping centers: Monday–Saturday 9:30am to 8pm or 9pm, Sun 11am–6pm. Banking hours: Monday–Thursday 10am to 3pm or 4pm, Fri 10am–5pm; some banks stay open later on Friday. Banks in larger cities may open on Saturday morning.

What to Buy

New Englanders have unique habits when it comes to shopping—residents buy more ice cream and less gold jewelry than the rest of America, for example—but shopping options suit all tastes. You'll find everything from quaint general stories to mega-outlet malls, as well as a Boston street that rivals New York's Fifth Avenue.

If you're seeking that classic "country store" experience, visit the region's villages and small towns. Vermont, as expected, has lots of country stores, some quite posh, and full of local cheeses and other foodstuffs. The ultimate is the **Vermont Country Store**, in Weston, which stocks everything from penny candy to flannel night-gowns, plus a range of hard-to-find gadgets and gizmos.

Another shopping standout, this one in Maine, is **L.L. Bean**'s mammoth flagship store in Freeport, open 365 days a year. This store is such a tourist attraction, a whole neighborhood of outlet stores has grown up around it. Maine is also home to the **Kittery Outlets**, in Kittery, making the state a go-to shopping destination, especially for outdoor gear and clothing. Look for other major outlet shopping zones and malls in North Conway, New Hampshire, Manchester, Vermont, Clinton, Connecticut, and Wrentham, Massachusetts.

If your idea of shopping bliss is finding that fabulous designer jacket marked down to nearly nothing, you'll experience shopping nirvana at the original **Filene's Basement**. Located in Boston's **Downtown Crossing**, "the basement" features clothing, shoes, accessories, and housewares culled from high-end stores such as Barney's New York and Neiman Marcus. All price tags have a date stamped on the back, and the price drops as time passes. Again, a whole zone of discount stores has flourished around Filene's Basement, with everything from shoes to diamonds offered at

a discount at Downtown Crossing, a pedestrian-friendly shopping zone. If price is no object, or you simply like the ambience of picturesque brown-stone townhouses chock-a-block with stores and boutiques, head to Boston's **Newbury Street**. Interspersed with shopping places are sidewalk cafes and galleries, making up an eight-block stretch that's also prime for people-watching.

New England's huge population of college students has also had an impact on the shopping scene. College towns, in particular, offer lots of shopping in the "cheap-and-chic" category, and lots of used book and music stores, vintage clothing stores, and places to drape your dorm room in neo-bohemian style. One example: the **Garment District**, "an alternative department store" in Cambridge, Massachusetts, where you can buy recycled clothing by the pound.

Savvy shoppers also take advantage off New England's **museum shops**. Nearly every museum, even the smallest, has a store that features unique gift items, books, and other merchandise you won't find in your local shopping mall.

What are some "uniquely New England" things to buy? **Food** plays a big part: Vermont cheese and maple syrup, of course, and products made from Maine blueberries and Massachusetts cranberries. Rhode Island's gift shops (and some grocery stores) offer take-home mixes for local treats such as Del's Lemonade and johnnycakes and coffee syrup, so Ocean State visitors can whip up coffee milk (coffee syrup mixed with milk) once

🙂 A Bit of Advice 🙂

If you see a small storefront shop that says "Spa" but doesn't look like a place to get a facial, it's because convenience-type stores were called "spas" back in the old days. And if you hear someone from Massachusetts mention "the packy" or "package store," they're referring to a liquor store. (Alcohol isn't sold in grocery stores in the state.)

Antiquing in New Hampshire

they return home. Maine and New Hampshire have a lock on the "moose" category. Local gift shops will help you decorate your entire home in a moose theme, should you desire, or you can simply pick up a pair of earrings adorned with moose droppings (true!). **Wineries** in Vermont, Rhode Island and Massachusetts offer wines made with local grapes. Meanwhile, Connecticut is home to scores of antique shops; shops and galleries in coastal towns specialize in nautically-themed art and artifacts.

Some of New England's most interesting shopping opportunities can be found in antique shops and farmers' markets. Here's where to find both.

ANTIQUING

Displayed in elegant Boston shops or in simple roadside stands along rural roadways, New England antiques will delight both the seasoned and novice collector in variety and quality. **Auctions**, typically listed in the Thursday and weekend editions of local newspapers, are a bargain-hunter's dream. The following organizations provide dealer listings:

- Woodbury in Litchfield County is one of Connecticut's best antiquing towns: www.antiqueswoodbury.com.
- *Antique Hunter's Guide to Route 7*, A&L Travel Guides, P.O.

Box 488, Waitsfield, VT 05673; ☏ 802-496-3062.
- Maine Antique Dealers' Association Directory; www.maineantiques.org.
- New Hampshire Antiques Dealers' Association, www.nhada.org.
- Vermont Antiques Dealers' Association Directory, c/o Elizabeth Harley, Yellow House Antiques, 88 Reading Farms Rd., Reading, VT 05062 *(include a self-addressed-double stamped envelope)*; www.vermontada.com.

FARMERS' MARKETS AND MAPLE SUGARING

During the New England harvest season (mid- to late June through early October), many farmers sell fresh-grown **produce** at modest prices at roadside stands. Visitors can also pick their own fruits and vegetables (for a small fee) at farms open to the public. Look in the Thursday calendar sections and weekend editions of daily newspapers for listings.

Maple syrup is harvested in the spring. Farmers collect sap from maple trees and boil down the watery substance into syrup. Visitors are welcome at a number of sugarhouses. For listings, contact the Vermont Dept of Agriculture *(www.vtmaple.org)* or the New Hampshire Dept. of Agriculture *(www.nhfarms.com)*.

BASIC INFORMATION

Electricity

Electrical current in the US is 110 volts AC, 60 Hz. Foreign-made appliances may need voltage transformers and North American flat-blade adapter plugs (available at specialty travel and electronics stores).

Emergencies

In all major US cities, you can call the police, an ambulance or the fire department by dialing **911**. Emergencies may also be reported by dialing **0** for the operator.

Liquor Laws

The legal age for the purchase and consumption of alcoholic beverages is 21 throughout New England; proof of age may be required. Liquor stores and many grocery and drug stores sell liquor. Almost all grocery stores sell beer and wine.

Major Holidays

Most banks and government offices in the New England states are closed on the legal holidays shown in the chart below (many retail stores and restaurants remain open on days indicated by an asterisk*):

Mail

First-class postage rates within the US: letter 39¢ (1oz), postcard 24¢. Overseas: letter 84¢ (1 oz), postcard 75¢ (see the Yellow Pages phone directory under "Mailing Services" or "Post Offices"; www.usps.gov). Most post offices are open Monday–Friday 9am–5pm; some are open Saturday 9am–noon.

Money

CURRENCY

The American **dollar** is divided into 100 cents. One **penny** = 1 cent; one **nickel** = 5 cents; one **dime** = 10 cents; one **quarter** = 25 cents.

Holiday	States Observing	Date
New Year's Day		January 1
Martin Luther King's Birthday*		3rd Monday in January
Presidents' Day*		3rd Monday in February
Town Meeting Day*		1st Tuesday in March
Patriots' Day*		3rd Monday in April
Memorial Day		Last Monday in May or May 30
Independence Day		July 4
Victory Day*		2nd Monday in August
Bennington Battle Day*		August 16
Labor Day		1st Monday in September
Columbus Day*		2nd Monday in October
Veterans Day*		November 11
Thanksgiving Day		4th Thursday in November
Christmas Day		December 25

BANKS

Most banks are members of the network of Automated Teller Machines (ATMs), allowing visitors from around the world to withdraw cash using bank cards and major credit cards. ATMs can usually be found in banks, airports, grocery stores and shopping malls. To inquire about ATM service, locations and transaction fees, contact your local bank; Cirrus (☎ 800-424-7787); or Plus (☎ 800-843-7587). You can send money, have money wired to you, or send a **telegram** via **Western Union** (☎ 800-225-52274; www.westernunion.com).

CREDIT CARDS AND TRAVELER'S CHECKS

Most banks will cash traveler's checks and process cash advances on major credit cards with proper identification. Traveler's checks are accepted at most stores, restaurants and hotels. To report a lost or stolen **credit card**, call the issuing bank or credit card company: American Express (☎ 800-668-2639; www.americanexpress.com); Diners Club (☎ 800-234-6377; www.dinersclub.com); MasterCard (☎ 800-622-77478; www.mastercard.com); Visa (☎ 800-847-2911; www.visa.com).

CURRENCY EXCHANGE

Most main offices—and some branch offices—of national banks will exchange foreign currency for a small fee. Boston's Logan International Airport has several currency-exchange offices (Travelex World Wide Money; ☎ 800-228-9792 www.travelex.com). **Thomas Cook Currency Services** (☎ 800-223-7373; www.thomascook. com) and **American Express Travel Services** (☎ 800-346-3607; www. americanexpress.com) operate exchange offices throughout New England.

Senior Citizens

Many of New England's attractions, parks, hotels and restaurants offer discounts to visitors age 62 and older (proof of age may be required). Discounts on lodging, car rentals and other travel-related services are available to members of the Alliance for Retired Americans (8403 Colesville Rd., Suite 1200, Silver Spring, MD 20910; ☎ 301-578-8422; www.retiredamericans.org). Discounts are also available to members of AARP, formerly the American Association of Retired Persons (601 E St. NW, Washington, DC 20049; ☎ 202-434-2277; www.aarp.org).

Smoking Regulations

Many cities throughout New England have ordinances that prohibit smoking in public places or confine smoking to designated areas.

Taxes and Tipping

Prices displayed or quoted in the US do not generally include the **sales tax**. Sales tax is added at time of purchase and is not reimbursable as in other countries (it can sometimes be avoided if the buyer requests purchased items be shipped to another state or country).

State taxes vary from state to state (☙ see chart above). New Hampshire has no sales tax.

In the US it is customary to give a **tip** (a small gift of money) for services

Equivalents									
Degrees Fahrenheit	95°	86°	77°	68°	59°	50°	41°	32°	23°	14°
Degrees Celsius	35°	30°	25°	20°	15°	10°	5°	0°	−5°	−10°

1 inch = 2.54 centimeters	**1 quart** = 0.946 liters
1 foot = 30.48 centimeters	**1 gallon** = 3.785 liters
1 mile = 1.609 kilometers	**1 pound** = 0.454 kilograms

State Sales Tax				
State	General Sales Tax	Room Tax	Restaurant Tax	Exemptions
⊛	6%	12%	6%	Clothing purchases under $50, grocery items
⊛	5%	7%	7%	Grocery items
⊛	5%	5.7–12.4%	5%	Articles of clothing under $175, grocery items
⊛	none	8%	8%	None
⊛	7%	7%	7%	Clothing and grocery items
⊛	6%	9%	9%	Articles of clothing under $110, grocery items

received from restaurant servers, porters, hotel maids and taxi drivers. It is customary in restaurants to tip the server 15–20% of the bill (unless the menu specifies that the gratuity is included). At hotels, porters should be tipped $1 per suitcase, and hotel maids $1 per night of stay. Taxi drivers are usually tipped 15% of the fare.

Telephones

To place an **international call**, dial **011**+country code+number. The cost for a local call from a pay phone is typically 25¢. Most hotels add a costly surcharge for local and long-distance calls. Telephone numbers that start with **1-800, 1-866, 1-877** or **1-888** are toll-free *(no charge)* and may not be accessible outside North America.

Time Zone

New England is on Eastern Standard Time (EST), 5hrs behind Greenwich Mean Time. Daylight Saving Time *(clocks advanced 1hr)* is in effect from the second Sun in Mar to the first Sun in Nov, beginning in 2007.

Typical New England Fishing Village
©PhotoDisc, Inc.

NATURE

Framed by the White Mountains to the north and the Green Mountains to the west, New England's gently rolling hills and valleys taper off to an irregular rockbound coastline edged with sandy beaches to the south. Vast woodlands coupled with an extensive river and stream system complete the picture. The region's major mountain ranges are remnants of higher peaks that were formed 300 million to 500 million years ago. Much younger in geologic age, the numerous ponds, lakes, U-shaped valleys and winding ridges owe their existence to the Laurentide ice sheet and associated glaciers that covered this portion of the North American continent until about 10,000 years ago.

Geographic Features

APPALACHIAN MOUNTAINS

The Appalachians, extending about 1,600mi from Canada's St. Lawrence Valley to Alabama, form the spine of New England. Several parallel ranges with a primarily north-south orientation make up the northeastern Appalachian system.

THE WHITE MOUNTAINS

These once heavily glaciated mountains, characterized by rocky, cone-shaped summits and U-shaped valleys, claim the highest peak in the northeastern US: Mt. Washington (6,288ft).

THE GREEN MOUNTAINS

The most prominent peaks in Vermont form a north-south ridge through the center of the state. Composed of ancient metamorphic rocks, including Vermont's rich marble deposits, this mountain chain extends into Massachusetts, where it is known as the Berkshires.

THE TACONIC RANGE

Extending along the common border of New York and Massachusetts, and into southern Vermont, this range, comprised primarily of schist, includes Mt. Equinox in Vermont and Mt. Greylock in Massachusetts.

THE MONADNOCKS

Several isolated mountains, called monadnocks, the remnants of ancient crystalline rock more resistant to erosion than the surrounding rock strata, dominate the countryside. Mt. Monadnock in New Hampshire exemplifies this type of relief; its name has been adopted by geographers to describe similar formations found elsewhere. Other monadnocks include mounts Katahdin and Blue in Maine, mounts Cardigan and Kearsage in New Hampshire, and Mount Wachusetts in Massachusetts.

THE CONNECTICUT VALLEY

New England is bisected by this 400mi-long, north-south incision carved by the Connecticut River. The valley follows a fault that is punctuated by several craggy basalt ridges (mounts Sugarloaf and Holyoke) rising above the valley floor in Massachusetts and north of New Haven, Connecticut.

Bass Harbor, Maine

Brigitta L. House/MICHELIN

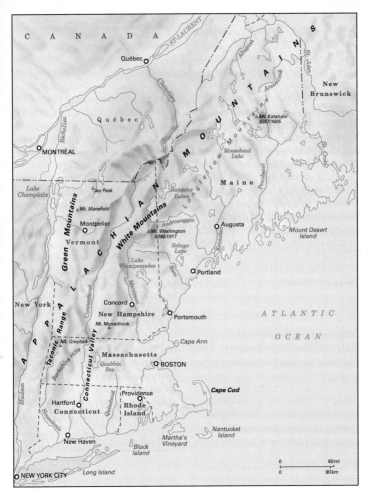

THE COAST

In the north the coast is jagged and indented, with countless peninsulas and bays and hundreds of offshore islands. Melting glacier waters, together with a rising sea level, inundated this land, hiding most of the glacial landforms and creating a coastline of elongated bays and hundreds of offshore islands. South of Portland, Maine, the broad, flat coastal plain gives way to sandy beaches. The estuaries and lagoons of quiet water protected by barrier beaches have given rise to vast salt marshes that provide food and resting grounds for birds and waterfowl in the Atlantic Flyway. Farther south, enormous accumulations of sand cover the glacial moraines of Cape Cod and the islands, creating the landscape that typifies the Cape.

Climate

Mark Twain once observed that "there is a sumptuous variety about the New England weather, that compels admiration—and regret....In the spring I have counted 136 different kinds of weather inside of 24 hours." This varied climate results from the fact that the region lies in a zone where cool, dry air from Canada meets warm, humid air from the southeast. Annual precipitation averages 42in, and the seasons are sharply defined.

Winter is cold, particularly in the north, where temperatures can range from –10°F to 10°F (–23°C to –12°C).

A pattern of hazy or foggy days alternating with showers and followed by clear weather characterizes the humid **summer**. Daytime temperatures peak at 90°F (32°C); evenings are cool along the coast, in the mountains and near the lakes. **Autumn**, with its sunny days and cool nights, is the season when "leaf lookers" inundate New England to view the spectacular fall foliage. A cool spell in late September is often followed by **Indian summer**, a milder period when the leaves take on their most brilliant color.

Northeasters, coastal storms accompanied by high tides, heavy rain (or snow in winter) and gale-force winds, can occur at any time of year, especially off the coast of Maine.

Vegetation

With more than 70 percent of the region's surface covered by woodlands, New England's landscape is appealing in the summer for its thick cover of green, and even more so in the fall for its blazing leaf colors. The forests consist of a combination of deciduous trees and evergreens. The most common deciduous trees are beech, birch, hickory, oak, and sugar or rock maple. Among the conifers, the white pine is found while hemlock, balsam fir and spruce forests abound in the north.

FALL FOLIAGE

Dramatic and unforgettable, the colorful New England foliage transforms the countryside into a palette of vivid golds (birches, poplars, gingkos), oranges (maples, hickories, mountain ash) and scarlets (red maples, red oaks, sassafras and dogwoods), framed by the dark points of spruce and fir trees. What makes the scene especially impressive are the flaming crimsons of the maple trees that cover New England. The Indian summer climate, with its crisp, clear sunny days followed by increasingly longer and colder nights, catalyzes the chemical reaction that halts the production of chlorophyll in the leaves, and causes the previously concealed pigments—yellowish carotene, brown tannin, and red anthocyanin—to appear.

Leaves begin to change color in the northern states in mid-September and continue to change until mid-October, and until late October farther south. However, the first two weeks in October remain the most glorious period, when bright color blankets the New England landscape. In all six states, information centers provide foliage reports by telephone. *See p33 and fall foliage driving itineraries pp16-19.*

SUGAR MAPLES

Capable of adapting to a cold climate and rocky soil, the sugar or rock maple

Fall Foliage, Vermont

Vermont Department of Tourism and Marketing/ Andre Jenny

Jack-in-the-Pulpit

Aster

Wild Lupine

Lady's Slipper

R. Corbel/MICHELIN

is found throughout Vermont and New Hampshire. In early spring, when the sap begins to rise in the maple trees, farmers insert a tube, from which a bucket is suspended, into the trunk. The sap that collects in the bucket is transferred to an evaporator in a nearby wooden shed called a sugarhouse, where it is boiled down into syrup. It takes about 40 gallons of sap to produce one gallon of syrup. Modern technology has simplified this process; now, plastic tubes lead directly from the tree to the sugarhouse. *Visitors can watch this process at many New England sugarhouses;* *see p 40.*

MARSHES AND BOGS

Because of its glacial origin, the soil in New England is often swampy. Vast marshlands, distinguished by tall grasses and reedy plants, line the region's coast. Bogs, wetlands characterized by the high acid content of the soil, support plants such as sedges, heaths, orchids, Labrador tea, sphagnum moss and, in low-lying sandy areas, cranberries. Dead matter that accumulates in the bog is prevented from decaying because of the acidic environment, and over a period of time this material is transformed into peat. Gradually the surface of the bog may be covered with a thick, soggy mat of sphagnum moss. Peat deposits will support trees and shrubs, and eventually vegetation will fill in the bog, converting it into dry, forested land.

WILDFLOWERS

By late spring the mantle of snow has almost disappeared and the flowers in the woods, along the roadside and in the fields and mountains burst into bloom. The magnificent **rhododendron** and **laurel** bushes lend pink accents to the dark green woods. During the summer the roadsides are alternately tinted with the orange of the flowering **Turk's-cap lily**, the yellow of the tall-stemmed **goldenrod**, the pale blue of the multitude of tiny **asters** and the purplish hue of broad, swaying patches of **lupine**. Maine's mountains and woods are filled with wild blueberries. Hundreds of species of more familiar wildflowers, including buttercups, daisies, sunflowers, Queen Anne's lace and lily-of-the-valley, adorn the fields and grassy meadows. In moist, marshy areas, look for the delicate **lady's slipper**, a small pink or white member of the orchid family, and the greenish **Jack-in-the-pulpit**, so named because of the curved flap that gives the flower its appearance of a preacher in a pulpit.

Rhododendron

Turk's-Cap Lily

Mountain Laurel

Goldenrod

R. Corbel/MICHELIN

Wildlife

There are virtually no forms of wildlife unique to New England, yet several species are typical of the region's fauna.

THE FORESTS

The **white-tailed deer**, characterized by its white, bushy tail, inhabits the northern spruce and fir forests together with **black bears** and **moose**. The region's largest mammal and the state animal of Maine, moose may be encountered in the middle of forest roads, along marsh lands and boggy areas. Outfitters in northern New Hampshire and Maine offer a variety of moose-watching excursions, including guided kayak, canoe, pontoon, seaplane, and bus trips. Greenville, Maine, near Moosehead Lake, hosts MooseMainea, a popular festival held each fall.

In ponds and streams, colonies of **beavers** toil, felling trees with their teeth to build dams. Their structures often create deep ponds or cause flooding in low-lying areas.

Among the other forest inhabitants are the masked **raccoon**, the **porcupine** with its protective bristly quills, the black-and-white-striped **skunk**, and the **red squirrel**. The **chipmunk**, a member of the squirrel family, is a small mammal that frequents settled areas as well as woodlands.

THE COAST

Seagulls and **terns** are ever-present along the coast, always searching for food on boats, on the beaches, in inlets and marshes and on the piers that line the waterfront. The **great cormorants** are larger in size and live principally on the rocky sea cliffs that they share with several species of seals.

Coastal marshes serve as the feeding and resting grounds for hundreds of species of birds. Located along the Atlantic Flyway, broad stretches of salt marshes, such as those west of Barnstable Harbor on Cape Cod, are frequented by large numbers of bird-watchers during the spring and fall migrations. Flocks of Canada geese, their graceful V-formation a familiar sight in the New England sky during migratory seasons, rest in these tranquil areas. Puffins have nesting and feeding grounds on northern Maine islands and bald eagles and hawks can be seen along the coastline.

New England waters are home to a variety of species of **whale, dolphin and porpoises**. Whales migrate here to their feeding grounds at Stellwagen Bank, a 19-by-5-mile underwater plateau between Gloucester and Provincetown, Massachusetts, that is the centerpiece of the Stellwagen Bank National Marine Sanctuary. The region has been called one of the best places in the world to see whales in the wild. Several whale watching cruises sail from major towns along the coast, including Boston, Gloucester, Provincetown, Plymouth, Newburyport and Salem, Massachusetts; Portsmouth, New Hampshire; and Ogunquit, Maine.

Moose in a Bog

HISTORY

Time Line

EXPLORATION

1497   **John Cabot** explores the coast of North America.

1602   The English explorer **Bartholomew Gosnold**, sailing south along the New England coast, names Cape Cod, the Elizabeth Islands and Martha's Vineyard.

1604   The Frenchmen **Samuel de Champlain** and **Pierre de Gua, Sieur de Monts**, explore the Maine coast.

1607   Virginia Colony, the first permanent English settlement in North America, is established at Jamestown.

1613   The Jesuits establish a mission on Mt. Desert Island, Maine.

1614   **Captain John Smith** returns to England with a cargo of fish and furs. The term "New England" is used for the first time in his account of the voyage.

COLONIZATION

1620   The Pilgrims arrive on the **Mayflower** and establish Plymouth Colony.

1630   **Boston** is founded by Puritans led by **John Winthrop**.

1635   **Thomas Hooker** leads a group of settlers from Massachusetts Bay Colony to the Connecticut Valley and founds Hartford Colony.

1636   **Harvard College** established. **Roger Williams** flees the intolerance of Massachusetts Bay Colony and establishes Providence, Rhode Island.

1638   **Anne Hutchinson** settles on an island near present-day Portsmouth, Rhode Island.

1639   The **Fundamental Orders of Connecticut**, the governing document drawn up by members of Hartford Colony, is regarded as the New World's first constitution.

1701   Yale University is founded.

1763   The Treaty of Paris ends the French and Indian War (1756-63). France cedes Canada and territories east of the Mississippi to Britain.

INDEPENDENCE

1765   The **Stamp Act**, a direct tax levied by Britain on the American colonies, is passed.

1766   The Stamp Act is repealed.

1767   Parliament passes the **Townshend Acts**.

Landing of the Pilgrims, after a painting by H. Sargent

Library of Congress

1770 The majority of the Townshend Acts are repealed, but the tax on tea remains.

1773 Colonists stage the Boston Tea Party at Boston Harbor.

1774 Parliament passes the four **Coercive Acts**—called the **Intolerable Acts** by the colonists. Colonists who oppose Britain's policies hold the **First Continental Congress**.

1775 Outbreak of the **American Revolution**:
April 18 – Ride of Paul Revere.
April 19 – Battles of Lexington and Concord.
May 10 – Siege of Fort Ticonderoga by Ethan Allen and the Green Mountain Boys, along with Benedict Arnold and his men.
June 17 – Battle of Bunker Hill.

1776 British troops evacuate Boston on March 17. The **Declaration of Independence** is adopted on July 4.

1777 Vermont declares its independence and adopts its own state constitution.

1780 French forces led by General Rochambeau arrive in Newport, Rhode Island, to aid the American revolutionaries.

1781 Colonists defeat British troops led by General Cornwallis at Yorktown, Virginia.

1783 End of the American Revolution.

1788 The US Constitution is ratified. Connecticut, Massachusetts and New Hampshire are admitted to the Union as the fifth, sixth and ninth states, respectively.

1789 **George Washington** is chosen as the first president of the US.

1790 Rhode Island becomes the 13th state.

1791 Vermont, the last New England colony to join the Union, is admitted as the 14th state in the US.

19C AND 20C

1812 Britain declares war on the US.

1814 The Treaty of Ghent ends the War of 1812 on Christmas Eve.

1820 Maine enters the Union as the 23rd state.

1861-65 **Civil War**

1905 The Treaty of Portsmouth, ending the Russo-Japanese War, is signed at the Portsmouth Naval Base in Kittery, Maine.

1914-18 **World War I**

1929 Stock market crash signals the start of the Great Depression.

1939-45 **World War II**

1944 Bretton Woods Conference is held in New Hampshire.

1954 World's first nuclear-powered submarine is constructed in Groton, Connecticut.

1961 At age 43, John F. Kennedy from Massachusetts becomes the youngest man ever to be elected US president.

1963 On November 22, President Kennedy is assassinated in Dallas, Texas.

1966 Massachusetts attorney general Edward W. Brooke is the first African American elected to the US Senate since Reconstruction.

1976 The Liberian tanker **Argo Merchant** runs aground near Nantucket Island and spills 7.5 million gallons of crude oil into the North Atlantic.

1980 Boston celebrates its 350th anniversary.

1983 **Australia II** wins the America's Cup by defeating the American yacht **Liberty** in the best of seven races off the coast of Newport, Rhode Island.

1985 Vermont voters elect the nation's first foreign-born woman governor, Madeleine M. Kunin.

1988 Democratic candidate Michael Dukakis, former governor of

Massachusetts, loses the US presidential election to George Bush.

1990 Twelve works of art, valued at $100 million, are stolen from the Isabella Stewart Gardner Museum in Boston.

1992 Mashantucket Pequot Indians open Foxwoods, a resort casino in Connecticut.

1993 The Norman Rockwell Museum at Stockbridge opens in Massachusetts.

1994 **Harvard University**, the most generously endowed of private universities ($6 billion), launches largest fundraising drive in the history of higher education.

1995 **Boston Garden**, one of the oldest sports arenas in the nation, is torn down and replaced by a new sports and entertainment complex.

Part of the largest public works project in the US (the "Big Dig"), Boston's new Ted Williams Tunnel opens, connecting the city to Logan Airport.

1997 From its Charlestown berth, the **USS Constitution**, America's oldest commissioned warship afloat, sails under its own power for the first time in 116 years.

1998 The worst ice storm of the century hits the Northeast, killing trees and causing power outages in Maine, New Hampshire and Vermont.

1999 The **Massachusetts Museum of Contemporary Art** (MASS MoCA) opens in a renovated factory in North Adams.

The second major milestone of the Big Dig project—the Leverett Circle Connector Bridge—opens, connecting downtown Boston to I-93 in Charlestown.

THE NEW MILLENNIUM

2000 The first US census of the new century is conducted, revealing the growth patterns of the towns and cities of New England as well as the nation.

Nearly 5,000 workers are employed in the $14 billion Big Dig project.

2001 On September 11, two Boeing 767s departing from Boston's Logan Airport are hijacked by terrorists and crashed into the World Trade Center in New York City.

2002 **New England Patriots** win the Super Bowl.

Leonard P. Zakim Bunker Hill Bridge, part of the Big Dig project, is completed.

2003 New Hampshire's **Old Man in the Mountain** rock formation collapses.

100 people killed in **Rhode Island** night club fire. Anglicans elect first openly gay bishop in New Hampshire.

2004 **New England Patriots** win the Super Bowl.

Massachusetts is first in the nation to recognize gay marriages.

Massachusetts senator John Kerry accepts the Democratic presidential candidate nomination.

Boston Red Sox win the World Series, the team's first title in 86 years.

George W. Bush defeats Kerry in presidential election.

Boston's new Convention and Exhibition Center opens.

2005 **New England Patriots** win the Super Bowl.

2006 A ceiling panel in Boston's Ted Williams Connector Tunnel collapses, killing one woman and forcing Logan airport traffic to be rerouted until repairs on this section of the Big Dig are completed.

New England and the Sea

New England has been closely related to the sea ever since the colonists turned from the rocky soil to the off-shore waters for their food. At first the colonists erected weirs, similar to those used to this day by the Indians in Maine to snare fish near the shore. Not until the mid-17C did Yankee vessels sail in large numbers to the Grand Banks, the fishing grounds off the southern coast of Newfoundland, which teemed with cod, haddock and pollack. The Sacred Cod, hanging in the Massachusetts State House in Boston, symbolizes the important role played by the cod fisheries in the history of Massachusetts. New England's fisheries became the backbone of the region's trade with Europe, and boatyards sprang up along the coast from Connecticut to Maine to construct fishing and cargo vessels.

Fisheries, trade and shipbuilding prospered, reaching their zenith in the mid-19C. The south (Connecticut, Rhode Island and southeastern Massachusetts) was home to the Yankee whaling fleet; ports along the northern coast of Massachusetts and New Hampshire led the trade with the Orient (the China trade) and the ship-building industry. With its protected inlets and thick forests, the Maine coast focused on wooden shipbuilding. Between 1830 and 1860, nearly one-third of the boats launched in the US were built in Maine.

Small coastal villages grew into sophisticated urban centers, as merchants, ship-masters and sea captains accumulated great wealth and built the handsome Federal and Greek Revival homes that still stand in Salem, Nantucket, Portsmouth, Newburyport, New Bedford, Providence and other seaport cities.

Several large museums preserve New England's seafaring past. Mystic Seaport and the whaling museums in New Bedford, Nantucket and Sharon recall the Yankee whaling tradition. In Salem the Peabody Essex Museum presents the story of New England's trade with the Orient, and the Maine Maritime Museum (Bath) and the Penobscot Marine Museum (Searsport) portray the history of shipbuilding in Maine.

WHALING

During the 19C whale oil was used to light homes and streets across America and Europe. New Bedford and Nantucket, leading whaling centers, were busy day and night with vessels arriving, departing or preparing for whaling voyages. Herman Melville's novel *Moby Dick* (1851) vividly re-creates New England's whaling days.

A Prized Catch

The sperm whale, averaging 63 tons, was hunted in large numbers; it was the species on which New England's whaling industry depended for candles, fuel, and perfumes.

A Meteoric Industry

Indians were hunting whales long before the first settlements were established. The colonists learned how to hunt inshore whales by observing the Indians. They built tall watchtowers and set up large black cauldrons, called try-pots, in which the whale fat was melted down, on the beaches. In the 18C the discovery of sperm whales in deep ocean waters led to the construction of larger vessels that were outfitted for long ocean voyages. By 1730 Yankee whalemen had moved the tryworks from the beaches to the decks of whaling vessels so they could process whales at sea.

In the late 18C Nantucket boasted a fleet of 150 whaling vessels; in its heyday, New Bedford was the home port of nearly 400. New London, Provincetown, Fairhaven, Mystic, Stonington and Edgartown also launched fleets. Shipyards turned out sturdier ocean-going vessels, factories manufactured spermaceti candles, tons of baleen were dried in the fields and thousands of barrels of whale oil were stored along the wharves. Whaling ships built, owned and commandeered in New England sailed the oceans from Greenland to the North Pacific, from the Azores to Brazil, and from Polynesia to Japan. Many languages could be heard as seamen from international ports of call walked the streets of New England's waterfront districts.

The decline of the whaling industry in New England was precipitated by the discovery of petroleum in Pennsylvania in 1859 and the loss of nearly half of New England's whaling fleet during the Civil War years. In 1861 the Union Navy purchased 39 whaling ships to form the "Stone Fleet," a group of vessels that were loaded with blocks of granite and sunk in the harbors of Savannah, Georgia, and Charleston, South Carolina, to prevent blockade runners from entering those channels. The Confederate ship *Shenandoah* destroyed an additional 21 whaling vessels in the north Pacific Ocean in 1865. After the war New England sent out fewer and fewer whalers. In 1971, whale hunting was finally outlawed in the US.

MARITIME COMMERCE

New England's maritime commerce with Africa, Europe and the West Indies brought prosperity to many of its coastal ports in the early 18C, but not until after the Revolution, when Americans were free to trade with the Orient, did Boston, Providence, Portsmouth, Salem and other cities develop into rich centers of the China trade.

China Trade

Boats sailing to the Far East rounded Cape Horn, then generally made detours to ports along the way to obtain returns—goods that could be traded in China for silk, porcelain and tea. Furs were acquired along the northwest Pacific coast, sandalwood from the Sandwich Islands, and the delicacy *bêche-de-mer* (sea grub) from the Polynesian Islands. Later, when opium replaced furs, boats called at ports in India and Turkey to barter for the illicit drug before continuing to China.

Other exotic products obtained along the route were pepper purchased in Sumatra, sugar and coffee from Java, cotton from Bombay and Madras, ivory from Zanzibar, spices from Indonesia and gum arabic from Oman.

Until 1842 Canton was the only Chinese port open to foreign trade. Vessels anchored about 10 miles outside the city at **Whampoa Reach**. Several weeks or even months could be spent visiting shops and factories and bartering with Chinese merchants before the foreign vessel, filled with a cargo of luxury items, set sail for home.

The museums and historical houses of New England exhibit countless examples of Chinese decorative arts and furnishings brought back to America from the Orient during the years of the China trade.

Ice: A New England Industry

The ice trade developed in the 19C when ice was harvested north of Boston and in Maine, and shipped to the southern states, the West Indies and as far away as Calcutta to be used for refrigeration. Ice was harvested in the winter, when the rivers, lakes and ponds were frozen over. Snow was cleared with the aid of oxen or horses. The ice field, marked off into squares, was cut into blocks weighing up to 200 pounds each. Packed in sawdust and stored in nearby icehouses until the first thaw, the ice was then transported by boat to its destination. Boats with specially constructed airtight hulls were used to prevent the ice from melting. The ice business prospered until the introduction of mechanical refrigeration in the late 19C.

SHIPBUILDING

The wooden sailing vessel has been the basis of New England's shipbuilding tradition since 1607, when the pinnace *Virginia* was built by the short-lived Popham colony on the banks of the Kennebec River in Maine.

Early Days

As the colonists established their first settlements, shipyards began to dot the coast. At first they built small, one-masted ketches and fishing sloops, followed in the early 18C by two- and three-masted schooners capable of crossing the Atlantic. The schooner enjoyed a long and glamorous career in the waters off the New England coast. When English dominance of American trade led to widespread smuggling by the colonists, it was the schooner, with its simple rigging, ease of handling, and ability to evade British revenue ships, that carried many an illicit cargo safely into port. During the American Revolution, armed, privately owned schooners (privateers) were authorized by the Continental Congress to capture enemy vessels. The schooner remained in service as a cargo carrier until the end of World War I.

Age of the Clipper Ship

With the opening of Chinese ports in the 1840s, Americans clamored for Chinese goods. Knowing that American customers would pay high prices for the freshest teas from the Orient, shrewd shippers demanded faster vessels to transport this perishable commodity in the shortest possible time. The clipper—derived from the word *clipper,* which was used to describe any person or thing that traveled quickly—was designed to meet their needs. Between the mid-1840s and the mid-1850s, these three-masted vessels, with their lean hulls, narrow bows and acres of canvas sails, became famous for the great speeds they could attain. During the California Gold Rush, clippers with names such as *Lightning, Flying Cloud* and *Eagle Wing* carried miners and supplies from the Atlantic coast, around Cape Horn, to San Francisco, and sailed the long ocean routes to the Orient.

The major boatyards working to turn out these ships were located in New York, Boston, and Bath, Maine, and the master designer was **Donald McKay** of East Boston. Of the approximately 100

vessels that made the voyage around Cape Horn in less than four months, 19 of them, including the *Flying Cloud,* were built by McKay. The first ship to round the Cape to San Francisco in under 90 days, the *Flying Cloud* set a record of 89 days on her maiden voyage in 1851, and repeated it three years later. The record has since surpassed.

Last Sailing Ships

From the 1850s to the early 1900s, the ports of Maine specialized in the production of commercial wooden sailing vessels: the **down-easter** and the **great schooner**. The down-easter, a three-masted square-rigger, had the long, clean lines of a clipper, and could attain comparable speeds. Unlike the clipper, the down-easter had a large, deep hull that offered greater carrying space.

The down-easters and two- and three-masted schooners were used in shipping until the 1880s, when boat builders discovered that four-masted schooners, though larger, cost little more to operate. The construction of the great schooners—four-, five- and six-masted vessels—followed. These ships hauled large bulk cargoes (coal, lumber, granite, grain) from the East Coast, around Cape Horn and up to the West Coast. Striving to compete with the steamboat, Maine shipyards turned to the production of a small fleet of steel four-, five- and six-masters. The profitable days of sailing were numbered, however: the efficient, regularly scheduled steamer triumphed.

ART AND CULTURE

Best known for its Colonial architecture, New England nevertheless retains a rich heritage of building traditions from all periods, ranging from practical Indian dwellings to the magnificent seaside estates of the Gilded Age and the high rises of post-Modernism. A plethora of art museums, artist galleries and studios, gardens, historic homes, antique shops, and more showcase New England's rich artistic heritage and thriving arts community. New England has been home to some of America's greatest writers, from Henry David Thoreau and Robert Frost to popular modern-day authors, like Robert Parker and Stephen King. Some of the region's famous writers are laid to rest on Authors' Ridge at the Sleepy Hollow Cemetery in Concord, Massachusetts.

Architecture

NATIVE AMERICAN

The traditional Algonquin dwelling was not the familiar tepee of the Great Plains but the **wigwam**, a domed or conical hut made of bent saplings covered with reed mats or bark. Quick and easy to build, these snug shelters were adopted as temporary housing by the first Massachusetts colonists until they could construct timber-framed homes. Wigwams built in the traditional manner may be seen at Salem's Pioneer Village and at the Institute for American Indian Studies in Litchfield Hills.

EARLY COLONIAL

The prevailing early-Colonial dwelling was the two-story post-and-beam house, characterized by a steeply pitched roof originally designed to support thatch. Several examples dating from about 1660 to 1720 still exist in Connecticut (Buttolph-Williams House in Wethersfield) and in the early Massachusetts Bay town of Ipswich (Parson Capen House) and at Plimoth Plantation in Plymouth. Settlers, finding an unlimited timber supply in the new country,

continued a building technique that was already familiar. The typical house plan comprised two large, multipurpose rooms with exposed beams and a massive center chimney hugged by a narrow stairway leading to chambers above. Clad in shingles or clapboard siding, the exterior featured small casement windows with diamond-shaped glass panes imported from England. When the steep roof extends almost to the ground over a rear kitchen lean-to, the house is known as a **saltbox**. Built low to brace against shoreline winds, the smaller, one-and-a-half-story **Cape Cod cottage** features a pitched or bowed roof.

By court decree all 17C New England villages were laid out according to a similar plan, with the houses set around a park-like central **green**, or common, to provide protection against Indians and assure close proximity to the **meeting house**, the largest building in a settlement.

GEORGIAN

This term generally refers to an English architectural style developed by such noted architects as Christopher Wren and James Gibbs and popularized in America from about 1720 until the Revolution (during the reigns of Kings George II and III) largely through pattern books and British-trained builders. Based primarily on the design principles of ancient Rome, this style incorporated the Classical orders, especially Doric, Ionic and Corinthian.

Dignified and formal, the high-style Georgian house proved ideally suited to the tastes of a growing mercantile class. Mansions in wood, stone or brick

R. CORBEL/MICHELIN

Early Colonial

Georgian

R. CORBEL/MICHELIN

soon appeared in every major port city. Crowned by a pitched, hipped or gambrel roof, the Georgian house featured a symmetrical facade accentuated with even rows of double-hung windows. Often a central projecting pavilion front with a Palladian window and a pedimented portico graced the entryway. Heavy quoins (stone or wood blocks) typically marked the corners, and the elaborate front door was topped by a round-arched fanlight and a sculptural pediment.

A central-hall plan with end chimneys accommodated larger rooms (now with specific uses such as dining and music), robust wood carving and plaster decoration, and colorful paint treatments. In rural farm towns the Georgian house frequently retained the old center-chimney plan but boasted ornate exterior features, such as the heavy swan's-neck door pediments used in the Connecticut River Valley (Deerfield). Several Georgian public buildings were designed by **Peter Harrison** (1716-75), perhaps America's most important colonial architect. Harrison's Redwood Library in Newport is based on a Roman temple. His Touro Synagogue, also in Newport, and King's Chapel in Boston are notable for their interior paneling.

During this period many New England churches gained their familiar front towers and steeples, often adapted from the published designs of Wren (Trinity Church) or Gibbs (First Baptist Church in America).

FEDERAL

Popular from about 1780 to 1820, this British Neoclassical style, sometimes called Adam style, was first adopted in America by an affluent merchant class, primarily Federalists who retained close trade ties to England even after the Revolution. Bostonian **Charles Bulfinch** (1763-1844) was New England's best-known Federal-period architect, responsible for Beacon Hill's Massachusetts State House, while **Samuel McIntire** (1757-1811) designed Federal-style structures for the city of Salem.

Like its Georgian counterpart, the high-style Federal mansion, often with bowed or rounded walls, was symmetrical, and its central door was topped by a Palladian window (Harrison Gray Otis House in Boston). But the overall appearance was far lighter and more conservative, with proportions elongated, exterior decoration reduced and fanlights flattened from half-rounds into ellipses.

The style is most notable for its refined interior decor, influenced by the work of British architect **Robert Adam**. Oval and round rooms were introduced, along with graceful freestanding staircases and exquisitely decorated fireplace mantels and surrounds. Extremely popular, Federal-style design eventually spread to even the most modest of farm- and village houses and churches throughout New England (look for the telltale elliptical front-door fanlight).

GREEK REVIVAL

The Greek Revival style was popular from about 1820 to 1845. While the Georgian and Federal styles were based on Roman prototypes, the new architectural mode adhered to ancient Greek orders and design principles, notable for squarer proportions, a more monumental scale and less surface ornament. Imitative of Greek temples, buildings in

Federal

R. CORBEL/MICHELIN

Greek Revival

the style were almost always white and usually featured the so-called "temple front." This two-story portico with Doric, Ionic or Corinthian columns supported an unbroken triangular pediment at the roof line.

Among the educated elite the Greek Revival style represented a symbolic link between the republic of ancient Greece and the new American nation. It was adopted for many impressive public buildings, including marble or granite courthouses, banks, libraries (Providence's Athenaeum), churches (United First Parish Church) and temples of trade (Providence's Arcade), as well as for domestic architecture. Elegant Greek Revival-styled mansions appeared in affluent towns and seaports (Whale Oil Row in New London).

Among the major designers of the period were **Alexander Parris** (Quincy Market in Boston) and **Robert Mills** (Custom House). **Asher Benjamin**, who wrote some of the most influential builder's handbooks in America, designed many New England churches (Boston's Old West Church) and fine Bostonian homes (Nos. 54-55 Beacon Street).

19TH-CENTURY VERNACULAR

A distinctive feature of rural New England is the **covered bridge** (West Cornwall and Windsor). In 1820 noted New Haven architect Ithiel Town (Center and Trinity Churches in New Haven) patented the **lattice truss**, the interwoven framework visible on the inside of the bridge. The roof, of pine or spruce, was designed to protect the structural elements from harsh weather. The **connected farm**, a complex of attached houses, barns and animal sheds prevalent in northern New England in the mid-19C, developed as old outbuildings were moved from farm property and added to the main residence.

Along the coast, 19C **lighthouses** mark harbor entrances and dangerous shoals. These structures originally included a tower and beacon, first lit with oil lamps and parabolic reflectors, as well as housing for the keeper, who was often a US customs agent. Many lights can be visited by the public (Sheffield Island in Norwalk; Owl's Head in Rockland).

Still visible in many industrial towns are 19C **textile mills**, originally powered by water turbine (steam power became common in the 1850s). Manned largely by cheap immigrant labor, mills were designed as self-contained complexes and typically included railroads, parks, canals, churches and employee housing. Punctuated by rhythmic rows of windows and an occasional clock tower or smokestack, these granite- or brick-walled buildings, usually five or more stories, can stretch for miles along a riverfront. Some complexes now contain museums (the National Historic Park in Lowell); others have been converted to house small business and retail outlets (Lowell's Amoskeag Manufacturing Complex).

VICTORIAN ECLECTICISM

During the Victorian era (1837-1901), classical design was abandoned in favor of a broad range of styles, many inspired by the dark, romantic architecture of medieval Europe. Pointed-arch windows, steeply pointed gables and gingerbread cornice boards are hallmarks of the picturesque **Gothic Revival** style (Kingscote) that is also seen in board-and-batten **Carpenter's Gothic** villas and cottages. Other Victorian-era styles include **Italianate** (square towers, flat or low-pitched roof and broad porch; Victoria Mansion); **Second Empire** (mansard roof, ornate cornice and round dormers; Boston's Old City Hall); and **Queen Anne** (turrets, spindlework, asymmetrical porches, bay windows and gingerbread trim; Oak Bluffs, Martha's

Italianate

R. CORBEL/MICHELIN

Vineyard). In the early 1870s Boston architect **Henry Hobson Richardson** developed Romanesque Revival (also known as Richardsonian Romanesque), a distinctly American style rooted in the Medieval architecture of France and Spain. His masterpiece, Trinity Church in Boston, incorporates the characteristic squat columns, round arches and heavy, rough-cut stone. Favored for seaside resorts were the **Shingle** style (dark wood shingles, towers and piazzas, steeply pitched roofline and asymmetrical facade; Newport's Hammersmith Farm and Casino) and **Stick** style (gabled roof, rustic woodwork with diagonal bands, contrasting paint colors, decoratively shaped shingles; Newport's Art Museum and Mark Twain House in Hartford).

TURN OF THE CENTURY

Late in the 19C architects trained in the academic principles of the prestigious École des Beaux-Arts in Paris rejected the eccentric Victorian styles. Typical of the highly decorative **Beaux-Arts** style are great estates such as The Breakers and Marble House (both in Newport) by the fashionable society designer **Richard Morris Hunt**, and grandiose public buildings (Boston Public Library).

Developing at the same time was the **Colonial Revival** style, which drew on America's own Colonial architecture, reinterpreted on a larger scale. A Palladian window, classical columns, swan's-neck pediments and a large entry portico are typical features. Promoted by

such prestigious architectural firms as **McKim, Mead and White** (Rhode Island State House), the style was used primarily for Georgian Revival town houses and country estates from about 1900 to 1920 (North and South Streets in Litchfield).

CONTEMPORARY ARCHITECTURE

New England attracted many of the European architects who brought the **International Style** to America in the 1930s, including **Walter Gropius** (1883-1969), founder of the German design school known as the **Bauhaus**. Representative of **early Modernism**, which rejected ornament and historical references and embraced machine-age technology and materials, is the 1938 Gropius House, a streamlined cubic design incorporating the then-new materials of glass block, acoustical plaster and chrome. Among other innovative modernist works is **Eero Saarinen's** 1955 M.I.T. Chapel in Cambridge. The heir of early Modernism was the so-called **glass box** design, ubiquitous in the 1960s in the construction of multistoried urban apartments and public buildings. An unusual example is the 1963 Beinecke Library at Yale University by **Gordon Bunshaft** of **Skidmore, Owings and Merrill**, designed with self-supporting walls of translucent marble. Many glass boxes appeared in New Haven, Boston and other New England cities during periods of widespread urban redevelopment that resulted in the demolition of older buildings. In concert with the growing preservation movement of the last two decades, innovative design programs have, however, helped save endangered structures .

Since the early 1970s innovators Robert Venturi, Robert Stern, Philip Johnson and others have developed **post-Modernism**, a movement promoting a deliberate return to ornament. Familiar historical motifs such as the classical pediment are often playfully exaggerated, used as the dominant crowning element of a building, for example. The Palladian window is simplified, even caricatured, or the classical column is reduced to a plain shaft, topped by a ball rather than a traditional capital. Unexpected exterior color combinations are another feature. In recent years New England campuses and city skylines, notably Boston (222 Berkeley Street and 500 Boylston Street), Providence and Hartford, have become national showcases for buildings in the style, which emphasizes scale, compatible materials and the relationship of a building to its neighbors.

Visual and Decorative Arts

PAINTING

From the beginning of the colonial period to the late 17C, painting was appreciated primarily for its practical uses for trade signs and portraiture.

18th-Century Development

The arrival of Scottish painter **John Smibert** (1688-1751) in America in 1729 initiated the era of professional painting. His works, such as *Bishop Berkeley and his Entourage* (Yale University Art Gallery, New Haven), served as models for the Americans who studied with him, including **John Singleton Copley** (1738-1815), America's first important portraitist. Copley painted the well-known persons of his day (*Paul Revere*, Museum of Fine Arts, Boston), rendering his subjects amazingly lifelike.

Rhode Islander **Gilbert Stuart** (1755-1828) was the most important American painter of the period. Although he is best remembered for his portraits of George Washington, Stuart in fact painted only three portraits of the president from life, using these as models for his later works. The most well-known of these, *George Washington (The Athenaeum Portrait)*, was begun in 1796 and never finished. It now hangs in the Smithsonian's National Portrait Gallery in Washington, D.C.

19th Century

Following the American Revolution, the opening of the West led to an increased awareness of the vast scale and beauty of the nation, and the American scene became a popular theme for artists. Painters of the **Hudson River school** in the 1820s followed the lead of **Thomas Cole** and **Albert Bierstadt** by setting up their easels outdoors and painting directly from nature. Their favorite New England subjects were the White Mountains and the Connecticut Valley. The sea was a source of inspiration for other artists. **Fitz Hugh Lane** (1804-65), living in Gloucester, illustrated in soft, glowing tones the serene beauty of the sea and the offshore islands. New Bedford artist **William Bradford** (1823-92), fascinated by maritime themes and the northern lights, depicted the rising and setting of the arctic sun, and whalers sailing among icebergs (New Bedford Whaling Museum).

Beginning in the 1860s, Americans began to live and study abroad for longer periods of time. Italian-born **John Singer Sargent** (1856-1925) traveled extensively in Europe and won acclaim as the portraitist of the international social set. The career of the self-taught watercolorist and master of the naturalist movement, **Winslow Homer** (1836-1910), began during the Civil War, when Homer served as an illustrator for *Harper's Weekly*. He is known for large canvases of the sea that he painted during summers at Prout's Neck, Maine.

20th Century

Several painters,have been identified with New England. **Grandma Moses** (1860-1961) illustrated themes associated with rural New England (*Sleigh Ride; Sugaring-Off*).

Norman Rockwell (1894-1978), for many years an illustrator for the *Saturday Evening Post,* painted a chronicle of American life. His principal works can be viewed in Stockbridge. Born in 1917, **Andrew Wyeth** has spent several summers in Maine. The Wyeth Family Center at the Farnsworth Art Museum in Rockland exhibits a large group of his works.

SCULPTURE

Sculpture consisted predominantly of folk art—shop and trade signs, weather vanes, figureheads—until the 19C, New Hampshire-born **Daniel Chester French** (1850-1931) and **Augustus**

Saint-Gaudens (1848-1907), who lived his later years in New Hampshire, trained abroad and exerted a strong influence on American sculpture from the period following the Civil War until the early 20C. French became known for his statue *The Minute Man* (Concord, MA), while the monumental seated *Lincoln* (Lincoln Memorial in Washington, DC) is recognized as his most impressive achievement.

Saint-Gaudens executed delicate, bas-relief portrait plaques and monumental sculptures, such as the Shaw Memorial in Boston, for which he is best remembered.

In more recent times, award-winning sculptor **Louise Nevelson** (b. 1900), who was born in Russia, grew up in Rockland, Maine. By the mid-1950s, she had developed the style for which she is best known: open boxes of monochromatically painted wood stacked to form a freestanding wall. Her work may be seen at the Farnsworth Art Museum in Rockland. Among other New England locations, sculptural works (particularly contemporary sculpture) are on view at the DeCordova Sculpture Park in Lincoln, Massachusetts and the sculpture garden at the Aldrich Museum of Contemporary Art in Ridgefield, Connecticut, as well as on the campuses of Yale University and Massachusetts Institute of Technology.

FURNITURE

American furnishings were influenced from colonial days through the 19C by European, and particularly English, designs.

Pilgrim

Furniture made between 1620 and 1690—tables, chairs, Bible boxes and chests—reflect the Medieval influences of the English Tudor and Jacobean styles. Oak is the principal wood used. The Connecticut-made Hadley, Guilford and Sunflower chests ornamented with carved and painted floral designs or geometric motifs are characteristic of this period.

William and Mary

This style was in vogue from 1689 to 1702 during the reign of William of Orange and his wife, Mary. The Flemish influence and contact with the Orient introduced such techniques as japanning (floral or scenic designs on lacquered wood surfaces) and turning (wooden pieces shaped on a lathe). Japanned highboys, chests with bold turnings, and chairs with caned or leather backs were popular during these years.

Queen Anne

Curved lines, such as the gracefully shaped cabriole leg, are a stylistic feature of furniture made between 1720 and 1750. Maple, walnut and cherry are the woods typically used; decoration is minimal.

The **Windsor chair**, unrelated to the Queen Anne style, was imported from England in the early 18C and remains popular in America.

Chippendale

London cabinetmaker Thomas Chippendale borrowed elements of French Rococo and Chinese art in creating the

William and Mary

Queen Anne

Windsor

R. CORBEL/MICHELIN

Chippendale

wide range of furniture forms illustrated in his design manuals. Pieces from 1750 to 1785 are generally fashioned of mahogany, with curved legs (ending in the ball-and-claw foot) and chair backs pierced with lacy fretwork. The **Goddard and Townsend** families of Newport, Rhode Island, were among the most celebrated cabinetmakers working in this style.

Federal

Inspired by British architect **Robert Adam** and English cabinetmakers **George Hepplewhite** and **Thomas Sheraton**, the style that won favor from 1785 to 1815 is defined by light, straight lines and refined decoration: veneers, inlay and marquetry in contrasting woods. The square, tapered leg—fluted, reeded or ending in a spade foot— is common. Cabinetmakers working in the Federal style included John and Thomas

Seymour and John and Simeon Skillin of Boston.

Empire

Imported from Europe, this heavy, massive style, popular from 1815 to 1840, was inspired by Greek and Egyptian antiquity. Bronze, gilt, winged and caryatid supports, lion's-paw feet, rolled backs on chairs, and sofas with upswept ends distinguish this style.

Victorian

Furniture of the period between 1840 and the late 19C, inspired by a variety of styles including Gothic, Elizabethan, Renaissance and French Rococo, is heavy and ornate. Upholstered chairs and sofas are overstuffed, and velvet coverings are typical. Balloon-back and fiddleback chairs, and tables with marble tops were popular.

Shaker Furniture

Produced primarily from 1800 until the middle of the 19C, Shaker chairs, tables and cupboards, simple and functional, are admired for their clean, pure lines and superb craftsmanship. Shaker chairs are recognized by their ladder backs, and seats made of rush, cane, splint or woven webbing.

FOLK ART

In rural New England, necessities for daily living were handmade by the farmers themselves or by tradesmen who received a modest fee for their services. The tools, household utensils, cloth, weather vanes and furniture they produced revealed the tastes, flair and loving attention to detail of their creators. Today these items are admired for their unsophisticated charm, and for the picture of early rural American life they present.

Quilts

Quilted bed coverings were essential during the long, cold New England winter. Often finished in a geometric or floral motif, the quilt became one of a rural household's few decorative accessories. Quilting had a pleasant social aspect as well: the **quilting bee**.

Hepplewhite

Vermont Department of Tourism/ Andre Jenny

Pumpkin Farm, VT

Stencils

This early decorative technique, which uses paint and precut patterns to embellish furniture, implements, cloth, floors and walls, brightened the interiors of many homes. Wall stenciling added color to the otherwise plain white plaster or wooden plank surfaces, and in the 19C it was a low-cost alternative to expensive imported wallpapers.

Weather Vanes

When most New Englanders farmed or went to sea, weather vanes were important as indicators. The simple profile of a weather vane topped most buildings of any significant height. A weather vane made to crown a church spire might be in the shape of a cockerel or fish, the symbols of early Christianity. In rural areas the silhouette of a cow, horse or sheep rose above farm buildings, while along the coast, the whale, clipper ship and mermaid were popular. New England's famous grasshopper weather vane, atop the cupola of Boston's Faneuil Hall, has been the symbol of the port of Boston since the 18C.

Figureheads, Trade Signs and Shop Figures

During the age of sailing, carvers sculpted figureheads, sternboards and other accessories for new vessels. Excellent examples of figureheads can be found in the maritime museums in

Mystic, CT; New Bedford, Nantucket and Salem, MA; and Shelburne, VT.

Ship carvers also produced trade signs and shop figures. The streets of the Old Port Exchange in Portland are lined with such eye-catching signs.

Glass

Until the mid-19C most glass manufactured in New England was in the form of window glass and glass containers. Handmade glassware was a luxury only a few could afford. However, Deming Jarves and his workmen at **Sandwich** made available, for the first time, attractive glassware at affordable prices. The factory at Sandwich became famous for pressed glass with patterns that resembled lace. Despite large-scale production of pressed glass, the art of glassblowing continued to thrive. Items varied from tableware to decorative art glass and may be seen at the Glass Museum in Sandwich, and at the Bennington Museum in Vermont.

Scrimshaw

Perfected by New England sailors in the 19C, scrimshaw, the art of etching the surface of the teeth or jawbone of a whale, or the tusks of a walrus, is considered by some the only art form indigenous to America. The tooth or tusk was allowed to dry, then the surface was polished with shark skin, and the picture or design to be etched was incised onto

Courtesy Mystic Seaport Museum

Scrimshaw - Whale's Tooth

the bone with a jackknife or sail needles. Ink, soot or tobacco juice was applied for color. Exceptional scrimshaw collections can be found at the whaling museums in New Bedford, Nantucket and Sharon.

Decoys

Wooden decoys sculpted and painted to resemble geese, ducks, shorebirds and waterfowl have been used since colonial times to lure birds within range of the hunter. By the 19C decoy-making had developed into an art form. Craftsmen portrayed birds with increasing realism, taking into consideration the natural conditions where the decoys would be used. Craftsmen along the coast from Cape Cod to Maine still engage in producing these lures. The Shelburne Museum in Vermont owns a fine collection of over 1,000 decoys.

Gravestones

The Puritans have left outstanding examples of the skill of their early stonecutters in the gravestones that stand in New England's old burial grounds. The designs were initially symbolic and plain. In the 17C the hourglass, sun, scythe, winged skull, hearts and cherubim (symbols for life, death and resurrection) were typical motifs. Throughout the 18C realistic portraits and detailed scenes of the death of the deceased became popular. The romantic tendencies of the 19C were represented by extensive use of the weeping willow and the urn, classical symbols for death.

The old cemeteries in Boston, Lexington, Newburyport and Salem (MA), and in New London (CT) and Newport (RI) contain splendid examples of gravestone art.

Literature

The literature produced in the colonies in the 17C and 18C consisted primarily of histories and religious writings. The *History of Plimoth Plantation* by William Bradford, governor of Plimoth Plantation between 1621 and 1657, remains one of the principal records of this period.

COMING OF AGE

In the 19C a literature distinctly American emerged in New England. The transcendentalist movement gained popularity under the leadership of **Ralph Waldo Emerson** (1803-82.) **Henry David Thoreau** (1817-62) recounts his life in the woods in *Walden* (1854.) **Louisa May Alcott** (1832-88) became famous for her novel *Little Women*. Other writers included **Nathaniel Hawthorne** (1806-64), author of *The Scarlet Letter* (1850) and *The House of the Seven Gables*, and **Herman Melville** (1819-91), who wrote *Moby Dick* in 1851 while living in the Berkshires. Hartford resident **Mark Twain** (1835-1910) was a master of the new regional literature. His most popular works, *The Adventures of Tom Sawyer* (1876) and *Adventures of Huckleberry Finn* (1885), portrayed life on the Mississippi River. In 1828 **Noah Webster** (1758-1843), a native of New Haven, published the first *American Dictionary of the English Language*.

20TH CENTURY

In the 20C the American theater won international acclaim through the works of playwright **Eugene O'Neill** (1888-1953). New England was the setting for his *Desire Under the Elms, Mourning Becomes Electra* and the Pulitzer Prize-winning *Beyond the Horizon*. Other New England authors include native-born John P. Marquand, Kenneth Roberts, William Dean Howells and Jack Kerouac as well as writers who adopted New England as their second home, including Edith Wharton, Pearl Buck, Norman Mailer and Alexander Solzhenitsyn. Harvard graduate **John Updike**, perhaps best known for his novels *Rabbit Run, Rabbit Redux* and Pulitzer

Prize-winning *Rabbit is Rich* (1981) and *Rabbit at Rest* (1990), moved to Ipswich in the 1960s. He used New England as the setting for much of his later fiction, including *The Witches of Eastwick* (1984). Best-selling author **Stephen King**, a master of the horror genre, was born in Portland. The prolific writer has used New England, and in particular Maine, as the background for many of his short stories and novels, such as *Salem's Lot*, *It*, and *The Girl Who Loved Tom Gordon*. Former New Hampshire resident Bill Bryson has attracted more attention to the popular Appalachian Trail with his humorous best-seller *A Walk in the Woods* (1998).

POETRY

Henry Wadsworth Longfellow (1807-82), born in Portland, was one of the most widely read poets of his day. **Emily Dickinson** (1830-86), an Amherst resident, wrote verses rich in lyricism and sensitivity. Known for his poems about nature, **Robert Frost** (1874-1963) lived on a farm in New Hampshire from 1901 to 1909, and later spent his summers in Vermont. The poetry of **e.e. cummings** (1894-1962), a native of Cambridge, is distinguished by his unconventional use of typography and punctuation. Another New England-born poet whose work has made a significant impact on modern poetry is **Robert Lowell** (1917-77).

THE REGION TODAY

The economic evolution of New England paralleled that of the area's mother country. A period of intense agricultural activity was followed by maritime prosperity and then by industrialization, which formed the backbone of the economy through the 19C and into the 20C. After World War II the region fell into an economic slump, due to the movement of many of its factories to the South. As a result New England turned to new, diversified, high-value industries, such as electronics, as its principal sources of revenue.

New England's population of 13 million inhabitants is unevenly distributed; the majority live in the southern half of the region, where the largest cities (Boston, Worcester, Providence, Springfield, Hartford and New Haven) are found. The large waves of immigrants who arrived in the 19C brought with them a diversity of cultures that is still reflected in the ethnic character of the population today.

Economy

INDUSTRY

In the 19C profits from trade, shipping and whaling, together with the influx of immigrants from Europe and Canada—which provided the large labor force needed for industrialization—fostered New England's transformation into one of the world's leading manufacturing centers.

The Mill Towns

The region's many waterways compensated for the lack of raw materials and fuel by providing the power necessary to operate factory machinery. Mill towns, supporting factories that specialized in a single product, sprung up on the banks of rivers and streams. Textiles and leather goods were made in Massachusetts and New Hampshire, precision products such as clocks and firearms were manufactured in Connecticut, and machine tools were produced in Vermont. The large manufacturing centers in the Merrimack Valley—**Lowell**, Lawrence and **Manchester**—developed into world leaders in textile production. Strings of brick factories, dwellings and stores still dominate these cities.

During the 20C most of these industries moved south to the Sun Belt, but the region remained a leader in the manufacture of woolen cloth. The production of machine tools and fabricated metals has now replaced textiles, and the shoe industry is important in New Hampshire and Maine.

The New Industries

The rebirth of New England after World War II was linked to the development of its research-oriented industries, which could draw on the region's excellent educational institutions and highly trained personnel. These new industries, located essentially in the Boston area (on Route 128), in southern New Hampshire and in Hartford, contributed to advances made in space and computer technology and electronics. Their existence gave rise to the production of high-value goods, such as information systems, precision instruments and electronic components, and provided an increasing number of jobs. **Boston**, known for its medical research firms, is also home to producers of medical instruments and artificial organs.

AGRICULTURE

Despite the poor soil and rocky, hilly terrain, subsistence farming was an important activity until the mid-19C. In the spring settlers cleared land to ready it for planting. The mounds of rock they removed from the soil were used to build the low stone walls that appear to ramble aimlessly through the woods. Farming reached a peak in New England between 1830 and 1880 with 60 percent of the region under cultivation. After 1880 the opening of the fertile plains south of the Great Lakes drew farmers westward. They abandoned their farms, and the forests gradually reclaimed the land. Today only 6 percent of the surface of New England continues to be devoted to agriculture, while 70 percent of the region's land (90 percent in Maine and 80 percent in New Hampshire) remains covered with woodlands. Despite this fact, certain areas have been successful in cultivating single-crop specialties.

Dairy and Poultry Farming

The major portion of income from agriculture is provided by dairy and poultry farming. The region's dairy farms supply milk products to the sprawling urban areas of southern New England. Dairy farms, well suited to the terrain, predominate in Vermont, where large red barns with their shiny aluminum silos dominate the landscape.

Poultry farming is practiced throughout the region. Connecticut and Rhode Island focus on raising chickens. In fact, Rhode Island is famous for raising a breed of chicken called the Rhode Island Red.

Specialty Crops

Shade-grown **tobacco** is raised in the fertile Connecticut River Valley. Firm and broad-leafed, this tobacco, grown beneath a layer of netting and hung in large sheds to dry, is used as the outer wrapping of cigars. Fruit is cultivated in many areas: apple, peach and pear orchards extend along the banks of Lake Champlain and abound on the sunny slopes of New Hampshire, in the Connecticut and Nashua valleys and in Rhode Island. Maine leads all other states in production of lowbush **blueberries**, and the sandy bogs on Cape Cod and in nearby areas yield the nation's largest crop of **cranberries**, the small, red berries traditionally served as part of the Thanksgiving Day feast.

Maine's other specialty crop is potatoes, grown in the fertile soil of Aroostook County. The state's potato industry ranks in the top ten in the nation.

Forests

Despite the enormous area that they cover, New England's deciduous and coniferous forests are not significant as sources of income because of large-scale deforestation of the region throughout the 19C. Today vast tracts of land are under federal and state protection. Only the commercial timberlands owned by the large paper companies in northern Maine and New Hampshire constitute important sources of revenue. A major portion of the timber harvested is processed into wood pulp for the mills in Maine and New Hampshire, with Maine's factories ranking among the world's leading paper producers. Other plants and mills transform timber into a variety of wood products, including lumber, veneer, furniture and boxes. The production of **maple syrup** is a traditional springtime activity in Vermont, New Hampshire and Maine.

FISHING

As early as the 15C, European fishermen were drawn to the rich fishing grounds off the coast of New England. These shallow, sandy banks (such as George's Bank), extending 1,500mi east-to-west off Cape Cod, teemed with fish. The fishing industry was so vital to New England that fishermen were exempt from military service, and Massachusetts Bay Colony adopted the cod as its symbol. Commercial fishing has been especially important to the ports of Gloucester, New Bedford and Boston. Modern techniques of filleting, freezing and packaging fish, and larger, more efficient vessels have made New England a leader in the packaged and frozen seafood industry. However, the region's fishing industry has seen dramatic curtailment over the past three decades, stemming from overfishing (particularly of cod, flounder, tuna and haddock), pollution and insufficient conservation. More recently, stringent federal regulations have been proposed to reduce stock depletion.

Lobstering ranks as an activity approaching an art in Maine, where it is practiced by thousands of Down East lobstermen, who can often be observed in a variety of craft, checking their traps in the off-shore waters. Maine lobster is a delicacy that is shipped to markets across the nation.

INSURANCE

Insurance has been an important business in New England since the 18C, when investors offered to underwrite the risks involved in international shipping. With the decline of sea trade, the insurance industry expanded to include losses due to fire, and the center of the industry shifted inland. Hartford, Connecticut, a national insurance center, is the seat of a substantial number of insurance companies. The modern office towers built in Boston to serve as headquarters of the John Hancock and Prudential insurance companies are the tallest structures in New England, symbolizing the importance of this industry to the economy.

EDUCATION

Traditionally renowned as a national center of culture and learning, New England is home to four prestigious Ivy League universities (Harvard, Yale, Brown and Dartmouth) and two choice preparatory schools (Phillips Exeter Academy in Exeter, New Hampshire, and Phillips Academy in Andover, Massachusetts). The concentration of schools, academies and some 258 institutions of higher learning in the six-state area makes education a significant contributor to the economy. Small businesses in cities (Worcester, New Haven, Providence) and towns (Middlebury, Hanover, Brunswick, Amherst) depend on the revenue generated by the schools within their borders. In Massachusetts, the state's 80 private colleges alone have generated $10 billion in revenue.

TOURISM

Tourism ranks with manufacturing as one of New England's major industries. Mountain and seaside resorts in New England have been welcoming visitors

Lobster Traps

for over a century, and with the growing popularity of winter sports since the 1940s, the region has developed into a year-round vacation area. Fine handicrafts, fashioned by artisans working in New Hampshire, Vermont and along the coast, abound throughout New England. Their sale depends to a great extent on tourists.

Population

The **Indians** of the Algonquian Nation were the first to inhabit the region. They were woodland Indians, who farmed, hunted, fished and camped along the coast. The largest group, the **Narragansett** tribe of Rhode Island, was virtually wiped out by the English colonists in the Great Swamp Fight during King Philip's War. Similarly the **Pequot** tribe of Connecticut was decimated by colonists and enemy tribes in the Pequot War of 1637. Today the Mashantucket Pequot Indians operate a number of successful enterprises near Mystic. Present-day descendants of the **Passamaquoddy** and **Penobscot** tribes live on reservations at Pleasant Point and Old Town in Maine. Members of the **Wampanoag** tribe make their home on Cape Cod and Martha's Vineyard.

Descendants of the 17C and 18C Puritan settlers dominated New England's population until the mid-19C. Hard work, frugality and "Yankee ingenuity"—the talent for making the best of any situation—characterized these early New Englanders, some of whom amassed great fortunes in trade and shipping, and later in industry and finance.

The population remained basically homogeneous until the 1840s, when the potato famine in Ireland caused thousands of **Irish** to emigrate to New England, where they found work in the mills. The **Italians** followed in the 1870s, and at the end of the 19C **French Canadians**, attracted by jobs in the region's factories, began to settle here. Communities of **Portuguese** fishermen from the Azores developed in coastal ports such as Gloucester, Provincetown and Quincy, while successive waves of immigrants brought **Swedes**, **Russians** and other **Eastern Europeans** to the cities and factory towns. As Boston's **African-American** community vacated the North End for Beacon Hill, the Irish, followed by the Jews and eventually the Italians, made the North End their home. Each ethnic group formed its own cohesive neighborhood, where the unity of language, culture and religion drew them together. Irish, Italians and Jews tended to settle in or near the large cities, while the Portuguese continue to reside in the coastal areas. French names are common in northern New England, where French Canadians form a significant part of the population. The majority of the region's black and **Hispanic** populations reside in southern New England.

Culinary Traditions

New England has a well-deserved reputation for simple, hearty fare. In addition to seafood, the region boasts regional specialties ranging from maple syrup and Vermont cheddar cheese to Boston cream pie. Country inns and taverns serve traditional Yankee fare, while waterfront clam shacks and dockside lobster pounds offer the best in seafood dining experiences. In Boston, you'll find a big-city array of fine restaurants and ethnic food.

NATIVE AMERICAN TRADITIONS

Many local dishes trace their roots to the New England Indians, who were the first to make maple sugar, **cranberry sauce**, **Johnnycakes** (fried cornmeal patties) and **Indian pudding**. Slow-cooked **Boston baked beans** flavored with molasses and salt pork also derive from a native recipe, as does their traditional accompaniment, **brown bread**.

FISH AND SHELLFISH

Brook trout is a popular freshwater fish, while swordfish and tuna, **bluefish** and **striped bass** are saltwater favorites. **Lobster** is the king of shellfish, **Blue mussels** grow in clusters around shoreline rocks; try them steamed in wine and herbs. Equally popular are **clams**, harvested by rake from the sandy bottoms

©Comstock Images

Lobster Dinner

of warm-water bays and salt ponds. Fall and winter are the seasons for tiny, delicate **bay scallops** and **oysters**. Another Indian custom, the famous New England **clambake** is served up from a beach-dug pit where potatoes, onions, unhusked corn, chicken, lobsters and clams are layered in seaweed over heated stones for hours of slow steaming.

CHOWDERS AND STEWS

Thought to have originated with settlers from the Channel Islands, **chowders** are thick, slow-simmered soups traditionally made with milk and vegetables. Corn chowder is a regional specialty. Fish chowder usually features cod or haddock; steamers or quahogs, potatoes and onions—never tomatoes—are key ingredients of **clam chowder**.

FRESH PRODUCE

Seasonal favorites include wild fiddlehead ferns (spring), and strawberries (early summer). Maine is famous for its wild lowbush blueberries. Late summer produces vine-ripened tomatoes, corn on the cob and pumpkins. In autumn, stop at a pick-your-own orchard for cider and some of the best apples grown in the US.

MAPLE SYRUP

Come early spring, maple trees are tapped for sap, which is cooked down into a sweet syrup used for baking and as a topping for pancakes, waffles and ice cream. Vermont and New Hampshire lead New England in maple syrup production. The best quality is Grade A light amber, followed by Grade A medium and dark ambers.

Personalized gifts are an important part of any relationship.

Your company's name here

For reaching your customers, driving sales to your business, go for Michelin customized road maps and travel guides. Contact us via **www.b2b-cartesetguides.michelin.com** and we will work out with you a business solution to meet your needs.

Autumn in New Hampshire
©PhotoDisc, Inc.

CONNECTICUT

POPULATION: 3,405,565
AREA: 5,018SQ MI
CAPITAL: HARTFORD
OFFICIAL DESIGNATION: THE CONSTITUTION STATE
NICKNAME: THE NUTMEG STATE
STATE FLOWER: MOUNTAIN LAUREL
OFFICIAL WEB SITE: WWW.CTBOUND.ORG

This rectangle extending about 90mi east to west and 55mi north to south bears the name of the river that divides it almost in half: the Connecticut, an Indian word meaning "beside the long tidal river." Small colonial villages scattered throughout the state offer a pleasing contrast to the densely populated, industrialized centers in the Hartford region and to the cities of Stamford, Bridgeport, Stratford and New Haven on the south shore. The affluent communities in southwestern Connecticut's Fairfield County (Greenwich, Ridgefield, New Canaan) are, in essence, suburbs of New York City.

Connecticut is predominantly rural; two-thirds of its woodlands are included in the state park and forest system. To the south, on the shores of Long Island Sound, sandy beaches separate the former whaling ports of New London, Mystic and Stonington. The idyllic Litchfield Hills, rising in the northern part of the state, are an extension of the Green Mountains and the Berkshire Hills.

The Constitution State – The area's first permanent settlers were staunch Puritans who arrived from Massachusetts in 1633. The **Fundamental Orders of Connecticut**, statutes drawn up and adopted January 14, 1639, was the first constitution drafted in the New World—thus the state's nickname, the Constitution State.

Economy – Connecticut has traditionally been a prosperous manufacturing center. Connecticut clock makers created one of the state's earliest industries. The Colt .45 revolver, developed by **Samuel Colt**, and the Winchester rifle were made in Connecticut. During the same period, **Eli Whitney** manufactured his revolutionary cotton gin in New Haven. Connecticut continues to obtain a great part of its income

Mystic Seaport

Mystic Seaport, Mystic CT

from manufacturing. The Electric Boat Division of General Dynamics at Groton builds submarines for the nation's fleet. A number of corporations (General Electric, Union Carbide, Xerox) and more than 100 insurance companies maintain headquarters in the state.

Locally marketed dairy products, poultry, and fruits and vegetables are major sources of agricultural income. Broadleaf tobacco, used for cigar wrapping, is shade-grown in the Connecticut and Farmington valleys. Look for the picturesque tobacco sheds that dot the flat valley landscapes.

CONNECTICUT VALLEY★

MAP P 76

TOURIST INFORMATION ☎ 800-793-4480 OR WWW.CTTOURISM.ORG

Wide, shallow and bordered by unspoiled countryside, the Connecticut River flows into a multitude of coves and boat harbors on its more than 400mi journey downstream to Long Island Sound. Villages such as Old Lyme and Old Saybrook have retained their early character thanks to a sandbar at the mouth of the river that has always prevented deep-draft vessels from entering these waters.

The best ways to explore the valley are by following the suggested driving itinerary through small riverside towns, or by taking a cruise from East Haddam, Deep River or Essex. In the summer, ferry rides (3 hrs) from Haddam to Long Island are also available.

Driving Tour *26mi. Map p 76.*

▶ *From I-95, take Exit 69 (Old Saybrook), and follow Rte. 9 to Exit 3 in the direction of Essex.*

Connecticut CCT

Griswold Inn, Essex

Essex★

Established in 1645, Essex developed into an important shipbuilding center by the early 18C, and in 1775 produced Connecticut's first warship, the *Oliver Cromwell*. Today Essex attracts a sophisticated summer crowd who berth their yachts and cabin cruisers at local marinas. The town's main street consists of interesting shops, art galleries and the Griswold Inn, which has been operating since 1776. A former warehouse at Steamboat Dock houses the **Connecticut River Museum,** with maritime exhibits that include a model of the *Oliver Cromwell* (67 Main St.; ◷ open year-round Tue–Sun 10am–5pm; ◷ closed Jan 1 & Dec 25; ⌾ $7; ♿ ℗ ☎ 860-767-8269; www.ctrivermuseum.org).

Essex Steam Train and Riverboat

🄺 *Exit 3 off Rte. 9 Train departs from Essex Station mid-Jun–early Sept daily. Limited service rest of the year. Train to Chester (1hr round-trip) with connecting river cruises from Deep River to East Haddam (train & cruise: 2hr 30min round-trip). ⌾ $17.00 (train only), $26.00 (train & cruise). ℗ ✗ (riverboat). For schedules and information, contact Valley Railroad Co.; ☎ 860-767-0103; www.essexsteamtrain.com.* Rides on the railroad's early-20C steam train afford views of the bucolic valley landscape and the Connecticut River.

▶ *From Essex take Rte. 9 to Exit 6, then Rte. 148 to the ferry that crosses the river.*

Chester-Hadlyme Ferry

◷ *Departs from Chester Apr–Nov Mon–Fri 7am–6:45pm, weekends & holidays 10:30am–5pm.* ◷ *Closed Thanksgiving Day. One-way 5min. ⌾ $2.25 (car & driver). State Bureau of Aviation & Ports. ☎ 860-443-3856. www.chesterct.com/ferry.htm.*

During the crossing there is a good view of Gillette Castle, perched high on a hilltop above the east bank.

▶ *Take Rte. 148, then turn left, following the signs for Gillette Castle.*

Gillette Castle State Park★

◷ *Park open daily year-round 8am–dusk.* ◷ *Castle open Memorial Day-Columbus Day daily 10am–4:30pm. ⌾ $5 ✗ ☎ 860-526-2336. www.dep.state.ct.us/stateparks.*

The castles of the Rhine Valley inspired the design of this bizarre

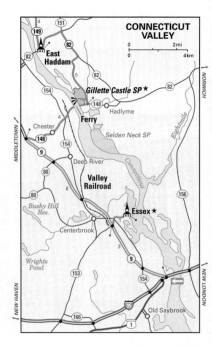

Gwen Cannon/ MICHELIN

Gillette Castle State Park

stone castle built in 1919 by actor **William Gillette**, who drew up the plans for the castle and decorated each of the 24 rooms himself. Furniture that slides on metal tracks and other devices were developed by Gillette, who had a fascination for gadgetry. The 190-acre estate offers splendid **vistas**★ of the Connecticut River and the valley below. On the grounds you'll find picnic areas and hiking trails.

▶ *Take Rte. 82 to East Haddam.*

East Haddam

This small town with beautiful old homes is proud of its little red **schoolhouse** where Nathan Hale once taught, and of being the site of the **Goodspeed Opera House**, a Victorian opera house dating from the era when New York-to-Connecticut steamers called at East Haddam. *Musicals are presented from Apr–Dec Wed-Sun. Ticket information: ☎ 860-873-8668, www.goodspeed.org.*

▶ *Follow Rte. 149, which offers good views of the river before turning northeast.*

HARTFORD★★

POPULATION 121,578
MICHELIN MAP 581 J 10 AND MAPS PP 78 AND 82
TOURIST INFORMATION ☎ 860-728-6789 OR WWW.ENJOYHARTFORD.COM

Rising beside the Connecticut River, the state capital also bears the nickname "Insurance Capital of the Nation." The headquarters of several major insurance companies are located here. The downtown holds a tight cluster of skyscrapers, a sprawling convention center and indoor shopping mall, several landmark buildings and some striking examples of 1980s architecture such as One Corporate Center.

▶ **Orient Yourself:** Bisected by east-west I-84/US6, the central core of the city lies off the west bank of the Connecticut River. The state Capitol building and spacious grounds dominate the southwestern corner of downtown. Diagonally to the northwest, across Asylum Ave., lies Constitution Plaza. Adjacent to it, in a southerly direction, sits the Old State House, on Main St.

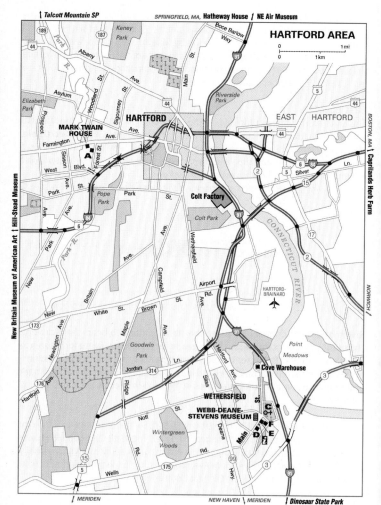

Parking: Parking is available off Market St. opposite Constitution Plaza and behind it, off Columbus Blvd.

Don't Miss: Wadsworth Atheneum Museum of Art (especially the Wallace Nutting furniture collection) and the Mark Twain House.

Organizing Your Time: After stopping in the Old State House (be sure to see the museum of curiosities), walk to the Wadsworth Atheneum and allow at least an hour to view the exhibits. An hour minimum is needed for Mark Twain House.

Especially for Kids: Children will love the house of the author of *Tom Sawyer*, especially Mark Twain's bed, in which he slept backward.

Also See: The historic village of Wethersfield, located 5mi south of Hartford.

A Bit of History

From Good Hope to Connecticut Colony – Hartford's location on a waterway navigable to the sea led the Dutch to establish a trading post, named Fort Good Hope, on this site in the early 17C. In the 1630s, the region's abundant supply of furs and timber attracted Puritans from the Massachusetts Bay Colony. Their village grew quickly, and in 1638 it joined with Wethersfield and Windsor to form Hartford Colony. In 1662 Hartford Colony joined New Haven Colony to become the Colony of Connecticut.

An Insurance Center – Hartford's insurance industry originated in the 18C when a group of men agreed to cover a ship owner's losses if his vessel did not return home safely. As shipping began to decline in the 19C, the industry shifted from marine to fire insurance.

Today's Economy – Manufacturing plays an important role in the city's economy. Pratt and Whitney Aircraft, the Colt Industries and producers of typewriters, precision instruments and computers are located in the Greater Hartford region. In recent years, the city has become a center for managed-health companies.
Extensive revitalization of Hartford's downtown area during the past several decades includes the construction of new shopping and business complexes, notably Constitution Plaza and the Civic Center. A new Convention and Exposition Center, along with a hotel, an entertainment complex, shops and restaurants recently opened on the banks of the Connecticut River.

Downtown *Map p 82.*

A staffed visitor center is located a half-block south of the Civic Center (31 Pratt St.). Downtown visitors can also obtain directions and information from the cadre of Hartford guides, recognizable by their red coats.

Hartford Civic Center
One Civic Plaza. ☎ 860-249-6333. www.hartfordciviccenter.com.
Completed in 1975, this concrete-and-glass structure is one of Hartford's premier entertainment venues. A pedestrian walkway links the center to CityPlace, designed by Skidmore, Owings and Merrill; exhibits and concerts are offered year-round in the atrium.
Diagonally across from the Civic Center, on Church Street, is the award-winning **Hartford Stage Company**. *Performances are presented by the company year-round. For specific information, call ☎ 860-527-5151 or access www.hartfordstage.org.*

Old State House★
800 Main St. Open year-round Tue–Fri 11am–5pm, Sat 10am–5pm. Closed major holidays. Visitor center has maps and brochures for Hartford and the state. ☎ 860-522-6766. www.ctosh.org.
This elegant Federal-style building (1792) with its graceful staircases, arches, balustrades and classical pediments was designed by Charles Bulfinch, the architect of the state houses of Maine and Massachusetts. Second-floor legislative chambers contain original furnishings; the Amistad trial began in the Senate chamber here. Don't miss the small Steward's Museum of Curiosities containing such oddities as a two-headed calf, also on the second floor.

Old State House

Address Book

The properties listed below were selected for their ambience, location and/or value for money. Prices reflect the average cost for a standard double room (two people) in high season (not including any applicable city or state taxes). Room prices may be considerably lower in off-season, and many hotels offer discounted weekend rates. The presence of a swimming pool is indicated by the ☃ symbol.

☙ *For price ranges, see the legend on the cover flap.*

WHERE TO STAY

The Goodwin Hotel – *Goodwin Square, 1 Haynes St. (opposite Civic Center), Hartford.* ⚒♿🅿☃ ☎ *860-246-7500 or 800-922-5006. www.goodwinhotel.com. 124 rooms.* **$$$$** A National Historic Landmark, this centrally located, bright-red brick 1881 Queen Anne building is the city's premier hotel. Many of the rooms have unusual features (fireplaces, marble baths, sleigh beds). Most luxurious: the J.P. Morgan Suite, so-named because the hotel was, indeed, the home of the famed financier.

Avon Old Farms Hotel – *279 Avon Mountain Rd., Avon.* ⚒♿🅿☃ ☎ *860-677-1651. www.avonoldfarmshotel.com. 157 rooms.* **$$$** Down the road from the Hill-Stead Museum, this attractive hotel features rooms ranging from motor-inn basic to country-inn luxury. Setting the tone are 400 local artists' watercolors depicting the Farmington River Valley, a three-story staircase worthy of Scarlett O'Hara, and an enchanting restaurant-in-the-round overlooking a mountain stream. An English-style pub, health club, pool and 20 acres of woods, trails and gardens round out the facilities.

Centennial Inn Suites – *5 Spring Lane, Farmington.* ♿🅿☃ ☎ *860-677-4647 or 800-852-2052. www.centennialinn. com. 112 units.* **$$$** A refreshing alternative to chain hotels and B&B's, the Centennial offers homey comforts in a modern all-suite complex that resembles a condominium development set on 12 rolling acres. Suites range from studio to two-bedroom, with fireplaces, cathedral ceilings with skylights, and well-equipped eat-in kitchens. Continental breakfast is offered in the

main building, a 200-year-old restored carriage house, as are weekday guest receptions. Dog lovers rejoice: Fido is welcome here.

WHERE TO EAT

The venues listed below were selected for their ambience, location and/or value for money. Rates indicate the average cost of an appetizer, an entrée and dessert for one person (not including tax, gratuity or beverages). Most restaurants are open daily—except where noted—and accept major credit cards. Call for information regarding reservations and opening hours.

Additional restaurants are listed throughout this guide in the form of sidebars.

☙ *See Index for a complete listing of eateries described in the text.*

☙ *For price ranges, see the legend on the cover flap.*

Max Downtown - *185 Asylum St., Hartford.* ♿ *Reservations recommended.* ☎ *860-522-2530. www.maxrestaurantgroup.com.* **$$$ Continental**. The flagship of Hartford-area restaurant impresario Rich Rosenthal, Max Downtown is the place for chophouse classics, creative New American fare (pan-seared swordfish with caramelized orange sauce), Max's famous chopped salad and memorable desserts—all in a city-chic setting. With streetside windows and a stunning three-wall mural, there's ample food for the eye as well.

Ann Howard Apricots – *1593 Farmington Ave., Farmington.* ♿ ☎ *860-673-5405.* **$$$ American**. Hartford's special-occasion restaurant for the past 20 years, Apricots overlooks the rushing Farmington River, with romantic décor and classic cuisine. In good weather, enjoy drinks or light fare on the riverfront terrace.

Peppercorn's Grill – *357 Main St., Hartford. Closed Sun.* ♿ ☎ *860-547-1714. www.peppercornsrestaurant.com.* **$$$ Italian**. In a city where Italian cuisine is numero uno, Peppercorn's does it proud. Two generations of an Italian restaurant family do a splendid job updating classical Italian fare here. The stylish décor features a Roman street-scene mural—just the backdrop for your duet of carpaccios (seared veal and smoked swordfish), veal filet with truffle-and-porcini-scented glaze, lobster risotto, ethereal tiramisu, and warm-chocolate Valhrona cake with homemade gelato.

Black-eyed Sally's Bar-B-Que & Blues – 350 Asylum St., Hartford. ♿ ☎ 860-278-7427. www.blackeyedsallys. com. **$$ Southern**. Hartford's take on a Memphis juke joint, Sally's offers an authentic Southern dining experience, complete with colorful Southern folk art on the walls, a velvet Elvis above the bar and live blues that keep the joint jumpin' into the wee hours (Thu–Sat). Fare is down-home delicious, from the signature fallin'-off-the-bone ribs to "Cajun popcorn" (fried crawfish tails), to jambalaya and cornmeal-crusted cat-

fish, accompanied by corn bread, fried okra and collard greens. For dessert, what else but bourbon pecan pie and Mississippi mud pie?

First and Last Tavern – *939 Maple Ave., Hartford.* ♿ ☎ 860-956-6000. **$ Italian**. Think Cheers, add Italian comfort food and you'll have a sense of this beloved 65-year-old tavern in Hartford's Little Italy, with its warm family atmosphere and friendly staff. Unpretentious fare ranges from superior brick-oven breads and pizza to the original house special spaghetti with meatball, sausage and salad (all served on the same plate). Save room for homemade desserts: cannoli, bread pudding or, for true pizza aficionados, apple or cherry pie pizza.

Constitution Plaza★

▶ *Across from the Old State House, bordered by Market St. and Columbus Blvd.*

The modern 12-acre plaza completed in the 1960s provided Hartford with new office buildings, shops and an open mall, and added a striking landmark to the city's skyline: the **Phoenix Mutual Life Insurance Building**. This elliptical, glass-sheathed tower is referred to as "the Boat" because of its shape. The plaza is the site of the **Hartford Festival of Light**, an annual lighting display held every evening from late November to the first of January.

Travelers Tower

1 Tower Sq.

This building is the home of the Travelers Insurance Company. From the **observation deck** there is a **view**★★ of the Hartford region (👁 *visit by 30min guided tour only, mid-May–mid-Oct Mon–Fri 10am–2:30pm;* 🕐 *closed major holidays;* 👣 *advance 1-day reservations suggested;* 👣 *72 steps to climb;* ☎ 860-277-4208; www.travelers.com).

Wadsworth Atheneum Museum of Art★★

600 Main St. 🕐 *Open year-round Wed–Fri 11am–5pm, weekends 10am–5pm.* 🕐 *Open the first Thu of each month until 5pm.* 🕐 *Closed major holidays.* 💲 *$10.* ✗ ♿ ☎ 860-278-2670. www.wadsworthatheneum.org.

Founded in 1842, this formidable museum, whose initial collection consisted of landscapes by such artists as John Trumbull, Frederic Church and Thomas Cole, now houses some 50,000 works spanning more than 5,000 years. In addition to paintings by the Hudson River school, highlights include European porcelain, 19C European paintings and the comprehensive Nutting collection of 17C American furniture.

Outside the museum stands the giant **Stegosaurus (1)** by Alexander Calder. Across from the Atheneum, note Carl Andre's controversial sculpture **Stone Field (2)**, a group of 36 boulders arranged in a geometrical pattern.

MODERN PASTRY SHOP, INC.

422 Franklin Ave. ☎ 860-296-7628. It's worth the drive to South Hartford to the Italian neighborhood located along Franklin Avenue, where there's a wide choice of good dining establishments. But if time is short, stop at this bakery, where over 30 Italian and French pastries awaits you.

The Charter Oak

The independence of the Hartford Colony was guaranteed by the Royal Charter of 1662. In 1687, however, the royal governor, Edmond Andros, demanded the return of the charter. According to legend, during a meeting that took place one evening to discuss the matter, someone fled with the document. The charter was hidden in an oak tree where it remained until Sir Edmond returned to England a few years later. The tree, which became known as the Charter Oak, fell during a storm in the 19 C. The original charter remains intact and is on display with the Fundamental Orders at the State Library *(231 Capitol Ave.)*.

Connecticut State Capitol★

210 Capitol Ave. ◷ *Open Apr–Oct Mon–Fri 8am–5pm, Sat 10:15am–2:15pm (tours only). Rest of the year Mon–Fri 8am–5pm.* ◷ *Closed major holidays.* ✕ ♿ 🅿 ☎ *860-240-0222. www.cga.ct.gov/capitol/tours.*

This array of turrets, finials, gables, porches and towers, designed by Richard Upjohn, was the talk of the town when it was built in 1879. Rising above heavily sculpted walls, the capitol's golden dome overlooks **Bushnell Park**, designed originally by Frederick Law Olmsted.

State Library

231 Capitol Ave. ◷ *Open year-round Mon–Fri 9am–5pm, Sat 9am–2pm.* ◷ *Closed major holidays.* ♿ ☎ *860-757-6500. www.cslib.org.*

This building, across from the capitol, houses the State Library *(east wing)*, the state's Supreme Court *(west wing)* and the State Museum *(center;* ◷ *open Mon–Fri 9am–4pm; Sat 10am–4pm)*. Museum exhibits include Colt firearms, revolving displays of Connecticut history and the original Fundamental Orders of Connecticut.

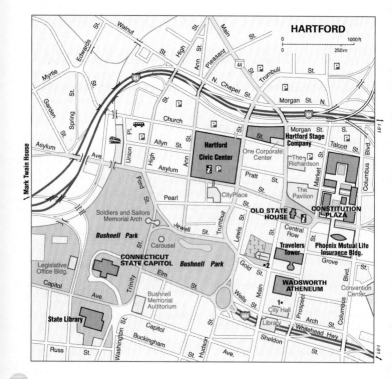

Mark Twain

Among America's best-loved authors and humorists, Mark Twain (1835-1910) gave voice through his writings to the burgeoning culture of America's heartland. Born Samuel Langhorne Clemens in Florida, Missouri, Twain moved with his family to the Mississippi River town of Hannibal, Missouri when he was four years old. Here the young Twain was bewitched by the river life, which he brought to life so artfully in his most famous works, *The Adventures of Tom Sawyer* and *The Adventures of Huckleberry Finn*. As an adult, the high-spirited and good-natured individualist smoked 20 cigars a day, slept backward in his bed in order to face its carved headboard, and did most of his best writing in the Billiard Room of his Hartford home.

Additional Sights Map p 78.

Mark Twain House★★

351 Farmington Ave. ▶ *From downtown Hartford, take I-84 west to Exit 46. Turn right on Sisson Ave., then right on Farmington.* ⬤ *Visit by guided tour (1hr) only, May–Oct & Dec Mon–Sat 9:30am–5:30pm, Sun noon–5:30pm. Rest of the year Mon & Wed–Sat 9:30am–4pm, Sun noon–4pm.* ◷ *Closed major holidays.* ⬤ *$12.* 🅿 ☎ *860-247-0998. www.marktwainhouse.org.*

This Stick-style house, commissioned by Twain in 1874, was one of the Victorian dwellings that stood on **Nook Farm**. In the 19C a community of writers lived in this pastoral setting, including Twain and Harriet Beecher Stowe. Outside, open porches, balconies, towers and steeply pitched roofs give the structure an irregular shape. Silver stenciling, carved woodwork and elaborate wall coverings adorn the inside.

Harriet Beecher Stowe Center (A)

77 Forest St. ⬤ *Visit by guided tour (1hr) only, Jun–Columbus Day & Dec Mon–Sat 9:30am–4:30pm, Sun noon–4:30pm. Rest of the year Tue–Sat 9:30am–4:30pm, Sun noon–4:30pm. Last tour 30min before closing.* ◷ *Closed major holidays.* ⬤ *$8* 🅿 ☎ *860-522-9258. www.harrietbeecherstowecenter.org.*

This simple 1871 Victorian cottage was home to writer Harriet Beecher Stowe (1811-96) from 1873 until her death. Stowe, whose 1852 book *Uncle Tom's Cabin* served to solidify Northern feelings against slavery, also wrote several novels about New England. Lacy gingerbread motifs adorn the plain facade of her former home. The airy interior contains Stowe family furnishings and memorabilia.

Mark Twain House

Mark Twain House, Hartford CT

Excursions

Wethersfield★
5mi south of Hartford via I-91. 🚶 *See entry heading.*

Dinosaur State Park★
10mi south of Hartford, in Rocky Hill. 400 West St. ▶ *Take I-91 North to Exit 23; turn left onto West St. at the light.* 🕐 *Open year-round Tue–Sun 9am–4:30pm.* 🕐 *Closed major holidays.* 🎫 *$5.* 🧒 🚶 🅿 ☎ *860-529-8423. www.dinosaurstatepark.org.*

The park offers a good opportunity to observe, intact and at their original site, more than 500 dinosaur tracks. A full-scale model of Dilophosaurus and a model of Coelophysis, some skeletal remains of which have been found in the Connecticut Valley, are part of the exhibit. In the casting area, visitors may make plaster casts of actual tracks (🕐 *May–Oct daily 9am–3:30pm; visitors must provide their own materials; call for information*).

Hill-Stead Museum★
35 Mountain Rd., in Farmington. 🕐 *Open May–Oct Tue–Sun 11am–4pm.* 🕐 *Closed major holidays.* 🎫 *$9.* 🅿 ☎ *860-677-4787. www.hillstead.org.*

In 1900 Theodate Pope, one of America's early female architects helped design this Colonial Revival country house for her father, Cleveland iron industrialist Alfred Atmore Pope. Pope's passion for Impressionist art led him to purchase a large number of the works displayed here, notably fine paintings by Monet, Manet, Degas and several canvases by Whistler and Mary Cassatt. Centerpiece of the 152-acre grounds is the sunken garden, designed c.1920 by Beatrix Jones Farrand.

New Britain Museum of American Art★
15mi southwest of Hartford, in New Britain. 56 Lexington St. 🕐 *Open year-round Tue–Fri noon–5pm (Thu til 7pm), Sat 10am–5pm, Sun noon–5pm.* 🕐 *Closed Mon & major holidays.* 🎫 *$9.* 🚶 ☎ *860-229-0257. www.nbmaa.org.*

The holdings of this small museum illustrate trends in American art from the colonial period to the present. The 18C portraitists (Trumbull, Stuart, Smibert), the Hudson River school, the eight artists of the Ashcan school (including Sloan, Henri, Luks) and such renowned 19C and 20C masters as Homer, Whistler, Wyeth and Cassatt dominate the collection.

Talcott Mountain State Park
8mi northwest of Hartford. ▶ *Leave Hartford on Rte. 189, then follow Rte. 185 to park entrance.* 🕐 *Grounds open year-round daily 8am–dusk. Tower open Labor Day–Oct daily 10am–5pm; late May–early Sept Thu–Sun 10am–5pm.* 🅿 ☎ *860-242-1158. http://dep.state.ct.us/stateparks/parks/talcott.htm.*

Nathan Hale

The small town of **Coventry** in rural northeastern Connecticut was the birthplace of the American patriot **Nathan Hale** (1755-76). During the Revolutionary War, he volunteered for the perilous mission of gathering intelligence about the British troops on Long Island. Young Hale was discovered by the British and hanged as a spy on September 22, 1776. The last words he spoke on the scaffold, "I only regret that I have but one life to lose for my country," are among the most memorable in American history.

Today the **Nathan Hale Homestead** (*23mi east of Hartford in Coventry; 2299 South St.;* 🕐 *open mid-May–mid-Oct Wed–Sun 1pm–4pm;* 🕐 *closed major holidays;* 🎫 *$4;* 🅿 ☎ *860-742-6917; www.hartnet.org/als*) stands on the site of the home where Hale was born.

Located on the site of the former summer home of a Hartford family, the park is noted for a trail (1.5mi) that leads up to the 165ft-high Heublein Tower. From the top of the tower, you can enjoy sweeping **views**★.

New England Air Museum

14mi northeast of Hartford, in Windsor Locks. On the grounds of Bradley International Airport. ▶ *Take I-91 North to Exit 40 (Rte. 20 West), then right on Rte. 75 North for 3mi.* ◷ *Open year-round daily 10am–5pm.* ◷ *Closed Jan 1, Thanksgiving Day & Dec 25.* ⌖ *$9.* Kids *&* P *☎ 860-623-3305. www.neam.org.*
Located in two spacious hangars on the west side of Bradley airport, the museum displays some 70 aircraft that trace the history of aviation.

Hatheway House

18mi north of Hartford, in Suffield. ▶ *Take I-91 North to Rte. 20 West, then Rte. 75 North. 55 S. Main St.* ↝ *Visit by guided tour (1hr) only, Jul & Aug Thu–Sun 1pm–4pm, mid-May–Jun & Sept–mid-Oct Wed & weekends 1pm–4pm.* ◷ *Closed major holidays.* ⌖ *$4.* ☎ *860-668-0055. www.hartnet.org/als.*
The house, actually three structures in one, owes its present size to Oliver Phelps, a merchant and land speculator who acquired the property in 1788. Phelps enlarged the main section of the house (c.1760) by adding a single-story structure to the south end. About 1795 Phelps had the Federal-style north wing built. The central section is simple and functional, furnished with William and Mary and Queen Anne pieces. In contrast, the Federal wing is elegant, decorated with Adamesque ornamentation and fine Hepplewhite, Sheraton and Chippendale furnishings. The original 18C hand-blocked French wallpapers in the Federal wing add a special touch to the house.

Caprilands Herb Farm

23mi east of Hartford in Coventry. Take I-384 East to US-44 East; past Bolton Notch, take Rte. 31 South to Coventry. 534 Silver St. ◷ *Open year-round daily 10am–5pm.* ◷ *Closed major holidays.* ⅋ P *☎ 860-742-7244. www.caprilands.com.*
More than 300 different types of herbs are cultivated in more than 30 gardens that fill the 20 acres of this farm, which has been the family estate of Adelma Grenier Simmons (1903-97) since 1929. Visitors are free to wander through the restored 18 C barn, the specialty gardens and the greenhouse.

LITCHFIELD HILLS★★

POPULATION 1,328
MICHELIN MAP 581 H, I 9, 10 AND P 86
TOURIST INFORMATION ☎ 860-567-4506 OR WWW.LITCHFIELDHILLS.COM

The area known as the Litchfield Hills, situated in Connecticut's northwest territory just south of Massachusetts' Berkshire Hills, covers some 1,000sq mi of countryside and woodland—much of it preserved as state parks and wildlife sanctuaries. Some 30-odd towns, such as Litchfield, Norfolk, Woodbury and Washington, distinguished by pristinely preserved main streets and 18C homes, dot the region. Comely country inns and B&Bs, antique shops, art galleries and craft stores greet visitors to this tranquil corner of New England.

The broad **Housatonic River** quietly traverses the thickly wooded and hilly extreme northwest section of Connecticut, between the foothills of the Taconic Mountains and the Berkshire Hills. The beauty of Housatonic Valley and its proximity to New York have made Litchfield Hills a favorite destination of artists, writers and visitors.

Litchfield★★

A photographer's paradise in Indian summer when the trees flame with color, Litchfield is a small, reserved New England village with broad streets and stately clapboard dwellings dating from the 18C.

In the 19C, both the railroad and industrial development bypassed the center of town, a fact that accounts for Litchfield's having one of the loveliest and best-preserved ensembles of early-American architecture in Connecticut.

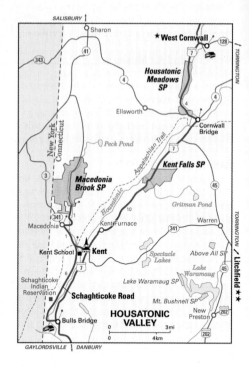

The Green

North, South, East and West Streets meet at the green, which is dominated by Litchfield's **First Congregational Church.**

Nearby, the **Litchfield History Museum**★ organizes exhibits related to early life in the town (7 South St.; ⊘ open mid-Apr–Nov Tue–Sat 11am–5pm, Sun 1pm–5pm; ⊘ $5; ♿ ☎ 860-567-4501; www.litchfieldhistory.org). Many handsome dwellings can be found along **North Street** and **South Street**; most are privately owned and are accessible to the public only during the historic homes tour in mid-July.

White Memorial Foundation Wildlife Sanctuary★

80 Whitehall Rd., 2.5mi west of Litchfield center via Rte. 202 West. ⊘ *Grounds open daily year-round.* 🅿 ☎ 860-567-0857. www.whitememorialcc.org.

Varied vegetation and landscapes abound on this 4,000-acre preserve, which is owned and operated by the White Memorial Foundation. A map of the hiking trails and historic buildings may be purchased on the grounds at the museum (⊘ open year-round Mon–Sat 9am–5pm, Sun noon–5pm; ⊘ closed major holidays; ⊘ $5) or at the Foundation office.

WHITE FLOWER FARM

Rte. 63, 3mi south of Litchfield. ☎ 800-503-9624. www.whiteflowerfarm.com. Exploring this quintessential Connecticut landscape of tree-shaded lanes, meadows and perennial gardens is more like visiting a botanical park than a working nursery. Among the highlights of the self-guided walking tour are the rose arbor, a spring cottage garden, an all-white moon garden and a greenhouse display of lush tuberous begonias. The 63-acre farm sells every imaginable type of bulb, perennial, shrub and ornamental species.

Address Book

⚑ *For price ranges for hotels and restaurants, see the legend on the cover flap.*

WHERE TO STAY

The Mayflower Inn – *118 Woodbury Rd. (Rte. 47), Washington.* ✗♿🅿⊒ ☎ *860-868-9466. www.mayflowerinn.com. 31 rooms.* **$$$$$** This onetime New England inn has been dramatically reinvented as a grand English-style country house, and has been accepted into the prestigious Relais & Châteaux group. Inside, you'll be surrounded by fine art and antiques; outside, you'll find a Shakespearean garden, bocce court and pool, all on 28 wooded acres.

Dolce Heritage – *522 Heritage Rd., Southbury.* ✗♿🅿⊒ ☎ *203-264-8200 or 800-932-3466. www.dolce.com. 183 rooms.* **$$$** In a beautifully landscaped setting overlooking the Pomperaug River, Dolce Heritage is a comfortable contemporary country resort, with a health club, indoor and outdoor pools, tennis and racquetball courts, a nine-hole golf course and cross-country ski trails. Spacious rooms with river or golf course views sport country décor.

WHERE TO EAT

Carole Peck's Good News Café – *694 Main St. S. (Rte. 6), Woodbury.* 🕐 *Closed Tue.* ♿ ☎ *203-266-4663. www.goodnewscafé.com.* **$$$ American**. The atmosphere is funky and fun (art exhibits vie for space with Peck's antique radios); the menu is creative and healthful. Peck, who prides herself on combining fresh, local (often organic) ingredients in original ways, is known for her onion bundles, pecan-crusted oysters, globally inspired entrées, and desserts.

West Street Grill – *West Street, on the green, Litchfield.* ♿ ☎ *860-567-3885.* **$$$ American**. Not only the place to see and be seen, this stylish restaurant is also the place for reliably excellent, often ahead-of-the-curve New American cuisine. Best of show are the signature grilled calamari, superb soups, and fresh seafood dishes.

Hopkins Inn – *22 Hopkins Rd., New Preston.* 🕐 *Closed Mon & Jan–Mar.* ☎ *860-868-7295. www.thehopkinsinn. com.* **$$ Austrian**. Commanding the area's best lake views, this 1847 Federal-style hilltop inn features Old World fare such as backheldl (breaded chicken cutlets) with lingonberries and roesti (roasted potatoes) and schnitzel with spaetzle.

Driving Tour: Along the River *24mi.*

This itinerary follows Route 7, once a major route linking Montreal and New York City, from Bulls Bridge along the Housatonic River north to West Cornwall. Three state parks are included in the tour as well as the towns of Kent and West Cornwall.

▶ *Begin at Bulls Bridge, 3mi north of Gaylordsville on US-7. Turn left onto Bulls Bridge Rd., which passes over a covered bridge that spans the Housatonic River. After crossing a second bridge, turn right onto Schaghticoke Rd.*

Schaghticoke Road

⊙ *The first mile of this narrow road is largely unpaved.*

The road follows the river as it winds through wooded terrain that is offset by patches of gnarled ledges and rock formations bordering the riverbed. After 1mi, the road arrives at the Schaghticoke Indian Reservation and passes an old Indian burial ground. The road also passes the buildings of **Kent School**, a prestigious private secondary school.

▶ *Turn left onto Rte. 341 and follow it north for 1mi to Macedonia. Turn right and follow signs to Macedonia Brook State Park.*

RIVER RECREATION

April is the time to shoot the rapids on the Housatonic River. Just when the waters are wildest, trained guides from **Clarke Outdoors** *(163 US-7, West Cornwall;* ☎ *860-672-6365; www.clarkeoutdoors.com)* offer class IV-V whitewater rafting trips through the Bulls Bridge Gorge (call for reservations). For a calmer paddle in summer or autumn, rent a canoe or kayak and travel a 6mi stretch of flat water. A shuttle returns upriver at the end of the run.

STROBLE BAKING CO.

14 N. Main St., Kent; ☎ *860-927-4073.* By the time the doors open every morning at 8am, Patsy Stroble and her crew of bakers have been up for hours preparing the Linzertortes, croissants, miniature cheesecakes and giant sugar cookies that make this tiny bakery a local landmark. If you arrive early enough, the muffins and bread will still be warm. Stroble's also offers sandwiches, salads and homemade soup at lunch time.

Macedonia Brook State Park

Off Rte. 341, 4mi north of Kent in Macedonia. ◷ *Open year-round daily 8am–dusk.* ⛺ 🅿 *(seasonal)* ☎ *860-927-3238. http://dep.state.ct.us/rec.*
With its rocky gorge, streams, and web of trails, this state park offers recreation galore in the form of camping, fishing and hiking.
▹ *Take Rte. 341 South back to Kent.*

Kent

Nestled among the hills bordering the Housatonic River, Kent is the home of artists and craftspeople whose works are often displayed in shops in the village center.
▹ *Follow US-7 North.*

Kent Falls State Park

Entrance on US-7. ◷ *Open year-round daily 8am–dusk.* 💰 *$7-$10/car on weekends.* 🅿 ☎ *860-927-3238. http://dep.state.ct.us/stateparks/parks/kentfalls.htm.*
To view the falls from above, climb the steps to the right of the falls. From this vantage point, you can cross the bridge and descend to the parking lot by following a path through the woods.
North of Kent Falls, Route 7 passes through the hamlet of Cornwall Bridge, where the local general store is a welcome sight to hikers on the Appalachian Trail.

West Cornwall

Gwen Cannon/ MICHELIN

Antiquing in Woodbury

Settled in 1673, Woodbury already ranks as an antiquarian treasure. But antiquers prize it most for the 50-plus 18C and 19C houses lining Main Street (Rte. 6), which double as quality antiques emporia. Among the most highly regarded dealers are **Wayne Pratt**, a regular on Antiques Roadshow, for New England furniture; **Thomas Schwenke**, for Federal pieces; **G. Sergeant**, for English and Continental antiques; **Eleish-Van Breems**, for Scandinavian furniture; **Joel Einhorn**, for American clocks, maps, toys and ship paintings; and **Monique Shay**, for French-Canadian painted pieces.

Housatonic Meadows State Park

Entrance on US-7, 1mi north of Cornwall Bridge. ○ *Open year-round daily 8am–dusk.* P ⚠ *(seasonal)* ☎ *860-927-3238. http://dep.state.ct.us/stateparks/parks/housatonic. htm*

The Pine Knob Loop Trail 🚶 (round-trip 2hrs from the parking lot on the west side of US-7) leads to the summit of Pine Knob (1,160ft) where there are views across the Housatonic Valley.

▶ *Return to US-7 and continue north to West Cornwall.*

West Cornwall★

This tiny village is known for its picturesque covered bridge, built in 1864 and recently restored.

Additional Sights

American Clock and Watch Museum★

100 Maple St., Bristol. ▶ *Take I-84 East to Exit 31. Follow Rte. 229 North to the right for 5.5mi. Turn left on Woodland St. and follow signs.* ○ *Open Apr–Nov daily 10am–5pm. Open Dec Dri-Sat 10am-5pm Sun 1pm-5pm.* ○ *Closed Easter Sunday & Thanksgiving Day.* ✆ *$5.* P ☎ *860-583-6070. www.clockmuseum.org.*

In the 19C America's clockmaking industry was centered in the Bristol area, where in 1860 alone, more than 200,000 clocks were produced. Most of the clocks and watches in the museum's collection were produced in Connecticut.

HICKORY STICK BOOKSHOP

At the junction of Rtes. 47 & 109, in Washington. ☎ *860-868-0525. www.hickorystickbookshop.com.* Although one of the many nationally known authors living in Litchfield Hills—which have included Philip Roth and Arthur Miller—might be on hand for a signing, the real draw at this welcoming bookstore is the vast selection of current books, plus the personal service. People come from all over the state to browse the well-stocked sections on sports, photography, nature, cooking, music, biography, history, reference, fiction, poetry and drama.

Bellamy-Ferriday House and Garden★

9 Main St. North, Bethlehem (at the intersection of Rtes. 61 & 132). 🕿 *Visit by guided tour (45min) only, mid-May–mid-Oct Wed, Fri & weekends 11am–4pm.* ○ *Closed major holidays.* ✆ *$5.* P ☎ *860-247-8996. www.hartnet.org/als.*

Located on the village green, this two-story Georgian-style clapboard house, graced with a Palladian portico, was built c.1745 and enlarged and embellished over the next 200 years. The interior includes vernacular furnishings from the area.

Dotted with white barns and orchards, the grounds feature a 1912 garden where lilacs, peonies, magnolias and roses bloom in season.

Institute for American Indian Studies

38 Curtis Rd., Washington. ▶ *Take Rte. 199 South 2mi to Curtis Rd. and follow signs to the institute.* ○ *Open year-round Mon–Sat 10am–5pm, Sun noon–5pm.* ○ *Closed major holidays.* ◒ *$4.* ☎ *860-868-0518. www.birdsong.org.*

This small museum in a peaceful woodland setting honors the culture and history of Connecticut Indians. Exhibits include archaeological artifacts, handcrafted splint baskets and a longhouse room. Outside, a short nature trail leads to a re-created Algonquin encampment, complete with a longhouse and several **wigwams**.

Glebe House Museum and Jekyll Garden

49 Hollow Rd. off Rte. 6, Woodbury. ○ *Open May–Oct Wed–Sun 1pm–4pm. Nov weekends 1pm–4pm.* ◒ *$5.* 🅿 ☎ *203-263-2855. www.theglebehouse.org.*

Considered the birthplace of the Episcopal Church in this country, the restored c.1750 gambrel-roof dwelling built on a **glebe** (land set aside for the parish priest) reflects the Revolutionary period.

Surrounding the house, perennial borders brim with lupines and hollyhocks. They were planted in the 1990s in accordance with plans designed for the property in the 1920s by English garden designer Gertrude Jekyll, but not implemented at the time.

Connecticut Impressionist Art Trail

Follow the Art Trail to visit any or all of 11 sites that showcase the work of American painters. *For a color brochure with map, contact one of the Connecticut tourism districts listed on the Web site www.arttrail.org.*

Bruce Museum – *One Museum Dr., Greenwich.* ☎ *203-869-0376.* Represents several artists who painted in Cos Cob and Greenwich, an area particularly important to the development of the American Impressionist movement.

Bush-Holley House Museum – *39 Strickland Rd., Cos Cob.* ☎ *203-869-6899.* Takes visitors back to the 19C, when this Colonial saltbox was a gathering place for Hassam, Twachtman and others.

Weir Farm National Historic Site – *735 Nod Hill Rd., Wilton.* ☎ *203-834-1896.* Preserves the bucolic landscapes that inspired American Impressionist J. Alden Weir.

Yale University Art Gallery – *1111 Chapel St., New Haven.* ☎ *203-432-0600.* See entry heading New Haven.

Florence Griswold Museum – *96 Lyme St., Old Lyme.* ☎ *860-434-5542.* Presents the studio of William Chadwick and a collection of works by artists belonging to the famous 19C Lyme art colony.

Lyman Allyn Art Museum – *625 Williams St., New London.* ☎ *860-443-2545.* See entry heading New London.

William Benton Museum of Art – *University of Connecticut at Storrs.* ☎ *860-486-4520.* Showcases works by Emil Carlsen, Mary Cassatt, J. Alden Weir and more.

Wadsworth Atheneum of Art – *600 Main St., Hartford.* ☎ *860-278-2670.* See entry heading Hartford.

Hill-Stead Museum – *35 Mountain Rd., Farmington.* ☎ *860-677-4787.* See entry heading Hartford/Excursions.

New Britain Museum of American Art – *56 Lexington St., New Britain* ☎ *860-229-0257.* See entry heading Hartford/Excursions.

Mattatuck Museum – *144 W Main St., Waterbury.* ☎ *203-753-0381.* The state's only museum devoted exclusively to Connecticut history and artists.

MYSTIC SEAPORT★★★

MICHELIN MAP 581 L 11
TOURIST INFORMATION ☎ 888-973-2767 OR WWW.VISITMYSTICSEAPORT.COM

The village of Mystic, on the Mystic River, has been a shipbuilding center since the 17C. Today Mystic (population 4,000) is known primarily as the site of Mystic Seaport, an interpretive museum that re-creates the atmosphere of America's maritime past. This living replica of a 19C waterfront community features tall ships, a village center and a working shipyard, all of which add to the authenticity of the setting. Museum buildings house extensive collections of marine art and artifacts, providing visitors with insight into America's seagoing past.

▶ **Orient Yourself:** Mystic Seaport sits on the Connecticut waterfront, easily accessed by north-south I-95 and east-west I-91.

🅿 **Parking:** Ample parking is available at the museum.

🖐 **Don't Miss:** The waterfront area, filled with 19C shops.

🕐 **Organizing Your Time:** Start at the Visitor Center where you can view a brief video presentation, pick up maps and check out what events and activities are scheduled for the day. Allow at least a day to tour the museum.

Especially for Kids: Youngsters will particularly enjoy the **Children's Museum**, where they will find child-size fishing boats and a gallery store.

🖐 **Also See:** The vintage ships moored at the waterfront; consider a boat ride on one of the historic ships for a view of the waterfront.

Visit

From I-95 Exit 90, follow Rte. 27 south. 🕐 *Open year-round Apr–Oct 9am–5pm. Rest of the year daily 10am–4pm.* 🕐 *Closed Dec 25.* ⊕ *$17.50, good for two consecutive days. Schedule of daily events and map are available at the entrance.* ✕ 🅿 ☎ *860-572-5315 or 888-973-2767. www.visitmysticseaport.com.*

The museum has grown from a collection of nautical memorabilia displayed in a renovated mill to a complex of some 60 buildings covering 17 acres, formerly the site of timber ponds and shipbuilding yards. In 1978 the name Mystic Seaport was adopted and today the popular attraction is maintained as a private, nonprofit

Mystic Seaport

Address Book

WHERE TO STAY

For price ranges for hotels and restaurants, see the legend on the cover flap .

Inn at Stonington – *60 Water St., Stonington Borough.* ♿ 🅿 ☎ *860-535-2000. www.innatstonington.com. 12 rooms.* **$$$$** It's rare that a "new" country inn is built on a prime waterfront site in an old seafaring town, but here is one and it's a gem. After a centrally located harborside restaurant burned down, this white Greek Revival inn was built in its place. Luxurious antiques-appointed guest rooms with fireplaces and harbor views await visitors here. Facilities include a common room with a bar (for breakfast and evening wine and cheese), an exercise room, bikes at the ready, and kayaks to launch from the inn's own deepwater dock. Restaurants, shops, historic houses and secret gardens lie within an easy walk or bike ride away.

Steamboat Inn – *73 Steamboat Wharf, Mystic.* ♿ 🅿 ☎ *860-536-8300. www.steamboatinnmystic.com. 10 rooms.* **$$$$** Originally a ship's store, today it's a luxury B&B on the Mystic River in downtown Mystic. Each room is unique in configuration and décor, all are designer-decorated and equipped with whirlpool baths (some with baths for two), and most have fireplaces and river views (the Mystic Suite has views on two sides). The pretty common room is open for serve-yourself "continental-plus" breakfast, afternoon tea and evening sherry.

The Inn at Mystic – *US-1 and Rte. 27, Mystic.* ✗ ♿ 🅿 ⛵ ☎ *860-536-9604 or 800-237-2415. www.innatmystic.com. 67 rooms.* **$$$** Set high on a hill with stunning views of Mystic harbor, this unique inn has multiple personalities: a modern motor inn and deluxe harbor-view wing (both sporting colonial décor), and the 1904 Colonial Revival-style Haley Mansion and gatehouse with nine more rooms between them—including one where Bogart and Bacall honeymooned. Bonuses are tennis, boating, terraced gardens, and the romantic Flood Tide restaurant, where Caesar salad is tossed tableside, twin lobster tails are stuffed with herbed shrimp, and a bountiful Sunday buffet brunch is served.

The Old Mystic Inn – *52 Main St., Old Mystic.* ♿ 🅿 ☎ *860-572-9422. www.old-mysticinn.com. 8 rooms.* **$$$** Two miles down the road from bustling Mystic Seaport, the charming Old Mystic Inn is a red 1784 Colonial surrounded by gardens. Guest rooms in the house, and in the 1988 carriage house, are named after New England writers and boast canopy beds and fireplaces, wide-plank or inlaid floors, stenciling and wainscoting. The owner, a graduate of the Culinary Institute of America, turns out lavish breakfasts like scrambled eggs in puff pastry with steamed asparagus and Mornay sauce, and strawberry-stuffed French toast with maple-pecan syrup. No children under 15 years allowed.

Brigadoon Bed & Breakfast – *180 Cow Hill Rd., Mystic.* ♿ 🅿 ☎ *860-536-3033. www.brigadoonofmystic.com. 8 rooms.* **$$** You'll find a touch of Scotland a mile from downtown Mystic at this rambling 250-year-old farmhouse-turned-bed-and-breakfast located on a quiet side street. Hosted by Scottish-born Kay and her husband Ted, their labor of love offers charming light-filled rooms in pretty pastels, with king- or queen-sized beds, air conditioning and often oversized private baths. The honeymoon suite features a brass-and-iron bed, cathedral ceiling, French doors and a separate entrance. Complimentary breakfast is served in the dining room overlooking the garden or, in season, under a tree in the garden itself.

WHERE TO EAT

Restaurant Bravo Bravo –*E. Main St., Mystic. Closed Mon.* ♿ ☎ *860-536-3228.* **$$$ Italian**. The name may seem a bit self-congratulatory, but in this case it is warranted. This 50-seat restaurant overlooking Mystic's Main Street sidewalk scene wins steady applause for its contemporary takes on pasta and seafood, often creatively combined. Typical are the tomato-tarragon fettuccine with lobster, scallops, mussels and asparagus in lobster-cream sauce; baked crab cakes; or lobster ravioli with lobster-chive sauce, zuppa de pescado and champagne risotto. In summer there may be a wait, but it's worth it.

Seamen's Inne – *105 Greenmanville Ave. (Rte. 27), Mystic.* ✆ *860-572-5303. www.mysticseaport.org. (click on dining)* **$$$ American**. This nautically themed Colonial inn abutting Mystic Seaport is not a place for seamen (or anyone else, for that matter) to overnight. Rather, it's a restaurant and pub overlooking the Mystic River that turns out classic New England fare—creamy clam chowder, fresh fish, prime rib, chocolate bread pudding—in a series of tavern-style rooms, most with fireplaces.

Captain Daniel Packer Inne – *32 Water St., Mystic.* ✆ *860-536-3555 or 800-536-3555. www.danielpacker.com.* **$$ American**. Across from the marina, this 1756 National Historic Register inn still caters to travelers, but today they're more likely to come by car than by boat or stagecoach. It remains a step back

in time, with oversized hearths, stone interior walls and wide-plank floors. The lower-level rathskeller is a cozy spot for updated New England fare creatively interpreted (portobello mushroom topped with Alouette cheese); and fresh fish, notably Cajun-style Stonington scallops and stuffed blackback flounder.

Mystic Pizza – *56 W. Main St., Mystic.* ✆ *860-536-3700 or 536-3737. www.mysticpizza.com.* **$ Italian**. Yes, there really is a Mystic Pizza and, yes, it starred in the popular 1988 movie of the same name that launched Julia Roberts. The place that boasts of "the pizza that made the movie famous" still features the secret-recipe thick-crust pie that the Zelepos family opened with in 1973. Beyond pizza (pepperoni is the most popular), there's a full menu from fried calamari to burgers, salads to chicken-Parmesan.

educational facility. The **waterfront** is lined with wharves and adjacent streets where shops and businesses commonly found in a 19C seaport abound. Three such tall ships and a vintage steamboat are moored at the waterfront. In addition, Mystic Seaport preserves nearly 500 small craft and more than one million maritime photographs—the largest two collections of their kinds in the world.

The Charles W. Morgan

This 133ft-long whaleboat, sole survivor of America's 19C whaling fleet, has been declared a National Historic Site. Fully rigged, the Morgan can carry 13,000sq ft of sail. Visitors may board the 1841 ship to examine the crew's quarters and gigantic try-pots, the cauldrons used to boil the oil out of whale fat.

The Joseph Conrad

This Danish-built training vessel, built as the Georg Stage in 1882 and designed to accommodate a crew of 80, has sailed under the Danish, British and American flags. Renamed in 1934 and now the property of Mystic Seaport, the 117ft-long schooner serves its original function as a training ship.

The L.A. Dunton

This graceful 124ft schooner, built in 1921, typifies the round-bow fishing vessels that sailed from New England to Newfoundland in the 19C and early 20C.

Sabino

Built in 1908, the steamboat Sabino is the last wood-hulled, coal-fired passenger-carrying steam vessel operating in the US today. Visitors can board the Sabino for 30min waterfront tours from the river (⟵ *depart from the Sabino dock near the main entrance to Mystic Seaport mid-May–mid-Oct daily 10:30am–3:30pm, every hour on the hour;* ⟵ *$5.25).*

Henry B. du Pont Preservation Shipyard

All kinds of boats from the museum's vast collection are restored here. Visitors may observe craftsmen at work from a platform on the second level.

Mallory Building

A collection of ships' models, half-models and portraits here traces the growth of America's maritime industry through the life of one prominent shipping family.

Mystic River Scale Model

The Mystic River area appears in small scale here as it did in the 1870s. At more than 50ft long, the model features some 250 detailed structures.

Wendell Building

The first exhibit building at Mystic Seaport, the Wendell Building houses the seaport's rich collection of wooden **figureheads** and **ships' carvings**.

Also on-site is the **Schaefer Building**, which contains special exhibitions from the museum's collection of maritime art and artifacts; and the **Planetarium**, where programs under the dome focus on sailors' dependence on celestial navigation.

Additional Sight

Mystic Aquarium and Institute for Exploration★★

Kids 55 Coogan Blvd. in Mystic. ◷ Open Mar-Oct daily 9am–6pm (Fri & Sat til 6pm). Open Dec–Feb Mon–Fri 10am–5pm. Rest of the year daily 9am–6pm. ◷ Closed Jan 1, Thanksgiving Day & Dec 25. ☜ $19.75. ✗ 🄿 ♿ ☎ 860-572-5955. www.mysticaquarium.org.

More than 6,000 sea creatures, including four-eyed fish and Australian mudskippers, make their home here. It's one of the largest and most ecologically minded aquariums in the nation.

Living specimens of marine animals and plants are grouped into some 45 major exhibits demonstrating aquatic communities, habitat and adaptation. In the Ocean **Planet Pavilion**, bonnethead sharks prowl a 30,000-gallon tank along with 500 exotic fish, while the **Sunlit Seas** exhibits feature species that thrive in ecosystems such as estuaries and coral reefs. Atlantic bottlenose dolphins, known for their sunny dispositions, play in the World of the Dolphin tank *(daily demonstrations are held in the theater)*. Another favorite is the Hidden Amazon with electric eels, poison dart frogs, and more. Outside, view the underwater world of northern fur seals and graceful beluga whales in settings constructed to resemble their habitat, the **Alaskan Coast**; and watch African black-footed penguins frolic above and below the water in the **Roger Tory Peterson Penguin Exhibit**.

KITCHEN LITTLE

135 Greenmanville Ave. ☎ *860-536-2122.* Located near Mystic Seaport, this tiny, waterside eatery is well known for its huge and inventive breakfasts (6:30am–2pm; breakfast only on weekends), featuring such egg dishes as the Mystic Melt, the Portuguese Fisherman or the Kitchen Sink. If indoor seating is not available, share a picnic table outside at the rear with the seagulls.

ABBOTT'S LOBSTER IN THE ROUGH

117 Pearl St., Noank (2.5mi southwest of Mystic via Rte. 215). ◷ *Open daily Memorial Day–Labor Day, noon-9pm.* ☎ *860-536-7719. www.abbotts-lobster.com.* The large parking lot is a clue that Abbott's is indeed a popular place to eat. This rambling lobster shack right on the waters of Fishers Island Sound boasts great views, especially while you're consuming some of the best—and biggest lobsters around.

Excursions

Mashantucket Pequot Museum★★

🧒 *7mi northeast of Mystic.* ▶ *From I-95, take Exit 92, then Rte. 2 West and follow signs to museum.* ◷ *Open year-round daily 10am-4pm. Last admission 1hr before closing.* ◷ *Closed major holidays.* ⊛ *$15.* ✕ ⃝P ⃝& ☏ *800-411-9671. www.pequotmuseum.com.*

This tribally owned and operated museum —the largest Native American museum in the country— is devoted to the native and natural history of southern New England, including the history and culture of the Mashantucket Pequot Indians. Located on the original reservation, the glass and concrete facility pays homage to nature by embracing woodland views and integrating stone and gurgling streams into the modern structure. Inside the museum, dioramas, interactive videos, films, campfire aromas and recorded bird songs create a multisensory experience that focuses on the Pequots' day-to-day life from prehistoric times to the present. The highlight of the museum is the indoor 16C **Pequot Village**, a 22,000sq ft re-creation of a native dwelling site.

Algonquian Man (1645) Engraving by Wencelaus Hollar

Curtis Moussie/ Courtesy of MPMRC

Stonington★

4mi east of Mystic on Rte. 1, then Rte. 1A.

Overlooking a tranquil harbor studded with boats, Stonington is justly known as one of the prettiest coastal villages in Connecticut. The early character of this former shipbuilding center is preserved in the lovely 18C and 19C homes lining the tree-shaded streets of Stonington borough. Spend some time browsing through the antique shops and boutiques clustered on Main Street.

Captain Palmer House★

40 Palmer St. 🔍 *Visit by guided tour (45min) only May–Oct Thu–Sun 1pm–5pm.* ⊛ *$5 (includes Lighthouse Museum).* ☏ *860-535-8445. www.stoningtonhistory.org/palmer.htm.*

Perched on the highest hill in Stonington, this Greek Revival manse is crowned with an octagonal cupola that commands water views in all directions.

CLYDE'S CIDER MILL

On Rte. 201 in North Stonington. Open Sept–Dec. ☏ *860-536-3354.* Making fresh apple cider is an autumn tradition throughout New England, but perhaps nowhere more than at Clyde's, where six generations of the Clyde family have steadfastly upheld the practice of cider-pressing that their grandfather started in 1881. It's the oldest steam-powered cider mill in the US. Designated a National Historical Mechanical and Engineering Landmark, the mill still employs its all-steel screw cider press.

Besides sweet cider and a wide variety of apple wines, Clyde's sells myriad seasonal goodies as well: apples, pumpkins, gourds, homemade apple butter and johnnycake meal ground on the premises.

The Nutmeg State

In the 1830s a series of essays satirizing the proverbially dishonest Connecticut peddler by Canadian writer Thomas Haliburton included the apparently false accusation that crafty Yankee salesmen were passing off wooden nutmegs. Cheap and plentiful, nutmegs were imported from the West Indies to Connecticut ports, and it is doubtful that anyone would bother to carve wooden imitations when the real thing was so easily accessible. Nevertheless, the story stuck. One entrepreneur did sell wooden nutmegs as Connecticut souvenirs at the 1876 Philadelphia Centennial Exhibition—claiming they were made from Hartford's famed Charter Oak. For their own part, Connecticut residents took characteristically perverse pleasure in the sobriquet **Nutmeg State** and adopted the nickname as their own.

Old Lighthouse Museum

7 Water St. 🕐 *Open Jul–Aug daily 10am–5pm. May–Jun & Sept–Oct Tue–Sun 10am–5pm.* 🎟 *$5 (including Captain Palmer House.)* ☎ *860-535-1440. www.stoningtonhistory.org/light.htm.*

Seasonal exhibits in the 1840 stone lighthouse serve as nostalgic reminders of Stonington's past as a shipbuiding center.

NEW HAVEN★★

POPULATION 123,626
MICHELIN MAP 581 J 11 AND MAPS P 97 AND P 101
TOURIST INFORMATION ☎ 203-777-8550, 800-332-7829 OR WWW.NEWHAVENCVB.ORG

Seen from I-95, New Haven's skyline is pierced by tall office structures, such as the 23-story, glass-faced Knights of Columbus Building (L), set off by four 320ft brown tile towers. On closer look, however, quaint commercial districts, serene residential streets, a historic green and the ivy-covered buildings of prestigious Yale University characterize Connecticut's third-largest city.

▶ **Orient Yourself:** Situated on New Haven Harbor on the northern coast of Long Island Sound, New Haven is halfway between the New York City metro area and New England metro areas. The city is easily assessible off north-south I-95 and I-91. Route US34 travels east-west.

🅿 **Parking:** Metered parking is available along Elm, Orange and Court Streets. Lots can also be found on Elm Street (between Orange and State Streets) and Orange Street (between Elm and Wall Streets). Yale University opens its lots to the public free of charge on weekends.

🅐 **Don't Miss:** A walking tour of the prestigious Yale University.

🕐 **Organizing Your Time:** Begin your visit at **INFO New Haven** *(1000 Chapel St.)* where you can pick up information and maps, purchase ticket for local events, make restaurant and theater reservations and access an interactive Web station. The tour of Yale will take half a day; save an hour or two to visit the University Art Museum.

🄺 **Especially for Kids:** Take a hike on the 1.6-mile Tower Path in nearby Sleeping Giant State Park.

🅐 **Also See:** The Yale Center for British Art, known for its comprehensive collection, and the Peabody Museum of Natural History.

A Bit of History

The first planned city in America was founded as an "independent kingdom of Christ" in 1638 by a group of Puritans. In the late 18C and early 19C, New Haven became an important seaport. The War of 1812 brought an end to this prosperous period in New Haven, as it did in other ports throughout New England.

The face of the town changed forever with the arrival of the railroad in the 19C. Industry and manufacturing developed, and immigrants came by the thousands to work in Connecticut's clock, firearms and carriage factories. In New Haven today you'll find a mix of traditional and contemporary architectural styles.

Yale University★★★ *Map below.*

This Ivy League school is one of the oldest and most distinguished institutions of higher learning in the US. The university was founded in 1701 by a group of Puritan clergymen who wished to provide Connecticut with an institution where young men could be trained to serve the church and state.

Yale gained university status in 1887, long after its Medical School (1810) and Law School (1824) were established. The nation's first Ph.D. degrees were awarded by Yale in 1861.

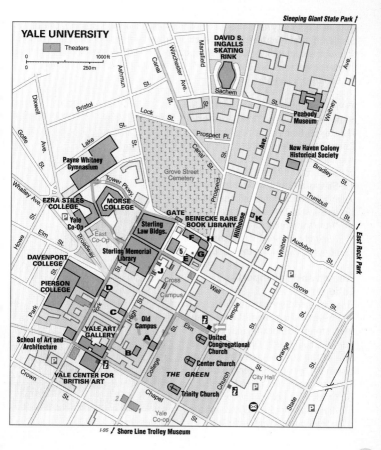

Sleeping Giant State Park /

YALE UNIVERSITY

Theaters

0   1000 ft
0   250 m

DAVID S. INGALLS SKATING RINK

Peabody Museum

New Haven Colony Historical Society

Payne Whitney Gymnasium

Grove Street Cemetery

EZRA STILES COLLEGE

MORSE COLLEGE

Yale Co-Op

East Co-Op

GATE

Sterling Law Bldgs.

BEINECKE RARE BOOK LIBRARY

Sterling Memorial Library

DAVENPORT COLLEGE

PIERSON COLLEGE

Cross Campus

YALE ART GALLERY

Old Campus

School of Art and Architecture

United Congregational Church

Center Church

YALE CENTER FOR BRITISH ART

THE GREEN

City Hall

Trinity Church

Yale Co-op

I-95 / Shore Line Trolley Museum

East Rock Park

Walking Tour

▶ *Begin at the visitor center on Elm St. See map.*

Visitor Center

149 Elm St. ⏱ *Open year-round Mon–Fri 9am–4pm, weekends 11am–4pm.* ⏱ *Closed Jan 1, Thanksgiving Day, Dec 24, 25 & 31.* 🚶 *Guided tours (1hr 15min) of the campus available Mon–Fri 10:30am & 2pm, weekends 1:30pm.* ☎ *203-432-2300. www.yale.edu/visitor.*

Historically known as the Pierpont House, this two-story Georgian Colonial white frame structure (1767) is the oldest surviving house in New Haven. Here visitors can obtain a fact booklet and other brochures about the university.

▶ *Proceed to Phelps Gate (A) on College St. and enter the Old Campus.*

Old Campus

This is the site of Yale's earliest college buildings, including **Connecticut Hall (B)**, the university's oldest structure. A statue of Nathan Hale, a Yale alumnus, stands in front of this simple Georgian hall where Hale lived as a student.

▶ *Cross the Old Campus and exit onto High St.*

Across High Street is the landmark **Harkness Tower (C)** (1920), a 221ft Gothic Revival bell tower heavily ornamented with carved figures of famous Yale alumni, among them Noah Webster and Eli Whitney.

▶ *Turn left on High St., pass under an arch, then turn right onto Chapel St.*

The **Yale University Art Gallery,** Louis Kahn's first major work, stands facing his last creation, the **Yale Center for British Art.** Both buildings present interesting conceptions of museum architecture from the point of view of building materials, light and the use of space. 👁 *See descriptions of the museums' collections, pp 102-104.*

▶ *Continue to York St.*

The former Gothic Revival-style church on the left is now the **Yale Repertory Theater (3),** home of the Yale Repertory Company, a professional acting troupe in residence at the university. Diagonally opposite stands Paul Rudolph's high-rise **School of Art and Architecture**. Seemingly seven stories tall, the building actually has 36 levels that are visible only from the interior.

▶ *Turn right onto York St. and continue about halfway down the street.*

Pierson and Davenport Colleges★

These elegant Georgian buildings hidden beyond the colleges' Medieval-style, street-side facades may be seen from the courtyards. On the opposite side of the street stands **Wrexham Tower (D),** designed after the church in Wales where Elihu Yale is buried.

▶ *Cross Elm St. and continue on York St. At no. 306 York St., walk through the narrow passageway on the left.*

Harkness Tower

Michael Marsland/ Yale University

Cultural New Haven

The presence of Yale University has made New Haven a prominent cultural center. New Haven's theaters, once a proving ground for Broadway productions, have become well known in their own right. Numbers and letters in parentheses refer to the New Haven map.

Long Wharf Theater – *222 Sargent Dr.* ☎ *203-787-4282. www.longwharf.org.* Located in a former warehouse, this theater received a regional Tony award.

Shubert Performing Arts Center (1) – *247 College St.* ☎ *203-562-5666. www. shubert.com.* The Shubert's varied program of performances includes Broadway-bound productions, Broadway road shows and concerts.

Palace Performing Arts Center (2) – *246 College St.* ☎ *203-789-2120.* Musicals and classical and popular concerts are presented at this 2,037-seat concert hall.

Yale Repertory Theater (3) – *1120 Chapel St.* ☎ *203-432-1234. www.yale.edu/yalerep.* The "Rep" focuses on plays written by young playwrights and on modern interpretations of the classics.

New Haven Symphony Orchestra – *70 Audubon St.* ☎ *203-776-1444. http://new-havensymphony.com.* One of the finest in the nation, the city's resident symphony orchestra performs at **Woolsey Hall (G)** on the Yale campus.

Yale students stage concerts at the **Yale School of Music (4)** ☎ *203-432-4157.*

Morse and Ezra Stiles Colleges★

Eero Saarinen's design for this ensemble of contemporary buildings was inspired by an Italian hill town. A continuous play of light and shadows is created throughout the day by the maze of stone passages with their vertical planes, geometric forms and sharp angular turns.

Nearby is another of Saarinen's works, the **Yale Co-op** (now known as the West Co-op, since an adjacent building, the East Co-op, has been constructed).

On Tower Parkway, across the street from Morse and Ezra Stiles Colleges, is the **Payne Whitney Gymnasium**, one of Yale's cathedral-like structures.

▶ *Continue along Tower Pkwy., which becomes Grove St., to High St.*

Note the massive Egyptian Revival-style **gate**★ at the entrance to Grove Street Cemetery. Its architect, **Henry Austin,** was responsible for several of the 19C houses on Hillhouse Avenue.

▶ *Return via Grove St. to York St. Turn left onto York St., then left onto Wall St.*

Sterling Law Buildings

Law students live in this group of buildings, which are similar in design to the English Inns of Court where students studied law from the 16C to the 18C. Portraits of police and robbers have been carved in stone above the windows.

▶ *Cross High St.*

The Yankee Peddler

No figure of Connecticut lore better personifies the New Englander's reputation for driving a hard bargain than the **Yankee peddler**. By 1800 the word was used as a verb specifically meaning "to cheat." As the western frontier opened up in the 19C, Yankee became synonymous with the peripatetic Connecticut salesmen who set out for remote rural areas with wagons and wicker baskets full of locally made goods—and the occasional broken watch, stagnant barometer and magic nostrum said to cure everything from bunions to head colds.

Address Book

For price ranges for hotels and restaurants, see the legend on the cover flap.

WHERE TO STAY

Omni New Haven Hotel at Yale – *155 Temple St.* ☎ *203-772-6664 or 800-THE-OMNI. www.omnihotels.com. 306 rooms.* **$$$** Just a block from the Yale campus, the New Haven Green and New Haven's museums and shops, it can't be beat for convenience. You also get the guest-friendly amenities such as a fully stocked refreshment center in your room, a well-equipped fitness center, and a fine-dining rooftop (19th floor) restaurant, Galileo's, with dramatic views of the city skyline and harbor.

Three Chimneys Inn – *1201 Chapel St.* ☎ *203-789-1201 or 800-443-1554. www.threechimneysinn.com/ct. 10 rooms.* **$$$** Just blocks up from the Yale campus, the New Haven Green and downtown, this imposing multicolored B&B (known as the "painted lady" in 1870) is perfect for those looking for a homey place with character. A Victorian-era feel pervades here, with vintage paneling, tapestries and Oriental rugs, antiques-filled guest rooms (some with four-poster or canopy beds), complimentary port and sherry in a library filled with Old Eli memorabilia, and a gracious dining room where a full breakfast is served each morning.

WHERE TO EAT

Roomba – *1044 Chapel St.* ☎ *203-562-7666. Closed Sun & Mon.* **$$$ Latin.** Like the dance, Roomba is one seductive number. Credit goes to chef-owner Arturo Franco-Camacho, whose Latin-fusion cuisine has woken up taste buds around the state and whose dramatic presentations have inspired area restaurants to ratchet up their creativity. Ordering here is like exploring a tantalizing foreign land, with endless variations on ceviche, coconut-crusted shrimp with mango-horseradish sauce, Caribbean grilled salmon with lemongrass sauce and fried banana, and incredible chocolate lava cake.

Tre Scalini – *100 Wooster St.* ☎ *203-777-3373. www.trescalinirestaurant.com.*

$$$ Italian. This upscale trattoria is a primo choice in a city rich with Italian restaurants. You'll find classic Italian fare here, but the real allure runs to the more inventive dishes—grilled lamb chops with figs and pignoli nuts and pork chops stuffed with Parma prosciutto, mozzarella and wild mushrooms.

Zinc – *964 Chapel St.* ☎ *203-624-0507. www.zincfood.com.* **$$$ American.** The city-sleek restaurant has won a following among diners with a taste for New American fare with Asian accents. The menu offers a nice assortment of small plates, like smoked duck nachos and lobster and salmon gravlax summer rolls. Entress are equally inventive with dishes like Moroccan spiced lamb, seared black cod and white cornmeal crusted red trout with Hoja Santo butter sauce.

Claire's Corner Copia – *1000 Chapel St. Open daily from 8 a.m.* ☎ *203-562-3888. www.clairescornercopia.com.* **$$ Vegetarian.** Anyone who has passed through New Haven in the past 25 years knows Claire's. Owner Claire Chriscuolo, a pioneer of vegetarianism, learned to cook at her Italian grandmother's knee and blended what she learned with her own belief in healthy eating and an interest in international cuisine. Her restaurant is casual; customers line up to order and serve themselves. Popular choices are eggplant Veracruz, Cuban black bean soup, pasta Amalfitana and Lithuanian coffeecake. (Claire's is also certified kosher.)

Louis' Lunch – *261-263 Crown St. Closed Sun, Mon & month of August.* ☎ *203-562-5507. www.louislunch.com.* **$ American.** One of New Haven's main claims to fame—after Yale—is this tiny eatery, with a menu that redefines "limited." Louis' is considered the birthplace of the hamburger and is on the National Register of Historic Places. The burger is served here today as it was 100 years ago: straight up, on toast, with cheese, tomatoes, onions, chips, even potato salad if you like, but no fries or—perish the thought—ketchup. Soups and pies round out the menu.

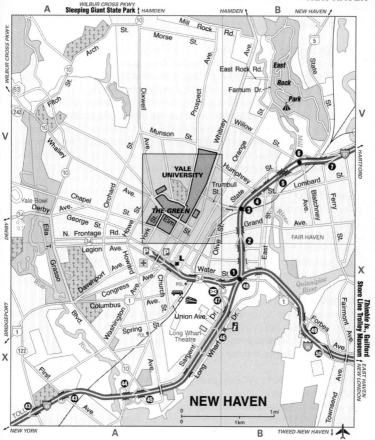

Beinecke Rare Book and Manuscript Library★

121 Wall St.

The exterior walls of this library (1961, Gordon Bunshaft) are composed of a granite framework fitted with translucent marble panels. Enter the library and observe the unusual effect produced by the sunlight streaming through the marble slabs. A **Gutenberg Bible** and changing exhibits are displayed on the mezzanine.

Isamu Noguchi's **sculptures (5)** of geometric shapes anchor the sunken courtyard that fronts the library.

Facing the library are several buildings erected to celebrate Yale's bicentennial: **Woodbridge Hall (E)** offices, the **University Dining Hall (F)** and **Woolsey Hall (G)** auditorium. The rotunda, **Memorial Hall (H)**, contains a large group of commemorative plaques. On the plaza, near Woodbridge Hall, note Alexander Calder's red stabile *Gallows and Lollipops*.

▶ *Return to the corner of Wall and High Sts. and turn left onto High St. A number of small statues ornament the rooftops of buildings along this street.*

Sterling Memorial Library

120 High St. At first glance, Yale's main library, with its stained-glass windows, frescoes and archways, resembles a cathedral.

The **Cross Campus Library (J)**, located beneath Cross Campus *(to the left)*, was built underground to allow the green to remain intact.

Museums

Yale University Art Gallery★★

1111 Chapel St. ◷ *Open year-round Tue–Sat 10am–5pm, Sun 1pm–6pm, Thu 10am–8pm. (Sep-Jun).* ◷ *Closed major holidays.* ♿ ☎ *203-432-0600. www.artgallery.yale.edu.* ◔ *Detailed floor plans are available at the information desk.*

This gallery was founded in 1832 with a gift of some 100 works of art by the Patriot artist **John Trumbull**. Today selections from an 80,000-piece collection ranging from early Eqyptian times to the present are displayed in two interconnected units: a 1928 Gothic-style building and a 1953 addition designed by Louis Kahn. Particularly strong are the holdings of American decorative arts, which focus on the colonial and federal eras, and American painting and sculpture.

Ground Floor

The collection of **ancient Mediterranean art** featured here comprises more than 12,000 objects and spans 5,000 years. Artifacts include a Mithraic shrine *(Temple to the Sun God)* with elaborate paintings and reliefs from **Dura-Europos**, an ancient Roman town in Syria; and *Leda and the Swan* (370 BC), a Roman copy of a Greek sculpture attributed to Timotheos. Equally noteworthy are the stone, clay, and jade artifacts in the growing **pre-Columbian** collection.

First Floor (special exhibits and contemporary art)

Noteworthy in the Sculpture Hall is Richard Serra's site-specific *Stacks* (1990), two steel monoliths placed 60ft apart. The Albers Corridor features a rotating selection of the gallery's 74 paintings and 110 prints by the German-born artist Joseph Albers, who chaired Yale's art department for 10 years (1950–60).

Second Floor (11C to 19C European painting and sculpture; African sculpture)

In addition to Impressionist paintings, the 19C collection includes works by Manet *(Young Woman Reclining in Spanish Costume)*, Courbet *(Le Grand Pont)*, Van Gogh *(Night Café)*, Millet, Corot, Degas and Matisse.

In the section devoted to early modern art, the visitor will find works by Marcel Duchamp *(Tu'm)*, Stella *(Brooklyn Bridge)*, Magritte *(Pandora's Box)* and Dalí *(The Phantom Cart)* and canvases by Tanguy, Ernst, Klee and Kandinsky.

The collection of **African art** highlights masks and ceremonial and royal objects.

Third Floor (late-19C European and Contemporary art; American art)

The **Jarves Collection** of early Italian painting (13–16C) includes such jewels as da Fabriano's *Madonna and Child* and Ghirlandaio's *Portrait of a Lady with a Rabbit*. The adjacent galleries, devoted to European art, contain the Medieval collection. Among the European paintings are portraits by Holbein and Hals, an oil sketch by Rubens, Correggio's *Assumption of the Virgin*, and the *Allegory of Intemperance* attributed to Hieronymus Bosch.

The **Garven Collection** of colonial and early-19C Americana is arranged didactically for the university's teaching purposes. Furniture, silver, pewter and ironware are used to illustrate the

NEW HAVEN PIZZA

New Haven claims to be the home of America's primo pizza—thin-crusted Neapolitan style, with brick-oven flavor. Competing for top honors on Wooster Street, the city's Little Italy, are Pepe's, (established 1925) and Sally's (established 1938). Pepe's partisans claim Pepe's white-clam-with-garlic is top pie; Sally's supporters swear by Sally's white-broccoli-rabe pie (seasonal). **Frank Pepe's Pizzeria Neapolitan** *(157 Wooster St.;* ☎ *203-865-5762);* **(Pepe's) The Spot** *(163 Wooster St.; closed Mon & Tue;* ☎ *203-865-7602);* **Sally's Apizza** *(237 Wooster St.; closed Mon;* ☎ *203-624-5271).*

development of American art forms and their relationship to the society that produced them.

On view in the gallery of American paintings and sculpture from the 19C and 20C are masterpieces by, among others, Eakins, Homer, Church, Cole, Remington, Hopper and O'Keeffe. One section of the gallery displays works of John Trumbull including the original paintings *The Battle of Bunker Hill* and *Signing of the Declaration of Independence*, used as models for copies later produced by Trumbull for the Capitol in Washington, DC. Hiram Powers' sculpture *The Greek Slave* is also on display.

Fourth Floor (Asian art; prints and drawings)

Japanese sculpture and Chinese bronzes, ceramics and paintings span the period from the 12C BC to the present. You can trace the history of the graphic arts by way of 25,000 prints, 6,000 drawings and 3,000 photographs that date from the 15C to the 20C.

Yale Center for British Art★★

1080 Chapel St. ◷ *Open year-round Tue–Sat 10am–5pm, Sun noon–5pm.* ◷ *Closed major holidays.* ♿ ☎ *203-432-2800. www.ycba.yale.edu/index.asp.*

Established by a gift from philanthropist Paul Mellon in 1966, the Yale Center for British Art possesses the most comprehensive collection of British art outside Great Britain.

The Collection

Based on Mellon's original donation of more than 60,000 works—including 1,300 paintings, 10,000 drawings, 20,000 prints, and 20,000 rare books—the collection illustrates British life and culture from the 16C to the present. The museum also organizes large, often provocative temporary shows of British art (both contemporary and historical), as well as related lectures and film screenings.

On the fourth floor, paintings and sculpture are installed chronologically to provide a survey of British art from the late 16C through the early 19C. Several rooms on this floor are reserved for the works of **Gainsborough**, **Reynolds**, **Stubbs**, **Turner** and **Constable**. A selection of 19C and 20C paintings and sculpture fill the second floor.

Peabody Museum of Natural History

Kids *170 Whitney Ave.* ◷ *Open year-round Mon–Sat 10am–5pm, Sun noon–5pm.* ◷ *Closed major holidays.* ⇌ *$7 Free on Thu 2pm-5pm.* ♿🅿 ☎ *203-432-5050. www.yale.edu/peabody.*

FINER DINING

Scoozzi Trattoria & Wine Bar – *1104 Chapel St.* ☎ *203-776-8268. www. scoozzi.com.* **$$ Italian**. This trattoria and wine bar features innovative pasta and risotto dishes (like the Aragosta risotto with lobster, scallops, asparagus, mushrooms and sweet corn, finished with lemon-mascarpone cheese) and thin crust pizzas (try the Firenze with chicken sausage, asparagus, artichokes, tomatoes, smoked mozzarella and basil pesto).

Union League Café – *1032 Chapel St.* ◷ *Closed Sun.* ☎ *203-562-4299. www. unionleaguecafe.com.* Treat yourself to a bit of New Haven history along with fine cuisine at this French brasserie located just off the Green. The graciously restored Sherman Building incorporates the former home of Roger Sherman, a signer of the Declaration of Independence. Inside, the restaurant offers an elegant setting for enjoying gourmet fare such as terrine of venison and duck foie gras, wild striped bass on a bed of dried fennel and roasted Long Island duck with fresh corn croquettes and figs.

Endowed in 1866 by financier George Peabody, Yale's natural history museum showcases more than 11 million specimens. In the first-floor **Great Hall**, you'll find the Peabody's famous collection of **dinosaurs**, featuring the first *Stegosaurus* ever mounted, the ever-popular *Apatosaurus* (67ft long, 35 tons), and the 10ft *Archelon* (75 million years old), a giant sea turtle. Spanning the Great Hall is Rudolph Zallinger's mural *The Age of Reptiles*, which vividly summarizes over 300 million years of animal and plant evolution. The first floor also houses a collection of mammals, primates and artifacts representing the cultures of Mesoamerica, the Plains Indians and New Guinea. Rocks and minerals, the Hall of Connecticut Birds and dioramas of North American flora and fauna can be found on the third floor. The second floor is reserved for special exhibits.

Yale Collection of Musical Instruments (K)

15 Hillhouse Ave. 🕐 *Open Sept–Jun Tue–Thu 1pm–4pm.* 🕐 *Closed Jul & Aug, Thanksgiving Day, Dec 25, and during academic holidays.* ⊗ *$2 contribution requested.* ☎ *203-432-0822. http://www.yale.edu/musicalinstruments.*

Established in 1900, this rare collection assembles more than 800 fine and decorative musical instruments documenting the European music tradition from 1550 to 1900. Here you'll find violins by Jakob Stainer (1661) and Stradivari (1736) and an outstanding array of keyboard instruments dating back to 1569. *A series of concerts is held annually featuring restored instruments from the collection (for information, call ☎ 203-432-0822).*

Additional Sights *Map p 97*

The Green★

When New Haven was a Puritan colony, the town was laid out as a large square subdivided into nine smaller squares. Now a National Historic Landmark, the center square, or green, was reserved for the use of the entire community as pastureland, parade ground and burial ground, and has served as the heart of the downtown district since 1638. The upper green is characterized by its three early-19C churches: 1752 **Trinity Church** *(129 Church St.;* ☎ *203-624-3101; www.trinitynewhaven.org),* the first Gothic-Revival church built in the US; Georgian **Congressional United Church of Christ**, or **Center Church** *(250 Temple St.;* ☎ *203-787-0121),* whose present structure dates to 1812 and lies over part of the old burial ground; and the Federal-style **United Congregational Church**, or North Church *(323 Temple St.;* ☎ *203-787-4195),* whose steeple has been replicated in churches across the country.

Center Church, Town Green

Hillhouse Avenue

Most of the beautiful mansions on this street were built in the 19C by wealthy industrialists and merchants and are now owned by Yale University. Architectural styles represented include Greek Revival (no. 46), High Victorian Gothic (no. 43), Beaux-Arts Revival (no. 38) and Italianate (no. 24).

David S. Ingalls Skating Rink★
Corner of Sachem and Prospect Sts.
One of the most distinguished collegiate hockey facilities in the country, this lantern-shaped rink (1958) was designed for Yale by the Finnish-born architect Eero Saarinen. Its 300ft-long curved, arched roof accounts for its nickname, the Yale Whale.

New Haven Colony Historical Society
114 Whitney Ave. 🕐 *Open year-round Tue–Fri 10am–5pm, Sat noon–5pm.* 👓 *$4.* ♿🅿 ☎ *203-562-4183. www.nhchs.org.*
Recounting 300 years of New Haven's history, exhibits in 11 galleries here display antique pewter, china and toys dating from the period of the New Haven Colony, among other items. The society also preserves notable artifacts, including an original model of Eli Whitney's cotton gin and one of Samuel F.B. Morse's first code receivers.

East Rock Park
▶ *Follow Orange St.; cross Mill River and turn left, then bear right. The road leads to the summit parking lot.* 🕐 *Open year-round daily 8am–dusk. Summit drive open Apr-Oct 8am–dusk; Nov-Mar weekends 8am-4pm.* 🅿 ☎ *203-946-6086. www.city-ofnewhaven.com/parks.*
New Haven's oldest park features walking trails, a road to the summit of East Rock, and the Giant Steps up the cliff, as well as a rose garden and athletic fields. From the summit of this basalt ridge stretches a **view**★★ of the New Haven area with Long Island Sound in the distance.

The Amistad Affair, 1839–1841

For more than two years, New Haven was the focal point of the Amistad Affair, a major milestone in the long struggle to end slavery in the US. In August 1839, the officers of the US brig *Washington* discovered a Spanish ship anchored off the coast of Long Island. On board were 53 native Africans who had been kidnapped from their home in West Africa by Spaniards and sold into slavery in Cuba. En route from Havana to Puerto Principe, Cuba, aboard the schooner Amistad, the captives—under the leadership of a slave who came to be known as "Cinque"—overcame their captors and attempted to sail home with the help of two Spanish passengers whose lives they spared. The Spaniards, however, surreptitiously guided the ship northward and westward by night in hopes that the Amistad would be intercepted. After being recaptured by the Americans, the slaves were taken to New Haven, where they were charged with piracy and murder.

Yale professor Josiah Willard Gibbs gave the Africans a voice to defend themselves. Gibbs searched the wharves of New York City until he found an African sailor who could serve as an interpreter for the captives. Antislavery leaders aroused the public to raise funds to return them to their homeland, and promote the abolitionist cause. The Africans were finally granted their freedom by courts in the Connecticut co-capitals of Hartford and New Haven; soon after, the decision was upheld by the Supreme Court, thanks to the persuasive arguments of former president John Quincy Adams.

Today a 14ft bronze sculpture in front of New Haven City Hall (165 Church St.) pays tribute to the 53 Africans aboard the Amistad. The **Amistad Memorial** marks the former site of the New Haven Jail, where the Africans were incarcerated while awaiting trial.

Shore Line Trolley Museum

Kids *5mi east of New Haven. 17 River St., in East Haven.* ▶ *Take I-95 North to Exit 51; turn right onto Hemingway Ave., then left onto River St.* 🕐 *Open Jun–Aug daily 10:30am–4:30pm. Sept–mid-Dec & May weekends only 10:30am–4:30pm.* ⊝ *$6.* ♿ 🅿 ☎ *203-467-6927. www.bera.org.*

Primarily the work of volunteer trolley buffs who have restored one-third of the nearly 100 vintage street, subway and elevated railway cars on the grounds, the museum features a collection of trolley cars from 1878-1962. Visitors can ride restored cars on a 3mi trolley excursion along the Connecticut shore.

Sleeping Giant State Park

6mi north of New Haven, in Hamden. ▶ *Take Whitney Ave. to Hamden and turn right on Mt. Carmel Ave.* 🕐 *Open year-round daily 8am–dusk. Trail maps and information available at ranger headquarters.* ⊝ *$7 fee per in-state vehicle, $10 for out-of-state vehicle.* 🅿 ☎ *203-789-7498. www.dep.state.ct.us/ stateparks/parks/sleepinggiant.htm.*

Carved by glaciers more than 15,000 years ago, the rocky sandstone and trap rock ridge known as the Sleeping Giant resembles a colossal man lying on his back. The park is threaded by 30mi of trails, including the popular **Tower Path** 🔋 *(1.6mi round-trip),* which leads to Mt. Carmel, the highest point in the park. From a stone observation tower here stretch **views**★★ of New Haven, Long Island Sound and the Connecticut hills.

The Thimble Islands

Legend has it that Captain Kidd buried treasure on one of the 365 Thimble Islands that lie off the coast of Stony Creek *(12mi east of New Haven).* The miniature islands range in size from a few boulders to several acres of farmland. Twenty-five of the Thimbles are inhabited and many are privately owned. Narrated boat tours of the islands on the **Sea Mist** *(45 min;* ⊝ *$10; schedules:* ☎ *203-488-8905 or www.seamistcruises.com)* and the **Volsunga IV** *(45min;* ⊝ *$9; schedules:* ☎ *203-481-3345 or http:// thimbleislands.com)* leave from the Stony Creek town dock from May to Columbus Day.

Guilford

13mi east of New Haven. ▶ *Take I-95 North to Exit 58 and follow Rte. 146 South to Guilford.*

In 1639 Minister Henry Whitfield arrived here with 25 families and bought the land that became Guilford from the Menunketuck Indians. Today his 1639 home—the oldest stone dwelling in New England—has been restored to its 17C appearance as the **Henry Whitfield State Museum** *(248 Old Whitfield St.;* 🕐 *open Apr–mid-Dec Wed–Sun 10am–4:30pm, rest of the year by appointment;* ⊝ *$4;* 🅿 ☎ *203-453-2457; www.chc.state.ct.us/whitefieldhouse.htm).*

Guilford's early prosperity is reflected in its lovely green and its 18C and 19C homes. Noteworthy among them are two typical saltbox structures, the late-17C **Hyland House** *(84 Boston St.;* 👣 *visit by 45min guided tour only, Jun–Labor Day Tue–Sun 10am–4:30pm Labor Day-Columbus Day weekends 10am-4:30pm;* ☎ *203-453-9477; www.hylandhouse.com),* and the **Thomas Griswold House** *(171 Boston St.;* 👣 *visit by 45min guided tour only, Jun–Sept Tue–Sun 11am–4pm Oct weekends 11am-4pm;* ⊝ *$2;* 🅿 ☎ *203-453-3176; www.thomasgriswoldhouse.com).* Inhabited by five generations of the same family (1774-1958), the beautifully restored Griswold House features its original double-batten door (solid vertical planks held by horizontal boards), constructed for defense against Indian attacks. Period furniture includes two fine examples of the "Guilford" corner cabinet.

NEW LONDON

POPULATION 25,671
MICHELIN MAP 581 K 11 AND MAP BELOW
TOURIST INFORMATION ☎ 860-444-2206 OR WWW.MYSTICMORE.COM

Located on a harbor at the mouth of the Thames River, New London has always depended on the sea for its livelihood. Home to the US Coast Guard Academy, the city retains its ties with the ocean today. The shipping industry and the US Naval Submarine Base located across the Thames River in Groton are major contributors to the local economy.

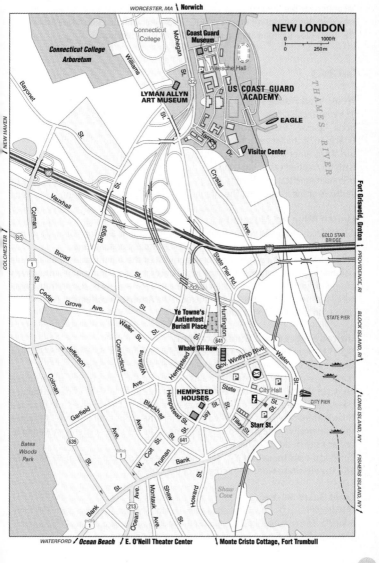

A Bit of History

New London's deep-water port was a haven for privateers during the Revolution, a fact that led to the British attack on New London and Groton in 1781. During this assault, led by Benedict Arnold, **Fort Trumbull** (🕐 *open year-round as Fort Trumbull State Park, 90 Walbach St.;* ☎ *860-244-3203)* and **Fort Griswold** *(preserved as Fort Griswold State Park, Monument St. & Park Ave., Groton;* ☎ *860-445-1729)* fell to the enemy, and nearly all of New London was destroyed by fire. In the mid-19C the city was a principal whaling port. Elegant homes built from the profits of whaling, such as the four white Greek Revival mansions in **Whale Oil Row** *(nos. 105–119 Huntington St.)*, still stand in neighborhoods that have remained residential, despite the development of onshore industry.

Scientists and engineers at the Naval Underwater Systems Center, on the grounds of Fort Trumbull, develop technology related to modern undersea warfare. Some 1,600 men and women attend Connecticut College, a four-year, liberal arts school located near the Coast Guard Academy. Revitalization of the downtown area has included the renovation of several 19C Greek Revival houses on **Starr Street** and the 19C Union Railroad Station (designed by H.H. Richardson).

Sights

Hempsted Houses★
11 Hempstead St. 🚶 *Visit by guided tour (45min) only, mid-May–mid-Oct Thu–Sun noon–4pm.* 🎫 *$4.* 🅿 ☎ *860-443-7949. www.hartnet.org/als.*
Built in 1678, the timber-framed Joshua Hempsted House provides a splendid example of 17C American architecture. The walls are insulated with seaweed and pierced with tiny leaded casement windows. Inside, the low-ceilinged rooms contain fine, primitive American furnishings. The granite Nathaniel Hempsted House was built by Joshua's grandson in 1759. The interior features an unusual projecting bake oven.

Lyman Allyn Art Museum★
625 Williams St. 🕐 *Open year-round Tue–Sat 10am–5pm, Sun 1pm–5pm.* 🕐 *Closed major holidays.* 🎫 *$5.* 🅿 ♿ ☎ *860-443-2545. http://lymanallyn.org.*
This small museum, established by a bequest of the Allyn family, specializes in paintings by Connecticut artists and in the decorative arts of the state. Attractively arranged furnishings, paintings, sculpture and decorative arts, dating from classical civilizations to the present, complement the **American collection** (1680-1920), housed in the first-floor Palmer Galleries.

United States Coast Guard Academy
🔲 *15 Mohegan Ave.* 🕐 *Open year-round daily 9am–dusk.* ♿ ☎ *800-883-8724. www. uscga.edu. Contact the academy for special events and parade dates.*
A four-year military college that trains officers for the Coast Guard, the academy began in 1876 when the schooner *Dobbin* was chosen to serve as a floating training school to prepare cadets for the Revenue Marine (which later evolved into the Coast Guard). The *Dobbin* was succeeded by several other ships until the early 20C, when the academy was established at Fort Trumbull. In 1932 the academy moved to its present site beside the Thames.
Begin at the **visitor center** (🕐 *open May–Sep Wed–Sun 9am–4:30pm;* ☎ *860-444-8611)* by viewing a video about the life of the cadets.

Coast Guard Museum
In Waesche Hall. 🕐 *Open year-round Mon–Fri 9am–4:30pm, Sat 10am–5pm, Sun noon–5pm.* 🕐 *Closed major holidays.* ♿ ☎*860-444-8511. www.uscg.mil/hg/9-cp/museum.*
The museum's exhibits recount the history of the Coast Guard.

The Waterfront

The academy's training vessel, the **USCG Barque Eagle**★, is occasionally berthed at the waterfront. German-built, the *Eagle* (1936) is a graceful, three-masted square-rigger used for cadet training cruises to Europe and the Caribbean in the summer. When in port, the *Eagle* may be visited by guided tour (☎ 860-444-8595).

Connecticut College Arboretum

Williams St. ○ *Open year-round daily dawn–dusk.* ✎ *Sun free guided tours May-Oct at 2pm.* ☎ *860-439-5020. http:// arboretum.conncoll.edu. A self-guided tour brochure is available at the main entrance to the Native Plant Collection.*
This 750-acre preserve consists of three major plant collections. Covering 20 acres, the Native Plant Collection

---

Cross Sound Ferry

For a scenic alternative to the lengthy drive from Long Island to coastal Connecticut, try the Cross Sound ferry. The company offers both vehicle and passenger transportation from Orient Point, Long Island to New London, Connecticut. The high-speed Sea Jet I accommodates passengers only and makes the crossing in 40 minutes.

One-way 1hr 30min. ⊸ *$44 (car and driver) Reservations required for vehicles.* ✗ 🅿 *For seasonal schedules, contact Cross Sound Ferry Services, Inc. (☎ 860-443-5281 in Connecticut or ☎ 631-323-2525 on Long Island; www. longislandferry.com).*

---

features shrubs, trees and wildflowers indigenous to eastern North America. The main trail *(2mi)* circles a marsh; two optional loops lead to a bog and a hemlock forest. A variety of woody plants occupy the three-acre Caroline Black Garden. The Campus Landscape comprises 120 acres with over 200 trees from different parts of the world.

Ye Towne's Antientest Burial Place

Huntington St. Enter from Hempstead St.
In this old burial ground you'll find many early New England slate tombstones carved with winged angels, skulls and crossbones, geometric patterns and other designs.

Monte Cristo Cottage

325 Pequot Ave., off Howard St. ✎ *Visit by guided tour (1hr) only Memorial Day–Labor Day Thu–Sat noon–4pm, Sun 1pm–3pm; Labor Day-mid-Oct; Thu-Sun 1pm-5pm.* ⊸ *$7.* 🅿 ☎ *860-443-0051. www.oncilltheatercenter.org*
The unpretentious two-story frame dwelling looking out on the Thames was the boyhood summer home of playwright **Eugene O'Neill** (1888-1953). Now a Registered National Landmark, Monte Cristo Cottage was the setting for O'Neill's two most autobiographical works: *Ah, Wilderness!* (1932) and the Pulitzer Prize-winning *Long Day's Journey into Night* (1956). A short *(18 min)* film serves as an introduction to the years the O'Neills spent here.

Excursions

Ocean Beach

5mi south of New London on Ocean Ave.
This wide, sandy beach, edged with a pleasant boardwalk, offers an amusement arcade, miniature golf, archery, swimming and boating.

Eugene O'Neill Theater Center

6mi south of New London, in Waterford. 305 Great Neck Rd. Take Bank St., and turn left at Ocean Ave.; continue to Rte. 213 (Niles Hill Rd.) and follow signs. ○ *Performances Jun–late Aug.* ✗ ♿ *For schedules, call* ☎ *860-443-5378; www.oneilltheatercenter.org.*
Named in honor of the 20C playwright Eugene O'Neill, the center is devoted to the development of new talent for the American stage. Activities on the center's 10-

acre grounds include the National Playwrights Conference and the National Music Theater Conference. The center also sponsors the National Theater Institute and the National Critics Institute.

Groton

3mi east of New London. ▶ *Take I-95 North to Exit 86 and follow Rte. 12 South to Groton.* Set opposite New London on the east bank of the Thames River, this small industrial city with its deep-water harbor is the home to the US Naval Submarine Base *(o─ᴥ not open to the public)*. Subs are berthed and repaired at the Lower Base beside the river. Groton's largest employer, the Electric Boat division of General Dynamics, is known for building the world's first nuclear-powered submarine. Each year in June, the Thames River is the site of the colorful **Yale-Harvard regatta**.

Historic Ship Nautilus★

📷 *Berthed adjacent to the Submarine Base.* 🕓 *Open mid-May–late Oct Wed–Mon 9am–5pm, Tue 1pm–5pm. Rest of the year Wed–Mon 9am–4pm.* 🕓 *Closed Jan 1, Thanksgiving Day, Dec 25 & first week in May.* 🅿 ☎ *860-694-3174 or 800-343-0079. www.ussnautilus.org.*

With the launching of the world's first nuclear-powered vessel, the *Nautilus*, in New London in 1954, submarine technology entered the atomic age. The *Nautilus* established new submerged records for speed, distance and underwater endurance, and in 1958 it became the first submarine to reach the North Pole.

Decommissioned in 1980, the 320ft ship is now the principal attraction at the USS Nautilus/Submarine Force Library and Museum complex. The torpedo room, control room and other sections of the vessel may be viewed. Changing exhibits in the **Submarine Force Museum** draw from the museum's collection of more than 18,000 artifacts, 20,000 documents and 30,000 photographs. The story of underwater navigation, the construction of the *Nautilus* and life aboard a sub are among the subjects presented. In April 2000, a new wing added space for expanded exhibits, a theater, archival storage and a new museum store.

Norwich

18mi north of New London via Rte. 32 West to I-395 North. Take Exit 81 and follow Rte. 2 East.

Situated where the Yantic and Shetucket Rivers meet to form the Thames, Norwich has been an important industrial center since the 18C. Birthplace of Benedict Arnold, the city's historic district radiates out from a prim triangular **green** and claims a fine group of early dwellings. One of these, the 18C **Leffingwell Inn** *(348 Washington St.)* was the site of many political meetings during the Revolution.

NORWALK

POPULATION 82,951
MICHELIN MAP 581 I 12
TOURIST INFORMATION ☎ 203-853-7770, 800-866-7925 OR WWW.COASTALCT.COM

Long famed for its oyster industry, this once lively 19C seaport has revived its spirit in SoNo (an acronym for South Norwalk) along the Norwalk River. Here, restored Victorian buildings lining Washington Street between Main and Water Streets house attractive restaurants, shops, clubs and galleries. This area is also the site of the annual SoNo Arts Celebration *(early Aug; www.sonoarts.org)*. Along the riverfront Heritage State Park incorporates museums, an amphitheater, a visitor center, fishing piers and playgrounds.

▶ **Orient Yourself:** Norwalk sits on the Connecticut coastline on the northern reaches of Long Island Sound. North-south I-95 and US-7 provides easy access.

🅿 **Parking:** There are several parking lots scattered throughout downtown, including the Main St. lot (on Main St. near the Wall St. intersection), Maritime Parking Garage (on Water St.) and the North Water lot (at junction of Liberty and Washington Streets), which gives easy access to the aquarium.

☺ **Don't Miss:** A stroll through bustling Heritage State Park.

🕐 **Organizing Your Time:** Start at the Maritime Aquarium (allow an hour or two), hop aboard the ferry to Sheffield Island Lighthouse, and when you return explore the docks, piers and boardwalks that lace through Heritage State Park.

Kids **Especially for Kids:** The Maritime Aquarium is top-notch; its exhibits, touch tanks and IMAX theater will fascinate children.

♿ **Also See:** Cruises leave from Hope Dock *(132 Water St., adjacent to the gazebo at the Maritime Aquarium)* for the historic 1868 **Sheffield Island Lighthouse** *(30 min one-way; commentary;* ⌚ *$18;* ✕ 🅿 *; for current schedules, contact Norwalk Seaport Assn.;* ☎ *203-838-9444; www.seaport.org)*.

Sights

Maritime Aquarium★

Kids *10 N. Water St.* 🕐 *Open daily 10am–5pm. Jul-Aug 10am–6pm.* 🕐 *Closed Thanksgiving Day & Dec 25.* ⌚ *$10.50. Combination tickets available for aquarium & IMAX theater.* ✕ ♿ 🅿 ☎ *203-852-0700. www.maritimeaquarium.org.*

A renovated 19C brick warehouse on the river houses this three-story complex, which features an aquarium devoted to Long Island Sound habitats, a new environmental education center and an IMAX theater *(*⌚ *$8.50).* Aquarium exhibits highlight life in the Sound, from tidal shellfish to sharks and rays, housed in the 110,000gal **Open Ocean** tank. Harbor seals, river otters and a ray touch-pool round out the attractions here.

Lockwood-Mathews Mansion Museum

295 West Ave. 🚌 *Visit by guided tour (1hr) only, mid-Mar–Dec Wed–Sun noon–4pm. Jan & Feb open by appointment only.* 🕐 *Closed major holidays.* ⌚ *$8.* ☎ *203-838-9799. www.lockwoodmathewsmansion.org.*

The three-story, turreted Victorian summer "cottage" of investment banker LeGrand Lockwood was completed in 1869 in granite with a mansard roof. The 62-room interior, including an art gallery, children's theater and Moorish sitting room, boasts marble floors and mahogany and walnut woodwork crafted by Italian artisans. The grand staircase alone, with 266 balusters, reportedly cost $50,000.

Address Book

For price categories for hotels and restaurants, see the legend on the cover flap.

WHERE TO STAY

West Lane Inn – *22 West Lane (Rte. 35), Ridgefield.* 🅿 ☎ *203-438-7323. www. westlaneinn.com. 14 rooms.* **$$** Passersby often stop to admire this gracious mansion, an 1849 Colonial surrounded by towering maples. All rooms have queen-sized four-poster beds, air conditioning and private baths, and some have fireplaces (a favorite is the semicircular front room—no fireplace, but three windows in a bay). Continental breakfast, available in the breakfast room in winter, is served on the expansive front porch in summer.

WHERE TO EAT

Bernard's Inn at Ridgefield – *20 West Lane, Ridgefield.* 🕐 *Closed Mon.* ♿ ☎ *203-438-8282. www.bernardsinnatridgefield.com.* **$$$ French**. Stellar dishes, courtesy of Bernard, who has cooked at Le Cirque, include the foie-gras trio (sautéed, poached with Sauternes gelée, and smoked with horseradish aspic), potato crusted salmon, crispy sweetbreads or braised veal cheeks.

Elms Restaurant & Tavern – *500 Main St., Ridgefield.* 🕐 *Restaurant open for dinner only Wed–Sun.* 🕐 *Restaurant & tavern closed Mon.* ♿ ☎ *203-438-9206. www.elmsinn.com.* **$$$ American**. This restored 1799 inn offers an updated Yankee menu in its dining room, more casual—and less expensive—fare in its tavern. TThe award-winning chef is known for his skillful renditions of soups (curried apple-butternut squash and hunter's consommé with pheasant quenelles), meats (lamb two ways—grilled rack and roasted loin) and game (roasted pheasant).

Habana – *70 N. Main St., South Norwalk. Dinner only.* ☎ *203-852-9790.* **$$$ Latin**. Habana breaks two cardinal restaurant rules: it's too dark and too loud. So why is it wildly successful? The secret is New Cuban cuisine dramatically presented. One taste of plantain-coated sea bass with black bean risotto and mango wine sauce, or filet mignon with purple potato hash and mariachi sauce, and you rationalize the dim lighting as romantic, the loudness as the Latin heartbeat, and count yourself lucky to be dining next to the potted palms.

Meigas Restaurant – *10 Wall St., Norwalk.* 🕐 *Closed Mon.* ♿ ☎ *203-866-8800. www.meigasrestaurant. com.* **$$$ Spanish**. This warmly lit, white-tablecloth restaurant has lured gourmets from Manhattan and beyond, thanks to the polished Spanish regional cuisine of chef-owner Ignacio Blanco. You'll likely become a convert, too, once you taste his roasted piquillo peppers stuffed with lamb or his marinated fresh anchovies with salmon caviar, and his grilled rib-eye with potato confit and mojo de ajo sauce.

Silvermine Tavern – *194 Perry Ave., Norwalk.* 🕐 *Closed Tues.* ☎ *203-847-4558. www.silverminetavern.com.* **$$$ American**. If ever a place looked straight out of central casting, it's the Silvermine Tavern. Set on a mill pond complete with waterfall and gliding swans, this rambling white clapboard 1785 landmark practically screams "country inn." It is known for lunch in season on the tree-shaded deck, its chicken potpie (dinner only), New England seafood stew, and its tasty honey buns, but you'll find an extensive menu of traditional steaks, poultry, and fish dishes, too.

Excursions

New Canaan

10mi north of Norwalk, via Rte. 123.

This choice suburb in Connecticut's Fairfield County has been an arts center since 1922, when the **Silvermine Guild of Artists** was founded here. The guild—which currently has 300 members—maintains a complex of studios, galleries and a year-round art school on a five-acre wooded site *(1037 Silvermine Rd., east of Rte. 123;* ☎ *203-966-9700; www.silvermineart.org).* Highlighting its program of events is the annual spring exhibition **Art of the Northeast**.

Barnum Museum

Kids *15mi east of Norwalk in Bridgeport.* ▶ *Take I-95 North to Exit 27 (Lafayette Blvd.); turn left at the fifth traffic light on Main St. to no. 820.* 🕐 *Open year-round Tue–Sat 10am–4:30pm, Sun noon–4:30pm.* 🕐 *Closed major holidays.* ⊗ *$5.* ♿ ☎ *203-331-1104. www.barnum-museum.org.*

This ornate building is as eccentric as its creator, showman-promoter **Phineas T. Barnum** (1810-91). Barnum's world-famous three-ring circus toured America and Europe in the 19C and won acclaim as "The Greatest Show on Earth." Highlights among the exuberant collection of circus memorabilia housed here include costumes and furnishings that belonged to Tom Thumb, the first major star attraction of the circus; and the **Brinley Miniature Circus** of more than 3,000 hand-carved figures. A contemporary wing features changing exhibits of art and American popular culture.

Ridgefield

15mi northwest of Norwalk. ▶ *Take US-7 North to Branchville and pick up Rte. 102 West to Rte. 35 North.*

Although Ridgefield lies just an hour's drive from the hustle and bustle of Manhattan, this charming town, with its tree-shaded avenues, shops and mansions, retains a distinctly New England character.

Keeler Tavern Museum

132 Main St., at the intersection of Rtes. 33 & 35. 🐾 *Visit by guided tour (45min) only, Feb–Dec Wed & weekends 1pm–4pm.* 🕐 *Closed major holidays.* ⊗ *$5.* 🅿 ☎ *203-438-5485. www.keelertavernmuseum.org.*

The Keeler Tavern operated as an inn from colonial days through the early 20C. During the Battle of Ridgefield, April 27, 1777, a cannonball lodged in the wall post, where it remains to this day. This fact accounts for the tavern's nickname, the Cannonball House.

BALDUCCI'S

21 Governor St., Ridgefield. ☎ *203-431-4400. www.balduccis.com.*

A feast for the eyes as well as the palate, this emporium for fresh garden produce is more than its name implies. In addition to an astounding selection of fresh fruit and vegetables, the store offers meat, seafood, breads, cheeses, confections, condiments and gifts. If you're overwhelmed by the selection and artful displays, take a restorative espresso break in the cafe, where a rack of daily newspapers is on hand. *There is also a Westport Balducci's (1385 Post Rd. East) and a Greenwich Balducci's (1050 E. Putnam Ave., Riverside).*

Aldrich Museum of Contemporary Art

258 Main St. 🕐 *Open year-round Tue–Sun noon–5pm.* 🕐 *Closed major holidays.* ⊗ *$7.* 🅿 ☎ *203-438-4519. www.aldrichart.org*

Changing exhibits by both established and upcoming contemporary artists are presented in this handsome Colonial dwelling. The **sculpture garden** displays changing works by such sculptors as Sol LeWitt, Tony Smith and others *(🕐 open year-round daily dawn to dusk).*

"The very warm heart of 'New England at its best,' such a vast abounding Arcadia of mountains and broad vales and great rivers and large lakes and white villages embowered in prodigious elms and maples. It is extraordinarily beautiful and graceful and idyllic—for America."
Henry James' impression of Connecticut, May 1911

WETHERSFIELD ★

POPULATION 26,271
MICHELIN MAP 581 J 10 AND MAP P 78
TOURIST INFORMATION ☎ 860-525-4451 OR WWW.HISTORICWETHERSFIELD.ORG

Unspoiled by industry throughout the 20C, Wethersfield remains a pleasant suburb of Hartford. Approximately 200 dwellings in the town's picturesque historic district, Old Wethersfield, date from the 17C and 18C. A number of these houses, built by wealthy merchants and shipowners, have been restored.

Established in 1634 along a natural harbor in the Connecticut River, Wethersfield was an important center of trade until the 18C, when floods changed the course of the river, leaving only a cove at the original harbor site. This change drastically affected the town's commercial activity, which decreased rapidly until, by the late 18C, farming had replaced trade as the economic mainstay.

Old Wethersfield ★★

Main Street
This wide street is lined with attractively restored 18C houses, many of which boast monumental double doors with carved swan's neck pediments distinctive to the Connecticut River Valley. The 1764 brick **Congregational Meetinghouse (C)** adjoins an early burial ground that contains tombstones dating from the 17C.

Webb-Deane-Stevens Museum ★★
211 Main St. Visit by guided tour (1hr) only, May–Oct Wed–Mon 10am–4pm. Rest of the year weekends only 10am–4pm. Closed Jan 1, Thanksgiving Day & Dec 25. $8. ☎ 860-529-0612. www.webb-deane-stevens.org.
Owned by the National Society of the Colonial Dames of America, these three houses allow a study in architectural styles and decorative arts from 1752 to 1840, and a comparison of the lifestyles of a wealthy merchant, a politician and a modest craftsman.

Webb House
This elegant Georgian residence (1752), built by the prosperous merchant Joseph Webb Sr., was the scene of a four-day conference in May 1781 between Gen. George Washington and the French Count Rochambeau. Plans for the Yorktown campaign, which led ultimately to the defeat of the British in the American Revolution, were discussed by the two military leaders during this time.
The house contains a fine collection of period furnishings and decorative arts. Highlights include the south parlor where Washington and Rochambeau met—note the Colonial Revival mural (c.1916) that depicts Revolutionary events—and the bedchamber used by General Washington, who lodged at the Webb House during his stay in Wethers-

Old Wethersfield

field. The bedroom features the original flocked wool wallpaper, which Washington admired and noted in his diary.

Deane House

This house was built in 1766 for Silas Deane, an American diplomat who traveled to France during the Revolution to negotiate arms and equipment for the Continental Army. While abroad, Deane became involved in business deals that aroused suspicions about his loyalty, and he was accused of treason. He returned home and spent the rest of his life attempting, unsuccessfully, to clear his name. The entry hall is notable for the splendid side stairway with its carved cherrywood balusters, stained to imitate more expensive mahogany. The off-center stairway is unusual for a house of its period.

COMSTOCK, FERRE & CO.

263 Main St. ☎ *860-571-6590 or 800-733-3773. www.comstockferre.com.* This venerable seed company dates back to 1820, reputedly the oldest in the country. Its retail seed business and garden center began in 1958. Today a large selection of bedding plants, shrubs and flowers as well as the famous seeds, available in packets or in bulk, attract backyard gardeners and nurserymen alike. Old-fashioned wooden pull-down seed bins line the interior of the 18C structure, and an adjoining gift shop brims with crafts and keepsakes. The center is an especially colorful place to browse in fall, when pumpkins and squash, cornstalks and chrysanthemums surround decorative scarecrows dressed in denim overalls.

Stevens House

Isaac Stevens was a leather worker who built this house in 1788 for his bride. The dwelling passed by marriage to the Francis family, many of whose possessions are on view. Among the typical mid-19C furnishings are the Hitchcock chairs. The modest interiors make an interesting contrast to those of the more richly embellished Webb and Deane houses.

Wethersfield Museum (D)

200 Main St. ○ *Open year-round Mon–Sat 10am–4pm, Sun 1pm–4pm.* ○ *Closed major holidays.* ∞ *$3.* ♿ ▣ ☎ *860-529-7161. www.wethhist.org.*
A former schoolhouse, this Victorian-era brick building (1893) serves as a visitor center and features a thematic exhibit that brings Wethersfield's history alive with interactive displays and artifacts ranging from a tiny arrowhead to a massive Connecticut Valley doorway. Two galleries are devoted to changing exhibits.

Hurlbut-Dunham House★ (E)

212 Main St. 👣 *Visit by guided tour (45min) only, mid-May–mid-Oct Sat 10am–4pm, Sun 1pm–4pm.* ○ *Closed major holidays.* ∞ *$3.* ▣ ☎ *860-529-7656. www.wethhist.org.*
During the early 1900s Jane and Howard Dunham, a prominent Wethersfield couple, traveled the world to collect furnishings for the gracious brick house that had been in their family since 1875. The Georgian-style house, which passed to the Wethersfield Historical Society with the Dunham belongings intact, has been restored to reflect the period of 1907–1935. Rococo Revival wallpapers, trompe l'œil cornices and crystal chandeliers are among the featured appointments.

Buttolph-Williams House★ (F)

249 Broad St. 👣 *Visit by guided tour (45min) only, May–Oct Wed–Mon 10am–4pm.* ○ *Closed major holidays.* ∞ *$4.* ☎ *860-529-0612. www.hartnet.org/als.*
This center-chimney house (c.1720), distinguished by oak clapboards, casement windows and a hewn overhang, is considered to be one of the most faithful restorations of an early Colonial dwelling in Connecticut. Particularly evocative of the Pilgrim era, the house served as the inspiration for the popular children's book *The Witch of Blackbird Pond* (1958) by Elizabeth George Speare.

Cove Warehouse

At Cove Park, north end of Main St. ⏱ *Open mid-May–mid-Oct Sat 10am–4pm, Sun 1pm–4pm.* 🎫 *$1 (donation).* 🅿 ☎ *860-529-7656. www.wethhist.org.*

Goods that arrived by sea in the 17C were stored in Wethersfield's seven warehouses before they were transported inland. About 1700, floods demolished six of the warehouses, leaving only Cove Warehouse intact. The structure houses an exhibit on the town's maritime trade between 1650 and 1830.

Connecticut Firsts

The State of Connecticut distinguishes itself by claiming many firsts in US history. Among them are:

1639 – America's first Constitution, the Fundamental Orders of Connecticut, established a representative government.

1764 – The *Connecticut Courant* is the first newspaper published in America. The paper, still published today, is now called the *Hartford Courant*.

1794 – First cotton gin is patented by Eli Whitney and produced in New Haven.

1796 – Amelia Simmons of Hartford publishes the first cookbook in America.

1806 – Hartford native Noah Webster publishes his first dictionary.

1810 – The country's first insurance company, ITT Hartford Group, Inc. is established.

1836 – Samuel Colt, another Hartford native, patents the first revolver.

1860 – The corkscrew is patented by Philios Blake of New Haven.

1861 – Yale University awards the country's first Doctor of Philosophy degree.

1865 – Howe Machine Company is founded in Bridgeport to manufacture sewing machines, the first of which was patented by Elias Howe in 1846.

1868 – Alvin Fellows of New Haven is granted a patent for the first tape measure.

1908 – The first lollipop is made in New Haven by the Bradley and Smith Company.

1919 – Hartford's Traveler's Insurance Company becomes the first to issue aircraft liability insurance.

1939 – Russian-born engineer and US émigré Igor Sikorsky designs the first successful helicopter in the Western Hemisphere. It is produced by the United Aircraft Corporation in Bridgeport.

1949 – The prototype for the heart-lung machine is developed at Yale New Haven Hospital.

1954 – First nuclear submarine, the USS *Nautilus*, is launched in New London.

1975 – Ella T. Grasso becomes the first woman in America to be elected governor in her own right. She serves two terms as Governor of Connecticut.

1982 – Stamford native Dr. Robert K. Jarvik invents the world's first artificial heart.

1988 – The first heart-lung transplant is performed at Yale New Haven Hospital.

MAINE

AREA: 33,215SQ MI
POPULATION: 1,274,923
CAPITAL: AUGUSTA
NICKNAME: THE PINE TREE STATE
STATE FLOWER: WHITE PINE CONE AND TASSEL
OFFICIAL WEB SITE: WWW.VISITMAINE.COM

Equal in surface area to the combined size of the other five New England states, Maine is a vast, thickly forested region fringed with a 3,500mi coastline. The origin of the name Maine is uncertain. Attributed by some historians to the Maine region in western France, the name is believed by others to derive from "the main," a term used by fishermen to distinguish the mainland from the offshore islands. Maine is also referred to as Down East because of the winds that carry sailing vessels eastward along this section of the coast.

Offshore, hundreds of islands, the peaks of submerged mountains, dot the water. Pine trees grow on the islands, along the shore and across the interior to the north, giving the state its nickname.

A Succession of Owners – The Maine coast was explored by the Vikings in the 11C and several centuries later by European fishermen. In 1605 Pierre de Gua, Sieur de Monts, and Samuel de Champlain founded the Acadian territory. An English settlement, the Popham Colony, was established at the mouth of the Kennebec River in 1607; then in 1635 the English monarch Charles I gave the region of Maine to Sir Ferdinando Gorges, appointing him "Lord of New England." From this time on, the coast was the scene of constant battles between the French and the English. In 1677 the Massachusetts Colony bought Maine from the descendants of Sir Gorges, and the region remained under the jurisdiction of Massachusetts until 1820, when Maine was granted statehood under the conditions of the Missouri Compromise.

Economy – The state of Maine has a diversified economy. In the early days the state's wealth depended on its forests. Timber was harvested to supply masts for the Royal Navy during the colonial period, when all pine trees 24 inches or greater in diameter belonged to the Crown. In the 19C wooden **shipbuilding** in Maine peaked at Wiscasset, Bath and Searsport, where boatyards turned out four-, five- and six-masted vessels. With nearly 89 percent of the state covered with forests, Maine claims some of the country's largest **paper** and **pulp mills** at Jay, Millinocket, Rumford, Westbrook and Woodland.

Fishing, especially **lobstering**, is a major industry. The state leads the US in the sardine-packing industry.

Textiles, shoes and boots are also Maine-made products. Maine's potato crop ranks within the country's top ten, and the state produces 98 percent of the country's lowbush blueberries.

Beale's Lobster Pier, Southport

©JoAnn Taylor

ACADIA NATIONAL PARK★★★

MAPS P 121 AND P 124
TOURIST INFORMATION ☎ 207-288-3338 OR WWW.NPS.GOV/ACAD

This popular national park, set on an island along Maine's northern rocky coast-line, boasts an abundance of scenic riches. Glacier-carved mountains and rugged cliffs rise from the sea; crystal-clear lakes and ponds dot inland valleys and lush forests. The island, attached to the mainland by a bridge, is also home to sleepy fishing villages, harbor towns and the bustling resort town of Bar Harbor.

▶ *Entrance located on Rte. 3 just south of Bar Harbor.*

Located primarily on **Mount Desert Island**★★★ (pronounced "dessert"), with smaller sections on **Isle au Haut** and **Schoodic Peninsula** across Frenchman Bay, Acadia National Park welcomes some four million visitors each year.

Gateway to Acadia National Park, the village of **Bar Harbor**★ *(on Rte. 3 south of US-1 on Mount Desert Island)* serves as the commercial center for visitors to the park. Hotels, motels and guest houses line the road approaching the business district; the center of town *(follow Main St.)* holds many fine shops and restaurants. Information regarding area accommodations and recreational opportunities is also available from local chambers of commerce: **Bar Harbor** *(93 Cottage St.; P.O. Box 158, Bar Harbor ME 04609;* ☎ *288-2404 or 800-288-5103);* **Mount Desert** *(🕐 open Jun–Oct; P.O. Box 675, Northeast Harbor, ME 04662;* ☎ *276-5040);* and **Southwest Harbor/Tremont** *(P.O. Box 1143, Southwest Harbor, ME 04679;* ☎ *244-9264 or 800-423-9264).*

▶ **Orient Yourself:** Route 3 is the only road onto the island. The scenic Park Loop Road weaves through the park, with overlooks and stops at major sights and attractions. Bar Harbor sits on the eastern edge of the island, just over the bridge. Secondary roads spiderweb the island, providing access to other resort villages and towns, like Northeast Harbor, Southwest Harbor, Bass Harbor and Seal Cove.

🅿 **Parking:** Parking is available at major sights and attractions throughout the park. Street and lot parking is offered in downtown Bar Harbor. In summer, the Island Explorer shuttle bus provides free transportation around Mount Desert Island and other parts of the national park *(www.exploreacadia.com).*

👁 **Don't Miss:** Loop Drive; the 29mi scenic road takes you past sweeping vistas and many of the park's major attractions and sights.

🕐 **Organizing Your Time:** Stop at the Hull's Visitor Center on Route 3 before entering the park for information on events and programs. Proceed to Loop Road for the park's scenic drive. Plan the better part of the day for the drive, allowing time to stop at sights along the way.

Kids **Especially for Kids:** A variety of kid-focused ranger-led programs are offered at the park. Also, rent bikes in Bar Harbor to pedal some of the more than 45mi of carriage roads that weave through the interior of the park.

👶 **Also See:** The Cadillac Mountain summit. Set the alarm clock and drive the twisty, altitude-gaining road to the top to be one of the first to view the day's sunrise.

©National Park Service

Acadia National Park

A Bit of History

Measuring 108sq mi, Mount Desert Island once served as the summer campgrounds of the Penobscot and Passamaquoddy Indians. In September 1604 French explorers **Samuel de Champlain** and Sieur de Monts anchored in what is now **Frenchman Bay**. Champlain's impression of the largest island in the bay as a line of seven or eight mountains with rocky, treeless summits led him to name the island Isle des Monts Deserts ("Island of Deserted Mountains").

In the mid-19C the area's beauty was discovered by artists. The enthusiasm expressed in their writings and paintings enticed the wealthy to vacation on Mount Desert Island and Bar Harbor developed into a resort community, while Northeast and Southwest harbors became popular yachting centers.

Over one-third of the park's 35,000 acres were donated by John D. Rockefeller, Jr. In fact, it was Rockefeller who created the 45mi of carriage paths that crisscross the eastern side of the island.

Park Loop Road★★★ *29mi. Map p 124.*

The many scenic outlooks, turnoffs and parking areas along the park's coastal road afford vistas ranging from sweeping seascapes to panoramas of pink granite mountains and island-studded waters. *Road may be fogbound during morning hours.*

▶ *Begin at the Hulls Cove Visitor Center on Rte. 3. Then follow signs for the Loop Road .6mi to Frenchman Bay Overlook.*

Frenchman Bay Overlook★

From the overlook here you have an unobstructed **view** to Schoodic Peninsula and across Frenchman Bay.

▶ *The Loop Road is one-way from the Spur Rd. entrance to just south of Jordan Pond. After 3mi turn right for Sieur de Monts Spring.*

Sieur de Monts Spring

Named for Sieur de Monts, leader of the 1604 expedition to North America, the spring and surrounding area constituted one of the first parcels of land set aside as part of the nature preserve that became Acadia National Park. The nearby **Nature Center**

© National Park Service

Thunder Hole, Acadia National Park

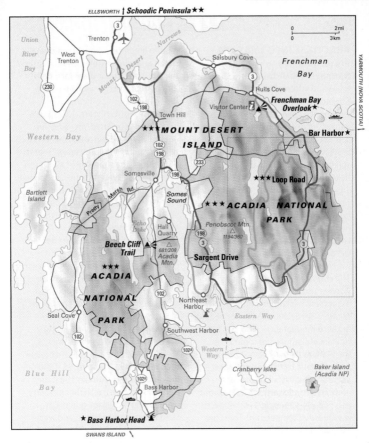

contains displays related to the park and its preservation (🕐 *open Jun–Sept daily 9am–5pm*). In the **Wild Gardens of Acadia**, regional trees, flowers and shrubs are arranged according to their natural habitat: marsh, bog, beach or mountain.

Abbe Museum [M]

🕐 *Open mid-May–mid-Oct daily 9am–5pm, rest of year Thu–Sun 9am–5pm.* 👓 *$6.* ♿📶 ☎ *207-288-3519. www.abbemuseum.org.*

Dioramas and prehistoric artifacts (Stone Age tools, pottery) in this small pavilion evoke the life of Maine's earliest inhabitants, who occupied the Frenchman Bay and Blue Hill Bay areas prior to European colonization.

▶ *Return to the Loop Road.*

To the left stand the buildings of **Jackson Laboratory**, internationally known for its role in cancer research. The cliffs of Champlain Mountain loom on the right. Along the road you'll see scenes typical of Acadia: pink granite peaks, tall evergreens and natural roadside rock gardens.

▶ *Follow signs to Sand Beach.*

Sand Beach★

Composed of ground seashells, the only saltwater beach in the park provides a pleasant swimming spot for those who don't mind the bracing water temperature (50-60°F in summer). To see some spectacular scenery, walk **Shore Path** *(1.8 mi)*

Address Book

PRACTICAL INFORMATION

Visitor Information – Acadia National Park Visitor Center provides maps and information about the park *(3mi north of Bar Harbor at Hulls Cove entrance; ◷ open mid-Apr–Jun daily 8am–4:30pm Jul-Aug daily 8am.-6pm Sep-Oct daily 8am-4:30pm; ☎ 207-288-3338; www.nps.gov/acad).* In off-season information is available at park headquarters at Eagle Lake *(Rte. 233, 3mi west of Bar Harbor; P.O. Box 177, Bar Harbor, ME 04609; ◷ open Nov–mid-Apr daily 8am–4:30pm).* Acadia National Park is open daily year-round. The park Loop Road is closed Nov–Apr, but the Ocean Drive section is open year-round *(◉ entrance fee $20/vehicle for 7 days, $10/vehicle off-season).*

Accommodations – *☝ For specific suggestions of accommodations and restaurants, see below.* Information regarding accommodations is also available from local chambers of commerce: **Bar Harbor** *(☎ 207-288-5103; www. barharborinfo.com);* **Mount Desert** *(☎ 207-276-5040; www.mountdesertchamber.org);* and **Southwest/Tremont** *(☎ 207-244-9264 or 800-423-9264; www.acadiachamber.com).* There are two **campgrounds** in Acadia National Park: Blackwoods *(Rte. 3, 5mi south of Bar Harbor; ◷ open year-round; $20/ day; reservations: ☎ 800-365-2267)* and Seawall *(Rte. 102A, 4mi south of Southwest Harbor; ◷ open late May–Sept; ◉ $14–$20/day).* Camping on **Isle au Haut** requires a special-use permit *(◉ $25; available from park headquarters).* For a list of private campgrounds in the area, contact the area chambers of commerce.

WHERE TO STAY

☝ For price categories for hotels and restaurants, see the legend on the cover flap.

Chiltern Inn – *3 Cromwell Harbor Rd., Bar Harbor.* ※🅿 ☎ *207-288-3371 or 800-709-0114. www.chilterninn.com. 4 suites.* **$$$$** This four-suite property is a pampering oasis within walking distance to Compass Harbor in Acadia National Park and downtown Bar Harbor. The spacious —and very romantic—rooms feature fireplaces, window seats with ocean and garden views, and oversized marble baths. Public areas include an indoor pool and spa, art gallery, and lush gardens.

The Claremont – *On Rte. 102 in Southwest Harbor.* ◷ *Closed Nov–early Jun.* ※🅿 ☎ *207-244-5036 or 800-244-5036. www.theclaremonthotel.com. 42 rooms.* **$$$$** Set on the shoreline of Mt. Desert Island, the Claremont seems unchanged since it first opened in 1884. The four-story wooden hotel with its wide veranda overlooks lovely Somes Sound and its surrounding mountains. Two facts speak volumes about the genteel attitude here: Croquet is the sport of choice, and men are requested to wear jackets and ties at dinner. Rooms are simply furnished, as they would have been a century ago, although all now have private baths.

Acadia Hotel – *20 Mount Desert St., Bar Harbor. Closed Nov–mid-Mar.* ※🅿 ☎ *207-288-5721 or 888-876-2463. www. acadiahotel.com. 11 rooms.* **$$** If you're looking for value, you can't beat this prime downtown Bar Harbor property overlooking the village green. Bar Harbor shops, restaurants, and waterfront are within easy walking distance from the front door. Rooms have been recently renovated with tasteful floral and print wallpapers, quality beddings and furnishings. Friendly, accommodating service adds to the value—and your experience!

WHERE TO EAT

Havana – *318 Main St., Bar Harbor. Dinner only.* ☎ *207-288-2822. www. havanamaine.com.* **$$$ Cuban.** A zesty alternative to boiled lobster, Havana takes New American concepts and deftly overlays them with Latino influences. The oft-changing menu is filled with creative selections, like coconut-and-curry infused white beans served with vegetable brochettes, and chili-dusted salmon served over Cuban black beans with a cilantro-tomato salsa.

Jordan Pond House – *Park Loop Rd, Acadia National Park (north of Seal Harbor).* ☝🅿 ☎ *207-276-3316. www. jordanpond.com.* **$$ Regional New**

England. Popovers and tea on the lawn of the Jordan Pond House is one of the great Acadia National Park traditions. Buttery popovers are served afternoons at rustic wooden tables with a view up the pond to a pair of perfectly rounded mountains. But don't overlook the rest of the menu; the lobster rolls and lobster stew are filled with succulent lobster chunks, and are among the best on the island. In the evening and on rainy days, indoor seating is offered. Dress is mixed but casual—mountain bikers off the trail sit next to well-coiffed tea sippers.

West Street Cafe – *76 West St., Bar Harbor.* ☎ *207-288-5242. www.weststreet-cafe.com.* **$$$ American**. Fresh quality and a casual, friendly atmosphere have made this a favorite with locals and visitors alike for more than a quarter-century. Emphasis is on seafood and traditional New England fare, like clam chowder, lobster every which way (the shore dinner comes with mussels and a slice of blueberry pie), crab cakes, and shrimp. Is there a non-seafood lover in your group? There are sandwiches, beef, pasta and poultry dishes, too.

Cafe Bluefish – *122 Cottage St., Bar Harbor.* ☎ *207-288-3696. www.cafe-bluefishbarharbor.com.* **$$ American**. You'll find upscale dining— predominately fresh seafood dishes with gourmet touches— in a cozy, charming atmosphere. Slip into one of the dark booths, listen to soft jazz in the background, and feast on the award-winning lobster strudel, followed by a hunk of German chocolate mud pie.

---

from the upper parking level along the rocky coast past Thunder Hole *(below)* to the end of Otter Point.

▶ *Continue south on Loop Rd.*

Thunder Hole★

🅿 *Parking on the right.* Over the years the ocean has burrowed into the rock here. At high tide the surf crashes through this narrow chasm, creating a thunderous roar.

▶ *Continue .3 mi on Loop Rd.*

Otter Cliffs★★

The next stop takes in the sheer cliffs just north of Otter Point, which rise 110ft above the ocean. Here, on the highest Atlantic headlands north of Rio de Janeiro, dramatic **views**★★ encompass the splintered coast and the vast sea beyond.

Loop Road winds around Otter Point and Otter Cove, intersects with the road to Seal Harbor, then follows the shore of **Jordan Pond**, which lies below the cliffs of Penobscot Mountain. At the northern end of the pond, note the large boulder balanced precariously atop one of the two rounded hills known as **The Bubbles**. For a closer look, stop at The Bubbles parking area.

▶ *Continue on the Loop Road 1.4mi past The Bubbles parking area and turn right at sign for Cadillac Mountain.*

Cadillac Mountain★★★

The 3.5mi drive to the top of Cadillac Mountain (1,530ft) affords views of Eagle Lake—the largest body of freshwater in the park—Bar Harbor and the islands below. Cadillac Mountain ranks as the highest point on the Atlantic Coast. Easy **Summit Trail**, which winds for less than

Bass Harbor Head Lighthouse, Acadia National Park

©PhotoDisc, Inc.

a mile around the barren mountaintop, offers breathtaking 360-degree **views**★★★ of Frenchman Bay and the park.

▶ *Return to the Loop Road, then turn right to complete the circle.*

Other Areas of the Park★★

Beech Cliff Trail

▶ *From Somesville take Rte. 102 South, turn right, then left onto Beech Cliff Rd. and continue to the end of the road.*

This easy trail *(30min round-trip)* leads to the crest of Beech Cliff, where magnificent **views**★★ reach from freshwater Echo Lake to Acadia Mountain.

Bass Harbor Head★

▶ *At the end of Rte. 102A, 4mi south of Southwest Harbor.*

Towering above the rocky shore of a remote headland, the **Bass Harbor Head Lighthouse** (1858) makes a delightful sight, especially at sunset.

Sargent Drive

▶ *Runs between Northeast Harbor and Rte. 3/198. Passenger cars only.*

For views of the East Coast's only true fjord—a deep glacial valley now flooded by the ocean—take Sargent Drive as it traces the eastern shore of Somes Sound.

Schoodic Peninsula★★

▶ *From Mount Desert Island, take Rte. 3 North to US-1. Follow US-1 North to West Gouldsboro and turn right on Rte. 186. Just past Winter Harbor, look for signs to Acadia National Park and turn right. Road becomes one-way at park entrance.*

Two thousand acres of Acadia National Park occupy the southern tip of this peninsula, which juts out from the mainland east across the bay from Mount Desert Island. Scenery along the park road takes in a kaleidoscope of tall stands of fir trees rimmed by pink granite ledges and encircled by the blue waters of the bay.

Isle au Haut★

Boats depart from Stonington (on Rte. 15) to Isle au Haut Harbor. One-way 45min. $16. *Isle au Haut Co.* Call for seasonal schedules: ☎ 207-367-6516; www.isleauhaut. com. *One of the morning boats continues on to Duck Harbor (late Jun–early Sept only).*

Located south of Stonington on Deer Isle, tiny Isle au Haut measures just 6mi long and 3mi wide. The island is private, except for the 2,800 acres of woodland that belong to Acadia National Park. To best sample its beauty, spend some time hiking the web of trails that traverse the park.

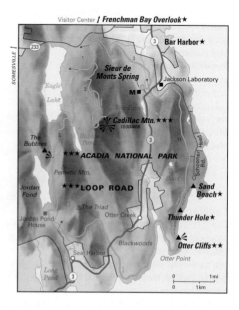

Visitor Center / **Frenchman Bay Overlook★**

AUGUSTA

POPULATION 18,560
MICHELIN MAP 581 O 2
TOURIST INFORMATION ☎ 207-623-4559 OR WWW.CI.AUGUSTA.ME.US

Situated on the banks of the Kennebec River, Maine's capital is a bustling industrial and residential city. The river and its adjacent woodlands have been a source of wealth to Augusta ever since the 17C, when the Pilgrims established a trading post on its east bank. In the 18C and 19C the Kennebec River served as an important avenue for boat traffic, as well as a source of ice in winter. Wood cut from the forests bordering the river also contributed to the region's prosperity.

▶ **Orient Yourself:** I-95 provides quick access to Augusta. The capitol district, located in the State Street area on the west bank of the Kennebec River, includes the State House, the State Museum and other attractions.

🅿 **Parking:** Free parking is available in lots west and north of the State Capitol and Maine State Museum. A free parking garage is located at the corner of Capitol and Sewall streets.

🅐 **Don't Miss:** A free tour of the Bullfinch-designed State Capitol and a visit to the Maine State Museum.

🕓 **Organizing Your Time:** Allow a half day to see the sights in the capitol district, then plan a day or so to explore outlying areas and to be outdoors

Kids Especially for Kids: Whitewater rafting on the Kennebec River is a popular adventure for older children. Get a list of professional outfitters from Raft Maine (☎ 800-723-8633; www.raftmaine.com).

🕭 **Also See:** The nearby town of Hallowell, two miles south of the State Capitol on Rte. 201, has been dubbed the state's "antique capitol." Browse shops and galleries on Water St.

Sights

State House

State and Capitol Sts. 🕓 *Open year-round.* *Free guided tours Mon–Fri 9am–1pm.* 🕓 *Closed major holidays.* ♿ ☎ *207-287-2724. www.maine.gov.*
The domed capitol building is best viewed from the riverside park across from the front entrance of the State House. Constructed between 1829 and 1832 according to the design of eminent Boston architect Charles Bulfinch, the major portion of the State House was later remodeled and enlarged. Despite this change, the columned facade and other characteristic Bulfinch elements were preserved. The House, Senate and Executive chambers are all located in the State House. Twenty acres of garden and green space decorated the front.

Maine State Museum

83 State House Station, just south of the State House. 🕓 *Open year-round Mon–Fri 9am–5pm, Sat 10am–4pm. Sun 1pm-4pm.* 🕓 *Closed major holidays.* ⊜ *$2.* ♿ ☎ *207-287-2301. www.state.me.us/museum.*
This modern building houses the State Library and Archives as well as the State Museum. Exhibits on the history, life and environment of Maine and its residents are on view in the museum's three levels. Dioramas, period rooms, artifacts and equipment tell the story of state industries, past and present, such as agriculture, lumbering and shipbuilding. **Made in Maine** includes mill and factory machinery plus more than 1,000 samples of products manufactured in the state. Archaeological artifacts document the life of the area's first inhabitants and an interactive display

traces early exploration routes. Maine's geographical and political histories from the early 17C to 1842 are also featured.

Blaine House

192 State St. ✏ Visit by guided tour (20min) only, year-round Tue–Thu 2pm–4pm.
 ☎ *207-287-2121. www.blainehouse.org.*
Built for a Bath sea captain in the 1830s, this Colonial mansion was the home of James G. Blaine (1830-93), congressman, secretary of State and presidential candidate in 1884. The house has served as the governor's mansion since 1919. The tour includes public and family rooms on the main floor.

BETHEL

POPULATION 2,411
MICHELIN MAP 581 M 2
TOURIST INFORMATION ☎ 207-824-2282 OR WWW.BETHELMAINE.COM

Bethel's distinguished inn and prep school are enhanced by the town's magnificent setting in the White Mountains. Here opportunities abound for hiking, biking, hunting, fishing, golfing, rock-hounding in the abandoned mines in the area, and excursions into the surrounding White Mountains.

▶ **Orient Yourself:** The historic village is located at the intersection of Route 26 and Route 2 in western Maine, just east of the New Hampshire border. The village is small, dominated by the commons and the historic Bethel Inn and Country Club. Sunday River Ski Resort is located about five miles east of the village.

🅿 **Parking:** On-street parking is available in the village. Several large lots are available for visitors at Sunday River. The *Mountain Explorer* offers free shuttle service between Bethel Village and Sunday River Resort, November-early April.

😊 **Don't Miss:** A visit to scenic Grafton Notch State Park. The drive along east-west Route 26, through mountain notches and alongside waterfalls, is especially beautiful in fall.

🕐 **Organizing Your Time:** Spend your time on outdoor adventures; hiking, skiing, fishing, and nature walks abound here. Grafton Notch State Park, with waterfalls and hiking trails, can take the better part of a day.

🧒 **Especially for Kids:** Sunday River Resort offers kid-pleasing activities, including tubing, skiing, nature hikes, biking and more. Also, take a hike on the easy Androscoggin River Trail.

👟 **Also See:** A walk around Bethel Commons, with historic buildings, shops and galleries. A walking-tour brochure for the village is available from the Bethel Historical Society (☎ 207-824-2908; www.bethelhistorical.org).

Legendary Logger

The state of Maine is largely forested land: logging has long been a big part of the economy. Popularized by professional writers and lumber-industry publicists, the legend of Paul Bunyan tells how he and Babe the Blue Ox felled trees an acre at a time. Paul was known for his gigantic size and feats of strength as well as his lumbering prowess. He and Babe dug the Grand Canyon and formed the Black Hills of South Dakota. No lumberman claimed as voracious an appetite as Paul; when he was a boy, he would eat 40 bowls of porridge. As a man, Paul ate so many pancakes that his cook required 50 men with slabs of bacon tied to their feet just to grease the humongous griddle.

A Bit of History

Permanent settlement in the area dates from 1774, when a sawmill and then a gristmill were established on a brook flowing into the Androscoggin River. In 1796 the town was incorporated and named Bethel, a Biblical term meaning "house of God." With the arrival of the railroad in 1851 connecting the community to Portland and then to Montreal, the timber industry began to dominate Bethel's economy. Lumber and dairy products are major sources of area income today.

Today a National Historic District, the village of Bethel is a quiet residential hamlet, attracting visitors to the recreational facilities of the Bethel Inn and Country Club, co-ed students to its **Gould Academy**. The surrounding mountains and forests are magnets for outdoor enthusiasts and skiers are drawn to the slopes of nearby **Sunday River Resort**.

Sights

Dr. Moses Mason House

On the Green. ☞ *Visit by 30min guided tour only Jul–Labor Day Tue–Sun 1pm–4pm.* ☞ *$3.* 🅿 ☎ *207-824-2908. www. bethelhistorical.org/museum.*

This is one of the carefully preserved houses fringing the village green. Built in 1813 for a prominent physician, the house features period furnishings and colorful folk-art murals (c.1835) adorning the central staricase.

Artist's Covered Bridge

Sunday River Rd., Newry 4mi northwest of North Bethel. 🅿 ☎ *207-624-3490. www. maine.gov/mdot/covered-bridges.*

It's said that no covered bridge in Maine is more photographed, sketched or painted than this 1872 gem. It features an arched entrance and latticework sides.

EATING OUT

Bethel Inn & Country Club – *Broad St.* ☎ *207-824-2175, or 800-654-0125. www.bethelinn.com.* An ensemble of large yellow houses and service buildings, the inn fronts the village green and welcomes the public at breakfast, lunch and dinner. The main dining room provides the setting for dinner specialties and traditional New England dishes, such as fresh Maine lobster, rack of lamb or seafood stuffed sole. *Dinner reservations required.* Family fare (sandwiches, ribs, burgers) is served in the more casual **Millbrook Tavern**. Have lunch on the screened-in terrace, overlooking the 18-hole golf course.

Excursions

Grafton Notch State Park★

25mi northwest of Bethel via Rte. 26 West. 🕐 *Open mid-May–mid-Oct daily dawn–dusk.* ☞ *$2.* ☎ *207-824-2912 or 207-624-6080 (off season). www.state.me.us/doc/parks.*

Route 26 heads through the Bear River Valley and into Grafton Notch State Park, an unspoiled area in the White Mountains. An auto tour through the park offers views of the notch dominated by **Old Speck Mountain** (4,180ft) to the west and **Baldpate Mountain** to the east. Take time to visit lovely **Screw Auger Falls** and **Mother Walker Falls** *(1mi north of Screw Auger Falls)*.

Evans Notch★

18mi southwest of Bethel. Follow Rte. 2 West for 10mi, then turn left onto Rte. 113.

Fine **views** of the Cold River Valley abound on the drive from Gilead to North Chatham through this notch in White Mountain National Forest (☞ *see entry heading The White Mountains in New Hampshire*).

COBSCOOK BAY

MICHELIN MAP 583 V 4 AND MAP BELOW
TOURIST INFORMATION ☎ 207-853-4644 OR WWW.EASTPORT.NET

Emptying into Passamaquoddy Bay, Cobscook Bay is a natural basin that is almost entirely landlocked. The coastal fishing towns of Eastport and Lubec, separated by less than 3mi of water but nearly 40mi apart by land, stand sentinel over the channels linking the two bay areas. The exceptionally high tides (18-24ft) for which this bay and its neighboring shores are known so impressed the local Indians that they named it Cobscook, meaning "boiling waters."

Driving Tour: Lubec to Eastport 60mi.

Lubec

During the 17C and 18C, this small fishing port was a center for goods smuggled into the US from Canada. Ships authorized to sail to Europe set out from Lubec and returned several days later with cargoes of rum, sugar and other staples. The record-breaking time of these highly profitable round-trip "transatlantic voyages"—in fact only short trips to Canada where goods were available at low prices—was never questioned. By the late 1800s, 20 sardine-packing factories had been established in Lubec, forming the basis of the town's economy. Only two of these factories remain.

▷ *From Lubec, cross the Franklin Delano Roosevelt International Bridge to Campobello Island and follow the signs to Roosevelt Campobell International Park.*

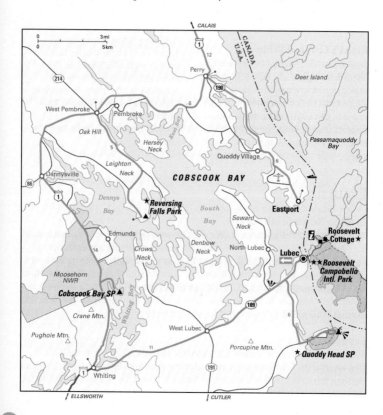

Roosevelt Campobello International Park★★

Campobello Island is part of the Canadian province of New Brunswick. US citizens must present a passport at the border. 🕐 *Park grounds open daily year-round dawn–dusk. Buildings open late May–Columbus Day daily 10am–6pm. (Atlantic time)* 🅿 ♿ ☎ *506-752-2922. www.nps.gov/roca.*

Campobello Island, at the mouth of the Bay of Fundy in the Canadian province of New Brunswick, is linked to Lubec Maine by the Franklin Delano Roosevelt Memorial Bridge. An agreement by Canada and the U.S. established an international park dedicated to Franklin Delano Roosevelt on the island.

Roosevelt, whose four terms as president of the US were unprecedented in the nation's history, spent his early summers at Campobello, his "beloved island." He continued to vacation on the island with his wife, Eleanor, and their children until August 1921 when, following a swim in the icy waters of the Bay of Fundy, he was suddenly stricken with polio.

The vast 2,800-acre international park exhibits a variety of magnificent landscapes, including forests, bogs, cliffs, lakes and beaches. From **Friars Head** *(south of the visitor center turn right at the sign marked Picnic Area)* there is a view west to Lubec and the Maine coast. A sweeping vista along the shore of **Herring Cove** to **Herring Cove Head** is visible from **Con Robinson's Point** *(follow Glensevern Rd. east to the end)*. At **Lower Duck Pond** a pebble beach borders the rocky shore. Dubbed "fog forests," the island's woodlands are often enshrouded in a thick mist.

Facing Eastport across the bay, the 34-room **Roosevelt Cottage**★ displays many personal mementos that recall the vacations the Roosevelts spent at Campobello. A short distance north of Wilson's Beach *(take the gravel road)*, **East Quoddy Head Lighthouse**★ looks out on Head Harbor Island.

▶ *Return to Lubec and follow Rte. 189 some 4mi to the gas station. Turn left at the park sign.*

Quoddy Head State Park★

6mi south of Lubec. 🕐 *Open mid-May–mid-Oct daily 9am–dusk. Rest of the year call for hours.* ☎ *$2.* 🅿 ☎ *207-733-0911 or 207-941-4014 (off season). www.state.me.us/doc/parks.*

In this park you'll find red-and-white-striped **Quoddy Head Lighthouse**, which marks the easternmost point of the US. From the lighthouse there is a view of the island of Grand Manan in New Brunswick, Canada.

A coastal **footpath** *(*🚶 *round-trip 1hr 15min)* beginning at the parking lot *(to the right of the lighthouse, arriving from Rte. 189)* affords a superb **view** of the sea and the granite ledges.

▶ *Return to Rte. 189 and head west. The road climbs to a point that offers a view of Passamaquoddy Bay and the harbor. At Whiting take US-1 North.*

Cobscook Bay State Park

🕐 *Open mid-May–mid-Oct daily 9am–dusk. Rest of the year call for hours.* ☎ *$3.* △ 🅿 ☎ *207-726-4412. www.state.me.us/doc/parks.*

Set on the shores of Cobscook Bay, the park boasts some lovely scenery, such as the tall stands of evergreens that grow out of crevices in the coastal ledges.

▶ *Continue on US-1. In West Pembroke take the unmarked road on the right (opposite Rte. 214) and follow signs for Reversing Falls Park.*

Reversing Falls Park★

This is one of the best places from which to admire Cobscook Bay's pine-covered islands and secluded coves. Twice daily, with the changing of the tides, the current is so strong in one area that the rushing waters form a .5mi-long falls.

▶ *Return to US-1. Continue through Perry, then take Rte. 190 south.*

Eastport

This small community, the easternmost city in the US, is located on Moose Island between the entrances to Cobscook and Passamaquoddy bays. Exceptionally high tides invade the shore at Eastport, making it necessary for the city's wharves to be built on unusually tall piles.

Today the aquaculture industry has emerged as a major economic activity.

MAINE COAST★★

MICHELIN MAP 581 N-P 3-6 AND MAPS P 131 AND P 144
TOURIST INFORMATION ☎ 207-439-1319 OR WWW.MAINETOURISM.COM

Tumbling down glacier-sculpted cliffs of jagged rocks to meet the Atlantic Ocean, the coast of Maine defines the eastern edge of the state, stretching 3,500mi from Kittery north to the border of New Brunswick, Canada. This is a wind-whipped landscape, where fierce storms called "nor'easters" batter the shore in winter, and summer visitors are hard-pressed to find sandy beaches. Driving this rugged coast along US-1, with its tranquil harbors and lonely lighthouses, is its own reward.

Sights within this entry are organized from south to north beginning at the southern border of Maine in Kittery. Mileages given are for travel on US-1 unless otherwise specified.

▶ **Orient Yourself:** Scenic US-1 traces the entire length of the Maine coastline, beginning just north of Portsmouth, NH. For quicker travel, I-95 cuts inland and travels north from Kittery to Bangor. A plethora of secondary roads access jutting peninsulas and small coastal towns.

🅿 **Parking:** On-street parking and designated lots are located in top resort towns along the coast, but, in general, parking can be tough to find. In the busiest towns: follow the parking signs, make a few passes, and hope for the best.

🅰 **Don't Miss:** The sandy beaches of York and Ogunquit; the bustling, hip seaside city of Portland; picturesque Boothbay Harbor, Rockland and Camden; pristine Blue Hill —and lobster-in-the-rough anywhere along the way.

🕐 **Organizing Your Time:** You won't be able to see and do it all. Driving from one town to another can be time-consuming with traffic and slow-moving secondary roads. Try to spend at least a couple days each exploring the southern, mid-, and downeast coastal regions. Then reserve a day to relax on the beach or at a picnic spot overlooking the spectacular rocky Maine coastline.

🧒 **Especially for Kids:** Hop on a lobster boat excursion offered by outfitters along the coast; walk the boardwalk and swim in the calm waters at Old Orchard Beach.

👓 **Also See:** Popham Beach State Park in mid-coast Maine.

Kittery

ℹ *Tourist Information: ☎ 207-363-4422 or www.gatewaytomaine.org.*

Shipbuilding, fishing and tourism are the mainstays of this village located just north of the New Hampshire line. Private boatyards turn out pleasure craft, adding to the town's role as a shipbuilding center. A drive along tree-shaded Route 103 leading to the 18C settlement of Kittery Point affords glimpses of the river and some of the area's original Colonial homes.

Fort McClary State Historic Site

On Rte. 103 east of Kittery in Kittery Point.
🕐 *Open Memorial Day–late Sept daily 10am–8pm.* 💵 *$2.* 🅿 ☎ *207-384-5160. www.maine.gov/doc/parks.*
A hexagonal-shaped 1846 blockhouse in an oceanfront park setting is all that remains of the stockade first christened Fort William in the early 18C. During the Revolutionary War, the fort was renamed for Major Andrew McClary, who was killed at the Battle of Bunker Hill.

Kittery's Outlet Malls

From I-95, take Exit 3 to US-1. ☎ *800-548-8379. www.thekitteryoutlets.com.*
More than 120 outlet stores cluster along a 1.5mi stretch of Route 1 in Kittery. Offering a wide range of items including clothing, shoes, crystal, silver, housewares and furnishings, Kittery's outlets constitute a shopper's delight. Such designers as Anne Klein, Liz Claiborne, Ralph Lauren and Tommy Hilfiger are represented.

York★

9mi north of Kittery. 🛈 *Tourist Information:* ☎ *207-363-4422 or www.gatewayto-maine.org.*
York is splintered into so many separate villages that Mark Twain once wryly observed, "It is difficult to throw a brick … in any one direction without disabling a postmaster." Today the area known to locals as "the Yorks" include Colonial **York Village**; **York Harbor**, a low-key resort at the mouth of York River; **York Beach**, with its boardwalk amusement park; and the sheltered beach of **Cape Neddick**.

Colonial York★★

Along Rte. 1A in York Village, just off US-1. 🕐 *Open early-Jun–Columbus Day Mon–Sat 10am–5pm.* 💵 *$10 (tickets available at Jefferds Tavern, which serves as the visitor center).* ☎ *207-363-4974. www.oldyork.org.*

Address Book

PRACTICAL INFORMATION

Visitor Information – The **Maine Office of Tourism** (59 State House Station, Augusta, ME 04330; ☎ 207-287-5711; www.visitmaine.com) and the **Maine Tourism Association** (325B Water St., Hallowell, ME 04347; ☎ 1-888-624-6345; www.mainetourism.com) both provide a wealth of information to visitors. An official **Maine State Visitor Information Center** is located in Kittery at I-95 and US-1 (☎ 207-439-1319). *For specific suggestions of accommodations and restaurants, see below.*

WHERE TO STAY

For price ranges for hotels and restaurants, see the legend on the cover flap.

Black Point Inn – 510 Black Point Rd., Prouts Neck. ☎ 207-883-2500 or 800-258-0003. www.blackpointinn.com. 80 rooms. **$$$$$** A classic Maine seaside resort, the delightfully old-fashioned Black Point Inn dates to 1873. Guest rooms in the shingled main lodge, or in one of the cottages, are spacious and decorated in a simple shore-house style. Two beaches lie adjacent to the property for those of stout constitution; for others, the inn has two heated pools.

Captain Lord Mansion – Green St. (at Pleasant St.), Kennebunkport. ☎ 207-967-3141 or 800-522-3141. www.captainlord.com. 16 rooms. **$$$$$** This regal, three-story Federal-style house holds a mix of historic opulence with modern comforts. Filled with period antiques, guest rooms—even the smallest ones—have charm and amenities to spare.

Five Gables Inn – 107 Murray Hill Rd., East Boothbay. *Closed Nov–mid-May. Children under 12 not welcome.* ☎ 207-633-4551 or 800-451-5048. www.fivegablesinn.com. 16 rooms. **$$$** Sitting a few miles drive from Boothbay Harbor, this century-old Victorian has been attractively updated. Some first-floor rooms lack privacy, but all guest rooms are appointed with country charm, such as spindle beds and wingback chairs, and boast views of Linekin Bay.

Harraseeket Inn –162 Main St., Freeport. ☎ 207-865-9377 or 800-342-6423. www.harraseeketinn.com. 84 rooms. **$$$** This venerable 1798 inn offers early-American ambience, enhanced by 23 fireplaces. Bedrooms with modern amenities feature traditional dark-wood furnishings. Enjoy regional cuisine in the inn's formal dining room or Downeast specialties in the tavern.

Inn Britannia – 132 W. Main St., Searsport. ☎ 207-548-2007 or 866-466-2748. www.innbritannia.com. 6 rooms. **$$$** This bright blue former sea captain's house (1830) opens onto spacious grounds, complete with a hen house. Enamored of all things British, the friendly innkeepers have named the individually decorated guest quarters after places in England. Boldly painted walls backdrop iron, brass or wood beds topped with quilts, lace or other attractive coverings.

Whitehall Inn – 52 High St., Camden. *Closed late Oct–late May.* ☎ 207-236-3391 or 800-789-6565. www.whitehall-inn.com. 50 rooms. **$$$** A Steinway piano in the lobby sets a perfect tone for this longtime Camden institution. Choose from homey rooms in the main building (1834) or in two Victorian houses across the street. The restaurant serves traditional New England fare concentrating on local seafood. Rates are less if you share a bathroom (eight rooms share four baths).

Alden House – 63 Church St., Belfast. ☎ 207-338-2151 or 877-337-8151. www.thealdenhouse.com. 7 rooms. **$$** Inside this stately Greek Revival house, high ceilings, twin parlors and marble fireplaces grace the public spaces, while lace bed covers and antique furnishings decorate each pleasant bedroom (all but two have private baths).

Homeport Inn – 121 E, Main St., Searsport. ☎ 207-548-2259 or 800-742-5814. www.homeportbnb.com. 10 rooms. **$$** Once a sea captain's home (1861), this spacious, two-story dwelling welcomes travelers to its landscaped grounds and antique-filled interior. Cozy rooms, some with canopy beds and fanciful wallpaper, are furnished to make guests feel at home (three rooms share a bath).

The Lodge at Turbat Creek – *Turbat Creek Rd., Kennebunkport.* ○ *Closed Dec–Apr.* 🅿 🖵 ☎ *207-967-8700 or 877-594-5634. www.kingsportinn.com/turbatshome. 26 rooms.* **$$** This two-story motel tucked away in a quiet neighborhood is a pleasant surprise. With rates much lower than many Kennebunkport inns, Turbat Creek offers simple rooms painted a sherbet yellow, and a continental breakfast. The motel's location at the north end of Ocean Avenue makes it a good base for exploring.

WHERE TO EAT

White Barn Inn – *37 Beach Ave., Kennebunkport. Dinner only. Jackets required.* 🅿 ☎ *207-967-2321. www. whitebarninn.com.* **$$$$ New American**. Considered by many to be Maine's best restaurant, this Relais & Châteaux property juxtaposes Old-World formality in a casual setting. Housed in a handsome old barn, the dining room is appointed with country antiques and richly upholstered chairs. The four-course prix-fixe menu frequently changes to reflect availability of local produce and meats. Guests can spend the night in one of the inn's 25 oh-so-romantic rooms *($320–$370)*.

Robinhood Free Meetinghouse – *210 Robinhood Rd., Georgetown (southeast of Bath). Dinner only.* 🅿 ☎ *207-371-2188. www.robinhood-meetinghouse.com.* **$$$ International**. The menu is as elaborate as the décor is simple in this architecturally striking 1855 meeting-house set on a country lane. The chef displays a remarkably broad repertoire, with dishes reflecting cuisine from Thailand to Italy. Such wide-ranging interests can be a recipe for mediocrity in less sure hands, but they work with aplomb here. Even the between-course sorbets are homemade.

Twilight Cafe – *70-72 Main St., Belfast. Dinner only.* ○ *Closed Sun.* ☎ *207-338-0937. www.thetwilightcafe.com.* **$$$ Continental**. Adorned with bold artwork, a fresh, contemporary setting greets diners within these side-by-side storefronts. The food is equally appealing. Start with the seared garlic scallops with sautéed cucumbers, then choose a creative entrée like the pecan-crusted lobster cakes with pumpkin-ginger crème fraiche or the blueberry chicken with wild blueberry chutney.

Anglers Restaurant– *Rte. 1, Searsport.* 🅿 ☎ *207-548-2405.* **$$ Seafood**. This friendly family dining spot is a perennial favorite with the locals. Tasty food, generous portions and reasonable prices are the attractions. Lobster, haddock, scallops, salmon, clam, shrimp or trout—baked, broiled or fried—come with all the trimmings. Ribs, sirloin and chicken are also on the menu.

Fisherman's Friend – *School St., Stonington.* 🅿 ☎ *207-367-2442.* **$$ Seafood**. Lobster lovers trek to this down-home spot far off the beaten track for one reason—the velvety rich lobster stew. While the place won't win any awards for décor and the waitstaff fails to exude much congeniality, this is the real thing. Bring your own beer or wine, and leave room to select from the extensive menu of traditional New England desserts, like blueberry pie and grapenut pudding.

Bob's Clam Hut – *Rte. 1, Kittery.* ♿🅿 ☎ *207-439-4233; www.bobsclamhut. com.* **$ Seafood**. A local favorite since 1956, Bob's retained its take-out bonhomie even after adding indoor seating (patrons must still buy sodas from a vending machine). Fried foods at other places can be leaden; here, they're light and crispy.

Dolphin Marina – *515 Basin Point Rd, South Harpswell.* 🅿 ☎ *207-833-6000. www.dolphinchowderhouse.com* **$ Seafood**. It may not be the easiest place to find but it's worth the hunt for the splendidly uncomplicated food served up with a sweeping view of Casco Bay. Diners eat at plain wooden tables or a tiny counter. Especially popular, the chowders are rich and tasty, and most meals come with homemade blueberry muffins.

Sarah Orne Jewett

The second of three daughters born to a country doctor and his wife, Theodora Sarah Orne Jewett began life in 1849 in South Berwick, Maine. She grew up in the Georgian house (1774) that her grandfather—a wealthy sea captain and merchant—had purchased in 1819. As a young girl Jewett began writing sketches of the life she observed around her. Her first story, "Jenny Garrow's Lovers," was published in 1868, and the following year Jewett's stories began appearing in *The Atlantic* magazine. In 1877 a collection of her stories was published as the book *Deephaven*. Perhaps her best-known work, *The Country of the Pointed Firs,* an expression of her admiration for Maine and its people, came out in 1896.

Today admirers of this Victorian author can visit the house where Jewett was born and died. Furnishings and 18C antiques in the **Sarah Orne Jewett House** *(5 Portland St. in S. Berwick, 10mi north of Kittery on Rte. 236; visit by 45min guided tour only, Jun–mid-Oct Fri–Sun 11am–5pm; $5; ☎ 207-384-2454; www.spnea. org)* are arranged as they were when the author lived here.

Nearby, on a site overlooking the Salmon Falls River, the stately Georgian **Hamilton House**★ *(40 Vaughan's Lane in S. Berwick, 9mi west of Kittery via Rte. 236; ⏱ same hours and fee as Jewett House; ☎ 207-384-2454; www.spnea.org)* and its formal riverside gardens provided the setting for much of Sarah Orne Jewett's historical romance *The Tory Lover* (1901), set in Berwick during the Revolution.

A group of early structures flanks the village green, giving visitors a glimpse of Colonial times. On the north side of Route 1A stands the 18C **First Parish Church**, with its cock weathervane, and the **Town Hall**, which served for a time as the York County courthouse. Across Route 1A flanking the **Old Burying Ground** you'll find the **Jefferds Tavern** and schoolhouse, the **Emerson-Wilcox House,** and rising from the top of a small hill, the **Old Gaol**. Nearby are the George Marshall Store (a craft shop) and fishermen's sheds covered with lobster buoys. The inviting red Colonial dwelling (c.1730) beside the river was the home of **Elizabeth Perkins** (1879-1952), one of York's prominent residents.

The **John Hancock Warehouse** *(on Lindsay Rd.)* is one of several coastal warehouses owned by John Hancock, Revolutionary War patriot, signer of the Declaration of Independence and prosperous merchant.

York Harbor

Follow Rte. 1A South from York Village. This landlocked boating center is a haven for small craft. Beautiful homes grace the harbor's tree-covered shores. The **Sayward-Wheeler House** contains family heirlooms accumulated by prosperous trader Jonathan Sayward and his descendants *(79 Barrell Lane Extension; visit by 45min guided tour only, Jun–mid-Oct weekends only 11am–5pm; $5; ☎ 207-384-2454; www.spnea.org).*

▶ *Route 1A leads past Long Sands Beach, which stretches 2mi from York Harbor to Cape Neddick and is bordered by summer cottages.*

Maine Office of Tourism

Nubble Light

Nubble Light★
Leave Rte. 1A and turn right on Nubble Rd.; continue to the tip of Cape Neddick.
From the shore here you'll get a good view of 1879 Nubble Lighthouse on its offshore island; the Isles of Shoals lie in the distance.

Ogunquit★

8mi north of York. 🛈 *Tourist Information:* ☎ *207-646-2939 or www.ogunquit.org.*

In the Algonquin language, *ogunquit* means "beautiful place by the sea." The artists who discovered this little beach town undoubtedly agreed with the description, for by the turn of the century many painters and writers had come to live and work close to Ogunquit's rocky shores. Today, Ogunquit attracts hordes of summer crowds who come for the 3.5mi-long sugar white beach, upscale restaurants and resorts, and shops and galleries. Works by members of the town's present-day artists' colony are exhibited in galleries scattered throughout the village, including the **Ogunquit Art Association Gallery** *(on US-1 south of Ogunquit Sq.)* and the rustic **Barn Gallery** *(Bourne's Lane at Shore Rd.)*. Overlooking the sea, the small, modern **Ogunquit Museum of American Art** *(on Shore Rd. just south of Perkins Cove;* ☎ *207-646-4909)* showcases the work of 20C American artists. During the summer a different play is presented every week at the **Ogunquit Playhouse** *(*☎ *207-646-5511).*

Perkins Cove★
From Rte 1, take Shore Rd. and follow signs to cove. 🅿 *Parking is limited.*
This charming man-made anchorage harbors dozens of shops and several seafood restaurants along its shores. A footbridge across the entrance to the cove can be raised to accommodate local traffic. Perkins Cove is also the departure point for a variety of excursion and fishing boats.

Marginal Way★
🅿 *Parking available at Perkins Cove and at Israel's Head lighthouse.*
Beginning at Perkins Cove, this scenic coastal footpath leads around the windswept promontory called Israel's Head and ends near the center of Ogunquit. Originally a cattle path for a local farmer, Marginal Way now provides visitors with striking **views**★ of the rocky coast and Perkins Cove.

Excursion

Wells Auto Museum
Kids *5mi north of Ogunquit. 1811 US-1.* 🕐 *Open Memorial Day–Columbus Day daily 10am–5pm.* 👓 *$5.* 🅿 ☎ *207-646-9064. www.wellsauto.com.*
Car buffs will find more than 80 vintage cars here dating from 1900 to 1963. And kids will enjoy the collection of antique toys and bicycles.

The Kennebunks★

Kennebunk is 12mi north of Ogunquit. 🛈 *Tourist Information:* ☎ *207-967-0857 or www.visitthekennebunks.com.*
Popular with artists and writers, the resort villages of the Kennebunk region include **Kennebunk, Kennebunkport, Cape Porpoise** and their associated beaches. This area owes its early prosperity to the shipbuilding industry. In later years, from the late 19C through the early 20C, this stretch of Maine coast reigned as a fashionable resort area, with grand hotels and summer mansions.

Kennebunkport★

Take Rte. 9 East off US-1.

The town's narrow streets swell with tourists in the summer months; its most famous summer resident is George Bush, 41st president of the US, whose family estate on Walker Point is visible from Ocean Drive. When you tire of sunbathing on **Kennebunk Beach**, Kennebunkport's commercial center, **Dock Square**, harbors a variety of charming shops set along the tidal Kennebunk River.

Seashore Trolley Museum

📷 *On Log Cabin Rd., about 2mi southeast of US-1.* 🕐 *Open late-May–mid-Oct daily 10:00am–5:00pm.* 💵 *$8.* ♿ ☎ *207-967-2712. www.trolleymuseum.org.*

Take a 3.5mi ride back in time here on a restored antique electric trolley car. After the tour, stroll through the car barns to see additional trolleys, and watch artisans involved in the painstaking process of restoration in the workshop.

Portland★★   *23mi north of Kennebunk. See entry heading.*

Freeport

15mi north of Portland. 🏢 *Tourist Information:* ☎ *207-865-1212, 800-865-1994 or www.freeportusa.com.*

A favored shopping spot, the comely town of Freeport is the home of L.L. Bean, the famous sporting goods mail-order enterprise, as well as the more than 85 brand-name factory outlets that have sprung up along Main Street (Route 1) and its capillaries. During Freeport's early days, the logs for ships' masts and spars were harvested from the surrounding forests and shipped to England from the town's open harbor, or "free port." In 1820 Freeport earned its sobriquet, "Birthplace of Maine," when the treaty agreeing to separate Maine from Massachusetts—and subsequently granting Maine statehood—was signed in a local tavern here.

Wolfe's Neck Woods State Park★

5mi from the center of Freeport. From Main St., turn right onto Bow St. (across from L.L. Bean); take the third right on Flying Point Rd. and veer right on Wolfe's Neck Rd. 🕐 *Open Apr-Oct daily 9am–dusk.* 💵 *$3.* ♿ 🅿 ☎ *207-865-4465 (in season) or 207-624-6080 (off-season). www.state.me.us/doc/parks.*

The beauty and calm of the park's wooded picnic sites and trails overlooking Casco Bay offer a pleasant diversion from the shop-lined streets of Freeport village. The Casco Bay Trail *(.5mi)*, which provides close-up views of Googins Island, is especially scenic.

FREEPORT FINDS

Master craftsmen are hard at work at **Brown Goldsmiths** *(11 Mechanic St.;* ☎ *207-865-4126 or 800-753-4465; www.browngoldsmiths.com),* turning out customized baubles and restoring heirlooms for clients as far away as Manhattan, Boston and even the West Coast. Certified gemologists Stephen and Judith Brown have satisfied customers' jewelry needs for gold, platinum and diamond pieces, Mikimoto pearls, Maine tourmaline or other exquisite adornments. The upscale firm opens its studio and gem lab for a fascinating behind-the-scenes tour *(15min, upon request).* An offshoot of Jackson Hole's namesake emporium, the **Mangy Moose** *(112 Main St.;* ☎ *207-865-6414 or 800-606-6517; www.themangymoose.com)* offers all things mooselike: lampshades, pillows, furniture, frames, dishware, blankets, doormats and bed linens, as well as toys, jewelry and clothing—all emblazoned with images of, or shaped like, Maine's beloved state animal. If, by some remote possibility, you don't find what you fancy, ask to see the 5,000-item catalog.

L.L. BEAN

On Main St. at Bow St. ☎ *800-341-4341.*
www.llbean.com. Outdoorsman and
inventor Leon Leonwood Bean (1872-
1967) began his merchandising empire
in 1912 making and selling hunting
boots. His success led him to expand his
enterprise into a mail-order business
specializing in outdoor clothing and
equipment. The modest factory show-
room blossomed over time into the
firm's flagship 119,000sq ft store, where
five levels—including an indoor trout
pond, hiking ramps and a cafe—display
equipment for nearly every outdoor
sport imaginable. It is not unusual to
see the parking lot crowded at 3am; the
store is open 24 hours a day year-round, as it has been since 1951, when its founder
tired of customers knocking on the door of his residence before dawn.

Courtesy L. L. Bean. Inc.

Brunswick

9mi north of Freeport. 🛈 *Tourist Information:* ☎ *207-725-8797, 877-725-8797 or www.*
midcoastmaine.com.
This attractive community, with its wide avenues, is the home of Bowdoin (BO-din)
College. Shade trees and handsome mansions line Federal Street and other streets
nearby. Small manufacturing plants and the US Naval Air Station are the chief contributors to the local economy, which supports a population of some 14,800 people.
The Bowdoin campus, in the heart of Brunswick, radiates outward from the town's
pleasant green, which was laid out by citizens in the early 18C.

Bowdoin College

The main campus is bounded by Maine St., Bath Rd. & College St. 🛈 *Information and tours*
available at the Moulton Union on College St. ☎ *207-725-3000. www.bowdoin.edu.*
Established in 1794, this well-regarded small liberal arts college spreads across 110
acres and enrolls some 1,600 students. Bowdoin counts among its alumni authors
Nathaniel Hawthorne and Henry Wadsworth Longfellow, explorers Robert Peary
and Donald MacMillan, and the nation's 14th president, Franklin Pierce. Harriet
Beecher Stowe penned *Uncle Tom's Cabin* while she and her husband, a professor
at Bowdoin, lived in Brunswick.

Peary-MacMillan Arctic Museum

Hubbard Hall. 🕐 *Open year-round Tue–Sat 10am–5pm, Sun 2pm–5pm.* 🕐 *Closed*
major holidays. ♿ 🅿 ☎ *207-725-3416. www.academic.bowdoin.edu/arcticmuseum.*
This museum, dedicated to admirals **Robert Peary** (1856-1920) and **Donald Mac-
Millan** (1874-1970), presents the history of polar exploration from the early 1800s
through the Arctic expeditions made by Peary, who is credited with being the first
man to reach the North Pole (1909), and his assistant, MacMillan.

Bath★

8mi north of Brunswick. ⓘ *Tourist Information:* ☎ *207-443-9751 or www.mid-coastmaine.com.*

Named for its sister city in England, Bath has been a shipbuilding center since the 18C, when its coveted location on a channel to the sea provided the town with advantages over other regional boatbuilding centers. Boatyards along the Kennebec River turned out square-riggers, down-easters, and some of the largest schooners ever constructed. The buildings of the Maine Maritime Museum and the graceful old homes on Washington Street date from this time.

Maine Maritime Museum★★

Kids *243 Washington St.* ⓧ *Open year-round daily 9:30am–5pm.* ⓧ *Closed Jan 1, Thanksgiving Day & Dec 25.* ⊚ *$10.* ✕ Ⓟ ☎ *207-443-1316. www.bathmaine.com.* ⌫ *Boat rides (additional fee) on the Kennebec River are offered late Apr–Oct.*

The museum, devoted to preserving Maine's maritime heritage, maintains a historic shipbuilding complex and a boatbuilding shop where visitors can watch wooden boats being restored and built.

Percy and Small Shipyard

Large wooden schooners were the specialty of the Percy and Small Shipyard, which operated on this site from 1897 to 1920. The six-masted, 3,720-ton *Wyoming*, the largest wooden sailing vessel ever to fly the US flag, was built here. Today five of the shipyard's original buildings remain and contain exhibits on Maine's boatbuilding past. Visitors can also observe craftsmen constructing and restoring wooden boats; board a 1942 wooden schooner, and learn about the lobstering industry.

WISCASSET SNACKS

Whether you're just passing through or lingering in Wiscasset, two informal spots downtown along US-1 are worth a stop. **Red's Eats** *(Water St. near the bridge;* ☎ *207-882-6128)* is a tiny but bright roadside stand that specializes in lobster rolls—they're overflowing with lobster meat, served with just a dab of mayo on the side. Across the street is **Sarah's** *(Water St;* ☎ *207-882-7504; www.sarahscafe.com),* where you can be sure of fresh-caught lobster (Sarah's father and brother are both lobstermen), or select from other finger-friendly fare like burritos or overfilled sandwiches on pita or croissants. Most everything is fresh and homemade.

Popham Beach

Excursion

Popham Beach★

16mi south of Bath on Rte. 209.

Situated at the tip of a finger-like peninsula reaching into the ocean, this resort village lies between the Kennebec River and the sea. At the northern tip of Popham Beach, **Fort Popham**, the granite and brick fortress overlooking the point where the Kennebec River meets the Atlantic Ocean, was built during the Civil War.

Nearby, at **Popham Beach State Park**, a broad sandy beach—rare for this section of the coast—lies on the ocean side of the point (🕐 *open mid-Apr–Oct daily 9am–5pm;* 🚗 *$3;* ☎ *207-389-1335; www.state.me.us/doc/parks).*

Boothbay Harbor★★

14mi east of Wiscasset via Rte. 27. ℹ️ *Tourist Information:* ☎ *207-633-2353 or www. boothbayharbor.com.*

Boothbay Harbor lies at the tip of one of the craggy peninsulas that extend into the sea from the deeply indented, mid-coast section of Maine. Protected headlands sheltering deep natural anchorages make the region a major boating center and a popular summer resort (ℹ️ *for information, call* ☎ *207-633-2353, 800-266-8422 or access www.boothbayharbor.com).*

Small shops line the streets leading down to the wharves, and motels, hotels and inns nestle in the snug coves and along the rugged stretches of shore leading down to **Ocean Point**★ *(5mi east of Boothbay Harbor via Rte. 96)* and Southeast Island, connected to the mainland by a short bridge.

Cruising the Bay and Islands

Boothbay Harbor serves as the departure point for a number of different cruises around the Boothbays and day trips to Monhegan Island. Cruises leave from several piers in the center of Boothbay Harbor *(along Commercial St.)* For information, contact the **Boothbay Harbor Chamber of Commerce** (☎ *207-633-2353; www.boothbayharbor.com)* or one of the following companies: *Cap'n Fish's Boat Trips at Pier 1,* ☎ *207-633-6605 or 800-633-0860; www.capnfishmotel.com;* or *Balmy Days Cruises at Pier 8,* ☎ *207-633-2284 or 800-298-2284; www.balmydayscruises.com.*

Brigitta L. House/ MICHELIN

Pemaquid Point Lighthouse

Pemaquid Point★★

20mi northeast of Wiscasset via US-1 North to Rtes. 129 & 130 South.
🛈 *Tourist Information:* ☎ *207-563-8340 or www.drcc.org.*
Carved by glaciers centuries ago, the gnarled ledges at Pemaquid Point are especially spectacular for their pegmatite formations—long, narrow bands of black and white rock that jut into the sea. The point is renowned for its lighthouse, which rises on the bluff above, standing guard over this dramatic section of coastline.

Pemaquid Point Lighthouse Park★★

At the end of Rte. 130 South in Bristol. 🕐 *Open Mother's Day–Columbus Day daily 9am–5pm.* ⊚ *$2.* ♿ 🅿 ☎ *207-677-2492. www.pemaquidlighthouse.com.*
Commissioned by President John Quincy Adams in 1827, Pemaquid Point Lighthouse *(interior closed to the public)* helped sailors—as it still does today—avoid the jagged rocks which divide the opening between Muscongus and John's bays. From this site stretches a photographer's dream **view**★★★.

Rockland

34mi north of Wiscasset via US-1. 🛈 *Tourist Information:* ☎ *207-596-0376 or www. therealmaine.com.*
Commercial center for the mid-coast, Rockland bustles as a modern seaport and one of the leading exporters of lobsters in the world today. Rockland is also home port to Maine's largest fleet of **windjammers**. During the summer months, visitors can cruise Penobscot Bay on one of these tall-masted schooners *(🛈 for information, contact the Maine Windjammer Association in Blue Hill:* ☎ *800-807-9463).*

Farnsworth Art Museum★★

356 Main St. 🕐 *Open Memorial Day–Labor Day daily 10am–5pm. Rest of the year Tues–Sun 10am–5pm, Sun 1–5pm.* 🕐 *Closed major holidays.* ⊚ *$10 (includes admission to Wyeth Center & Farnsworth Homestead).* 🅿 ♿ ☎ *207-596-6457. www.farnsworthmuseum.org.*
Recent renovations and additions have catapulted the Farnsworth from its status as a modest gallery for Maine art to a nationally acclaimed center for the study of Maine artists, particularly the three generations of Wyeth painters—**Newell Convers** (1882-1945), **Andrew** (b.1917), and **Jamie** (b.1946)—who have derived inspiration from the state's rugged land- and seascapes.

Wyeth Center★★

The former Methodist church chosen in 1997 to house hundreds of canvases by all three Wyeth painters is itself a work of art. Its stark, white clapboard exterior

Art Museum Neighbors

Across the street from the Farnsworth, stop in for press-pot coffee and a pre-owned paperback at **Second Read** *(328 Main St.;* ☎ *207-594-4123; www.secondreadbooks.com).* This café/bookstore encourages eaters to read and readers to eat. Used books at reduced prices fill the ceiling-high shelves and specialty coffees are the highlight of the menu.

Just around the corner is **Café Miranda** *(15 Oak St.; dinner only;* ☎ *207-594-2034; www.cafemiranda.com).* This quirky spot declines to take itself too seriously (dress code: "loin cloths and tool belts discouraged"), but does wonders with its wide-ranging menu inspired by cuisine from around the globe. Look for selections such as pierogies, Thai beef steak, BBQ and sweet potato burrito, and more.

has, in fact, been painted by Jamie Wyeth. The stunning interior has been renovated to accommodate 3,500sq ft of naturally lit exhibition space, where scores of Wyeth paintings from Andrew and Betsy Wyeth's personal collection allow visitors to compare and contrast the styles, subjects, and visions of these three tremendously talented artists.

Vinalhaven and North Haven Island Ferries

Depart from the foot of Main St. in Rockland and run to to Vinalhaven and North Haven. Ferry takes both passengers and vehicles. ♿ *For seasonal schedules and rates, call the Maine State Ferry Service* (☎ *207-596-2202 or 800-491-4883; www.state.me.us/mdot).*

Ferries cruise among the serene tree-clad Fox Islands in Penobscot Bay. Largest of these islands at 14mi long, quaint **Vinalhaven** was incorporated in 1789. Here lobster boats anchor in peaceful inlets, and fishing sheds furnished with stacks of lobster traps and brightly painted buoys dot the island. Several of Vinalhaven's abandoned granite quarries provide a place to swim and fish in summer. From the northern end you can spot **North Haven**, a quiet island that swells with summer residents.

Owl's Head Transportation Museum

2mi south of Rockland via Rte. 73, on grounds adjacent to Knox County airport. ○ *Open Jun–Sept daily 10am–5pm. Rest of the year daily 10am–4pm.* ○ *Closed Jan 1, Thanksgiving Day & Dec 25.* ⊙ *$7.* ✕ *(summer only)* 🅿♿ ☎ *207-594-4418. www.owlshead.org.*
The museum's core collection of pre-1930 aircraft is complemented by antique aircraft, automobiles, bicycles, motorcycles and engines dating from the early 20C. Demonstrations of automobiles and airplanes from the collection are held at special summer events on the museum grounds *(call for events schedule).*
Nearby on the coast, the Owl's Head Lighthouse *(follow signs to Owl's Head State Park from Rte. 73 South)* perches atop a 100ft cliff overlooking West Penobscot Bay.

Camden★★

8mi north of Rockland. ℹ *Tourist Information:* ☎ *207-236-4404 or www.visit-camden.com.*
Snuggled at the foot of the Camden Hills, surveying the island-speckled waters of Penobscot Bay, Camden ranks as one of the loveliest towns on the New England coast. It is easy to while away a day here, exploring the shops and galleries in the attractive village center and dining leisurely in waterfront restaurants. Mansions that wealthy summer residents built still line the streets around the center of town. In the harbor, sleek yachts are anchored amid the tall

Maine Lobster Festival

Held in Harbor Park in early August. ☎ *800-562-2529.* *www.mainelobsterfestival.com.* For more than 50 years, this five-day festival has been held each year in Rockland. There are seafood-cooking contests, music, exhibits, arts and crafts, and plenty of lobster—nearly eight tons—as well as other seafood to enjoy. Hardy souls can attempt to run the **Lobster Crate Race** atop 50 bobbing crates partially submerged in the cold harbor waters. The winner is the contestant who crosses the most crates without falling into the bay. There's a lobster diaper derby and cod-fish carry for the kids, among other games.

Camden

©PhotoDisc, Inc.

BAYVIEW STREET DINING

Camden's colorful waterfront is the big draw for residents and tourists alike, especially when it comes to eating. At the marina-side **Waterfront** restaurant *(Bayview St. at Camden Harbor; ☎ 207-236-3747; www.waterfrontcamden.com)*, with its superb seafood servings—such as haddock stuffed with shrimp, crabmeat and spinach—you'll enjoy efficient service and dining on the harborside deck. Also at water's edge is **Atlantica** *(Bayview St.; ☎ 207-236-6011; www.atlanticarestaurant.com)*, which offers creative regional cuisine with an international twist (the seasonal menu may include ceviche of scallops with Maine crab, seared Szechwan salmon, and rosemary-crusted rack of lamb) in a bistro-style setting. **Peter Ott's** *(16 Bayview St.; ☎ 207-236-4032)* may have a no-frills, ale-house interior, but it con-sistently impresses diners with its fare, which ranges from charbroiled black Angus steaks to carefully prepared seafood. Save room for dessert.

THE LOBSTER POUND

US-1, 5mi north of Camden in Lincol-nville Beach. ☎ 207-789-5550. www.lobsterpoundmaine.com. Situated right on the beach, this popular, rambling restaurant offers great views and delicious seafood for lunch and dinner. Family-owned for three generations, the complex has a separate picnic area *(open in summer)* for more casual dining and take-out. Steaks, chicken and roast turkey take a back seat to the likes of Maine shrimp, clams, haddock, Atlantic scallops, swordfish and halibut served blackened, broiled or grilled. Center stage, however, are the lobster dinner selections: served any way you like!

two-masted windjammers, which offer a variety of pleasure cruises in season *(for information & schedules, contact the Maine Windjammers Association, ☎ 207-374-5400 or 800-807-9463; www.sailmaine.com).*

Camden Hills State Park★★

2mi north of Camden off US-1. ⏲ *Open mid-May–mid-Oct daily 9am–dusk.* ⬤ *$3.* △ P
☎ *207-236-3109 (in season),* ☎ *207-236-0849 (off season). www.state.me.us/doc/parks.*
A narrow road snakes up 1mi to the top of Mt. Battie (800ft), where a spectaular **view**★★★ of Camden harbor, Penobscot Bay and the bay islands unfolds below. The park also includes a 25mi network of trails .

Belfast

21mi north of Camden. 🛈 *Tourist Information: ☎ 207-338-5900, www.belfastmaine.org.*
Overlooking Penobscot Bay, this quaint town has managed to retain its historic appearance and community atmosphere despite being a popular tourist stop. Hand-some brick buildings, many over a century old, and old-fashioned street lamps line Main Street. Here you'll find interesting antique stores, art galleries, gift shops, cafes, coffeehouses and other businesses.

Searsport

3mi northeast of Belfast. 🛈 *Tourist Information: ☎ 207-338-5900, www.belfastmaine.org.*
Located near the head of Penobscot Bay, this seafaring town was a boatbuilding center and home to more than ten percent of the nation's merchant marine captains in the late 19C. The beautiful dwellings built for these seamen still adorn the streets near the waterfront.
Second-busiest harbor in the state today, Searsport serves as an export center for manufacturing and agricultural products, notably the potato crop raised to the north in Aroostook County.

Penobscot Marine Museum★

Church St., just off US-1. ⏰ *Open May–Oct Mon–Sat 10am–5pm, Sun noon–5pm.* 💰 *$8.* 🅿 ☎ *207-548-2529. www.penobscotmarinemuseum.org.*
A complex of eight buildings on site includes several restored sea captains' homes, the former Town Hall, the Phillips Memorial Library and adjoining Douglas and Margaret Carver Memorial Gallery. Arranged throughout the buildings, the museum's rich collection of marine paintings, models and artifacts illustrates the era of sail and trade.

Excursion

Fort Knox State Historic Site★

10.5mi north of Searsport on Rte. 174. ⏰ *Open May–Oct daily 9am–dusk.* 💰 *$3.* ☎ *207-469-7719.*
Named for General Henry Knox, chief of artillery under General Washington during the Revolution, the fort—never completed—served as a military training ground during the Civil War. The enormous granite fortress, with its archways, buttresses and winding staircases, is a model of 19C American military architecture. From the top of the ramparts there is a **view** of the town of Bucksport and the Penobscot River.

Fishing Shack

Blue Hill and Deer Isle★

Map p 144. Blue Hill is 31mi northeast of Searsport via US-1 and Rte. 15 South. 🛈 *Tourist Information: ☎ 207-374-3242 or www.bluehillme.com.*
The quiet, breeze-swept peninsula that reaches from Route 3 down to Stonington seems to have been overlooked by modern civilization. Small, secluded villages and cozy inlets harboring lobster boats nestle in woodlands that hug the water's edge. Views of Penobscot Bay and Mount Desert Island are especially striking on a clear day, when the blue sky frames the dark green spruces.

Driving Tour *96 mi circuit from Bucksport*

Bucksport

This small town lies on the east bank of the Penobscot River at the point where Verona Island divides the river. Bucksport's main street, lined with shops and the historic **Jed Prouty Tavern**, runs parallel to the river.

▶ *From Bucksport take Rte. 1/3 North, then turn right onto Rte. 175 South. Continue straight on Rte. 166, then Rte. 166A to Castine.*

Castine

www.bluehillme.com. Pristine tree-lined streets and stately 18C and 19C Georgian and Federal homes create the first impression for visitors to this quiet town. Stroll along Main Street past small shops and down to the waterfront. Some of Castine's earliest architecture, including the 1790 Unitarian Church and the 1840 Ives house, later home to poet Robert Lowell, lines the charming **village green** *(on Court St. just off Main St.)*. The large brick buildings along Pleasant Street belong to the Maine Maritime Academy. The **State of Maine**, the academy's 499ft training vessel is berthed at the waterfront and can be toured when the ship is in port *(⏰ visit by*

30min guided tour only, mid-Jul–Aug Mon–Fri 10am–noon & 1pm–4pm; mid-Sept–mid-Dec & Feb–mid-Apr weekends only 10am–noon & 1pm–4pm; 🕐 *closed academic & major holidays;* ☎ *207-326-4311).*

▶ *Take Rte. 166 and Rte. 199 North around the east side of the peninsula. At Penobscot, take Rte. 175 South.*

Reversing Falls

Five miles south of South Penobscot there is a picnic area where an unusual phenomenon can be seen, a reversing falls. At this point, the waterway is very narrow. When the tide changes, the narrow passage creates a bottleneck, causing the water to rush in (or out, depending on whether the tide is rising or falling) with such great force that a series of falls is formed. The best view of the reversing falls is from the bridge on Route 175.

▶ *Continue south on Rte. 175 to Rte. 176/15. At the junction of Rtes. 175 and 15, cross the bridge to Little Deer Isle, then continue to Deer Isle. Rte. 15 passes through the village of Deer Isle and follows the eastern shore to Stonington.*

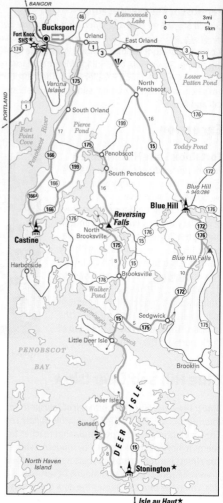

Stonington★

www.deerislemaine.com.

This tranquil fishing village at the tip of the peninsula typifies the picturesque towns along the coast. Boats to **Isle au Haut**★, part of which lies in Acadia National Park, leave from Stonington.

Continue along the western shore of the island, where a beautiful **view** unfolds as you approach the town of Sunset.

▶ *After Sunset head east and take Rte. 15 North. Cross the bridge to Little Deer Isle and pick up Rte. 175 East in Sargentville. In Sedgwick turn left onto Rte. 172. At the town of Blue Hill Falls turn right onto Rte. 175. Cross two bridges to Blue Hill Falls, another reversing falls. Return to Rte. 172 and follow it northeast to Blue Hill.*

Blue Hill

Named for the hill that dominates the town and yields a hearty annual blueberry harvest, this pretty village is home to many craftsmen, including a well-known cache of potters. A trail *(from the village drive north on Rte. 172 and turn left across from the fairgrounds; continue .8mi to trail marker)* leads to the top of Blue Hill (940ft), where you can look out across Blue Hill Bay to Mount Desert Island.

▶ *Take Rte. 15 North.*

The road climbs, passes along the base of Blue Hill, then gradually descends toward Route 1/3 offering beautiful **views** as it leads north.

Lobster Pounds

As you drive the coast of Maine, you'll see thousands of small, colorful, torpedo-shaped buoys bobbing in Maine's coves and off rocky headlands. These are lobster buoys, and each is attached to a lobster trap—or a line of traps—that sits on the seabed and is designed to capture the state's most popular crustacean.

Large and succulent, lobsters love the brisk waters of Maine, which produces more lobsters than any other state in the nation.

Much of the catch makes its way to Maine's shorefront lobster restaurants, where the lobsters are served up simply—boiled, with butter for dipping, corn on the cob, and maybe a baked potato or steamed clams. If you're on the go, the best option is a **lobster roll.** Available from myriad waterside shacks, lobster rolls consist of chunks of fresh lobster meat usually served on a simple hot dog roll. Sometimes the lobster is tossed in mayonnaise and embellished by bits of celery; sometimes the meat is just tossed in melted butter.

Maine's dozens of lobster restaurants range from the very simple—a shack with a couple of picnic tables and a vat of boiling water over an open fire—to more fancy waterfront establishments. *The following restaurants operate seasonally; call first to ensure they're open if you're traveling in the spring or after Columbus Day. (Venues are listed in geographical order, from south to north.)*

Chauncey Creek Lobster Pier – *16 Chauncey Creek Rd., Kittery Point.* ☎ *207-439-1030. www.chaunceycreek.com.* Just a short hop from the factory outlets of Kittery, Chauncey Creek lies a world apart from modern America. Place your order, then stake out one of the colorful picnic tables on the pier overlooking a quiet ocean inlet. Bring your own beverages and sides, if you like.

Two Lights Lobster Shack – *225 Two Lights Rd., Cape Elizabeth.* ☎ *207-799-1677. www.lobstershack-twolights.com.* This shack occupies a rocky point with a view of two lighthouses made famous by the painter Edward Hopper. It's about a 15-minute drive from Portland; dining is offered indoors and out.

Five Islands Lobster Co. – *Rte. 127, Georgetown.* ☎ *207-371-2990. www.fiveisladn-lobster.com.* At the very end of a scenic, winding drive south of Woolwich *(follow Rte. 127 to the water)* you'll find Five Islands Lobster Co. Ask for your lobster at the pier; while it's cooking, order onion rings and drinks at the adjacent snack bar.

Boothbay Region Lobsterman's Co-op – *Atlantic Ave., Boothbay Harbor.* ☎ *207-633-4900. www.mainelobstercoop.net.* Picnic tables atop a pier boast fine views of Boothbay Harbor. The co-op is run by lobstermen and their families.

Thurston's Lobster Pound – *Steamboat Wharf Rd., Bernard.* ☎ *207-244-7600.* Across from Bass Harbor on Mt. Desert Island, Thurston's is a stunning spot at sunset, when lobster boats at their moorings are touched with a burnished glow. Diners eat under a canary yellow awning atop a tall pier.

MONHEGAN ISLAND★★

POPULATION 70
MAPS P 131 AND P 147
TOURIST INFORMATION ☎ 207-439-1319 OR WWW.VISITMAINE.COM

Edged by steep, rocky cliffs, Monhegan Island appears, from the mainland 12mi away, to be the dark, curved back of a huge whale. Of the more than 4,600 islands off the Maine coast, Monhegan is one of only 14 that boasts a year-round island community. The resident population swells from 65 hardy souls in winter to some 200 people in summer. The island's magical beauty and its 17mi of trails attract both photographers and hikers.

Ledge markings discovered on Manana, the islet across the harbor from Monhegan, are considered by some as evidence that the Vikings landed here in the 11C. Several centuries later Monhegan served as a fishing station for European fishermen. Most of the island's small year-round population earns its living from fishing and lobstering. A law prohibiting fishermen from trapping lobsters in Monhegan waters between June 25 and January 1 allows Monhegan lobsters to grow bigger and thus bring a better price. In the summer the island is a haven for daytrippers and artists.

▶ **Orient Yourself:** Monhegan is best explored on foot. Trails are numbered and can be identified by tiny wooden blocks placed on tree trunks where two or more trails meet. We have described three trails to give you an overview.

Address Book

PRACTICAL INFORMATION

Getting There – From **Portland, ME** to all ferry departure points, take I-295 North to I-95 North to US-1 North: to **Port Clyde** (81 mi), take US-1 North to Rte. 131 South; to **New Harbor** (57 mi), take US-1 North to Rte. 130 South to Rte. 32; to **Boothbay Harbor** (49 mi), take US-1 North to Rte. 27 South.
Ferry Schedule (Make reservations 2 to 3 months in advance.) **Monhegan Boat Line** – ☎ 207-372-8848. www. monheganboat.com. Departs from **Port Clyde** May–mid-Nov, daily; Rest of the year Mon, Wed & Fri only. Duration: 1hr, Adult fare (roundtrip) $30.
Hardy Boat Cruises – ☎ 207-677-2026 or 800-278-3346. www.hardyboat.com. Departs from **New Harbor** mid-Jun–Sept daily; mid-May–early Jun & early Oct–mid-Oct. Wed & weekends only. Duration: 1hr, Adult fare (roundtrip) $28.
Balmy Days Cruises – ☎ 207-633-2284 or 800-298-2284. www.balmyday-scruises.com. Departs from **Boothbay Harbor** Memorial Day–Sept, once daily; first 2 weeks of Oct, weekends only. Duration: 1hr 30min, Adult fare (roundtrip) $32.

Visitor Information – Monhegan Island is easily visited by foot or bicycle. No cars or public transportation is available on the island (there are no paved roads); bicycles are prohibited on trails. For more information, contact the Maine Office of Tourism (59 State House Station, Augusta, ME 04333-0059; ☎ 888-624-6345; www.visitmaine.com).

Accommodations – Lodging information is available from the Maine Tourism Association (above) and from the Maine Innkeepers Association (☎ 207-773-7670; www.maineinns.com). Accommodations on Monhegan Island are limited, so reserve well in advance (in summer reserve 3 to 4 months ahead). No camping allowed.

Recreation – **Swimming** at Swim Beach only, near the village of Monhegan. Seventeen miles of **hiking** trails lace the island. You can see a host of birds at Lobster Cove; harbor seals can usually be found at half-tide on Duck Rock.

Sights

Burnt Head

Follow Trail 4 to Burnt Head for a **view**★★ of the White Head cliffs.

White Head★★

From Burnt Head follow Trail 1, which straddles the cliff ledges alongside an evergreen forest. White Head's 150ft cliffs are generally blanketed with seagulls.

Cathedral Woods

Trail 12 runs along Long Swamp to Cathedral Woods, an inland forest of evergreens towering above a lush under-growth of fern and moss.

Monhegan Lighthouse★

Overlooking the village from the top of Lighthouse Hill, the Monhegan Light was originally built in 1824, then rebuilt in 1850 and automated in 1959. From this vantage point, you can enjoy a **panorama** of Monhegan, the harbor and the deserted islet of Manana. The lighthouse keeper's house has been transformed into a **museum** that displays photographs, artifacts and prints related to animal, plant and human life on the island (○ *open Jul–Labor Day daily 11:30am–3:30pm; ☞ $2 contribution requested*). There is also an exhibit relating to Ray Phillips (1897-1975), the hermit of Manana, whose house still stands on the island's hillside.

THE NORTH WOODS★

MICHELIN MAP 583 U 4
TOURIST INFORMATION ☎ 888-624-6345 OR WWW.VISITMAINE.COM

A vast forested wilderness laced by miles of waterways, Maine's North Woods is a recreational paradise. Canoeing, kayaking, whitewater rafting, hunting, fishing, hiking, skiing and snowmobiling are just a sampling of the activities that visi-tors to this region can enjoy. Moose, deer and black bears abound in the forests, and wild brook trout, bass and landlocked salmon run in the rivers, lakes and streams. Here you will find Maine's largest lake (Moosehead Lake) and tallest peak (Mt. Katahdin), along with more than 200,000 acres of parkland. So tread lightly, and revel in one of the last real pockets of wilderness along the East Coast.

Baxter State Park★★

20mi north of Millinocket, ME; follow signs from Rte. 11/157. The main entrances to the park lead to narrow, unpaved Park Road, the only route through Baxter. The park's interior is accessible only by hiking trails. ○ *Open mid-May–mid-Oct daily 6am–10pm. Rest of*

Baxter State Park

the year call for hours. 🚗 *$10 nonresident vehicle fee.* 🏕 *Park headquarters: 64 Balsam Dr., Millinocket.* ☎ *207-723-5140. www.baxterstateparkauthority.com.*

Dominated by the state's highest peak, **Mount Katahdin** (5,267ft), Baxter State Park is a densely forested rectangular tract of land (204,733 acres) in the heart of the Maine wilderness. The park is named for **Percival Proctor Baxter** (1876-1969), who devoted much of his life and fortune to acquiring this land, which he deeded to the people of Maine under the condition that the park be preserved "forever in its natural wild state."

Accordingly, the park has remained primarily a wildlife sanctuary for deer, moose and bear. Here, roads are narrow and unpaved *(speed limit 15-20mph),* camping facilities are primitive, and there are no motels, shops or restaurants within the park boundaries.

Hiking Trails

🔲 *Before starting out, hikers should register with a ranger and check on area weather and trail conditions. Baxter Park and Katahdin, by Stephen Clark, is a comprehensive guide to the park trails. Trail maps are available at the 10 park campgrounds, the visitor center at Togue Pond (south entrance), and at the park headquarters in Millinocket. Most trails are located in the south section of the park. Baxter's trails are blazed blue; white blazes mark the Appalachian Trail.*

While only a few scenic attractions can be observed from the park road, Baxter's 175mi trail system, which includes the northern end of the Appalachian Trail *(which*

Mount Katahdin

A giant granite monolith, Katahdin (an Indian name meaning "the greatest mountain") has long figured in local Indian mythology. One Abnaki legend tells of Pamola, a deity with the wings and claws of an eagle, the arms and torso of a man, and the enormous head of a moose, who lived on the peak of Mt. Katahdin. Whenever he was angry, Pamola cast violent rainstorms onto the lands below.

Baxter Peak is the highest of Katahdin's four summits. Observed from the east, the **Great Basin**, a glacier-shaped formation scoured out of the mountain, is Katahdin's most distinguishable feature. Seen from the west, the **Knife Edge**—a narrow, serrated, 4,000ft-high granite ridge that joins Pamola and South Peaks—cuts a jagged profile across the sky.

Tips for Spotting Wildlife

- Learn about the animals you are hoping to see. Visiting the right habitat increases your chances of sightings.
- Look early in the morning and in the evening, when most animals are active.
- Walk slowly and quietly. The slightest sound can alert an animal to your presence.
- Be alert to the smallest movements; animals are well camouflaged in the dense brush.
- Look up to spot birds or small mammals on tree limbs.
- Stay on trails and watch for paths through the brush cut by animals.
- Keep a safe distance from all wildlife. If an animal signals fear by means of its vocalizations or body language, move away immediately.

cuts through the southwest section of the park) leads to points that afford spectacular views of this remote region.

For those who wish to scale Mt. Katahdin, the challenging **Hunt Trail** *(5.2mi; begin at Katahdin Stream Campground and follow the white blazes)* rewards the experienced and well-conditioned hiker with panoramic **views**★★ of the surrounding region.

Two easier hikes to other points in the park both begin at Roaring Brook Campground: **Sandy Stream Pond Trail** *(1.5mi)* and **Chimney Pond Trail** *(ascent 3.3mi)*. Lovely Chimney Pond, located on the floor of the Great Basin, is the site of one of the park's many campgrounds. A pleasant 1mi hike on the Hunt Trail leads to **Katahdin Stream Falls**.

Excursion

Patten

8mi east of Baxter State Park via Rte. 159.

This small agricultural community straddles the border between the rich potato fields of Aroostook County and the forests of northern Maine. High-powered diesel trucks hauling wood pulp and logs are a familiar sight on local roads. Lumbering is an important business in Patten, even though the era of lumber camps and river drives has long since ended.

At the **Lumbermen's Museum** *(.5mi west of Patten on Rte. 159)*, exhibits ranging from crooked knives to steam log-haulers, a sawmill and reconstructed lumber camps tell the story of the lumberjack's life. The 1820 bunkhouse replicates the type shared by as many as a dozen woodsmen during the lumbering season (🕐 *open Jul–Aug Tue–Sun 10am–4pm; late May–Jun & Sept–mid-Oct Fri–Sun 10am–4pm;* 🎟 *$7;* 🅿 ☎ *207-528-2650; www.lumbermensmuseum.org).*

Moosehead Lake Region★

ℹ *Tourist Information:* ☎ *207-695-2702 or www.mooseheadlake.org.*

Centered on remote inland **Moosehead Lake**★, this region has been a paradise for sportsmen since the 19C. Easy-to-reach ponds and lakes, as well as isolated lakeshore sporting camps *(accessible only by plane)*, attract fishermen and hunters. Canoe and raft trips, including those on the magnificent 98mi-long stretch of white water known as the **Allagash Wilderness Waterway**, begin on the shores of Moosehead Lake (🔆 *for access and information, see the Address Book).*

New England's largest lake (117sq mi), Moosehead is dotted with hundreds of islands and surrounded by timberlands that reach as far as the Canadian border. Numerous bays and coves indent the lake's 350mi shoreline, making it look from the air like a wide set of antlers.

Address Book

PRACTICAL INFORMATION

Getting There – Millinocket is the gateway to the Mt. Katahdin region; the Moosehead Lake area is accessible from Greenville. From **Bangor** to **Millinocket** *(71mi)*, take I-95 North to Exit 56 and follow Rte. 11 South. From **Quebec City** to **Millinocket** *(329mi)*, take I-73 South to Rte. 173 South; at the US border, take US-201 South to Rte. 16 East to Rte. 11 North. From **Bangor** to **Greenville** *(72mi)*, take Rte. 15 North. From **Quebec City** to **Greenville** *(219mi)*, take I-73 South to Rte. 173 South to Rte. 6/15.

Getting Around – Public roads in northern Maine are scarce. Many areas are accessible only by seaplane or canoe. Lumber companies maintain private roads; many of which are unpaved; four-wheel-drive vehicles are recommended.

Scenic flights in the Moosehead Lake area are provided by Folsom's Air Service *(P.O. Box 507, Moosehead Lake, Greenville, ME 04441; ☎ 207-695-2993)* and Currier's Flying Service *(P.O. Box 351, Greenville Junction, ME 04442; ☎ 207-695-2778; www.curriersflying-service.com)*. Jack's Air Service *(P.O. Box 338, Greenville, ME 04441; ☎ 207-695-3020)* provides **fishing trips** to remote camps. Fly-in camping and fly fishing trips to the Katahdin region are offered by Katahdin Air Service Inc. *(P.O. Box 171, Millinocket, ME 04462; ☎ 888-742-5527; www.katahdinair.com)* and Scotty's Flying Service *(RR 1, Box 256, Patten, ME 04765; ☎ 207-528-2626; www.katahdinoutdoors.com)/scottys)*. *Listed services are offered May–Oct only.*

Visitor Information – **North Maine Woods** provides information about access to wilderness areas, camping and guide services as well as detailed topographic maps *(P.O. Box 425, Ashland, ME 04732; ☎ 435-6213; www.northmainewoods.org)*.

Moosehead Lake Area – The following organizations provide information about area attractions, accommodations and recreational opportunities:

Moosehead Lake Region Chamber of Commerce *(visitor center on Rte. 15; P.O. Box 581, Greenville, ME 04441; ☎ 207-695-2702 or 888-876-2778; www.mooseheadlake.org);* and **Moosehead Vacation & Sportsmen's Association** *(P.O. Box MTG, Rockwood, ME 04478; ☎ 207-534-7300)*.

Katahdin Region – **Katahdin Area Chamber of Commerce** visitor information kiosk operates seasonally on Rte. 11 *(1029 Central St., Millinocket, ME 04462; ☎ 207-23-4443; www.katahdin-maine.com)*.

Accommodations – *For suggestions for accommodations and restaurants, see opposite.* Area accommodations are concentrated in Greenville and Millinocket. **Sporting camps** are located in Greenville, Rockwood and Millinocket. **Camping** is available at Lily Bay State Park *(☎ 207-695-2700; www.state.me.us/doc/parks)* and Baxter State Park *(reservations in person or by mail only; 64 Balsam Dr., Millinocket, ME 04462; ☎ 207-723-5140; www.baxterstateparkauthority.com)*. Camping information is available from the **Maine Forest Service** *(P.O. Box 1107, Greenville, ME 04441; ☎ 207- 287-2791; www.maine.gov/doc/mfs)*.

Recreation – Opportunities for **fishing**, **ice-fishing** and **hunting** abound throughout the region. Contact **Maine Fisheries and Wildlife** for seasons and information *(284 State St., Augusta, ME 04333; ☎ 207-287-8000; www.maine.gov/fw)*. The Kennebec, Penobscot and Dead rivers provide challenging **whitewater rafting**, and guided raft trips are offered Apr–Oct. **Raft Maine** *(331 Paradise Rd., Bethel, ME 04217; ☎ 800-723-8633; www.raftmaine.com)* is an association of whitewater outfitters conducting raft trips on all three rivers. The **New England Outdoor Center** *(P.O. Box 669, Millinocket, ME 04462; ☎ 207-723-5438 or 800-766-7238; www.neoc.com)* and **Professional River Runners** *(P.O. Box 92, Rte. 201, West Forks, ME 04985; ☎207-663-2229 or 800-325-3911; www.proriverrunners.com)* both organize kayaking and whitewater-rafting trips in Maine.

Cross-country ski rentals, trail maps and sporting supplies are available in both Greenville and Millinocket. **Snowmobilers** can use Maine's Interconnection Trail System (ITS).

The 92-mi-long **Allagash Wilderness Waterway** is accessible only by **canoe**. For information, contact the Maine Dept. of Conservation, Bureau of Parks & Lands *(State House Station 22, Augusta, ME 04333, ☎ 207-287-3821; www.maine.gov/doc/parks)*.

WHERE TO STAY

☝ *For price ranges for hotels and restaurants, see the legend on the cover flap.*

Blair Hill Inn – *Lily Bay Rd., Greenville.* ⚄ 🅿 ☎ *207-695-0224. www.blairhill. com. 8 rooms.* **$$$$** Set high on a hillside overlooking Moosehead Lake, the Blair Hill Inn is an oasis of sophistication amid the rustic North Woods. This 1891 Queen-Anne-style manor house has been lovingly restored with an eye to comfort, but neither the gracious living room nor the well-appointed guest rooms can begin to compete with the sweeping view of lake and rolling mountains.

Bradford Camps – *40mi west of Ashland via logging roads off Rte. 11.* 🕐 *Closed Dec–May.* ⚄ 🅿 ☎ *207-746-7777 (May–Nov) or 207-439-6364 (Dec–Apr). www.bradfordcamps.com. 8 rooms.* **$$$$** This is a destination for the truly adventurous. Although the camp is accessible by car from Ashland, guests usually arrive via chartered floatplane from Millinocket. All eight log cabins lie steps from pristine Munsungan Lake, and all have private baths. Spend your days here canoeing or kayaking on the lake, fly fishing, hiking, or on a photo safari in search of moose. Meals are served in the main lodge.

Little Lyford Pond Camps – *17mi east of Greenville via unpaved logging roads.* ⚄ 🅿 ☎ *207-280-0016. www. littlelyford.com. 8 rooms.* **$** Originally an 1870s logging camp, Little Lyford now offers guests the chance to stay in woodsy-rustic cabins, while getting a full immersion in backwoods living. Cabins are simply decorated, and each has cold running water, a woodstove and a private outhouse. (There's also a communal shower and sauna.) Meals are served family-style in the log lodge, and during the day guests can canoe nearby ponds, or hike along the Appalachian Trail to a river gorge for an afternoon of swimming. Access to the camp is via logging road.

WHERE TO EAT

Greenville Inn at Moosehead – *Norris St., Greenville. Dinner only.* 🅿 ☎ *207-695-2206 or 888-695-6000. www. greenvilleinn.com.* **$$$ Continental**. In 1895 a local lumber baron spared little expense building a Victorian mansion in Greenville, complete with interior cherry and mahogany woodwork fashioned by local ships' carpenters. Today this is the appealing Greenville Inn, which claims one of the region's two best dining rooms *(the other is at the Blair Hill Inn, above, which serves dinner Fri & Sat in summer and on Sat in winter).* The chef often lends a regional twist to dishes like wild mushroom crepes and pan roasted halibut.

Greenville

Situated at the southern end of Moosehead Lake, Greenville is a resort center, headquarters for two large paper companies and a major outfitting center for sportsmen heading into the north country. Winter skiing is offered at Big Squaw Mountain Ski Area northwest of town. A short distance to the northeast, **Lily Bay State Park** *(on Lily Bay Rd.)* features a lakefront beach and facilities for camping, boating and picnicking.

Mount Kineo

Rising abruptly from the waters of Moosehead Lake, Mt. Kineo reaches an altitude of 1,806ft. There is a good view of Kineo from Route 6/15 just north of Rockwood. Many area tribes knew this flint mountain as a source of the hard, durable stone needed to make weapons, tools and other implements.

PORTLAND★★

POPULATION 64,300

MICHELIN MAP 581 O 4 AND MAPS P 131 AND P 153

TOURIST INFORMATION ☎ 207-772-5800 OR WWW.VISITPORTLAND.COM

The largest city in Maine, Portland is located on Casco Bay, known for its picturesque Calendar Islands. The city is an important oil and fishing port and the financial, cultural and commercial center of northern New England's major metropolitan area.

A Bit of History

True to its motto, *Resurgam* ("I shall rise again"), Portland has risen like a phoenix from its ashes after being almost entirely destroyed on three different occasions. During the early 17C, the English established a trading post here, which developed into the village of Falmouth by 1658. Abandoned in the 1670s after Indian raids caused the inhabitants to flee, the village was resettled in 1716 and supported itself by its mast trade with England. Falmouth's strong anti-Loyalist sentiments led the British to bombard the town in October 1775, as an example to the other colonies. Following the war, the few hundred colonists who remained in Falmouth gradually rebuilt the city, and in 1786, ten years after the birth of the nation, they renamed it Portland.

The city served as the capital of Maine between 1820 and 1832. After the railroad linked Portland to Montreal in the mid-19C, the former capital grew into a prosperous shipping center. A fire swept through the downtown area on July 4, 1866, leveling most of the buildings in the business district; from these ashes rose the city's rich group of Victorian structures.

In the 1970s and 80s, Portland experienced a major economic and cultural rebirth. Today the city ships petroleum products to Canada via the Portland pipeline, while renewal of the Old Port Exchange and new construction projects continue to attract new businesses and visitors to the area.

The metropolitan area, cutting into Casco Bay, is rimmed with pleasant parks and strolling paths. The Eastern and Western promenades, both designed by the nation's preeminent landscape architect, Frederick Law Olmsted, offer panoramic views of the bay and the surrounding region. Portland's skyline is best viewed from the walking path around Back Cove.

▶ **Orient Yourself:** Maine's largest city is nestled on the southern coastline, bisected by north-south I-95 and I-295. The waterfront, boasting a busy, working port and cluster of fishing piers, is along Commercial St. From here, walk west, up the hill, to Old Port.

🅿 **Parking:** Metered on-street parking is available downtown (☞ *25¢/30min)* Public parking lots are located throughout the city (☞ *fees average $8–$12/day).* Many sights downtown are easily visited on foot. Greater Portland Transit (☞ *$1 one-way;* ☎ *207-774-0351)* bus lines operate within Portland and the outlying areas.

👓 **Don't Miss:** One of the many architectural and historical walking tours offered by Greater Portland Landmarks (☎ *207-774-5561; www.portlandlandmarks.org).*

🕐 **Organizing Your Time:** Stop by the Convention and Visitors Bureau (*245 Commericial St.*) for city maps and to get tickets for the Old Port Walking Tour (☞ *offered Mon-Sat, 10:30am; 60- to 90-minute tours leave from the Visitor Center).* Spend the remainder of the day browsing galleries and craft shops of historic downtown and visiting the Portland Museum of Art (allow one to two hours at the museum).

Kids Especially for Kids: Children's Museum of Portland is a hit with young children; also a cruise around Casco Bay is a fun water excursion.

Also See: The views from atop the Portland Observatory, the last remaining maritime signal tower in the U.S.

Sights

Old Port Exchange★★

The warehouses, offices and shops in this old waterfront district were run-down and deteriorating rapidly when, in the early 1970s, several people decided to open a few small restaurants and shops in the area. Their immediate success encouraged other merchants to move into the district and renovate neighboring buildings into attractive specialty shops, professional offices and living spaces.

Stroll along **Exchange, Middle and Fore Streets** and admire the window displays, art galleries and craft shops, and try some of the dozens of restaurants in this area. The 19C architecture here highlights diverse styles and decorative brickwork.

The **block [A]** encompassing nos. 103-107 of Exchange Street is inspired by the Italianate style. Note the **building [B]** on the corner of Middle and Exchange Streets, which has a trompe l'œil mural; several of the windows, though they appear to be part of the mural, are actually real. Along Middle Street note the mansard roof on the elaborately arched and arcaded **block [C]** that includes nos. 133-141. At no. 373 Fore Street, the **Seaman's Club** restaurant **[D]**, exemplifies the Gothic Revival style. Down the street, **Mariner's Church [E]** *(no. 368)*, with its tall windows and triangular pediment, illustrates the Greek Revival style. The Second Empire-style **Custom House** *(no. 312)* reflects the maritime wealth of 19C Portland.

Portland Museum of Art★

7 Congress Sq. ◷ *Open Memorial Day–Columbus Day daily 10am–5pm (Fri til 9pm). Rest of the year Tue–Sun 10am–5pm (Fri til 9pm).* ◷ *Closed Jan 1, Thanksgiving Day & Dec 25.* ⊛ *$10.* ⚆ ♿ ☏ *207-775-6148. www.portlandmuseum.org.*

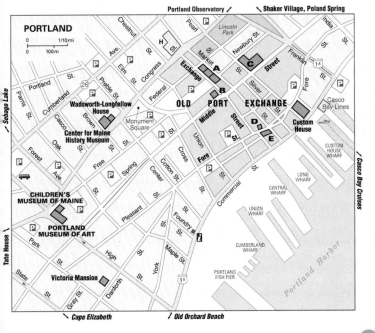

Address Book

PRACTICAL INFORMATION

GETTING AROUND

Visitor Information – The **Convention and Visitors Bureau of Greater Portland** offers maps and information regarding attractions, accommodations and recreational opportunities in the Greater Portland area. They maintain a visitor center downtown *(305 Commercial St.; ○ open mid-May–mid-Oct Mon–Fri 8am–6pm, weekends 10am–6pm; rest of the year Mon–Fri 8am–5pm, weekends 10am–3pm; ☎ 772-5800; www.visitportland.com)*.

Accommodations – *For specific suggestions of accommodations and restaurants, see below.* **Portland Youth Hostel** is located in Portland Hall *(645 Congress St.; ○ open Jun–late Aug; ☎ $17/night; ☎ 874-3281; www.hi-travel.com)*.

Recreation – Shops abound at the Old Port Exchange and on Congress Street. *Discover Historic Portland on Foot (☜ $4.95)*, containing self-guided walking tours and maps of four of the city's historic areas is available from **Greater Portland Landmarks** *(165 State St.; ☎ 774-5561; www.portlandlandmarks.org)*. You can walk along the Eastern and Western promenades, overlooking Casco Bay and the Fore River respectively, or hike the **Back Cove Trail,** which traces Portland's coastline from Maine State Pier *(Commercial & Franklin Sts.)* around Casco Bay and Back Cove. Biking trails run along the Eastern Promenade. Crescent Beach State Park *(☝ see text listing)* on nearby Cape Elizabeth offers a sandy Atlantic beach.

STAYING IN PORTLAND

☝ *For price ranges for hotels and restaurants, see the legend on the cover flap.*
The Danforth – *163 Danforth St.* ☐ ☎ *207-879-8755 or 800-991-6557. www.danforthmaine.com. 10 rooms.* **$$$$**
Among Portland's wealth of regal 19C homes, The Danforth ranks as one of the most handsome. Dating to 1821, this Federal-style brick residence capped with a cupola has been meticulously restored and filled with pastel colors, understated furnishings and modern amenities like hair dryers and ironing boards in each room. Among the inviting touches are the working fireplaces in every guest room but one, and a wood-paneled billiards room in the basement. The inn is a short walk (about 10 minutes) from Portland's Old Port.

Portland Regency Hotel – *20 Milk St.* ※☝☐ ☎ *207-774-4200 or 800-727-3436. www.theregency.com. 95 rooms.* **$$$$**
What began as an 1895 armory has morphed into an attractive and comfortable hotel situated in the heart of Portland's historic Old Port district. The designers have done a nice job converting this unique space into guest rooms, although idiosyncrasies remain—witness the odd little windows at knee height in some rooms. Guest quarters are done in Colonial style—four-poster beds, cherry wood, flowered fabrics—and feature high-speed internet access, nightly turn-down service and complimentary newspaper and coffee with your wake-up call. Just outside you'll find the numerous restaurants and shops of the Old Port (the neighborhood bar scene can be rowdy on weekends). Fitness fans will relish the hotel's health club, which features aerobic classes and a well-equipped exercise room.

Pomegranate Inn – *49 Neal St.* ☎ *207-772-1006 or 800-356-0408. www.pomegranateinn.com. 8 rooms.* **$$$** The staid facade of this handsome 1884 Italianate house in Portland's Western Promenade Historic District gives no hint of what you will find inside. Guest rooms and common rooms are chock-full of wildly whimsical art and antiques that allow the eyes little rest—it's a bit like residing in a mildly daft museum. Boldly painted by a local artist—some with faux vines, others with cartoonish Roman capitals—rooms are decorated in a boisterous mix of patterns and colors. Guests gather each morning in the cheery dining room for wonderfully filling breakfasts that range from blueberry pancakes to grilled stuffed tomatoes.

DINING IN PORTLAND

Fore Street – *288 Fore St. Dinner only.* 🅿 ☎ *207-775-2717.* **$$$ New American**. Noted chef Sam Hayward was hailed in both *Saveur* and *Gourmet* magazines in 2001 for the extraordinary things he accomplishes at this inviting Portland eatery. Housed in a loft-like industrial space, the restaurant centers on an open kitchen with a wood grill and wood-fired oven. Fore Street specializes in grilled fish and meats, purchasing from local purveyors when available. The restaurant and its staff have a decidedly unstuffy attitude, which makes the exceptional fare stand out all the more.

Street & Co. – *33 Wharf St. Dinner only.* ☎ *207-775-0887.* **$$$ Seafood**. This intimate bistro occupies a warren of low-ceilinged rooms off a cobblestone alley in the Old Port. Dining spaces are filled with copper-topped tables and bundles of herbs hanging from the rafters—you may feel like you've slipped across the Atlantic and back about a century. Seafood is the draw here—it's prepared grilled, sautéed, or however else you'd like. The evening specials offer the freshest catches, and rarely fail to impress. During the summer, you can dine outside in the alley.

Silly's – *40 Washington St.* ☎ *207-772-0360. www.sillys.com.* **$ American**. Pizza, jerk chicken, and lamb kabobs are a few of the items you'll find in this funky hole-in-the-wall in a part of town tourists don't often frequent. This is a neighborhood joint with an attitude (one apparently influenced by Elvis), which serves up some of the town's zestiest meals at a good price. Most everything is homemade, from the hand-cut french fries to the thick milkshakes. Eat in, or pack a lunch and head up and over nearby Munjoy Hill for a picnic on the grassy Eastern Promenade.

Founded in 1882, Portland's art museum is the largest and oldest public museum in Maine. Noted for its 19C and 20C American art, the museum showcases the **Elizabeth B. Noyce Collection** of works by American artists who painted in Maine. Winslow Homer *(Weatherbeaten)*, Andrew Wyeth (*Maine Room*), Fitz Hugh Lane (*Castine Harbor*) and Frederick Childe Hassam (*Isles of Shoals*) number among the artists represented who drew their inspiration from the Maine landscape. The collection, which began in 1888 with Benjamin Akers' sculpture *Dead Pearl Diver,* has grown steadily and has been enriched in recent years by the gifts of 17 canvases by Homer and more than 50 works by early-20C artists associated with the Ogunquit art colony.

Several galleries contain sections devoted to American glass *(lower level)*, American and English ceramics and the decorative arts *(4th floor)*. Highlighting the displays are cases of Portland glass, and the Pepperrell collection of silver presented to Maine-born Sir William Pepperrell—leader of the successful siege in 1745 of the French fortress of Louisbourg. A regular schedule of changing exhibits of American and international art supplements the permanent collection.

Children's Museum of Maine★

Kids *142 Free St.* 🕐 *Open Memorial Day–Labor Day Mon–Sat 10am–5pm, Sun noon–5pm.* 🕐 *Rest of the year, closed Mon.* 💰 *$6.* ☎ *207-828-1234. www.childrensmuseumofme.org.*

Children of all ages will find something to amuse them in this 17,250sq ft museum located next to the Museum of Art. On the first level—Maine Street, USA—kids can experience the daily routines of a farm, supermarket, bank and fire department. The second level is devoted to hands-on science exhibits ranging from a model space shuttle to a weather station. Highlight of the third level, the **Camera Obscura★** projects a panoramic view of Portland.

Center for Maine History Museum

489 Congress St. 🕐 *Open May–Oct Mon–Sat 10am–5pm, Sun noon–5pm. Rest of the year Mon–Sat 10am–5pm.* 💰 *$4.* ☎ *207-774-1822. www.mainehistory.org.*

Casco Bay Cruises

Depart from Maine State Pier at Commercial & Franklin Sts., Portland. For schedules & reservations, contact Casco Bay Lines: ☎ *207-774-7871; www.cascobaylines.com. The Bailey Island Cruise (🕐 late Jun–Labor Day daily 10am; 5hr 45min round-trip; commentary;* ⛴ *$18.50;* ✕ ♿ 🅿 *) allows for a stopover at Bailey Island. The Mail Boat Run stops at several islands, but passengers are not permitted to disembark (🕐 mid-Jun–Labor Day; round-trip 3hrs;* ⛴ *$13.* ✕ ♿ 🅿 *).*

The islands in Casco Bay are so numerous that 17C explorer John Smith dubbed them the **"Calendar Islands,"** since it seemed to him that there was one for each day of the year. Current counts range from 130 to 220, but Smith's label stuck nonetheless. Today, their history remains steeped in tales of pirates and other colorful characters.

From the boat, the houses and shops on heavily populated **Peaks Island** and the beaches of **Long Island** are visible. The population of **Great Chebeague**, the largest of the Calendar Islands (3mi wide and 5mi long), increases from 400 in winter to some 3,000 during the summer. The solitary stone tower on **Mark Island** commemorates shipwrecked sailors. At **Bailey Island** note the granite cribwork bridge constructed to allow the surf to pass freely through the openings.

Exhibit galleries in the Center for Maine History chronicle the history of Portland and the surrounding region.

Victoria Mansion (Morse-Libby House)

109 Danforth St. 🚶 *Visit by guided tour (45min) only, May–Oct Mon–Sat 10am–4pm, Sun 1pm–5pm. Day after Thanksgiving–Dec 31 Tue–Sun 11am–5pm.* 🕐 *Closed Jul 4 Dec 25 & Labor Day.* ⛴ *$10.00.* ☎ *207-772-4841. www.victoriamansion.org.*

Designed by architect Henry Austin for wealthy local hotelier Ruggles Morse, this brownstone mansion (c.1860) reflects the sumptuous design, décor and furnishings characteristic of the Italianate style. Inside, the lavish decoration, which includes trompe l'œil murals, elaborately carved woodwork and stained glass, suggests that of a luxury hotel.

Wadsworth-Longfellow House

489 Congress St. 🚶 *Visit by guided tour (45min) only May–Oct Mon–Sat 10am–5pm, Sun noon–5pm.* ⛴ *$7.* ☎ *207-774-1822. www.mainehistory.org.*

This 1785 brick dwelling—the first built in Portland—was the childhood home of poet **Henry Wadsworth Longfellow** (1807-82). Longfellow's simple narrative poems, recounting legends from America's past, won him fame across the nation and abroad. After his death he was the first American to be memorialized in the Poet's Corner in Westminster Abbey. Recently restored, the house displays furnishings and memorabilia relating to the poet and his family.

Tate House★

1270 Westbrook St. Drive west on Congress St., turn right on St. John St., then left on Park Ave. At I-295 overpass, continue on Congress St. to Westbrook St. 🚶 *Visit by guided tour (45min) only, mid-Jun–mid-Oct Tue–Sat 10am–4pm, open first Sun of the month only 1pm–4pm.* 🕐 *Closed Jul 4 & Labor Day.* ⛴ *$7.* 🅿 ☎ *207-774-6177. www.tatehouse.org.*

Located in Stroudwater beside the Fore River, this unusual gambrel-roofed dwelling (1755), was the home of George Tate, the king's mast agent. Tate's duties included making shipping arrangements for trees selected as masts for Royal Navy ships. All trees higher than 74ft and at least 24in at the base were marked as royal property, not to be felled by colonists. The trees were transported by oxen and then by ships custom-built to ferry the masts to England. The attractively furnished interior contains fine paneling, cornices, doorways and furniture that recall those in an 18C London town house.

Portland Observatory

138 Congress St., northeast of downtown on Munjoy Hill. ◷ *Open Memorial Day–mid-Oct daily 10am–5pm.* ◷ *Closed Jul 4 & Jul 28.* ⌨ *$5.* ☎ *207-774-5561. www.portland-landmarks.org/portland-observatory.htm.*

Last surviving 19C signal tower on the Atlantic Coast, this octagonal shingled observatory dates back to 1807. Prior to the days of the telephone and telegraph, shipowners would use this vantage point to signal (with flags) to Portlanders that ships were entering the harbor. Climb the 102 steps to the upper deck for a beautiful **view** of Portland and Casco Bay.

Excursions

Cape Elizabeth★

10mi south of Portland. Take Rte. 77 to South Portland. At the library turn right onto Cottage Rd., which becomes Shore Rd.

A drive around Cape Elizabeth's wild and rocky shoreline provides a scenic excursion from Portland. On the northeast end of the cape sits **Portland Head Light**★ *(located in Fort Williams Park on Shore Rd.)*, the first lighthouse constructed on the East Coast after the Revolution (1791). Climb up to the lighthouse deck for a panoramic **view**★ of Casco Bay. Housed in the former lightkeeper's quarters, the **Museum at Portland Head Light** *(*◷ *open daily Memorial Day–mid-Oct 10am–4pm, rest of the year weekends only;* ⌨ *$2; www.portlandheadlight.com)* details the history of the lighthouse and of adjacent Fort Williams.

On the southeastern section of the cape stand the Cape Elizabeth Light and its inactive twin at **Two Lights State Park**, surrounded by 40 acres of shoreline for picnicking and fishing *(access via Rte. 77 South to Two Lights Rd.;* ◷ *open year-round 9am–dusk;* ⌨ *$3;* 🅿 ☎ *207-799-5871; www.state.me.us/doc/parks)*. Boasting one of the best sand beaches in Maine, 243-acre **Crescent Beach State Park** lies just .5mi west of Two Lights *(access via Rte. 77/Bowery Beach Rd.;* ◷ *open Memorial Day–Columbus Day 9am–dusk;* ⌨ *$4.50;* ✕ ☎ *207-799-5871; www.state.me.us/doc/parks)*.

Just south of Cape Elizabeth, **Old Orchard Beach** *(access via Rte. 1 South and Rte. 9 East)* has attracted Americans and Canadians to its sandy shore for more than 100

Portland Head Light

Poland Spring

29mi north of Portland via Rte. 26. This mountain and lake hamlet became famous in the 19C after a man who had been seriously ill drank from the spring and quickly regained his health. A small factory was established to bottle the water, and a lavish hotel complex developed near the spring. The resort, which burned down in 1975, catered to dignitaries who came "to take the waters." Poland Spring water is still bottled at a factory and sold in stores and supermarkets around the world.

years. Motels, cottages, trailer parks and restaurants front the broad, 7mi-long saltwater beach, and carnival rides animate the pier in summer.

Sabbathday Lake Shaker Village and Museum★

25mi north of Portland in New Gloucester. Take I-95 North to Exit 11, then follow Rte. 26 8mi north. 🕐 *Open Memorial Day–Columbus Day Mon–Sat 10am–4:30pm.* 🍴 *Guided tours $6.50.* 🅿 ☎ *207-926-4597. www.shaker.lib.me.us.*

This hilly lakeside property is the site of the Sabbathday Lake Shaker Village, the last active Shaker community in America. Founded in the late 18C by Shaker missionaries, the settlement continued to exist throughout the 19C and 20C, a period when most other Shaker villages became extinct. Although there are only four Shakers now living here, the principles of Shakerism, "hands to work and hearts to God," and a strong devotion to the Shaker religion continue to guide their lives.

The Shakers occupy a number of the 18 buildings on site, only 6 of which are open to the public. With its granite trim and delicate wooden porch, the **Brick Dwelling House** appears elegant when contrasted with the simple white clapboard structures found throughout the village. Inside, simple furnishings and examples of clothing illustrate the Shakers' uncomplicated way of life. Shaker industries and inventions are depicted in the **Meeting House**, the first building (1794) erected in the village.

Sebago Lake

20mi north of Portland via US-302.

Portlanders who enjoy swimming, boating and fishing favor Sebago Lake, the second-largest inland body of water (45sq mi) in Maine after Moosehead Lake. Bordering the lake, **Sebago Lake State Park** *(off US-302 between South Casco and Naples)*, offers picnic areas, campsites and a sandy beach *(🕐 open May–mid-Oct 9am–dusk; 🎟 $4.50; △ ☎ 207-693-6613; www.state.maine.us/doc/parks).*

RANGELEY LAKES REGION★

MICHELIN MAP 581 M 1
TOURIST INFORMATION ☎ 207-864-5571 OR WWW.RANGELEYMAINE.COM

Nestled in the wooded mountains of western Maine, this region is characterized by its 111 lakes and ponds, the largest being the lakes of the Rangeley chain. Long before the area saw its first settlers, Abnaki Indians set up hunting and fishing camps on the lakeshores. Today visitors escape to this year-round recreational haven to go skiing, snowshoeing and snowmobiling on 150mi of trails in winter; to hunt deer, pheasant and bear in autumn amid a spectacular display of blazing foliage; and to go swimming, boating, canoeing and mountain climbing in summer. Anglers come in spring for the world-class brook trout and salmon fishing.

Scenic turnoffs on Route 17, south of tiny Oquossoc, afford great **views**★★★ of the area's largest lakes. And rewarding vistas abound along Route 4 South between Oquossoc and the sleepy village of **Rangeley** (population: 1,200 permanent residents), which claims no traffic lights to disrupt traffic along its Main Street. Moose can often be seen at dawn or dusk along Route 16, heading out of Rangeley. For those who prefer the solitude of the woods, abundant trails lead to quiet brooks and awe-inspiring mountaintops.

Sights

Rangeley Lake State Park

From Rte. 4 or Rte. 17, take Southshore Dr. and follow signs to park in Rangeley. 🕐 *Open mid-May–Sept daily 9am–dusk.* 📷 *$3.* ⚠ ☎ *207-864-3858 or 207-624-6080 (off season). www.state.me.us/doc/parks.*

Set on 869 remote acres on the south shore of Rangeley Lake, this park includes a beach area with boat ramps, docks and secluded campsites. The lake is renowned among anglers for its landlocked salmon and trout fishing.

Eustis Ridge★★

26mi north of Rangeley by Rte. 16. Turn left onto Rte. 27. After 3mi turn left onto the unmarked road.

From this vantage point there is a **view** of the region. Route 27 continues north to the Canadian border *(30mi)* through unspoiled countryside.

Mount Blue State Park★

31mi southeast of Rangeley in Weld. Take Rte. 4 East, then Rte. 142 South. 🕐 *Open mid-May–Oct 1 daily 9am–dusk. Rest of the year call for hours.* 📷 *$4.* ⚠ ☎ *207-585-2347 or 207-585-2261 (off season). www.state.me.us/doc/parks.*

A mountain panorama rings Mt. Blue State Park, with its 5,021 acres on the shores of **Lake Webb**★. Recreational opportunities here include hiking, boating, swimming, and sunbathing on the sandy beach. Enjoy mountain and lake vistas from **State Park Beach Road**.

Rangeley Lake

Brigitta L. House/MICHELIN

MASSACHUSETTS

AREA: 7,838SQ MI
POPULATION: 6,349,097
CAPITAL: BOSTON
NICKNAME: THE BAY STATE
STATE FLOWER: MAYFLOWER
OFFICIAL WEB SITE: WWW.MASSVACATION.COM

Extending from the Atlantic Ocean to the border of New York state, Massachusetts reflects the region's varied topography. The tree-covered Berkshire Hills in the west gradually slope down to the fertile meadows of the Connecticut Valley in the center of the state. Miles of sandy beach lie south of Boston, while to the north the coast is irregular and rocky. The state is rectangular in shape, except for the southeast section that juts into the ocean, adding hundreds of miles to the Massachusetts coastline.

Birthplace of American Independence – New England's earliest permanent settlements were in Massachusetts. In search of religious freedom, the Pilgrims established Plymouth Colony in 1620, followed within 10 years by the Puritans, who founded Boston. As the population expanded and prospered, the British parliament's taxation policies placed an increasing financial burden on the colonists. Angered by England's policy of "taxation without representation," and inspired by the oratory of **Samuel Adams**, **James Otis** and **John Hancock**, the colonists reacted by staging the **Boston Tea Party**, which, along with the **Boston Massacre** in 1770, proved to be the prelude to the confrontations at Lexington and Concord, and the ensuing battle for American independence.

Economy – For two centuries Massachusetts earned its living from the sea by fishing, whaling and trade. Great fortunes were made in the China trade, and when maritime commerce declined in the 19C, this wealth provided the capital needed for the shift to industrialization.
Thanks to abundant waterpower and the increasing waves of immigration that provided a large labor force, the Berkshires, the southern coast and the Merrimack

Falmouth Chamber of Commerce

Falmouth Lighthouse, Cape Cod

Boston Harbor

©Photo Disc, Inc.

Valley were soon dotted with many small industriall centers. Massachusetts developed into a prominent manufacturer of textiles and leather goods. By 1850 **Lowell**, the first planned industrial city in the nation, was the world's leading producer of textiles. In the 20C these industries migrated to the South and were supplanted by the manufacture of electronics, machine tools and electrical equipment. Today Massachusetts' most important source of revenue is its **"brain power,"** represented by the state's excellent educational institutions and technological and financial services industries.

Massachusetts continues to lead the New England states in commercial fishing, with Gloucester and New Bedford ranking among the nation's major ports. The Bay State's **cranberry crop**, cultivated in the regions of Cape Cod and Plymouth, is the nation's largest.

THE BERKSHIRES★★★

MICHELIN MAP 581 H, I 8, 9 AND MAP P 163
TOURIST INFORMATION ☎ 413-443-9186 OR WWW.BERKSHIRES.COM

In westernmost Massachusetts lies a valley ribboned with the streams of the Housatonic River and bordered by the foothills of the Taconic and Hoosac ranges. Known as the Berkshires, this region mixes small 19C mill towns with comfortable residential communities that blend gracefully with their surroundings. Home of the tallest peak in Masschusetts, Mt. Greylock, the region is a happy blend of natural beauty and cultural offerings. Hiking in the Berkshires is superb; fall and winter entices leaf-peepers and snow skiers.

▶ **Orient Yourself:** A fun way to get your bearings: Bike, stroll, in-line skate, or cross-country ski the Ashuwillticook Rail Trail, a partially-paved path that runs from the Pittsfield-Cheshire town line through the town of Adams.

Berkshire Visitors Bureau/ A. Blake Gardner

View of Mt. Greylock

- **Don't Miss:** MassMOCA, in North Adams, a sprawling center for contemporary art, and, in summer, the Tanglewood Music Festival for the Boston Symphony Orchestra at its summer home.
- **Organizing Your Time:** The museums are great, but don't leave without hiking or snowshoeing one of the beautiful trails around Mt. Greylock.

A Bit of History

The Mohegans – The Mohegans traveled from the Hudson River to the Housatonic Valley, "the place beyond the mountains" as they called it, to hunt. In time, reduced in number by disease and warfare, they abandoned the lowlands for the thickly wooded hills, where they lived peacefully until the arrival of the colonists in the 18C. Devoted to Christianizing the Indians, the colonists established Stockbridge in 1734 as an Indian mission.

To the north lived the **Mohawks**, enemies of the Mohegans and the French, and allies of the British. Today, the Mohawk Trail (Route 2) traces an old Indian trail blazed by the Mohawks as they journeyed through the Appalachian Mountains to the Great Lakes. The Mohawk Trail is an exceptional route for viewing fall foliage.

Great Barrington Region★★

Great Barrington

Located at the junction of US-7 and Route 23, Great Barrington serves as the commercial center for the many vacation homes on the outskirts of this pleasant town. The Great Barrington Rapids, once the site of Mohegan camps, were the major power source for local mills in the 18C. On March 20, 1886, Great Barrington became one of the first cities in the world to have its streets and homes lit by electricity.

Bartholomew's Cobble

11mi south of Great Barrington. ▶ *Take US-7 South to Sheffield Center and continue south 1.6mi. Turn right on Rte. 7A and continue .5mi; take a right on Rannapo Rd. and go 1.5mi; then right on Weatogue Rd.* ◷ *Open year-round daily 9am–5pm.* ◉ *$5.* ☎ *413-229-8600. www.thetrustees.org.*

This natural rock garden, covered with a variety of trees, wildflowers and ferns, rises above the Housatonic River. The **Ledges Trail** *(round-trip 45min)* passes through

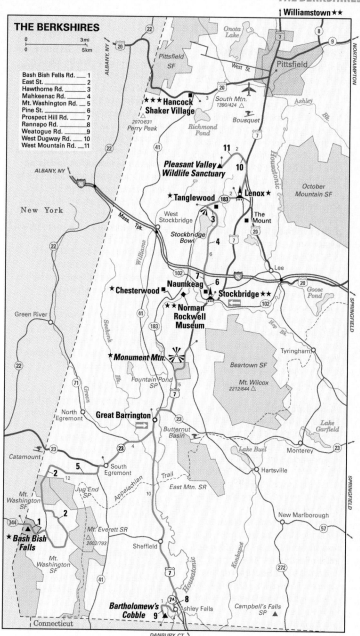

THE BERKSHIRES

Bash Bish Falls Rd.	1
East St.	2
Hawthorne Rd.	3
Mahkeenac Rd.	4
Mt. Washington Rd.	5
Pine St.	6
Prospect Hill Rd.	7
Rannapo Rd.	8
Weatogue Rd.	9
West Dugway Rd.	10
West Mountain Rd.	11

★★★ Hancock Shaker Village

★ Pleasant Valley Wildlife Sanctuary

★ Tanglewood

Lenox ★

★ Chesterwood

Naumkeag

Stockbridge ★★

★★ Norman Rockwell Museum

★ Monument Mtn.

Great Barrington

★ Bash Bish Falls

Bartholomew's Cobble

the cobble and follows the river. At station 17, cross the road and continue on Hulburt's Hill Trail to an open pasture on Miles Mountain (1,050ft) with a view of the Housatonic Valley.

Bash Bish Falls★

16mi southwest of Great Barrington. ▶ *Follow Rte. 23 West to South Egremont, then Rte. 415 at the pond, then immediate right onto Mt. Washington Rd., East St., West St.*

Address Book

PRACTICAL INFORMATION

Getting There – From the east, take I-90 (Mass Turnpike) West to Rte. 102 West *(Boston to Stockbridge 154mi)*. From the south, take I-684 East to US-7 North *(NYC to Stockbridge 130mi)*. From the west, take I-90 West to Rte. 102 South to US-7 North *(Albany to Stockbridge, 57mi)*. From the north, take US-7 South *(Burlington, VT to Stockbridge, 162mi)*. International and domestic flights service **Bradley International Airport** (BDL) in Windsor Locks, CT (☎ *860-292-2000; www.bradleyairport. com)* and **Albany International Airport** (ALB) in Albany, NY *(☎ 518-242-2200; www.albanyairport.com)*. If you're driving from Bradley airport, take I-91 North to I-90 West *(Hartford, CT to Stockbridge, 88mi)*. Major rental-car agencies are located at the airports. Amtrak *(☎ 800-872-7245; www.amtrak. com)* provides **train** service between Boston and Pittsfield. Greyhound *(☎ 800-231-2222; www.greyhound.com)* provides **bus** service from both Boston and Albany (NY) to Lenox and Pittsfield, MA.

Visitor Information – The **Berkshires Visitor's Bureau** in Adams provides maps and information about area attractions, accommodations, dining, recreation and annual festivals *(☎ 413-743-4500 or 800-237-5747; www. berkshires.org)*. For specific suggestions of area accommodations and restaurants, see below.

Entertainment and Recreation – Among Massachusett's most well-known events are the **Tanglewood Music Festival** *(☎ 413-637-1600 ; www. bso.org)* and the **South Mountain Concert Festival** *(☎ 413-442-2106)*. The **Jacob's Pillow Dance Festival** *(Jun–Aug; ☎ 413-243-0745; www. jacobspillow.org)* brings together international performers of ballet, modern dance and mime. Summer theater is offered at the **Berkshire Playhouse** in Stockbridge and at the **Williamstown Theater** in Williamstown *(see entry heading)*. Classical Shakespearean theater is presented in Lenox at **The Mount**, once the summer home of novelist Edith Wharton.

In winter, you can **ski** at: **Ski Butternut** in Great Barrington *(☎ 413-528-2000; www.skibutternut.com)* and **Jiminy Peak** in Hancock, the region's largest ski/snowboard resort *(☎ 413-738-5500; www.jiminypeak.com)*. **Snowy Owl Resort**, in New Ashford *(☎ 413-443-4752 ; www.jiminiypeak.com)*, offers snow tubing down 800-foot lanes. Trek with a woolly companion on a **llama hike** in October Mountain State Forest *(Berkshire Mountain Llama Hike, 322 Lander Rd., Lee, MA; ☎ 413-243-2224; www.hawkmeadowllamas.com)*.

One-Day Itinerary – If you only have one day in the Berkshires, begin in **Stockbridge** and take US-7 North to Lenox. Continue north and visit **Hancock Shaker Village** outside Pittsfield, and the **Clark Art Institute** in Williamstown.

The map in this section covers only the southern part of the Berkshires. For attractions in the northern part of the region, see entry headings for **Mohawk Trail** *and* **Williamstown**.

WHERE TO STAY

👌 *For price ranges for hotels and restaurants, see the legend on the cover flap.*

The Blantyre – *16 Blantyre Rd., Lenox. Open May–early Nov.* ✗👌♿❒☒ ☎ *413-637-3556. www.blantyre.com. 25 rooms.* **$$$$$** A Scottish castle in the Berkshires may be unexpected, but somehow the Blantyre looks right at home, set on 100 acres of woodlands. The hotel's amenities—a pool, tennis courts, a hot tub, sauna, a croquet lawn and hiking trails—are suitable for royalty too. Built in 1901, the house was modeled after a castle in Lanarkshire, Scotland, complete with towers, turrets and gargoyles. The Fitzpatrick family bought the manor in 1980, restoring it to its Gilded Age grandeur. Rooms in the main house sport lavish touches such as hand-carved beds, parquet floors, oriental rugs, marble sinks and walk-in steam showers. The Paterson Suite offers the best views, but the mid-priced Corner Room has charm to spare. The 1,200sq ft Ice House suite, decked out in rich period décor, was added in 2001.

Gateways Inn – *51 Walker St., Lenox.* ✗ 🅿 ☎ *413-637-2532. www.gateways-inn.com. 12 rooms.* **$$$$** Built in 1912 as the summer cottage of Harley Procter of Procter & Gamble, this Federal-style structure has been carefully renovated with a new bar and lounge and other accessories by innkeepers Fabrizio and Rosemary Chiariello. Some rooms reflect the names of famous guests: Norman Rockwell used to show up for lunch and the waitstaff would fight over his sketched-upon napkins; the late Boston Pops conductor Arthur Fiedler favored the suite now named for him, which is outfitted with an extra-long bathtub that suited his tall stature. Rooms are decorated with canopied four-poster beds, brass beds or sleigh beds, and gas fireplaces .

Hampton Terrace – *91 Walker St., Lenox.* 🕐 *Closed Thanksgiving & Christmas week.* ♿ 🅿 ☎ *413-637-1773 or 800-203-0656. www.hamptonterrace.com. 12 rooms.* **$$$** Located 1mi from Tanglewood, this homey B&B occupies an 1897 Dutch Colonial-style house. The house offers noteworthy architectural features such as the three-story suspended staircase, but it's the use of color that really grabs you—vivid yellows, reds, greens and blues make the walls pop. Comfortable rooms, split between the main house and the carriage house, have been re-done in vintage fabrics and antiques. Rates include a breakfast of fresh pastries, fruit and warm, seasoned grits (a nod to the owners' southern heritage). On weekends, they add a hot entrée, perhaps a frittata or French toast.

The Porches Inn – *231 River St., North Adams.* ♿ 🅿 🏊 ☎ *413-664-0400. www.porches.com. 37 rooms.* **$$$** Paint-by-numbers art and claw-foot bath tubs? Somehow it works, with stunning effect, at The Porches. Fashioned from six 1890's row houses, formerly the homes of mill workers in blue-collar North Adams, the inn sits directly across the street from MASS MoCA. Individual houses are painted different colors; catwalks span the open spaces in the back of each horseshoe-shaped building. Wood floors sport coats of bright paint, while mirrors above bathroom sinks have distressed frames, salvaged from the exteriors of the original buildings. Jacuzzi tubs, high-speed internet connections and DVD players pump up the comfort level. Outside, heated slate surrounds a pool and hot tub.

WHERE TO EAT

Red Lion Inn – *30 Main St., Stockbridge.* 🕐 *Open for breakfast, lunch and dinner daily.* ♿ *No shorts, jeans or sneakers in Dining Room.* ☎ *413-298-5545. www.redlioninn.com.* **$$-$$$ American**. Looking at this c. 1773 inn, you might expect a dinner menu that leaned toward Yankee pot roast and Indian pudding. You'd be wrong. Local ingredients go contemporary here; think lobster and scallop cakes in a saffron cream, roasted tomato and basil foam, for example. Even the ubiquitous Caesar salad gets a twist, with manchego cheese and white anchovies. The Red Lion's apple pie is a true classic, served warm with a dollop of ice cream, but adventurous palates opt for the tangy blood orange bisque. The Widow Bingham's Tavern serves more casual fare, like fish and chips.

Gideon's Restaurant – *34 Holden St., North Adams.* 🕐 *Open for dinner Tues.-Sun.* ☎ *413-664-9449. www.gideonsrestaurant.com.* **$$ Eclectic**. Chef Bill Gideon has hung his toque at five Four Seasons hotel restaurants, cooking for celebrities and presidents. Now, he's doing his own thing in North Adams, offering a tasty fusion of Mediterranean/Asian/New England fare. Appetizers might include grilled lamb lollipops or BBQ duck spring rolls; follow these tasty bites with, perhaps, grilled vegetable risotto. For dessert, few diners can resist the lure of molten chocolate cake, but Gideon's vanilla "scrunch" offers just the right blend of velvety ice cream and cinnamon-walnut crunch.

Spigalina – *80 Main St., Lenox.* 🕐 *Open for dinner Thu-Mon; open nightly in season.* ♿ ☎ *413-637-4455; www.spigalina.com.* **$$$ Mediterranean**. Spain meets Southern France meets Greece meets Morocco here, and the results couldn't be more delicious. Spaghetti with clams gets a swoon-worthy kick with the addition of sweet and hot Italian sausage, broccoli rabe and a strong dose of garlic.

and Bash Bish Falls Rd. ○ *Open year-round daily dawn–dusk.* ☺ *Can be dangerous when icy.* ☎ *413-528-0330.*
From the parking area, a steep trail marked with blue triangles and white blazes leads to the falls. Down the road 1mi there is another parking area; from there, a longer, but easier, path leads to the falls. Bash Bish Brook flows over a 275ft gorge, creating a 50ft waterfall and natural pool amidst a forested setting.

Monument Mountain★

4.5mi north of Great Barrington on US-7.
From the parking area on the west side of US-7, two trails lead to the summit. Off **Indian Monument Trail**, look for a cairn about 100yds off the trail that marks the grave of the Indian maiden for whom Squaw Peak is named. Turn right and continue, always selecting the right spur. The second, more difficult trail *(ascent 45min)* begins to the right of the parking area and is blazed with round white markers. From the rocky summit, called Squaw Peak after an Indian maiden who leaped to her death from this point, you will behold a sweeping view of the Berkshires.

JOHN ANDREW'S RESTAURANT

Rte. 23 in South Egremont. ☎ *413-528-3469, www.jarestaurant.com.* It's worth the drive to this somewhat isolated house in South Egremont for the elegant, understated décor and delectable cuisine. Superbly prepared and presented entrées, low-key jazz and a peaceful country setting greet diners here. Try the lobster ravioli to start, followed by pan-roasted cod, clams, chorizo and saffron rice or perhaps risotto of duck confit with leeks and parmigiano reggiano.For dessert, sample the carmelized bananas with chestnut ice cream and caramel sauce.
○ *Open for dinner daily; reservations advised.*

Driving Tour: From Stockbridge to Lenox★★★

Stockbridge★★

Located at the junction of US-7 and Rte. 102. See entry heading.

▶ *In Stockbridge, take Pine St. opposite the Red Lion Inn. Turn left onto Prospect St. (Mahkeenac Rd.) and drive along the lakeshore of Stockbridge Bowl; continue on Hawthorne Rd. At the junction of Hawthorne Rd. and Rte. 183 there is a good view of the lake.*

Tanglewood★

Tanglewood is the summer home of the Boston Symphony Orchestra and the site of one of the nation's most famous musical events, the **Tanglewood Music Festival** *(for schedules, visit www.bso.org).* More than 300,000 music lovers attend every year. The festival was inaugurated in 1934 with concerts by the New York Philharmonic Symphony Orchestra. In 1936 the New York Philharmonic was replaced by the Boston Symphony Orchestra, which has presented the summer series of concerts ever since.

Tanglewood, formerly the residence of the Tappan family, was given to the Berkshire Festival Society in 1937 to serve as the festival's permanent home. Buildings on the 500 acres include the main house; the 5,000-seat Koussevitzky Music Shed, designed by Eliel Saarinen; and the 1,180-seat Seiji Ozawa Hall, opened in 1994.

From the gardens there is a **view** of the **Stockbridge Bowl** and **Hawthorne Cottage** *(not open to the public),* a replica of the dwelling where Nathaniel Hawthorne lived for 18 months while writing *The House of the Seven Gables* (👣 *see entry heading Salem).*

▶ *Take Rte. 183 North to Lenox.*

The Grand Estates

Glowing descriptions of the Berkshires, written by Nathaniel Hawthorne and others, attracted wealthy families to summer here in the mid 19thc. These families built the handsome residences that still grace the countryside outside Great Barrington, Lee, Lenox and Stockbridge. At the beginning of the 20C, Lenox alone could count 75 of these magnificent properties, including the estate of Andrew Carnegie

Spiraling costs and the Great Depression brought an end to the luxuries of the era, and most of the estates were abandoned or sold. Several have found new life as year-round inns.

Lenox★

Surrounded by estates that have been transformed into schools and resorts, Lenox, with its inviting inns and restaurants, is a delightful place to stay.

▶ Take US-7 North and turn left opposite the Quality Inn onto W. Dugway Rd.; then bear left at the fork on W. Mountain Rd.

Pleasant Valley Wildlife Sanctuary

3mi north of Lenox at 472 W. Mountain Rd. ◷ *Open May–Oct Mon–Sat dawn–dusk, Sun 10am–4pm.* ⊗ *$4. Trail map available at office.* ⊡ ☎ *413-637-0320. www.massaudubon.org.* The refuge boasts 7mi of trails that lead through forest, wetlands and meadows, and along the slopes of Lenox Mountain. A beaver colony occupies the string of ponds in the valley; look for lodges along Yokun Brook. Canoe trips on the Housatonic River are offered from mid-May to Columbus Day. Come winter, the sanctuary is a favorite spot for snowshoers and cross-country skiers.

Pittsfield Area

Hancock Shaker Village★★★

3mi west of Pittsfield via US-20. ◷ *Open early April-mid- Oct daily 10am-4pm.* ⊗ *$12.50-$15.* ☛ *Mid-Oct-Dec open for guided tours only, daily 10am-4pm.* ◷ *Closed Jan 1, Thanksgiving Day & Dec 25.*

Hancock Shaker Village, an active Shaker community between 1790 and 1960, is today a museum village that relates the history of this sect, which for more than two centuries has practiced a form of communal living. Some 1,200 acres of farmland, meadow and woodland and more than 20 structures (those original to the site, some reconstructed and others moved from Shaker sites elsewhere) compose the museum. Exhibits interpret life as the Shakers lived it through more than 10,000 objects, and demonstrations of daily tasks such as gardening, milking cows, spinning wool and cooking.

Round Stone Barn

Built in 1826, the barn is a masterpiece of Shaker architecture and functionalism. Wagons entered the third level and emptied their hay into the central haymow. On the middle level, stables radiated out from the central manger,

DAKOTA

1035 South St. (US-7), in Pittsfield. Dinner and Sunday brunch. ☎ *413-499-7900. www.dakotarestaurant. com.* Enjoy seafood, steaks or Maine lobster in this authentic, re-created hunting lodge, with its fieldstone fireplaces and walls decked with moose heads and Plains Indian pottery. Wood-grilled chicken and Atlantic salmon are available from the menu as well as prime rib and aged, hand-cut steaks. Selections from a sizable farm-fresh salad bar complete your dinner, along with home-baked whole-grain bread. You probably won't have room for Dakota's signature mud pie!

making it easy for one person to feed the entire herd. Manure pits were located on the lower level.

Barn Complex
(1910-1939) Formerly a stable for livestock and hay storage, the barn includes the Good Room, where baked goods and beverages are served, and the **Discovery Room**. Here, visitors can make a Shaker basket, milk a "cow," weave a scarf and don period Shaker clothing, among other hands-on activities.

Meetinghouse
The Shakers met here every Sunday for their religious services. The meeting room, a large open hall on the first floor, provided ample space for dancing. Singing (a cappella) was customarily part of the worship as well.

Williamstown★★
22mi north of Pittsfield via US-20.  *See entry heading.*

BOSTON★★★

POPULATION 559,036
MICHELIN MAP 581 M 8 AND MAPS PP 174-175 AND PP 206-207
TOURIST INFORMATION B 617-536-4100 OR WWW.BOSTONUSA.COM

A bright, chaotic melding of old and new, modern Boston bears little resemblance to the spindly peninsula the Indians called Shawmut prior to the 17C. The city that was once the hotbed of American independence is today a renowned center of learning and culture, as well as being the administrative and financial nexus of New England. As "the hub" of the culturally diverse Greater Boston Metropolitan Area, Boston claims several universities—Harvard, Massachusetts Institute of Technology, University of Massachusetts and Boston University—along with a host of world-class museums.

Some five million people representing diverse ethnic backgrounds reside in the Boston metropolitan area; more than half a million of them live within the 46sq mi of the city proper. While offering all the advantages of a modern metropolis, Boston retains a strong sense of history, which is preserved in the city's museums, tiny villages and architecturally significant neighborhoods such as Beacon Hill, the Back Bay and the North End.

▶ **Orient Yourself:** Boston's financial district (including Downtown Crossing's retail stores and several hotels), unofficially "downtown," is framed by Chinatown, the Theater District and South Station to the south, Faneuil Hall to the north, the Boston Common and Tremont St. to the west, and the waterfront to the east.

🅿 **Parking:** For good rates and a handy location, try the Boston Common Garage (*enter on Charles St.*). Other big parking lots are located at Government Center/Quincy Market and Post Office Square.

👁 **Don't Miss:** For art lovers, the Isabella Stewart Gardner Museum is a treat, plus the exceptional Museum of Fine Arts (MFA) is nearby. (Don't miss the MFA's Egyptian burial treasures.) For baseball lovers (and every true Bostonian is in this camp), a tour of beloved Fenway Park is a highlight of the Boston experience.

🕐 **Organizing Your Time:** Put on those walking shoes—this city is best explored by foot. Spend a day wandering through the Public Garden and Boston Common, and then stop at the State House. Resume your tour on the brick sidewalks of

Beacon Hill to admire the stately brownstones (residences are interspersed with cafes and boutiques). From there, jog across the Common to take in the sights along Freedom Trail (Faneuil Hall and Quincy Market are located along the way), or turn right to stroll Newbury Street, the city's most upscale shopping district.

Especially for Kids: If you're visiting in summertime, treat the little ones to a ride on Boston's famous swan boats, plying the lagoon in the Public Garden. Anytime, the Children's Museum—one of the best in the US—is a wonderland of hands-on exhibits. The Museum of Science is always a huge hit with kids of any age.

Also See: Boston's cemeteries are an attraction in their own right. Visit Granary Burying Ground to see the final resting places of Paul Revere and John Hancock.

A Bit of History

European Settlement – In 1630 about 1,000 Puritans led by **John Winthrop** arrived on the coast of Massachusetts to establish a settlement for the Massachusetts Bay Company. Disenchanted with the living conditions in Salem and Charlestown, they set their sights on the peninsula the Indians named Shawmut, then inhabited by an eccentric Anglican clergyman, **Rev. William Blackstone**. The Englishman welcomed the Puritans, who proceeded to establish a permanent settlement on the small peninsula. When the Puritans tried to make Blackstone a member of their church, he sold them his remaining 50 acres and left for the more peaceful atmosphere of Rhode Island.

The new colony, known as Trimountain because of its hilly topography, was soon renamed Boston after the town in Lincolnshire from which many of the Puritan-shailed. Under the firm guidance of Governor Winthrop, the settlement developed as a theocratic society where church and state were one. A rigid moral code was enforced and a pillory was built on the common to punish offenders, among them the carpenter whose price for constructing the pillory was deemed too high. Because of its maritime commerce and shipbuilding, Boston rapidly became the largest town in the British colonies—a distinction it held until the mid-18C.

Cradle of Independence – In an attempt to replenish the Crown's coffers in the wake of the costly French and Indian War, the British parliament voted to enforce high taxes and harsh trade regulations against the American colonies. This policy enraged the colonists, who, as British citizens, claimed that their rights to representation were being denied. The **Stamp Act** (1765), a tax on publications and official documents in Massachusetts, public reaction became violent. Mobs roamed the streets, the governor's mansion was burned and a boycott was organized. Although parliament repealed the Stamp Act the following year, renewed demonstrations erupted in 1767 with the passage of the **Townshend Acts**, which regulated customs duties. England responded immediately by sending troops to enforce British law. The colonists, especially those who were forced to lodge and feed soldiers, grew increasingly hostile. Steadily mounting tensions eventually exploded into clashes between Bostonians and the British.

Mark Read ©APA

Acorn Street, Beacon Hill

The **Boston Massacre** was the first of these clashes. On March 5, 1770, a group of Bostonians gathered at the State House to protest recent events. When a British officer answered the insults of a member of the crowd with the butt of his musket, the crowd became abusive and the guard was called out. Several Redcoats, provoked by the civilians, loaded their weapons and fired, killing five men. Political activist **Samuel Adams** seized on this incident to rally the citizens to his cause.

Three years later the **Boston Tea Party** further aggravated the situation. By 1773 parliament had repealed all the Townshend Acts except the tax on tea, which gave the East India Company a monopoly to sell tea in the colonies. This tax so angered colonists that in November 1773 Bostonians refused to allow the captains of three of the company's tea-laden ships to unload their cargo. At a well-attended meeting held December 16, 1773, in the Old South Meeting House, an attempt was made to resolve the issue. When British compromise was not forthcoming, Samuel Adams concluded with his famed cue: "This meeting can do nothing more to save the country." Thereupon 90 Bostonians disguised as Indians fled the building with a war cry, trailed by a large crowd, and proceeded to board the ships and dump the tea into the harbor. In retaliation England closed the Port of Boston in 1774 and invoked punitive measures—known to colonists as the **Intolerable Acts**—that served only to further unite the colonists against the British.

Ride of Paul Revere – In April 1775 Gen. Thomas Gage dispatched 800 British soldiers to the outlying towns of Concord and Lexington to seize the colonists' stash of arms and arrest patriot leaders **John Hancock** and Samuel Adams. The patriots, forewarned by their network of spies, were prepared. According to a prearranged plan, on the night the British began to move toward Concord, the sexton of Old North Church hung two lanterns in the steeples to signal the Redcoats' departure by boat. In the meantime Paul Revere safely crossed the river to Charlestown and set out to Lexington on horseback to warn Hancock and Adams. Thanks to the legendary ride by Revere, William Dawes and Dr. Samuel Prescott, the militia was ready when the British arrived at Lexington, and later at Concord.

Siege of Boston and the Battle of Bunker Hill – Following events at Lexington and Concord, the British retreated to Boston, where they were surrounded by rebel forces. While the British eyed the strategic heights around Boston, colonial leaders, informed of the British plan to fortify Bunker Hill in Charlestown, hastened to occupy nearby Breed's Hill before the arrival of the British. On June 17, 1775, when the British awoke and discovered an American redoubt had been built on Breed's Hill during the night, a force of 5,000 soldiers was sent out to capture the site. Although the colonists' position was defended by only 1,500 militiamen, the British failed in their first two attempts to secure the fort. They then set fire to Charlestown and launched the third and final attack against the rebels. Colonial leader William Prescott, aware that his men were low on ammunition, gave his famous order: "Don't fire until you see the whites of their eyes!"

The British succeeded in capturing the fort, but in doing so, they lost over 10 percent of all the British officers killed during the Revolution. Although it took place on Breed's Hill, this struggle is known by the misnomer the Battle of Bunker Hill.

British Evacuation – During the early months of 1776, the supplies captured by the colonists at Fort Ticonderoga were hauled across New England to Boston. American artillery began to bombard Boston on March 2. By March 5 the colonists had fortified Dorchester Heights to the south with the cannons from the fort and the British were forced to accept a compromise. The colonial troops peacefully reclaimed Boston, and British General Howe and his men were permitted to evacuate the city unharmed. Soon after, General Washington made a triumphant entry into Boston, which saw little subsequent war activity as the theater of operations shifted to New York, Pennsylvania and the southern colonies.

"Cutting Down the Hills to Fill the Bays" – Modern Boston is the product of transformations wrought by two centuries of prodigious landfill projects. Familiar place names such as Back Bay, the South End and Dock Square recall features of the area's original 783-acre landmass, which has increased almost fourfold through landfill alone since the early 19C.

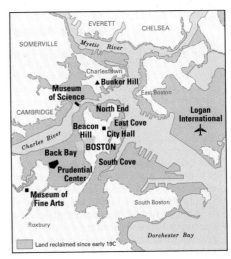

The Puritans who settled Shawmut found an irregularly shaped peninsula joined to the mainland by a natural causeway (the "neck") stretching along a section of present-day Washington Street. On the western side rose a three-peaked ridge (Trimountain) dominated by Beacon Hill. Extending south of Beacon Hill, the tract purchased from Reverend Blackstone was set aside as "Common Field," and remains parkland to this day as the Boston Common. The eastern shore facing the harbor was indented by Town or East Cove, which divided the residential North End from commercial and public sectors that burgeoned in the vicinity of the harbor, the original South End.

Over the course of the 19C, Boston's population increased dramatically, rising from 18,000 in 1790 to 54,000 in 1825. By the turn of the century, it totaled over half a million. The pressing need for more living space prompted a flurry of landfill projects that forever transformed the city's topography. These ambitious programs, characterized by historian Walter Muir Whitehill as "cutting down the hills to fill the bays," involved hauling colossal quantities of earth into the waters around the city, thus transforming the spindly peninsula into an extension of the mainland. The filling in of the waters on either side of the narrow neck was crucial to the city's growth, for it enabled a network of railroad lines to penetrate the downtown area. Boston's great 19C transformation began with the development of the Beacon Hill district in the early 19C. In the following decades the areas on the peninsula's east and

Boston Waterfront

Unique Museums

Looking for something different? Massachusetts is home to a medley of intriguing museums. The **Fuller Craft Museum** *(450 Oak St., Brockton;* ☎ *508-588-6000; www.fullercraft.org)* is New England's home for collecting, exhibiting and experiencing contemporary craft. Forget the macrame plant holders and potholders; items shown here are often avant-garde, eye-popping creations like baskets made of measuring tapes, pine needles, or pencil stubs. This one is definitely worth a stop, especially if you're a crafter looking for inspiration. If you have children, you've probably read *The Very Hungry Caterpillar* by Eric Carle, with its bold, colorful illustration. Author Carle, a resident of Northampton, MA, is part founder of the **Eric Carle Museum of Picture Book Art** *(124 West Bay Rd., Amherst;* ☎ *413-658-11100; www.picturebookart.org)*. This engaging museum showcases the work of Carle (author of 70 children's books) and other illustrators. Part of the fun is seeing the artist's sketches, and watching how they evolved into the finished product. In the town of Harvard, **Fruitlands** *(Prospect Hill Rd.;* ☎ *978-456-3924; www.fruitlands.org)* is a 218-acre farm that hosted one of America's first Utopian communities, founded by Bronson Alcott in 1843. The community's goal was to "live off the fruit of the land." Most members had little experience in farming, and the venture lasted only seven months. The farmhouse is now a museum of transcendentalism.

south sides were filled in, leading to the expansion of the waterfront area and the creation of the residential district now called the South End. The century's most spectacular landfill project took place in the Back Bay on the neck's north side. This 40-year project increased the city's area by 450 acres and resulted in one of the nation's finest planned residential districts. After the Great Fire of 1872 leveled 776 buildings downtown, many residents and churches resettled in the fashionable Back Bay, precipitating the development of the downtown as a commercial district. Landfill projects continued to increase the city's area throughout the 19C and into the present century, particularly around Charlestown and East Boston, site of Logan International Airport.

The city's system of public parks, parkways and tree-shaded malls, designed in the 19C by the nation's premier landscape architect, **Frederick Law Olmsted**, encircles the city with a nearly continuous swath of greenery. The so-called **Emerald Necklace** begins at Boston Common and stretches southwest along the Public Garden, Commonwealth Avenue, the Fenway, Jamaica Park, the Arborway, Arnold Arboretum and Franklin Park.

The New Boston – By the mid-20C Boston was deteriorating. Rising property taxes, the exodus of businesses to the suburbs or out of state and the general population decline had taken their toll. Faced with problems associated with urban blight, the city reacted by establishing the **Boston Redevelopment Authority** in 1957. Under the leadership of **Edward Logue**, BRA inaugurated a program aimed at "revitalizing" one-fourth of the city. The plan generated much controversy since it mandated the bulldozing of entire neighborhoods, including Scollay Square and the adjacent Jewish and Italian enclave known as the West End.

Architect **I.M. Pei**, who had trained at the Massachusetts Institute of Technology, was among the experts called upon in the 1960s to draw up designs for the new **Government Center** on the site of Scollay Square, Boston's bawdy entertainment district. This $260 million project called for an enormous brick-paved expanse showcasing the award-winning City Hall building alongside several contemporary structures of varying architectural merit and a 19C commercial building. In the following decades Pei contributed to reshaping Boston's built environment by executing such important commissions as the John Hancock Tower, the Kennedy Library and the West Wing of the Museum of Fine Arts.

A major renewal project of the 1960s, the mixed-use Prudential Center created controversy, largely because it failed to create a human scale compatible with surrounding Back Bay neighborhoods. More successful was the 1970s renovation of the Faneuil Hall Marketplace, which dramatically revived the ambience of downtown Boston by injecting new vitality into the city's historic heart.

In the 1980s the **Financial District**, long established in the vicinity of Federal and Congress Streets, began expanding in the direction of the rejuvenated harbor district. The waterfront's redevelopment, which was boosted by the rehabilitation of the adjacent Faneuil Hall area, has reestablished Boston's historic link to the sea. This area is being further enhanced with the dismantling of the unsightly, traffic-clogged Central Artery that has long severed the waterfront and the North End from the downtown proper. Begun in the early 1990s, the **Central Artery/Tunnel Project**, a.k.a. the Big Dig, created a multilane underground expressway beneath the site of the former Central Artery. The goal of this ambitious, multi-billion-dollar public-works program was to alleviate Boston's infamous traffic snarls and create over 150 acres of new parkland. Serious safety issues surfaced in mid-2006, when a portion of the Ted Williams Tunnel's ceiling collapsed, fatally killing a commuter en route to Logan International Airport. At this writing, repair work continues and a stronger, reinforced tunnel is expected to reopen.

Boston Today

Bostonians – Today the city is a product of the twin poles of the Boston psyche: Puritan preservationism and Patriot progressivism. The "proper Bostonian," or **Brahmin**, descends from New England's early Puritan settlers who shared a common language and culture, and whose close-knit society set Boston apart by the 19C as the city where "the Lowells talk only to the Cabots, and the Cabots talk only to God." Stereotyped as refined, conservative and Harvard-educated, the proper Bostonian today represents an ever-decreasing percentage of the city's population.

Boston's large **Irish** population began arriving by the thousands in the wake of the 1840s potato famine. Penniless yet hardworking, the Irish integrated into mainstream American life, and many succeeded in rising to positions in local and federal government. One of Boston's most famous Irish Americans was former US president John Fitzgerald Kennedy.

Toward the end of the century, many **Italian** immigrants, particularly from southern Italy, settled in Boston. The Italians eventually replaced the Irish and Jewish populations in the North End and the now-destroyed West End.

The **African-American** community, once concentrated on Beacon Hill, represents a large presence in Roxbury and the adjacent neighborhoods of Dorchester and Mattapan. Boston is home to one of the oldest black communities in the US. The first blacks were brought to colonial Boston as slaves from the West Indies in 1638, just eight years after the colony's establishment. A growing number of freed blacks settled in the North End. Many of them worked as barbers, sailors, laborers and coachmen and many, including **Crispus Attucks**, an assassinated hero of the Boston Massacre, served in the Revolution. In the 1780s the slave trade was legally abolished in Massachusetts—a reflection of the state's staunch abolitionist position. In the 19C, with the dedication of the African Meeting House on Beacon Hill, the black community moved to the north slope of the Hill in search of improved living conditions. Better housing, job opportunities and schools led blacks to move gradually out to Cambridge, the Back Bay and the South End.

Boston's rapidly growing **Hispanic** population has settled in pockets such as the South End, Jamaica Plain and East Boston. It is estimated that these and other minority groups, such as Asians, now make up about one-third of the city's population. In the 1970s and 80s, Boston became a national testing ground for controversial busing policies. In an attempt to provide quality education for students of all socio-

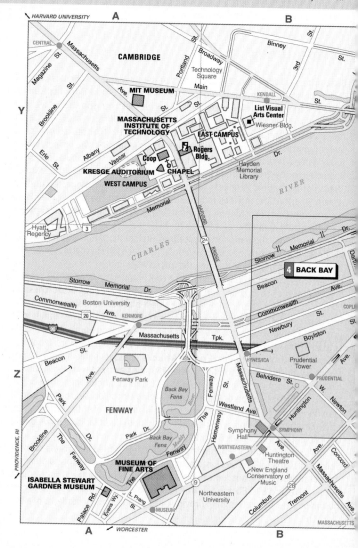

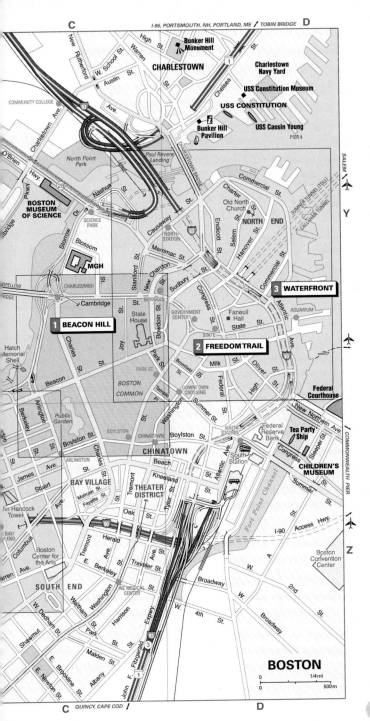

BOSTON

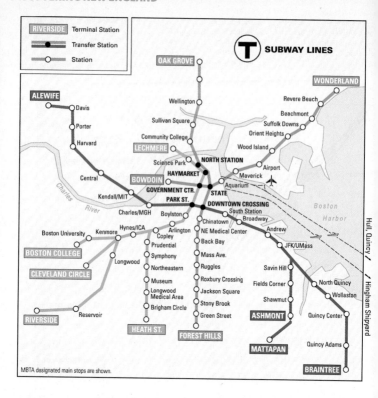

MBTA designated main stops are shown.

economic classes and particularly blacks, the federal government attempted with limited success to integrate the city's public schools.

Each year the area's colleges and universities draw a new influx of students and professors from across the country and abroad. The large **student population**, estimated in recent years at over 200,000, lends great diversity to the area's social and cultural fabric. Students reside on and around the numerous urban and suburban campuses scattered throughout the area, and they constitute a strong presence in large sections of Cambridge, Brookline and Allston-Brighton.

Economy – Since the days of the Bay Colony, shipping and trade have been the mainstays of Boston's economy. Following a period of decline in the early 20C, modernization of the port's services and of the 25mi of docking space in the 1950s and 60s increased the amount of cargo the port could handle. Today, however, Boston is not among the 20 top-ranking ports in the country.

A similar surge of growth was experienced in the business sector, particularly in the insurance industry. Insurance giants Prudential and John Hancock have established a towering presence in the Back Bay through the construction of the area's two tallest skyscrapers. Boston financiers, guardians of the Yankee fortunes made in shipping and industry, continue to generate a large share of New England's economic activity from their offices in the Financial District.

Industrially, a new era was born in the 1950s with the construction of Route 128, a circumferential highway outside the downtown area, and the emergence along this highway of about 700 research and development firms. Boston is a recognized world leader in this field; its universities are training grounds for scientists and research specialists, especially in electronics and computer technology. Boston is also a world leader in health care; the city's medical facilities, notably **Massachusetts General Hospital**, are internationally recognized centers of research and treatment. The

Address Book

BASIC INFORMATION

GETTING THERE

By Air – International and domestic flights service **Logan International Airport** (BOS) *(2mi northeast of downtown;* ☎ *617-561-1800 or 800-235-6426; www.massport.com)*. From the airport, you can get downtown via taxi. The **Massachusetts Bay Transportation Authority** (MBTA) subway's Blue Line services Logan Airport. The MBTA's Silver Line, a rapid-transit bus, runs from downtown to Logan Airport. Free shuttle buses run between the terminal and the airport station. The **Rowes Wharf Water Taxi** *(Mon–Fri 7am–7pm, every 15min, daily 7am–7pm, year-round;* ☞ *$10 one-way;* ☎ *617-406-8584)* makes the short trip between Logan dock and Rowes Wharf *(Atlantic Ave., downtown)*; shuttle bus 66 provides free service from the airport to the dock. Boats travel from Logan Airport to the South Shore and downtown *(year-round daily;* ☞ *$12 one-way; for schedules contact* **Harbor Express** ☎ *617 -376-8417; www.harborexpress.com)*. Major rental-car agencies are located in the baggage-claim area at all terminals.

By Bus and Train – Amtrak **trains** leave from South Station *(Atlantic Ave. & Summer St.;* ☎ *800-872-7245; www. amtrak.com)*. Suburban MBTA trains depart from North Station *(150 Causeway St.)* and South Station *(for schedules and fares, call* ☎ *617-222-3200; www. mbta.com.)*. **Bus** service is provided by Greyhound from South Station *(*☎ *800-231-2222; www.greyhound.com)* and Peter Pan Bus Line *(700 Atlantic Ave.;* ☎ *800-237-8747; www.peterpanbus. com)*.

GETTING AROUND

By Public Transportation – Commuter **ferry** service is available between Long Wharf, Lovejoy Wharf and Charlestown Navy Yard, North Station and World Trade Center *(year-round daily, except major holidays; Mon–Fri 6:30am—8pm, weekends 10am–6pm;* ☞ *$1.25 one-way; for schedules contact Boston Harbor Cruises:* ☎ *617-227-4321; www. bostonharborcruises.com)*.

Subway and Buses – The MBTA operates underground and surface transportation in the greater Boston area. The Red, Blue, Orange and Green subway lines radiate out from the four central downtown stations: Downtown Crossing, Park Street, State, and Government Center. Subway stations are indicated by the ⊤ symbol at street level. Most MBTA lines operate Mon–Sat 5am–12:45am, Sun 6am–12:45am. Timetables are posted at the Park Street Station. An in-city **subway** token costs $1.25; basic local **bus** fare is 90¢ *(token or exact change required)*. MBTA Visitor Passports are good for one *($7.50)*, three *($18)*, or seven *($35)* consecutive days of unlimited travel on all MBTA subway and local bus lines. Passports can be purchased at available at subway stations, Logan Airport and at the information kiosks at Boston Common and Quincy Market. Free MBTA public-transportation maps are available at North and South stations, at area hotels and at branches of Citizens Bank. MBTA system maps can be purchased at the Globe Corner Bookstore *(1 School St.)*. For MBTA route, schedule and fare information, call ☎ *617-722-3200; www. mbta.com*.

By Car –For updates on road closings and detours, call ☎ *617-228-4636 or visit www.BigDig.com*. Use of public transportation or walking is strongly encouraged within the city as roads are often congested and street parking may be difficult. Parking garages range from ☞ *$6/hr—$35/day*. Garages at Boston Common, John Hancock and Prudential Center are open 24/hrs daily. Some facilities give "early-bird" discounts before 10:30am.

By Taxi – **Boston Cab Association** ☎617-536-3200; **Red Cab** ☎ 617-734-5000; **Green Cab** ☎ 617-625-5000; **Town Taxi** ☎ 617-536-5000

GENERAL INFORMATION

VISITOR INFORMATION

Greater Boston Convention and Visitors Bureau, Inc. offers maps and the *Boston Travel Planner (free)*, with information regarding area attractions, accommodations, dining, festivals and recreation *(2 Copley Pl., Suite 105, Boston, MA 02116; ☎ 617-536-4100 or 888-SEE BOSTON; www.bostonusa.com)*. Several additional visitor centers are located throughout the city: **Boston Common Visitor Information Center** *(🕐 open Mon–Sat 8:30am–5pm, Sun 9am–5pm)*; **Prudential Center Visitor Information Center** *(800 Boylston St.; 🕐 open Mon–Sat 8:30am–5pm, Sun 10am–6pm)*; and the **National Park Service Visitor Center** *(15 State St.; 🕐 open year-round daily 9am–5pm; 🕐 closed Jan 1, Thanksgiving Day & Dec 25; ☎ 617-242-5642; www.nps. gov/bost)*.

Accommodations *– For specific suggestions of accommodations and restaurants, see pp 180-183.* Accommodations downtown range from pricey elegant hotels to less expensive motels. Rates vary depending on the season and the day of the week; many downtown hotels offer discounted rates on weekends. Most bed-and-breakfasts inns are located in residential areas of the city *(many B&Bs require a two-night minimum stay)*. A 12.4% room tax is added to the room rate in Boston.

Reservation services – Boston Reservations Inc., *1643 Beacon St, Suite 23, Waban, MA 02168, ☎ 617-332-4199; www.bostonreservations.com.* Reservation services specializing in B&B's and private homes: **Host Homes of Boston**, *P.O. Box 117, Waban Branch, Boston, MA 02468, ☎ 617-244-1308 or 800-600-1308; www.hosthomesofboston.com;* **Bed and Breakfast Cambridge & Greater Boston**, *☎ 617-720-1492 or 800-888-0178.*

Hostelling International maintains two youth hostels in Boston: Near the Museum of Fine Arts *(12 Hemenway St.; 🕐 open year-round; 👛 $28–$45 (private rooms, 👛 $70-$100); ☎ 617-536-9455)*; and the Fenway Summer Hostel *(575 Commonwealth Ave.; 🕐 open June 1–Aug 20; $35 (private rooms, 👛 $89; ☎ 617-267-8599). Reservations are suggested for all Boston hostels (www. bostonhostel.org).*

LOCAL PRESS
Daily news: *Boston Globe* (morning), Thursday entertainment section; *Boston Herald* (morning). Weekly entertainment: *Boston Phoenix.*

FOREIGN EXCHANGE OFFICES
Travelex World Wide Money *(☎ 617-567-2153)* operates currency-exchange offices in Logan International Airport: Terminal B *(🕐 open daily 6:30am–9pm)*, Terminal C *(🕐 open daily 6am–8pm)* and Terminal E *(🕐 open daily 7am–10:30pm)*. **American Express Travel Services** *(☎ 800-297-3429)* has exchange offices downtown *(1 State St.; 🕐 open Mon–Fri 8:30am–5:30pm; ☎ 617-723-8400)*, and at 432 Stuart St. *(🕐 open Mon–Fri 8:30am–5:30pm; ☎ 617-236-1331)*.

USEFUL NUMBERS
Police/Ambulance/Fire ☎ 911
Police (non-emergency) ☎ 617-343-4240
Dental Emergency *(24hrs)* ☎ 800-917-6453
Medical Emergency Inn-House Doctor *(24hrs)* ☎ 617-859-1776
Massachusetts General Hospital ☎ 617-726-2000
CVS Pharmacy ☎ 617-437-8414 *(587 Boylston St.; open 24hrs)*
Weather ☎ 617-936-1234

SIGHTSEEING
CityPassBoston *(valid for 1 year; 👛 $39)* available at visitor information centers, participating attractions and major hotels, covers reduced admission to six attractions. **Old Towne Trolley Tours** offers 1hr 40min narrated tours of the city *(daily year-round; starting at 9am; 👛 $26)* ☎ 617-269-7150; www.historicboston.com); visitors can board at major attractions along the route. Inner harbor sightseeing **cruises** depart from Long Wharf *(daily; 👛 $10–$18)*. A high-speed ferry offers service to Provincetown, Cape Cod *(daily May–Oct; 90min one-way; 👛 $90 round-trip; for schedules contact Boston Harbor Cruises: ☎ 617-227-4321; www.bostonharborcruises.com)*. Narrated lunch and dinner cruises leave from Commonwealth Pier at the World Trade Center year-round *(lunch cruises depart 11:30am, 👛 $48; dinner cruises depart 6:30pm, 👛 $70; for reservations contact Spirit of Boston Harbor Cruises: ☎ 617-748-1450 or 866-211-3807; www.spiritcruises.com)*. **Odyssey Cruises** depart from Rowes

Wharf *(daily May–Sept; 2hr lunch cruises* 🕿 *$35-$55; 3hr dinner cruises* 🕿 *$94-$112;* ☎ *888-741-0281; www.odyssey-cruises.com).* Sailing cruises leave from Long Wharf *(daily Jun–Sept for 2hr sails in Boston Harbor aboard Schooner Liberty Tall Ship;* 🕿 *$30:* ☎ *617-742-0333; www.libertyfleet.com).*

Whale-watching cruises – *See p 34.*

ENTERTAINMENT

Consult the arts and entertainment sections of local newspapers for schedules of cultural events and addresses of principal theaters. **BosTix Ticket Booths** *(locations at Faneuil Hall Marketplace and Copely Square)* offer half-price tickets for selected local events on the day of the performance, as well as full-price advance tickets (🕐 *open Mon–Sat 10am–6pm, Sun 11am–4pm; purchases must be made in person; cash only;* ☎ *617-482-2849; www.artsboston. org).* **Ticketmaster** also offers tickets to local events *(*☎ *617-931-2000; www. ticketmaster.com).*

MUSIC, DANCE AND THEATRE
Boston Center for the Arts (BCA) – 539 Tremont St., ☎ 617-426-5000, www.bcaonline.org

Boston Ballet – 270 Tremont St., ☎ 617-695-6955, www.bostonballet.org

Boston Lyric Opera – 265 Tremont St., ☎ 617-542-6772, www.blo.org

Charles Playhouse, Blue Man Group Boston – 74 Warrenton St., ☎ 617-426-6912, www.blueman.com or www.Broadwayinboston.com

The Colonial Theatre – 106 Boylston St., ☎ 617-880-2495, www.Broadwayin-boston.com

Emerson Majestic Theatre – 219 Tremont St., ☎ 617-824-8000, www.emerson.edu

Hatch Memorial Shell – Charles River Esplanade, ☎ 617-626-1470

Huntington Theatre – 264 Huntington Ave., ☎ 617-266-0800, www.hunting-tontheatre.org

New England Conservatory of Music – Jordan Hall, 290 Huntington Ave., ☎ 617-536-2412, www.newenglandcon-servatory.edu

Shubert Theatre – 265 Tremont St., ☎ 617-482-9393, www.boston.com

Symphony Hall – 301 Massachusetts Ave., ☎ 617-266-1492, www.bso.org

Wang Center for the Performing Arts – 270 Tremont St., ☎ 617-482-9393, www.wangcenter.org

Wilbur Theatre – 246 Tremont St., ☎ 617-423-4008, www.Broadwayinbos-ton.com

SPORTS
Tickets for major sporting events can be purchased at the venue, or through Ticketmaster outlets *(above).* The 26mi **Boston Marathon**, run every year from Hopkinton to the Back Bay, takes place on Patriots' Day *(3rd Mon in Apr).*

⚾ **Major League Baseball,** Team: Red Sox (AL), ☎ 617-267-1700, www.redsox.com, Season: Apr–Oct, Venue: Fenway Park

🏈 **Professional Football,** Team: New England Patriots (NFL), ☎ 617-543-1776, 800-543-1776;www.patriots.com, Season: Sept–Dec, Venue: Gillette Stadium

🏀 **Professional Basketball,** Team: Celtics (NBA), ☎ 617-523-3030, www.celtics.com, Season: Oct–Apr, Venue: TD Banknorth Garden

🏒 **Professional Hockey,** Team: Bruins (NHA), ☎ 617-624-1000, www.boston-bruins.com, Season: Sept–Apr, Venue: TD Banknorth Garden

SHOPPING IN BOSTON

DOWNTOWN
Downtown Crossing *(Washington & Summer Sts.)* is an outdoor walking mall anchored by Macy's department store. In the lower level of the Filene's Building *(426 Washington St.),* **Filene's Basement** is renowned for its great bargains. Across Congress Street from City Hall, **Faneuil Hall Marketplace** *(Dock Sq.; www.faneuilhallmarketplace.com)* comprises a lively cluster of more than 50 specialty shops, 14 full-service restaurants, 40 food stalls and a comedy club in three restored 19C buildings. The nearby **Haymarket** *(Blackstone St. between Hanover & North Sts.; open Fri & Sat only)* is a popular outdoor farmers' market featuring local produce and fresh fish.

BACK BAY
Opened in 1984, **Copley Place** *(Huntington Ave. & Dartmouth St., located between and connected to the Westin and Boston Marriott hotels in Copley Place; www.shopcopleyplace.com)* boasts two levels of upscale shops and

restaurants, among them such well-recognized names as Neiman-Marcus, Tiffany, Gucci, and Barney's. An enclosed walkway links the Copley Place shops to **Prudential Center** (800 Boylston St. between Gloucester & Exeter Sts.; www. prudentialcenter.com), with its own host of retailers and restaurants featuring Lord & Taylor, Saks Fifth Avenue and Legal Sea Foods.

Boston's answer to Rodeo Drive, tony **Newbury Street** (www.newbury-st.com) is lined with art galleries, designer boutiques, antique shops and some of the city's best restaurants. As you stroll the seven blocks of Newbury Street from the Public Garden to Hereford Street, be sure to notice the lovely 19C architecture. At no. 175, the **Society of Arts and Crafts** (☎ 617-266-1810; www.societyofcrafts.org) operates a gallery where artisans sell their handmade furniture, textiles, glass and jewelry.

BEACON HILL

Antiquers can browse to their heart's content on **Charles Street**, which claims more antique shops than any other part of the city. Don't expect to find too many bargains in this upscale Beacon Hill neighborhood.

CAMBRIDGE

The original site of the town of Cambridge (c.1630), **Harvard Square** (Massachusetts Ave. & John F. Kennedy St.; www.harvardsquare.com) today teems with trendy shops, bookstores, eateries and clubs. Dominating the square is the **Harvard Coop** (www.thecoop.com), where you can buy a plethora of gifts and apparel bearing the Harvard or MIT logo. Nearby you'll find the venerable **Club Passim** (47 Palmer St.; www. clubpassim.org), which, since 1958, has hosted such folk-music luminaries as Joan Baez and Bob Dylan.

If malls are more your style, the three-level **CambridgeSide Galleria** (100 CambridgeSide Pl., at Memorial Dr. & Edwin Land Blvd.; www.shopcambridge-side.com) houses more than 100 apparel and specialty stores.

STAYING IN BOSTON

For price ranges for hotels and restaurants, see the legend on the cover flap. Properties listed are in Boston unless otherwise specified.

Boston Harbor Hotel – 70 Rowes Wharf. ☎ 617-439-7000 or 800-752-7077. www.bhh.com. 230 rooms. **$$$$$** Perched dramatically overlooking Boston Harbor, this grand hotel—marked by an 80-foot archway—boasts some of the city's best water views. Although relatively new (it opened in 1987), it feels classically elegant, with chandeliers, marble floors, and plush upholstered furnishings. Guest rooms are comfortably posh, outfitted in 300-thread-count sheets and featherbeds, with marble countertops in the bathroom. **Meritage Restaurant,** with windows facing the water, showcases contemporary New England cuisine,

Fairmont Copley Plaza Hotel

Fairmont Hotels & Resorts

presented as small plates paired with fine wines. During the summer months, the hotel hosts jazz concerts al fresco.

Eliot Hotel – *370 Commonwealth Ave.* ⊠♿🅿 ☎ *617-267-1607 or 800-443-5468. www.eliothotel.com. 95 rooms.* **$$$$$** In this regal 1925 building overlooking tree-lined Commonwealth Avenue in the Back Bay, most guest accommodations are two-room suites, with French doors separating the sitting rooms and bedrooms. Furnishings are traditional, with floral spreads and down comforters; in the lobby, marble floors and chandeliers set the dignified mood. The hotel's top-rated **Clio Restaurant** serves imaginative contemporary French fare.

Fairmont Copley Plaza – *138 St. James Ave.* ⊠♿🅿 ☎ *617-267-5300 or 800-257-7544. www.fairmont.com. 383 rooms.* **$$$$$** Back Bay's palatial property has been the home base for visiting US presidents and foreign dignitaries since 1912. A look at the lobby's gilded coffered ceilings, crystal chandeliers, and ornate French Renaissance-style furnishings may explain why Elizabeth Taylor and Richard Burton spent their second honeymoon here. Sedate plaid or floral fabrics and Louis XIV reproductions adorn the large guest rooms. The **Oak Room** restaurant serves steaks and other traditional American fare in a similarly sumptuous environment.

Lenox Hotel – *61 Exeter St.* ⊠♿🅿▨ ☎ *617-536-5300 or 800-225-7676. www. lenoxhotel.com. 216 rooms.* **$$$$** Built in the 1901, this historic property, close to Boston's prime shopping zones (Newbury Street and Copley Place), has won awards for the restoration of its handsome facade. Several rooms boast working wood-burning fireplaces. The hotel's City Bar and Solas pub are popular with locals as well as hotel guests.

XV Beacon – *15 Beacon St.* ⊠🅿 ☎ *617-670-1500 or 877-982-3226. www. xvbeacon.com. 63 rooms.* **$$$$$** This Beacon Hill hotel offers unsurpassed luxury. Past the intimate lobby's "living room" alcove, the Beaux-Arts building's original cage elevator (1903) takes guests up to oversized rooms, studios and suites, all of which are outfitted with canopy beds, gas fireplaces and

mahogany paneling. Amenities include fresh flowers, 300-thread-count sheets, and surround-sound stereo. Guests have free access to a nearby health club. The **Federalist** restaurant serves contemporary French cuisine under silver chandeliers in a coolly elegant beige dining room paneled in dark wood.

Beacon Hill Hotel and Bistro – *25 Charles St.* ⊠♿ ☎ *617-723-7575 or 888-959-2442. www.beaconhillhotel.com. 13 rooms.* **$$$$** If the weather is mild, slip up to the roof terrace at this swank small hotel on Beacon Hill's main street to sip a glass of wine and watch the world go by. The property blends seamlessly with neighoring antique shops and boutiques along Charles Street. Like the terrace, the property feels like a stylish urban oasis. Rooms are sleek, almost spare, sporting fluffy duvets and hi-tech flat-screen TVs. Rates include a full breakfast in the Parisian-style bistro, which also serves French -inspired cuisine at lunch and dinner.

Clarendon Square Inn – *198 W. Brookline St.* ☎ *617-356-2229. www. clarendonsquare.com. 3 rooms.* **$$$-** Not our grandmother's B&B, this South End brownstone is stylishly appointed with a mix of Victorian antiques and contemporary designer touches. Contemporary art adorns the parlor walls, and marble mantles surround the fireplaces. Hotel-style amenities—in-room data ports, DVD players, a guest refrigerator—abound, and Continental breakfast is served in the sunshine-yellow dining room. You can soak away the stresses of the day in the hot tub up on the roof deck.

Gryphon House – *9 Bay State Rd.* ☎ *617-375-9003. www.gryphonhouseboston. com. 8 suites.* **$$$** There's nothing cookie-cutter about this four-story, 19th century brownstone—each suite is decorated with its own theme. The house evokes a quieter era, and it's easy to picture ladies wearing gloves ascending the staircase, but this inn doesn't stint on modern amenities, like data ports, CD players and oversize tubs. Adding to the charm is the vintage wallpaper mural and trompe-l'oeil paintings in common areas.

John Jeffries House – *14 David G. Mugar Way, at Charles Circle.* ♿ ☎ *617-*

367-1866. www.johnjeffrieshouse.com. 46 rooms. **$$$** At the foot of Beacon Hill, this solid-looking four-story redbrick building, built in the early 1900s, sits opposite a bustling traffic circle and the Charles Street T station. Despite its busy location, the inside is surprisingly serene. Well-maintained rooms are furnished with period reproductions, and most have kitchen facilities. Although the guest rooms are not large, many have separate sitting and sleeping areas. Enjoy a Continental breakfast in the sizable parlor, which is stocked with oversize chairs and offers views of the Charles River. Another plus: Charles Street's inviting cafes, boutiques and antique shops are right outside the door.

Newbury Guest House – *261 Newbury St.* P ☎ *617-437-7666. www.newburyguesthouse.com. 32 rooms.* **$$$** You can't beat the location on Boston's prime shopping street, so savvy travelers book this one months in advance. And, on a street filled with names like Valentino, here's a surprise: Newbury Guest House is an excellent value. The property comprises three attached 1880s brownstones, enhanced by fine furnishings and prints from the Museum of Fine Arts. Guest rooms, some with bay windows, are attractively furnished with Victorian-style reproductions and Oriental rugs atop natural pine floors. A Continental breakfast is served in the petite parlor.

Omni Parker House – *60 School St.* P ☎ *617-227-8600 or 800-843-6664. www.omniparkerhouse.com. 35 rooms.* **$$$** John F. Kennedy proposed to Jackie at table 40 at Parker's Restaurant, and Charles Dickens gave his first reading of "A Christmas Carol" here—how's that for star power? (If you want rock stars, stay at the Four Seasons) Quintessentially Boston, the Omni Parker House is the oldest continuously operating hotel in the U.S. You'll be transported back in time when you enter the lobby, with its gleaming wood and ornately-carved ceilings. But they've added lots of contemporary luxuries here, like feather duvets and Wi-Fi. Yes, Parker House rolls were invented here, as was Boston cream pie, and that pie is in such high demand, guests can even order it for breakfast.

DINING IN BOSTON

B & G Oysters – *550 Tremont St..* ♿ ☎ *617-423-0550; www.bandgoysters.com.* **$$$$ Seafood.** At this sleek, subterranean restaurant, waitpeople describe briny bivalves with the same reverence sommeliers have for wine. Nobody cares if you ultimately order the lobster roll instead! Chef Barbara Lynch of No. 9 Park, brings her magic touch to fresh seafood here, where the room is as sparkling as the food. It's all white marble, black stools, and silvery candlelight that evokes the inside of an oyster shell.

Grill 23 & Bar – *161 Berkeley St. Dinner only.* ♿ P ☎ *617-542-2255. www.grill23.com.* **$$$$ American.** Filled with martini-quaffing power suits, this clubby Back Bay expense-account haven built its reputation on top-quality steaks— but Grill 23 also made its mark as a seafood destination. Preparations range from straightforward filet mignon, New York sirloin, or grilled swordfish to more imaginative choices that might include cedar-roasted salmon with a warm snap pea and potato salad.

Hamersley's Bistro – *553 Tremont St. Dinner only.* ♿ P ☎ *617-423-2700. www.hamersleysbistro.com.* **$$$$ French.** Hamersley's helped establish the South End as a prime dining destination, and this petite bistro, where patrons turn up in everything from sweaters to suits, is still going strong after more than a decade. The menu stresses creative comfort food with a French flair, from the wholesome cassoulet to the signature garlicky roast chicken. Although it is cheery with its yellow walls, the dining room is a bit tight for a private tête-à-tête. Stop by in summer for a bite outside on the patio.

Radius – *8 High St. Closed Sun. No lunch Sat.* ♿ P ☎ *617-426-1234.* **$$$$ New French.** Perenially one of Boston's top tables, this sleek Financial District dining room exudes a mix of efficiency and Zen-like composure, from the staff's Nehru-style jackets to the artfully prepared contemporary French fare. Business types share space with foodies here, but the opulent experience comes at a price. The menu brims with luxury ingredients: seared foie gras with tropical fruits, Maine diver scallops with heirloom squash and black trumpet mushrooms, or Colorado lamb paired with barley risotto. And who could pass up such tempting finales as warm palm-sugar cakes with chilled pineapple soup or Tahitian vanilla crème brûlée?

Bomboa – *35 Stanhope St. Dinner only.* ☎ *617-236-6363. www.bomboa. com.* **$$$ French-Brazilian.** Find your way down a Back Bay side street near the John Hancock Tower to this French-Brazilian hot spot, where stylish twenty-somethings crowd the sleek zinc bar, *mojitos* or *caipirinhas* in hand. Beyond the bar, in the narrow dining room lit by space-age fixtures and the glow of a tropical fish tank, some dishes take their inspiration from France (duck breast and duck confit pairing) or Brazil (*feijoada*), while others (*steak frites* with *chimichurri* sauce) span both cultures.

Ginza – *16 Hudson St. Open until 2am nightly.* ☎ *617-338-2261.* **$$ Japanese.** Tucked away in Chinatown, Ginza serves up top-quality sushi and sashimi. The menu includes Japanese standards, from tempura to teriyaki to sukiyaki, but the raw fish is the main catch here. Look for the unusual maki rolls, like the B-52 roll (yellowtail layered with tempura) or the shaped-like-its-name caterpillar maki. Traditional low tables in the back room, where you sit on floor pillows, are quieter than the standard seating in the busy front room.

Legal Sea Foods – *26 Park Sq.* ☎ *617-426-4444; Copley Place, 100 Huntington Ave.* ☎ *617-266-7775; Prudential Center, 800 Boylston St.* ☎ *617-266-6800; 255 State St.* ☎ *617-227-3115. www.legalsea-foods.com.* **$$ Seafood.** This Boston classic stays on the map thanks to its fresh, straightforward seafood. The clam chowder is a New England favorite, and you can try new items at Legal's Test Kitchen.

Artu – *6 Prince St.* ☎ *617-742-4336.* **$ Italian.** You have to squeeze past the narrow open kitchen to enter this traditional trattoria just off Hanover Street, the North End's main drag. Yet once you're inside the simple but cozy dining room, you can feast on reason-ably-priced Italian fare—perhaps fusilli mixed with broccoli rabe and sausage, eggplant parmigiana, or chicken marsala—in portions that are more ample than the space.

Pho Pasteur – *119 Newbury St.* ☎ *617-262-8200.* **$ Vietnamese.** If you're looking for Boston's best inexpensive eats, you won't go wrong with Pho Pasteur, on posh Newbury Street and quickly cropping up elsewhere around the city. Pho (Vietnamese noodle soup) is presented in a big bowl—you can choose among types of noodles and select the meat you'd like to toss into the tasty, delicate broth, along with a nice sampling of fresh sprouts and other veggies. One bowlful makes a meal for most diners (if not, there are stirfries on the menu as well).

Sultan's Kitchen – *116 State St. Closed Sun. No dinner Sat.* ☎ *617-570-9009.* **$ Turkish.** A modest take-out spot with just a handful of tables, this tiny Turkish eatery is an excellent option for vegetarians or for anyone looking for a fast, flavorful meal in the Financial District. The speedy staff will pack your choices to go, if you prefer to picnic at the waterfront, just a short walk away. Middle Eastern salads and sandwiches, including several types of kebabs, are featured, but be sure to leave room for a piece of the syrupy baklava.

---

nationwide recession of the 1980s dealt a serious blow to Boston's economy as evidenced by skyrocketing unemployment and a sagging real-estate market. Signs of recovery were apparent in the 1990s, however, and, by the end of the decade, Boston's financial and high-tech industries were booming. The city positioned itself to take on major convention business with the opening of a new 1,700,000sq ft convention center in 2004. The Boston Convention and Exhibition Center (BCEC) is located in the Seaport District, near the South Boston waterfront and Boston's World Trade Center. The Westin Waterfront Hotel opened in mid-2006, and several other new hotels are currently under construction, including InterContinental, Mandarin Oriental, and Renaissance properties. A new hotel is also opening up at the former site of the Charles Street Jail.

A Cultural Hub – *For the locations of theaters and concert halls see map pp 174-175.* By the 19C Boston had become a gathering place for intellectuals and writers, earning the sobriquet "the Athens of America." Well-heeled and cultivated Bostonians traveled extensively, returning home with treasures that initiated the collections of the Museum of Fine Arts, the Isabella Stewart Gardner Museum and the museums of Harvard University. In 1881 philanthropist Henry Lee Higginson founded the **Boston Symphony Orchestra** (BSO). Today the BSO and the **Boston Pops**, with its repertoire of lighter music, perform seasonally in Symphony Hall. In the summer the Pops presents free concerts on the Charles River Esplanade. The heart of the **Theater District** lies in the area near Tremont and Stuart Streets. Boston is a testing ground for Broadway productions. The Colonial Theater, the Shubert Theater and the Wilbur Theater present musicals and comedies. Dramas are staged at the Charles Playhouse and at numerous university theaters, such as Boston University's Huntington Theatre and the American Repertory Theatre in Harvard Square. Performances by the **Boston Ballet Company** occur seasonally at the Wang Center.

Education – A principal concern of the Puritans was the establishment of a sound educational system. Ever since the founding of Boston Public Latin School (c.1630), the first public school in America, and Harvard College (1636), the first college in the colonies, Boston has remained a leader in the field of education. The metropolitan area's roster of some 68 colleges and universities includes Harvard, Massachusetts Institute of Technology, Boston University, New England Conservatory of Music, Boston College, Brandeis University, Tufts University and Wellesley College.

1 Beacon Hill★★ *Map opposite*

Historically the home of Boston Brahmins and the city's early black community, the "Hill" preserves an Old World ambience undisturbed by the bustle of the surrounding metropolis.

A Remarkable Transformation

Today's Beacon Hill is the only remnant of the three peaks comprising the Trimountain ridge. Its name derives from the primitive beacon that the Puritans raised on its summit in 1634 to warn of invasion. From 1795 to 1798 preeminent architect Charles Bulfinch oversaw the erection of his golden-domed State House on the Hill's southern slope. Construction of this grand building spurred Bulfinch, Harrison Gray Otis and their business associates to create an elegant residential district on a nearby tract purchased from painter John Singleton Copley. From 1799 until the mid-19C, these developers transformed the entire face of the Trimountain area: Beacon Hill's summit was lowered 60ft and the two neighboring peaks were leveled, creating abundant landfill for the surrounding marshlands; the present street system was laid out; and the charming enclave of English-style brick residences that we know as Beacon Hill came into being.

The sunny south slope, between Pinckney Street and the Common, became the bastion of Boston's affluent society and the center of its respected intellectual and artistic community, whose members included Daniel Webster, Julia Ward Howe and the Alcotts. The more modest north slope, spilling into Cambridge Street, became the center of Boston's black community in the 19C, many of whose members worked for the well-to-do on the the the Hill. Today Beacon Hill reigns as one of Boston's most desirable addresses. A stroll along its serene streets lined with gas lamps and brick facades transports the visitor to a bygone era.

An Architectural Showcase

Created almost entirely in the first half of the 19C, Beacon Hill constitutes a living museum of the period's architectural heritage, showcasing the works of the city's

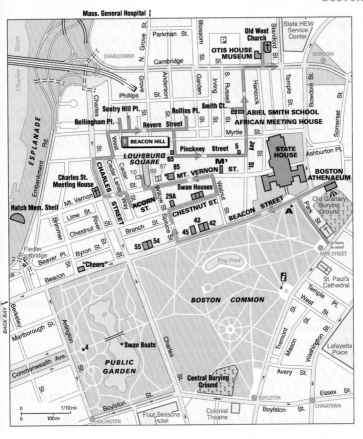

leading 19C architects. The work of Charles Bulfinch is well represented by the State House and some 15 Federal-style town houses found primarily on the fashionable south slope. The Hill's streetscape is noteworthy for its extraordinary visual unity, resulting from the predominant use of brick, a uniform three- to four-story building height, and harmonious blending of flat and bowed facades. Quaint service lanes are lined with former stables and servants' quarters, while intimate culs-de-sac evoke a sense of mystery. The Hill's designation as a historic district in 1955 and the determination of residents to safeguard its precious architectural heritage have been instrumental in the preservation of this urban jewel. *Beacon Hill's private gardens are revealed to the public in May by special tour.* For information, call the Beacon Hill Garden Club: ☎ 617-227-4392.

Walking Tour ⓣ *Park St.*

☺ *Exercise caution in inclement weather; brick sidewalks can be slippery when wet.*
▶ *Begin at the corner of Park and Tremont Sts. and walk up the hill on Park St.*

Gently sloping Park Street provides a pleasant approach to the gold-domed State House crowning **Beacon Street**★. Writer Oliver Wendell Holmes dubbed Beacon "the sunny street that holds the sifted few." The Hill's southern facade offers coveted views of Boston Common. Beyond the Common, this fashionable thoroughfare stretches west into the Back Bay and points beyond.
▶ *Turn right on Beacon St.*

Boston Athenaeum★

10 1/2 Beacon St. ◷ *Open year-round Mon–Fri 8:30am–5:30pm (Mon til 8pm), Sat 9am–4pm.* ◷ *Closed Sat. in summer.* ⟡ ☎ *617-227-0270. www.bostonathenaeum.org.*

This venerable Boston institution was established in 1807 as one of the nation's first private lending libraries. Later in the century numerous important works from the Athenaeum's art trove formed the core of the Museum of Fine Arts' world-class collection. The library's present home on Beacon Hill was built in the 1840s to accommodate its growing holdings, which today total some 600,000 volumes and works of art. Walking through the hallowed reading rooms packed with leather-bound volumes and fine sculptures, paintings and prints, visitors are ushered into a rarefied atmosphere. Works by Gilbert Stuart, Thomas Sully and Jean-Antoine Houdon highlight the collection. The art gallery *(1st floor)* features changing exhibits from the collection. Several rooms and terraces provide lovely **views** of the Old Granary Burying Ground.

State House★★

24 Beacon St. at the corner of Park St. ◷ *Open year-round Mon–Fri 10am–3:30pm.* ◷ *Closed Jan 1, Thanksgiving Day & Dec 25.* ⟡⟡ ☎ *617-727-3676.*

The golden dome of Massachusetts' capitol building dominates Beacon Hill, enduring as a cherished Boston landmark for more than two centuries. Completed in 1798 by Charles Bulfinch, the original brick building, fronted by a projecting portico, was extended in 1895 and 1916 by large additions to its sides and rear. Statues on the front lawn depict Anne Hutchinson, banished from the 17C colony for her theological views; Mary Dyer, hanged for her Quaker beliefs; orator Daniel Webster; and Horace Mann, a pioneer in American education.

The main entrance of the State House leads into **Doric Hall**, named for its rows of Doric columns. The 19C addition **Nurses Hall**, with its marble walls and floors, displays paintings immortalizing Paul Revere's ride, James Otis' oratory against the Writs of Assistance, and the Boston Tea Party. Paintings in the **Hall of Flags**, which was built to house a collection of Civil War battle flags, portray the Pilgrims on the *Mayflower*, John Eliot preaching to the Indians, and the scene at Concord Bridge on April 19, 1775.

The main staircase leads to the **Third Floor Hall**, dominated by Daniel Chester French's statue of Roger Wolcott, governor of Massachusetts during the Spanish-American War. The Senate Chamber, Senate Reception Room, Governor's Office and House Chamber occupy this floor. Before leaving the domed House Chamber, note the **Sacred Cod**, a gilded, carved-wood symbol of the fish that supported Massachusetts' early fishing industry.

Upon exiting the State House, cross Beacon Street to admire the **Shaw Civil War Monument**★ (**A**), a bronze relief by Augustus Saint-Gaudens that honors Col. Robert Gould Shaw and the 54th Massachusetts Colored Infantry, the Union's first regiment of free black volunteers. Shaw was killed in 1863 during the Union assault on Fort Wagner in South Carolina.

▸ *Continue walking down Beacon St.*

Among the street's noteworthy buildings are the exclusive Somerset Club at **nos. 42-43**, a double-bowed granite structure whose right half is attributed to Alexander Parris (1819); and **no. 45**

Black Heritage Trail

The Black Heritage Trail is a 1.6mi walking tour that identifies 15 significant African-American historic sites Highlights include the African Meeting House, the oldest standing African-American church in the U.S. Several sites along the trail are included in the walking tour here; for more details, contact the Boston African-American National Historic Site *(14 Beacon St., Suite 503;* ☎ *617-742-5415; www.nps.gov/boaf).* The National Park Service conducts free tours of the Black Heritage Trail *(Memorial Day–Labor Day daily).*

(1808), the last of three houses that Bulfinch designed and built for Harrison Gray Otis on Beacon Hill.

▶ *Cross Spruce St.*

The handsome pair of bowfront Greek Revival houses at **nos. 54-55** are attributed to Asher Benjamin, architect of the Charles Street Meeting House and the Old West Church *(both described later on the tour)*. The state chapter of the National Society of Colonial Dames occupies no. 55.

▶ *Return to the corner of Beacon and Spruce Sts., turn up Spruce and take a right on Chestnut St.*

As you pass narrow Branch Street on the left, note the modest buildings that once housed servants.

Chestnut Street★

This picturesque street presents a fine assortment of houses reflecting architectural styles dating from 1800 to 1830. At **no. 29A** (1800, Charles Bulfinch), note the distinctive purple glass in the house's bowfront. Other examples of the Hill's famed 18C purple window panes—resulting from the glass' manganese dioxide content—may still be seen in a few other dwellings on the Hill (including 63-64 Beacon St.). The graceful trio at nos. 13-17, known as the **Swan Houses** (c.1805), further illustrates Bulfinch's preference for a restrained Federal style.

▶ *Continue one block up Chestnut St., turn left on Walnut St. and continue one block to Mount Vernon St.*

Mount Vernon Street★★

Qualified by writer Henry James as "the only respectable street in America," this gracious thoroughfare boasts some of the Hill's finest residences. At no. 55 stands the **Nichols House Museum**★ (**M¹**), the Hill's only residence open to the public (⟲ *visit by 30min guided tour only, May–Oct Tue–Sat noon–4pm; rest of the year Thu–Sat noon–4pm;* ◷ *closed major holidays;* ⌨ *$7;* ☎ *617-227-6993)*. Designed by Bulfinch in 1804, the house preserves the possessions and spirit of a colorful Beacon Hill lady, Miss Rose Standish Nichols. The spacious interior contains late-19C and early-20C furniture carved by Nichols herself, as well as Flemish tapestries, needlepoint, ancestral paintings, and sculptures she collected on trips abroad.

On your way down the hill, pause to admire the freestanding building at **no. 85** (1802) set back some 30ft from the street line. Faced with slender pilasters and topped by a wooden balustrade and an octagonal tower, this handsome residence was the second of three mansions Bulfinch designed for Harrison Gray Otis. Bulfinch also conceived the neighboring mansions at nos. 87 and 89.

Louisburg Square★★

On Mount Vernon St. at Willow St.

Named in honor of the victorious siege of the French fortress at Louisbourg (Nova Scotia, Canada) led by the Massachusetts militia in 1745, this enclave epitomizes Beacon Hill's refined lifestyle. The appearance of the elegant Greek Revival bowfront row houses and the small private park have changed little since their creation in the 1830s and 40s. Writer Louisa May Alcott lived in no. 10 from 1880 until her death eight years later. Christmas Eve caroling on the square is a cherished Bostonian tradition.

▶ *Leave the square via Willow St. and turn right onto Acorn St.*

Acorn Street★

This romantic cobblestone passage is the most photographed street on the Hill.

▶ *At the end of Acorn St., turn right on West Cedar St., then left on Mount Vernon St. to Charles St.*

Charles Street★

Antique shops, art galleries and coffee shops line the Hill's bustling commercial thoroughfare. At the corner of Mount Vernon Street stands the **Charles Street Meeting House** (c.1807). This popular forum for 19C abolitionists William Lloyd Garrison, Frederick Douglass and Sojourner Truth was converted into offices in the 1980s.

▶ *Continue one block on Charles St. and turn right on Pinckney St.*

Pinckney Street

This lovely, sloping street was the dividing line between the affluent neighborhood on the sunny south slope and the more modest community on the north slope.

▶ *Turn left on West Cedar St. After one block, go right on Revere St.*

Revere Street

The street's left side is interrupted by a series of intimate private courts: **Bellingham Place**, **Sentry Hill Place** and **Rollins Place**. At Rollins Place the white "house" at the end of the court is not a house at all, but rather a decorative wall at the head of a drop.

▶ *Walk back to Anderson St. and turn left.*

The imposing brick building (1824) crowning the corner of Pinckney and Anderson Streets **(no. 65)** formerly housed the Phillips Grammar School (1844-61), the city's first racially mixed school.

▶ *Continue uphill on Pinckney St.*

The small clapboard house at **no. 5**, built for two black men in the 1790s, is one of the Hill's oldest surviving structures.

▶ *Turn left onto Joy St.*

Joy Street

This long street descends the north slope of the Hill, the center of Boston's historic black community from the late 18C to the 19C.

Smith Court

About halfway down Joy St. past Myrtle St.

This small cul-de-sac was the heart of the black community following the Revolution. Many of its residents worked for wealthy families who lived on the elite south slope. At no. 46 Joy Street stands the 1834 **Abiel Smith School**★ (○ *open Memorial Day–Labor Day daily 10am–4pm; rest of the year closed Sun;* ○ *closed Jan 1, Thanksgiving Day & Dec 25;* ⏶ ☏ *617-742-5415; www.nps.gov/boaf),* an elegant pedimented structure that housed the city's first black school, the first publicly funded school for black children in the country. Recently renovated, the building today contains a restored schoolroom and exhibits on African-American history.

Behind the school stands the nation's oldest remaining black church, the **African Meeting House**★ *(8 Smith Ct.;* ○ *same hours as Abiel Smith School).* Built in 1806 by black Baptists disenchanted with the discrimination encountered in the white churches, this handsome brick building provided a forum for supporters of the anti-slavery movement.

For most of the 20C, the meeting house served as a synagogue. Today it is preserved as a privately owned historic site managed by the National Park Service. The lower floor houses the **Museum of Afro-American History**, a small showplace for exhibits on themes relating to New England's black community. The meeting house proper occupies the upper floor.

▶ *At the foot of Joy St., cross busy Cambridge St.*

Otis House Museum★

141 Cambridge St. ⬙ *Visit by guided tour (45min) only, Jun–mid-Oct Wed–Sun 11am–4:30pm. Rest of the year weekends only, 11am–5pm.* ○ *Closed major holidays.* ⬙ *$8.* ☏ *617-227-3956. www.spnea.org.*

The house (1796) was the creation of two men who permanently influenced Boston's urban landscape: architect Charles Bulfinch and Harrison Gray Otis, lawyer, speculator and politician. The first of three houses Bulfinch designed for Otis on Beacon Hill, this Federal-style dwelling reflects the refined taste of the upper classes during the early years of the Republic. A second-story Palladian window softens the facade. Exquisite period furniture, ornate moldings, hand-blocked borders and a freestanding staircase adorn the interior.

The house serves both as a museum and as the headquarters of the Society for the Preservation of New England Antiquities. Founded in 1910, the society administers 36 house museums in five states.

Old West Church
Next door to Harrison Gray Otis House.

Complementing its Federal-style neighbor, the Otis House, this handsome structure with its strong vertical lines was designed by Asher Benjamin in 1806. In 1775 British troops razed the original meetinghouse that stood on this site when they suspected the patriots of using its steeple to signal American troops.

2 The Freedom Trail★★★ *Map below.* Ⓣ *Park St.*

The following walk includes most of the historical monuments along the Boston section of the Freedom Trail, a popular itinerary linking major Revolutionary and other sites of the **Boston National Historical Park**. The route is indicated on the pavement by red brick or a painted red line. 👁 *See Charlestown for additional Freedom Trail sights.*

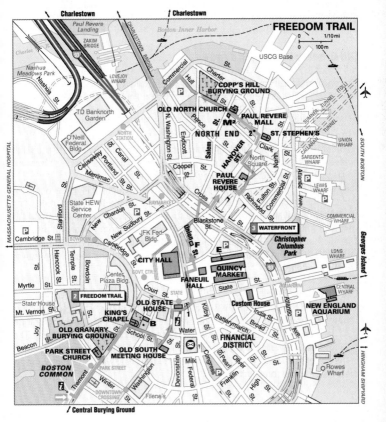

Begin at the visitor center on Boston Common (147 Tremont St., at West St.; ○ *open year-round daily 8:30am–5pm;* ○ *closed Thanksgiving Day & Dec 25;* ⛬ ☎ *617-536-4100).* 🛈 *For information about the Freedom Trail, call* ☎ *617-242-5642 or visit www.nps. gov/bost or www.thefreedomtrail.org.*

Downtown

Boston Common★ *Map p 189.*
This 50-acre park in the heart of the city has belonged to the people of Boston since the 1630s, when Reverend Blackstone sold the tract to the Puritans. Designated by these early Bostonians as "Common Field" forever reserved for public use, this Boston landmark has served over the centuries as pastureland, military training ground, public execution site, rallying ground and concert venue.

The park's hilly terrain is crisscrossed by tree-lined paths linking downtown to Beacon Hill and the Back Bay. The **Central Burying Ground** (1756), fronting Boylston Street, contains the unmarked grave of the preeminent early American portraitist Gilbert Stuart (1755-1828).

▶ *Proceed to the corner of Tremont and Park Sts. and follow the Freedom Trail red line for the rest of the tour.*

Park Street Church★
One Park St., facing Boston Common. ○ *Open Jun–Aug Tue-Sat 9:30am–3:30pm.* ○ *Closed Jul 4.* ⛬ ☎ *617-523-3383. www.parkstreet.org.*
The graceful, 217ft wooden steeple of this 1809 brick edifice, inspired by the work of English architect Christopher Wren, is one of Boston's loveliest landmarks. The church carillon chimes the melodies of familiar hymns on the hour. William Lloyd Garrison delivered his first anti-slavery speech in this meetinghouse in 1829, and "America" ("My Country 'tis of Thee") was sung for the first time here on July 4, 1831.

Old Granary Burying Ground★
Next door to Park Street Church, this burial ground was named for the 17C granary that once stood nearby. Here you'll find the tombstones of the great Revolutionary War orators James Otis and Samuel Adams, as well as Paul Revere and John Hancock. An obelisk in the center of the cemetery honors Benjamin Franklin's parents.

King's Chapel★
Corner of Tremont and School Sts. ○ *Open Labor Day–Memorial Day, Sat 10-4; summer hours vary (check website for details.* ○ *Closed during religious services.* ⌦ *Contribution requested.* ⛬ ☎ *617-227-2155. www.kings-chapel.org.*
New England's first Anglican church, this granite structure (1754, Peter Harrison) replaced the original wooden chapel built on the site in the 1680s. Only nine years after the British evacuation of Boston, the structure was reborn as the first Unitarian church in America. Enter the church to admire its outstanding Georgian **interior**. The adjoining **King's Chapel Burying Ground**★, Boston's oldest (1630), is the final resting place of John Winthrop (the colony's first governor) and John Alden (son of Priscilla and John).

Old City Hall (B)
45 School St. Constructed on the site of America's first public school (c.1630), this stately granite building (1865) is Boston's finest example of the Second Empire style. Its architect, Arthur Gilman, is also credited with planning the Back Bay. The structure was converted to commercial use in the late 1960s following completion of the present City Hall. A statue of Benjamin Franklin, who was born nearby, graces the left side of the forecourt.

Old South Meeting House★★

310 Washington St., at Milk St. ◐ *Open Apr–Oct daily 9:30am–5pm. Rest of the year daily 10am–4pm.* ◐ *Closed major holidays.* 🔊 *$5.* ♿ ☎ *617-482-6439. www. oldsouthmeetinghouse.org.*

Noted orators Samuel Adams and James Otis led many of the protest meetings held at Old South prior to the Revolution. The momentous rally that took place on the evening of December 16, 1773, gave rise to the Boston Tea Party.

Sporting a plain brick facade and a tower surmounted by a wooden steeple, the edifice was inspired by the designs of Christopher Wren. Its expansive interior was transformed by the British into a riding stable during the siege of Boston.

Old State House★★

206 Washington St., at State St. ◐ *Open year-round daily 9am–5pm.; extended hours in summer.* ◐ *Closed Jan 1, Thanksgiving Day & Dec 25.* 🔊 *$5.* ☎ *617-720-1713. www.bostonhistory.org.*

Boston's oldest public building (1713) was the British government headquarters in the colonies until the Revolution and was the site of several crucial events. In 1770 the Boston Massacre erupted on this site. On July 4, 1776, the colonies declared their independence in Philadelphia. Two weeks later the Declaration of Independence was read from the balcony here, inciting the crowds to topple and burn the lion and unicorn—symbols of the British Crown—perched on the building's gables (reproductions now adorn the building). The Massachusetts government met in this building until the new State House was completed in 1798; the Old State House was later converted into shops

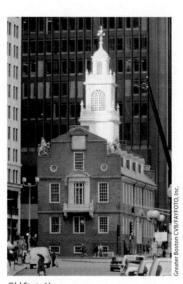

Old State House

and subsequently housed the city government. In 1881 the Bostonian Society was founded to maintain the site as a museum devoted to Boston's history.

Inside, two floors accessed by a spiral staircase feature excellent exhibits on the city, past and present. The historic balcony can be seen from the Council Chamber.

To the rear of the State House, note the circle of cobblestones embedded in the traffic island in the busy intersection of Congress and State Streets, marking the actual **Boston Massacre site (1)**. Farther down State Street rises the tower of another enduring Boston landmark, the **Custom House**★ (base: c.1840, A.B. Young; tower: c.1910, Peabody and Stearns).

After negotiating the intersection of Congress and State Streets, turn around to admire the east facade of the Old State House against the dramatic backdrop of a looming black metal tower (One Boston Place).

City Hall★★

Congress & State Sts., across from Faneuil Hall. ◐ *Open year-round Mon–Fri 8:30am–5:30pm.* ◐ *Closed major holidays.* ♿ ☎ *617-635-4000. www.cityofboston.gov.*

Rising from its brick base, this top-heavy concrete pile has remained one of Boston's controversial architectural statements since its completion in 1968. Designed by Kallman, McKinnell and Knowles, the structure recalls the works of the influential Modernist Le Corbusier and helped to bring the so-called Brutalist style to prominence in the US. City council meetings may be observed from the fifth-floor galleries *(Wed 4pm).*

Faneuil Hall★★★

Dock Sq., main entrance facing Quincy Market. ◔ *Open year-round daily 9am–5pm.* ◔ *Closed Jan 1, Thanksgiving Day & Dec 25.* ♿ ☎ *617-242-5675. www.nps.gov/bost/faneuil.*

Presented to Boston in 1742 by wealthy merchant Peter Faneuil, this revered landmark served as the town meeting hall throughout the Revolutionary period. Among the noted American leaders who have addressed groups here over the years are Samuel Adams, Wendell Phillips, Susan B. Anthony and John F. Kennedy. Damaged by fire in 1762, the building was reconstructed according to the original plans. In 1806 a major renovation supervised by Charles Bulfinch doubled the building's size.

Faneuil Hall's cupola is crowned with the grasshopper weather vane commissioned by Peter Faneuil in 1742. Modeled after the gilded bronze weather vanes that top the Royal Exchange in London, the grasshopper has symbolized the Port of Boston since the 18C. A statue of Samuel Adams stands in front of the building.

A staircase leads up to the large meeting hall on the second floor, where George P. A. Healy's painting *Daniel Webster's Second Reply to Hayne* covers the front wall. The **Ancient and Honorable Artillery Company**, America's oldest military organization, maintains a museum of historical arms, uniforms, flags and paintings on the third floor

KINGFISH HALL

At Faneuil Hall Marketplace, 188 S. Market Bldg. ☎ *617-523-8862.* Chef Todd English moved into the seafood arena with this flashy fish emporium at Faneuil Hall Marketplace. Its location lures in a mixed crowd, from downtown singles to tourists with kids in tow, and the Disneyesque interior—with its open kitchen, spear-like fish grill, and glittery lights—has enough dazzle for them all. The menu adds a fresh spin to New England seafood, tempting diners with dishes like crispy lobster with ginger and scallions, and bouillabaisse made with Northern fish and mussels, lobster curry broth, and Chinese eggplant.

Quincy Market★★

Behind Faneuil Hall. ◔ *Open year-round Mon–Sat 10am–9pm, Sun noon–6pm.* ◔ *Closed Thanksgiving Day & Dec 25.* ♿ ☎ *617-523-1300. www.faneuilhallmarketplace.com.*

The lively Faneuil Hall Marketplace complex, known as Quincy Market exemplifies the successful revitalization of a formerly blighted urban area. Run-down market buildings and warehouses have been restored, and the renewed commercial complex has become one of the most popular sections of the city. Day and night, tourists flock to its numerous restaurants, outdoor cafes and specialty shops.

The heart of the development consists of three granite buildings constructed in 1825 by Alexander Parris. The centerpiece, Quincy Market proper, is a long arcade in the Greek Revival style. Glass enclosures from the 1970s restoration flank its sides and contain dozens of small shops and eateries. The North and South Street buildings adjoining Quincy Market house upscale specialty stores. North Market is home to the family-style restaurant (known for communal tables and jokingly grouchy waitstaff) **Durgin Park (E)**.

Union Street

During the late 18C this street was lined with taverns and pubs. The Duke of Orleans, later King Louis-Philippe of France, lived for several months on the second floor of the venerable institution **Ye Olde Union Oyster House (F)** (still in operation as a restaurant), where he gave French lessons to earn his keep. Daniel Webster was also a frequent patron here.

▸ *Cross Blackstone St. to Haymarket, site of a colorful farmers' market on weekends, and continue through the pedestrian tunnel and into the North End.*

North End★

This colorful district has been continuously inhabited since 1630. Throughout the 17C and 18C, the North End reigned as Boston's principal residential district and included a community of free blacks. Irish and Jewish immigrants who settled here in the 19C. Eventually they moved on, replaced by Southern Italian immigrants, who have maintained a strong presence here, although this quaint neighborhood has been discovered by young urban professional couples in recent years. Rooftop gardens; shops bulging with fresh meats, poultry and vegetables; and restaurants and cafes that serve home-cooked pasta, pizza, pastries and espresso crowd **Hanover**★ and **Salem Streets**, the main thoroughfares. The local community continues to celebrate numerous saint's days throughout the year *(schedules of feasts are posted in storefronts and churches)*. These lively events feature religious processions, outdoor entertainment and an abundance of food sold by street vendors.

Paul Revere House★

19 North Sq. ◷ Open mid-Apr–Oct daily 9:30am–5:15pm. Nov–Dec daily 9:30am–4:15pm. Rest of the year Tue–Sun 9:30am–4:15pm. ◷ Closed Jan 1, Thanksgiving Day & Dec 25. ⬮ $3. ☎ 617-523-2338. www.paulreverehouse.org.
This two-and-a-half-story wooden clapboard house is the only extant 17C structure in downtown Boston. The dwelling was already 90 years old when silversmith Paul Revere bought it in 1770. The house was the starting point of Revere's historic ride to Lexington on April 18, 1775. Furnishings include items owned by the Revere family.

St. Stephen's Church★

Hanover and Clark Sts. ◷ Open year-round daily 7am–dusk.
Of the five churches designed by Charles Bulfinch in Boston, St. Stephens (1806) is the only one still standing. The well-preserved stark interior is flanked with a delicate colonnade that supports the balcony.

Paul Revere Mall★

This intimate brick pedestrian mall links St. Stephen's and the Old North Church. Beyond Cyrus Dallin's equestrian **statue (2)** of Paul Revere looms the spire of Old North Church. A series of bronze plaques set into the brick walls that enclose the mall traces the role of the North End's residents in Boston's history.

Old North Church ★★★ (Christ Church)

193 Salem St. ◷ Open Jun–Oct daily 9am–6pm. Rest of the year daily 9am–5pm. ◷ Closed Thanksgiving Day & Dec 25 (except for services). ⬮ $3 contribution requested. ♿ ☎ 617-523-6676. www.oldnorth.com.
It was here, on the evening of April 18, 1775, that the sexton displayed two lanterns in the steeple to signal the departure of the British from Boston by boat, on their way to Lexington and Concord. A century later this church was immortalized by Longfellow in his poem *Paul Revere's Ride.* Built in 1723, Old North was surmounted by a spire that was destroyed and replaced twice following violent storms. The present

Paul Revere Mall

Greater Boston CVB/FAYFOTO, Inc.

spire dates from 1954. Inside, the box pews, the large windows and the pulpit, from which President Gerald Ford initiated the celebration of the nation's bicentennial, are characteristic features of New England's colonial churches. The four wooden cherubim near the organ were among the bounty captured from a French vessel. Replicas of the famous lantern are for sale in the combination gift shop and **museum (M²)** adjacent to the church.

Copp's Hill Burying Ground★

Next to Old North Church, bordered by Hull and Charter Sts. ◷ *Open year-round daily dawn–dusk.* ☎ *617-536-4100.*

This cemetery contains the graves of noted Bostonians, including three generations of the prominent Mather family: Increase Mather (1639-1723), minister and Harvard president; Cotton Mather (1663-1728), clergyman and writer; and his son, Rev. Samuel Mather (1706-85). *The Mather plots are located in the northeast corner near the Charter Street gate.* Also interred here are the remains of hundreds of black Bostonians who settled in the North End in the 18C.

▹ *Return to Hanover St. to sample some Italian specialties or simply to enjoy the ambience. Note that the red line of the Freedom Trail continues to Charlestown.*

3 The Waterfront★ *Map p 189.* Ⓣ *Aquarium.*

During Boston's long period of maritime prosperity, sailing ships brimming with exotic cargoes frequented the busy harbor. To accommodate the port's burgeoning shipping industry, the original harborfront was dramatically transformed in the first half of the 19C via a landfill project that added more than 100 acres. After 1900 Boston's shipping activities sharply declined, and the waterfront area deteriorated . The construction of two traffic arteries (Atlantic Avenue in the 1860s and the elevated Central Artery in the 1950s) severed the area from the rest of the city.

Long-awaited rehabilitation of this historic area did not begin in earnest until the 1960s. Renovation of several wharf buildings injected new commercial and residential activity, and in the 1970s the Quincy Market restoration created a crucial link between downtown and **Christopher Columbus Park** (1976), a harborside promenade extending from Commercial Wharf to Long Wharf. A flurry of new residential and hotel complexes in the 1970s and 1980s significantly enhanced the waterfront's cachet while giving new texture to Boston's skyline. In 1998 the $112 million World Trade Center East Office Tower added its 16 stories to the landscape. From the harbor there is a commanding view of the new 10-story **federal courthouse** (1998).

Sights

New England Aquarium★★

Kids *On Central Wharf.* ◷ *Open Jul–Labor Day Mon–Fri 9am–6pm (Wed & Thu til 8pm), weekends 9am–7pm. Rest of the year Mon–Fri 9am–5pm, weekends 9am–6pm.* ◷ *Closed Thanksgiving Day & Dec 25.* ⊜ *$17.95* ♿ ☎ *617-973-5200. www.neaq.org.*

This large aquarium, the first of its kind in the nation, displays wonders of the underwater world in simulated natural environments. Interpretive panels, demonstrations and special exhibits help foster understanding of the 600 species of fish, inverte-, brates, mammals, birds, reptiles and amphibians found around the world. Dominating the center of the aquarium is a four-story, cylindrical **ocean tank** containing a re-creation of a Caribbean coral reef. As visitors descend the ramp encircling the 200,000 gallon tank, they can watch sharks, sea turtles, moray eels and the many species of fish that inhabit this glass-enclosed world as well as some 3,000 corals and sponges. In the Edge of the Sea tide pool, youngsters are invited to handle crabs, sea stars and urchins. A glass-enclosed lab permits observation of routine and emergency care of sea creatures. The large-format IMAX® theater is a big draw.

Ocean Tank, New England Aquarium

Boston Tea Party Ship and Museum

Map (**DZ**). *Congress Street Bridge.* *Reopening summer 2007; call for hours.* 617-338-1773. www.bostonteapartyship.com.

Due to extensive fire damage, this attraction is being completely rebuilt, and will be expanded to twice its former size. The museum will tell the story of the Boston Tea Party with an array of video presentations, living history programs, exhibits and memorabilia. A full-size replica of the brig *Beaver*, one of the original tea ships that was boarded by marauding "Indians" on December 16, 1773, is berthed at the pier on Congress Street. Two traditional tall ships will join the brig *Beaver* when the renovation is complete, replicas of the *Dartmouth* and the *Eleanor* (all three ships took part in the Tea Party). Visitors will be welcome to explore the ships' decks, crew's quarters and cargo holds. In addition, a new Boston Tea Room (of course!) will offer food service for Tea Party visitors.

Cruises

Sightseeing cruises and excursion boats that depart from the waterfront are a wonderful way to see the harbor and view the Boston skyline.

Georges Island

Cruises depart from Long Wharf Memorial Day–Labor Day daily 10am–5pm. Mid-Sept–mid-Oct daily 10am–4pm. Round-trip 40min. Commentary. $10 *Boston Harbor Cruises* 877-733-9425. www.bostonharborcruises.com.

This 28-acre island, inhabited during colonial times and later fortified due to its strategic location, is a public recreation site with picnic areas at the water's edge. Dominating the island is well-preserved Fort Warren, used during the Civil War to incarcerate some 2,000 Confederate military prisoners. The fort never saw battle. The fort's observation tower offers **views** of the Boston skyline and the many islands and islets composing the Boston Harbor Islands, which are now a national park.

Free water taxis run from Georges Island to several nearby islands during the summer season.

4 Back Bay★★ *Map opposite.*

Hailed by architectural critic Lewis Mumford as "the outstanding achievement in American urban planning for the 19C," Boston's Back Bay is a stunningly attractive, well-preserved historic district of 19C town houses, lined with flowering dogwood trees. Architectural styles run the gamut, including Gothic, Italian Renaissance and Georgian. At its east end, Back Bay meets the Public Garden; to the north, the riverfront Esplanade is Boston's premier park and outdoor concert site.

From Swamplands to Mansions
The Back Bay was once an expanse of mud flats submerged at high tide by the Charles River estuary. In the early 19C, construction of a 1.5mi tidal mill dam along present-day Beacon Street disrupted the area's natural drainage, creating acres of foul swampland. By mid-century this threat to public health and the need for additional housing provided the impetus for the most ambitious of Boston's landfill projects. From 1857 to the 1890s, more than 450 acres—contained within the present-day boundaries of the Charles River, the Public Garden, Huntington and Massachusetts Avenues—were reclaimed. For over 30 years, 3,500 carloads of earth a day were dumped into the swamp. Eventually, stately rows of four- and five-story mansions and townhouses would be built on the former swamplands of Back Bay.

Large-scale Contrast
South of the fast-paced Boylston Street corridor, the Back Bay takes on a dramatically different appearance. Monumental redevelopment schemes of varying quality, such as the Prudential Center, Copley Place and the Christian Science Center, create a decidedly 20C scale and flavor. Here, buildings of cement and steel offer a striking counterpoint to the low-scale brick universe of the 19C residential streets.

Walking Tour ⓣ *Copley.*

Copley Square★★
Named for painter John Singleton Copley, the Back Bay's principal public square showcases some of the city's most celebrated architectural treasures. The former railroad yard was transformed into the Back Bay's civic center in the 1870s and 80s with the construction of Boston's finest 19C public buildings. Today the square's east end is dominated by the contrasting silhouettes of massive Trinity Church and soaring John Hancock Tower. To the south rises the limestone facade of posh

View from Back Bay

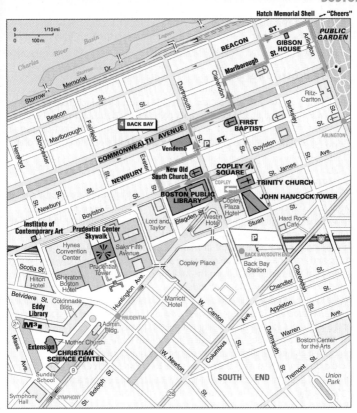

Copley Plaza Hotel (1912), designed in the Renaissance Revival style by Henry J. Hardenbergh, architect of New York's Plaza Hotel. The handsome 19C facade of the Boston Public Library graces the west side, while the New Old South Church, in the northwest corner, adds an exotic note to the ensemble.

Trinity Church★★

Copley Sq. ◷ *Open year-round for self-guided tours, Mon–Sat 9am–5:30pm, Sun 1pm–5pm.* ⊙ *$5.* ⊶ *Free guided tours every Sun following 11:15am service.* ☎ *617-536-0944. www.trinitychurchboston.org.*

Recognized as the masterpiece of architect Henry H. Richardson, this imposing granite and sandstone pile (1877) initiated the popular style known as Richardsonian Romanesque in America. A massive central tower, inspired by one of the towers of the Old Cathedral in Salamanca, Spain, dominates the church; the west porch, influenced by the church of St. Trophime in Arles, France, is carved with statues and friezes representing biblical figures.

Trinity Church and John Hancock Tower

197

Richardson chose John La Farge to oversee the decoration inside. The lavishly painted walls, murals, paneled ceilings and small lunettes above the high, tower windows, are among the best works executed by La Farge.

John Hancock Tower★★

St. James Ave.
This striking 60-story slab, sheathed in 10,344 units of half-inch-thick tempered glass, was designed by I.M.Pei. Since its completion, Hancock Tower (1975) has reigned as New England's tallest skyscraper. Walk around the building; from certain angles it is a gigantic mirror reflecting the sky and its esteemed neighbors, notably Trinity Church.

Boston Public Library★★

700 Boylston St. on Copley Sq. ○ *Open year-round Mon–Thu 9am–9pm, Fri & Sat 9am–5pm.* ○ *Closed major holidays.* ⚇ & ☎ *617-536-5400. www.bpl.org.*
This handsome Renaissance Revival style building (1895, McKim, Mead and White) influenced countless public buildings in the US for over half a century. The granite facade sports elaborate wrought-iron lanterns, relief panels by Augustus Saint-Gaudens, and an elegant row of second-story arched windows. Daniel Chester French, sculptor of the seated Lincoln on the Mall in Washington, DC, crafted the bronze doors dominating the vestibule. Wander through the cavernous rooms on the upper floors to admire murals executed by Edwin Abbey *(Quest of the Holy Grail; delivery room, 2nd floor)* and John Singer Sargent *(Judaism and Christianity; 3rd-floor corridor)* and the library's Joan of Arc collection *(Cheverus Room, 3rd floor).*
Fronting Boylston Street, the stark granite addition to the library was designed by renowned architect Philip Johnson as a contemporary complement.
Across Boylston Street rises the picturesque **New Old South Church** (1874, Cummings and Sears), with its lofty bell tower, Venetian-style cupola and a profusion of Italian Gothic detailing. The Boston Marathon ends here.
▷ *Turn right on Exeter St. and right on Newbury St.*

Newbury Street★

Originally a quiet residential street, Newbury now reigns as the city's most exclusive shopping district. Converted town houses sport glass storefronts showcasing the city's finest boutiques, antique shops, specialty stores and cafes *(www.newbury-st.com).*
The block between Exeter and Dartmouth Streets boasts a cluster of art galleries and a lively street scene, making it one of the Back Bay's most pleasant pockets.
▷ *Turn left on Dartmouth St. and continue to Commonwealth Ave.*

Commonwealth Avenue★★

Inspired by the grand boulevards laid out in late-19C Paris under Napoléon III, this 200ft-wide thoroughfare was reputedly the address of choice for Boston's nouveau riche. Today "Comm Ave," as it is known locally, still connotes elegant living.

SONSIE

327 Newbury St. ☎ *617-351-2500. www.sonsieboston.com.* Stylish Newbury Street, with its profusion of posh boutiques, sports a number of cafes and outdoor eateries, but none is more popular or more ingeniously versatile than Sonsie. In the morning, white-aproned staff glide between the marble tables and wicker chairs to deliver espressos, cappuccinos and croissants, while lunchtime pastas, grilled sandwiches and brick-oven pizzas provide the fuel needed for a shopping splurge. Dinner can be either casual in the cafe, where the floor-to-ceiling window-doors (folded back in summer) provide ample opportunities for people-watching, or more intimate in the restaurant, decorated in artful Mediterranean style.

On the southwest corner *(no. 160)* extends the sprawling **Vendome** (1871, W.G. Preston), once the Back Bay's most luxurious hotel and temporary home to such celebrities as Oscar Wilde, Mark Twain, Sarah Bernhardt and Ulysses S. Grant.

▶ *Cross to the planted mall and continue east one block.*

Commonwealth Avenue's pleasant **mall**, lined with elm trees and punctuated by commemorative statues, offers a good vantage point to view a characteristic sampling of Back Bay houses on either side of the wide avenue.

Just before reaching the next corner, glance to the right for a view of **First Baptist Church**★ (1872), a pivotal work by H.H. Richardson. The **frieze** adorning the upper portion of the bell tower is attributed to Frédéric-Auguste Bartholdi, designer of the Statue of Liberty.

▶ *Turn left on Clarendon St. and right on Marlborough St.*

> ### FINALE
> *One Columbus Ave.* ☎ *617-423-3184.* If you have a serious sweet tooth, make tracks to this swank dessert café, where the Theater District meets the Back Bay. There are sandwiches and light meals available, but the real reason to stop here is for the decadent, if pricey, desserts. Molten chocolate cake is a real crowd-pleaser, but for a true chocoholic, only the Chocolate Obsession, an orgy of a tasting plate, for two, will do.

Marlborough Street

This generously shaded residential street lined with brick sidewalks and gas lamps exudes a romantic 19C ambience.

▶ *Turn left on Berkeley St. and right on Beacon St.*

Beacon Street★

Favored by Boston's old-money families in the 19C, this distinguished thoroughfare is flanked by grand town houses, many converted to colleges and cultural institutions. North-side residences are prized for their views of the Charles River. The **Gibson House Museum**★ *(no. 137)*, built in 1859, has retained its Victorian flavor and offers a rare glimpse into the lifestyle of an affluent Back Bay family (visit by 45min guided tour only, year-round Wed–Sun 1pm–4pm; ◷ closed major holidays; $7; ☎ 617-267-6338; www.thegibsonhouse.org). Elaborate woodwork, 15ft ceilings, imported carpets, faux-leather wallpaper and scores of curios attest to the family's tastes and financial means.

▶ *Continue to the corner of Beacon and Arlington Sts.*

At this point TV fans will enjoy making a detour to the nearby Bull and Finch Pub *(84 Beacon St.)* to glimpse the familiar stone and brick facade popularized by the 1980s television series **"Cheers."**

Near the corner of Beacon and Arlington Streets, the Fiedler footbridge leads to the Charles River **Esplanade**. Landscaped in the early 1930s, this delightful waterfront park extending over 10mi attracts joggers, in-line skaters, cyclists, picnickers and

Go Sox

To the Fenway Faithful, Boston's ballpark is hallowed ground. Opened in 1912, Fenway, the home of the Boston Red Sox, is the smallest park in the major league. Tours are offered Mon through Sun year-round, from 9am-4pm. (If there's a home game, the last tour starts three hours before game time.) Highlights include a walk around the playing field (except during inclement weather), sitting in the dugout, and posing for a photo in front of the Green Monster. The walk-up ticket sales office near Gate A sells Fenway Park tour tickets. It's still possible to get tickets for a game, unless you have your heart set on a Red Sox-Yankees matchup. Opening Day is like a holiday here. www.redsox.com.

Swan Boats, Boston Public Garden

sailing enthusiasts. Outdoor performances given at the **Hatch Memorial Shell** are popular in summertime.

▶ *Return to the corner of Beacon and Arlington Sts. Continue on Arlington St.*

Public Garden★★ *Map p 185.*

Entering from the Arlington Street gate, your eye is drawn to the equestrian **statue (4)** of George Washington (1878, Thomas Ball), facing Commonwealth Avenue. This 24-acre rectangular park, bounded by a handsome cast-iron fence, was reclaimed from the swampy Back Bay in the 1830s to create a botanical garden. Today the popular retreat charms visitors with its lush plantings, tree-lined footpaths and commemorative statuary. First launched in the 1870s, the beloved **swan boats** ply the tranquil waters of an artificial pond traversed by a whimsical suspension bridge and bordered with weeping willows. The *Make Way for Ducklings* statue grouping in the northeast section re-creates the title characters of Robert McCloskey's classic children's book.

Additional Sights in Back Bay

Prudential Center Skywalk

800 Boylston St. ☎ 617-236-2335. www.prudentialcenter.com/play/skywalk. Purchase tickets at the kiosk at Prudential Arcade; if kiosk is closed, buy tickets at the Skywalk entrance. ◷ Open March-Oct. year-round daily 10am–9:30pm; open other times of year, 10am–8pm. ◷ Closed Thanksgiving Day & Dec 25. ⌾ $10.50 ♿🅿 ☎ 617-859-0648.
An observation deck on the 50th floor of the 52-story Prudential Tower offers sweeping 360-degree **views** of the Greater Boston. An audio tour provides commentary on landmarks and local history.

Christian Science Center★★

175 Huntington Ave. ◷ Open year-round. Free tours of the church Thurs–Sat noon–4pm (on the hour), Sun at 11:30am. No tours major holidays. ✗♿🅿 ☎ 617-450-2775. www.tfccs.com.
This stunning ensemble houses the world headquarters of the Christian Science Church. The Christian Science religion was founded in 1866 by New Hampshire native Mary Baker Eddy following a serious injury from which she quickly recovered after meditating on a Gospel account of one of Jesus' healings. After extensive study of the Bible, she felt she had discovered a science, or provable laws, behind Jesus' healing works, which still can be practiced today. She named her discovery

Christian Science and wrote about this system of divine healing in her best-selling book *Science and Health with Key to the Scriptures*.

Facing Massachusetts Avenue the grandiose **Mother Church Extension** (1906) features Renaissance-inspired elements such as the expansive entrance portico and a central dome rising 224ft. It holds one of the 10 largest organs in the country, with over 13,000 pipes. The Romanesque-style original church (1894), with its rough granite facade and bell tower, is connected to the rear of the extension. The interior is adorned with mosaics and stenciled frescoes.

The complex was expanded in the 1970s by a group of architects led by **I.M. Pei**. Three bold concrete structures—the 26-story Administration Building, the porticoed Colonnade Building and the fan-shaped Sunday School—stand like abstract sculptures around an enormous **reflecting pool** (670ft by 100ft). Step inside the **Mary Baker Eddy Library for the Betterment of Humanity** to experience the **Mapparium** (M³), a 30ft walk-through glass-paneled globe that represents the worldwide scope of the church's publishing activities.

The Museums

Museum of Fine Arts★★★   *Floor Plan p 203.*

*Map p 174 (**AZ**). 465 Huntington Ave. ⓣ Museum. ◷ Open year-round Mon–Tue 10am–4:45pm, Wed–Fri 10am-9:45pm, weekends 10am–4:45pm. ◷ Closed major holidays. ⊜ $15. Concert and film information: ☎ 617-369-3300 ⚒ ♿ 🅿 ☎ 617-267-9300. www.mfa.org.*

One of the country's leading museums, the Museum of Fine Arts (MFA) houses a comprehensive collection, organized into eight departments: Art of the Americas; Art of Europe; Contemporary Art; Art of Asia, Oceania and Africa; Art of the Ancient World; Prints, Drawings and Photographs; Textiles and Fashion Arts; and Musical Instruments. The 1909 Neoclassical building and a 1981 addition designed by I.M.Pei and Partners includes exhibitiion space, dining facilities, the MFA Bookstore and Shop and the Remis Auditorium. Items in the permanent collections are rotated throughout the year, and are complimented by an ongoing schedule of special exhibitions.

The museum's three enchanting **gardens** are the setting for outdoor concerts and alfresco dining, and provide a tranquil landscape for reflection. ⚒ *Dining facilities at MFA range from the informal Courtyard Café (lower level, West Wing); the Galleria Café; and Bravo, whose varying, eclectic menu is often tailored to complement special exhibitions. Bravo features a rotating collection of the MFA's masterpieces.*

Art of the Americas

American Paintings★★
The American collection of art is represented primarily by paintings, furniture and silver. Prominent among the 18C portraitists were Gilbert Stuart, whose paintings of George and Martha Washington *(Athenaeum Portraits)* are exhibited alternatively at the National Portrait Gallery in Washington, DC and at the MFA; and John Singleton Copley, who painted noted Bostonians of his day *(Samuel Adams* and *Paul Revere)*. In the 19C painters turned their attention to nature, and in particular to the sea. The adventure and beauty of the sea were portrayed on canvas by Fitz Hugh Lane *(Boston Harbor; Owl's Head Penobscot Bay, Maine)* Albert Pinkham Ryder and Winslow Homer *(Fog Warning: Lookout—All's Well)*.

Art of Europe

European Paintings★★
Principal European schools from the Middle Ages to the present are represented. A Catalonian chapel with a 12C apse fresco and the 15C panel painting of *St. Luke*

Drawing the Virgin by Rogier van der Weyden are noteworthy early works. The lovely **Koch Gallery** holds double-hung, gilt-framed works of the 16C and 17C, including the Rosso's renowned *Dead Christ with Angels;* El Greco's *Fray Hortensio Felix Paravicino; Don Baltasar Carlos with a Dwarf* by Velazquez; and two significant history paintings by Poussin. The Dutch gallery boasts five Rembrandts as well as Tiepolo's majestic allegory of *Time Unveiling Truth.* Among the 19thC French masters represented are Renoir *(Bal a Bougival)*, Monet *(La Japonaise; Haystacks; Rouen Cathedral)*, Degas *(Carriage at the Races)*, Manet *(Execution of Maximillian; The Street Singer)*, Van Gogh *(Postman Joseph Roulin)*, and Cessna *(Madame Cessna in a Red Armchair)*.

Art of Asia, Oceania and Africa★★★

For over a century, the MFA's collection of Arts of Asia, Oceania and Africa has been described as "the finest collection of oriental art under one roof in the world." **Indian Art** holdings include sculpture (2C BC–5C AD), miniature paintings from the courts of North India (16C–19C), and works of various metals, jade and ivory.

The MFA also houses one of the finest collections of **Japanese Art** in the world. Highlights include Buddhist and Shinto paintings and sculpture, scroll and screen paintings, ceramics, lacquerware, swords, metalwork, inro (medicine boxes), and netsuke (toggle weights), as well as woodblock prints by ukiyo-e masters, ranging from 17C works by Moronobu to those of contemporary

Statue from Asian Collection

Courtesy Museum of Fine Arts, Boston

artists. Most recently, the collection has been expanded to represent the art of Africa and Oceania.

The MFA boasts one of the few important museum collections of **Korean Art** in the Western world, comprised of high-quality stoneware and lacquerware of the Koryo and Yi dynasties, Buddhist paintings and sculptures, and Bronze Age funerary objects.

Art of the Ancient World

Ancient Egyptian, Nubian and Near Eastern Art★★

The bulk of the MFA's superb collection of Egyptian art, spanning 4,000 years of civilization, came to the museum as a result of a 40-year MFA/Harvard expedition to Egypt and the Sudan beginning in 1905. Excavations conducted at Giza yielded **Old Kingdom** treasures (2778–2360 BC) rivaled only by the Egyptian Museum in Cairo. Among the many pieces of sculpture excavated from the tombs and temples of Dynasty IV is **King Mycerinus** and his queen, one of the oldest extant statues portraying a couple. Dating from the same period is the realistic portrait bust of **Prince Ankh-haf**.

The expedition's digs at El Bersheh and in the Sudan produced treasures from the more recent Dynasty XII: the well-preserved paintings on the coffins of **Prince Djehutynekht** and his wife, the black granite statue of **Lady Sennuwy**, and painted wooden servant models designed to serve the dead in eternity.

Treasures from ancient Nubia (the region that today comprises southern Egypt and northern Sudan) include boldly painted pottery from the first Nubian Kingdom (3100–2800 BC) and intricate jewelry, such as blue faience beaded necklaces and ivory inlay, from the Kerma Kingdom (2000–150 BC).

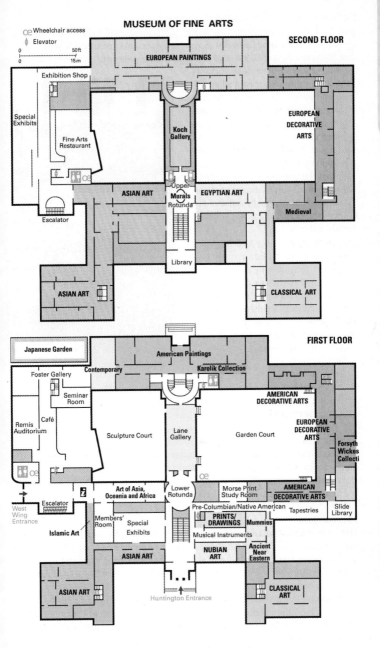

MUSEUM OF FINE ARTS

SECOND FLOOR

- ♿ Wheelchair access
- ⬆ Elevator

EUROPEAN PAINTINGS

Exhibition Shop

Special Exhibits

Fine Arts Restaurant

Koch Gallery

EUROPEAN DECORATIVE ARTS

Escalator

ASIAN ART

Upper Murals Rotunda

EGYPTIAN ART

Medieval

Library

ASIAN ART

CLASSICAL ART

FIRST FLOOR

Japanese Garden

American Paintings

Karolik Collection

Foster Gallery

Contemporary

Seminar Room

Remis Auditorium

Café

Sculpture Court

Lane Gallery

Garden Court

AMERICAN DECORATIVE ARTS

EUROPEAN DECORATIVE ARTS

Forsyth Wickes Collecti

West Wing Entrance

Escalator

Islamic Art

Art of Asia, Oceania and Africa

Lower Rotunda

Morse Print Study Room

AMERICAN DECORATIVE ARTS

Members' Room

Special Exhibits

Pre-Columbian/Native American

PRINTS/ DRAWINGS

Mummies

Tapestries

Slide Library

Musical Instruments

ASIAN ART

NUBIAN ART

Ancient Near Eastern

CLASSICAL ART

Huntington Entrance

Classical Art★★

The celebrated collection includes cameos, bronzes and Greek vases and a series of original Greek marble sculptures, including a head of Aphrodite in the style of Praxiteles and a three-sided marble bas-relief from the Greek island of Thasos. The museum has also built up its strength in mythological vases and Roman sculpture in silver and marble.

Isabella Stewart Gardner Museum★★★

*Map p 178 (**AZ**). 280 The Fenway.* Ⓣ *Museum.* Ⓒ *Open year-round Tue–Sun 11am–5pm.* Ⓒ *Closed Thanksgiving Day & Dec 25.* ☞ *$12 (All persons named Isabella are admitted free, forever).* 🍴 ♿ ☎ *617-566-1401. www.gardnermuseum.org.*

Isabella Stewart, born in New York City in 1840, became a Bostonian when she married financier Jack Lowell Gardner. Daring and vivacious, Mrs. Gardner was a free spirit whose actions were often frowned upon by other members of Boston's staid society. Art and music were her lifelong delights, and in 1899 she initiated the construction of **Fenway Court** to house her fabulous art collection, part of which she gathered in Europe, and part of which was acquired for her in the US.

The galleries of Fenway Court, permanently arranged by Gardner herself, opened to the public in 1903 and contain furnishings, textiles, paintings and sculpture from her collections. Nothing has been changed since her death (1924); the galleries, opening onto flower gardens in the courtyard, create an impression of continual summer.

Courtyard, Isabella Stewart Gardner Museum

Isabella Stewart Gardner Museum/ John Kennard

Ground Floor

In the **Spanish Cloister** ceramic tiles from a 17C Mexican church cover the walls, enhancing John Singer Sargent's dramatic painting *El Jaleo*.

The **courtyard**, with its refreshing gardens, Venetian window frames and balconies brimming with fresh flowers, provides a graceful haven in the city. Classical sculptures surround an ancient Roman mosaic pavement (2C AD) from the town of Livia. In the **small galleries** off the courtyard is an exhibit of 19C and 20C French and American paintings, including portraits by Degas and Manet, and landscapes by Whistler, Matisse and Sargent. The Yellow Room houses *The Terrace of St. Tropez,* the first canvas by Henri Matisse ever to enter an American museum.

Second Floor

The room of **early Italian paintings** contains Simone Martini's altarpiece *Madonna and Child with Four Saints,* two allegorical panels by Pesellino, Fra Angelico's *The Dormition and Assumption of the Virgin* and Constanzo da Ferrara's delicately executed *Turkish Artist*. The fresco of Hercules is the only fresco by Piero della Francesca outside of Italy.

The **Raphael Room** exhibits two of the Italian painter's works: a portrait of Count Tommaso Inghirami and a *pietà*. The *Annunciation* exemplifies the technique of linear perspective developed in the 15C. Other works in the room include Botticelli's *Tragedy of Lucretia* and Giovanni Bellini's *Madonna and Child*.

▶ *Continue through the Little Salon, decorated with 18C Venetian paneling and 17C tapestries, to the Tapestry Room.*

The **Tapestry Room** is the setting for concerts held at Fenway Court. On an easel sits *Santa Engracia* by Bermejo (15C Spain). There are also lovely 16C tapestries from France and Belgium.

Rubens' masterful portrayal of Thomas Howard, Earl of Arundel, and works by Hans Holbein and Anthony Van Dyck *(Lady with a Rose)* grace the **Dutch Room**.

Third Floor

From the **Veronese Room**, with its Spanish and Venetian tooled and painted leather wall coverings, enter the **Titian Room**, which contains one of Titian's masterpieces, the sensual *Rape of Europa,* painted for Philip II of Spain. In the **Long Gallery** the life-size terra-cotta statue *Virgin Adoring the Child,* attributed to Matteo Civitale, provides a beautiful example of Renaissance sculpture. On the wall above a large sideboard hangs Botticelli's *Madonna and Child of the Eucharist* (c.1470s, the "Chigi Madonna"). The **Gothic Room** contains a full-length portrait (1888) of Mrs. Gardner painted by her friend John Singer Sargent.

Children's Museum★★

Map p 175 (**D2**). 300 Congress St. at Museum Wharf. South Station. Open year-round daily 10am–5pm (Fri til 9pm). Closed Thanksgiving Day & Dec 25. $9 ($7 for kids age 15 and under; $1 Fri after 5pm). 617-426-8855. www.bostonkids.org. Conceived exclusively for children (but a delight to adults as well), the museum concentrates on visitor programs, teacher resources and early childhood education. In 1999, the museum announced plans to expand its waterfront site through the purchase of 60,000sq ft previously occupied by the adjacent Computer Museum, which merged with the Boston Museum of Science. The new space, currently under construction, will house a new lobby, exhibit halls and additional eating facilities. The complex contains four floors, three of which house interactive exhibits, many with a decidedly educational or multicultural twist, such as **Teen Tokyo** *(4th floor),* where visitors can ride a Japanese subway car; the Supermercado *(3rd floor)* stocked with Latin American foods; and a Native American wigwam and storage area *(3rd floor)* containing artifacts of Southern New England tribes. Among other galleries, the second floor features Boats Afloat with water exhibits that invite kids to play with toy boats or pilot harbor vessels and **Science Playground**, where children can experiment with physics. PlaySpace *(2nd floor)* welcomes toddlers and preschoolers. Participatory theater shows and other displays on Boston's ethnic groups round out the mix. There's even a recycle shop, where you can buy bags of foam, paper goods, decorative materials and other reusable items for kids to make their own creations.

Boston Museum of Science★★

Map p 175 (**CY**). Rte. 28. Science Park. Open daily 9am–5pm (Fri til 9pm); extended summer hours (Jul to Sep), 9am-7pm. Closed Thanksgiving Day & Dec 25. $16. 617-723-2500. www.mos.org.

Festivals for Kids

Boston sponsors a host of events that are geared toward children. Grab your parents and come on down!

Harborfest Children's Day – Balloons, face painting, educational activities and more as part of Harborfest *(City Hall Plaza; early July ☎ 617-227-1528).*

Franklin Park Kite & Flight Festival – Kite making, kite flying, music and family fun *(Franklin Park Golf Course; late May; ☎ 617-635-4505).*

Halloween Parade – Join the boys and ghouls who parade their costumes around the Common *(starts at Boston Common Playground; Oct 27; ☎ 617-635-4505).*

Duckling Day Parade – Dress as your favorite character from the children's classic *Make Way for Ducklings (Boston Common; Mother's Day; ☎ 617-426-1885).*

First Night Boston – Bundle up for Boston's family-friendly New Year's Eve festival, starting at 1 pm, with music, ice sculptures, a Grand Procession from Boylston St. to the Boston Common (5:30 pm) and a fireworks display; *☎ 617-542-1399; www.firstnight.org).*

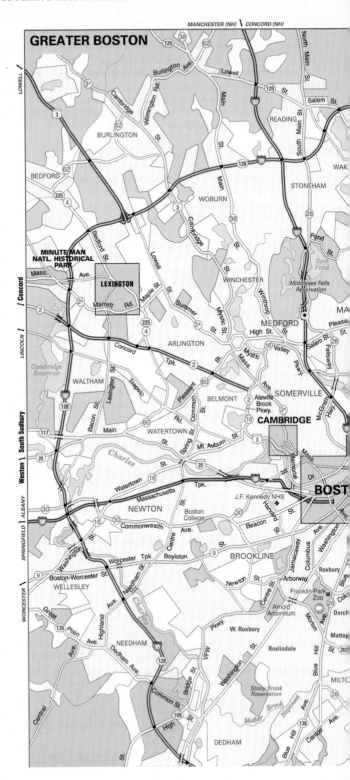

GREATER BOSTON

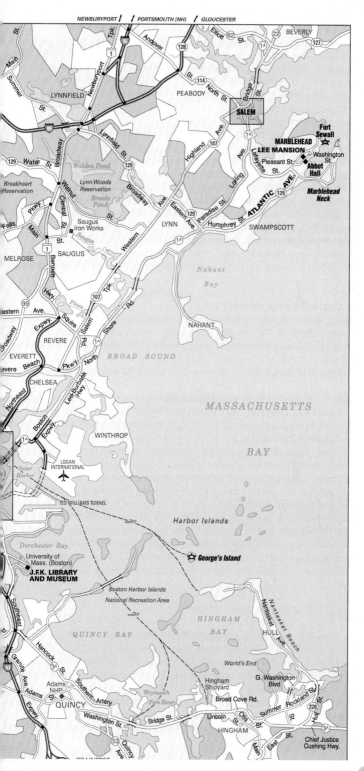

Located alongside the Charles River, the museum explores the world of science and technology through cutting-edge, hands-on exhibits. Though the museum traces its roots to the 1830 founding of the Boston Society of Natural History, it now embraces all areas of science, including computer technology, under one huge roof.

> ### Sailing Vessels
> Sailing vessels are distinguished by the type of sail and the number of masts they carry. A **sloop** is a one-masted, fore-and-aft-rigged vessel. A **schooner** carries two or more masts; all its sails are fore-and-aft rigged.

More than 600 interactive exhibits, a planetarium and observatory, and theater with a five-story screen greet visitors to the museum. The kaleidoscopic array of push-button displays and life-size models allows visitors to participate in activities ranging from playing with lightning produced by a Van de Graaff generator to pretending to fly through the cosmos in models of American spacecraft. Exhibits include a full-scale model of a *Tyrannosaurus rex*, musical stairs, and a **mathematics lab** that melds classical thought with modern-day applications. A current exhibit, Body Wars 2, looks at human and comparative anatomy through the use of real, preserved human bodies. In the first-floor atrium, the **Charles Hayden Planetarium** presents programs that explore the world of stars, galaxies, pulsars, clusters, quasars and other phenomena of outer space. There are usually two or more programs daily, in addition to laser shows (☞ $9; discounted combined admission available; call for schedule).

Institute of Contemporary Art
www.icaboston.org. Formerly located on Boylston Street, the ICA has relocated to Boston's waterfront The new, 65,000sq ft site will feature a facade of translucent and transparent glass, wood and metal, and a dramatic folding ribbon shape. A cantilever will extend to the water's edge, creating a sheltered but open space for visitors to enjoy views of Boston Harbor. The new ICA is scheduled to open in late 2006.

John F. Kennedy Library and Museum★
Columbia Point in Dorchester, near the University of Massachusetts. Ⓣ *JFK/UMass, .5mi from the museum; free shuttle bus available.* Ⓞ *Open year-round daily 9am–5pm.* Ⓞ *Closed Jan 1, Thanksgiving Day & Dec 25.* ☞ *$10.* ✗ ♿ 🅿 ☎ *866-JFK-1960. www.jfklibrary.org.*
This sleek, white concrete and glass structure, a monument to the late President John F. Kennedy, was designed by architect I.M. Pei. Approximately one-third of the library building is reserved for the **contemplation pavilion**, a nine-story gray glass pavilion that contains simply an American flag, a bench and quotations from President Kennedy on the wall.
The visit begins with a film on the early life of JFK. In a series of 25 exhibit bays, personal memorabilia and historic videos trace the life and accomplishments of John F. Kennedy. Included here are rare film and television footage, historic presidential documents, and personal Kennedy family keepsakes. The archives on the upper floors house thousands of photos, tapes and taped interviews.

Charlestown★ *Map p 175* (CD).

Ferries depart from Boston's Long Wharf to Pier 4 in the Charlestown Navy Yard year-round Mon–Fri 6;30am–8pm, weekends 10am–6pm. No service Jan 1 & Dec 25. ☞ *$1.25 (one-way).* ♿ *Boston Harbor Cruises.* ☎ *877-733-9425. www.bostonharborcruises.com.*
The Freedom Trail continues across Boston Harbor in Charlestown, easily recognized by its prominent stone obelisk, the Bunker Hill Monument. During the Battle of Bunker Hill in 1775, Charlestown's colonial dwellings were destroyed by the British and replaced following the Revolution by the rows of Federal-style houses that line Main and Warren Streets. The opening of the Navy Yard in 1800 made Charlestown a renowned shipbuilding center.

Greater Boston CVB/FAYFOTO, Inc.

USS Constitution and Bunker Hill Monument

Bunker Hill Monument

Adjacent to the Navy Yard on Constitution Rd. 🕐 *Open year-round daily 9am–5pm. Monument open to climb daily 9am–4:30pm.* 🕐 *Closed Jan 1, Thanksgiving Day & Dec 25.* ☎ *617-242-5641. www.thefreedomtrail.org.*

This 221ft Quincy granite obelisk (1842), designed by Solomon Willard, marks the site of the American redoubt during the 1775 Battle of Bunker Hill. The observatory, reached by a 294-step winding stairway, offers a **view** of Charlestown, Boston and the harbor. Exhibits and a scale model of the historic battle are contained in a meeting house made of Carrera marble.

Bunker Hill Pavilion

Visitor center 🕐 *open year-round daily 9:30am–4:30pm.* 🕐 *Closed Jan 1, Thanksgiving Day & Dec 25.* ♿ 🅿 ☎ *617-242-5641. www.nps.gov/bost.*

Information on the Navy Yard, Freedom Trail and Boston National Historic Park is available here. Park rangers conduct free tours of the Navy Yard *(call for schedule)*. The historic Battle of Bunker Hill, as seen through the eyes of an American militiaman and a British soldier, is presented in a multimedia program entitled "The Whites of their Eyes" *(20min)*, 👓 *$4.*

Charlestown Navy Yard

East of Bunker Hill Pavilion along Constitution Rd.

More than 200 warships were built—and thousands more maintained—here from the Navy Yard's establishment in 1800 to its closing in 1974. Following its closing, 30 of the former US Naval Shipyard's 130 acres were designated as part of Boston National Historical Park. Today the USS *Constitution* sits in its permanent berth at a wharf here in testament to the Navy Yard's glory days.

The USS Constitution★★

Kids 🚢 *Visit by guided tour (30min) only, mid-Jun–Oct Tues-Sun 10am–4pm; rest of the year Thu–Sun 10am–4pm.* 🕐 *Closed Jan 1, Thanksgiving Day & Dec 25.* 🅿 ☎ *617-242-5641. www.nps.gov/bost.*

The USS *Constitution,* the pride of the American fleet, is the oldest commissioned warship afloat. Authorized by Congress in 1794, this 44-gun frigate won her greatest victories during the War of 1812 against the British: capturing the HMS *Guerrière* and the *Java* in 1812, and simultaneously seizing the *Cyane* and the *Levante* three years later. It was during the battle with the *Guerrière*, when enemy fire seemed to bounce off her planking without causing damage, that the *Constitution* was given her

WARREN TAVERN

2 Pleasant St., Charlestown. ☎ *617-241-8142. www.warrentavern.com.* With its low timbered ceilings, snug fireplace and long mahogany bar, this tavern may resemble an English pub, but in fact it's just as American as they come—Patriot, that is. Constructed c.1780, the structure was one of the first to be rebuilt after the British torched Charlestown in 1775. Doubling as a Masonic hall, the alehouse was a favorite of Paul Revere. George Washington was known to quaff a few here, too. Today Warren Tavern remains a cozy place for a beer and sandwich or Shepherd's Pie (a house specialty), and a cup of cocoa after a long day on the Freedom Trail.

nickname "Old Ironsides." By 1830, after having survived 40 military engagements, the *Constitution* was declared unseaworthy and destined for the scrap heap. Oliver Wendell Holmes' poem "Old Ironsides" aroused such strong popular sentiment in favor of the ship that funds were appropriated to rebuild it. Reconstructed in 1905, 1913 and 1973, the ship got A $12 million overhaul in 1997, in honor of its 200th birthday. This was the ship's first sailing under its own power since 1881.

Berthed a short distance from the USS *Constitution* is the **USS Cassin Young**, a World War II destroyer similar to the type built here in the 1930s and 40s.

USS Constitution Museum

Kids *Pier 1.* ⏱ *Open April 15–Oct 15 daily 9am–6pm. Rest of the year daily 10am–5pm.* ⏱ *Closed Jan 1, Thanksgiving Day & Dec 25.* ♿ 🅿 ☎ *617-426-1812. www.ussconstitutionmuseum.org.*

Exhibits in the granite building (designed by Alexander Parris) trace the history of Old Ironsides from 1794 to the present. The collection of some 3,000 artifacts here includes ship's logs, charts, decorative arts and paintings. Kids will enjoy hands-on activities such as hoisting a sail, steering a ship, and fighting the British in a computerized battle.

Excursions

Lexington★★

11mi northwest of Boston. See entry heading Concord and Lexington.

Concord★★

17mi northwest of Boston. ♿ *See entry heading Concord and Lexington.*

CAMBRIDGE★★

POPULATION 101,355
MICHELIN MAP 581 M 8 AND MAP BELOW
TOURIST INFORMATION ☎ 617-441-2884 OR WWW.CAMBRIDGE-USA.ORG

Located on the Charles River across from Boston, Cambridge is the home of Harvard University and the Massachusetts Institute of Technology (MIT). Massachusetts Avenue, the state's longest thoroughfare, extends the length of Cambridge from Harvard Bridge, past MIT and through the city's center, Harvard Square, with its lively coffeehouses, restaurants and theaters. Memorial Drive borders the Charles River, with great views of downtown Boston and Back Bay.

▶ **Orient Yourself:** The key to getting around Cambridge (and ending up at your chosen destination) is knowing which "Square" (neighborhood) you're looking for. There's Central Square, Harvard Square, Inman Square, Kendall Square, and Porter Square.

🅿 **Parking:** Now here's a great idea: a Web site with maps to help locate parking garages in Harvard Square, plus rates and hours: www.harvardsquare.com/parking. Plan to pay a daily rate of about $20; hourly rates are around $7 or $8.

👓 **Don't Miss:** Mt. Auburn Cemetery is, believe it or not, a wonderful place to walk, especially in spring and fall. This beautifully landscaped garden cemetery (the first of its kind in the US) is the final resting place of Henry Wadsworth Longfellow, Isabella Stewart Gardner and Winslow Homer. Look for the giant Sphinx and other sculptural headstones.

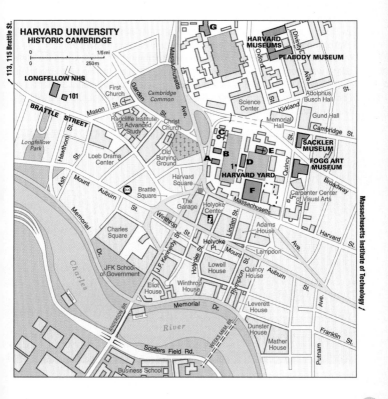

🕐 **Organizing Your Time:** You could easily spend a day walking around Harvard Square, browsing the bookstores, the giant HMV music store, and "experienced clothing" (second-hand) shops like the Garment District. Have lunch at Bartley's Burger Cottage and take in one of Harvard's museums.

A Bit of History

From New Towne to Cambridge – In 1630 New Towne, the small settlement across the river from Boston, was chosen as the capital of the Bay Colony. Fortifications were built to protect the town, and six years later, when the Puritans voted to establish a college to train young men for the ministry, New Towne was selected as the site. Leaders of the Bay Colony agreed to give the college a sum of money equal to the total colony tax. In 1638, recognizing the close bond between the college and thecolony, they changed the name of New Towne to Cambridge, after the English university town. The school was called Harvard, in honor of the Charlestown pastor **John Harvard**, who died later that year, leaving half his estate and library to the college.

Harvard University★★★ *Map p 211.* Ⓣ *Harvard.*

☎ *617-495-1000. www.harvard.edu. Campus borders the Charles River off Memorial Dr. (west of MIT).*

Harvard College
Established in 1636, America's first college is one of the world's leading institutions of higher learning. Harvard developed as a modern university in the 19C, as professional schools were added to the original college: Medicine (1782), Divinity (1816), Law (1817), School of Dental Medicine (1867) and Arts and Sciences (1872). Harvard's $25.9 billion endowment is the largest of any university in the world.

Women were first admitted to the Harvard community in 1879, when Radcliffe College was founded to provide women with equal access to a Harvard education. Today, Harvard's undergraduate program is completely coeducational. Students live in one of thirteen Harvard Houses, many of them lovely Georgian-style buildings that surround courtyards.

Courtesy Harvard University/Joe Wrinn

Harvard's Crew Team Practices on the Charles River

Address Book

For price ranges for hotels and restaurants, see the legend on the cover flap.

STAYING IN CAMBRIDGE

Charles Hotel – *One Bennett St.* ✗ ♿ 🅿 💻 ☎ *617-864-1200 or 800-882-1818. www.charleshotel.com. 293 rooms.* **$$$$** Shaker-style furnishings and quilts blend with modern blond-wood fixtures at this contemporary luxury hotel, an understated oasis in hopping Harvard Square. Dining options include Mediterranean cuisine at **Rialto** or more traditional New England fare at Henrietta's Table; at the Regattabar jazz club, you can catch noted national and local musicians.

A Cambridge House B&B – *2218 Massachusetts Ave.* 🅿 ☎ *617-491-6300 or 800-232-9989. www.acambridgehouse.com. 15 rooms.* **$$$$** Small touches, like bowls of M&Ms and homemade cookies win over guests at this gracious 1892 Greek Revival inn and adjacent carriage house. Set on busy Massachusetts Avenue, near Davis Square, the inn is lushly turned out with cherry panellng, Victorian antiques, oriental rugs and canopy beds. Carriage house rooms are smaller, but each has a fireplace.

Hotel at MIT – *20 Sidney St.* 🅿 ☎ *617-577-0200. www.hotelatmit.com. 210 rooms.* **$$$-$$$$** This is what happens when high-tech meets high style. Art on loan from the MIT collection has an artificial intelligence theme; early robotic specimens serve as sculptures. The elevator is carpeted with a pattern of stylized molecules, while bed coverings sport a scientific equation motif. Rooms are simple and sleek with maple armoires, inlaid with computer circuit boards. Rooms have floor-to-ceiling windows withwood shutters, ergonomically designed furniture, and high-speed Internet. This hotel is a top choice for techie business travelers and a bargain for weekend vacationers.

DINING IN CAMBRIDGE

Rialto – *One Bennett St., in the Charles Hotel. Dinner only.* 🅿 ☎ *617-661-5050. www.rialto-restaurant.com.* **$$$$ Mediterranean.** Consistently ranked among the Boston area's top restaurants, Rialto serves up epicurean elegance in a snazzy setting, with striped lamp shades and two-toned wood floors complementing curvaceous Art Deco-style seating and floor-to-ceiling windows. Chef Jody Adams' food derives its inspiration from southern Europe, updated with Boston gourmet panache: Expect savory seafood dishes, pastas, and game prepared with seasonal vegetables and plated with artful precision. Leave room for the rich chèvre cheesecake or the decadent "Three Degrees of Chocolate."

East Coast Grill & Raw Bar – *1271 Cambridge St. Dinner & Sunday brunch only.* ☎ *617-491-6568. www.eastcoast-grill.net.* **$$ American.** Chef Chris Schlesinger continues to draw happy crowds with his innovative touch with fresh fish, often paired with intriguing fruit salsas.You can still get his famous southern-style barbecue, but fish reigns supreme at this ultra-casual spot. And "Hell Night" draws fans of super-hot chile dishes, including the notorious habanero-spiked "pasta from Hell."

Harvest – *44 Brattle St.* 🅿 ☎ *617-868-2255. www.the-harvest.com.* **$$ American.** Salt- and pepper-colored upholstery punctuates the pale corn-yellow walls and dark woods in this classy space on Harvard Square. The menu reflects Northeastern bounty, served with a twist; dinner entrees might include miso-glazed salmon with fermented black bean beurre blanc or roasted halibut in a salt-cured olive sauce. The rack of pork is a perennial favorite, and who can resist sharing a plate of chili-spiced fries with lime-chipotle aioli? Chocolate espresso torte makes a great finale.

Mr. & Mrs. Bartley's Burger Cottage – *1246 Massachusetts Ave. Closed Sun.* ☎ *617-354-6559.* **$ American.** Thick, juicy hamburgers, paired with crisp onion rings or sweet-potato fries, entice crowds of students, locals, and tourists to this bustling Harvard Square institution. To drink? A lime rickey or a thick frappe (a milk shake to Bostonians).

Massachusetts Hall, Harvard University

The Campus

Harvard is a city within a city with some 500 buildings. These reflect a variety of architectural styles, from Colonial residences to public buildings by prominent 20C figures such as Gropius (Harkness Commons and the Graduate Center, 1950; (**G**), and Le Corbusier (Carpenter Center of Visual Arts).

▶ *Begin at Harvard Information Center at 1350 Massachusetts Ave.*

Harvard Yard★★
Bounded by Massachusetts Ave., Quincy St. and Cambridge St.
Harvard Yard is the oldest part of the university. Administration buildings, dormitories and Holden Chapel, Harvard's first official chapel, are located here. To the left is **Massachusetts Hall** (**A**) (1720), the oldest Harvard building still standing; across from it sits **Harvard Hall** (**B**) (1766). Beyond Harvard Hall is **Holden Chapel** (**C**). **University Hall** (**D**) (1815), a granite building designed by Charles Bulfinch, occupies the other side of the Yard. Daniel Chester French's **statue of John Harvard** (**1**) stands in front of University Hall. Because of the plaque on the statue that reads "John Harvard, founder 1638," the statue is known as the "statue of the three lies": the college was founded in 1636, John Harvard was the school's benefactor, not its founder, and the figure portrays a student who attended Harvard in 1882. To the rear of University Hall stands **Memorial Church** (**E**), dedicated to Harvard men killed in the world wars. Opposite rises the **Widener Memorial Library** (**F**), with its imposing stairway. Named for Harry Widener, a former Harvard student who lost his life in the Titanic tragedy, Widener Memorial is the largest university library in the world.

The Museums *Map p 211.*

Harvard Museum of Natural History★★
26 Oxford St. ⏲ *Open year-round daily 9am-5pm.* ⏲ *Closed Jan 1, Jul 4, Thanksgiving Day & Dec 25.* ∞ *$9.* 🅿 *617-495-3045. www.hmnh.harvard.edu.*
Grouped under one roof, these four museums serve as the repository for the 21 million specimens and artifacts that make up Harvard's research collections. Many of the galleries, dimly lit and packed with simple glass-and-wood display cases, have retained the old-fashioned charm of a 19C exhibition hall. Don't be put off by the no-frills presentation; the collections merit a look.

Peabody Museum of Archaeology and Ethnology★

Founded in 1866 by George Peabody, this large museum displays objects and works of art brought back from the early-20C Harvard-sponsored exhibitions. The ground floor contains a delightful museum shop and an exhibit that explores the evolution of North American cultures to the present day. The Victorian-style **Oceania** exhibit *(4th floor)* reveals a variety of exquisitely crafted artifacts from the Pacific Rim. *The other museums are accessible from the third-floor gallery.*

Among the numerous minerals, gemstones and meteorites featured in the three galleries of the **Mineralogical and Geological Museum** do not miss the eye-catching giant gypsum crystals from Mexico.

The world-renowned collection of **Blashka Glass Flowers** occupies the **Botanical Museum's** two galleries. Crafted in Germany by Leopold and Rudolph Blashka between 1886 and 1936, the nearly 3,000 hand-blown glass models accurately represent some 830 species of flowering plants and are prized for their scientific and aesthetic value.

Some of the rare finds on view in the fossil collections of the **Museum of Comparative Zoology** are the 25,000-year-old Harvard mastodon, unearthed in New Jersey; a *Paleosaurus*, one of the oldest fossil dinosaurs (180 million years old); and a *Kronosaurus* (120 million years old), perhaps the largest marine reptile to have ever lived. In the adjacent galleries, scores of large glass cases enclose specimens of animals from around the globe. Note the impressive North American bird collection representing 650 species.

Fogg Art Museum★

32 Quincy St. ◷ *Open year-round Mon-Sat 10am-5pm; Sun 1pm-5pm.* ◷ *Closed major holidays.* ⬡ *$7.50 (includes admission to Sackler Museum).* ♿⬡*617-495-9400. www.artmuseums.harvard.edu.*

On entering the museum, take a moment to admire the Italian Renaissance-style courtyard. Exhibits on two levels surrounding the courtyard span all periods of Western art from the Middle Ages to the present and include notable examples of **Italian Renaissance** painting, Impressionist and post-Impressionist painting and sculpture, and classical art.

A corridor on the second floor leads to the **Busch-Reisinger Museum★**, specializing in the art of 20C German-speaking Europe *(◷ same hours as Fogg Art Museum;* ♿⬡ *617-495-9400; www. artmuseums.harvard.edu).* Its renowned collection, displayed on a rotating basis in six galleries, boasts works by Expres-

Bookish Cambridge

Cambridge claims more bookstores per capita (30, in 6sq mi radius) than any other US city. **Harvard Book Store** *(1265 Massachusetts Ave.;* ☎ *617-661-1515 www.harvard.com)* is considered the best of the big independents. Founded in 1927, **Grolier Poetry Book Shop** *(6 Plympton St.;* ☎ *617-547-4648)* is one of only two stores in the US devoted solely to poetry. **Schoenhof's Foreign Books** *(76-A Mt. Auburn St.;* ☎ *617-547-8855; www.schoenhofs.com),* contains some 56,000 titles representing more than 400 languages and dialects, while the **Globe Corner Bookstore** *(28 Church St.;* ☎ *617-497-6277 www.globecorner. com)* specializes in travel literature and maps to many countries.

sionists such as Max Beckmann and members of the Die Brucke and Der Blaue Reiter (Kandinsky, Klee, Feininger) groups. Another gallery is reserved for temporary exhibits.

Sackler Museum★

485 Broadway. Same hours as Fogg Art Museum.   *$7.50 (includes admission to the Fogg Art Museum).* &617-495-9400. www.artmuseums.harvard.edu.
A dramatic post-Modern building designed by James Stirling (1985) houses this companion museum to the Fogg. The Sackler focuses on Ancient, Near Eastern and Far Eastern Art. Asian ceramics, sculpture, Japanese prints and a noteworthy group of Chinese bronzes and jades highlight the collection. In addition, temporary exhibits on a variety of subects are presented in the ground-floor galleries.

HI-RISE BREAD CO.

56 Brattle St. &617-492-3003. Tucked back from the street, in the canary-yellow 1808 Dexter Pratt House (the former abode of the village blacksmith immortalized by Longfellow) stands a humble cafe that sells some of the best baked goods in Harvard Square. Piled up next to the front counter is a cornucopia of brownies, cookies, scones and brioches (if you arrive early enough), as well as a selection of breads (brown, semolina, corn, country) baked daily at the main bakery/cafe on Concord Avenue in West Cambridge. For lunch there's a creative assortment of deli sandwiches quiche, and soups. souhearty soups. Eat upstairs or take a picnic to go.

Historic Cambridge★ *Map p 211.*

Brattle Street★

Loyalists to the British Crown, wealthy Tories built homes here in the 18C, thus the street's former name, Tory Row. The stately residences now lining Brattle Street date primarily from the 19C. Note **no. 101** (Hastings House) and **nos. 113** and **115** (these two structures belonged to Longfellow's daughters).

Longfellow National Historic Site★

105 Brattle St.   *Visit by guided tour (1hr) only, mid-May–Oct Wed–Sun 10am–4:30pm.*   *Closed major holidays.*   *$3* &617-876-4491. www.nps.gov/long.
This Georgian dwelling, built in 1759 by the Loyalist John Vassall, served as the headquarters of General Washington during the siege of Boston. In the 19C **Henry Wadsworth Longfellow** lived in the house between 1837 and 1882, the period during which he wrote *Evangeline* (1847) and *The Song of Hiawatha* (1855). Today the house contains many of the Longfellows' original furnishings, including 10,000 books, artworks by such noted painters as Gilbert Stuart and Albert Bierstadt and, in the poet's study, a chair crafted from the wood of the "spreading chestnut tree," made famous by Longfellow's *The Village Blacksmith*. A small garden graces the rear of the house.

Massachusetts Institute of Technology★

Map p 178.   *Kendall Center/MIT. Campus borders the Charles River along Memorial Dr. and Massachusetts Ave.* &617-253-1000. www.mit.edu.
One of the nation's premier science and research universities, Massachusetts Institute of Technology (MIT), overlooks the Charles River. Inviting green spaces, broad concrete plazas and vast recreational fields interweave with a variety of architecturally styled buildings, from Neoclassical to post-Modern.
The school was established as the Massachusetts Institute of Technology in 1861 by **William Barton Rogers**, a natural scientist who stressed the practical application of knowledge as the institute's principal goal. Guided through its early years

Literary Cambridge

Cambridge developed as a publishing center in the 17C, when the first printing press in the colonies was established here. A Bible in an Indian language, an almanac and the *Bay Psalm Book* were among the first works printed. As the seat of Harvard College, Cambridge became the home of many leading educators and scholars. By the mid-19C the city had developed into a center of progressive thought, attracting a circle of prominent writers, reformers and intellectuals. Among the more famous figures associated with Cambridge are Henry Wadsworth Longfellow, Oliver Wendell Holmes, Margaret Fuller and Dorothea Dix.

by Rogers, MIT continued to pursue its original objective in the 20C and is today a leader in modern research and development, with schools of Engineering, Science, Architecture and Planning, Management, and Humanities and Social Science. The international character of the institute is reflected in its enrollment of some 10,000 students from 50 states and 100 foreign countries.

East Campus

▶ *To the right of Massachusetts Ave., arriving from Harvard Bridge.*

A low dome tops the **Rogers Building** *(77 Massachusetts Ave.)*, where a visitor center stocks free maps of the campus. Next door at the **Hart Nautical Gallery**, part of the MIT Museum, you can view more than 40 ship models dating from the late 19C through the 20C *(55 Massachusetts Ave.;* 🕐 *open year-round daily 9am–7pm;* 🚻 ☎ *617-253-5942; www.mit.edu/museum).*

Contemporary art is displayed in the **List Visual Arts Center** on the main floor of the Wiesner Building, a Postmodern structure by MIT graduate I.M. Pei. The three galleries hold temporary exhibits curated with an eye toward aesthetic experimentation and political engagement *(20 Ames St.;* 🕐 *open Sept–Jun Tue–Sun noon–6pm, Fri until 8pm;* 🕐 *closed major holidays;* ☜ *$5 contribution suggested;* 🚻🚻 ☎ *617-253-4680; http://web.mit.edu/lvac).*

Between the Hayden Memorial Library and the Earth Sciences Center looms Alexander Calder's stabile *LaGrande Voile (The Big Sail)*. Nearby stands *Transparent Horizon*, a black steel sculpture by Louise Nevelson.

Farther north on Massachusetts Avenue *(no. 265)*, the **MIT Museum** is a fun-house of eye-catching, mind-boggling art *(*🕐 *open year-round Tue–Fri 10am–5pm, weekends noon–5pm;* 🕐 *closed major holidays;* ☜ *$5;* 🚻 ☎ *617-253-4444; http://web.mit.edu/museum).* Defying the truism that art and science don't mix, permanent exhibits include an array of stop-motion photographs, mobiles based on geometric principles, kinetic sculptures and **holograms.**

West Campus

▶ *To the left of Massachusetts Ave., arriving from Harvard Bridge.*

The modern Student Center houses the **Tech Co-op**, the student union and restaurants. **Kresge Auditorium**★ and the **MIT Chapel**★ were designed by **Eero Saarinen** in 1956. The interfaith chapel, a cylindrical brick structure, is topped with an aluminum sculpture by Theodore Roszak.

CAPE ANN★★

MICHELIN MAP 581 N 7 AND MAP OPPOSITE
TOURIST INFORMATION ☎ 978-977-7760 OR WWW.NORTHOFBOSTON.ORG

Salty sea air, exhilarating and clear, pervades the fishing villages, coastal estates and harbors of this rocky peninsula north of Boston. A 32mi road (Routes 127 and 127A) rings the periphery of Cape Ann and offers stunning views of the beaches, cliffs and towns that make this area a summertime vacation classic.

▶ **Orient Yourself:** The towns of Manchester-by-the-Sea, Magnolia, Gloucester and Rockport are located on Cape Ann.

🅿 **Parking:** Parking isn't a big issue in these seaside communities—unless you're looking for a spot at the beach in summertime. Arrive early to beat the crowds (most beach lots close after they reach capacity). You don't need a car to get to Singing Beach, in Manchester-by-the-Sea; the commuter rail from Boston *(MBTA; www.mbta.com)* has train service to the town; from there, it's a 1mi walk to Singing Beach.

🅐 **Don't Miss:** A stroll around Rockport's Bearskin Neck, where old fishing sheds have been converted to shops, galleries and restaurants.

🕐 **Organizing Your Time:** A driving tour of Routes 127 and 127A offer a great overview of Cape Ann, with plenty of opportunities to stop for a clam roll, an ice cream cone, or a cup of chowder. Plan to overnight at one of the local inns, such Emerson Inn by the Sea *(www.emersoninnbythesea.com;* ☎ *800-964-5550).*

🄺🄸🄳🅂 **Especially for Kids:** Good Harbor Beach is great for kids, and parking is free after 4pm.

🅐 **Also See:** Gloucester's Ravenswood Park, on Route 127, has easy-going hiking trails (good for snowshoeing and cross-country skiing in winter.)

A Bit of History

The cape was explored in 1604 by Samuel de Champlain, then in 1614 by Capt. John Smith, who mapped and named the area in honor of Queen Anne, wife of James I of England. A small colony was established in 1623 at Gloucester by a group of Englishmen who had come "to praise God and catch fish." Their descendants were the generations of cape-born sailors who have made the region one of the world's largest fishing centers.

Bostonians frequent Cape Ann, seeking out its maritime atmosphere, art galleries and fine seafood restaurants. Browsing in the shops and enjoying the area's ruggedly beautiful scenery are among the popular pastimes. **Whale-watching cruises** *(p 34)* offer visitors the opportunity to observe these great creatures in their summer feeding grounds just off the coast. Artists delight in the magnificent natural light, which strikes the rocky shores and transforms the landscape into a changing spectrum of color and shadows throughout the day.

Driving Tour★★ *32mi.*

This itinerary follows Routes 127 and 127A around Cape Ann, passing through quaint fishing villages and offering views of the coast and the ocean. Begin on the southern shore of the cape in Magnolia.

Magnolia

▶ *Take Magnolia Ave. toward the coast off Rte. 127.*

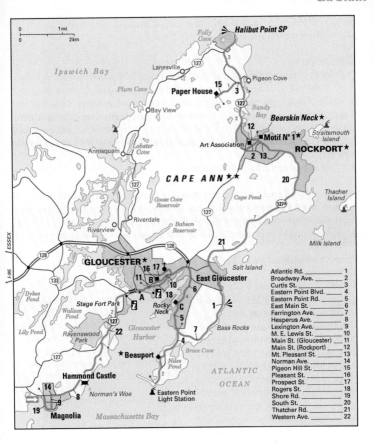

This former fishing village developed into a summer resort in the 19C. Shore Road follows the coast, presenting views of the modest harbor and, in the distance, the Boston skyline.

▶ From Magnolia Center, take Hesperus Ave. 1mi east toward Gloucester and follow signs to Hammond Castle.

Hammond Castle Museum

Kids 80 Hesperus Ave. ◷ Open April–Sept. Mon–Thurs, 10am–5pm; Fri–Sun, 10am–3pm. ◷ Closed major holidays. ⊗ $8.50. ⊓ ☎ 978-283-7673. www.hammondcastle.org.
Inspired by castles built in the Middle Ages, this stone castle was completed in 1929 by the eccentric inventor John Hays Hammond, Jr. On one side, twin towers rise 80ft above terraced gardens, a drawbridge and an enclosed exercise yard that Hammond built for his 18 cats. Below the opposite towers lie the treacherous rocks of Norman's Woe, the setting for Longfellow's poem *The Wreck of the Hesperus*. The interior contains Hammond's collection of medieval furnishings, paintings and sculpture. The **Great Hall**★ houses an 8,200-pipe organ that Hammond constructed over a period of 20 years.

▶ Return to Hesperus Ave.; follow it northeast to Rte. 127 (Western Ave.) and turn right toward Gloucester.

Just before Gloucester, you'll pass **Stage Fort Park**, site of the settlement established in 1623. Cross the drawbridge that links the cape to the mainland. To the right is Leonard Craske's statue the **Gloucester Fisherman**★ **(A)**, a tribute to the thousands of Gloucestermen who have died at sea, and the nearby Fishermen's Wives Memorial, erected in 1999.

Gloucester★

The oldest seaport in the nation, Gloucester is one of the world's leading fishing ports. Its fleet of schooners, which once sailed between Virginia and Newfoundland in search of cod, halibut and mackerel, was immortalized by Rudyard Kipling in his novel *Captains Courageous* (1897). Gloucester's fishermen, many of whom are of Portuguese or Italian descent, remain devoted to their traditions, and especially to the annual **Blessing of the Fleet**, which takes place during the last weekend in June on the feast of St. Peter.

▶ *Enter Gloucester on Rte. 127 (Rogers St.).*

Crowning a knoll above a small park stands the austere stone house of noted 19C maritime artist Fitz Henry (Hugh) Lane *(not open to the public; grounds open year-round daily dawn–dusk)*. Views from the knoll sweep across the harbor.

▶ *Turn left on Manuel E. Lewis St., left on Main St. and right on Pleasant St.*

Cape Ann Historical Museum (B)★

27 Pleasant St. ⏲ *Open year-round except Feb, Tue–Sat 10am–5pm; Sun, 1-4.* ⬭ *$6.50.* ♿ ☎ *978-283-0455. www. capeannhistoricalmuseum.org.*

The museum is dedicated to the sea-faring, granite quarrying and artistic traditions of Cape Ann. Three levels of large, sunlit galleries trace the history of the fisheries and maritime industries here and highlight works of 19C and 20C artists. Among the museum's holdings are works by Maurice Prendergast, John Sloan, Stuart Davis and Marsden Hartley as well as the nation's largest collection of **seascapes** by 19C American marine painter **Fitz Henry (Hugh) Lane** (1804-65). His paintings of Gloucester Harbor and of local scenes are admired for their luminous colors, serene atmosphere and attention to detail.

WOODMAN'S

121 Main St., in Essex; about 6mi northwest of Gloucester via Rte. 133. ☎ *978-768-6057. www.woodmans. com.* Woodman's doesn't merely serve up fried clams—Lawrence "Chubby" Woodman claims to have *invented* them back in 1914. Today this sprawling clam shack is a North Shore fixture. Lines of eager diners snake out the door on summer weekends (it's a post-beach/post-antiquing favorite). Once you're inside at the order counter, you have your choice of all things clam: fried clams, fried clam strips, award-winning clam chowder, clam cakes and other items, including whole boiled lobster, scallops, corn on the cob and onion rings.

▶ *Return to Rte. 127 (Rogers St.) by Prospect St. You will pass the Portuguese-inspired* **Our Lady of Good Voyage Church**, *which is surmounted by two blue cupolas.*

▶ *Follow Rte. 127 North to E. Main St. and bear right.*

East Gloucester

Among East Main Street's restaurants and art galleries is the **North Shore Arts Association (C)**, *(11 Pirate's Lane.;* ⏲ *open mid-May–mid-Oct Mon–Sat 10am–5pm, Sun noon–5pm;* ♿ ▣ ☎ *978-283-1857; www.northshoreartsassoc.org).* The association features the work of local artists. Nearby, jutting out into the water, **Rocky Neck** has harbored an artists' colony since the 19C.

▶ *Follow Eastern Point Rd. to Eastern Point (private). Visitors to Beauport are permitted access via the private road.*

Beauport★

75 Eastern Point Blvd., in Eastern Point. 🕊 *Visit by guided tour (1hr) only, Jun–mid-Sept Mon–Fri 10am–5pm (last tour 4pm). Mid-Sept–mid-Oct daily 10am–5pm.* ⏲ *Closed major holidays.* ⬭ *$10.* ☎ *978-283-0800. http://www.historicnewengland.org.*

Rockport

Overlooking Gloucester Harbor and the distant Boston skyline, this 40-room summer residence of architect-decorator Henry Davis Sleeper (1878-1934) contains an imaginative mix of period styles and décors. Sleeper wished to create a different mood and character in each room. Thus, beneath the varied roofline of chimneys, turrets, spiral flues and towers, he designed a Colonial Paul Revere Room, an Indian Room, a Byron Room and a China Trade Room, among others. His creations here made him one of the most celebrated decorators of his day.

At the tip of Eastern Point is **Eastern Point Light Station**, dominating a long, granite breakwater at the entrance to Gloucester Harbor.

▶ *Return along Eastern Point Blvd. to the entrance of the private road, then turn right onto Farrington Ave. and left onto Atlantic Rd.*

The drive east along Atlantic Road offers a good **view** of the coast and, across the water, of the twin lights on Thatcher Island.

▶ *Follow Atlantic Rd. to Rte. 127A (Thatcher Rd.), which skirts beaches, occasional salt marshes and rocky, wooded areas. Thatcher Rd. becomes South St. as you approach the town of Rockport.*

Rockport★

During tourist season, downtown parking is difficult to find. A shuttle bus operates every 15min between the parking lot outside of town (free parking) and the town center.

This tranquil fishing village, which developed as an artists' colony in the 1920s, enjoyed its industrial heyday in the 19C, when granite quarried from its shores was shipped to ports as far away as South America. Rockport's art galleries and shops *(in the vicinity of Main St.)*, and its seaside charm attracts many visitors.

The village is especially picturesque in the late afternoon, when the setting sun illuminates the sea, the granite ledges, the boats anchored offshore and the red fishing shed **Motif No. 1**★, named for the many paintings it has inspired. The shed is accessible from **Bearskin Neck**★, a small promontory where old fishing sheds have been converted into shops. Narrow walkways lead to the end of the neck, a good vantage point from which to observe the rocky shore and the harbor. On Main Street *(no. 12)*, the **Rockport Art Association** exhibits the works of regional artists. A public oceanside pathway passes through private lawns and leads to Garden, North and South beaches.

▶ *Leave Rockport on Mt. Pleasant St., which turns into Main St. and leads back to Rte. 127 (Railroad Ave.). Just before Pigeon Cove, turn left onto Curtis St., then left onto Pigeon Hill St. Stop for a look at #52, the **Paper House**, a house made almost*

North Shore Best Bets

Here's what North Shore insiders (Cape Ann and the coastal communities north of Boston are considered the North Shore) recommend to visitors:

- **Singing Beach in Manchester-by-the-Sea**: Take the commuter rail, then take a pleasant 1mi walk to the beach (squeaky sand makes it 'sing') Stop for an ice cream at Cap'n Dusty's.
- **Le Grand David and His Own Spectacular Magic Company**: Old-fashioned vaudevillian-style magic show at an historic theater in Beverly
- **Myopia Polo**: Sunday afternoon polo matches are a tradition in Hamilton. From late May-mid-Oct. Bring a picnic.
- **Wenham Museum**: This charming little museum will delight small fry.

---

entirely of newspapers (furnishings, too). Return to Rte. 127; continue north for almost 1mi and turn right on Gott Ave.

Halibut Point State Park

🕐 *Open May–Labor Day daily 8am–8pm. Rest of the year daily dawn–dusk.* 🕭 *$2/ vehicle.* ♿🅿 ☎ *978-546-2997. www.state.ma.us/dem/parks/halb.htm.*

From the parking lot, numerous self-guided trails wind through the woods and past granite quarries (🕭 *guided 2hr quarry tour Memorial Day–Columbus Day, Sat 10am*) to the northern tip of Pigeon Cove. Vantage points on the rocky shore provide extensive **views**★ across Ipswich Bay to the south, and as far as Maine to the north. The Halibut Point State Park headquarters incorporates a concrete World War II watchtower.

CAPE COD★★★

MICHELIN MAP 581 N-P 9, 10 AND MAP PP 230-231
TOURIST INFORMATION ☎ 508-862-0700 OR WWW.CAPECODCHAMBER.ORG

Shaped like a muscular arm curled in a flex, celebrated Cape Cod is fringed with 300mi of sandy beaches, whitewashed fishing villages, towering dunes, salt marshes and windswept sea grasses. The product of a fascinating geological and human past, the cape has been a favorite resort since the development of the automobile.

▶ **Orient Yourself:** Route 6A, a National Scenic Byway, runs nearly 35mi from Bourne to Orleans. The Upper Cape is the section that's closest to the Sagamore Bridge (and the rest of MA); the Mid-Cape is the part in the middle (Hyannis, Barnstable, Yarmouth, Dennis); the Lower Cape (Harwich, Brewster, Chatham, Orleans); and the Outer Cape (Eastham, Wellfleet, Truro and Provincetown).

🅿 **Parking:** Parking isn't the issue; driving is. The Cape's roadways get crowded in summertime. Ride your bike when you can, or, if you're visiting the Upper Cape, take the Whoosh Trolley, running from Falmouth to Woods Hole.

🐚 **Don't Miss:** A walk along Cape Cod National Seashore, in the steps of Henry David Thoreau (enchanting in every season).

🕐 **Organizing Your Time:** Don't try to squeeze in all of the Cape's highlights in one visit. Choose an area, and get to know it well; Cape Cod is best when savored.

🧒 **Especially for Kids:** Whale-watching trips out of Provincetown are a good choice for kids, since the trip to see them is only 6 mi out to sea (vs. much longer trips from other MA locales). The whales' main feeding grounds are close to P'town.

🎐 **Also See:** The Wampanoag Powwow is held during the first weekend of July at the Tribal Grounds in Mashpee. Festivities include native crafts and foods, drumming, dancing, and singing, capped with a clambake on the last day.

A Bit of History

Cape Cod was named by explorer **Bartholomew Gosnold**, who landed here in 1602 and was impressed by the cod-filled waters that surrounded the peninsula. Eighteen years later, the **Mayflower**, en route to its original destination in Virginia, anchored at the present site of Provincetown, and the Pilgrims spent five weeks exploring the region before continuing on to Plymouth.

The earliest permanent settlements on the cape were established around 1630 with fishing and farming as the mainstays. In the 18C whaling grew into a principal industry on the cape, as vessels sailed out of Barnstable, Truro, Wellfleet and Provincetown for the open sea. The rocky, treacherous shoals, a challenge to even the most expert seamen, posed a great danger to all shipping in these waters. Traces of several of the hundreds of vessels that sank off the cape before the construction of the Cape Cod Canal are occasionally revealed on the beach during low tide; as the tide rushes in, they are again hidden by the shifting sands.

The Cape Today – In the summer, traffic along the cape's two main thorough-fares—US-6 and Route 28—can slow to an agonizing crawl and the strip malls that flank the roads provide little diversion. Despite the numerous motels, fast-food places, souvenir shops and clusters of condominiums found in or near the old fishing ports, the cape has managed to preserve pockets of its natural beauty and seafaring charm. Small colonial and fishing villages dot the bay side; to the east, miles of windswept dunes are protected in the Cape Cod National Seashore (CCNS). Acres of low-lying cranberry bogs and salt marshes, pine and scrub oak forests, and dozens of lakes, ponds and small, gray-shingled "Cape Cod" cottages offer a pleasing relief to the sandy landscape of this peculiar Atlantic peninsula.

A large number of craftspeople live on Cape Cod. Local shops feature their handmade creations including glassware, leather goods, candles and pottery. For details, pick up a copy of *Arts & Artisans Trails of Cape Cod (www.CapeAndIslandsArtsGuide.com).*

The Islands – The Cape islands, **Martha's Vineyard**, **Nantucket** and the **Elizabeth Islands**, lie to the south. Purchased by Englishman Thomas Mayhew in 1642, the

Cape Cod National Seashore

Address Book

PRACTICAL INFORMATION

GETTING THERE

From **Boston** to **Sagamore Bridge** (*72mi*), take I-93 South to Rte. 3 South, continue east on US-6. From **Providence** to **Sagamore Bridge** (*66mi*), take I-195 South to Rte. 25 East and follow US-6 East across the Sagamore Bridge. International and domestic flights service **Logan International Airport** (BOS) in Boston (☎ 617-561-1800 or 800-235-6426; www.massport.com) and **T.F. Green Airport** (PVD) in Warwick, RI, near Providence (☎ 401-737-8222; www.pvdairport.com). Major rental-car agencies are located at the airports. Year-round **shuttle** service between Logan Airport, Plymouth and Provincetown is provided by Plymouth & Brockton Street Railway Co. (*17 Elm Ave., Hyannis, MA;* ☎ *508-746-0378; www.p-b.com*).

Closest Amtrak **train** station is in Boston (☎ 800-872-7245; www.amtrak.com). Bonanza Bus Lines (☎ 888-751-8800; www.bonanzabus.com) and Peter Pan Bus Lines (☎ 800-237-8747; www.peterpanbus.com) offer **bus** service from Boston to points on the Cape. **Ferry** service between Boston (Commonwealth Pier, World Trade Center) and Provincetown is provided by Bay State Cruise Company via excursion boat (*Provincetown II, late-Jun–Sept, weekends , 3hrs,* ☎ *$30 round trip) and high-speed ferry, mid-May to Oct. daily, 1hr 30min,* ☎ *$58 round-trip; Provincetown II, mid-Jun–Labor Day Fri–Sun only, 3hrs,* ☎ *$69 round-trip; reservations suggested,* (☎ *617-748-1428; www.baystatecruisecompany.com*).

GETTING AROUND

Cape Cod is easily navigated by car or bicycle. Bicycle rentals are available in most Cape towns; cars can be rented in Hyannis.

VISITOR INFORMATION

Cape Cod Chamber of Commerce Visitor Center offers additional information on attractions, lodging, dining, shopping and recreation (*Junction, Routes 6 & 132, Hyannis MA 02601;* ☎ *508-362-3225; www.capecodchamber.*

org). Kiosks operate seasonally at both the Sagamore and Bourne bridges.

ACCOMMODATIONS

For specific suggestions of accommodations and restaurants, see the opposite page. The **Outermost Hostel** (*closed in winter*) is located in Provincetown (*28 Winslow St.;* ☎ *508-487-4378*).
American Youth Hostels are located in Eastham (*75 Goody Hallet Dr., open late-May–mid-Sept;* ☎ *$20-22;* ☎ *508-255-2785; www.capecodhostels.org*) and Truro (*N. Pamet Rd.; open late-Jun–early Sept;* ☎ *$25-32;* ☎ *508-349-3889; www.usahostels.org*).
Reservation services: **Bed & Breakfast Cape Cod**, Box 1312, Orleans, MA 02653, 508-255-3824 or 800-541-6226 www.bedandbreakfastcapecod.com; **Destination Insider**, 10 State Rd., Tisbury, MA 02568, 508-696-3900; www.destinationinsider.com.

RECREATION

Saltwater and freshwater **beaches** are located throughout Cape Cod. Most beaches are owned and administered by the individual towns. Waters on the Atlantic Ocean are cooler than waters along the south shore, and, unlike the calmer waters of Cape Cod Bay, the ocean has a strong undertow. A parking fee (☎ *$10-12*) is charged at public beaches in the summer. **Bicycle** trails abound on the Cape (☎ *see Cycling the Cape in North Shore entry*). Bike maps (including the **Cape Cod Rail Trail** from South Dennis to S. Wellfleet) are available at the visitor centers in Eastham and Provincetown. Public **golf** courses are located in Brewster, Falmouth, Dennis and Mashpee. Along the eastern peninsula you'll find excellent opportunities for **bird-watching**. Other outdoor activities include walking the numerous nature trails along the national seashore, sailing, sea-kayaking, deep-sea fishing and whale-watching. For old-fashioned fun, you can't beat the **Wellfleet Drive-In**, a drive-in movie theater by night, and the Cape's biggest flea market by day. Located on Route 6 on the Eastham-Wellfleet line, this family-fun favorite also has a dairy bar and mini-golf.

STAYING ON CAPE COD

For a description of price categories for hotels and restaurants, see the legend on the cover flap.

Wequassett Inn – *Pleasant Bay, Chatham.* 🍴♿🅿️🛏️ ☎ 508-432-5400 or 800-225-7125. *104 rooms.* **$$$$$** Welcoming guests for more than 50 years, this sprawling upscale resort—with several town house- or cottage-style buildings decorated with spring colors, patchwork quilts and flower-filled wicker baskets—is an inviting place to escape from the Cape's bustle. The main dining room, contained in a 19C house transported here from nearby Brewster, features floor-to-ceiling windows overlooking the bay, and the reception building dates back to c.1740. You'll find a beach and tennis court on the neatly landscaped grounds.

Belfry Inne & Bistro – *8 Jarves St., Sandwich.* 🍴🅿️ ☎ 508-888-8550 or 800-844-4542. *www.belfryinn.com. 14 rooms.* **$$$** Just off Main Street, this 1902 former church and adjacent "painted lady" rectory have been converted into a dramatically different B&B, with a bistro serving contemporary American fare in the former sanctuary. Six sizable guest rooms in the abbey are stylishly appointed with antiques, two-person whirlpool tubs, and gas fireplaces, as well as architectural elements retained from the church—vaulted ceilings, arches, stained-glass windows. Rooms in the Drew House next door are attractive, if more conventional, with Laura Ashley bedding, hand-painted furniture and vintage bathtubs.

Crowne Pointe Historic Inn & Shui Spa – *82 Bradford St., Provincetown.* 🅿️ ☎ 508-487-6767. *www.crownepointe. com. 40 rooms.* **$$$$** Feeling a bit frazzled and in need of serious pampering? This 140-year-old sea captain's estate makes the perfect escape. Rooms are spread among six restored buildings, and done up in soft hues of sand and aqua that reflect the colors of the Cape's dunes, sea and marshlands. All have hardwood floors and many have fireplaces and whirlpool tubs for two. It's in the amenities category that Crowne Pointe really shines. Complimentary goodies include a daily wine/cheese/beer social, home-baked treats in the afternoon, a hot buffet breakfast each morning, high-speed Internet, and shuttles via SUV to the beach. Also included are spa facilities (not treatments), including a eucalyptus-infused steam room. The property is a short walk from MacMillan Wharf. The Bistro dining room is a Wine Spectator award winner.

Spring Garden Inn Motel – *578 Rte. 6A, East Sandwich.* 🅿️🛏️ ☎ 508-888-0710 or 800-303-1751. *www.springgarden.com. 11 rooms.* **$$** The tidy rooms at this gray-shingled motel aren't large, but the flower-patterned comforters and knotty-pine walls give them a cozy feel. Two of the units are efficiency apartments with kitchenettes, and there's also a two-room suite with a sleep sofa in the sitting room. But the best feature is around the back, where the lush green yard, dotted with hammocks, swings and picnic tables, overlooks acres and acres of marsh.

DINING ON CAPE COD

Cape Sea Grille – *31 Sea St., Harwich Port. Dinner only.* 🕐 *Closed Nov–mid-Apr.* 🅿️ ☎ 508-432-4745. *www.capeseagrille.com.* **$$$** **Seafood.** You don't have to love fish to eat here, but if you do, the contemporary seafood preparations are definitely worth a detour to Harwich Port. Filling an old sea captain's house, the dining rooms—with white tablecloths and captain's chairs—are not spacious. Better to focus on the food: seafood paella with clams, shrimp, and chorizo; a crispy seafood piccata with capers and olives; or halibut in an Asian-inspired coconut milk sauce. The warm chocolate truffle cake is a decadent finale.

Cap'n Frosty's – *219 Main St. (Rte. 6A), Dennis.* 🕐 *Closed Labor Day–Mar.* 🅿️ ☎ 508-385-8548. **$** **Seafood.** Fried seafood is a Cape specialty, and this Dennis clam shack draws crowds for crispy-battered clams, fish, scallops, and other creatures of the deep. Place your order at the counter, then hunt for a seat at one of the Formica-topped tables in the bare-bones dining room. Of course there's ice cream for dessert.

islands developed into whaling centers in the 18C and 19C and remained unspoiled by industry into the 20C. Bordered by magnificent beaches bathed by the warm Gulf Stream waters, the islands today are devoted primarily to tourism.

Driving Tour: Along the Bay★★ 30mi. Map pp 230-231.

Route 6A follows the north shore (known as the **Bay Side** because it fronts Cape Cod Bay), passing through tiny villages that were prosperous 19C ports.

▶ *Begin at the intersection of US-6 and Rte. 6A; take Rte. 6A east for .5mi.*

Pairpoint Glass Works

851 Sandwich Rd. (Rte. 6A), in Sagamore. Glassblowing demonstrations Mon-Fri 9am-4pm. ♿ P ☎ 508-888-2344. www.pairpoint.com.

At America's oldest glassworks, visitors may observe skilled glassblowers as they produce, then decorate, pieces of Pairpoint crystal according to the methods traditionally employed in the production of handmade glassware through the 19C.

▶ *From Rte. 6A bear right onto Rte. 130 (Main St.).*

Sandwich★

The first settlement on Cape Cod—founded in 1637—Sandwich has long been famous for the manufacture of glass. Today the town is known for its glass museum and picturesque spots such as Shawme Pond, created by the early settlers to power their mills. Clustered around the willow-shaded pond are several 17C sites that evoke the colonial charm of Sandwich; these include the **Hoxie House** and **Dexter Mill**. In 1825 Boston entrepreneur Deming Jarves chose the village as the site of his Boston and Sandwich Glass Company because the region's vast forests provided the wood needed to fuel the furnaces in which he fired glass. With the help of skilled craftsmen from Europe, Jarves reintroduced the use of the three-part mold that had been used centuries before by the Romans, and developed a process to mass-produce clear, cut glass in a variety of shapes, forms and patterns. The delicate lacy pattern of the glass Jarves made became known as **Sandwich glass** and brought fame to the town. By 1850, 500 workers were employed at the factory, but labor disputes in

Cycling the Cape

Shining Sea Bikeway *(3.1mi, Depot Ave. in Falmouth to Locust St., Woods Hole)* borders the water's edge for about 1mi, otherwise it leads through townscape and wetlands. This bike trail is being extended, hurrah. For specifics, contact Falmouth Town Hall (☎ 508-548-7611; http://www.town.falmouth.ma.us).

Cape Cod Rail Trail *(19.6mi, South Dennis to Salt Pond Visitor Center in Eastham or 25.8mi to South Wellfleet)* follows a paved, former rail bed along some busy city streets, but also through forests and along the ocean, with occasional views of cranberry bogs. For updates on trail expansion, contact Nickerson State Park (☎ 508-896-3491; http://www.state.ma.us/dem/parks/ccrt.htm).

Nauset Trail *(1.6mi, Salt Pond Visitor Center to Coast Guard Beach)* winds through the forests and marshlands of Cape Cod National Seashore to reach the beach. CCNS Headquarters can provide details about this trail (☎ 508-349-3785; www. nps.gov/caco). Bicycle trail maps are available at visitor centers in Eastham and Provincetown.

Bike Rentals: Holiday Cycles *(465 Grand Ave., Falmouth Heights; ☎ 508-540-3549)* offers free parking for the Shining Sea Bikeway with rental. **Little Capistrano Bike Shop** *(Salt Pond Rd., US-6, Eastham; ☎ 508-255-6515)* rents helmets, car racks and bikes equipped with baby seats as well the usual array of bicycles. This one's close to the Cape Cod Rail Trail.

1888 eventually forced the company to shut its doors permanently.

Sandwich Glass Museum★

129 Main St. ◷ *Open Apr–Dec daily 9:30am–5pm. Feb & Mar Wed–Sun 9:30am–4pm.* ⊙ *$4.75.* ⧆ ℗ ☎ *508-888-0251. www.sandwichglassmuseum.org.*
Located across from the village green, the museum was founded in 1907 and owns an extensive collection of the glass made in Sandwich between 1825 and 1888. Moderately priced when it was produced in the 19C, Sandwich glass is today highly valued by collectors.
Exhibits display a variety of patterns in a wide range of Sandwich glass items, such as candlesticks, tableware, vases, and furniture knobs. Examples of early pressed lacy glass, the colorful (canary, blue, green, opalescent) mid-period pattern glass, and the lesser-recognized blown, cut and engraved glassware are included.

Heritage Museums and Gardens

Heritage Museums and Gardens★

🧒 *67 Grove St. From the Sandwich town hall, turn left onto Grove St.* ◷ *Open April–Oct daily 10am–5pm; Fri-Sun, Nov 1-Dec 31 , 5-9pm Fri & Sun; 5-10pm Sat, for Spectacle of Lights holiday display.* ⊙ *$12.75.* ⧑ ℗ ☎ *508-888-3300. www.heritagemuse-umsandgardens.org.*
This impeccably maintained, 76-acre park setting includes three museums as well as an expansive rhododendron garden. The museum's collections of early-American historical artifacts and folk art are arranged in several buildings designed to harmonize with the landscape. Formerly the estate of horticulturist Charles Dexter, who performed extensive research on rhododendrons in the 1920s and 1930s, the plantation is especially lovely from mid-May through mid-June, when the plants are in bloom.
The **Automobile Museum**, a replica of the Round Stone Barn constructed by the Shakers at Hancock, contains antique automobiles in mint condition dating from 1899 to the 1962.
The Cape Cod Baseball League Hall of Fame and exhibit, antique toys and Native American artifacts are among the intriguing items you'll discover at the **American History Museum**—a re-creation of the Publick House (1783) built by the Continental Army in New Windsor, New York.
A superb collection of folk art fills the **Art Museum**, including primitive portraits, wood carvings, metalwork, glass, scrimshaw, and decoys. 🧒 Children will enjoy riding on the vintage 1906-1912 carousel.
▸ *As you continue east on Rte. 6A toward the town of Barnstable, cranberry bogs, then sand dunes and salt marshes become visible. Beyond the dunes lies* **Sandy Neck***, a 7mi strip of land that protects Barnstable Harbor. At one time, whalers boiled down whale blubber in cauldrons that lined the shores of* **Sandy Neck Beach***, now a popular swimming area. Continue east through the towns of Yarmouth Port and Dennis.*

Yarmouth Port

The beautiful sea captains' homes on Main Street are reminiscent of Yarmouth's era as a busy port. For a close-up look at the home of an 18C trader, tour the c.1780 **Winslow-Crocker House** *(250 Rte. 6A;* ⟿ *visit by 45min guided tour only, Jun–mid-Oct* weekends 11am–5pm; ⬛ $4; ☎ 617-227-3957, ext.256; www.spnea.org).

Dennis

Musicals, dramas and comedies are presented at the **Cape Playhouse**, a well-known summer theater. From **Scargo Hill Tower** (from Rte. 6A, turn right after the cemetery, then left onto Scargo Hill Rd.) there is a **view** that extends from Plymouth to Provincetown.

▶ From Dennis, continue east along Rte. 6A to the town of Brewster.

Brewster★

Extending 8mi along Cape Cod Bay, this charming resort town, first settled in the mid-17 C, has preserved many of the stately residences built by prosperous sea captains in the 19C. The town's eight public beaches (accessible from various points along Main St./Rte. 6A) are noteworthy for the 2mi garnet-tinted flats that are uncovered at low tide.

Sydenstricker Glass Factory (A)

490 Main St. in Brewster. ⏰ Open year-round daily 9am–5pm. ⏰ Closed Jan 1, Thanksgiving Day & Dec 25. 🅿 ☎ 508-385-3272. www.sydenstricker.com.
The late artist Bill Sydenstricker developed an original technique in glassmaking. Two sheets of glass are used to make each item; one of the sheets is decorated, then joined to the second according to the principles used in the enameling process. See examples of this at the gallery, where artisans continue the tradtion (Sydenstricker glass is also on display at the Museum of Modern Art in New York).

Cape Cod Museum of Natural History (B)

Kids 869 Main St. ⏰ Grounds open year-round daily. Museum open daily June–Sept. 9:30am–4:30pm, April-May, Wed-Sun 10am–4pm, Oct-Mar, Wed-Sun, 11am-3pm. ⏰ Closed major holidays. ⬛ $8. 🅿 ☎ 508-896-3867. www.ccmnh.org.
This learning center featuring interactive exhibits on the flora, fauna and geology of the cape appeals to visitors of all ages. Three **nature trails** crisscrossing the museum's 80-acre property allow exploration of typical Cape Cod landscapes, such as salt marshes, cranberry bogs and a pristine beach. Tours of Monomoy Island are conducted by museum naturalists.

Nickerson State Park

On Rte. 6A. ⏰ Open Apr–Sept daily 8am–8pm; Oct–Mar daily dawn–dusk. ⛰ ♿ 🅿 ☎ 508-896-3491. www.mass.gov/dcr/parks.
Picnic grounds, bicycle rentals and a small store are located in the park, the former estate of pioneer railroad-builder Roland Nickerson. Swimming is permitted in Flax Pond, and boat rentals are available.

▶ Follow Rte. 6A east to its end at Orleans.

Orleans

Orleans is the first town on the cape where you will see ocean beaches. **Nauset Beach**, about 10mi long, protects Nauset Harbor, Pleasant Bay, Orleans and Chatham from the violent storms called nor'easters that pound this section of the coast.

Cape Cod National Sea Shore★★★ *Map p 231.*

In 1961 the eastern coast of Cape Cod, with its fragile dunes, cliffs, marshes and woodlands, became a federally protected area: the Cape Cod National Seashore (CCNS). Since that time bicycle trails, nature trails and dune trails for over-sand vehicles (dune buggies, four-wheel-drive vehicles and jeeps) have been created, allowing visitors to enjoy the magnificent landscape. A visitor center is located at each end of the 27,000-acre seashore, and lifeguard services are available at the CCNS beaches: **Coast Guard Beach**, **Nauset Light Beach**, **Marconi Beach**, **Head of the Meadow Beach**, **Race Point Beach** and **Herring Cove Beach** (☜ *$15/day parking fee is charged at all CCNS beaches; seasonal pass is ☜ $45; ☏ 508-349-3781; www.nps.gov/caco).*

Salt Pond Visitor Center★

Kids *On US-6 in Eastham.* 🕐 *Open year-round daily 9am–4:30pm. Extended summer hours.* 🕐 *Closed Dec 25.* ♿🅿 ☏ *508-255-3421. www.nps.gov/caco.*
Rangers dispense information regarding seashore regulations, trails, facilities and programs. A large room contains exhibits on Cape Cod's natural history.

Nauset Marsh Trail
🚶 *1mi. Access near the visitor center.*
Beautiful views of the pond and marshes can be seen from the trail.

Marconi Station
The area was named for **Guglielmo Marconi**, the Italian physicist who established the transatlantic wireless station that operated here between 1901 and 1917. The first formal transmission from this station was a communication between President Theodore Roosevelt and King Edward VII on January 19, 1903. Scattered remnants of the station remain; other sections have been destroyed by shore erosion, which is especially evident along the cliffs and beach here.

Atlantic White Cedar Swamp Trail
🚶 *1.25mi. The trailhead is located at Marconi Station parking lot.*
The trail reveals various aspects of the vegetation on Cape Cod as it leads through the low brush, where beach grasses prevent erosion, then passes into an area of scrub oaks and pitch pines. The trail continues through a white cedar swamp before opening out onto the road that formerly led to the wireless station.

Pilgrim Spring Trail
🚶 *.5mi from the interpretive shelter near the Pilgrim Heights parking lot.*
The trail leads through a section of scrub pines and brush to the site of a spring where the Pilgrims are believed to have first found drinking water in 1620.

Cranberry Bogs

Half of the nation's cranberries come from southeastern Massachusetts and Cape Cod, where natural conditions such as marshy areas and sandy bogs lend themselves to the production of this small red berry. Named by Dutch settlers for the likeness of its flower's stamen to a crane's beak, the cranberry is used to make juice, baked goods and jellies. Widespread cultivation of this fruit was begun in the early 19C, when a local resident, Henry Hall, discovered that the berries thrive best when covered with a layer of sand. Each spring sand was spread over the plants, and the berries were harvested in the fall. The process remains basically unchanged, although it is now mechanized. Festivals are held each fall on the Cape to celebrate the harvest of the cranberry crop from the region's bogs.

Province Lands Visitor Center★
Race Point Rd. outside Provincetown. ⏱ *Open May–Oct daily 9am–5pm.* ♿ 🅿
☎ *508-487-1256. www.nps.gov/caco.*

Sign up for a guided nature walk here. The observation deck atop the building provides a lovely **panorama★** of the dunes. After visiting the center, follow the road to **Race Point Beach**, where a two-mile walk leads to **Race Point Lighthouse**.

Beech Forest Trail
🚶 *1.5mi. Access from Beech Forest parking lot.*
The trail passes through a beech forest threatened at certain spots by the advancing dunes.

Provincetown★★
👣 *See entry heading.*

Along Nantucket Sound *Map below.*

Route 28 runs along the South Shore through Hyannis and Dennis Port, the major shopping centers of the cape. Extremely commercial and tourist-oriented, with its motels, shops and restaurants, this section of the cape also has a number of pretty villages, including Chatham, Harwich and Falmouth.

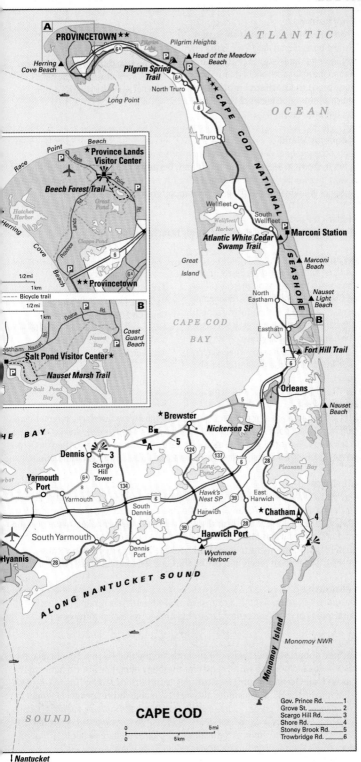

CAPE COD

Gov. Prince Rd. _____ 1
Grove St. _____ 2
Scargo Hill Rd. _____ 3
Shore Rd. _____ 4
Stoney Brook Rd. _____ 5
Trowbridge Rd. _____ 6

Nantucket

Chatham★

Chatham remains an active fishing port. Fishing boats depart daily from **Fish Pier** *(off Shore Rd.)* and return in the late afternoon. One mile south of Chatham, Shore Road leads to **Chatham Lighthouse**, which affords good **views** of both Pleasant Bay and Nauset Beach.

> **TIP**
>
> Visit on Friday nights *(July to Sept)* to take in a free concert at the bandstand of Kate Gould Park.

Monomoy Island

⛵ *Access by boat only.* 🚻 *Ferry & tour information* ☎ *508-945-0594.*

A fierce storm in 1958 created this island. Because of the island's importance as a stopover for birds in the Atlantic Flyway, it has been established as Monomoy National Wildlife Refuge *(🕐 open year-round daily dawn–dusk).*

Harwich Port

Picturesque **Wychmere Harbor** is visible from Route 28.

Hyannis

Situated midway along the South Shore, this town is the major commercial center of the cape. Hyannis is also a maor gateway to Cape Cod, with regularly scheduled airline and island ferry services. The **Cape Cod Melody Tent** *(21 W. Main St.; ☎ 508-775-5630; www.melodytent. com)* features live theater and children's shows.

> **TIP**
>
> For a fun, tasty freebie, tour the **Cape Cod Potato Chip Factory** *(off Breed's Hill Rd; ☎ 508-775-3358; www.capecodchips.com)*; weekdays, 9am-5pm.

Hyannis Port

This fashionable waterfront resort is the site of the Kennedy family's summer compound. *(The compound is not visible from the road, nor is it open to the public.)* The **John F. Kennedy Memorial**, a bronze medallion set in a fieldstone wall, is located on Ocean Street. **Craigville Beach** *(off Rte. 28)* is a pleasant place to swim and sunbathe.

Mashpee

On Rte. 130. Wampanoag Indians were already living on the Cape when the English settlers arrived. In the 17C Rev. Richard Bourne appealed to the Massachusetts legislature to set aside land for the Indians. In response, the lawmakers gave the large tract of land known as Mashpee Plantation to the native residents. In the 19C this parcel of land became the town of Mashpee. The **Old Indian Meeting House**, built in 1684, is the oldest meetinghouse on the Cape *(Meetinghouse Rd., off Rte. 28)*.

Falmouth★

Despite its development as a tourist town, Falmouth has retained a quaint 19C atmosphere in its village center. Lovely old homes stand near the green.

Woods Hole

Located about 2mi southwest of Falmouth, on the tip of a small peninsula, this former whaling port is a world center for the study of marine life. It's home to the **Woods Hole Oceanographic Institution**, the largest independent marine research laboratory in the US. The institute also maintains an **Exhibit Center** *(15 School St.; 🕐 open May-Oct, Mon–Sat 10am–4:30pm, Nov-Dec, Tues-Fri 10am–4:30pm; 🕐 open Apr by appointment; 🕐 closed Jan–Mar; ⛵ $2 contribution suggested; ♿ ☎ 508-289-2252; www.whoi.edu)*. Tours of the institute are offered in July and August *(⛵ 1hr; Mon–Fri 10:30am & 1:30pm; reservations required; see above)*.

PIE IN THE SKY BAKERY

10 Water St., Woods Hole, MA; next to the post office. ⏱ *Open for breakfast and lunch.* ☎ *508-540-5475.* Woods Hole residents are up and about early, between the marine center's activity and the constant arrival and departure of Martha's Vineyard ferries at the Steamship Authority. So buy a newspaper and head for this pleasant bakery/cafe for coffee and breakfast fare. Espresso, cappuccino, fresh-made muffins and pastries are served from 7am *(Sun 8am)*. Both outdoor and indoor seating are available.

The **Woods Hole Science Aquarium**, used by the National Marine Fisheries Service in its research, offers touch tanks full of sea reatures native to the Cape *(166 Water St., at Albatross St.;* ⏱ *open mid-June-Labor Day, Tue-Sat 11am–4pm, rest of the year Mon–Fri 11am–4pm;* ☎ *508-495-2001).*

Cruises – *Boats to Martha's Vineyard depart from the Steamship Authority Pier in Woods Hole.* ♿ *See entry heading Martha's Vineyard.*

Cape Cod Canal *Map p 230.*

Dug between 1909 and 1914, Cape Cod Canal separates Cape Cod from the rest of Massachusetts. The **Sagamore** and **Bourne bridges** (for vehicles) and a railroad bridge that resembles London's Tower Bridge links the Cape to the mainland.

Aptucxet Trading Post Museum (E)

24 Aptucxet Rd, Bourne. ⏱ *Open Memorial Day to Columbus Day, Tue–Sat 10am–4pm, Sun 2pm–5pm.* ⊗ *$4.* ♿🅿 ☎ *508-759-8167.*

The Pilgrims established this trading post in 1627 to promote trade with both the Dutch from New Amsterdam and the Wampanoag Indians. Furs, sugar, tobacco and cloth were bought and sold here, using wampum (beads cut and polished by the Indians from shells and used as currency).

The present building was reconstructed in 1930 on the foundations of the former trading post. Inside there are examples of the goods bartered. An ancient rune stone found in Bourne bears an inscription translated as: "God Gives Us Light Abundantly." A saltworks, similar to those used by early cape settlers to evaporate salt from sea-water, has been built near the canal.

CONCORD AND LEXINGTON★★

POPULATION: CONCORD 16,993; LEXINGTON 30,355
MICHELIN MAP 581 M 8 AND MAPS P 235 AND P 237
TOURIST INFORMATION ☎ 978-459-6150 OR WWW.MERRIMACKVALLEY.ORG

The thriving residential community of Lexington has been historically insepa-rable in the minds of most Americans from the small town of Concord since April 19, 1775, when British and colonial troops clashed at Lexington and at Concord, triggering the events that exploded into the American Revolution. The Revolutionary War sites and monuments preserved here allow visitors to retrace, step by step, the incidents that occurred on that day, over 200 years ago, when the British marched from Boston to Lexington and on to Concord.

Named in the 17C for the "concord" of peace established between the Indians and the settlers, the refined colonial town of Concord boasts a distinguished literary past, having been the home, in the 19C, of intellectuals and writers such as Ralph Waldo Emerson, Nathaniel Hawthorne, Henry David Thoreau and Bronson Alcott.

▶ **Orient Yourself:** Concord and Lexington are actually two neighboring towns. Many of the attractions you'll want to visit are located along Route 2A.

🅿 **Parking:** Most attractions offer on-site parking. Lexington has a big public parking lot off Mass. Ave.

🅰 **Don't Miss:** The terrific 25min multi-media show, "The Road to Revolution" at Minute Man National Historic Park, followed by a walk to Hartwell Tavern.

🅺 **Especially for Kids:** The Minuteman Bike Path is a fun way to travel through Lexington (the 10.5mi paved, multi-use trail runs from Cambridge to Bedford).

🅰 **Also See:** Drumlin Farm, in South Lincoln, is a great place for city folk to explore life on a New England farm; see kitchen gardens, livestock, and demonstrations.

A Bit of History

The Revolt Begins – Forewarned of the British soldiers' approach by Paul Revere and his riders, 77 minutemen who had spent the night of April 18 at **Buckman Tavern** in Lexington awaiting the enemy moved toward the **green** where their leader, Captain Parker, advised them: "Stand your ground and don't fire unless fired upon, but if they mean to have a war, let it begin here!" At about five o'clock in the morning, the British began to arrive, and Parker, realizing that his men were greatly outnumbered, gave the order to disperse. He was too late; a shot rang out, and during the skirmish that followed, eight minutemen were killed and ten others wounded. The British commander ordered his men to regroup and march on to Concord.

In Concord, the **minutemen**—untrained, poorly equipped farmers, so-called because of their readiness to take up arms to fight the British at a minute's notice—who had arrived from nearby villages observed from a hilltop as British soldiers began to search for the supplies. Aware that fires were burning in the town below, and fearful that the British would raze Concord, the patriots descended to the **Old North Bridge**, where they found themselves confronted by the enemy. There, a battle ensued until the British, weary and reduced in numbers, began their retreat to Boston along Battle Road. Snipers firing from the woods added to the day's British casualties; before nightfall another skirmish between the two forces took place at **Meriam's Corner**.

Old North Bridge

Greater Boston CVB/ FAYFOTO, Inc.

Concord ★★ *Map below.*

Tourist Information: ☎ *978-369-3120 www.concordchamber.org.*

Minute Man National Historical Park★

Visitor center located off Rte. 2A in Lexington (see Lexington heading). ☎ *978-369-6993. www.nps.gov/mima.*

This park was established to commemorate events that took place April 19, 1775 along Battle Road *(Rte. 2A between Lexington and Concord)* and in Lexington, Lincoln and Concord. The 1,000-acre park is essentially a contiguous strip of land 4mi long, stretching over the three townships, with additional sections in Concord. A 5.5mi interpretive trail running alongside Battle Road describes the patriots' guerrilla-style attacks on British troops retreating to Bunker Hill.

North Bridge Unit★★

A replica of the **Old North Bridge** marks the place where colonial farmers advanced on the British and fired the "shot heard 'round the world." Emerson immortalized the old "rude bridge" in his poem *Concord Hymn. (Brief interpretive talks are held at the North Bridge Apr–Oct, weather permitting).* Nearby, Daniel Chester French's famous statue of the **Minute Man (1)** honors the patriots who resisted the British at Concord. The **North Bridge Vistor Center** has exhibits detailing the battle and provides information regarding ranger talks and other special programs *(up the road from the North Bridge;* ◷ *open mid-Apr–Oct daily 9am–5pm; rest of the year daily 9am–4pm;* ◷ *closed Jan 1 & Dec 25;* ☎ *978-369-6993; www.nps.gov/mima).*

As you leave, note on the right the **Old Manse,** where Ralph Waldo Emerson, and later Nathaniel Hawthorne, lived *(269 Monument St.; visit by 45min guided tour only, mid-Apr–Oct Mon–Sat 10am–5pm, Sun noon–5pm; $8;* ☎ *978-369-3909; www.thetrustees.org).*

Concord Museum★

200 Lexington Rd. ◷ *Open Apr–Dec Mon–Sat 9am–5pm, Sun noon–5pm. Rest of the year Mon–Sat 11am–4pm, Sun 1pm–4pm.* ◷ *Closed major holidays. $8.* ☎ *978-369-9609. www.concordmuseum.org.*

Arranged in 19 galleries, many of which feature authentic period pieces, this extensive collection of artifacts, documents and period rooms provides visitors with an excellent survey of Concord's rich history. Opened in 1997, the six-gallery exhibit **Why Concord?** traces the growth of the town from prehistoric times to the 20C and includes the interior of **Emerson's study** and the renowned **Thoreau gallery**. One of the lanterns hung in the steeple of Old North Church to signal Paul Revere on April 18, 1775; a diorama of the battle at Old North Bridge; and objects used by Thoreau at Walden Pond are also on display. Upstairs, more than 1,500 objects illustrate trends in **American decorative arts** from the 17C to the 19C. Cummings E. Davis, a Concord merchant, amassed the collection in the mid-19C, mostly from local sources.

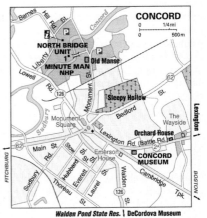

Walden Pond State Res. | DeCordova Museum

Orchard House

399 Lexington Rd. ✎ Visit by guided tour (45min) only, Apr–Oct Mon–Sat 10am–4:30pm, Sun 1pm–4:30pm. Rest of the year Mon–Fri 11am–3pm, Sat 10am–4:30pm, Sun 1pm–4:30pm. ⊘ Closed Jan 1–15 & major holidays. ☜ $8. ℗ ☎ 978-369-4118. www.louisamayalcott.org.

Orchard House was the home of the Alcott family from 1858 to 1877, the period during which Louisa May Alcott wrote her autobiographical novel *Little Women* (1868).

Walden Pond State Reservation★

1.5mi south of Concord center on Rte. 126 (Walden St.). ☜ $5 parking fee.

Henry David Thoreau built his cabin on the shore of this lake. To reach the cabin site (marked by a cairn), follow the trail signs to a granite post, where the trail turns right *(15 min)*. There's also a replica of the (amazingly small) cabin near the parking lot. Walden Pond is a busy swimming hole in summertime; in winter, there's ice fishing, as well as cross-country skiing and snowshoeing on trails that circle the pond.

Sleepy Hollow Cemetery

Bedford St. at Partridge Lane. From Concord center turn right onto Rte. 62. Enter the cemetery through the second gate on the left and follow signs for Author's Ridge. ⊙ Open year-round daily 7am–dusk. ℗

A short climb from the parking lot leads to **Author's Ridge**, where the Alcotts, Hawthorne, Emerson, Thoreau, Margaret Sydney and others are buried.

Excursion

DeCordova Museum and Sculpture Park★★

51 Sandy Pond Rd., Lincoln. ⊙ Sculpture park open year-round daily 6am–10pm. Museum open year-round Tue–Sun 11am–5pm. ⊙ Closed major holidays. ☜ $9 (museum). ✗ ♿ ℗ ☎ 781-259-8355. www.decordova.org.

Opened in 1950 on a lush lakeside estate bequeathed by Bostonian Julian de Cordova, this museum is a showcase for contemporary art by Americans, with particular emphasis on New England artists. The 35-acre sculpture park provides a sylvan setting for a rotation of 75 monumental works, made from everything from tree bark to anodized steel by nationally and internationally acclaimed artists. A new wing, added to the original mansion-museum in 1998, doubled gallery space and now hosts 18 temporary group and individual exhibits per year, along with selections

---

SALLY ANN FOOD SHOP

73 Main St., Concord. ☎ *978-369-4558.* To revive your flagging spirits while touring Concord's sights, stop into this inviting bakery for a quick pick-me-up. The kids will go for the peanut butter cookies (particularly the ones topped with a chocolate kiss), while Mom and Dad might prefer a pecan-studded sticky bun, a sweetly wholesome muffin, or a chocolate chocolate-chip cookie. Drinks and sandwiches are also available. *Takeout only.*

Freemasonry

Reputedly the world's largest and oldest global fraternal order, Freemasonry had its origins in the stonemason guilds of the late Middle Ages. Its official founding, however, was in England in 1717. Established in the American colonies in the late 1720s, it was embraced by prominent leaders of the Revolutionary period. George Washington is perhaps the best-known member of this society. In fact, 14 US presidents have been Masons. Though Freemasonry is not a secret society, as is often believed, it does maintain secrecy concerning its ritual practices, which include the symbolic use of architectural concepts and implements to recall stonemasonry.

Transcendentalism

Ralph Waldo Emerson (1803-82), a native of Concord, popularized transcendentalism (a philosophical movement characterized by the belief that God exists in both man and nature) and expressed his philosophical ideas in his *Essays on Nature,* a series of lectures he delivered across the US. Other writers and thinkers, attracted by the liberal ideas and the return-to-nature philosophy inherent in transcendentalism, came to Concord to live near Emerson. Among them was **Henry David Thoreau** (1817-62), who built a cabin in the woods near Walden Pond, where he lived from 1845 to 1847. Thoreau's book *Walden* recounts the author's personal experiences during this period.

Nathaniel Hawthorne, Margaret Fuller and others founded Brook Farm, an experimental community near West Roxbury that they envisioned as a retreat from Victorian society and a return to a simple life. **Amos Bronson Alcott**, a proponent of transcendentalism, established his School of Philosophy adjacent to Orchard House, where his daughter **Louisa May Alcott** penned an account of her childhood in *Little Women.*

from the museum's 2,000-piece permanent collection. The **Art ExperienCenter** is an interactive display that explains the theory and creation of abstract art.

Lexington★★

7.5mi east of Concord on Rte. 2A. Map below. 🚏 *Tourist information:* ☎ *781-862-2480. www.lexingtonchamber.org.*

Minute Man Visitor Center★

Off Rte. 2A in Lexington. ◐ *Open mid-Apr–Oct daily 9am–5pm. Rest of the year daily 9am–4pm.* ◐ *Closed Jan 1 & Dec 25.* ♿ ⓟ ☎ *978-369-6993. www.nps.gov/mima.* Exhibits and a state-of-the-art multimedia presentation entitled *The Road to Revolution (25min)* introduce visitors to the events of April 19, 1775, which occurred in the surrounding area.

Lexington Green★★

The first confrontation between the British soldiers and the minutemen on April 19 took place in this triangular park. Henry Kitson's statue **The Minuteman (1)** represents the leader of the Lexington militia, Captain Parker. Seven of the colonists killed here that day are buried beneath the **Revolutionary Monument (2)**.

Buckman Tavern★

1 Bedford St. 🚶 *Visit by guided tour (30min) only, mid-Mar–Nov Mon–Sat 10am–4pm, Sun 1pm–4pm.* ◐ *Open 1hr later in summer.* ⓢ *$5. Combination ticket*

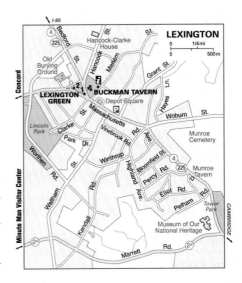

(✉ *$12) available for Buckman Tavern, Hancock-Clarke House & Munroe Tavern.*
☎ *781-862-5598. www.lexingtonhistory.org.*

The minutemen gathered here on the evening of April 18 to await the arrival of the British troops. Following the battle between the British and the militia on the green, the minutemen who had been wounded were carried to Buckman Tavern, where they were given medical care. Restored to its original 18C appearance, the tavern comprises a bar, bedchambers, a ballroom, separate rooms set aside for women, and an attic where, for a few pennies a night, drovers were permitted to sleep.

DEERFIELD ★★

POPULATION 4,750
MICHELIN MAP 581 J 8
TOURIST INFORMATION ☎ 413-665-7333 OR WWW.MASSVACATION.COM

Locally known as "The Street," Deerfield's mile-long main thoroughfare with its limited number of business establishments and many 18C and 19C dwellings, embodies a wealthy early-American farming community. The richness of the surrounding farmlands, threaded by the Deerfield River and nestled below the Pocumtuck Ridge, makes Deerfield's site one of the loveliest in the state. Today the village is known for Historic Deerfield, a collection of restored Colonial and Federal structures open to the public as a museum.

▶ **Orient Yourself:** Check out the day's activity schedule at Hall Tavern Information Center.

🚫 **Don't Miss:** Historic Deerfield's stunning house museums, and a visit to the Yankee Candle Company (*Route 5, S. Deefield.*)

🕐 **Organizing Your Time:** Don't try to see Historic Deerfield in one day; 3-4 houses will likely be more than enough at once! Admission tickets are good for 7 consecutive days.

🧒 **Especially for Kids:** Channing Blake Trail is a child-friendly half-mile meadow walk within the Historic Deerfield property.

A Bit of History

Deerfield was not always the tranquil town it appears to be today. Incorporated in 1673, Deerfield was abandoned two years later after Indians massacred 64 men at Bloody Brook in 1675, and again in 1704 when the village was burned down in a French and Indian attack during Queen Anne's War. A peace treaty signed in 1735 encouraged settlers to return, and during the following century the village grew into one of New England's most prosperous agricultural centers. As a result, many fine houses were built, particularly in the 1740s and 50s. The painstaking process of the renovation and redecoration of Deerfield's large Colonial and Federal structures began in 1848, the first project of its kind in the US. Of some 55 buildings in Deerfield that pre-date 1825, only two have been moved to the village from other Massachusetts locations.

Today the **Brick Church** (1824) and several buildings of **Deerfield Academy**, a prestigious prep school founded in 1797, stand on the grassy **common** near the post office, which is a replica of a Puritan meetinghouse. A little farther down the street is the well-appointed 1884 **Deerfield Inn**, a popular lodging and dining spot for residents and out-of-towners. Private residences are interwoven with the museum buildings along The Street and side roads.

Historic Deerfield★★

Of the more than 60 18C and 19C buildings in Deerfield, a total of 13 structures dating from c.1730 to 1850 are open to the public as house museums today. Many of the dwellings, all on their original sites, are topped with gambrel roofs and adorned with richly carved doorways characteristic of the Connecticut Valley style. The interiors are equally luxurious and elegant. More than 18,000 objects dating from 1600 to 1900 are on display.

Visit

Old Main St. ◷ *Open Apr–Dec daily 9:30am–4:30pm.* ◷ *Closed Thanksgiving Day, Dec 24 & 25.* ◠ *$14.* ✕ ♿ 🅿 ☎ *413-774-5581. www.historic-deerfield.org.*
ⓘ *Wear comfortable shoes, since buildings are some distance apart. Highlights of the museum are described below.*

Ashley House

Typical of the dwellings that were built in the Connecticut Valley in the 18C, Ashley House (1730) contains richly carved woodwork and beautiful furnishings. The house was home to Parson Jonathan Ashley, a devoted Tory who, despite threats from the townspeople to bar him from the meetinghouse, persisted in his loyalty to the Crown during the Revolution.

Asa Stebbins House

The Stebbins House (1810), with its distinctive arched doorway, was the first Deerfield residence to have a dining room. A splendid collection of wall coverings, including 19C French wallpaper illustrating Captain Cook's voyages to the South Seas, decorates the interior.

Frary House/Barnard Tavern

This late-18C dwelling was later enlarged to serve as a tavern. Inside is a ballroom with a fiddlers' gallery, and rooms filled with country antiques, pewter and ceramics.

Dwight House

A handsomely carved doorway ornaments the facade of this 1725 dwelling; this feature was typical of Connecticut Valley architecture.

Memorial Hall

This brick building houses the museum of the **Pocumtuck Valley Memorial Association**, a memorial to the Pocumtuck Indians and to the settlers of Deerfield. Exhibits are displayed over three floors and include a large assortment of quilts, household items, furniture, portraits, costumes, military memorabilia and period rooms.

DEERFIELD DINING

For traditional New England fare in a formal setting, the **Deerfield Inn** *(81 Old Main St.;* ☎ *413-774-5587; www.deerfieldinn.com)* will not disappoint. The spacious dining room reflects the charm of the Colonial décor found throughout the inn. The seasonal menu may include New England clam chowder, potato-crusted sea bass, steak au poivre or blackened red snapper. For dessert, try the Indian pudding served à la mode. In the village center of South Deerfield, the ground floor of an old house is the modern setting for **Sienna** *(6-B Elm St.; dinner only Wed–Mon* ☎ *413-665-0215; www.siennarestaurant.com)*. The ever-changing menu incorporates inspired pairings such as duck breast with roated shallot bread pudding, venison loin with smoked bacon-potato croquettes, and wild Alaskan salmon in a calamata tapenade.

FALL RIVER

POPULATION 91,938
MICHELIN MAP 581 M 10
TOURIST INFORMATION ☎ 508-997-1250 OR WWW.BRISTOL-COUNTY.ORG

The site of the famous 1892 trial of Lizzie Borden, who was accused of murdering her parents with an ax (she was ultimately acquitted), Fall River was a major textile center in the 19C and early 20C.

During the same period, luxuriant steamships of the Fall River Line linked New York to Boston and carried the wealthy to their summer cottages in Newport. The city was hard hit by the Great Depression, then by the migration of the textile mills to the South and the development of synthetic fibers. Despite these setbacks, the city's textile industry survived. Textiles and clothing are still produced here, and many of the old mill buildings have found new life as factory outlets. In the mid-1960s the state's slain World War II service personnel were commemorated at Fall River's waterfront, initiating what is now a naval museum.

▶ **Orient Yourself:** Fall River is 50mi southwest of Boston.
◉ **Don't Miss:** Battleship Cove is the top attraction here; if you're interested the the Lizzie Borden story, check out the Lizzie Borden Museum at 92 Second St. (also a B&B).
◷ **Organizing Your Time:** A driving tour from New Bedford (◖ *see entry heading*) to Fall River, along I-195, is a good way to see the sights. Or see the sample tour of Fall River at www.fallriverma.org/tourism.
▥ **Especially for Kids:** The Carousel at Battleship Cove is a delight for small fry (and nostalgic grownups).
◖ **Also See:** Horseneck Beach in Westport is a lovely 3mi stretch of sand, with oceanfront camping.

Battleship Cove★

In 1965 the battleship USS *Massachusetts* was moored at Fall River to serve as a permanent memorial to the 13,000 Massachusetts men and women who gave their lives in service to their country during World War II. In recent decades, several other naval ships have joined the *Massachusetts* as exhibits at this outdoor naval museum.

Lizzie Borden took an ax...

www.lizzie-borden.com. No doubt there are people in Fall River who'd rather forget their most infamous resident, **Lizzie Borden**. Lee-ann Wilber and Donald Wood are not among them! Wilber and Wood are proprietors of the **Lizzie Borden Bed and Breakfast and Museum** *(92 Second St.)*, a Greek Revival home with 7 guest rooms, where guests can sleep in the rooms where the murders were committed—the Andrew and Abbey Borden suite, where Lizzie's wealthy father was killed, and the John Morse room, where Lizzie's stepmother met her death. Guests are served a breakfast similar to the one the Borden's might have enjoyed, including jonny-cakes.

Visit

Kids *On Davol St. along the waterfront.* 🕐 *Open Apr–Jun 9am–5pm. Jul–Labor Day daily 9am–5:30pm. Rest of Sept–Mar 9am–4:30pm.* 🕐 *Closed Jan 1, Thanksgiving Day & Dec 25.* 🎟 *$12.* 🍴 ☎ *508-678-1100. www.battleshipcove.com.*

Berthed on the waterfront next to State Pier, five vessels are permanently preserved and open to the public as a means of exploring naval history.

Warships

Developed in Europe, small, fast PT (Patrol, Torpedo) boats first served the US Navy in World War II. Destroyers, among the fastest ships in the navy, were originally designed to protect the fleet's battleships from enemy torpedo boats. Because of their tactical flexibility, destroyers are now used offensively as well as defensively.

PT Boat 796
The ferocious shark painted on the hull symbolizes the threat these modest-sized boats posed to the enemy. PT boat memorabilia is displayed.

Submarine Lionfish
This World War II submarine carried 20 torpedoes and an 80-member crew. The vessel's sophisticated operating equipment, once considered classified, can be seen in the control room.

Destroyer USS Joseph P. Kennedy
The ship was named for Joseph, the eldest of the four Kennedy brothers, who was killed on a volunteer mission in World War II. A typical World War II destroyer, the Kennedy carried a crew of 275.

Battleship USS Massachusetts★
Remarkable for its enormous size (longer than two football fields) and the large crew required for operation (2,300 men), the 46,000 ton *Massachusetts* logged 225,000 mi in wartime service between 1942 and 1945 and was the first and last US battleship to fire 16-inch shells against the enemy.

LOWELL

POPULATION 105,167
MICHELIN MAP 581 M 7
TOURIST INFORMATION ☎ 978-459-6150 OR WWW.MERRIMACKVALLEY.ORG

One of the state's largest cities, Lowell originated as the earliest planned industrial city in the country. Proximity to the Merrimack River was a key factor in its development as a leading 19C producer of textiles. Lowell is also the birthplace of three famous personalities in the arts: painter James Abbott McNeill Whistler (birthplace/museum at 243 Worthen St., one block from the visitor center), writer Jack Kerouac and screen star Bette Davis.

▶ **Orient Yourself:** The city of Lowell is about 30 min northwest of Boston.
🚶 **Don't Miss:** A ride on a restored vintage trolley around downtown Lowell and the historical park.
🕐 **Organizing Your Time:** Plan your visit around the time of your canal tour *(must be reserved in advance).*
Kids **Especially for Kids:** The University of Massachusetts/Lowell campus offers six Sundays of family fun with its Discovery Series of performances. You might see

juggling, African dance, puppetry or Chinese acrobats (☎ 978-934-4444; www.
uml.edu/centerforarts/discovery).

⚓ **Also See:** Harold Parker State Forest, in nearby N Andover, is a great, woodsy
escape from the city, with swimming holes, hiking and camping.

A Bit of History

First Mill Town – Incorporated as a town in 1826, Lowell quickly rose to prominence
as the nation's largest cotton textile producer. Initially the city's labor force consisted
of young Yankee women from the farms of New England, but by the mid-19C, the so-
called "mill girls" were replaced by Irish and French-Canadian immigrants willing to
accept lower wages. Successive waves of newcomers from other European countries
followed. The early chapters of America's labor history unfolded in the mills of Lowell,
where strikes and social unrest periodically disrupted production. A number of fac-
tors, including increased competition from Southern mills, and the development of
steam as an alternative energy source, contributed to the city's decline in the late
19C. The economic crash of 1929 sounded the death knell for Lowell.

Diversification, and an influx of new industry, helped to turn Lowell's economy
around. To preserve the city's unique industrial heritage, local and state bodies, in
collaboration with the federal government, restored many of Lowell's 19C buildings
and its canal system. This successful restoration project has served as a model for
similar sights around the US, and has helped Lowell build a base for tourism.

Sights

Lowell National Historical Park★★

*246 Market St. Begin your visit at the visitor center at Market Mills to obtain a free map
and daily schedule of tours and to reserve a canal tour.* 🕐 *Visitor center open daily
July 1-Labor Day, 9am–5:30 pm. Rest of the year Mon–Sat 9am–5pm, Sun 10am–*

5pm. 🕐 *Closed Jan 1, Thanksgiving Day
& Dec 25.* 🍴♿🅿 ☎ *978-970-5000. www.
nps.gov/lowe.*
Established in 1978, the park comprises a
group of buildings, canals and walkways
scattered throughout Lowell's downtown
district. The park **visitor center**, located
in a renovated mill complex, offers an
introduction to Lowell's history through
an award-winning 20min video entitled
Lowell: The Industrial Revolution. Restored
vintage **trolleys** *(free)* run continuously

©National Park Service

Lowell National Historical Park

Urban Adventure:
Whitewater-Rafting in Lowell

Whitewater rafting, in the city? Only in Lowell. The same roiling rapids that
brought the textile industry to the city are sought out by fun seekers in April and
May, when dam releases create Class III and IV whitewater. A one-mile stretch of
the Concord River goes through the heart of the city; trips include being lifted 17ft
through an 1850 lock chamber. The three sets of rapids include "Twisted Sister,"
"Three Beauties" and "Middlesex Dam[n]." Trips are run on Sat and Sun in season,
led by rafting guides from Zoar Outdoors. Call ☎ 888-375-1115 or visit www.low-
elllandtrust.org for more information.

Outdoor Escapes

Whitewater rafting a bit too adventurous for your taste? Here are some tamer options:

Harold Parker State Forest, in North Andover, offers 3,500 acres of wilderness, within a forest dotted with nine ponds. ☎ 978-686-3391; www.massparks.org.

Bradford Ski Area, in Haverhill, is a favorite small ski area for local familles (night skiing and lessons, too); ☎ 978-373-0071; www.SkiBradford.com.

Stevens-Coolidge Place, in North Andover, is an historic house museum set on 95 acres. ☎ 978-682-3580; www.thetrustees.org.

Weir Hill, also in North Andover, offers pretty, easy-going hiking, cross-country skiing or snowshoeing along Lake Cochichewick. ☎ 978-682-3580; www.thetrustees.org.

around the downtown area and allow visitors to tour the attractions at their leisure.

Canal tours explore the remarkable man-made water network that channeled the waters of the Pawtucket Falls to the mill turbines (*🚌 depart from the visitor center daily late Jun–Labor Day; 🎫 $8-10; reservations required; ☎ 978-970-5000*).

Boott Cotton Mills Museum★★

🕐 *Open Nov–Feb Mon-Sat 9:30am–4:30pm, Sun 11am–4:30pm. Rest of the year daily 9:30am–5pm.* 🎫 *$6.* ♿.

Wedged between the Eastern Canal and the Merrimack River, this imposing industrial complex (1873) graced by a central bell tower houses the park's main exhibit. The first floor **weave room**, equipped with 88 operating power looms *(earplugs provided at entrance)*, re-creates the jarring atmosphere of a 1920s textile mill. The second floor features a series of exhibits focused on America's Industrial Revolution, Lowell's history, textile production and technology and labor relations, including a riveting labor-oriented film *(25min)* entitled *Wheels of Change: The First Century of American Industry*. Recorded oral histories of former mill workers provide poignant testimony to the grim realities of mill life.

Additional Sights

Fronting the long facade of the Massachusetts Mills, Eastern Canal Park contains an elegant group of marble monoliths inscribed with quotations from the works of native son and Beat Generation writer **Jack Kerouac** (1922-69). *A handout locating sights associated with Kerouac is available at the visitor center.*

American Textile History Museum★

491 Dutton St. 🕐 *Open year-round Tue–Fri 9am–4pm, weekends 10am–5pm.* 🕐 *Closed Jan 1, Thanksgiving Day & Dec 25.* 🎫 *$8.* ♿🅿 ☎ *978-441-0400. www.athm.org.*

Housed in a renovated 160,000sq ft brick warehouse, this engaging museum covers 300 years of American textile history. Exhibits proceed chronologically through early fabrics, spinning wheels, hand looms and dyes to the 20C weave shed, where visitors can see and hear cloth being made. Re-created interiors include as an 18C weaver's log cabin, 1820s general store and 1870s woolen mill.

New England Quilt Museum

18 Shattuck St. 🕐 *Open Tue–Sat 10am–4pm, Sun noon–4pm.* 🕐 *Closed major holidays.* 🎫 *$5.* ♿ ☎ *978-452-4207. www.nequiltmuseum.org.*

This two-level, sunlit gallery showcases traditional and contemporary quilts—some hung like paintings, some thrown over beds—on a rotating basis.

MARBLEHEAD ★

POPULATION 20,377
MICHELIN MAP 581 N 7 AND MAP P XXX
TOURIST INFORMATION ☎ 781-631-2868 OR WWW.VISITMARBLEHEAD.COM

Marblehead owes its prosperity as a resort and boating center to its magnificent harbor; this community continues to be one of the East Coast's major yachting capitals.

Prior to the Revolution, this small fishing port was a flourishing trade center. Marblehead vessels returned home with great wealth, and their owners and captains spent freely in building the Colonial and Georgian homes that line the narrow, winding streets of Old Town. Losses suffered during the war, competition from other ports, and the gale of 1846, which destroyed 10 Marblehead ships and killed 65 men, caused the inhabitants to turn to other industries to earn their living.

The sea again became the source of prosperity for Marblehead when, in the late 19C and early 20C, the town developed into a resort, with boating as a major attraction. The sailboats and motor yachts that crowd the harbor in season are especially impressive when viewed from **Fort Sewall** (at the end of Front St.), **Crocker Park** (off Front St.) or the lighthouse on **Marblehead Neck**. Meticulously preserved 18C and 19C structures along **Atlantic Avenue** ★ and surrounding side streets are crammed with both tony shops and laid-back bars and coffeehouses.

- ▶ **Orient Yourself:** Geographically, Marblehead is a prominent outcropping of land (the "head") between Boston and Gloucester. So connected is it with the ocean, the chamber of commerce Web site gives directions to M'head by sea.
- 🅿 **Parking:** Most parking is streetside in Marblehead.
- 🚫 **Don't Miss:** A walk to Fort Sewall, at the end of Front Street.
- 🕐 **Organizing Your Time:** After admiring the massive canvas, The Spirit of '76, in Abbott Hall (Washington St., Town Hall), wander along Marblehead's narrow streets, toward the water.
- 📷 **Especially for Kids:** A visit to Devereux Beach (go early or late) and a bite to eat at Flynnies at the Beach.

Sights

Jeremiah Lee Mansion ★

170 Washington St. 🚶 Visit by guided tour (50min) only, Jun–Oct Tue-Sat 10am–4pm. 💰 $5. ☎ 781-631-1768.

The wood blocks composing the exterior of this dignified 16-room Georgian dwelling, built in 1768 for the successful merchant Col. Jeremiah Lee, have been refinished with a mixture of paint and sand to resemble stone.

Inside, the immense **entrance hall**, with its grandiose proportions, highly polished mahogany woodwork and English mural wallpapers, makes this house one of the most memorable of the period in New England. Reproductions of two full-length portraits of the Lees by John Singleton Copley are hung in the hall. In several rooms, wallpaper hand-painted in the style of the 18C Italian artist Giovanni Pannini depicts classical ruins and fishing scenes. The house contains 18C and 19C furniture, silver, ceramics and textiles.

Across the street, the **Frost Folk Art Gallery** (no. 170) displays sculpture and a group of brightly colored primitive seascapes by self-taught Marblehead artist John Frost, formerly a Grand Banks fisherman (🕐 open Jun–Oct Tue-Sat 10am–4pm; Nov–May Tue-Fri 10am-4pm).

Abbot Hall

188 Washington St., in the Town Hall. ◷ *Open Jun–Sept Mon–Fri 8am–5pm (Wed til 7:30pm), weekends 11am–5pm. Rest of the year Mon–Thu 8am–5pm (Wed til 7:30pm), Fri 8am–1pm.* ◷ *Closed major holidays.* ♿ ☎ *781-631-0000. www.marblehead.org.*
The familiar patriotic canvas **The Spirit of '76**, painted by A.M. Willard to celebrate the nation's centennial, hangs in the Selectman's Room. The picture was given to the town by Gen. John Devereux, whose son was the model for the drummer boy in the painting.

MARTHA'S VINEYARD ★★

POPULATION 15,010
MICHELIN MAP 581 N, O 10, 11 AND MAP BELOW
TOURIST INFORMATION ☎ 508-693-0085 OR WWW.MVY.COM

This triangular-shaped island, 6mi south of Cape Cod, is blessed with a stunning landscape. Here, rolling heaths spotted with ponds and lakes give way to forests of oak and pine, seaside cliffs and broad beaches (both pebble and sand). The towns on the Vineyard are small fishing villages and summer resorts, each with its own history and character.

When Bartholomew Gosnold landed on this island in 1602, he found an abundance of wild grapes growing here. He thus named this land Martha's Vineyard, in honor of his daughter Martha. Today, however, wild grapes no longer cover the island.
As with the Cape and Nantucket, the population of Martha's Vineyard skyrockets in the summer, bringing a mix of day-trippers and wealthy second-home owners and making off-season visits particularly appealing.

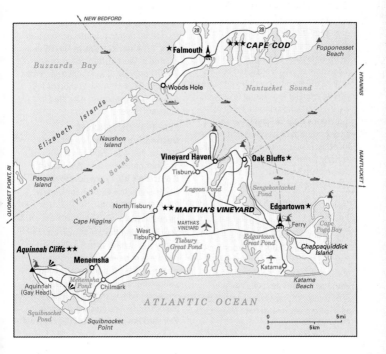

Address Book

PRACTICAL INFORMATION

GETTING THERE

Ferries for Martha's Vineyard depart from New Bedford, Falmouth, Woods Hole, Hyannis and Nantucket, MA, as well as from New London, CT and Montauk, Long Island. From **Boston** to **Woods Hole** (85mi), take Rte. 3 South to the Sagamore Bridge; then take US-6 West to Buzzards Bay, cross the Bourne Bridge and follow Rte. 28 South. From **New York City** to **Woods Hole** (271mi), take I-95 North to I-195 East to Rte. 25 East; cross the Bourne Bridge and follow Rte. 28 South. From **Providence** to **Woods Hole** (83mi), take I-195 South to Rte. 25 East across the Bourne Bridge, and follow Rte. 28 South.

International and domestic flights service **Logan International Airport** (BOS) in Boston (☎ 617-561-1800 or 800-235-6426; www.massport.com). Year-round service from Boston, Hyannis, Nantucket, New Bedford and Providence is provided by **Cape Air** (☎ 800-352-0714; www.flycapeair.com).

Bonanza Bus Lines offers **bus** service year-round daily from Boston to Woods Hole (☎ 888-751-8800; www.bonanzabus.com); Peter Pan Bus Lines (☎ 800-237-8747; www.peterpanbus.com) provides service from Boston to the ferry terminals on Cape Cod.

Ferry Service – Several ferry companies, three of which are listed below, service the island. Schedules and fares vary seasonally. In summer reservations are highly recommended. Ferries leaving Woods Hole sail daily year-round and carry both passengers and vehicles. All other ferries carry passengers only and run from spring through fall. The **Steamship Authority** (☎ 508-477-8600; www.islandferry.com) is the only company offering transportation daily year-round for cars, trucks (reservations required), passengers and bikes; departures from Woods Hole to Vineyard Haven and Oak Bluffs, and from New Bedford to Oak Bluffs (service to Oak Bluffs mid-May–Sept only). **Hy-Line Cruises** (☎ 508-778-2600 or 800-492-8082; www.hy-linecruises.com) offers seasonal service (May–Oct)

departing from Hyannis to Oak Bluffs and from Nantucket to Oak Bluffs. **New England FastFerry Co.** connects New Bedford to Vineyard Haven in just one hour (May–Oct; ☎ 866-683-3779; www.nefastferry.com). The Falmouth to Oak Bluffs route is run by the **Island Queen** (May–mid-Oct, 35min; ☎ 508-548-4800; www.islandqueen.com).

GETTING AROUND

Streets in Martha's Vineyard are often congested and parking may be difficult (especially in Jul & Aug). Getting around on foot or by bicycle is easy in the main towns. An island-wide **bus** service links island towns (limited service in off-season; ☎ 508-693-9440; www.vineyardtransit.com). **Shuttle** service between the main island towns of Vineyard Haven, Oak Bluffs and Edgartown runs from Apr–Oct (Island Transport; ☎ 508-627-8687; www.mvtour.com). Bicycle rentals are available in Vineyard Haven, Oak Bluff and Edgartown.

Visitor Information – **Martha's Vineyard Chamber of Commerce**, located on Beach Road, provides maps and information (☎ 508-693-0085; www.mvy.com).

ACCOMMODATIONS

🕯 For specific suggestions of accommodations and restaurants, see opposite page. An **American Youth Hostel** is located in West Tisbury (Edgartown-West Tisbury Rd. 525; 🕐 open Apr–Oct; ☎ 508-693-2665; www.usahostels.org). A family **campground** is located in Vineyard Haven.

RESERVATION SERVICES

Destination Insider, , ☎ 508-696-3900 or 866-696-3900; www.vineyard.destinationinsider.com; **Nantucket & Martha's Vineyard Reservations**, ☎ 693-7200 or 800-649-5671; www.mvreservations.com.

RECREATION

Southern **beaches** are known for their heavy surf, while northern and eastern beaches are more protected. Popular **water sports** include sea-kayaking, swimming and sailing. Boats can be rented in main island towns; windsurfing equipment rentals are available in Vineyard Haven. Paved **biking** trails are located throughout the island. There are two **golf** courses on the island: Farm Neck Golf Club in Oak Bluffs *(508- 693-3057)*, and Mink Meadows Golf Course in Vineyard Haven *(508-693-0600)*. **Felix Neck Wildlife Sanctuary** *(508-627-4850)* sponsors guided nature hikes and other programs. **Shopping** and art galleries and can be found in Edgartown, Vineyard Haven and Oak Bluffs.

STAYING ON MARTHA'S VINEYARD

For price ranges for hotels and restaurants, see the legend on the cover flap.

Charlotte Inn – *27 S. Summer St., Edgartown.* ✗ 🅿 ☎ *508-627-4751. 25 rooms.* **$$$$$** The white clapboards and black shutters on the exterior of this Edgartown inn may be traditional New England, but inside each of the five buildings, the luxurious décor is pure English manor house. Gilt-framed paintings of nobles and their regal steeds accent the polished antiques and crystal chandeliers, while the staff promises discreet, polished service. And if that's not beguiling enough, the inn's restaurant, **L'Etoile**, serves excellent contemporary American fare in a candlelit room facing the gardens.

Winnetu Oceanside Resort – *31 Dunes Rd., Edgartown.* 🅿 ☎ *978-443-1733 www.winnetu.com. 133 rooms.* **$$$$** With a variety of accomodations, from townhouses to suites, this property appeals to families who may not want small fry to mingle with antiques at local inns! All rooms are a 5-15 minute walk to South Beach. Resort guests

enjoy free use of the children's program and fitness center (including some classes, like yoga on the lawn.) All this comes with a price tag, but rates plunge during shoulder seasons.

DINING ON MARTHA'S VINEYARD

Alchemy – *71 Main St., Edgartown.* ☎ *508-627-9999.* **$$$ New French**. White walls and white-cloth-topped tables form the backdrop for the colorful French-inspired cuisine at this smartly casual Edgartown bistro. Dinner entrées run from pan-roasted cod to lobster risotto to sirloin paired with "cheezy fondue," while the lighter bar menu offers salmon cakes, Cuban sandwiches, and tequila-and-lime-glazed chicken.

Art Cliff Diner – *39 Beach Rd., Vineyard Haven.* 🕒 *Closed Wed.* 🅿 ☎ *508-693-1224.* **$ American**. Although the open rafters and old-fashioned checkered tablecloths would steer you to order plain old bacon and eggs or a burger and fries here, this diner's fare shows an innovative edge. Eggs might come in a chorizo frittata, waffles might be pumpkin, and lunch options include grilled eggplant sandwiches, and an asparagus-prosciutto salad.

Seafood Shanty – *31 Dock St., Edgartown.* 🅿 ☎ *508-627-8622.* **$$ Seafood**. Harbor, views, tasty seafood (the steamed mussels appetizer makes a meal,)reasonable prices and a festive vibe make this one a reliable choice.

▶ **Orient Yourself:** There are no bridges to the island. Arrive by sea (ferry) or by air (Cape Air). The ports of Hyannis, Woods Hole and New Bedford offer year-round ferry service to the island *(45min to 1hr 45min)* See www.mvy.com for details.

🅿 **Parking:** Woods Hole has the only car ferry to the island; reservations are required in high season. Tip: Skip the car and bring your bike, or rely on the VTA buses to get around (cheap and easy).

🐾 **Don't Miss:** A look at the gingerbread cottages of Oak Bluffs; also South Beach (also known as Katama Beach), south of Edgartown.

🕒 **Organizing Your Time:** If it's your first time here, spend some time getting to know the island. Getting around, remember this: *up island* means the southwest side; *down island* means the northeast area of the Vineyard.

Kids Especially for Kids: The Flying Horses Carousel (1876) is a delight for all.

Mark Read ©APA

Edgartown

Sights

Vineyard Haven

Ferries arrive at and depart from this upscale community. Shops and eateries border Main Street.

Oak Bluffs★

In the 1830s, the Methodists of Edgartown began to meet regularly in an oak grove at the northern end of town. Each summer the group attracted a larger number of followers who spent three months in a tent camp situated a short distance from the place where religious services were held.

By the 1850s more than 12,000 persons were attending the annual services at Cottage City (as the encampment came to be known), and by the end of the 19C the city had been renamed Oak Bluffs for the oak grove where the first revival meetings were held. At about the same time, small wooden cottages were built to replace the tents that stood near the tabernacle, the center of religious worship.

Trinity Park and Gingerbread Cottages★

▶ *Leave the car near the harbor and follow Central Ave. to Cottage City.*

Small ornate Victorian "gingerbread" houses, colorfully painted and decorated with lacy wooden trim resembling cake frosting, ring the tabernacle, a beautiful example of ironwork architecture.

Edgartown★

Most of tony Edgartown's large, handsome dwellings were built in the 1820s and 30s when the town was an important whaling center. A number of these homes line North Water Street and face Edgartown Harbor, once dominated by

> ### Mmmmarvelous
>
> We wonder why it is that so many of the Vineyard's Best Bets begin with the letter "m"? There's the **Marine Discovery Tour**, run by Felix Neck Wildlife Sanctuary; the Farmer's **Market** in West Tisbury; and **Menemsha**, a tiny fishing village that's a beloved subject of photographers. Finally, there's **Mad Martha's**, the local favorite ice cream emporium (several locales on the island), where you can get a Sinful Chocolate Sundae (President Bill Clinton was a fan).

a fleet of whaling vessels and now filled with modern pleasure craft. The 1672 **Vincent House** interprets island life and history *(Main St.;* 🕐 *open May–Oct Mon–Sat noon–3pm;* 🚻 *$3;* ☎ *508-627-8619).*

Opposite Edgartown is **Chappaquiddick Island**, where private homes and unspoiled natural areas are sheltered by thick woodlands. The ferry whose name is *On Time,* an ironic reference to its irregular schedule, provides service between Edgartown and Chappaquiddick.

Aquinnah Cliffs★★

Located at the western tip of the Vineyard, these 60ft cliffs are composed of striated layers of clay, appearing as heathery stripes of blue, tan, gray, red, white and orange. Dating back 100 million years, the cliffs contain fossils of prehistoric camels, wild horses and ancient whales. Today Aquinnah's Native American residents use the clay to make decorative pottery.

MOHAWK TRAIL★★

MICHELIN MAP 581 I, J 7, 8
TOURIST INFORMATION ☎ 413-773-5463 OR WWW.MOHAWKTRAIL.COM

The scenic 63 mi stretch of Route 2 through northwestern Massachusetts, running from Millers Falls to the New York border, is known as the Mohawk Trail. Following an old Indian path along the banks of the Deerfield and Cold rivers, through the Connecticut Valley and into the Berkshire Hills, this trail was used by the Mohawks as an invasion route during the French and Indian War. As the road passes through tiny mountaintop hamlets, sheer river gorges and dense forests, views from the highway and off-road overlooks are spectacular—especially in foliage season.

▶ **Orient Yourself:** The Mohawk Trail, a segment of Route 2, runs east and west.

🐾 **Don't Miss:** MassMOCA put North Adams on the map—see what the buzz is about.

🕐 **Organizing Your Time:** Make it a weekend getaway—take in the museums, hike Mt. Greylock, and stay at the happily hip Porches inn.

Kids **Especially for Kids:** The Freight Yard Restaurant, at **Western Gateway Heritage State Park,** has lots to look at, several TVs tuned to sports events, and pub-style food. Also, Kidspace at MassMOCA is the place for small fry to create cool art.

TRAIL TRINKETS

Like bookends for the Mohawk Trail, two large souvenir stores flank each end of Route 2. Distinguished by a huge statue (28 ft) of a Native American at the entrance, the **Big Indian Shop** **Kids** *(2217 Mohawk Trail;* ☎ *413-625-6817),* on the Shelburne Falls side, stocks toys and trinkets for the whole family. Jewelry, moccasins, T-shirts, prints, postcards, candy and much more are affordably priced, allowing kids to stretch their spending money. Near the North Adams side, the **Wigwam and Western Summit Giftshop** **Kids** *(*☎ *413-663-3205)* features rocks and minerals, native garb and jewelry, maple products, fudge and T-shirts.

Driving Tour 67 mi.

Greenfield

This agricultural town at the eastern end of the Mohawk Trail is named for its fertile green valley. The revitalized Main Street sports a tiny triangular common and handsome brick buildings housing a variety of shops and restaurants.

▶ *Follow Rte. 2. After 6 mi the road rises, affording views into the valley. Continue to the intersection of the road to Shelburne Falls (13.5 mi after Greenfield).*

Shelburne Falls★

This quiet mountain village is located beside the falls of the Deerfield River. Glacial potholes, ground out of granite during the last Ice Age, can be seen on the riverbank near Salmon Falls *(Deerfield Ave.).*

Bridge of Flowers

On the south side of the bridge over the Deerfield River.
Originally used by trolleys, this bridge has been transformed into a 400 ft-long path of flower beds above the Deerfield River.

▶ *Return to Rte. 2.*

Two miles past Charlemont the road enters **Mohawk Trail State Forest**. At the entrance to the forest stands a statue of an Indian brave titled **Hail to the Sunrise**. This bronze sculpture was created as a memorial to the five Indian tribes that once lived along the Mohawk Trail. The road continues through a mountainous and rugged section of Route 2. Between Florida and North Adams there are good views to the north of Mt. Monadnock and Mt. Greylock.

From **Whitcomb Summit** (the highest peak on the trail at 2,240 ft), the Green Mountains stretch into the distance; from **Western Summit** the Hoosac Valley is visible. A **hairpin curve** offers broad **views** across the Hoosac and Berkshire Valley to the Taconic Range.

▶ *Just before North Adams turn right onto Rte. 8 North, then turn left after .5mi.*

Natural Bridge State Park★

🕐 *Open Memorial Day–Columbus Day daily 9am–5pm.* 🚫 *$2/car.* 🅿 ☏ *413-663-6312. www.mass.gov/dcr/parks.*
The white marble natural bridge that gives the park its name rises 60ft above the churning waters of a narrow 475ft-long chasm. Glaciers sculpted and polished this marble, which was formed primarily from seashells deposited about 550 million years ago.

Massachusetts Museum of Contemporary Art (MASS MoCA)★★

87 Marshall St., North Adams. On Rte. 8, just north of Rte. 2. 🕐 *Open July–early Sept daily 10am–6pm. Rest of the year Wed–Mon 11am–5pm.* 🕐 *Closed Jan 1, Thanksgiving Day & Dec 25.* 🚫 *$10.* ✗ & 🅿 ☏ *413-664-4481. www.massmoca.org.*
Spread out within the spacious, renovated interiors of a former factory, complete with a clock tower, this sprawling modern art campus provides space for large installations of contemporary art. The museum takes advantage of the intimate courtyards and vast wood-floored rooms of the 19C brick buildings to display works that have gone largely unseen because their size and weight had made exhibition impossible. The complex occupies a 13-acre site in downtown North Adams, making it the biggest center for contemporary visual and performing arts in the US to date—indeed, one of the 19 galleries measures the length of a football field *(Building 5)*; another rises 40ft in height *(Building 4)*.

Works by such artists as Robert Rauschenberg, Mario Merz, Joseph Bueys and video artist Tony Oursler visit MassMOCA from studios and museums around the world.

▶ *Return to Rte. 2 West, then 1mi after North Adams center turn left onto Notch Rd. Follow the sign for Mt. Greylock Reservation.*

Mount Greylock★★

9mi ascent by car. 🅱 *Tourist information:* ☎ *413-499-4462. http://www.mass.gov/dcr/parks.*

Located between the Taconic and Hoosac Ranges, Mt. Greylock (3,491ft) is the highest point in Massachusetts. The mountain was named for chief Grey Lock, whose tribe once hunted on these lands. Near the top, the rustic **Bascom Lodge**, a haven for hikers and nature lovers, offers overnight accommodations, meals (🅐 *reservations required*), workshops, snacks, trail guides and maps. From the War Memorial Tower at the summit there are magnificent **views**★★★ of the entire region, including the Berkshire Valley, the Taconic Range and nearby Vermont and New York.

▶ *Descend to North Adams and continue on Rte. 2 west.*

Williamstown★★   🜂 *See entry heading.*

NANTUCKET★★★

POPULATION 3,830

MICHELIN MAP 581 O, P 11 AND MAPS P 253 AND P 256

TOURIST INFORMATION ☎ 508-228-1700 OR WWW.NANTUCKETCHAMBER.ORG

Lying 28mi south of Cape Cod, Nantucket is a triangular patch of land 14mi long and 3.5mi wide that Herman Melville described in Moby Dick as "a mere hillock and elbow of sand." The flat relief, sandy soil, rounded ponds and tree-studded moors are evidence of the island's glacial origins. The island of Nantucket—an Indian word meaning "distant land"—includes the village of the same name, situated on a magnificent harbor protected by a long, narrow barrier of beach.

▶ **Orient Yourself:** Set nearly 30 miles out to sea, Nantucket is reachable by air or by ferry.

🅿 **Parking:** Avoid bringing a car to the island, especially in season.

🅐 **Don't Miss:** Madaket Beach at sunset (bring a picnic of cooked lobsters or other treats from the supermarket in Nantucket Town).

🕓 **Organizing Your Time:** The island is at its most crowded in August. Consider coming in early June or late fall (typically, the weather is pleasant then).

Typical Nantucket architecture: The White Elephant Hotel

Nantucket Island Resorts

Mark Read ©APA

Nantucket

Kids **Especially for Kids:** Jetties Beach has a snack bar, restrooms, and a playground. Also, don't miss the tiny Toy Boat toy store, where a bubblegum machine dispenses marbles!

A Bit of History

The Rise and Fall of Whaling – The history of the island is interwoven with that of its famous port, which was the world capital of the whaling industry in the early 19C. In the 17C the Indians taught the settlers how to harpoon whales that passed close to shore. As hunting depleted the whale population in the Atlantic Ocean, Nantucketers sought their prey in the unexploited waters of the Pacific. For almost 100 years, between 1740 and the 1830s, Nantucket reigned as the preeminent whaling port. Merchants and ship owners grew rich by selling as many as 30,000 barrels a year of precious whale oil in London and other major cities. With their wealth, whalers built the magnificent homes that stand on Main Street near the wharves.

Then came the decline. A sandbar stretching across the mouth of Nantucket harbor prohibited the entrance of the deep-draft whaling ships that were being constructed in the early 19C, and the island's whaling industry gradually migrated to the deepwater port of New Bedford. A devastating fire in 1846, the California Gold Rush and to the discovery of oil in Pennsylvania, all conspired to bring Nantucket's golden era to a close.

Nicknamed "the little gray lady in the sea" by early sailors because of its weathered gray cottages covered with pink roses in the summer, Nantucket was spared the industrialization of the 19C. With its comfortable old homes, wharfside structures and cobblestone streets, Nantucket today reigns as one of the most charming, well-preserved towns on the East Coast.

Nantucketers – The difficult life led by seamen and their wives, and the Quaker religion many of them practiced, contributed to the simple, austere and strong character for which Nantucketers are known. **Peter Foulger**, the grandfather of Benjamin Franklin, and **Maria Mitchell**, the first American woman astronomer, were both from Nantucket.

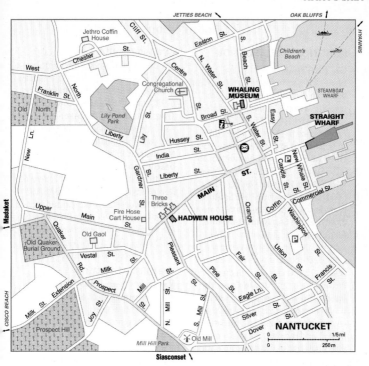

Nantucket Town★★★

The Nantucket Historical Association sells a combination History Ticket ($18), which admission to the Whaling Museum and four historic sites: the Hadwen House, Jethro Coffin House, Old Mill and the Quaker Meeting House. Purchase tickets at Hadwen House, the Jethro Coffin House or at the Whaling Museum. ☎ *508-228-1894. www.nha.org.*

Hadwen House★

96 Main St. Visit by guided tour (30min) only, Memorial Day–Columbus Day daily 10am–5pm.
This impressive dwelling, with its Neoclassical pediment and columns, was built in 1845 for the whale oil merchant William Hadwen. The house and its rich decor bear witness to the life of luxury led by its owner.

Whaling Museum★★

13 Broad St. ⏰ Open mid-May–Columbus Day Mon-Sat 10am–5pm, Sun noon-5pm; extended summer hours, Thurs 10am-8pm. Rest of the year, call for hours. $15.

CENTRE STREET BISTRO

29 Centre St. ☎ *508-228-8470. www.nantucketbistro.com.* Inventive New American food, a casual atmosphere, and moderate prices (at least for Nantucket) make this diminutive bistro worth a stop. The tiny dining room, with cheerful yellow walls and floral-cushioned chairs, is a tight squeeze--try the outdoor patio in good weather. At lunch, there are intriguing salads, perhaps couscous with roasted peppers, olives, and feta cheese, as well as updated sandwiches. Dinner follows the same contemporary lines: Seared salmon is paired with Asian veggies and wontons, and duck is served with fruited grains.

Address Book

PRACTICAL INFORMATION

GETTING THERE

Ferries for Nantucket depart from Hyannis. From **Boston** to **Hyannis** *(76mi)*, take Rte. 3 to the Sagamore Bridge and follow US-6 East to Rte. 132 East. From **Providence** to **Hyannis** *(82mi)* take I-195 South to Rte. 25 East to US-6 East; cross the Sagamore Bridge and follow US-6 East to Rte. 132 East. From **New York City** to **Hyannis** *(264mi)* take I-95 North and pick up I-195 South in Providence. International and domestic flights service **Logan International Airport** (BOS) in Boston *(☎ 617-561-1800 or 800-235-6426; www.massport. com)*. Year-round service from Boston, Hyannis, Nantucket, New Bedford and Providence is provided by **Cape Air** *(☎ 800-352-0714; www.flycapeair.com)*; **US Airways Express** *(☎ 800-428-4322; www.usair.com)* flies to Nantucket from Boston and Hyannis. Bonanza Bus Lines offers **bus** transportation from Boston to Woods Hole *(☎ 888-751-8800; www.bonanzabus.com)*; Peter Pan Bus Lines *(☎ 800-237-8747; www.peterpanbus. com)* provides service from Boston to the ferry terminals on Cape Cod.

Ferry Service – Three different ferries service the island. Schedules and fares vary seasonally; high-speed boats usually carry passengers only. Reservations are highly recommended in the busy summer season *(Jul–Aug)*. The **Steamship Authority** is the only company offering year-round transportation daily for cars, trucks *(reservations required)*, passengers and bikes; departures from Hyannis *(Jan–May)*, Woods Hole and Martha's Vineyard *(☎ 508-477-8600; www.islandferry.com)*. A high-speed ferry operates seasonally, making the trip in an hour.

Hy-Line Cruises carry passengers and bikes in season *(May–Oct)*; a high-speed ferry runs between Hyannis and Nantucket daily year-round *(no service on Dec 25; 508-778-2600 or 800-492-8082; www.hy-linecruises.com)*.

Freedom Cruise Line carries passengers and bikes, and departs from Harwich Port for Nantucket daily *(late May–mid-Oct; 508-432-8999; www. nantucketislandferry.com)*.

GETTING AROUND

The best way to get around Nantucket center is on foot or by bicycle, as streets are often congested and parking may be difficult. The **Nantucket Regional Transit Authority** (NRTA) operates a shuttle island-wide *(late May–early Oct, daily 7am–11:30pm)*, with routes to Madaket, Sconset, Surfside and Jetties beaches, and mid-island areas. Order shuttle passes from NRTA *(22 Federal St., Nantucket, MA 02554; ☎ 508-228-7025; www.nantucket.net)*. Bicycle and moped rentals are available from Island Bike Co. *(☎ 508-228-4070; www.islandbike.com)*; and Young's Bicycle Shop *(☎ 508-228-1151; www.youngsbicycleshop.com)*.

VISITOR INFORMATION

Nantucket Island Chamber of Commerce provides maps and information regarding attractions, accommodations, shopping and recreation on the island *(508-228-1700; www.nantucket-chamber.org)*. A visitor center is located at 48 Main St.; **Nantucket Visitor Services** office is at 25 Federal St. *(☉ open Jun–Sept daily 9am–6pm, rest of the year Mon–Sat 9am–5:30pm; 508-228-0925)*. Two information kiosks operate seasonally on the island.

ACCOMMODATIONS

👌 *For specific suggestions of accommodations and restaurants, see the opposite page.* A **youth hostel** is located 3.5mi from Nantucket ferry wharf *(31 Western Ave.; ☉ open mid-Apr–mid-Oct; ⇌ $24; ☎ 508-228-0433; www. usahostels.org)*. Camping is prohibited on the island.

Reservation services: Nantucket Accommodations, ☎ 508-228-9559; **Destination Insider**, ☎ 508-696-3900 or 800-258-1581, www.vineyard.destinationinsider.com; **Nantucket & Martha's Vineyard Reservations,** ☎ 508-693-7200 or 800-649-5671, www.mvreservations.com; **Nantucket Concierge**, ☎ 508-228-8400, www.nantucketconcierge.com.

Recreation – Swimming is permitted at all island beaches; you can **surf** at South Shore beaches. Twenty-four miles of **bicycle** paths and numerous **hiking** paths thread the island.

Specialty **shopping** and supplies can be found in Nantucket Town.

STAYING ON NANTUCKET

⚫ For price ranges for hotels and restaurants, see the legend on the cover flap.

Pineapple Inn – *10 Hussey St.*
🕐 *Closed Nov–mid-Apr.* ☎ *508-228-9992. www.pineappleinn.com. 12 rooms.*
$$$$ Tucked back on a narrow Nantucket Town street, this 1838 Greek Revival residence has been carefully restored with Federal antiques. Guest rooms, named for local whaling captains, come with handmade four-poster beds, goose-down comforters and cable TV. For breakfast, served in the formal dining room or outside in the garden, enjoy fresh-squeezed juice, cappuccino, fruit and fresh-baked pastries.

Union Street Inn – *7 Union St.*
🕐 *Closed Jan–Mar.* ☎ *508-228-9222 or 800-225-5116. www.unioninn.com. 12 rooms.* **$$$$** This dignified gray-shingled c.1770 house, one block from Main Street, pairs a stately Nantucket ambience with sumptuous appointments. Most rooms have wide-board floors topped with Oriental rugs and are done in muted colors (primarily quiet beiges and greens). Four-poster, canopy, or other antique beds are dressed with Frette linens; six rooms have working fireplaces. The full hot breakfast might include eggs Benedict or apple-cinnamon pancakes; guests can help themselves to coffee, tea, and cookies round the clock.

Cliff Lodge – *9 Cliff Rd.* ☎ *508-228-9480. www.nantucket.net/lodging/cliflodge. 12 rooms.* **$$$** In this former whaling captain's home, built in the late 1700s, the simple, country-style rooms are done in cheerful pastels, with quilt-topped beds, floral wallpapers, and splatter-painted wood floors. The rear-facing bedrooms have glimpses of the harbor, and although some rooms are quite small, the homey space is efficiently designed, with built-in drawers and shelves. The Continental breakfast buffet usually incorporates muffins or coffeecake, and afternoon tea brings cucumber sandwiches and fresh-baked cookies.

DINING ON NANTUCKET

The Pearl – *12 Federal St. Dinner only.*
🕐 *Closed Dec–Apr.* ☎ *508-228-9701.*
$$$$ Asian-fusion. Lavish, exotic and sensual, the Asian-fusion dishes at this tony hot spot are as wildly inventive as the tropical fish in the dining room's sparkling aquarium are luminous. From the yellowfin tuna martini to the salt-and-pepper lobster with Asian BBQ sauce to the sauté of prawns and sweetbreads served with sweet-potato mousse and beet greens, the Pearl packs plenty of excitement onto its plates. The young, the adventurous, and the trust fund-endowed are all here, making it the Scene—with a capital S.

Sfoglia – *130 Pleasant St. Dinner only.*
☎ *508-325-4500.* **$$$ Italian**. There's serious cooking going on in this mid-island house with its mismatched wooden tables and chairs and eclectic assortment of crockery. The menu of modern Italian regional cuisine may be small—several appetizers, a half-dozen pastas, and a few entrées—but husband-and-wife chef/owners Ron Suhanosky and Colleen Marnell-Suhanosky are unquestionably talented. Pastas are handmade (the potato gnocchi are lighter than air), and desserts are dynamite. If you're lucky, you might find hot peach and raspberry crostata or almond torte topped with cherries and rich chocolate.

Fog Island Cafe – *7 S. Water St. Breakfast & lunch year-round; dinner Jun–Labor Day.* ☎ *508-228-1818. www.fogisland.com.* **$$ New American**. On Nantucket, even down-home is relatively upscale—witness this inviting cafe, with its sturdy wooden tables, where owners Mark and Anne Dawson, graduates of the Culinary Institute of America, serve up American comfort food with a contemporary flair. Throughout the year, it's a popular spot for breakfast and lunch (try a "global roll-ups"); in the summer, you can get moderately priced American fare in the evenings as well.

Stop & Shop – Your best "cheap eats" on the island may well be a do-it-yourself beachside picnic, with prepared foods from the island's two supermarkets, in Nantucket Town and Madaket.

Recently renovated, the Whaling Museum is home to a 46 foot sperm whale skeleton, hanging from the ceiling. The 1847 factory, where candles were made from whale oil, has been brought back to authentic glory. Also featured are fine collections of scrimshaw, harpoons, models and paintings. Don't miss a trip to the rooftop observation deck for an overview of Nantucket Harbor.

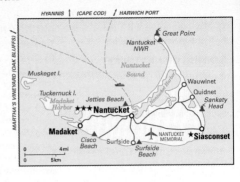

Main Street★★★

Shaded by venerable elms, paved with cobblestones and lined with captains' homes and shops, Main Street has preserved its colonial atmosphere despite the upscale boutiques and galleries that fill the storefronts. During the summer it is a delightful place for a leisurely stroll.

Straight Wharf★

This wharf at the eastern end of Main Street and its old fishing sheds have been transformed into modern marinas and shops, art galleries and restaurants. Yachts and other pleasure craft tie up here in summer.

Additional Sights

Siasconset★

Islanders call this village "Sconset." Fishermen who came here during the 17C to fish for cod built the sheds that were later converted into the **gray cottages** of Siasconset. Discovered at the end of the 19C by artists in search of unspoiled natural scenery, the area rapidly grew into a fashionable resort. A great summer bike ride: the seven -mile trip from Nantucket Town to Siasconset.

▷ *Continue to picturesque Sankaty Head Lighthouse, up to Quidnet and returning along Nantucket Harbor to the center of town.*

Madaket

A paved bike path leads through the moors to Madaket Beach on the western end of the island. Madaket is the perfect place to enjoy a romantic Vineyard sunset.

NEW BEDFORD ★

POPULATION 93,768

MICHELIN MAP 581 N 10

TOURIST INFORMATION ☎ 508-979-1745 OR WWW.CI.NEW-BEDFORD.MA.US

The whaling capital of the world during the mid-19C, New Bedford is still a working fishing port. Once the anchorage of majestic whaling ships, the wharves are now crowded with modern fishing craft.

Cobblestone streets lead down to the waterfront, where ships' supplies and antiques are sold. Follow one of these streets up from the waterfront to Johnny Cake Hill to discover memories of New Bedford's illustrious whaling days, which are well preserved in the Whaling Museum and the Seamen's Bethel, or mariner's chapel. In 1996 these and other sights were linked together as a national park.

▸ **Orient Yourself:** New Bedford is about 60 mi south of Boston.

🅿 **Parking:** The Elm Street Garage is located one block north of the National Park Visitor Center and two blocks from the Whaling Museum.

☺ **Don't Miss:** The collections of scrimshaw and sailor's valentines (woven from human hair) at the Whaling Museum.

🕐 **Organizing Your Time:** Visit the whaling museum in the morning, stop at Seamen's Bethel, and then have lunch at one of the city's fine Portuguese restaurants. (Leave the car in the lot and stroll to sites.)

🄺🄸🄳🄸 **Especially for Kids:** Little kids enjoy climbing aboard the replica of the whaleship **Lagoda**.

👍 **Also See:** Visiting from May-Sept? Take in a performance at the Zeiterion Theatre (the Z), New Bedford's last-remaining (c 1923) old-time movie palace. Catch Etta James, the Flying Karamazov Brothers, Suessical the Musical, and other big-name acts. *684 Purchase St.,* ☎ *508-994-2900; www.zeiterion.org.*

New Bedford Whaling National Historical Park

A Bit of History

Whaling's Golden Age – New Bedford's 30-year reign as the world capital of the whaling industry began in 1765 when Joseph Rotch, a Nantucketer who had established the whaling industry on his island, came to this fishing village. Rotch's efforts helped launch New Bedford's burgeoning whaling trade. By the late 1830s New Bedford had surpassed Nantucket as the center of the industry. In 1840 Herman Melville described the influence that whaling exerted on the quality of life in New Bedford: "All these brave houses and flowery gardens came from the Atlantic, Pacific and Indian Oceans, one and all they were harpooned and dragged up hither from the bottom of the sea."

Sperm-whale oil and bone formed the basis of the city's wealth. Factories worked day and night converting the oil into candles; whalebone, destined to be transformed into corset stays, umbrellas and walking sticks, was set out along the piers to dry. New Bedford's glory days peaked in the 1850s, when 80 percent of America's whale ships sailed from this town, and more than 10,000 men—about half the town's population—participated in whaling.

New Bedford Whaling National Historical Park

Created in 1996, the park encompasses a 13-block area adjacent to New Bedford's waterfront and preserves some 70 structures (most of them privately owned) related to the city's whaling heyday. The park visitor center offers maps, guided tours and information *(33 William St.;* 🕐 *open year-round daily 9am–5pm;* 🕐 *closed Jan 1, Thanksgiving Day & Dec 25;* ☎ *508-996-4095; www.nps.gov/nebe).*

New Bedford Whaling Museum★★

18 Johnny Cake Hill. From I-95 Exit 15, follow the signs to downtown New Bedford. Turn right on Elm St., then left on Bethel St. 🕐 *Open year-round daily 9am–5pm (open Thu til 9pm during summer months).* 🕐 *Closed Jan 1, Thanksgiving Day & Dec 25.* ⊜ *$10.* ♿ ☎ *508-997-0046. www.whalingmuseum.org.*

The museum's collections, which now include the 72,000 artifacts, prints, log books, journals and other objects from the Kendall Whaling Museum in Sharon, Massachusetts, are among the finest in the world. Here you'll find the history of whaling illustrated through artifacts, paintings, scrimshaw, glassware, textiles and photography. A highlight is the 89ft half-scale model of the fully rigged whaling bark **Lagoda**. Formerly a trade ship, the *Lagoda* made 12 whaling voyages out of New Bedford in the 1800s. Visitors may climb aboard the replica, which is the largest of its kind in the world, to examine the elaborate rigging and the tryworks.

Seamen's Bethel

15 Johnny Cake Hill. 🕐 *Open May–Oct, Mon–Fri 10am–5pm. Rest of the year call for hours.* ☎ *508-992-3295.*

This chapel (1832), described in Herman Melville's classic novel *Moby Dick,* was a necessary stop for the mariner who was about to embark on a perilous whaling voyage. Still used for services today, the chapel contains a pulpit shaped to resemble the hull of a whaleboat.

Rotch-Jones-Duff House and Garden Museum★

396 County St. 🕐 *Open year-round Mon–Sat 10am–4pm, Sun noon–4pm.* 🕐 *Closed Thanksgiving Day & Dec 25–Jan 1.* ⊜ *$4.* ♿ ☎ *508-997-1401. www.rjdmuseum.org.*

Located within walking distance of the Whaling Museum and the historic downtown district, this Greek Revival mansion (1834, Richard Upjohn) and its sylvan grounds typify the "brave houses and flowery gardens" of New Bedford that Herman Melville immortalized in *Moby Dick*. Sumptuous period rooms and historical exhibits chronicle 150 years of the economic and social evolution of the city as it was experienced by the New Bedford whaling elite.

NEWBURYPORT★

POPULATION 17,189
MICHELIN MAP 581 N 7
TOURIST INFORMATION ☎ 978-462-6680 OR WWW.NEWBURYPORTCHAMBER.ORG

This small city at the mouth of the Merrimack River was the home of a large fleet of merchant vessels in the 18C and 19C. The dignified Federal mansions built on High Street by sea captains, and the handsomely- restored Market Square area evoke Newburyport's heyday as a bustling shipbuilding port and trading center. Newburyport's 19C boatyards produced some of the finest clippers ever to sail the seas. Today, the city's lively waterfront is the setting for outdoor concerts, and the launching point for whale watching trips and sightseeing cruises.

▶ **Orient Yourself:** Newburyport is about 40 miles north of Boston, and just south of the New Hampshire border. The city (the smallest in Massachusetts) is reachable via commuter rail from Boston.

🅿 **Parking:** There is free parking *(3hr limit)* in the lot off Green St., and all-day parking on the waterfront lot *(Merrimac St.)*.

👁 **Don't Miss:** Exploring downtown on foot, especially during Yankee Homecoming week *(late July/early Aug)*.

🕐 **Organizing Your Time:** Newburyport is a popular day trip from Boston.

🧒 **Especially for Kids:** The Dragon's Nest toy store and Fowle's soda fountain.

🖐 **Also See:** Plum Island Kayak *(☎ 978-462-5510; www.plumislandkayak.com)* offers great guided sunset paddles.

Sights

High Street★

Ornamented with carved porches and columns, the houses represent the major styles of early American architecture: late Georgian, Federal and Greek Revival. **Frog Pond** and **Bartlett Mall**, fronting High Street, provide the setting for the **Court House** (1800) designed by Charles Bulfinch, and later remodeled.

At no. 98, the brick **Cushing House** *(👁 visit by 1hr guided tour only, May–Oct Tue–Fri 10am–4pm, Sat noon–4pm; ☎ $5; ☎ 978-462-2681; www.newburyporthist. org)*, built c.1808, was home to three generations of the Cushing family. The dwelling's most famous occupant, Caleb Cushing, was the first US envoy to China in 1842. Furnishings that Cushing acquired in Asia are exhibited.

Custom House

25 Water St. 🕐 *Open Apr–Dec Mon–Sat 10am–4pm, Sun noon–4pm.* ☎ *$5.* 🅿 ☎ *978-462-8681. www.essexheritage.org.*

Designed by Robert Mills, architect of the Washington Monument in the nation's capital, this granite structure once welcomed mariners returning from long sea voyages. Today it contains the **Museum of the Newburyport Maritime Society**, featuring exhibits on shipbuilding, the Coast Guard and foreign imports.

Excursions

Plum Island-Parker River National Wildlife Refuge★★

3mi south of Newburyport via Water St., then Plum Island Tpk. 🕐 *Open year-round daily dawn–dusk.* 🕐 *Refuge Beach closed Apr–Aug.* ☎ *$2/pedestrian or cyclist; ☎ $5/car. Refuge closes when parking capacity is reached. Park in the small lots off the road that* *leads through the refuge. Camping prohibited.* 🅿 ☎ *978-465-5753. www.parkerriver. fws.gov.*

The southern two-thirds of this island has been designated as a haven for waterfowl in the Atlantic Flyway. Opportunities for bird-watching abound (more than 350 species have been sighted), especially during the spring and fall migrations. The observation tower at Hellcat Swamp offers **panoramas** of the island's 4,662 acres of dunes, marshlands and oceanfront beach. Birding hikes are offered frequently.

Crane Beach★

4.5mi east of Ipswich. From Rte. 1A, take Rte. 133 east toward Essex. Turn left on Northgate Rd. At the end of Northgate Rd., turn right on Argilla Rd. The road ends at Crane Beach. 🕐 *Open year-round daily 8am–dusk.* 🚗 *$15–$22/car from Memorial Day-Labor Day; half price after 3 pm.* 🍴 ☎ *978-356-4354; www.thetrustees.org.*

This sandy beach stretches for more than 4mi along the Atlantic (Avoid the beach in July, when the greenhead flies make their annual, annoying appearance). Beyond the beach, the dunes are covered with a pitch-pine maritime forest and a red-maple swamp. The best way to explore the area is by following the **Pine Hollow Trail** *(access to the right of the parking lot)*. During the summer, concerts are presented at the mansion on **Castle Hill**, the former residence of the Crane family (🎫 *concert information:* ☎ *978-356-4351).*

RUSSELL ORCHARDS

143 Argilla Rd. 🕐 *Open May until the weekend after Thanksgiving Day.* ☎ *978-356-5366. www.russellorchardsma.com.* En route to Crane Beach, look for this delightful 125-acre farm amid the meadows, ponds and horse pastures of the lovely countryside. Produce-filled bins and fresh flower bouquets front the large 18C barn (there's a big pumpkin patch out front in autumn.) Inside, they sell a variety of farm-grown fruits and vegetables and other homemade treats. Don't miss a cider donut and a cup of hot or cold apple cider. Raspberries, strawberries, blueberries and apples are all ripe for the picking in season.

PIONEER VALLEY ★

MICHELIN MAP 581 J, K 7-9
TOURIST INFORMATION ☎ 800-723-1548 OR WWW.MASS-VACATION.COM

The fertile Connecticut River Valley was once the haunt of dinosaurs. Today the area is known particularly for its concentration of colleges and universities.

▶ **Orient Yourself:** Pioneer Valley, as this region is known, extends from north to south through the center of Massachusetts.

🅿 **Parking:** Parking is available at state reservations; the towns of Northhampton and Amherst have centrally-located parking lots.

☸ **Don't Miss:** Hiking or driving to the summit of Mt. Holyoke at Skinner State Park.

🕓 **Organizing Your Time:** Beware of spontaneous visits to the five-college area during Parents' Weekends (fall) and graduation season; parents book up local inns and restaurants during these times.

▨ **Especially for Kids:** The Eric Carle Museum of Picture Book Art is a hit with kids from ages 2 to 10.

☙ **Also See:** The Norwottuck Rail Trail, an 8.5mi bike path on the former Boston and Maine railway bed. The paved path goes through the towns of Northhampton, Hadley, Amherst and Belchertown, amid forest, pasture and residential areas.

Geological Notes

Valley of the Dinosaurs – Of great geological interest are the fine-grained sedimentary rocks containing the tracks of dinosaurs that roamed the Connecticut Valley approximately 200 million years ago. These footprints, pressed into the mud on the valley floor and baked by the sun, were later covered and preserved by additional layers of mud. Eventually, they became layers of sedimentary rocks, primarily sandstone and shale. Today these rocks reveal the fascinating story of the region's prehistoric past. The creatures that once roamed this area were small, about the size of a man, according to the size of their footprints. Dinosaurs did not attain their mammoth size until about 100 million years later.

Dinosaur tracks can be seen at the **Pratt Museum** at Amherst College, and in their original formation in Rocky Hill and at various other locations.

A Bit of History

Western Boundary – During the 17C the valley was one of the major axes settled by pioneers, who were attracted by its rich soil and plentiful water resources. It remained the western frontier of New England until the 18C, as the colonists did not dare risk crossing the Berkshire Hills and venturing into the Hudson River Valley, the domain of the Dutch.

A Center of Education – More than 60,000 students attend the numerous schools, colleges and the university in the Pioneer Valley. These include the **University of Massachusetts** at Amherst *(www.umass.edu)*; **Amherst College**, established in 1821; innovative **Hampshire College**; **Smith College** at Northampton, one of the most select colleges in the nation for women, founded in 1875; and **Mount Holyoke College**, across the river in South Hadley, established in 1837 as the first women's college in the US. The poet **Emily Dickinson** was a student at Mount Holyoke before she settled in Amherst, where she lived the remainder of her reclusive life.

Sights

Deerfield★★   ♿ *See entry heading.*

Quabbin Reservoir★

Access from Rte. 9. 2mi from Belchertown. Drive on Windsor Dam, then follow the signs for Quabbin Hill Tower.

Construction of the 28sq mi reservoir (storage capacity: 412 billion gallons) that serves the Boston region was accomplished by damming the Swift River and flooding four of the valley towns. The many islands that stud Quabbin's vast water reserves (*quabbin* in the Nipmuck language means "a lot of water") were created by hilltops jutting out of the submerged area. Impressive **views★★** are available from **Enfield Lookout** and from the **observation tower** on Quabbin Hill. The reservoir offers opportunities for fishing, hiking, picnicking and scenic shore drives *(swimming and hunting prohibited)*.

Mount Sugarloaf State Reservation

Follow the signs from Rte. 116. ☎ 413-545-5993. www.massparks.org.

Wind your way to the top of this basalt ridge for an expansive **view** of the Connecticut River as it meanders through open farmlands. Small towns fleck the valley landscape.

Mount Tom State Reservation

From Holyoke take Rte. 141 North 3mi. ◷ Open Memorial Day–Columbus Day Mon–Fri 8am–8pm, weekends 9am–8pm. Rest of the year daily 8am–4pm. ◷ Closed Jan 1, Thanksgiving Day & Dec 25. ⊜ $2/car (summer only). ♿ ☎ 413-534-1186. www.massparks.org.

Easthampton and Northampton can be seen in the valley below the access road to this 1,800-acre recreation area, which includes some 30 mi of hiking trails.

The summit of Mt. Tom commands a view of the curved arm of the Connecticut River, made famous by Thomas Cole's painting *The Oxbow* (in New York City's Metropolitan Museum of Art), as well as Northampton and the Berkshire Hills beyond. The slopes of Mt. Tom provide a venue for skiing in winter.

Pioneer Valley Picks

Here are some popular places in the valley to take a break from sightseeing:

In Amherst:
Judie's Restaurant – *51 N. Pleasant St. ☎ 413-253-3491. www.judiesrestaurant. com.* A student favorite, famous for giant popovers, burgers and big portions.
Amherst Bookstore – *8 Main St. ☎ 413-256-1547.* Great stock, helpful staff.
Atkins Farms Country Market – *1150 West St. ☎ 413-253-9528. www.atkinsfarms. com.* A complete produce store with a bakery (try the cider donuts) and deli.
In Northampton:
Paul and Elizabeth's – *150 Main St. ☎ 413-584-4832.* The go-to place for vegetarian cuisine, artfully prepared. They also serve fish, and killer fresh breads. *Open for breakfast, lunch and dinner.*
Spoleto – *530 Main St. ☎ 413-586-6313. www.fundining.com.*
A local institution for upscale Italian food, served in generous portions. Hillary and Chelsea Clinton dined here on their East Coast college tour.

In Holyoke:
Yankee Pedlar Inn – *1866 Northampton St. ☎ 413-532-9494. www.yankeepedlarinn.com.* A cozy 19C wayside inn with affordable, down-home cooking.

MUSEUM HOPPING

Shopping for colleges, or looking for something to do on a rainy day? Check out some of these museums:

Hampshire College Art Gallery, Amherst. ☎ 413-549-4600. www.library.hampshire.edu/gallery.

Mead Art Museum and **Pratt Museum of Natural History**, Amherst College, Amherst. ☎ 413-542-2335/413-542-2165. www.amherst.edu.

Mount HolyokeCollege Art Museum, South Hadley. ☎ 413-538-2245. www.mtholyoke.edu/offices/artmuseum.

Smith College Museum of Art, Northampton, ☎ 413-585-2760. www.smith.edu/artmuseum

University Gallery, U of MA, Amherst. ☎ 413-545-3670. www.umass.edu/fac.

Northampton★★

Northampton comes as a surprise to those expecting just another small town. Like a mini-Cambridge, the town has a diverse population, a lively vibe, and a vibrant cultural-and-nightlife scene. Northampton is known for its enticing collection of restaurants and for its burgeoning population of gays and lesbians. The **Smith College Museum of Art**, on Elm Street, owns a collection noted for its American and French works of the 19C and 20C (🕐 open Tues–Sat 10am–4pm, Sun noon–4pm; 🕐 closed Jan 1, Thanksgiving Day, & Dec 25; ♿ ☎ 413-585-2760; www.smith.edu/artmuseum).

Skinner State Park★

From Rte. 47 follow the signs for the Summit House. 🕐 Open Memorial Day–Labor Day Mon–Fri 8am–8pm, weekends 10am–8pm. Mid-Apr–Memorial Day & rest of Sept–Oct daily 10am–6pm. 🚗 $2/car (weekends & holidays May–Oct). ☎ 413-586-0350. www.massparks.org.

The old summit hotel (no longer in operation) sits atop Mt. Holyoke, a basalt ridge. This vantage point offers panoramic **views** of the valley. A variety of hiking/snowshoeing trails lead to the summit and extend on to Holyoke Range State Park.

PLYMOUTH★★

POPULATION 51,701
MICHELIN MAP 581 N 9 AND MAP P 265
TOURIST INFORMATION ☎ 508-747-7533 OR WWW.VISIT-PLYMOUTH.COM

This attractive town with hilly streets sloping down to the harbor is the site of the first permanent settlement in New England. The long voyage of the Mayflower, the hardships the Pilgrims endured and the eventual success of Plymouth Colony form part of the cherished story related in Plymouth's historic monuments and sites.

▶ **Orient Yourself:** Plymouth lies about 40mi southeast of Boston off Route 3. Plimoth Plantation is located 3mi south of downtown; the *Mayflower II* sits at the Plymouth waterfront.

🅿 **Parking:** There are several lots in town, including one near the visitor center on Water St.

🅰 **Don't Miss:** Plimoth Plantation is the major must-see here.

🕐 **Organizing Your Time:** After stopping at the visitor center at 130 Water St., figure out what you want to see and they'll point you in the right direction. Save at least a couple of hours for Plimoth Plantation.

Kids **Especially for Kids:** Lobster Tales Pirate Adventure (for ages 4-11) puts young ones in pirate hats and face paint, and lets them loose with water cannons. (☎ 508-746-5342; www.lobstertalesinc.com).

A Bit of History

A Colony Off Course – A group of English Puritans known as **Separatists** attempted to reform the Church of England in the 16C. To avoid persecution by the authorities, members of the group emigrated from Scrooby, England, in 1607 to Holland. They remained there until, impressed by favorable accounts of the New World, they decided to emigrate to America. Early in September 1620, 102 passengers, including 35 Separatists, boarded the *Mayflower* at Plymouth, England, and set sail for the Virginia Colony in North America. Diverted north by a storm, the settlers landed two months later on the shores of Cape Cod. They spent five weeks in the region before again setting sail for Virginia. Detoured a second time by strong winds, the Pilgrims headed for the bay that had been charted six years earlier by Capt. John Smith. It was on the shores of this bay that they established Plymouth Colony.

The First Winter – Harsh weather and a scarcity of food left almost half the colony dead by the end of the first winter. Burials were held at night on **Cole's Hill**, and graves were left unmarked to conceal the settlers' dwindling numbers from the neighboring Wampanoag tribe. The spring brought hope to the settlement along with a group of Indians who befriended the Pilgrims and taught them how to raise crops and to hunt and fish. After the harvest that fall, members of Plymouth Colony joined with the Indians in a three-day feast, the first American **Thanksgiving celebration**, in gratitude for their blessings.

From **Burial Hill**, where an old cemetery contains gravestones dating back to the Plymouth Colony, there are lovely views overlooking the town and out to sea. The **Town Brook**, close to the place where the Pilgrims built their first homes, runs through a lovely public park, **Brewster Gardens**.

Historic District

Begin at the visitor center at 130 Water St. 🕐 *Open Jul–Aug daily 8am–8pm; Sept–Nov & Apr–Jun daily 9am–5pm.* 🍴 🅿 ♿ ☎ *800-872-1620. www.visit-plymouth.com.*

Mayflower II★★

Kids *Berthed at the State Pier.* 🕐 *Open Apr–Nov daily 9am–5pm.* 🎫 *$8 (combination ticket with Plimoth Plantation $24).* ☎ *508-746-1622. www.plimoth.org.*
The *Mayflower II*, built in England (1957), is a full-scale replica of the ship that carried the Pilgrims to Plymouth in 1620.

Plymouth Rock★

Kids *On the beach at Water St.* Set at the harbor's edge, this boulder has traditionally been regarded as the stepping stone used by the *Mayflower* passengers when they disembarked at Plymouth. The boulder is sheltered by a multi-

Pilgrims' Progress

Every Friday in August and on Thanksgiving Day, modern Plymouth residents dress as Pilgrims and take part in a Sabbath procession up Leyden Street to Burial Hill, where a religious service is held.

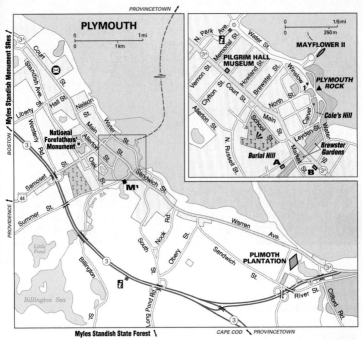

columned granite structure. Opposite is **The Pilgrim Mother (1)**, a fountain honoring the women of the *Mayflower*.

Richard Sparrow House (A)

42 Summer St. 🕐 *Open daily, Thu–Tue, 10am–5pm.* 🎟 *$2.* ☎ *508-747-1240. www. sparrowhouse.com.*

The oldest dwelling (1640) in Plymouth contains 18C furnishings. Locally-made pottery and artwork are on display and available for sale.

Jabez Howland House (B)

33 Sandwich St. 🚶 *Visit by guided tour (1hr) only, late May–mid-Oct daily 10am–4:30pm.* 🎟 *$4.* ☎ *508-746-9590.*

This is the only house remaining in Plymouth where Pilgrims are known to have lived.

Pilgrim Hall Museum★

75 Court St. 🕐 *Open Feb–Dec daily 9:30am–4:30pm.* 🕐 *Closed Dec 25.* 🎟 *$6.* 🅿 ☎ *508-746-1620. www.pilgrimhall.org.*

Built as a memorial to the Pilgrims and Plymouth Colony, this austere granite structure (1824), designed by Alexander Parris, contains original Pilgrim furnishings and artifacts, including chairs owned by Governors Bradford and Carver; the cradle of Peregine White, who was born on the *Mayflower;* Bibles belonging to John Alden and Governor Bradford; and a sampler made by Loara Standish, daughter of Myles Standish.

Jenney Grist Mill Museum (M¹)

6 Spring Lane. 🕐 *Open April–Nov, Mon-Sat 9:30am-5pm, Sun noon-5.* 🕐 *Closed Easter Sun.* 🅿 ☎ *508-747-4544. http://www.jenneygristmill.com.*

Located on Town Brook, where its water wheel grinds corn daily, the museum recreates the grist mill that John Jenney established in 1636. Visitors can watch the age-old process in the mill and purchase ground corn in the mill shoppe.

Courtesy Plimoth Plantation/ Ted Curtin

Plimoth Plantation

National Forefathers' Monument

Allerton St. off US-44. Representing the virtue Faith, this large monument (36ft) honors the Pilgrims and their small colony.

Additional Sight

Plimoth Plantation★★

Kids *3mi south on Rte. 3 from the center of Plymouth; take Exit 4.* ◷ *Open Apr–late-Nov daily 9am–5pm.* ◈ *$21 (combination ticket with Mayflower II, $24).* ✗ ♿ 🅿 ☎ 508-746-1622. www.plimoth.org.

The plantation is a reproduction of the Pilgrims' village as it appeared in 1627. (The spelling "Plimoth" was adopted from Governor Bradford's early journals by the museum curators.) The **Fort/Meetinghouse**, at the entrance to the plantation, offers a good vantage point from which to view the entire village, with its neat rows of thatched-roof cottages similar to those inhabited by the Alden, Carver, Bradford and Standish families. Rooms inside the houses are decorated with reproductions of 17C English furnishings. Throughout the village, costumed guides portray specific Pilgrim settlers, chatting with visitors while performing tasks such as gardening, cooking and harvesting crops according to the methods used in the early colony.

A path leads to **Hobbamock's Wampanoag Indian Homesite**, where the culture of this Native American group is interpreted by staff members engaged in raising crops, drying food, weaving and other chores traditionally performed by the Wampanoag people. The campsite includes examples of the *wetus*, a domed dwelling once built as shelter by the Wampanoag. Visitors can watch as workers use 17C methods to make handicrafts in the modern **Carriage House Crafts Center**. The walk-through exhibit **Irreconcilable Differences** tells the story of the colony through the perspectives of a *Mayflower* passenger and a Wampanoag sachem.

Excursions

Myles Standish Monument State Reservation

In Duxbury, 8mi from Plymouth via Rte. 3A to Crescent St. Turn right and enter through the gate at left. ◷ *Open Memorial Day–Labor Day daily 8am–8pm.* 🅿 ☎ 508-208-0676. www.mass.gov/dcr/parks/southeast.

Atop a 116ft granite shaft, a 14ft statue of Pilgrim leader Myles Standish overlooks the bay. Visitors can climb the 125 steps up to the observation area to enjoy a **view** of Plymouth, Cape Cod Bay and Provincetown.

Myles Standish State Forest★

Cranberry Rd., South Carver, 26mi from Plymouth via Rte. 3 south to exit 5, right onto Long Pond Rd. to entrance. 🅿 ☎ *508-866-2526. www.mass.gov/dcr/parks/southeast.* Bike, swim, fish, hike or camp at this 14,635-acre park, dotted with 15 ponds.

PROVINCETOWN★★

POPULATION 3,431
MICHELIN MAP 581 O 9 AND MAP BELOW
TOURIST INFORMATION ☎ 508-362-3225 OR WWW.PROVINCETOWN.COM

Extending to the tip of Cape Cod, Provincetown, or "P-town," as it is known to locals, combines elements of a fishing village, artists' colony and resort. During the summer, the arrival of large numbers of tourists, many gay and lesbian, swell the population of the town from 3,400 to 75,000.

▶ **Orient Yourself:** Provincetown is about 120mi from Boston. As Rte. 6 heads north through the Province Lands area of Cape Cod National Seashore, Provincetown Harbor is visible to the left.

🅿 **Parking:** The main town lot is located at the western base of MacMillan Pier.

⊘ **Don't Miss:** Art's Dune Tours are fun; on a clear day, climb to the top of the Pilgrim Monument and enjoy marvelous views.

🕐 **Organizing Your Time:** Getting to P-Town from Boston can take a long time in traffic (2.5hrs is a quick trip), so stay long enough to make the trip worthwhile.

🧒 **Especially for Kids:** With gentler waves than Race Point Beach, Herring Cove Beach is a good pick for families with young children.

A Bit of History

Pilgrims and Mooncussers – By the 18C, less than 100 years after the Pilgrims landed on the cape, Province-town had grown into the third-largest whaling center after Nantucket and New Bedford. In the mid-19C, 75 wharves could be counted along its shores, and the beaches were covered with fish flakes, or racks for drying fish, and saltworks, wooden structures used to filter salt from seawater. Provincetown vessels recruited seamen in the Azores and Cape Verde Islands, a factor

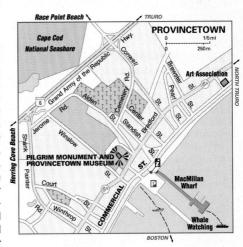

that accounts for the town's large Portuguese population and the traditions they have preserved.

Other Provincetowners found fortune closer to home. Villains known as mooncussers erected lights along the shore to lure unwitting ships into dangerous shoals where they ran aground. Mooncussers then boarded the vessels, killed the crew and stole the valuable cargo. The place where these rogues gathered was nicknamed "Hell-town" and was cautiously avoided by the village's more respectable citizens.

Provincetown of the Artists – At the beginning of the 20C, Provincetown's wild natural beauty attracted artists and writers to its shores. In 1901 Charles W. Haw-thorne founded the **Cape Cod School of Art** here, followed 15 years later by the establishment of the **Provincetown Players**, a group of playwrights and actors rebelling against the rigid criteria of the Broadway stage. **Eugene O'Neill**'s career as a playwright was launched at Provincetown in 1916 when his first play, *Bound East for Cardiff,* was produced at the Wharf Theatre. At about the same time, the town became a prestigious artists' colony, where writers and dramatists such as O'Neill, John Dos Passos, Sinclair Lewis and Tennessee Williams gathered. Over the ensuing decades, the town has hosted art-world celebrities such as Robert Motherwell and Mark Rothko. Today the numerous galleries along Commercial Street, the **Provincetown Art Association** and the **Provincetown Theater Company** carry out the cultural and artistic traditions so closely associated with the town's character.

🅘 *For a listing of current art shows, consult the free gallery guide available from the visitor center at MacMillan Wharf and from major galleries.*

Tourist Mecca – In the summer, crowds weave in and out of the shops, galleries and eating places that line the narrow streets, especially along **Commercial Street**, the main thoroughfare in town. Visitors and residents alike find the nearby beaches of the **Cape Cod National Seashore** (CCNS)—including **Herring Cove Beach** and **Race Point Beach** *(map p 231)*—a refreshing contrast to the hustle and bustle. *(In summer, shuttle buses run hourly along Bradford St. and to Herring Cove Beach.)* The **Province Lands Trail** (🚲 *7mi)* offers cyclists a challenging, but spectacular ride through forests and dunes with expansive views of the water (🅘 *for details, contact CCNS:* ☎ *508-255-3421; www.nps.gov/caco).*

Address Book

STAYING IN PROVINCETOWN

Fairbanks Inn – *90 Bradford St.* 🅿 ☎ *508-487-0386 or 800-324-7265. www.fairbanksinn.com. 14 rooms.* **$$$** Although this sea captain's house was built in the 18C and its antique furnishings recall that era, the feel is cozy rather than precious. In the main house, set one block back from busy Commercial Street, the larger front bedrooms sport four-poster beds and fireplaces; yet even the smaller rooms have distinctive touches like a carved-wood headboard or a marble-topped dresser. Continental breakfast is served on the cheery sun porch; fresh-from-the-oven scones or coffee cakes may lure you downstairs early.

DINING IN PROVINCETOWN

Front Street – *230 Commercial St. Closed Jan–Apr & Tue in season.* ☎ *508-487-9715.* **$$ Mediterranean**. Brick walls, antique wooden booths, and lacquered handmade tables give this dining room a romantic, yet informal, appeal. The menu—updated Continental fare with Mediterranean accents—changes every Friday. Herb-crusted rack of lamb is a specialty.

Sights

MacMillan Wharf

At the end of Standish St. Public parking lot on the wharf.

Late in the afternoon, fishing boats, announced by the procession of seagulls that greets them, return to the wharf, where their fresh catches are unloaded and shipped to markets in Boston and New York. On the last Sunday in June, the **Blessing of the Fleet**, a colorful and impressive Portuguese celebration, takes place in the harbor. This lively pier is also the departure point for ever-popular **whale-watching cruises** *(schedules are available from the visitor center).*

Pilgrim Monument & Provincetown Museum★

On High Pole Hill off Winslow St. ◷ *Open Jul–Aug daily 9am–6:15pm; Apr–Jun & Sept–Nov daily 9am–4:15pm. Last admission 45min before closing.* ⊙ *$7.* P ☎ *508-487-1310. www.pilgrim-monument.org.*

Inspired by the 14C bell tower in the Tuscan hill town of Siena, the Pilgrim Monument was completed in 1910 to commemorate the 1620 landing of the Pilgrims at Provincetown. The observation deck atop this 252 ft granite structure affords sweeping **views**★★ of Provincetown, its harbor, and the lower cape *(116 steps and 60 ramps).* Located near the tower, a small history museum serves as the entrance to the facility and houses a permanent collection of historic documents and artifacts, including a model of the *Mayflower.*

Dune Tours★★

Departs from Art's Dune Tours, corner of Standish and Commercial. ◷ *Mid-Apr–mid-Nov daily 10am–dusk. 1hr. Commentary.* ⊙ *$20. Reservations required.* ☎ *508-487-1950. www.artsdunetours.com.*

This tour by four-wheel-drive vehicle is a magnificent way to explore the spectacular Provincetown Dunes of the Cape Cod National Seashore, both of which are constantly being reshaped by the winds. Art's also offers sunrise and sunset tours.

SALEM★★

POPULATION 40,407

MICHELIN MAP 581 N 7 AND MAP P 271

TOURIST INFORMATION ☎ 877-725-3662 OR WWW.SALEM.ORG

Salem, a town tormented by its fear of witchcraft in the 17C, and a seaport that launched nearly 1,000 ships in the following centuries, is a bustling and pleasant city where historic districts adjoin industrial sites. While witch-related sites draw lots of tourists, Salem is rightly proud of its restored waterfront, stunning Federalist homes and first-class museum, the Peabody Essex Museum.

▶ **Orient Yourself:** Salem lies on the North Shore of Massachusetts, about 20mi north of Boston, off Rte. 128.

P **Parking:** There is limited metered parking around Salem Common, and a couple of central lots, on St. Peter and Derby Streets.

◉ **Don't Miss:** The Peabody Essex Museum's Yin Yu Tang House is fascinating.

◷ **Organizing Your Time:** Salem is a good central base for exploring the North Shore.

Kids **Especially for Kids:** Take a tour of Harbor Sweets *(85 Leavitt St.;* ☎ *978-745-4777; www.harborsweets.com)* to watch the chocolate-making process.

◔ **Also See:** The nautical town of Marblehead (◔ *see Entry).*

A Bit of History

A City of Peace – Founded in 1626 by Roger Conant, Salem derives its name from the Hebrew word *Shalom,* meaning peace. Ironically, intolerance and violence dominated the early days of this Puritan city. Roger Williams, persecuted by the authorities, fled to Rhode Island in 1636, and thereafter zealous Salemites devoted their energies to driving the "evil ones" from the colony. Intended to rid the colony once and for all of evildoers, the notorious witch-hunts began in the early 1690s.

The Witchcraft Hysteria – In 1692 several young girls, whose imaginations had been stirred by tales of voodoo told to them by the West Indian slave **Tituba**, began to have visions and convulsive fits. After examining the girls, a doctor declared them to be victims of "the evil hand." Impressionable and frightened, the youngsters accused Tituba and two other women of having bewitched them, and the women were immediately arrested and put into prison. From that point on, fear and panic spread through Salem, leaving no one free of suspicion. More than 200 persons were accused of witchcraft, 150 of whom were imprisoned and 19 found guilty and hanged. The hysteria, credited in retrospect to rivalries between several prominent Salem families, came to an abrupt end about a year later when Governor William Phips' wife was accused of witchcraft.

An Era of Maritime Glory – Salem's sizable fleet of vessels, important to colonial trade in the 17C, won special recognition during the Revolution. When the ports of Boston and New York were occupied by the British, it was Salem's ships that carried arms and supplies to the colonial troops. Operating as privateers, the town's vessels also weakened the enemy by raiding and capturing about 400 British ships before the war ended.

After the Revolution, Salem's merchant craft were prominent in worldwide trade. In 1786 the *Grand Turk,* sailing out of Salem to China, returned home to New England laden with luxury goods. To the many ships that followed the *Grand Turk,* the route to the Far East became a familiar one; "To the farthest port of the rich East!" became Salem's motto. The Chinese, who saw great numbers of vessels arriving in their ports bearing Salem's name, imagined Salem was a vast and magnificent country.

Two years after the *Grand Turk* set sail for China, trade between Salem and India was opened by another Salem ship, the *Peggy,* owned by Elias Hasket Derby. The China trade brought such enormous wealth to Salem that taxes paid in the town on imported goods alone provided eight percent of the nation's revenues. Salem merchants, including the Derbys, Peabodys and Crowninshields, were among the richest men in America; their mansions were filled with treasures retrieved from the Orient aboard their ships.

The decline of the port of Salem, due in part to the embargo on foreign trade enforced by President Jefferson in 1807, was hastened by the development of new, deep-draft clipper ships that could only be outfitted in deepwater ports such as those of Boston and New York.

Salem Today – Renewal programs in the heart of the downtown area, around **Essex Street**, have created the look of the colonial era with brick walkways and a pedestrian mall. A number of shops devoted to the occult offer tarot and psychic readings and sell witchcraft and New Age items. Operated by the National Park Service, the **visitor center**, housed in the town's renovated turn-of-the-century armory, just off Essex Street, features a 27min film, *Where Past is Present,* that details the history of Essex County (*2 New Liberty St.;* ◷ *open year-round daily 9am–5pm;* ◷ *closed Jan 1, Thanksgiving Day & Dec 25;* ♿ ☎ *978-740-1650; www.nps.gov/sama*).

Two Famous Men of Salem

Samuel McIntire (1757-1811), carpenter, wood carver, sculptor, builder and architect, influenced much of Salem's architecture. His solid, four-square wood and brick mansions, such as the Pierce-Nichols House (1782) on Federal Street (⚓ *not open to the public*), ornamented with handsome porches and balustrades, are among the finest examples of American Federal architecture. A leading 19C American literary figure, **Nathaniel Hawthorne** (1804-64) was born in Salem, where he wrote his earliest stories. Salem provided the inspiration or setting for many of Hawthorne's works, including *The House of the Seven Gables.* Much of the description in his novel *The Scarlet Letter,* especially that of the Custom House *(below),* was influenced by the years he spent as surveyor of the port.

Seaside Salem

The historic waterfront district may be visited on foot; begin at the orientation center (below) on Central Wharf.

After more than a century, Salem is once again alive with a vitality reminiscent of its days of maritime supremacy. **Pickering Wharf** boasts a concentration of restaurants and specialty shops; just beyond it, on Derby Street, is the Salem Maritime National Historic Site.

Salem Maritime National Historic Site★

🅺𝖎𝖉𝖘 *193 Derby St.* 🕐 *Open year-round daily 9am–5pm.* 🕐 *Closed Jan 1, Thanksgiving Day & Dec 25.* ☎ *978-740-1660. www.nps.gov/sama.*

The city's historic waterfront site is administered by the National Park Service; guided tours (🕶 *$5*) of the Custom House and Derby House are offer several times daily. The **orientation center** features a film *(17min)* recounting how Salem pioneered trade with the Orient. At one time more than 40 wharves reached out into the harbor from the town's shoreline. **Derby Wharf**, the longest (2,100ft), and for many years a busy mercantile center, still remains.

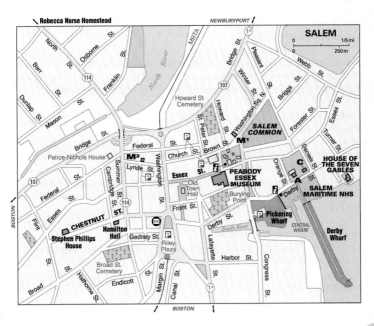

Address Book

For price ranges for hotels and restaurants, see the legend on the cover flap.

WHERE TO STAY

Hawthorne Hotel – *18 Washington Square West.* ✗ ♿ 🅿 ☎ *978-744-4080 or 800-729-7829. www.hawthornehotel. com. 89 rooms.* **$$$** Sitting opposite the town's Common, this sturdy brick dowager (1925) is a well-situated base for exploring Salem's historic attractions. The feel here is stately, if a bit old-fashioned. Guest rooms are furnished with 18C reproductions, brass lamps, and sedate paisley or geometric-patterned spreads. In the hotel's wood-paneled **Tavern on the Green**, you can get sandwiches, pastas and New England-style seafood; while Nathaniel's, the more formal dining room, serves updated Continental fare.

Amelia Payson House B&B – *16 Winter St. Closed late Nov–Mar.* 🅿 ☎ *978-744-8304. www.ameliapaysonhouse.com. 4 rooms.* **$$** It feels as if you should sit daintily sipping tea in the elegant parlor with its grand piano in this dignified 1845 Greek Revival home, but the warm welcome here reflects more of the present day. This long-established B&B, within a short walk of the historic sights, is furnished with period antiques, iron or brass beds, and plenty of pretty pink. Continental breakfast is served—along with sightseeing tips—in the formal dining room.

WHERE TO EAT

Strega – *94 Lafayette St. Dinner only.* 🅿 ☎ *978-741-0004. www.stregasalem. com.* **$$ Italian**. Strega is a favorite with local foodies thanks to its menu of small plates, great for sharing among friends. Mix and match dishes like mussels provencale, calamari fritti, and a tasty grilled apricot with gorgonzola, proscuitto and arugula; each $10 or so.

Lyceum Bar & Grill – *43 Church St.* 🅿 ☎ *978-745-7665. www.lyceumsalem. com.* **$$$ New American**. Lyceum remains the go-to, place to take clients and impress guest. Modern constructions as wasabi-crusted tuna share the menu with a tradtional baked stuffed lobster and a NY sirloin served with mashed potatoes and buttermilk onion rings. Lunch runs from Caesar salads and burgers, to grilled salmon and a shrimp BLT. Brick walls, large windows, and beige-toned upholstery feel both casual and comfortably up-to-date.

Custom House★ (A)

Visit by guided tour only.

This Federal-style building with its symbolic eagle was constructed in 1819 to house the customs offices of Salem. Inside, several of the offices, including the one used by Nathaniel Hawthorne when he was an officer of the port, have been restored.

Derby House (C)

Visit by guided tour only.

This brick mansion was built in 1762 for merchant Elias Hasket Derby, whose ships eventually opened trade with India and the Orient, making him very rich. From the waterfront location of this house, Derby could see his ships as they docked near Derby Wharf. Inside, the wave motif ornamenting the stairway and the staircase balusters, carved to resemble twisted rope, is an appropriate feature for the home of a man who earned his living from the sea.

House of the Seven Gables★

54 Turner St. *Visit by guided tour (45 min) only, July–Oct daily 10am–7pm; Oct weekends until 11pm. Rest of the year daily 10am–5pm.* ⏱ *Closed first 2wks of Jan, Thanksgiving Day & Dec 25.* ✄ *$12. Candlelight tours available.* 🅿 ☎ *978-744-0991. www.7gables.org.*

House of the Seven Gables

A rambling three-story Colonial with steeply pitched roofs, this house was immortalized by Hawthorne's novel of the same name. Built in 1668, the house was completely restored in 1968. Inside, scenes from Hawthorne's novel come alive as visitors pass from Hepzibah's Cent Shop to the parlor where the judge was found, and into Clifford's room, under the eaves, at the top of a secret staircase. Tours cover 6 of the 16 rooms, as well as Hawthorne's birthplace (c.1750, moved from its original location on Union Street).

Other buildings in this garden setting include the Retire Becket House (1655, which contains the museum shop), the Hooper-Hathaway House (1682) and a counting house (c.1830).

Peabody Essex Museum★★★

This illustrious museum focuses on America's maritime history from the 17C to the present, and on the historical significance of the city of Salem and Essex County. It pays special tribute to Salem's great 18C and 19C maritime era, during which

the town flourished as a major American port. The collections reflect the global range of Salem's ship captains, who returned from their travels with porcelain, carvings and other artifacts from the Far East, India, Africa and the Pacific Islands. In celebration of its bicentennial, the museum initiated a 250,000sq ft, $125 million expansion. Designed by renowned architect Moshe Safdie, a new 111,000sq ft wing, as well as the renovated facilities, opened in 2003. A 19C rural house, moved here from China's Anhui Province, with its original furnishings, is now open to the public. With its expanded space, the PEM can showcase the entire range of its collection, including African, Korean and Indian art, photography, architec-

Peabody Essex Museum

ture and design, and contemporary Native American Art. In Idea Studios, museum visitors can meet the artists and participate in making art.

Visit

🄺 *East India Square.* 🕐 *Open year-round daily 10am-5pm (Thu til 9pm).* 🕐 *Closed Jan 1, Thanksgiving Day & Dec 25.* 💲 *$13 (Admission to Yin Yu Tang, a Chinese House, is $4 plus museum fee).* ☎ *800-745-9500. www.pem.org.*

Museum
The collections are spread over three floors, and organized into several categories. Here are some highlights.

Maritime Art
The collection of marine paintings includes works by major artists, such as Fitz Henry Lane and Antoine Roux. Portraiture and other paintings by such famed artists as John Singleton Copley and Gilbert Stuart are also featured, as are rare nautical instruments and charts and a dramatic collection of carved ships' figureheads.

Asian Export Art
Considered one of the most complete collections of its kind in the world, the collection features 19C and early-20C decorative and utilitarian porcelain, silver, furniture, textiles and precious objects. Created in China, Japan, India, the Philippines and Ceylon (now Sri Lanka), the pieces were intended for export to England and America and therefore reflect a melding of Eastern artistry and Western tastes. The lacquer, ivory and mother-of-pearl pieces, as well as the items fashioned in gold and silver, are particularly impressive for their refined style and exquisite detail.

Asian, African and Pacific Islands Art
This section encompasses textiles, shields, ritual costumes, masks and pottery from the tropical Pacific Islands, Indonesia, Japan and Africa. The Edward S. Morse Collection of 19C Meiji costumes and crafts is reputedly the largest of its kind outside Japan.

Native American Arts and Archaeology
The collection includes artifacts from the Indian cultures of the Eastern seaboard, Great Lakes, Great Plains, Northwest Coast and South America.

Yin Yu Tang: A Chinese House
One of the highlights of a visit to this museum is a tour of a Chinese merchant's house from the Anhui province, more than 200 years old. The house has been reassembled here, on the museum's campus (🚶 *tours by reservation only;* 💲 *$4 fee applies, added to museum admission*).

Salem Bewitched

In recent years Salem has become a center for adherents of the ancient religion of Wicca, a belief system based on goddesses and nature. Several thousand witches, as followers of Wicca call themselves, currently live in the area, quietly practicing their religion and attempting to dispel long-held public opinions concerning witchcraft. Several points of interest in or near Salem individually re-create the tale of the witch-hunts and the story of their unfortunate victims. In 1992 the city celebrated the tercentenary of the witch trials. Each year at Halloween, Salem hosts Haunted Happenings, a month-long festival that recalls the city's past.

Additional Sights

Salem Common★

In the 19C a number of Federal mansions were built bordering the common of colonial Salem, called Washington Square. A notable group of these residences stands on Washington Square North.

Chestnut Street★★

This broad street lined with Federal-style mansions illustrates the wealth of 19C Salem. The majority of the dwellings on Chestnut Street were built between 1800 and 1820; their size and richly adorned facades are unrivaled. **Hamilton Hall** (no. 9) was designed by Samuel McIntire. The **Stephen Phillips Memorial Trust House** (no. 34), decorated with furnishings from around the world, is open to the public (*visit by 45min guided tour only, late May–Oct Mon–Sat 10am–4pm;* 978-744-0440; www.phillipsmuseum.org).

Salem Witch Museum (M¹)

19 1/2 Washington Square. Open Jul–Aug daily 10am–7pm. Rest of the year daily 10am–5pm (call for Jan hours). Closed Jan 1, Thanksgiving Day & Dec 25. $7.50. 978-744-1692. www.salemwitchmuseum.com.

The museum presents a multimedia program (30min) of 13 life-size scenes that sensationalize the major events of the witchcraft hysteria from 1692 to its final days in 1693. A permanent exhibit titled "Witches: Evolving Perceptions" traces the meaning of the word *witch* up to current times and includes a look at the Wicca movement. Across from the museum stands Henry H. Kitson's statue of Salem's founder, **Roger Conant**.

Witch Dungeon Museum (M²)

16 Lynde St. Visit by guided tour (25min) only, Apr–Nov daily 10am–5pm. $6. 978-741-3570. www.witchdungeon.com.

A live stage presentation, based on historic transcripts of a 1692 witch trial, captures the hysteria that swept Salem in the late 17C. Following the presentation, visitors tour a re-creation of the dank dungeon where local "witches" were jailed in tiny, unlit cells.

Rebecca Nurse Homestead

149 Pine St., in Danvers, 4mi north of Salem. Visit by guided tour (1hr) only, mid-Jun–Labor Day noon–4:30pm; Sept–Oct weekends only noon–4:30pm. $5. 978-774-8799. www.rebeccanurse.org.

Rebecca Nurse, a victim of the Salem witch-hunts, lived in this saltbox house (c.1678). Accused of being a witch, Rebecca was tried, convicted and hanged, despite a petition in her favor that had been signed by many of the townspeople. A short walk from the house leads to the Nurse Burial Ground, where a monument marks Rebecca's presumed grave.

SPRINGFIELD

POPULATION 152,082
MICHELIN MAP 581 J 9
TOURIST INFORMATION ☎ 413-787-1548 OR WWW.VALLEYVISITOR.COM

A rich industrial past has contributed to making Springfield the hub of business, finance and industry in the Pioneer Valley and the third-largest city in Massachusetts.

Established on the banks of the Connecticut River in 1636 as a trading post, Springfield grew into an industrial center by the 19C. For over 200 years the city was known for the **Springfield Armory**, the government arsenal that turned out the first American musket (1795) and weapons used by the Union troops in the Civil War.

Every September the Springfield area hosts the **Eastern States Exposition**, the largest fair in the northeast. Located on the 175-acre fairgrounds in West Springfield (*2mi west of the center of Springfield on Rte. 147*), the "Big E," as the annual fair is called, features exhibits, entertainment, the Eastern States Horse Show and a tour of **Old Storrowtown Village**, a restored colonial village on the grounds. In June the fairground is also the site of the annual **American Craft Fair**, formerly held in New York.

▶ **Orient Yourself:** Springfield is located in south-central Massachusetts, about 90mi southwest of Boston.

🅿 **Parking:** The city has several lots, usually charging $1.50 per half hour. The Dwight St. lot is $5 for all-day parking.

🏀 **Don't Miss:** Naismith Basketball Hall of Fame is a must for sports fans.

🕐 **Organizing Your Time:** Visit the b'ball hall first (it opens at 9am), and then head over to the quadrangle for lunch and museum-hopping.

📷 **Especially for Kids:** The Dr. Seuss National Memorial Sculpture Garden is a delight for small fry.

🕯 **Also See:** Six Flags New England, in nearby Agawam, is the region's largest amusement park.

Sights

Basketball Hall of Fame★

📷 *1000 W. Columbus Ave.* 🕐 *Open year-round Mon-Sat 9am–5pm, Sun 10am-5pm.* 🕐 *Closed Thanksgiving Day & Dec 25.* ☜ *$16.99.* ⚇ 🅿 ☎ *877-446-6752. www. hoophall.com.*

Basketball was originated by Dr. James Naismith, whose Springfield College team played the first game in 1891. Equipment consisted of a ball and a peach basket; each time a team scored, someone had to climb a ladder to remove the ball from the basket. The game was adopted by the YMCA three years later, and by 1936 it had gained international recognition and acceptance as an Olympic sport.

Exhibits trace the development of the sport from amateur to professional and international status. Life-size action photos of such basketball greats as Wilt Chamberlain and Bob Cousy, videotapes of unforgettable coaches in action on the sidelines, film clips of the celebrated Harlem Globetrotters, and a selection of uniforms, equipment and memorabilia constitute the displays. Recently refurbished, the Hall is loaded with state-of-the-at interactive exhibits. The main event here is the Center Court, a full-size basketball court and scoreboard, with viewing balconies on three levels, where visitors play and compete in shoot-out contests. Play one-on-one against former stars in the Virtual Reality area.

The Quadrangle

220 State St. ⏲ *Museums open Wed–Fri noon–5pm, weekends 11am–4pm.* 👓 *$7.* 🍴♿🅿 ☎ *413-263-6800. www.quadrangle.org.*

Four museums are grouped together on the Quadrangle bounded by Chestnut and State Streets. In the center of the action is the 🅺🅸🅳🆂 **Dr. Seuss National Memorial Sculpture Garden**, a series of bronzes of the beloved characters of Dr. Seuss's books. The statues were designed by sculptor Lark Grey Dimond-Cates, stepdaughter of Dr. Seuss. Seuss, whose real name was Theodor Seuss Geisel, was born in Springfield in 1904.

Museum of Fine Arts

Holdings include European paintings of the 17C Dutch, 18C Italian, and 18C and 19C French schools. The American section contains canvases by eminent 19C painters, such as Winslow Homer and Frederic Edwin Church.

George Walter Vincent Smith Art Museum★

This building, designed to suggest an Italian Renaissance villa, contains a collection of Oriental and American art and furnishings, and casts of ancient Greek and Roman statues.

The collection includes 19C American paintings, interesting examples of Japanese armor, screens, lacquers and ceramics and **Chinese cloisonné** (enamel poured into raised compartments).

Connecticut Valley Historical Museum

Changing exhibits of the museum's collection of furniture, pewter, silver and portraits depict the social and cultural development of the Connecticut Valley from the 17C.

Springfield Science Museum

🅺🅸🅳🆂 The museum contains a planetarium, a hands-on exploration center and the multilevel African Hall, as well as displays devoted to plant and animal life, geology and dinosaurs—including a full-size replica of a *Tyrannosaurus rex.*

Forest Park

Sumner Ave. ⏲ *Open Apr–mid-Oct, daily 10am–4:30pm; mid-Oct–Nov, weekends only, 10am-3:30 pm.* ⏲ *Closed Dec-·Mar & Thanksgiving Day.* ♿ ☎ *413-733-2251. www.forestparkzoo.com.*

🅺🅸🅳🆂 This pleasant city park features a small zoo, with barnyard animals, a petting zoo, and exotic species such as a South American capabara, emus and wallabies.

Excursion

Stanley Park

400 Western Ave. in Westfield. 15mi west of Springfield via US-20, then turn left onto Elm St., left onto Court St., and bear left onto Granville Rd. ⏲ *Open year-round daily 7am–dusk.* ♿🅿 ☎ *413-568-9312. www.stanleypark.org.*

A 61-bell Flemish carillon, an English herb garden and a rose garden are among the many attractions in this 275-acre park, an expansive recreational space for the surrounding communities. Located in the pond area are a covered bridge, an old mill and a blacksmith's shop.

STOCKBRIDGE★★

POPULATION 2,276
MICHELIN MAP 581 I 9
TOURIST INFORMATION ☎ 413-298-5200 OR WWW.STOCKBRIDGECHAMBER.ORG

Founded in the early 18C as an Indian mission, this quintessential New England town nestled in the heart of the Berkshires exudes a grace and charm that has traditionally endeared it to well-heeled Bostonians and New Yorkers as well as to artists and writers.

The town's **Main Street** ★ is lined with a picturesque row of pedimented buildings bounded to the west by the sprawling white facade of the **Red Lion Inn** (☎ 413-298-5545; www.redlioninn.com), a cozy country hostelry dating from colonial times. Beyond the inn, Main Street gives way to large clapboard dwellings rimmed by broad landscaped lawns.

Due to its prime location (less than 3 hours by car from both Boston and New York), Stockbridge welcomes a steady stream of visitors throughout the year. In the summer, performances of classic American drama are presented at the Berkshire Theater Festival.

▶ **Orient Yourself:** Stockbridge lies 3hrs west of Boston, off the Mass. Turnpike.
🅿 **Parking:** Free, street-side parking is available (check the side streets).
🔗 **Don't Miss:** The Norman Rockwell Museum offers a sweet slice of Americana.
🕐 **Organizing Your Time:** Stockbridge makes a great base for exploring Berkshires attractions, to the north or Connecticut's Litchfield Hills, to the south.

Sights Map p 163.

Norman Rockwell Museum★★

▨ 9 Glendale Rd. 2.5mi from Stockbridge center. ▶ Take Rte. 102 West (Main St., then Church St.). After 2mi turn left onto Rte. 183 and continue .6mi to museum entrance on left. 🕐 Open May–Oct daily 10am–5pm; rest of the year Mon–Fri 10am–4pm, weekends 10am–5pm. 🕐 Closed Jan 1, Thanksgiving Day & Dec 25. ⊛ $12.50. ⚅🅿 ☎ 413-298-4100. www.nrm.org.

Occupying a 36-acre estate overlooking the Housatonic River Valley, this immensely popular museum is the repository of the largest collection of original works by America's premier 20C illustrator.

Visit

The core collection comprises Rockwell's personal holdings along with his studio and personal library and archives. In addition, the museum has acquired works through gifts or purchases, bringing the total holdings to more than 500 paintings and drawings, including 172 large-scale works. The main building, containing nine galleries, was designed by the eminent post-Modern architect **Robert A.M. Stern** to provide a spacious setting for the collection. The Neoclassical style of the building brings to mind a New England town hall.

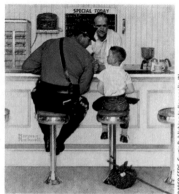

The Runaway (1958) by Norman Rockwell

©1958 SEPS, Curtis Publishing Indianapolis, IN

Norman Rockwell: Illustrator of American Life

Norman Rockwell (1894-1978) began his long and prolific career in his teens. At age 22 the artist drew his first cover for the *Saturday Evening Post*, thereby beginning a collaboration that would result in a total of 321 covers for the prestigious magazine over the next 47 years.

Rockwell's realistic paintings chronicle the changing times in America, while capturing the timeless essence of humanity—mankind's comic foibles, noble aspirations and wrenching tragedies. His homespun scenes, often depicting the routines of day-to-day living, are seasoned with a sense of humor and wonder. Rockwell often depicted children, and in many cases his subjects were modeled on family, friends or neighbors. When Rockwell embarked upon a 10-year association with *Look* magazine in the 1960s, he focused on contemporary political figures and American social issues, such as the civil rights movement and poverty. In 1978 Rockwell died in Stockbridge, his home since 1953.

On display inside is a sizable sampling of Rockwell's works, including *Stockbridge Main Street at Christmas*, *Triple Self-Portrait* and *The Problem We All Live With*. Also in the museum's collection is the celebrated **Four Freedoms Series** (1943) inspired by President Franklin Delano Roosevelt's 1941 landmark speech rallying the nation to defend the rights of all people menaced by the Axis powers: freedom of speech, freedom of worship, freedom from want and freedom from fear. During World War II, these poignant images toured the nation on posters that formed the centerpiece of a fund-raising drive that yielded over $130 million in government bonds to support the war.

The museum also features temporary exhibits focusing on the work and life of Rockwell and, more broadly, on the art of illustration.

Just a short stroll from the museum, on a rise overlooking the valley, stands **Rockwell's studio** (🕐 *open May–Oct*), a simple red wooden building relocated from its original site in downtown Stockbridge.

Chesterwood★

3mi from Stockbridge center. ▶ *Take Rte. 102 West and turn left onto Rte. 183. Continue .8mi and turn right onto Mohawk Lake Rd., then left on Willow St. and continue .5mi to Chesterwood.* 🕐 *Open May–Oct daily 10am–5pm.* 🕐 *$10.* ♿ 🅿 ☎ *413-298-3579. www.chesterwood.org.*

This large estate, formerly a farm, was acquired in the late 19C by the American sculptor **Daniel Chester French** (1850-1931). Although French achieved his first major success at the age of 25 with his *Minute Man* statue at Concord, he is probably best remembered for the impressive seated *Abraham Lincoln* he sculpted for the Lincoln Memorial in the nation's capital. French executed more than 100 public monuments during his lifetime.

Models and casts of French's works, including the Dupont Circle Fountain he sculpted for Washington, DC, occupy the **Barn Gallery**. The large Colonial Revival **house** (designed by Henry Bacon) replaced the farmhouse originally on the property. The house is furnished as it was when the artist lived here. Also on the grounds is French's spacious, well-lit **studio** (another Henry Bacon design), with its tall double doors and railroad tracks that allowed French to move large works outdoors, where he could work in natural light.

A woodland walk *(20min)* affords views of the hilly countryside.

Naumkeag

2mi from Stockbridge center on Prospect Hill Rd. ▶ *From the intersection of US-7 and Rte. 102 in Stockbridge center, take Pine St. north; bear left on Prospect Hill Rd. and* follow it .5mi to entrance. ✎ *Visit by guided tour (45min) only, late May–Columbus Day daily 10am–5pm. $10.* ⓟ ☎ *413-298-8146. www.thetrustees.org.*

This Norman-style mansion (1886, Stanford White) and its terraced hillside gardens were built for Joseph Choate (1832-1917), US ambassador to England. Naumkeag was the Choate family's summer cottage. The unusual design of the entrance to the Chinese garden was intended to keep the devil out.

WILLIAMSTOWN★★

POPULATION 8,424
MICHELIN MAP 581 I 7
TOURIST INFORMATION ☎ 413-458-9077 OR WWW.WILLIAMSTOWNCHAMBER.COM

This beautiful colonial village snuggles in the northwest corner of Massachusetts, at the place where the Mohawk Trail enters the Berkshires. The Berkshires' verdant rolling hills provide a lovely setting for Williams College, as well as for the Sterling and Francine Clark Art Institute and the Williamstown Theater Festival, which is held each summer.

In 1753 the early settlement of West Hoosuck was established here by soldiers from Fort Massachusetts. Later one of the soldiers, Col. Ephraim Williams Jr., bequeathed part of his estate for the founding of a free school in West Hoosuck—provided the town be renamed in his honor. Soon after the colonel's death, West Hoosuck was renamed Williamstown.

▶ **Orient Yourself:** Williamstown is located in Berkshire County, in the northwest corner of Massachusetts, just south of the Vermont border.

ⓟ **Parking:** Street parking is available here; check the side streets for spots.

☻ **Don't Miss:** The Clark Art Institute is one of the finest in the region; also, stroll the beautiful grounds of Williams College (1793), with more than 50 buildings from different historical periods.

🕐 **Organizing Your Time:** Museum-hopping and lunch on Spring Street, then a movie at Images Cinema—now that's a perfect day.

Spring Street Treats

A college town like Williamstown is bound to have a restaurant on the main shopping drag where the food is good, filling and cheap, and the lines spill out the front door. **Pappa Charlie's Deli** (28 Spring St.; ☎ 413-458-5969) fills the bill, with overstuffed sandwiches, home-made soups (leek and rice, tomato orzo, and *pasta e fagioli*), gargantuan slabs of veggie lasagna and eggplant parmesan—and a mean root beer float to wash it all down. The blackboard reveals dozens of selections, each named in honor of various celebrity patrons, many of which are alumni of the Williamstown Theater Festival.

Afterwards walk up the street to **Lickety-Split** (69 Spring St.; ☎ 413-458-1818), a popular student hangout, for an ice-cream cone. Then cross the street and duck into the intimate **Images Cinema** (☎ 413-458-5612; www.imagescinema.org) to see a foreign film. Housed in a historic brick building, this independent film house also offers film discussions over Sunday brunch, family films, and late-night bites as an alternative to cookie-cutter mall megaplexes.

Clark Art Institute★★★

The European and American paintings, sculpture, works on paper and decorative arts of the illustrious **Sterling and Francine Clark Art Institute** were gathered by Robert Sterling Clark and his wife, Francine, during the years between World War I and 1956. The collection, worthy of being compared with those of some of the world's finest museums, reflects the Clarks' early taste for classical art and, later, 19C paintings. The couple chose Williamstown as the site of their institute for its idyllic natural setting and its location far from urban centers (most likely to be threatened during wartime). The white marble building (1956), designed to house the collection, suggests a private residence and provides a splendid setting for the works. The red granite annex houses additional gallery space as well as the museum's auditorium.

Visit

225 South St. ◷ *Open Jul–Aug daily 10am–5pm. Rest of the year Tue–Sun 10am–5pm.* ◷ *Closed Jan 1, Thanksgiving Day & Dec 25.* ⚲ *$10 (free admission Nov–May).* ✕ 🅿 ♿ ☎ *413-458-2303. www.clarkart.edu.*

In a room off the entrance court dedicated to the works of Remington, Homer and Sargent. **Frederic Remington** (1861-1909) is known for his paintings of the American West. During his lifetime he created several thousand paintings and pieces of sculpture that portrayed his favorite subjects: cowboys, Indians and the cavalry, and their heroic way of life. **Winslow Homer** (1836-1910) chose to depict the rugged New England landscape—the White Mountains of New Hampshire and the rocky Maine coast—in his paintings. In contrast to Remington and Homer, **John Singer Sargent** (1856-1925) was a modern portraitist whose subjects, generally members of high society, were rendered with the artist's flair for sophistication. Sargent painted his famous *Fumée d'Ambre Gris* while on a voyage to Tangiers.

The museum's earliest works date back to the Renaissance period. Highlighting this section are the Italian paintings, including a seven-part panel altarpiece by Ugolino da Siena, and *Virgin and Child Enthroned with Four Angels* by **Piero della Francesca**. However, it is in the realm of 19C French and American art that the collection excels. In the section devoted to the French school, the group of paintings by **Corot** shows the artist's skill in executing landscapes as well as figures. *The Trumpeter of the Hussars* by **Gericault**, the Romantic painter, typifies his masterful style and contrasts with the muted tones used by **Millet**. Among the Impressionist canvases are more than 30 works by **Renoir**, including *Sleeping Girl with a Cat, The Blonde Bather, The Onions* and others painted between 1870 and 1890. **Degas'** treatment of his favorite subjects, dancers and horses, shows his extraordinary sense of movement. Shimmering with color, the paintings by **Monet** include one from his *Rouen Cathedral* series, and *The Cliffs at Étretat*. The post-Impressionist **Toulouse-Lautrec** is represented by several works, including his *Dr. Péan Operating*.

Williamstown Theatre Festival

Since 1955, this venerable festival has presented more than 500 plays and musicals, along with outdoor free theater, cabaret performances and readings. Its stage has hosted a cast of Hollywood and Broadway luminaries, including Gwyneth Paltrow, Joanne Woodward, Joel Grey and Calista Flockhart. Held in the Adams Memorial Theatre at Williams College, five Main Stage productions run for two weeks each *(mid-Jun–Aug)*. Plays include classic dramas as well as new works from promising young playwrights. 🎭 *For information, call* ☎ *413-597-3400 or www.wtfestival.org.*

Displays of porcelain, furniture and silver accompany the paintings and sculpture. The Clark collection of American and European silver, one of the finest in the world, includes pieces made by the 18C English silversmith **Paul de Lamerie**.

On the upper level of the granite building are recent acquisitions of early photography, featuring a selection of works by French, English and American photographers.

Additional Sight

Williams College Museum of Art★

On Main St. between Spring and Water Sts. ○ *Open year-round Tue–Sat 10am–5pm, Sun 1pm–5pm.* ○ *Closed Jan 1, Thanksgiving Day & Dec 25.* ☎ *413-597-2429. www.wcma.org.*

This building, one of the finest on the Williams campus, has evolved over the years from a brick Greek Revival octagon (1846) to its present size, which includes additions by renowned architect Charles Moore. The building's unassuming exterior belies the dramatic atrium and neatly sculpted, well-lit gallery spaces within.

The collection includes 12,000 works that span the history of art, with an emphasis in modern art from the late 18C to the present. It is particularly strong in American art: Copley, Homer, Eakins, Hopper, Inness, O'Keeffe and Wood are all represented. Art that represents world cultures is a growing category here.

WORCESTER

POPULATION 172,648
MICHELIN MAP 581 L 8
TOURIST INFORMATION ☎ 508-755-7400 OR WWW.WORCESTER.ORG

Worcester, the second largest city in New England, is a commercial and industrial hub. Its central location within the state has promoted the growth of a diverse economy, which includes retail and medical services.

▶ **Orient Yourself:** Worcester is located in central Massachusetts, about an hour west of Boston. Get your bearings at the visitor center at 30 Worcester Center Blvd.

🅿 **Parking:** There are several surface parking lots in and around the city.

☺ **Don't Miss:** Depending upon your interests, the Worcester Art Museum or the Higgins Armory.

○ **Organizing Your Time:** Plan your visit to the Worcester Art Museum for Saturday morning, when admission is free from 10am to noon.

Especially for Kids: The Ecotarium (☎ 508-791-9211; www.ecotarium.org) is a wonderful nature museum for families.

ᐞ **Also See:** Purgatory Chasm, in Sutton (☎ 508-234-3733; www.massparks.org) is an 80ft-deep hole in the ground, with granite walls that rise 70ft—a cool quirk of nature. The property includes "The Coffin," a small cave, and "Fat Man's Misery," a foot-wide, 10ft-long space between two boulders (☺ enter with care).

Sights

Worcester Art Museum★★

55 Salisbury St. ⏰ *Open year-round Wed–Sun 11am–5pm (Thu til 8pm), Sat 10am–5pm.* ⏰ *Closed major holidays.* ⌬ *$10 (free Sat. from 10am–noon).* 🍴 🅿 ☎ *508-799-4406. www.worcesterart.org.*

The museum owns collections of paintings, sculpture and decorative arts spanning 50 centuries from antiquity to the present. Displayed in a building inspired by Italian Renaissance architecture, the collections are arranged in galleries that surround an a central court/arcade. The space includes galleries for prints and drawings, 20C and contemporary art and changing exhibits, and an outdoor garden courtyard.

Mrs. Elizabeth Freake and Baby Mary (c.1674) Artist Unknown

Worcester Art Museum, gift of Mr. & Mrs. Albert W. Rice

The **first floor** is devoted to ancient art, the art of the Middle Ages, and Asian art, including extensive holdings of Japanese prints from the Edo period. Highlights include the 11-headed Japanese Kannon (9-10C AD); the 12C **Chapter House**, formerly part of a Benedictine priory in France; and *The Last Supper,* one of a group of c.1300 frescoes from Spoleto, Italy.

On the second floor, the European schools of painting from the Middle Ages through the 20C are represented. Highlights include El Greco's intense *Repentant Magdalene; The Flight into Egypt* by Nicolas Poussin; a portrait by Gainsborough of his daughters; Gauguin's *Brooding Woman;* and in the Italian section, the dramatic *Calling of St. Matthew* by Strozzi.

The third-floor **American wing** features the American school of painting with works by John Copley, Worcester native Ralph Earl, James McNeill Whistler, Winslow Homer, John Singer Sargent, Mary Cassatt, Childe Hassam and the landscapists George Inness, Albert Pinkham Ryder and Samuel Morse. The portrait of **Mrs. Elizabeth Freake and Baby Mary,** by an anonymous 17C artist, is considered one of the finest portraits of the colonial period. An unusual feature of the self-portrait by Thomas Smith (c.1680) is the naval battle scene that replaces the traditional landscape in the background. Another early work, *The Peaceable Kingdom* by Quaker Edward Hicks, is noteworthy for its simple, unsophisticated theme and treatment.

The museum's distinguished **pre-Columbian collection** *(4th floor)* is also worth viewing. Works in gold, jade, clay, stone and ceramics represent various pre-Columbian cultures, such as Zapotec and Chimu.

Higgins Armory Museum★

🧒 *100 Barber Ave.* ⏰ *Open year-round Tue–Sat 10am–4pm, Sun noon–4pm.* ⏰ *Closed major holidays.* ⌬ *$8.* ♿ 🅿 ☎ *508-853-6015. www.higgins.org.*

This multistoried steel and glass building was constructed by John W. Higgins, a Worcester native and former president of the Worcester Pressed Steel Co. It houses a prized collection of armor as well as early tools and weapons that Higgins gathered during his travels abroad and across the US. Presented in multimedia shows, live demonstrations and historical exhibits, these objects provide a unique perspective on knightly culture.

Principal displays are arranged in an enormous exhibit gallery, modeled after the Great Hall of an 11C Austrian castle. Paintings, furnishings, tapestries, banners and stained glass in the gallery add to the illusion of being in a medieval castle. Along the walls stand some 100 suits of parade, combat and jousting armor dating from the 14C to the 16C. Produced by highly skilled craftsmen, some of these suits are truly works of art, such as the suit of Maximilian armor named for **Emperor Maximilian**, who preferred fluted armor, and the **Franz von Teuffenbach** armor, with its elaborate decorative etching. Tools and weapons of the Stone and Bronze ages and a rare gladiator's helmet (1C AD) are included in the other exhibits. The fourth floor features a time line showing the evolution of armor; on the second floor, children can don medieval dress and a variety of helmets as well as participate in period board games.

Excursion

Old Sturbridge Village★★★

Kids *22mi southwest of Worcester, in Sturbridge, at Mass. Tpk. and I-84.* ⏱ *Open Apr–mid-Oct Tue–Sun 9:30am–5pm; rest of the year Tue–Sun 9:30am–4pm.* ⏱ *Closed major holidays.* ⌨ *$20 (valid for 2 days in a 10-day period).*

This living history museum re-creates life between 1790 and 1840 in a rural New England community. When the museum opened in 1946, historic houses, farm buildings and shops had been moved to and reconstructed on the Sturbridge site. En route to the Common, visitors pass the **Friends Meetinghouse** (1796), which typifies the austere piety associated with the Quakers. At the west end of the Common stands the Greek Revival-style **Center Meetinghouse**. The white "saltbox" **Richardson Parsonage** (1748) is the village minister's home. In the **Tin Shop** next door, a smith turns out wares like those used in early-19C households. Near the tiny **Law Office** sits the well-stocked **Knight Store**, typical of country stores of the period. The Federal-style **Towne House** (1796) is similar to dwellings built by prosperous rural families of the period. Beyond the bank lies an early-19C printing office.

With its livestock fields, **Freeman Farm** is a lively area. Activities performed here include plowing, harvesting field crops and milking cows.

A blacksmith shop, carding mill, gristmill and an 1820 water-powered sawmill are also on the premises.

Don't miss the Glass Exhibit; Firearms, Fibers and Fashion Exhibit; and the Lighting Exhibit. Adjoining the visitor center, the clock gallery contains more than 100 New England clocks. Family activities in the **Samson's Children's Museum** focus on younger children.

Children in the Fitch Garden

Thomas Neill/ Courtesy of Old Sturbridge Village

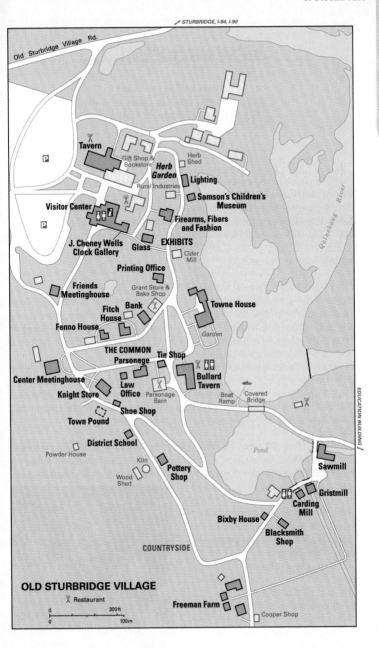

STURBRIDGE, I-84, I-90

Old Sturbridge Village Rd.

P

P

Tavern

Gift Shop & Bookstore

Herb Garden

Herb Shed

Lighting

Rural Industries

Samson's Children's Museum

Visitor Center

Firearms, Fibers and Fashion

J. Cheney Wells Clock Gallery

Glass

EXHIBITS

Cider Mill

Printing Office

Grant Store & Bake Shop

Friends Meetinghouse

Towne House

Fitch House

Bank

Fenno House

Garden

THE COMMON

Parsonage

Tin Shop

Center Meetinghouse

Law Office

Bullard Tavern

Knight Store

Parsonage Barn

Boat Ramp

Covered Bridge

Shoe Shop

Town Pound

District School

Powder House

Kiln

Wood Shed

Pottery Shop

Pond

Sawmill

Gristmill

Carding Mill

Bixby House

Blacksmith Shop

COUNTRYSIDE

OLD STURBRIDGE VILLAGE

Restaurant

0   300ft

0   100m

Freeman Farm

Cooper Shop

Quinebaug River

EDUCATION BUILDING

NEW HAMPSHIRE

AREA: 9,304 SQ MI
POPULATION: 1,235,786
CAPITAL: CONCORD
NICKNAME: THE GRANITE STATE
STATE FLOWER: PURPLE LILAC
OFFICIAL WEB SITE: WWW.VISITNH.GOV

Forests cover 80 percent of the land in this triangle measuring 168 miles long and 90 miles at its widest point. The mountainous relief of the Appalachian ridges to the west and north contrasts with the hilly coastal region that slopes gently down to the Atlantic Ocean. The southern section of the state is heavily industrialized and more densely populated than the rest of the state. Located here are New Hampshire's largest cities—Concord, Manchester, Nashua, Keene—as well as its only seaport, Portsmouth.

"Live Free or Die" – "Here no landlords rack us with high rents. Here every man may be master of his land in a short time," wrote John Smith about New Hampshire in 1614. Despite Smith's tribute, the colonization of New Hampshire proceeded slowly. The first settlement, established in 1623 on the coast, was followed by several other small settlements. New Hampshire was administered as a part of Massachusetts until 1679, when the region became a royal colony.

Its people, self-reliant, taciturn, industrious and independent, were staunch supporters of the Revolution. The New Hampshire colony declared its independence from Great Britain and set up its own government seven months before the Declaration of Independence was signed. The heroic words of Revolutionary War colonel John Stark, "Live free or die," are immortalized in the state motto.

Economy – In the 19C factory complexes such as the **Amoskeag Mills**, once the world's largest textile manufacturer, were built on the banks of the Merrimack River. Textiles are still produced but have been surpassed by machinery, electronic and computer equipment, and business and financial services as principal sources of income. Since the 1960s, many companies have established branches in New Hampshire, attracted to the state's favorable tax structure and proximity to Boston.

Today tourism and industrial development share equal importance in New Hampshire's economy.

Farming is oriented chiefly toward dairy products, Christmas trees, specialty products such as apples and maple sugar, and vegetables, livestock and poultry. Sand, gravel and feldspar are among New Hampshire's most important minerals, and building granite is quarried on a limited scale. The introduction of concrete and steel construction has resulted in a decline of the granite industry that gave the state its nickname.

NHDTTD/Dave Shafer

Gourds at a Farmers' Market

CONCORD

POPULATION 40,687

MICHELIN MAP 581 L 6

TOURIST INFORMATION ☎ 603-224-2508 OR WWW.CONCORDNHCHAMBER.COM

The capital of New Hampshire since 1808, Concord boasts the largest state legislature in the nation, with 424 representatives. The gilded dome of the State House dominates the cluster of buildings that rise alongside the Merrimack River. A modern center of government and commerce, the city is also the hub for railway and road systems linking all corners of the state.

Originally called Rumford, this town was claimed by both the colonies of New Hampshire and Massachusetts. In 1741 a royal declaration settled the dispute by granting Rumford to New Hampshire, and the town was renamed Concord. The city became known for its granite and for the **Concord coaches** that were built here from 1813 to 1900.

▶ **Orient Yourself:** Concord, in the heart of the state, is located at the intersections of I-89, 93 and 393 and of US Highways 3, 4 and 202. The Merrimack River runs through the downtown historic district.

🅿 **Parking:** All-day parking is available at the Firehouse (one block west of Main St. between State and Green) and Durgin Block (1/2 block west of Main St. between School and Warren) structures. Metered street parking is available throughout downtown; parking at meters is free after 5pm and on weekends and holidays.

😊 **Don't Miss:** Christa McAuliffe Planetarium (be sure to reserve show tickets).

🕐 **Organizing Your Time:** Start at the State House, then stroll Main Street for a look at historic houses, before heading out to the Christa McAuliffe Planetarium.

Kids **Especially for Kids:** Get up close and personal with more than 200 animals at nearby Charmingfare Farm.

👍 **Also See:** Canterbury Shaker Village, with 25 original buildings, hands-on craft workshops, and 694 acres of meadow and farmlands.

Sights

State House
107 N. Main St. 🕐 *Open year-round Mon–Fri 8am–4pm.* 🕐 *Closed major holidays.* 🍴♿ ☎ *603-271-2154. www.gencourt.state.nh.us/visitorcenter.*
Completed in 1819, the New Hampshire State House is the oldest state capitol building where the legislature still meets in its original chambers. A visitor center on the

Concord Comestibles

The popular and always bustling **Common Man** *(25 Water St.; lunch & dinner daily; ☎ 603-228-3463. www.thecman.com)*, mixes rustic charm with well-prepared American cuisine. It's famous for its lobster corn chowder, daily roasted prime rib and country meatloaf.

For a light bite downtown, look for **Bread & Chocolate** *(29 S. Main St.; ☎ 603-228-3330; www.breadandchocolatenh.com)*, a European bistro/bakery that serves a formidable array of cakes, tarts, breads, cookies and sandwiches. Before or after eating, take time to browse in adjoining, well-stocked **Gibson's Bookstore** *(27 S. Main St.; ☎ 603-224-0562; www.gibsonsbookstore.com)*.

Address Book

♿ *For price ranges for hotels and restaurants, see the legend on the cover flap.*

WHERE TO STAY

Colby Hill Inn – *.5mi west of Henniker Center on Rte. 114, Henniker (17mi west of Concord).* ✗ 🅿 ☎ *603-428-3281. www.colbyhillinn.com. 16 rooms.* **$$$** Just 20 minutes west of Concord, this quintessential New England inn offers elegant accommodations. The inn, originally a 1797 farmhouse, still sports some 18C woodwork and wide pine floorboards. Rooms are individually decorated with floral wallcoverings and early-American antiques and reproductions. The inn's **restaurant** is top-notch, well-known for its seasonal preparations and classic New England dishes.

The Centennial Inn – *96 Pleasant St., Concord.* ✗ 🅿 ☎ *603-225-7102 or 800-360-4839. www.someplacesdifferent.com. 32 rooms.* **$$** The restored brick Victorian Centennial Inn features both antiques and modern amenities. It's perfect for travelers who prefer a historical ambience but don't want to give up the creature comforts. If you're ready to splurge, stay in one of the suites located in the inn's towering turrets. There's also a lounge and an intimate dining room on site.

WHERE TO EAT

Angelina's Ristorante – *11 Depot St.* ♿ ☎ *603-228-3313. www.angelinasrestaurant.com.* **$$ Italian.** The focus at Angelina's is classic Italian fare: daily ravioli, soups, sauces and desserts are all homemade. Bounteous entrées come with soup or salad and a side of pasta.

Barley House – *133 North Main S.* ♿ ☎ *603-228-6363. www.barleyhouse.com.* **$ American.** This casual, local favorite features American classics with international twists, like the lobster rangoons with orange-chile sauce, chipolte bison sausage, Guinness beef stew, and beer-braise bratwurst platter. Other favorites include the Irish whiskey steak, Cuban mojito double chop and the 12-hour BBQ pork rack. Save room for the to-die-for chocolate cake.

Hermanos Cocina – *11 Hills Ave.* ♿ ☎ *603-224-5669. www.hermanos-mexican.com.* **$ Mexican.** One sip of a Hermanos margarita, made from just-squeezed lemons and limes, and a nibble of the crispy nachos dunked in freshly made salsa, and you'll know why this Mexican restaurant is always hopping. Authentic south-of-the-border fare, with fresh ingredients and on-the-spot preparation are key.

ground floor contains exhibits and dioramas of historic events. The House Chamber may also be viewed from a gallery off the third floor.

Museum of New Hampshire History

Kids *Eagle Sq.* 🕐 *Open Jul–mid-Oct & Dec Mon–Sat 9:30am–5pm (Thu til 8:30pm), Sun noon–5pm. Rest of the year closed Mon.* 🕐 *Closed major holidays.* ⬤ *$5.50.* ♿🅿 ☎ *603-228-6688. www.nhhistory.org.*
More than five centuries of the Granite State's history are depicted in the exhibits here. Items include a Concord coach made in the 19C; a sampling of New Hampshire-made furniture (1760–1915); and landscape paintings by such notables as Thomas Hill, Frederic Church and Albert Bierstadt.

Christa McAuliffe Planetarium

3 Institution Dr. 🕐 *Open year-round Mon–Sat 10am–5pm, Sun noon–5pm.* 🕐 *Closed major holidays.* ⬤ *$8.* ♿🅿 ☎ *603-271-7827. www.starhop.com.*
Named after one of the *Challenger* teacher-astronauts who was a Concord native, the museum is a pleasing mix of small hands-on exhibits and high-tech shows *(reserve show tickets ahead of time as these frequently sell out)*. Every Friday night, dusk until 10pm, telescopes are set out on the front lawn to view the constellations *(free)*.

The Dwelling House, Canterbury Shaker Village

Courtesy Canterbury Shaker Village

Excursions

Hopkinton

8mi west of Concord via Rte. 9.
Antique hunters haunt this appealing Concord suburb. The town's wide main street is lined with attractive dwellings and shops, the town hall and St. Andrew's Church.

Charmingfare Farm

20mi southwest of Concord in Candia. ▶ *Take I-93 south to Exit 9; follow Rte. 27E for 4.5mi.* 🕐 *Open May-Columbus Day daily 10am–4pm.* ⊜ *$11.* ♿ 🅿 ☎ *603-483-5623. www.charmingfarefarm.com.*
More than 200 animals, including black bear, lynx, cougar, wolf and porcupine, call this small farm home. There's also a large collection of friendly farm animals, petting areas, wildlife exhibits and a variety of daily demonstrations and exhibits.

Canterbury Shaker Village★★

20mi north of Concord. ▶ *From I-93 take Exit 15E; follow Rte. 393E to Exit 3 and follow signs to Shaker Village.* 🕐 *Open mid-May–Oct daily 10am–5pm. Nov & Dec weekends only 10am–4pm.* 🕐 *Closed Thanksgiving Day & Dec 25.* ⊜ *$15.* 🍴 🅿 ☎ *603-783-9511. www.shakers.org. Begin at the visitor center, where a site plan of the village and schedule of craft demonstrations are available.*
Attracted by the serene countryside and the gift of a large tract of land in Canterbury, the **Shakers** established a community near the small village of **CanterburyCenter**.

THE SHAKER TABLE

Built on the site of the historic 1811 Blacksmith Shop at Canterbury Shaker Village, this intimate restaurant, overlooking Village pastoral grounds, offers a unique dining experience. Entrées, based on Shaker recipes, are served with the freshest ingredients. Start with artisan flatbread topped with grilled apple and chicken sausage or smoked butter and garlic mussels. Follow with main dishes like honeyed duck, or bouillabaisse brimming with lobster, scallops, shrimp and mussels and smoked sausage. Looking for comfort food? Try the Shaker favorite Blond Mac & Cheese or slow-cooked Yankee pot roast. Special candlelight dinners are offered Thursday evenings, July-Oct. 🕐 *Open May–Oct. Lunch daily 11:30am–4pm; dinner Thu–Sat. 5pm-9pm; Sun brunch 9am–4 pm.* ☎ *603-783-9511. www.shakers.org.*

Founded in the 1780s, the village was formally organized in 1792, the year the meet-inghouse was built, and grew to include some 300 residents and 100 buildings on 4,000 acres at the height of the community in the mid-19C. Today 25 original build-ings still stand on 694 acres.

An idyllic atmosphere pervades the orchards, meadows, vegetable gardens and grassy yards that surround the community's dwellings and farm buildings. Bor-dered by nature trails, several man-made ponds dot the distant acreage, attracting waterfowl and deer. After your tour of the village, extend your stay in this peaceful area of New Hampshire by picnicking by a pond or strolling along one of the nature trails that run through the grounds, having lunch or dinner at the restaurant or participating in one of the many hands-on craft workshops.

HANOVER ★

POPULATION 10,850
MICHELIN MAP 581 J 4
TOURIST INFORMATION ☎ 603-643-3115 OR WWW.HANOVERCHAMBER.ORG

A regional commercial center for the Upper Connecticut River Valley, Hanover occupies a pretty site on the banks of the Connecticut River. Its claim to fame is Dartmouth College, one of the nation's prominent Ivy League schools. Despite the town's growth, Hanover's colonial charm and pleasant tree-lined streets remain essentially unspoiled.

▶ **Orient Yourself:** Hanover is the geographic center of the Upper Valley Region, located on the east side of the Connecticut River. It's about an hour's drive north of Concord, easily accessed off I-89.

🅿 **Parking:** All-day parking is available at the Market St. and Water St. parking structures, near the downtown mall. There is metered street parking throughout downtown.

👁 **Don't Miss:** A tour of Dartmouth College, with its picturesque Colonial buildings, Hood Art Museum and Parker Memorial Library.

🕐 **Organizing Your Time:** Start at the Dartmouth College Visitor Center, where you can pick up a campus map.

Especially for Kids: Dig for gems at Ruggles Mine.

⚲ **Also See:** Saint-Gaudens National Historic Site.

Hanover Hot Spots

Serving patrons since 1780, the upscale **Hanover Inn** *(Wheelock & Main Sts.; ☎ 603-643-4300; www.hanoverinn.com)* presents sumptuous breakfasts, lunches and dinners in the Edwardian elegance of its Daniel Webster Room. In summer, alfresco dining is popular on the flower-bedecked terrace, overlooking the col-lege green.

A favorite with students and young professionals, **Rosey Jeke's** *(15 Lebanon St.; ☎ 603-643-5282)* is a tiny cafe/deli that makes terrific panini (grilled sandwiches). Try the Norma (eggplant, feta, tomatoes and pesto on farm bread), the saucisson (herbed salami and provolone with Dijon mustard on a baguette) or the grilled tuna (white albacore with capers, dill and watercress on semolina bread).

Another popular spot is the **Dartmouth Co-op** *(27 S. Main St.; ☎ 603-643-3100; www.dartmouthcoop.com)*, where logo-laden college souvenirs come in all shapes and sizes, from door mats to desk pads, key chains to coffee mugs, as well as sweatshirts, socks and more—all in Dartmouth's school colors.

Address Book

🍴 *For price ranges for hotels and restaurants, see the legend on the cover flap.*

WHERE TO STAY

The Trumbull House Bed & Breakfast – *40 Etna Rd.* 🅿 ☎ *603-643-2370 or 800-651-5141. www.trumbullhouse. com. 5 rooms.* **$$** You'll feel comfortable the minute you walk into this country home-away-from-home. Set on 16 acres just outside downtown, the Trumbull House offers pastoral surroundings and luxurious accommodations. Take a dip in the swimming pond, or hike nearby paths that hook up with the Appalachian Trail. When you are ready to call it a day, sink into crisp sheets and wrap yourself in a soft down comforter.

WHERE TO EAT

Murphy's on the Green – *11 S. Main St.* ☎ *603-643-4075. www.murphys-onthegreen.com.* **$ American.** One of author Bill Bryson's favorite hangouts when he lived in Hanover, this popular neighborhood tavern located in the heart of downtown Hanover attracts a lively and loyal clientele. Menu items range from traditional pub food (Heap 'O Buffalo Wings) to more innovative offerings (spinach and wild mushroom fondue). There are also Irish stew and buffalo burgers, fiery fajitas and thick steaks. Check out the back room, which boasts wood wainscoting and c.1898 pews from Webster Hall at Dartmouth College.

Dartmouth College★

Main entrance off E. Wheelock St. ☎ *603-646-1110. www.dartmouth.edu.*
Established in 1769, Dartmouth today offers its 4,500 students undergraduate programs in the liberal arts and sciences, as well as graduate studies in medicine, engineering, sciences and business administration. Dartmouth's list of illustrious alumni includes lawyer and orator Daniel Webster (1782-1852) and Nelson A. Rockefeller (1908-79), the former governor of New York and US vice president. The popular Dartmouth **Winter Carnival**, held each February, features skiing, skating, art shows and other special events.

The Green★
Bounded by Main, Wheelock, Wentworth & College Sts.
The spacious green is bordered by the venerable **Hanover Inn** and a number of college buildings. The corner of Main and Wheelock Streets commands a good view of Dartmouth Row, a group of four Colonial buildings.

Hopkins Center
Recognizable by its multistoried windows, the performing-arts center (1962) houses theaters and two concert halls.

Hood Art Museum
On Wheelock St., behind the Hopkins Center facing the south side of Dartmouth Green.
🕐 *Open year-round Tue–Sat 10am–5pm (Wed til 9pm), Sun noon–5pm.* 🕐 *Closed major holidays.* ♿ ☎ *603-646-2808. www.hoodmuseum.dartmouth.edu.*
Dartmouth's art museum features Native American, American, European, African and ancient art. On the lower level, a special area displays a group of 9C BC Assyrian reliefs; on the upper level, contemporary art occupies a spacious loft gallery.

Baker Memorial Library
North end of the Green. 🕐 *Open year-round daily 8am–midnight.* 🕐 *Closed major holidays.* ♿ ☎ *603-646-2560.*

Saint-Gaudens National Historic Site

The library houses **Epic of American Civilization**★, a series of wall murals painted by the Mexican artist José Clemente Orozco (1883-1949). Powerful and often brutal in their expression of the forces of good and evil, the murals are Orozco's interpretation of the 5,000-year history of the Americas. *Interpretation pamphlet is available at the library information desk.*

Excursions

Saint-Gaudens National Historic Site★
20mi south of Hanover in Cornish. ▶ *From Hanover, take Rte. 10 south to Rte. 12A. Travel approximately 15mi on Rte. 12A and follow signs to the site.* ⓞ *Open Memorial Day–late Oct daily 9am–4:30pm. Visit of Aspet by 30min guided tour only.* ⌑ *$5.* ⓞ *Closed major holidays. Summer concerts Jul–Aug Sun 2pm.* 🅿 ☎ *603-675-2175. www.nps.gov/saga.*
Nestled in a wooded clearing bordering the Connecticut River, the former home and studio of America's foremost 19C sculptor, Augustus Saint-Gaudens, has been open to the public as a National Historic Site since 1965.
Saint-Gaudens is remembered for his monumental Civil War memorials—such as the Shaw Memorial on Boston Common—and for his portrait reliefs. During the two decades he lived in Cornish, Saint-Gaudens produced about 150 sculptures. Today five buildings as well as gardens and an 80-acre woodland are open to the public.

Ruggles Mine★
28mi southeast of Hanover. Take Rte. 120 South to I-89 South to Exit 17. Follow US-4 East to Grafton Center. Mine is 2mi from the Grafton Center village green; follow signs. ⓞ *Open mid-Jun–mid-Oct daily 9am–5pm. Mid-May–mid-Jun weekends only 9am–5pm. Last admission 1hr before closing.* ⌑ *$20.* ☎ *603-523-4275. www.rugglesmine.com.*
The mammoth abandoned pegmatite mine on Isinglass Mountain is a fun place to explore, with its huge arched stone tunnels, winding passageways and large open pits. Amateur rock hounds can rent equipment and dig for mica, feldspar or one of the other 150 minerals that have been found here. Kids love it!

Sunapee★
8mi south of New London on Rte. 11.
This diminutive, colorful lake resort community is dominated by lovely Sunapee Lake. Shops, restaurants and residential homes crowd its shore. The tiny hillside

Sunapee Sundries

The community of Sunapee Harbor offers a variety of shops and eateries, all clustered within walking distance of each other along short Main Street. After a relaxing afternoon of boating and sunning, browse in the **Wild Goose Country Store** *(77 Main St.; ☎ 603-763-5516)* for collectibles, gift items or penny candy. Then pull up a chair at **The Anchorage** restaurant *(Main St.; ☎ 603-763-3334)* for lakeside dining, dancing and live entertainment in the summer. For countryside dining, turn right after the bandstand onto Burkehaven Hill Road and proceed half a mile to **The Inn at Sunapee** *(☎ 603-763-4444; www.innatsunapee.com)*. Here guests enjoy classic, freshly prepared American cuisine in a dining room that provides year-round views of Mt. Sunapee. A spacious, comfortable lounge with a field-stone fireplace adjoins the dining area.

common sports a bandstand and the busy harbor teems with small pleasure craft, cruise boats and fishing vessels.

The best way to see the lake is to take a **cruise** aboard the *M.V. Sunapee II. (1hr 30min; commentary; ⊗ $17; ♿; for information and schedules, contact Sunapee Cruises, ☎ 603-938-6465 or www.sunapeecruises.com)*.

Mount Sunapee State Park

5mi south of Sunapee via Rte. 11 and Rte. 102 East. 🕐 *Open daily year-round.* ♿ ☎ *603-763-5561. www.nhstateparks.org/ParksPages/sunapee.*

Sunapee Lake and the mountain of the same name form the center of a year-round vacation resort. Opposite the entrance to the park is the entrance to the **Sunapee State Beach** on the shores of Lake Sunapee *(off Rte. 103 in Newbury;* 🕐 *open mid-Jun–Labor Day daily 9am–6pm; mid-May–mid-Jun weekends only 9am–6pm; ⊗ $3; ☎ 603-763-5561)*. The **chairlift** to the summit of Mt. Sunapee (2,700ft) operates from North Peak Lodge during the summer and early fall, offering good **views**★ of the region *(hours vary; call for information; lift rates vary; Mount Sunapee Resort, ☎ 603-763-2356; www.mtsunapee.com)*.

LAKE WINNIPESAUKEE REGION★

MICHELIN MAP 581 L, M 4, 5
TOURIST INFORMATION ☎ 603-744-8664 OR WWW.LAKESREGION.ORG

New Hampshire's largest lake covers an area of 72sq mi, has a shoreline of 283mi, and is dotted with more than 250 tiny islands. On a clear day, Lake Winnipesaukee, set against the backdrop of the White Mountains, makes a magnificent sight.

▶ **Orient Yourself:** The largest lake in the state lies south of the White Mountain region, and east of north-south I-93. Routes 11, 25, 113 and 109 circle the lake.

🅿 **Parking:** Free and metered street parking are available in towns and villages surrounding the lake. There is also limited parking at beach areas.

🅐 **Don't Miss:** A boat ride on the M/S *Washington* or M/V *Sophie C.*

🕐 **Organizing Your Time:** It's best to base yourself in one of the lakeside towns or villages (see descriptions below) and do daytrips from there.

🚸 **Especially for Kids:** The honky-tonk Weirs Beach area is a favorite with families for its rocking arcade, water park, and fast food stands.

🅐 **Also See:** Castle in the Clouds for some of the best Lake Winnipesaukee and mountain views.

Address Book

For price ranges for hotels and restaurants, see the legend on the cover flap.

WHERE TO STAY

The Inns at Mill Falls – *312 Daniel Webster Hwy., Meredith.* ☎ 800-622-6455. *www.millfalls.com. 101 rooms.* **$$$$** Once a 19C linen mill, this property on the southwest shore of Lake Winnipesaukee is now a replica New England village with four lodging choices. The Inn at Mill Falls offers modern guest rooms and is connected by a glass-enclosed bridge to Mill Falls Marketplace, where shoppers can explore boutiques and galleries. Adjacent is the lakefront Inn at Bay Point, surrounded by a formal park, with great views of the lake. Many of the guest rooms at Bay Point feature private balconies and fireplaces. Both the Chase House and the newest property Church Landing have modern lakeview rooms. You may be tempted to spend your entire getaway on the property. If you do decide to venture out, all of the lake's activities are just outside your doorstep.

Wolfeboro Inn – *90 N. Main St., Wolfeboro.* ☎ 603-569-3016 or 800-451-2389. *www.wolfeboroinn.com. 44 rooms.* **$$$$** This small, elegant hotel, nestled on the eastern shore of Lake Winnipesaukee, has been a mainstay in downtown for nearly two centuries. The original 1812 building has been updated with a soaring three-story addition. The inn's 44 guest rooms include restored rooms in the historic inn or modern suites in the addition, some with lake-view balconies and private decks. Throughout, you'll find classic country décor, antique furniture, handmade quilts and period reproductions. Be sure to visit **Wolfe's Tavern;** with its old wood beams and brick fireplaces, it's a popular local hangout.

The Margate on Winnipesaukee *Rte. 3, Laconia.* ☎ 603-524-5210 or 800-627-4283. *www.themargate. com. 141 rooms.* **$$$** Families looking for a bargain will want to consider this year-round resort on Lake Winnipesaukee. For the sports-minded, activities abound on-site, including indoor and outdoor pools, a health club, tennis courts, a sports bar and lounge, boat rentals and more. Guests wanting to relax can do so on the 400ft private sandy beach. Rooms are motel-style basic, spread across three separate buildings.

WHERE TO EAT

The Woodshed – *128 Lee Rd., Moultonboro. Dinner only.* ⏱ *Closed Mon.* ☎ 603-476-2311. *www.thewoodshedrestaurant.com.* **$$ American.** Meander inland from the lake and you'll discover backcountry roads, rolling pastures and rustic farmhouses, like the one that holds this lake region favorite. Most people come here for the homemade soups and breads and the Woodshed's famous prime rib or thick loin lamb chops, but you'll find seafood, too.

Hart's Turkey Farm – *Rte. 3, Meredith.* ☎ 603-279-6212. *www.hartsturkeyfarm.com.* **$ American.** Billboards throughout the area advertise Hart's home-style restaurant. Yes, it's a tourist trap (complete with its own gift store), but Hart's can't be beat for old-fashioned comfort food. Since 1954 the Hart family has been serving up turkey dinners with the works: salad, rolls, veggies, cranberry sauce, stuffing, potatoes, piping hot gravy, and dessert (think Jell-O). There are other selections, but why bother?

Lakeside Villages

Each of the villages on the lake possesses its own character. **Laconia** is the industrial and commercial center of the region. The small charming village of **Wolfeboro**★, with its large lakeside homes, has attracted summer vacationers for centuries; it's one of the prettiest communities on Lake Winnipesaukee. **Weirs Beach**, with its amusement arcade, souvenir shops and lakefront Victorian dwellings, is a lively family resort. Attractive **Center Harbor** and Meredith, both set on bays at the northern end of the lake, serve as shopping centers for the resort cottages and campgrounds nearby.

Lake Winnipesaukee Pier

Every summer thousands of vacationers enjoy boating on Winnipesaukee's waters. Public docks, marinas and launching ramps abound. Popular beaches include Weirs Beach and **Ellacoya State Beach**. For hikers, walking trails thread the surrounding hills. During the winter, **Gunstock Ski Area** and **Ragged Mountain Ski Area** teem with activity. Ice fishing, snowmobiling and the dogsled championships held each February in Laconia provide additional winter attractions.

Sights

Sightseeing Cruises★★

The best way to experience the lake is by cruising its waters. Winnipesaukee Flagship Corp. offers scenic cruises on several different excursion vessels, including the **M/S Mount Washington** and the **M/V Sophie C** mailboat. *(For seasonal schedules, rates and information, call ☎ 888-843-6686 or www.cruisenh.com).*

Castle in the Clouds★

On Rte. 171 East in Moultonborough. ○ *Open late May–Columbus Day daily 10am–4:30pm. Castle tour $10. Scenic drive, ⊙ $5 per person.* ╳ & ☐ ☎ 603-476-2352. www.castleintheclouds.org.

This 5,200-acre estate, overlooking Ossipee Mountains and the forests and lakes below, was acquired in 1910 by millionaire Thomas Plant. Lucknow Mansion, the residence Plant commissioned, has a distinctive red slate roof and its eclectic design incorporates elements from several different countries. From the terrace you can enjoy a **view★★** of Lake Winnipesaukee with its myriad tree-clad islands. Miles of foot and horse trails lace the property *(horse rental ⊙ $35/hr; reservations required)*; and a path *(.25mi)* beginning about 1mi from the entrance gate leads to two waterfalls.

> ## BROWSING IDEAS
>
> In Moultonborough, **Carriage House Crafters** *(Rte. 25; ☎ 603-253-9724)* tempts browsers with New England-made toys, baskets, pottery, clothing and a host of other handcrafted items all housed within a bright fuchsia-colored roadside carriage house. The **Old Country Store** *(Rtes. 25 & 109; ☎ 603-476-5750; www.nhcountrystore.com)* delights those who venture in with its bygone-era charm and cluttered array of penny candy, crocks full of pickles, aged cheddar cheese, New Hampshire maple syrup and a myriad of other products.

Loon Center and Markus Wildlife Sanctuary

In Moultonborough. From Rte. 25 turn onto Blake Rd. (look for Loon Center sign) and continue 1mi to the end, then turn right onto Lee's Mills Rd. Trails ⏰ open year-round daily dawn–dusk. Center open Jul–Columbus Day daily 9am–5pm; rest of the year Mon–Sat 9am–5pm. ☎ 603-476-5666. www.loon.org.

Begin your visit inside Loon Center to view the small exhibit area. In the 200-acre wildlife sanctuary, there's a short 🥾 **Forest Walk** through mixed woods and wildflowers; or opt for the longer **Loon Nest Trail** *(allow 1hr)* through marshland, streams and upland forests bordering Lake Winnipesaukee. Along the way, a lookout permits a view of a loon nesting site, and if your timing is right, an actual loon or two.

Center Sandwich★

5mi north of Moultonborough by Rte. 109.

Situated at the foot of the White Mountains, Center Sandwich is one of New England's prettiest villages. In the fall, a tapestry of brilliant autumn color frames its simple white clapboard structures.

MANCHESTER

POPULATION 107,006

MICHELIN MAP 581 L 6

TOURIST INFORMATION ☎ 603-666-6600 OR WWW.MANCHESTER-CHAMBER.ORG

In the 19C the largest textile factory in the world, the Amoskeag Mills, was built here beside the Merrimack River. The mile-long stretch of brick buildings still standing along the river proves an awesome sight. Financial services have replaced manufacturing as Manchester's main industry.

▶ **Orient Yourself:** Just over the Massachusetts border, this metropolis is bisected by I-93 and I-293. Route 101 runs east-west from the seacoast.

🅿 **Parking:** There are several downtown parking structures and metered street parking.

☻ **Don't Miss:** Currier Art Museum, with its fine collection of paintings, sculpture and decorative arts.

⏰ **Organizing Your Time:** Allow 2hrs to tour the Currier Museum of Art and nearly 3hrs for the excursion to Anheuser-Busch Hamlet (the tour is 90min).

Kids Especially for Kids: Anheuser-Busch Hamlet is a hit with families.

⚲ **Also See:** America's Stonehenge.

Sights

Currier Museum of Art★

201 Myrtle Way. ⚲ Temporarily closed in June 2006 for expansion and renovation. Check for updated opening schedule. ✗ ♿ 🅿 ☎ 603-669-6144, ext. 108. www.currier.org.

The museum is known for its fine collection of paintings, sculpture and decorative arts.

The main level is devoted largely to temporary exhibits, and in the Henry Melville Fuller Gallery, contemporary and 20C art.

On the second floor, the east gallery contains the **European collection:** early Italian paintings; drawings by **Tiepolo**; and canvases from the French, Spanish, English and Dutch schools. The west gallery showcases American paintings, and **American decorative art** from the 17-19C, with emphasis on New Hampshire pieces. Works by **Andrew Wyeth**, **Edward Hopper**, Georgia O'Keeffe, Louise Nevelson, Alexander Calder and others represent 20C American painting.

Zimmerman House★

🐾 *Visit by guided tour (1-2hrs) only, Apr–mid-Jan, Mon & Fri 2pm Thu 2pm & 4pm Sat 11:30, 1 & 2:30 pm, Sun 1 & 2:30pm.* 🚫 *$11–$17. Reservations required.* 🅿 ☎ *603-669-6144, ext. 108. www.currier.org.*

Designed by Frank Lloyd Wright in 1950, this low-roofed, single-story house made of brick, concrete and cypress typifies the famed architect's "Usonian" style—Wright's own term for the small, utilitarian, yet elegant houses he created late in his career to counter the housing shortage of the Great Depression. The interior contains Wright-designed textiles, and his built-in and freestanding furniture.

CHEZ VACHON

136 Kelley St. ☎ *603-625-9660.*
The mills of Manchester attracted foreign workers, particularly French Canadians from Quebec. The French influence is still evident today in the city's Franco-American Centre, with its public art gallery, and in this restaurant, which caters to the big appetites of locals and laborers alike. Its popular attraction is the array of *poutine* dishes (french fries in Canadian curd cheese with chicken gravy).

Excursions

Anheuser-Busch Hamlet

12mi south of Manchester in Merrimack. Take US-3 (Everett Turnpike) South to Exit 10 and go east on Industrial Dr. to the hamlet, which is located on the grounds of the Anheuser-Busch brewery at 221 Daniel Webster Hwy. 🐾 *Visit by guided tour (1hr 30min) only,* 🕐 *Jun–Aug daily 9:30am–5pm. May & Sept–Dec daily 10am–4pm. Rest of the year Thu–Mon 10am–4pm.* 🕐 *Closed major holidays.* ♿🅿 ☎ *603-595-1202. www.budweisertours.com.*

Budweiser Clydesdales clip-clop through the picturesque hamlet where they are raised and trained. The "white-stockinged" horses have been the symbol of Anheuser-Busch since 1933, when the company acquired its first team to celebrate the repeal of Prohibition. Today teams of Clydesdales tour the country, appearing in parades and other events.

America's Stonehenge

24mi southeast of Manchester in Salem. Take I-93 South to Exit 3. Follow Rte. 111 East 4.5mi; turn right onto Island Pond Rd. and follow signs to 105 Haverhill Rd. 🕐 *Open late Jun–Aug daily 9am–6pm. Rest of the year daily 9am–5pm (Nov–Dec til 4:30pm).* 🕐 *Closed Thanksgiving Day & Dec 25.* 🚫 *$9.* 🅿 ☎ *603-893-8300. www.stonehengeusa.com.*

The standing granite slabs of this stone complex give the site its name, although these stones are much shorter than their counterparts in England. Many theories exist concerning the site's origin and function; the aligned slabs led scientists to speculate that this may be the remnant of a calendar laid out 4,000 years ago by an advanced civilization with a knowledge of the movement of the stars, moon and sun.

MOUNT MONADNOCK REGION★

MICHELIN MAP 581 K 7 AND MAP P 300
TOURIST INFORMATION ☎ 603-352-1303 OR WWW.KEENECHAMBER.COM

The centerpiece of Monadnock State Park is Mt. Monadnock (3,165ft), looming above pastoral farmlands and tiny villages in southwestern New Hampshire. Hiking to the top of Mt. Monadnock for its spectacular view became popular in the 19C, and today it is one of the most frequently climbed peaks in the world. Each year some 125,000 persons scale its summit to enjoy the exhilarating view.

▶ **Orient Yourself:** Also known as "Currier & Ives" country, the region is tucked in the southwest corner of the state, a 70-minute drive from Manchester and two hours from the seacoast.

🅿 **Parking:** Street parking is available in Keene and other small towns throughout the area.

🚗 **Don't Miss:** A driving tour of the area; it's the best way to see classic New England villages and small towns.

🕐 **Organizing Your Time:** Allow the better part of a day to enjoy Monadnock State Park.

👧 **Especially for Kids:** Take a hike to the top of Mount Monadnock.

👤 **Also See:** The historic buidlings on Main Street in Keene on a self-guided walking tour.

Keene

Gateway to the Mount Monadnock region, this commercial and manufacturing center has grown rapidly during the past several decades. Tree-lined Main Street sports gift shops, restaurants and retail businesses, as well as several Georgian, Federal, Italianate and Second Empire structures dating from the 1760s *(a walking tour guide is available from the Historical Society of Cheshire County; ☎ 603-352-1895; www.hsccnh.org).* Main Street divides at **Central Square**, which is dominated at the north end by the stately United Church of Christ (1788). Opposite stands the community gazebo on the small common.

West of the downtown core lies the Ashuelot River, where 46 acres of riverfront were donated to the city for recreation. The gardens and woods of **Ashuelot River Park** offer opportunities to cycle, walk or jog. Covered-bridge enthusiasts will enjoy a side trip on Route 10 South to covered bridges **Nos. 2**, **4** and **5** that straddle the river *(roadside markers direct you to the bridges).*

Monadnock Memories

Sometimes it's the little things that make a trip memorable: a stop at a farm, a roadside ice-cream stand or a trail ride through the woods.

Two miles west of Dublin sits the five-acre **Friendly Farm** 👧 *(Rte. 101; closed in winter; 👁 $5. ☎ 603-563-8444; www.friendlyfarm.com)* filled with pigs, goats, sheep, ducks, chickens, rabbits and the like. Visitors are encouraged to feed and pet the animals. About a mile east of Jaffrey, along Route 124, **Kimball Farm Restaurant** 👧 *(open Memorial Day–Columbus Day; ☎ 603-532-5765; www.kimballfarm.com)* is a popular stop for ice cream or cold drinks. Across the road from Kimball's is **Silver Ranch** 👧 *(Rte. 124; reservations required; ☎ 603-532-7363),* a livery stable that offers trail, hay and sleigh rides, as well as scenic carriage tours.

Address Book

For price ranges for hotels and restaurants, see the legend on the cover flap.

WHERE TO STAY

Hancock Inn – *33 Main St., Hancock.* ⊠ 🅿 ☎ *800-525-1789. www.hancockinn.com. 10 rooms.* **$$$$** Lovers of historic houses will be enchanted with this inn, which has been in continuous operation since 1789. Although rooms have modern conveniences (besides private baths, air conditioning and cable TV, some also have gas fireplaces and private patios), there is much preserved in this old inn, including the original domed ceiling in the Ball Room and hand-painted murals in the Rufus Porter Room. The elegant on-site restaurant is popular with both inn guests and locals. Try its signature Shaker Cranberry Pot Roast, a favorite for more than 20 years. *Children under 12 are not welcome at the inn.*

Grand View Inn & Resort – *580 Mountain Rd., 4mi northwest of Jaffrey Center on Rte. 124.* ⊠ 🅿 ☎ *603-532-9880. www.thegrandviewinn.com. 9 rooms.* **$$$** Imagine being tucked away in a private outdoor spot overlooking Mt. Monadnock, and receiving a professional massage. Such fresh-air service is just one of the treatments offered by the spa at the Grand View Inn. In addition to elegant lodgings, this 1800 brick mansion offers a large equestrian center, restaurant, and top-notch personal service.

Woodbound Inn – *62 Woodbound Rd., Rindge.* ⊠ 🅿 ☎ *603-532-8341 or 800-688-7770. www.woodbound.com. 45 rooms.* **$$** Families looking for down-to-earth accommodations will find plenty to keep them happy at this Monadnock country estate. Set on 165 acres on the shores of Lake Contoocook, the resort attracts vacationers who enjoy the daily program of sports and activities—ranging from golf in summer (the inn has its own nine-hole course) to cross-country skiing in winter. Choose from airy, individually decorated rooms in the main inn (14 out of the 19 have private baths), more contemporary rooms in the Edgewood Building, and rustic lakefront cabins.

WHERE TO EAT

Acqua Bistro – *9 School St., Peterborough. Dinner only, Wed–Sun.* 🅿 ☎ *603-924-9905. www.acqua-bistro.com* **$$ New American.** The upper-level dining room, overlooking the Nubanusit River, is the epitome of casual elegance. Relying on simple dishes prepared with the freshest ingredients, the Mediterranean menu here lists top-selling gourmet pizzas as well as a daily changing selection of entrées, such as pan-seared scallops with saffron risotto.

Inn at Jaffrey Center – *379 Main St., Jaffrey Center.* 🅿 ☎ *603-532-7800 or 877-510-7019. www.theinnatjaffrey-center.com.* **$$ New American.** This restaurant, set in a rambling 1830s summer home, boasts fresh seasonal dishes, just-baked breads, and homemade desserts. Start with an appetizer (crab cakes with tomato-basil jam or wild mushroom and goat cheese strudel) and end with a slice of fresh berry pie. In between, you'll have a wide choice of entrées, including meat, poultry, fish and pasta. When a chill is in the air, cozy up to the wood-burning fireplace; in warm weather, dine on the screened porch and enjoy views of the inn's sweeping grounds.

Driving Tour: Mount Monadock Region

47mi. ▶ *Begin in the town of Fitzwilliam (14mi south of Keene via Rte. 12).*

Fitzwilliam

Large clapboard structures, an old meetinghouse, an inn and a Congregational church, which is crowned by a wedding-cake steeple, face the green. To the west

(2.5mi off Rte. 119), **Rhododendron State Park** encompasses 16 acres of wild rhododendrons that provide a colorful spectacle when they burst into bloom in July.

▶ *Take Rte. 119 East; after the intersection with Rte. 202, follow the signs for the cathedral.*

Cathedral of the Pines★

🕐 *Open May–Oct daily 9am–5pm. Contribution requested.* ♿ 🅿 ☎ 603-899-3300. www.cathedralpines.com.

Situated on the crest of a pine-carpeted hill, this outdoor cathedral, the work of a couple who lost their son in World War II, commemorates all Americans who were killed in battle. The **Memorial Bell Tower**, rising in a clearing, is dedicated to American women who served their country in wartime; Norman Rockwell designed the plaques above the tower arches. The **museum** contains artifacts from around the world, including medals from World War I.

▶ *Turn left when leaving the Cathedral of the Pines; 1.5mi farther, at the fork, bear right onto Rte. 124.*

New Ipswich

The **Barrett House**, a handsome Federal mansion on Main Street, and its sedate rustic surroundings have changed little over the years. Built in 1800 by wealthy mill owner Charles Barrett as a wedding gift for his son, the house is furnished with family pieces and features two late-19C bathrooms (👁 *visit by 45min guided tour only, Jun–Oct first Sat of the month 11am–4pm; ⏏ $5; 🅿 ☎ 603-878-2517; www.spnea.org).*

▶ *Follow Rte. 124 west to Jaffrey. Located at the foot of Mt. Monadnock, Jaffrey provides easy access to Monadnock State Park. Continue on Rte. 124.*

Jaffrey Center

A series of lectures held each year *(Jul–Aug Fri 8pm; ☎ 603-532-6527)* at the old meeting house on Route 124 honors **Amos Fortune**, a former slave who bequeathed a sum of money to the Jaffrey School when he died.

▶ *Take Rte. 124 west and .5mi after the meetinghouse turn right.*

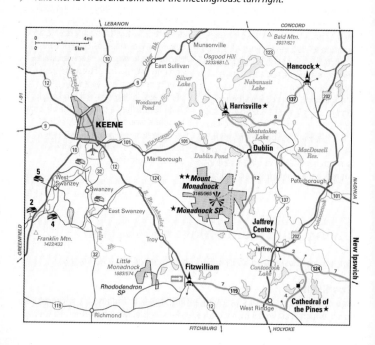

Monadnock State Park★

🕐 *Open year-round daily 8am–dusk.*
🚌 *$3.* ⚠ 🅿 ☎ *603-532-8862. www.
nhstateparks.org.*

Trails to the summit of Mt. Monadnock
begin at the end of the tar road beyond
the tollbooth.

Mount Monadnock★★

Of the 40 trails leading to this peak,
the trail most frequently taken is the
White Dot Trail 🏃*(several steep sections; round-trip 3-4hrs).* A similar route,
the **White Cross Trail** 🏃 is somewhat
more difficult. **Pumpelly Trail** 🏃 is the
longest, but easiest, path to the top. The
far-reaching **view**★★ from the summit
on a clear day includes Mt. Washington
(north) and the Boston skyline *(southeast).* The summit is the only place in New
England from which parts of all six of the region's states can be seen.

▶ *As you leave the park, turn left onto Upper Jaffrey Rd.*

Dublin

Mark Twain summered in this hillside hamlet, today the home of *Yankee Magazine*
and *The Old Farmers Almanac.*

▶ *Continue north on Upper Jaffrey Rd., turn right on Rte. 101, then left onto New Har-
risville Rd.*

Harrisville★

The handsome ensemble of modest brick buildings, dwellings, mills and Congregational church reflected in the village pond creates a pleasing tableau of an early
rural mill town.

▶ *Follow the unmarked road east along the lakes, then turn left onto Rte. 137.*

Hancock★

The tranquility of this colonial village is disturbed only once a year, on July 4th, when
the bells of the meetinghouse peal from midnight to one o'clock in the morning to
celebrate the anniversary of America's independence. The **John Hancock Inn** sits in
the center of the village, opposite the general store. Headstones in the old **cemetery**
at the end of the street provide good examples of the skill of early stonecutters.

HANNAH GRIMES MARKETPLACE

42 Main St., Keene. ☎ *603-352-
6862; www.hannahgrimes.com.* If
you're looking for evidence of the
creativity and productivity of Granite
State artists and craftspeople, this
well-stocked store—named after a
Keene woman born in 1776—brims
with regional crafts, furnishings and
foodstuffs. Wooden whirligigs and
jigsaw puzzles, woven scarves and
handmade quilts, packaged herbs
and baked goods, paintings and pottery, baskets, antiques, household
items and more are for sale.

NEW HAMPSHIRE COAST

MICHELIN MAP 581 N 6

TOURIST INFORMATION ☎ 603-436-1118 OR WWW.SEACOASTNH.COM

Sandy beaches, rocky ledges and state parks line New Hampshire's short 18mi coastline. Skirting the shore, Route 1A runs from Seabrook to Portsmouth past resort areas, elegant estates, and fine views of the ocean.

▶ **Orient Yourself:** North-south I-95 and Routes 1 and 1A provide access to seacoast towns and beaches.

🅿 **Parking:** Limited parking at public beaches along Route 1A. A large (paid) parking lot is available at Hampton Beach.

👁 **Don't Miss:** Rollicky Hampton State Beach with its sugar white sand and plethora of activities.

🕐 **Organizing Your Time:** Arrive at beaches early to snag parking spots and a place in the sand.

🧒 **Especially for Kids:** Tidepooling at pretty Odiorne Point State Park and a visit to the on-site Seacoast Science Center.

👆 **Also See:** Fuller Gardens.

Sights

Hampton Beach

On Rte. 1A, 1mi north of Seabrook.

This lively resort center claims a casino, large clusters of oceanfront hotels, motels and eating places, as well as a 3.5mi sandy beach. The **New Hampshire Marine War Memorial**, a granite statue of a seated maiden looking out to sea, borders Route 1A in the center of Hampton Beach. North of Hampton Beach the road passes the waterfront estates of **Little Boars Head**.

Fuller Gardens

🕐 *Open mid-May–mid-Oct daily 10am–5:30pm.* 🎫 *$6.50.* 🅿 ☎ *603-964-5414. www.fullergardens.org.*

The formal garden occupies the summer estate of Alvan T. Fuller, a former governor of Massachusetts. A stroll through the formal rose beds containing over 2,000 rosebushes, Japanese gardens, greenhouses and beds of annuals and perennials is punctuated with glimpses of the sea beyond.

Rye Harbor State Park

On Rte. 1A in Rye. 🕐 *Open year-round daily 8am–8pm.* 🎫 *$3 (mid-Jun–early Sept).* ♿ ☎ *603-436-1552. www.nhstateparks.org.*

This rocky headland overlooking the Atlantic Ocean provides good picnic and fishing grounds.

Wallis Sands State Park

On Rte. 1A in Rye. 🕐 *Open mid-Jun–Labor Day daily 8am–8pm. Mid-May–mid-Jun weekends only* 🎫 *$10/car.* ♿ ☎ *603-436-9404. www.nhstateparks.org.* A gentle surf breaks onto the park's quarter-mile-long beach, which is mobbed in summer.

Odiorne Point State Park

On Rte. 1A near Rye. 🕐 *Open year-round daily 8am-6pm.* 🎫 *$3 weekends Late-May–mid-jun and daily mid-Jun-mid-Oct.* ♿ ☎ *603-436-7406. www.nhstateparks.org.*

Address Book

For price ranges for hotels and restaurants, see the legend on the cover flap.

WHERE TO STAY

Wentworth By-the-Sea – *860 Wentworth Rd, New Castle.* P ☎ *603-422-7322 or 866-240-6313. www.wentworth. com. 205 rooms.* **$$$** Arguably the finest place to stay in the seacoast region, this luxury resort on New Castle island boasts ocean and harbor views. Rooms are bright and airy, with top-notch amenities. Full-service spa, tennis club, two pools, health club, marina and golf course are on-site; the dining room is a favorite among locals and visitors.

The Victoria Inn – *430 High St., Hampton.* P ☎ *603-929-1437 or 800-291-2672. www.thevictoriainn.com. 6 rooms.* **$$** Nestled among oceanfront mansions and stately homes, this small inn offers a quiet oasis from the bustling beach and boardwalk scene. Built in 1875 as a carriage house, the Victorian structure was later owned by New Hampshire governor George Ashworth. Today the renovated rooms are furnished with Victorian-era antiques and feature private baths, air-conditioning and cable TV. The sunny side porch, gazebo and landscaped grounds are fine places to linger on warm summer nights. Bikes are available for cycling New Hampshire's coastal roads.

Ashworth by the Sea – *295 Ocean Blvd., Hampton Beach.* ☎ *603-926-6762 or 800-345-6736. www.ashworthhotel.com. 105 rooms.* **$$** Oceanfront rooms on popular Hampton Beach and an indoor/outdoor pool make this resort hotel a magnet for vacationing families. Here you'll be in the middle of the action; the boardwalk, attractions and miles of sandy beach are right outside your room. Standard guest rooms are spacious, clean and bright. Some rooms claim ocean views and sun decks. The hotel's restaurants, including a formal dining room and the Hampton Room Buffet, have been favorites in the area for more than 20 years.

WHERE TO EAT

Betty's Kitchen – *164 Lafayette Rd., Rte. 1, North Hampton. Breakfast & lunch only.* ☎ *603-964-9870. www. bettyskitchen.com.* **$ American.** Betty's is famous for its extensive "breakfast served anytime" menu. Try the omelet creations (the Cordon Bleu, or the Florentine with artichokes, mushrooms and Boursin cheese) or new twists on eggs Benedict (Seafood with lobster, shrimp, scallops and crab). Bring your appetite!

Ron's Landing – *379 Ocean Blvd., Hampton Beach.* ☎ *603-929-2122;. www.ronslanding.com.* **$$ American.** Situated in the thick of the beachfront commercial strip, Ron's features two floors of dining, including an enclosed second-story deck overlooking the ocean. A wide selection of seafood, steaks and pastas is offered at this casual, full-service, family-friendly restaurant.

The ragged promontory of Odiorne Point was the site of the first settlement in New Hampshire, established in 1623. Today the park's 137 undeveloped acres are the domain of herons, harriers, egrets and other water birds. You'll have sweeping views of Altantic Ocean; it's also a great place for tidepooling. Be sure to visit the **Seacoast Science Center** at the park, with exhibits, aquariums and a touch tank (*separate admission fee*).

NORTHERN NEW HAMPSHIRE

MICHELIN MAP 581 L 1
TOURIST INFORMATION ☎ 603-237-8939 OR WWW.NORTHCOUNTRYCHAMBER.ORG

North of the White Mountains, a dense boreal forest stretches north into Canada. Although development of this sparsely settled region has historically been hindered by the challenging terrain of the White Mountains, sports enthusiasts have long been drawn here. Visitors come here to hunt, fish, snowmobile, or simply to enjoy the area's unspoiled natural beauty. Here you'll find scenic Dixville Notch, as well as the Connecticut Lakes, a series of wilderness waterways linked by the Connecticut River.

▶ **Orient Yourself:** North-south Route 3 snakes through the northern top of the state to the Canadian border. Scenic Route 26 travels east-west through the region.

🅿 **Parking:** Street parking is available in most small towns.

🔗 **Don't Miss:** A drive through spectacular Dixville Notch and a visit to the opulent Balsams Resort.

🕐 **Organizing Your Time:** Plan at least a day for outdoor adventure on the Connecticut Lakes or for a hike in the mountains.

Kids Especially for Kids: Several outfitters offer fishing and boating trips.

Connecticut Lakes Region

🛈 *Tourist Information:* ☎ *603-538-7118 or www.nhconnlakes.com.*
Rising in the narrow reaches of New Hampshire, the headwaters of the Connecticut River flow south through the **Third**, **Second** and **First Connecticut Lakes** before turning southwest to form the border between New Hampshire and Vermont. This region is a sportsman's paradise: Its woods are home to moose, black bear, whitetail

The White Mountains

deer, grouse and woodcock, and its lakes teem with trout and landlocked salmon. Along US-3, between the gateway township of Pittsburg and the Canadian border, you can glimpse the lakes through the trees. As you drive north on US-3 through Connecticut Lakes State Forest, it is not unusual to spot moose browsing along the sides of the road.

Lake Francis State Park

7mi northeast of Pittsburg via US-3. Turn right onto River Rd.; park entrance is 2mi past the covered bridge. ○ *Open mid-May–mid-Oct daily 8am-8pm.* ⊚ *$3* △ P ☏ *603-538–6965. www.nhstateparks.org.* Just south of First Connecticut Lake, man-made Lake Francis is southernmost in the chain of lakes connected by the Connecticut River. Surrounded by New Hampshire's northern wilderness, the scenic shores of Lake Francis provide an ideal spot to camp, picnic or fish.

Dixville Notch

ℹ *Tourist Information:* ☏ *603-237-8939, 800-698-8939 or www.northcountry-chamber.org.*

Route 26, between the towns of Colebrook and Errol, passes through Dixville Notch, the northernmost of the White Mountain notches. An area of steep jagged cliffs and thick stands of evergreens, much of the notch falls within the confines of **Dixville Notch State Park** (☏ *603-323-2087, www.nhstateparks. org*). On the shores of Lake Gloriette, near the highest point (1,871ft) in the notch, stands the grand resort hotel known as **The Balsams**.

Raft, Kayak & Canoe Trips

The small village of **Errol** *(southeast of Dixville Notch on Rte. 26 at the intersection of Rte. 16)* is an outdoor center for wilderness camps and river trips, given its proximity to the beautiful Androscoggin River. **Saco Bound** in Conway (☏ *603-447-2177; www.sacobound.com*) offers a host of water treks and camping trips, paddling and kayaking classes and pontoon boat cruises in the region. Touring kayaks and canoes can be rented as well as camping equipment.

Hiking Trails

🚶 Several trails compose the Dixville Notch Heritage Trail, which encompasses Dixville Notch State Park in a 51mi loop. Two of these trails are located east of the Balsams Hotel and lead to waterfalls. The first is an easy .3mi walk that begins at the **Flume Brook Parking Area** on Route 26. The second, the **Cascades-Waterfalls Trail** *(.5mi)* to **Huntingdon Falls**, begins 1mi east of the Flume Brook parking area at Dixville Notch State Park wayside. You can stop for refreshment at the Balsams Resort's spring house, located on the hotel's entrance road, were cold, spring water flows continuously from a drinking fountain during the summer months.

THE BALSAMS GRAND RESORT HOTEL

Rte. 26, Dixville Notch. ☏ *800-255-0600. www.thebalsams.com.* Built in 1866 as a modest 25-room summer guest house, this venerable hotel was first expanded in the 1890s and then again in 1918, when a new wing more than doubled the structure's size. Today the resort comprises 15,000 acres, affording guests the opportunity to ski, hike, golf and play tennis. The hotel's Ballot Room is famous as the place where the citizens of Dixville Notch gather just after midnight on election day to cast their ballots—the first votes that the candidates receive in presidential primaries and elections.

PORTSMOUTH★★

POPULATION 20,784
MICHELIN MAP 581 N 6 AND MAP OPPOSITE
TOURIST INFORMATION ☎ 603-436-1118 OR WWW.PORTSMOUTHCHAMBER.ORG

New Hampshire's only seaport and the colonial capital until 1808, when the seat of government was moved to Concord, Portsmouth is a small city on the banks of the Piscataqua River. In summer tourists flock to its waterfront, historic houses and numerous shops, galleries and restaurants. A number of Portsmouth's colonial structures and historic houses are open to the public as museums. The most interesting is Strawbery Banke, the city's early waterfront community that has been transformed into a living history museum.

- **Orient Yourself:** Portsmouth sits on the Piscataqua River, just off north-south I-95.
- **Parking:** A public parking garage is located on Hanover Street within walking distance to downtown sights and attractions.
- **Don't Miss:** Strawbery Banke Museum, with more than 35 historic buildings, formal gardens, and a host of demonstrations and activities.
- **Organizing Your Time:** Start at Market Square, the hub of downtown acitvity. You can purchase a Harbor Trail map at the information kiosk in the square and follow the self-guided walking tour of historic sites, or use the map opposite. Reserve a half to full day to visit Strawbery Banke museum.
- Kids **Especially for Kids:** Children will enjoy seeing the tugboats in the Old Harbor off Ceres Street.
- **Also See:** Prescott Park on the waterfront.

A Bit of History

In 1630 a group of English settlers arrived on the banks of the Piscataqua River. Noting that the riverbanks were covered with wild strawberries, they named their

Portsmouth Harbor

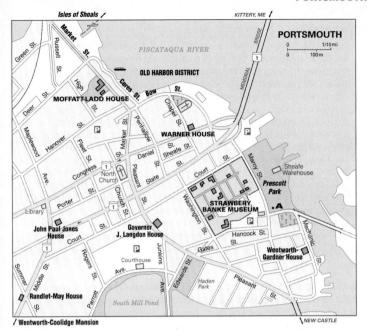

community "Strawbery Banke." Not until three decades later was the "port at the mouth of the river" renamed Portsmouth.

Vintage Georgian mansions, reminiscent of Portsmouth's past as a lumber and seafaring center, line the streets leading to the waterfront. In the **Old Harbor District—Bow**, **Market and Ceres Streets**—restored and freshly painted restaurants, art galleries and antique shops, as well as the tugboats tied up at the Ceres Street cove, remind visitors of a time when commerce was the mainstay of Portsmouth's economy. **Harbor cruises** on the Piscataqua River offer a pleasant way to view the city and its environs *(depart from Ceres Street Dock; 1hr 15min; commentary; reservations suggested; ⊛ $14; ╳; for seasonal schedules, contact Portsmouth Harbor Cruises: ☎ 603-436-8084 or www.portsmouthharbor.com).*

Strawbery Banke Museum★★

Entrance on Marcy St. 🕐 *Open May–Oct daily 10am–5pm; Nov–Apr Sat 10am-5pm Sun noon–2pm.* ⊛ *$15 (valid for 2 consecutive days). Site plan available at the entrance.* ╳ 🅿 ☎ *603-433-1106. www.strawberybanke.org.*

Overlooking lovely Prescott Park and the broad Piscataqua River beyond, this village-museum is a pleasant assembly of tree-shaded paths, historic houses and period gardens that border an expansive green. The slower pace of bygone eras envelopes visitors as they enter this remnant of yesteryear, which traces over 300 years of American architectural styles.

The tour of Strawbery Banke is self-guided. You may want to follow the sequence in which the buildings are numbered on the museum's site plan. Interpreters in period dress staff several of the structures and are available to answer questions. Conant House (c.1791), on the Washington Street side of the museum, serves lunch and light refreshments during the day. On the opposite end, bordering Marcy Street, the Dunaway Store now houses one of Portsmouth's finest restaurants. In addition, some eight period gardens grace the grounds—a kitchen garden, Victorian and victory gardens, and an herb garden among them.

MUNCHIES

Bordering North Church, the popular square at the intersection of Market, Pleasant, Daniel and Congress Streets, is a great place for people-watching, relaxing and eating. There are many restaurants to choose from downtown. European styled **Cafe Brioche** *(14 Market Square;* 🕐 *open Sun–Thu for lunch, Fri & Sat dinner only;* ☎ *603-430-9225; www.cafebrioche.com)* sits at the heart of the square, its outdoor tables and chairs populated with townspeople and tourists alike. Adjacent restaurant **Bella Luna** *(10 Market St.; dinner only Tue–Sat;* ☎ *603-436-9800)* serves up international cuisine in the evenings in its attractive, but small dining space just off the square.

The Friendly Toast – *121 Congress St.* ☎ *603-430-2154. www.friendlytoast.com.* This 1950s style eatery is popular for its funky garage-sale interior, creative menu and hours of operation *(*🕐 *open 7am–midnight Mon–Thu; open 24hrs Fri & Sat; 7am–9pm Sun).* Start the day with Almond Joy cakes (buttermilk pancakes, chocolate chips, coconut and almonds), or the Peasant (egg whites scrambled with Cuban brown rice, plus fresh spinach mixed with black beans and feta). Lunch brings a variety of salads, burgers and clubs, like the Matt #2 (grilled anadama bread with black beans, salsa, cream cheese, cheddar and avocado).

Between Strawbery Banke and the river lies **Prescott Park**, which is planted with lush flower gardens during the summer and filled with weekend picnickers, sunbathers, volleyball players and kite flyers. Opposite the entrance to Strawbery Banke is a **liberty pole** (A), similar to those raised by the patriots during Revolutionary days to signify their opposition to the Crown.

Historic Houses

Warner House★★

150 Daniel St. 🔍 *Visit by guided tour (45 min) only, Jun–Oct Mon–Sat 11am–4pm, Sun noon–4pm.* 🕐 *Closed major holidays.* 👓 *$5.* ☎ *603-436-8420. www.warnerhouse.org.*
This brick Georgian mansion was built in 1716 and is decorated with European- and New England-made furnishings. A series of 18C murals adorn the walls of the stairwell.

Moffatt-Ladd House★

154 Market St. 🔍 *Visit by guided tour (1hr) only, mid-Jun–mid-Oct Mon–Sat 11am–5pm, Sun 1pm–5pm.* 👓 *$6.* ☎ *603-436-8221. www.moffattladd.org.*
This elegant three-story Georgian mansion, built in 1763, includes a grand entrance hall with period wallpaper and elaborate wood paneling. A pleasant terraced garden (mid-19C) adjoins the house.

Wentworth-Gardner House

50 Mechanic St. 🔍 *Visit by guided tour (1hr) only, mid-Jun–mid-Oct Tue–Sun 1pm–4pm.* 🕐 *Closed major holidays.* 👓 *$5.* ☎ *603-436-4406. www.seacoastnh.com/wentworth.*
The facade of this lovely Georgian mansion, built in 1760, casts its reflection on the surface of the Piscataqua River. The pineapple carved above the doorway was the symbol of hospitality in colonial times. Inside, the paneling, balusters and cornices are flawlessly carved.

Governor John Langdon House

143 Pleasant St. 🔍 *Visit by guided tour (45min) only, Jun–mid-Oct Fri–Sun 11am–4pm (on the hour).* 🕐 *Closed Labor Day.* 👓 *$6.* ☎ *603-436-3205. www.spnea.org.*
This handsome Georgian mansion (1784) is known primarily for its original owner John Langdon, the first president of the US Senate and a former governor of New

Address Book

For price ranges for hotels and restaurants, see the legend on the cover flap.

WHERE TO STAY

Martin Hill Inn – *404 Islington St.* P ☎ 603-436-2287. *www.martinhillinn.com. 7 rooms.* **$$$** A longtime favorite, the Martin Hill Inn is recognizable by its canopied windows and white picket fence. Guest rooms occupy two adjoining historic buildings lined by a short brick pathway through perennial and water gardens. The large Master Bedroom, with original wide-board pine flooring, Federal-style canopy bed, and antique mahogany English armoire, is a favorite among guests. All rooms have queen-size beds, air conditioning and private baths.

Sise Inn – *40 Court Street.* ♿ P ☎ 603-433-1200 or 877-747-3466. *www.siseinn.com. 34 rooms.* **$$$** Once owned by wealthy Portsmouth merchant John Sise, this centrally located 1881 Queen Anne mansion is decorated in Victorian-era antiques, high-end reproductions and museum prints. Rooms have modern amenities mixed with period furnishings and historic surroundings. The parlor, with its intricate woodwork and paneling, and the sun-filled breakfast room are popular gathering spots.

The Inn at Christian Shore – *335 Maplewood Ave.* P ☎ 603-431-6770. *www.portsmouthnh.com/christianshore. 5 rooms.* **$$** This early 19C structure now houses a small bed-and-breakfast inn within walking distance of downtown and Portsmouth Harbor. Three guest rooms feature queen beds and private baths; two have double beds and shared bath. Don't expect traditional country décor: Innkeeper Mariaelena Koopman decorates with an unusual mix of antiques and objects from around the world, including African art, pre-Columbian ceramics, and contemporary drawings and paintings. Guests enjoy a daily gourmet breakfast (one of the best in town) in the rough-hewn, low-beamed dining room.

WHERE TO EAT

Anthony Alberto's – *59 Penhollow St. Dinner only, Mon–Sat.* ☎ 603-436-4000. *www.anthonyalbertos.com.* **$$$ Italian**. For special-occasion dining, you can't beat this tiny restaurant, housed in the cellar of the historic 1816 Custom House. The intimate dining room boasts its original water-struck brick walls, arches, and hand-hewn beams. The chef serves up excellent seasonal Italian cuisine.

Dunaway at Strawbery Banke – *66 Marcy St. Lunch daily 11:30am-2pm, Dinner Mon–Thu 5:30pm-9:30pm Fri-Sat 5pm-10pm Sun 5pm-9pm.* ☎ 603-373-6112. *www.dunawayrestaurant.com.* **$$$ American**. Chef Mary Dumont is a genius at pairing flavors; it's little wonder that *Food & Wine* magazine recently named her one of their top new chefs. The historic simple surroundings are warm and cozy, the creative American cuisine is made from freshest local fish and produce, often blended with historic and rare herbs and fruits grown at Strawbery Banke's own kitchen gardens. Fresh and innovative; it's *the* place to dine in Portsmouth!

Pesce Blue – *103 Congress St. Lunch Mon-Fri 11:45am-2pm Dinner daily 5pm-9pm, until 10pm Fri-Sat.* ☎ 603-430-7766. *www.pesceblue.com.* **$$$ Seafood**. This hip, upscale restaurant offers the freshest seafood prepared with simple Italian flavors. The menu changes daily but may include dishes like sea bass in salt crust or the house specialty Grigliata Mista, an assortment of grilled char, trout, swordfish, sardines and jumbo scallops.

Hampshire. The interior features wood-carved embellishments, as well as 18C and 19C furniture that was made in Portsmouth.

John Paul Jones House

43 Middle St. 🚶 *Visit by guided tour (30min) only, mid-May–mid-Oct Thu–Mon 10am–4pm, Sun noon–4pm.* 👜 *$5.* ☎ 603-436-8420. *www.seacoastnh.com/touring/jpjhouse.*

The American naval hero **John Paul Jones** stayed in this Colonial-style home on two occasions during the Revolution. Early furnishings, china, clothing and historical memorabilia are on display.

Rundlet-May House

364 Middle St. 🚳 *Visit by guided tour (45min) only, Jun–mid-Oct first Sat of the month 11am–4pm (on the hour).* 🕓 *Closed Labor Day.* 🎫 *$6.* ☎ *603-436-3205. www. spnea.org.*

This elegant three-story Federal residence reflects the taste and lifestyle of the merchant family who owned the property from its construction in 1807 until the 1970s. The interior is appointed with many of the original embellishments and amenities, such as fine pieces of Portsmouth furniture, English wallpaper and innovative early-19C kitchen conveniences. The attached outbuildings and garden further enhance the dwelling's charm.

Excursions

Cruise to Isles of Shoals★

Departs from Market St. dock mid-Jun–Labor Day daily. Limited schedule spring & fall. Round-trip 2hr 30min. Commentary. Reservations recommended. 🍴♿🅿 *Fees & schedules vary; call for information: Isles of Shoals Steamship Co.,* ☎ *603-431-5500, 800-441-4620 or www.islesofshoals.com.*

The 10mi boat trip to this group of nine islands follows the banks of the Piscataqua for 5mi before heading out to sea. There are good views of sights along the river, **Fort McClary** (Kittery, Maine), **Fort Constitution**, and the lovely homes in the island town of New Castle.

In the 19C the islands were popularized by author Celia Thaxter and other writers who gathered at her home on Appledore Island each summer.

Wentworth-Coolidge Mansion

On Little Harbor Rd. off Rte. 1A, 2mi south of downtown Portsmouth. Cross the Portsmouth city line (.25mi) and turn right just before the cemetery onto Little Harbor Rd. Continue 1mi and follow signs. 🚳 *Visit by guided tour (1hr) only, late-May–Sept Wed–Sat 10am–4pm, Sun 1pm–5pm.* 🎫 *$7.* ☎ *603-436-6607. www.nhstateparks.org.*

This 18C mansion on the banks of the Piscataqua River was the home of Benning Wentworth, the son of John Wentworth, New Hampshire's first colonial governor. Although only partially furnished today, the house remains an elegant example of the sophisticated early-American architecture of the Portsmouth region.

THE WHITE MOUNTAINS★★★

MICHELIN MAP 581 K-M 2-4 AND MAP PP 314-315
TOURIST INFORMATION ☎ 603-745-8720 OR WWW.VISITWHITEMOUNTAINS.COM

Spreading across northern New Hampshire and into Maine, the White Mountains make this region the most mountainous in New England. Included in this area, the federally managed White Mountain National Forest is renowned for its 772,000 acres of spectacular natural attractions, picnic areas, campgrounds and more than 1,200mi of hiking trails. The region's long winter offers numerous opportunities for skiing in the National Forest and in the valleys close by. Throughout the summer, hikers and motorists enjoy the cool woods and waterfalls and the views from the mountain summits; in the fall, nature transforms the White Mountains into a leaf-peeper's paradise.

▶ **Orient Yourself:** The popular White Mountain region dominates the central part of the state. Route 16 travels north-south on the eastern border; I-93 runs north-south on the west side of the region. Route 302 travels west and northwest; the scenic Kancamagus Highway (Rte. 112) runs east-west.

▣ **Parking:** You'll pay (👓 $5 a day) to park at some of the popular trailheads.

☺ **Don't Miss:** Flume Gorge, with towering waterfalls and cascades.

◷ **Organizing Your Time:** Plan at least a day for outdoor activities, like hiking, biking, or boating. Join a guided hike with the Appalachian Mountain Club; free daily trips are offered from the AMC Highland House in Crawford Notch.

▦ **Especially for Kids:** Young children love the characters and rides at Story Land. They'll also enjoy a ride on the Conway Scenic Railway.

⚲ **Also See:** The Mount Washington summit, via the Cog Railway or Auto Road.

Geological Notes

Named for the snow that blankets the area during most of the year, these mountains, dominated by Mt. Washington (6,288ft), are characterized by their rounded summits and deep, broad, U-shaped valleys known as **notches**.

The mountains are remnants of ancient, primarily granite, mountain ranges. During the last Ice Age, they were covered by an immense ice sheet, which ground and carved the summits until they were rounded. As the ice sheet retreated, glaciers created steep-walled valleys, polishing them to smooth U-shaped notches, while the swirling action of melting glacial water sculpted giant potholes, such as the basin found in Franconia Notch.

A Bit of History

Giovanni da Verrazzano sighted the White Mountains from the coast in 1524, and as early as 1642 a settler scaled the peak we now call Mt. Washington. The artists and writers who visited the region in the early 19C depicted the rugged beauty of the White Mountains in their paintings, novels, short stories and poetry. During the same period, New Hampshire residents named Mt. Washington and the other peaks

The Presidential Range

NHDTTD/Dale Lary

Address Book

PRACTICAL INFORMATION

GETTING AROUND

Many scenic routes traverse White Mountain National Forest, including I-93 from **Plymouth** to Exit 35 *(30mi)*; Rte. 112 from **Lincoln** to **Conway** *(37mi)*; and Rte. 15 from **Milton Mills** (south of the National Forest) to **Gorham** *(86mi)*.

The **Mount Washington Valley Chamber of Commerce** offers maps and information on attractions, accommodations, dining, and recreation in the area *(☎ 603-356-5701, 800-367-3364; www.mtwashingtonvalley.org)*.

The **Appalachian Mountain Club (AMC)** runs a visitor center at the base of Mt. Washington in Pinkham Notch and at the Highland House in Crawford Notch *(☎ 603-466-2721; www.outdoors. org)*. Trail maps and guide books are available at the visitor center. For information on campgrounds, hiking trails and scenic drives in the **White Mountain National Forest,** check with the forest headquarters *(719 N. Main St., Laconia NH 03246; www.fs.fed. us/r9/white)*.

ACCOMMODATIONS

👌 *For specific suggestions of accommodations and restaurants, see Where to Stay opposite.* Most lodgings are located in towns near the southeastern edge of the national forest. The **Appalachian Mountain Club** *(above)* administers a system of huts and shelters along the Appalachian Trail, a lodge at the base of Mt. Washington and in Crawford Notch. **Camping** is permitted year-round *(advance reservations available for many campsites through New Hampshire state parks; ☎ 603-271-3628; www.nhstateparks.org)*. Camping on Mt. Washington is not permitted. Permits are not required for **backcountry camping**.

RECREATION

There are more than 1,200mi of **hiking** trails in the national forest; trail maps are available at ranger stations and at the AMC visitor center. AMC also offers guided hiking trips throughout the year.

Hunting and **fishing** are permitted in some areas; licenses and rental equipment are available at sporting-goods stores in neighboring towns. **Swimming**, **canoeing** and **kayaking** are allowed on many lakes and rivers. **Cross-country skiing** trails lace the area; **downhill skiing** is available primarily in Mt. Washington Valley, Waterville Valley and Franconia Notch. Specialty **shopping**, sporting supplies and outlet stores are available in North Conway.

WHERE TO STAY

👌 *For price ranges for hotels and restaurants, see the legend on the cover flap .*

Dana Place Inn – *Rte. 16 in Pinkham Notch, Jackson.* ✕ ♿ 🅿 ⛷ ☎ *603-383-6822 or 800-537-9276. www.danaplace. com. 34 rooms.* **$$$** This sprawling 1890s resort sits on 300 acres, flanked by the meandering Ellis River and surrounded by the White Mountain National Forest. In summer, you can hike, bike, play tennis, and fish; when the mercury drops, try cross-country skiing, snowshoeing or sleigh riding—then warm up with a brandy next to the fireplace in the wood-paneled library.

The Franconia Inn – *1300 Easton Valley Rd., Franconia.* ✕ 🅿 ⛷ ☎ *603-823-5542 or 800-473-5299. www.franconiainn. com. 32 rooms.* **$$$** You'll think you've stepped into a Currier and Ives painting when you enter this pristine, three-story white clapboard Colonial, surrounded by the Franconia and Kinsman mountain ranges. In all seasons, the 100-acre property offers recreational activities galore—nature walks, horseback riding, tennis, hiking, cross-country skiing, gliding, sleigh rides and snowshoeing. All this, and fine cuisine, too—the inn's chef prepares gourmet fare using locally produced ingredients.

The Inn at Thorn Hill – *Thorn Hill Rd, Jackson Village.* 🅿 ☎ *603-383-4242 or 800-289-8990. www.innatthornhill.com. 36 rooms and three private cottages.* **$$$** Arguably the poshest —and most romantic— inn in the valley. This top-notch, upscale property offers luxurious accommodations (think: fine linens, fireplaces, jacuzzis, steam showers).

Located in postcard-pretty Jackson Village, the inn boasts breathtaking mountain views. Added bonus: reserve a table in one of the three elegant dining rooms for award-winning, creative cuisine.

WHERE TO EAT

Horsefeathers– *Main St., across from Schouler Park and the train station. North Conway.* 🕐 *Sun-Thu 11:30am-10pm Fri-Sat 11:30am-11pm* ♿ ☎ *603-383-4414. www.horsefeathers.com.* **$$ American**. This perennially popular eatery has been a North Conway mainstay for 30-plus years. The casual, friendly restaurant boasts an impressive menu. Munch on appetizers like spicy Maine lobster and crab cakes, salads (try the calamari caesar or the seared beef and snow pea), homemade soups, sandwiches (grilled crab and havarti or the best reuben in town) signature burgers, grilled fish, ribs, steaks and more.

Red Parka Pub – *Rte. 302, Glen. Open daily for dinner.* ♿ ☎ *603-383-3344. www.redparkapub.com.* **$$ American**. Popular with both locals and the après-ski crowd, this casual restaurant is named for the red parkas with yellow crosses once worn by members of the local ski patrol. Here you'll find traditional pub fare, from nachos and potato skins to ribs, chicken, pasta, salads, and the restaurant's signature massive burgers and steaks. Live music is featured downstairs on weekends.

Wentworth Inn –*Corner of Rte. 16A and Carter Notch Rd. in Jackson Village.* 🕐 *Open daily for dinner; reservations suggested.* ☎ *603-383-9700. www.thewentworth.com.* For country dining in the grand manner, stop in at this well-appointed resort hotel, established in 1869. In the formal dining room, chef-prepared appetizers such as New England game pie with pheasant sausage and currants, or roasted Mahogany clams prove a fitting precedent to entrées like roasted Australian lamb loin or white bean and tomato bruschetta. After dessert and coffee, linger beside the lobby fireplace or stroll the extensive grounds, which contain cottages and condominiums, a swimming pool, tennis court and 18-hole golf course.

in the Presidential Range after former US presidents. By the end of the century, with the construction of the railroad and the abundance of Victorian hotels that had sprung up in the valley, tourism had established itself on a grand scale in the White Mountains. Many of the fine old hotels have since been destroyed by fire and replaced by clusters of motels and cottages.

Mount Washington★★★

Mount Washington is the highest point in New England (6,288ft) and the principal peak in the Presidential Range. A subarctic climate—characterized by bitter cold, wind and ice—predominates in the higher altitudes of this peak. The strongest winds ever recorded (231mph) swept across Mt. Washington's summit on April 12, 1934. Snow has fallen on this peak during every month of the year. Fog-bound at least 300 days each year, the summit of Mt. Washington, with its group of mountaintop buildings, has been dubbed the "City Among the Clouds."

Dining with a View

The **1785 Inn** (☎ *603-356-9025; www.the1785inn.com*) is known for its award-winning cuisine and fine views of Mt. Washington from the dining room. Soak up the views and feast on creative dishes, like the veal-topped shiitake mushroom caps, sherried rabbit, veal and lobster saute or the melt-in-your-mouth medallions of deer venison with sun-dried cherry and bourbon demiglaze.

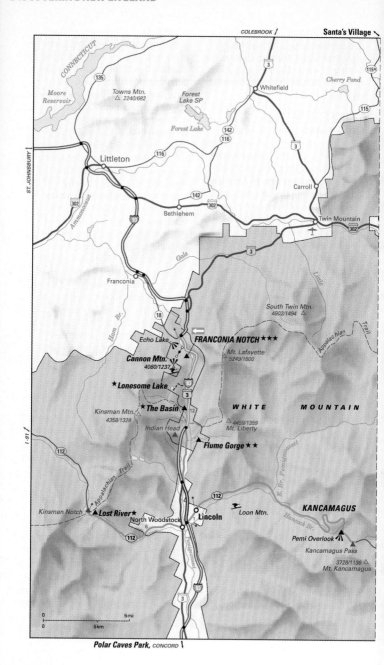

The Summit

The Mount Washington Cog Railway and the Auto Road (closed during severe weather) are the quickest means of reaching the summit. Hikers in good condition can try one of the four strenuous trails that lead to the summit.

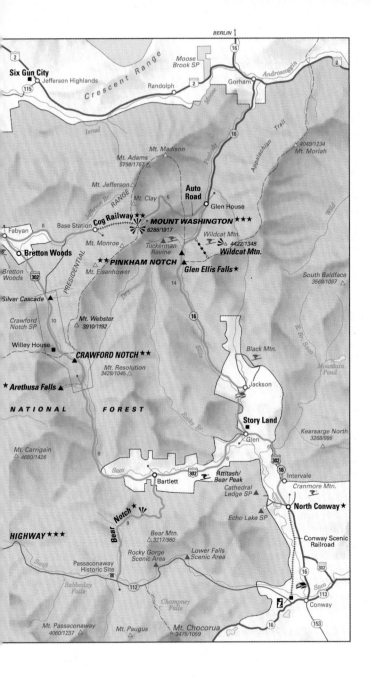

Among the half-dozen structures that cap Mt. Washington are the stone-walled Tip Top House (1853), radio and TV broadcasting facilities, and the Summit Building. The **Sherman Adams Summit Building** is the home to the Mt. Washington Weather Observatory (🕐 *open May–mid-Oct daily 8am–8pm;* 🍴♿🅿 ☎ *603-466-3347; www.nhstateparks.org.*) On a clear day, the rooftop deck of the building offers an impressive **panorama**★★★.

Mount Washington Cog Railway★★ – *6mi east of Fabyan.*   *See description.*

Pinkham Notch★★ – *North Conway to Glen House*

46mi via Rtes. 302 and 16.

North Conway★

Situated on the edge of the White Mountain National Forest, this bustling resort town is chockfull of restaurants, inns, outfitters and shops.

The Roman-style railroad station (1874) has been transformed into a museum and ticket office *(on Rte. 16)* for the **Conway Scenic Railroad** , which operates several different tours through the Saco Valley and Crawford Notch *(departs from North Conway depot mid-May–late Oct daily;* 🍴 🅿️*; call for information: Conway Scenic Railroad,* ☎ *603-356-5251, 800-232-5251 or www.conwayscenic.com).*

Story Land

On Rte. 16, Glen. 🕐 *Open mid-Jun-Labor Day daily 9am–6pm. May, Sept–mid-Oct weekends 9am–5pm.* 🚫 *$22.* 🍴&🅿️ ☎ *603-383-4186. www.storylandnh.com.*

This popular theme park features life-size characters and settings from children's stories and nursery rhymes, along with rides, a picnic grove and snack bars.

Glen Ellis Falls★

Off Rte. 16. Parking lot on left side of the road.

The falls and its pools, located on the east side of the road *(take the underpass)*, are formed by the Ellis River.

Wildcat Mountain

Parking area off Rte. 16.

Ski trails that look across Pinkham Notch to Mt. Washington have been cut on the slopes of Wildcat Mountain (4,422ft). An aerial gondola provides access to the summit, which offers **views**★★ of Mt. Washington and the northern peaks of the Presidential Range *(*🕐 *gondola operates mid-Jun–mid-Oct daily 10am–5pm; mid-May–mid-Jun weekends only;* 🚫 *$12.* 🍴& ☎ *603-466-5152 or 800-255-6439; www. skiwildcat.com).*

Auto Road

The 8mi trek to the summit of Mt. Washington begins at **Glen House**, from where you can drive your car or take a guided tour to the top. From the summit and scenic outlooks there are spectacular views of the Great Gulf Wilderness Area and the Presidential Range. *The road is open to private vehicles mid-May–mid-Oct daily 8am–4pm (weather permitting); extending hours in summer.* 🚫 *$20/car & driver. Guided van tours (1hr 30min) depart from Great Glen Lodge; $26.* 🍴& ☎ *603-466-3988. www. mountwashingtonautoroad.com.*

Tax-Free Shopping and Miniature Golfing

North Conway is a shopper's paradise, with top designer outlet shops and local specialty stores —and shopping is tax-free! Stop by the historic **North Conway 5¢ and 10¢** for penny candy, homemade fudge, and cheesy souvenirs. **Zeb's General Store** is a handsome emporium filled with maple syrup, jams, candy, books, puzzles and other New England-made products. **The Penguin Gallery** stocks wind chimes, banners, rocking chairs, hammocks, books and other merchandise. After your shopping spree, head for a round of miniature golf at **Banana Village** (☎ 603-356-2899) or **Pirate's Cove** (☎ 603-356-8807), both on Route 16.

Crawford Notch★★ – Glen to Fabyan

24mi via Rte. 302 from Glen. Route 302 follows the Saco River through Crawford Notch, a broad valley in the heart of the White Mountains. The road passes the **Attitash/Bear Peak**, a popular ski resort, and continues to Bartlett. In **Bartlett** a road located just past the library leads south through Bear Notch.

Bear Notch★

An additional 8mi between Bartlett and the Kancamagus Hwy.
This drive is especially scenic during the foliage season. At the point where the road leaves Crawford Notch *(3.5mi after Bartlett),* there is a beautiful **view** of the valley.

Crawford Notch★★

(1,773ft) This pass was named for the Crawford family, White Mountain pioneers who cut the first trail to the summit of Mt. Washington in the 19C, and whose home in the notch served as a shelter for hikers.

Arethusa Falls★

Parking lot on the left side of the road. Cross the railroad tracks, then follow the path (right) into the woods.
The trail *(round-trip 2hrs)* follows a brook, then crosses it just before reaching the falls, situated in a refreshing forest setting.
Route 302 passes in front of the rustic **Willey House** and **Mount Webster**, its slopes covered in places with the rocky debris of recent landslides. Farther on you will pass the **Silver Cascade**, a roadside waterfall tumbling from a high ledge.

Bretton Woods

The slopes of the Presidential Range form the backdrop for the **Mount Washington Resort**, a sprawling complex that is one of the few 19C grand hotels still in existence. In 1944 the hotel was the site of the United Nations Monetary and Financial Conference (Bretton Woods Conference), which established the American dollar as the medium of international exchange and developed plans to establish the World Bank.

▷ *Continue north on Rte. 302. At Fabyan, turn right onto the road leading to the Cog Railway.*

Mount Washington Cog Railway★★

Kids *Departs from Marshfield Base Station 6mi east of Rte. 302 mid-Jun–Labor Day daily 9am–5pm (hourly). Rest of the season departure times vary; call for hours. 3hrs round-trip (includes 20min stop at summit). Commentary. ⊜ $57. Reservations suggested.* P
☎ *603-278-5404 or 800-922-8825. www.thecog.com.*
This small steam train is almost as famous as the mountain itself. Built in 1869, the 3.5mi railway represents an outstanding technological achievement for its day, and still offers passengers a thrilling ride to the summit of the mountain, especially as the train ascends **Jacob's Ladder**, the steepest grade (37 percent) on the trestle. During the leisurely ride to the top, note how the vegetation and landscape change with increasing altitude.

MOUNT WASHINGTON RESORT

Kids *Rte. 302 in Bretton Woods.* ☎ *800-258-0330; www.mtwashington.com.* It's hard to miss this grand resort, resting at the bottom of the Presidential Mountain range, in the shadow of mighty Mount Washington. The historic 1902 hotel, with its 900-foot veranda, opulent lobby, and expansive grounds, retains much of its stately glamour. The resort features Indoor and outdoor pools, formal dining room, golf, tennis and daily activities; cross country/downhill skiing and sleigh rides are offered in winter.

Franconia Notch ★★★ *13mi via US-3.*

Running along the floor of this scenic notch cradled between the Franconia and Kinsman ranges, US-3 offers easy access to **Echo Lake** (Rte. 18) and to many of the area's natural attractions.

Cannon Mountain

An **aerial tramway** travels to the summit (4,060ft), of this ski mountain, which overlooks Echo Lake and affords a **view**★★ of the notch *(tramway operates Memorial Day–mid-Oct daily 9am–5pm; round-trip 15min; commentary;* ☞ *$11;* ♿ ☏ *603-823-8800; www.cannonmt.com).*

Located next to the Cannon Mountain tramway station, the **New England Ski Museum** illustrates skiing history with audiovisual presentations, photographs, equipment and memorabilia (🕐 *open Memorial Day–Columbus Day & Dec–Mar daily 10am–5pm;* 🅿 ☏ *603-823-7177; www.skimuseum.org).*

Covered Bridge in Franconia Notch

Lonesome Lake★

🥾 *Trail (3hrs) leaves from the parking lot at Lafayette Campground. Follow the yellow markers.*
This lake occupies a clearing 1,000ft above Franconia Notch. A trail around the lake leads to the Appalachian Mountain Club Hut, which accommodates hikers in the summer.

The Basin★

The action of churning waters rushing down from the falls above has formed this 30ft granite pothole.

Flume Gorge★★

On US-3/Franconia Notch Parkway in Franconia Notch State Park. 🕐 *Open May–mid-Oct daily 9am–5pm.* ☞ *$10. B* 🍴 🅿 ☏ *603-745-8391. www.flumegorge.com.*
Discovered in 1808, this natural gorge runs for 800ft along the base of Mt. Liberty. Its narrow walls of Conway granite rise to 90ft. Beginning at the visitor center, a series of connecting paths, boardwalks and stairways lead to falls and cascades.

Lincoln

Located at the southern entrance to Franconia Notch, Lincoln is a center for neighboring resorts, boasting a plentiful assortment of motels, restaurants, shops and commercial attractions.
En route to Lost River, travelers pass the colorful mountain community of **North Woodstock**, whose main street brims with shops and eateries.

LOVETT'S INN

1474 Profile Rd. off Rte. 18 in Franconia. 🕐 *Open daily for dinner and brunch on Sun; reservations suggested.* ☏ *603-823-7761. www.lovettsinn.com.* For superb dining in Franconia, look for the rambling Lovett's Inn on the left before you reach the village proper. Relax in the cozy lounge, with its marble bar. Then move to the spacious dining room for New England crab cakes or spinach ravioli, followed by entrees like the gorgonzola linguini with wild mushrooms, roasted duck, or herb crusted, pan-seared salmon.

WOODSTOCK INN

Stop for lunch at the **Woodstock Inn** (☎ 603-745-3951, 800-321-3985; www.
woodstockinnnh.com) on Main Street in North Woodstock. There's indoor dining
in the Clement Room and its glass-enclosed "petticoat porch" or an outdoor
umbrella-covered patio for warmer weather. Sandwiches and dinner are also
served evenings in the informal Woodstock Station. One of the inn's big attractions
is its brewpub, since the beer served is made on the premises in the Woodstock Inn
Brewery, a microbrewery that uses the traditional seven-barrel system.

Lost River★

7mi from Lincoln by Rte. 112 West. ○ *Open Jul & Aug daily 9am–6pm. May–Jun &
Sept–Oct daily 9am–5pm. Last ticket sold 1hr before closing.* ∞ *$11.50.* ⚒ ▣ ☎ *603-
745-8031. www.findlostriver.com.*

Located in Kinsman Notch, between the Connecticut and Pemigewasset valleys, the
Lost River Gorge is a steep-walled glacial ravine filled with enormous boulders that
have been sculpted into potholes by the river. A system of boardwalks and staircases
allows visitors to tour the caves, potholes and waterfalls in the gorge.

Kancamagus Highway★★★ *Lincoln to Conway 32mi.*

This road through the White Mountain National Forest follows the **Hancock Branch**
of the Pemigewasset River and the **Swift River**. It is one of the most spectacular
drives in New England during the foliage season, when the maples and birch trees
take on their fall colors. Picnic areas and campgrounds along the highways invite
visitors to relax by the clear mountain streams, waterfalls and scenic rapids.
The road passes in front of **Loon Mountain Recreation Area**, a year-round resort,
then begins to climb to Kancamagus Pass. During the ascent, there is an exceptionally
scenic **view★** from the **Pemi Overlook**. The road then dips into the Saco Valley.

Additional Sights

Santa's Village

Kids *Rte. 2 in Jefferson. Call for hours* ∞ *$21.* ▣ ☎ *603-586-4445. www.santasvillage.
com.*

You'll find Christmas 12 months a year at this theme park, set in a grove of tall evergreens. Here kids can ride roller coasters and log flumes, feed Santa's reindeer, and
help the "elves" working in Santa's workshop.

Six Gun City

Kids *.25mi west of the junction of Rtes. 2 & 115A, near Jefferson.* ○ *Open mid-Jun–Sept
daily 9am–6pm. Memorial Day–mid-Jun weekends only 10am–5pm.* ∞ *$18.95.* ▣
☎ *603-586-4592. www.sixguncity.com.*

This replica of a small western town includes a blockhouse, jail, saloon and 35 other
buildings. Visitors can enjoy the waterslide and ride logs through a mill.

Polar Caves Park

On Rte. 25, 5mi west of Plymouth. ○ *Open May–early Oct daily 9am–5pm.* ∞ *$12.*
⚒ ▣ ☎ *603-536-1888. www.polarcaves.com.*

The Polar Caves consist of a series of caves and stone passageways that were formed
during the last Ice Age, as freezing temperatures and ice caused gigantic boulders
to break loose from the mountain. Five conveniently placed stations with taped
commentaries allow visitors to tour the different chambers at their own pace along
wooden walkways.

RHODE ISLAND

AREA: 1,214SQ MI
POPULATION: 1,048,319
CAPITAL: PROVIDENCE
NICKNAME: THE OCEAN STATE
STATE FLOWER: VIOLET
OFFICIAL WEB SITE: WWW.VISITRHODEISLAND.COM

The smallest state in the nation, Rhode Island measures only 48 miles long and 37 miles wide. In 1524 Italian navigator Giovanni da Verrazzano sailed into Narragansett Bay and along the coast of the island known to the Indians as Aquidneck. Impressed by the brilliance of the natural light here, Verrazzano noted the similarity in appearance between Aquidneck and the Greek isle of Rhodes. More than a century later, Aquidneck was renamed Rhode Island. Its official name, the State of Rhode Island and Providence Plantations, reflects the state's origin as a series of independent settlements. The Royal Charter of 1644 united "Providence Plantations" at the head of the Narragansett Bay with settlements at Newport and Portsmouth on Aquidneck Island. Today the state ranks as the third most densely populated state in the US.

A Land of Tolerance – The earliest colonists came to Rhode Island in search of religious freedom they could not find in Massachusetts. The first to arrive, in 1630, was the **Rev. William Blackstone**, fleeing the Puritans' invasion of his privacy on the Shawmut Peninsula. He was followed by the minister **Roger Williams**, who founded Providence in 1636. Exiled from Massachusetts for his "new and dangerous opinions," Williams established Providence Plantations, a farming community, on lands that he purchased from the Narragansett Indians. Two years later a group of disgruntled Bostonians bought the island of Aquidneck and started the colony of Portsmouth (north of present-day Newport). The religious leader **Anne Hutchinson** joined them in 1638, with her own adherents in tow. Newport was founded in 1639 by 11 former Portsmouth colonists who left after a factional dispute. Relations between the colonists and the Indians remained friendly until 1675 when Philip, chief of the Wampanoags, led his tribe, along with the Narragansetts and Nipmucks, in raids against the settlers in **King Philip's War** (1675-76). During the Great Swamp Fight (in Mount Hope, Rhode Island) on December 19, 1675, colonists launched a surprise

Newport Bridge at sunset

©Photo Disc, Inc.

Rhode Island fishing village

attack on the Narragansetts, Rhode Island's most powerful tribe. The war dissipated the tribe's strength and greatly reduced the local Indian population.

Economy – Rhode Island's economy was at first based on the sea, with Newport and Providence vying for positions as the nation's leading seaports. By the 1650s Rhode Island had gained a portion of the trade between New England and the West Indies. The great fortunes made from trade provided capital for the textile industry, which had its beginnings at Pawtucket in 1793. One of the country's leading textile producers throughout the 19C, Rhode Island soon became the most heavily industrialized state in the US. The exodus of the textile factories to the South after World War II led to an emphasis on diversified manufacturing, which today ranks as the state's leading source of income and its largest employer. Rhode Island's early manufacture of machine tools gave rise in 1796 to the production of jewelry and silverware, now a major industry. Tourism generates over a billion dollars a year in revenues for the state.

BLOCK ISLAND ★

POPULATION 1,010
MICHELIN MAP 581 L 11
TOURIST INFORMATION ☎ 401-466-2982 OR WWW.BLOCKISLANDINFO.COM

This unspoiled island, 7mi long and 3mi wide at its widest point, is a delightful low-key getaway off the coast of mainland Rhode Island. Quaint Victorian hotels and storefronts hug the shore of Old Harbor, where the ferry comes in to port. Quickly, civilization gives way to a pastoral landscape of rolling hills and inland moors. The preferred mode of transport is a bicycle—you'll pedal past grazing sheep, kids with lemonade stands, and beautiful natural areas.

Block Island was named for Adriaen Block, the Dutch navigator who explored the region in 1614. The first permanent colonists arrived at the beginning of the late 17C to farm and fish. Following the advent of steamboat travel some 200 years later, the island developed into a summer resort, and Victorian-style hotels sprang up along Water Street in **Old Harbor.** Today, shops, inns and restaurants line the quaint streets of Old Harbor. **New Harbor,** the other hub of activity on the island, is home to a large marina for visiting pleasure boats. Great Salt Pond is a haven for paddlers. The island is ringed by 17mi of beaches.

> ▶ **Orient Yourself:** Block Island is located 12mi off the coast of Rhode Island, reachable by ferry from Pt. Judith, RI (2hrs from Boston), and New London, CT. (☎ *866-783-7996; www.blockislandferry.com).*

> 🅿 **Parking:** Unless you're spending the summer here, there's no reason to bring a car. Rent a bicycle to get around on-island *(rentals are available in Old Harbor and New Harbor, including kid-size bikes and tagalong systems)* or hire a taxi.

> ⊛ **Don't Miss:** Bicycling around the island, with stops at Mohegan Bluffs and Clay Head Preserve; visit Block Island Farmers' Market for local treats like cinnamon honey from Littlefield Bee Farm.

> 🕓 **Organizing Your Time:** Many inns have minimum-stay requirements in summertime; plan to stay for a week if you really want to unwind.

> 🄺🄸🄳🅂 **Especially for Kids:** Stop by the farm at the Hotel Manisses, where kids can visit with resident llamas.

Sights

Mohegan Bluffs★★★
Along the island's southernmost tip is a series of spectacular multi-colored cliffs known as Mohegan Bluffs. Climb up a path (about 200ft elevation) and gaze out over the Atlantic. Wooden stairs descend to Mohegan Bluffs beach, secluded but pebbly. Large, flat-topped boulders make a great place for a picnic.

Clay Head Preserve★★
Much of Block Island is protected space, including this lovely property maintained by the Nature Conservancy. After you pass Clay Head Swamp, bear right to get to the beach. Or, bear left to clmb up above the clay cliffs to "the maze," a series of interwoven nature trails lined with shrubs and filled with songbirds.

Crescent Beach★
Just north of Old Harbor, the eastern shore of Block Island is lined with a sandy stretch of beaches. Crescent Beach *(entrance off Corn Neck Rd.)* has dressing rooms, a snack bar, showers and a lifeguard.

NEWPORT★★★

POPULATION 26,475
MICHELIN MAP 581 M 10 AND MAPS P 327 AND P 332
TOURIST INFORMATION ☎ 401-845-9123 OR WWW.GONEWPORT.COM

Set on an island in Narragansett Bay, Newport has evolved from a bustling colonial port to a 20C resort for the fabulously rich and famous to its present incarnation as a modern tourist mecca. Now, as in bygone days, Newport's allure hails from the sea: Sailboats crowd the harbor in summer and visitors cruise the offshore waters in a variety of vessels. And, of course, the best of Newport's renowned mansions enjoy ocean views.

▶ **Orient Yourself:** Newport is an island, linked by bridges to mainland Rhode Island (there is also ferry service between Newport and Providence and Newport and Jamestown).

🅿 **Parking:** Parking lots are located on Church St. (off Thames St.), on America's Cup Ave. near Commercial Wharf and at the Gateway Visitors Center.

⊘ **Don't Miss:** A walk along Cliff Walk, Newport's 3.5mi oceanfront path, and a peek at a couple of the mansions.

🕐 **Organizing Your Time:** Make your first stop the Gateway Visitors Center a 23 America's Cup Ave, a great source for tours, tickets and advice on what to do.

🄺 **Especially for Kids:** The most fun mansion tour for kids is the Astors' Beechwood Mansion, where actors portray characters from 1891.

👣 **Also See:** Sachuest Point National Wildlife Refuge, in Middletown, is a great place for a scenic walk, or surf fishing from the shore line.

A Bit of History

A Harbor of Refuge – In the wake of a political dispute with Anne Hutchinson in Portsmouth, **William Coddington**, another Boston exile, led a group of settlers to the southern part of Aquidneck Island in 1639. There, on the shore of a large harbor, they founded Newport. Other religious minorities—Quakers, Baptists and Jews—soon followed, seeking the religious tolerance for which the Rhode Island settlements were known. These settlers were talented entrepreneurs, and with their help the colony rapidly developed.

Newport's fortunes were abruptly reversed with the outbreak of the American Revolution. Marked by the British for destruction, Newport was occupied from 1776 to 1779. Inhabitants were forced to house English soldiers, and looting and burning were widespread. Following the British defeat, French troops, allies of the Americans, occupied Newport. It was here that meetings between General Washington and Count Rochambeau took place. By the end of the war Newport lay in ruins. Most of its merchants had fled to Providence, and the colony would never again regain its commercial splendor.

Playground of the Wealthy – During the years before the Revolution, planters from Georgia and the Carolinas escaped the heat of the southern summer by vacationing in Newport. In the mid-19C, with the introduction of steamboat travel between New York and Newport, an increasing number of visitors arrived each year. Following

The Breakers

Courtesy Preservation Society of Newport County

the Civil War, America's wealthiest families—including the Astors, Belmonts and Vanderbilts—began to summer here. Impressed by the magnificence of the palaces and châteaux they had seen while touring Europe, they commissioned America's finest architects to design the enormous "cottages" (as they whimsically called them) that grace Ocean Drive and Bellevue Avenue.

In summer Newport's rich, part-time residents held fabulous picnics, dinner parties and balls, famed for their extravagance. Presiding over these events were Mrs. William Astor, Mrs. O.H. Belmont, Mrs. Hermann Oelrichs and other high-society matriarchs. During a single summer season, each social maven might spend as much as $300,000 just on entertaining. The search for unusual diversions led to such eccentricities as the champagne and caviar dinner given by Harry Lehr for his friends and their pets, during which masters and pets ate and drank at the same table; and the fleet of full-size model ships made for Mrs. Oelrichs and placed on the ocean to convey the impression of a harbor.

Attracted by the latest fads and inventions, the affluent residents of Newport drove the first motor cars, built the first roads, filled the harbor with princely mahogany and brass-trimmed yachts, and introduced boat racing to the town.

Newport Today

Newport provides an architectural sampler of the nation's most aesthetically pleasing building styles dating from the 17C to the 19C. The city's large group of colonial structures range from the simple and austere Quaker meetinghouse to Trinity Church, inspired by the work of renowned 17C British architect Christopher Wren. More than 100 restored dwellings stand in the **Historic Hill** *(in the vicinity of Trinity Church)* and **Easton's Point** *(the area along the harbor north of Bridge St. and west of Farewell St.)* neighborhoods. Most of the restored homes in The Point—as it's know to locals—date from the 18C, when the neighborhood prospered as a colonial mercantile community.

The city sponsors several notable music festivals, including the **Newport Music Festival**, a series of musical programs presented in the mansions (Rosecliff, Beechwood, The Elms and The Breakers) during the month of July. The **JVC Jazz Festival** draws thousands of fans to hear some of the music industry's top jazz musicians in a spectacular outdoor setting—Fort Adams State Park— in mid-August.

Newport and Sports

Several sports owe their development and popularity to Newport society, whose favorite pastimes included tennis, golf and boating. In 1881 the first US tennis championships were held on the courts of the Newport Casino; annual tennis tournaments, including the **International Tennis Hall of Fame Grass Court Championships** *(held in early July)*, are still played here. The first US amateur and open golf championships took place on a nine-hole course laid out on Brenton Point in 1894 by members of society's elite "400," as compiled by Mrs. William Astor.

It was, however, in the realm of sailing—especially yachting—that Newport became internationally famous. By the late 19C several yachting clubs had been established in Newport, and from 1930 to 1983 the city hosted the celebrated **America's Cup** races. These races, an international competition among the most sophisticated sailing yachts in the world, date from 1851. It was in that year that the New York Yacht Club sent the schooner *America* across the Atlantic to compete against the British for the prestigious Hundred Guinea Cup. The *America* won the race and returned home with the cup—actually an ornate silver pitcher thereafter known as the America's Cup. Newport is the starting point of the biennial 685mi **Newport-Bermuda Race** and the destination of the **Single-Handed Transatlantic Race** that begins in Plymouth, England.

Address Book

PRACTICAL INFORMATION

GETTING THERE

From the north, take I-95 South to US-1 South; follow US-1 to Rte. 138 East, cross the Claiborne Pell Bridge (☞ *$2 one-way for passenger vehicles)* and follow signs *(Boston to Newport, 74mi; Providence to Newport, 37mi)*. From the south or west, take I-95 North to Rte. 138 East across the bridge *(New York City to Newport, 181mi)*. Domestic and international flights service **T.F. Green Airport** (PVD) in Warwick (☎ 401-737-4000; www.pvdairport.com), located 27mi northwest of Newport *(Exit 13 off I-95)*. Taxis and van shuttles are available from the airport to downtown Newport. The nearest Amtrak **train** stations are in Providence *(37mi;* ☎ 800-872-7245; www.amtrak.com) and Kingston *(15mi;* ☎ 401-783-2913). Bonanza Bus Lines provides **bus** service from New York City and Boston to Green Airport (☎ 800-751-8800; www. bonanzabus.com).

GETTING AROUND

Walking is the best way to get around in the downtown and historic areas. Metered street parking and public lots are available, but in the summer season, spaces are at a premium. Rhode Island Public Transit Authority (RIPTA) buses offer service on the island. In season, RIPTA provides trolley service to Newport attractions, including the mansions and Cliff Walk *(trolleys depart from Gateway Center Memorial Day–Columbus Day;* ☞ *$6/all-day pass;* 🅿/☞ *$2;* ☎ 401-781-9400 or www.ripta.com).

VISITOR INFORMATION

The **Gateway Information Center**, run by the Newport County Convention and Visitors Bureau, provides maps and information about area attractions, accommodations, annual events and recreational activities *(23 America's Cup Ave., Newport, RI 02840;* ☎ 401-845-9123 or 800-976-5122; www.gonewport.com).

ACCOMMODATIONS

For specific suggestions of accommodations and restaurants, see Where to stay, opposite. **Reservation Services:** Bed & Breakfast Newport, Ltd. (☎ 401-846-5408 or 800-800-8765; www.bbnewport. com); or Historic Inns of Newport (☎ 800-427-9444; www.historicinnsofnewport.com).

CRUISES

A variety of sightseeing cruises, from 2hr sails aboard a 72ft schooner to 3-night excursions to Martha's Vineyard or Nantucket on a 160ft yacht, are available from Classic Cruises of Newport *(Christies Landing;* ☎401-849-3033; www.cruisenewport.com). Sailing enthusiasts can charter one of the 12-meter America's Cup winners for a sunset sail or a cruise of Narragansett Bay *(America's Cup Charters;* ☎ 401-849-5868 or ☎ 401-846-9886; www.americascupcharters.com).

WHERE TO STAY

For price ranges for hotels and restaurants, see the legend on the cover flap.
Inn at Castle Hill & Resort – *590 Ocean Dr.* 🍴👤🅿 ☎ 401-849-3800 or 888-466-1355. www.castlehillinn.com. *25 rooms.* **$$$$$** Originally the home of marine biologist Alexander Agassiz, this Victorian seaside inn, set on a 40-acre peninsula with sweeping ocean views, has moved up a notch after a restoration by new owners. Rooms in the Victorian mansion are the grandest, with sumptuous paneling, fireplaces and whirlpool tubs; though the harbor houses and the new beach houses possess charms of their own—and porches. Guests enjoy complimentary breakfast and afternoon tea. Dining in the sunset room *(open to the public),* whose curved window walls create the illusion of a ship's bridge, captures the magic of the site. *Jackets are requested at dinner; no denim or workout clothes.*
Vanderbilt Hall – *41 Mary St.* 🍴👤🅿🛎 ☎ 401-864-6200 or 888-826-4255. www. vanderbilthall.com. *52 rooms.* **$$$$$** The YMCA is not your usual first choice for an overnight, especially one built in 1909, but when it's one with the Vanderbilt imprimatur that has been transformed into a four-star mansion-hotel, well, that's a YMCA of a different color. From the billiards and card rooms to the music room and conservatory, the ambience is luxurious. Each of the 52 guest rooms has its own theme

(global traveler, Oriental, presidential) and is outfitted with features such as four-poster beds, spiral staircases, claw-foot tubs and marble mantels. Many rooms also enjoy harbor views. Rates include afternoon tea. Even if you stay elsewhere, it's worth coming by to see a YMCA in a class of its own.

Francis Malbone House – *392 Thames St.* ☐ ☎ *401-846-0392. www. malbone.com. 20 rooms.* **$$$$** Designed by Peter Harrison (architect of Touro Synagogue), the Georgian-style inn was built in 1760 for shipping merchant Francis Malbone. Today this historic hostelry wraps guests in comfort in large rooms decorated with period reproductions, gas fireplaces, down comforters and eyelet-trimmed sheets. If it's chilly, warm yourself by a crackling fire in one of the front parlors. Rates include afternoon tea and a hearty breakfast, served in the elegant dining room. For those desiring complete privacy, the refurbished c.1750 Benjamin Mason House next door features two luxury suites.

Cliffside Inn – *2 Seaview Ave. Open year-round.* ☐ ☎ *401-847-1811m 800-845-1811. www.LegendaryInnsofNewport.com. 16rooms.* **$$$** Located a few steps from Cliff Walk (near First Beach), this antique-filled Victorian inn is one of America's top 50 tea rooms, thanks to its decadent afternoon tea service (try the swoon-worthy macaroons). Breakfast is delightful as well. Guest rooms—oozing romance— have fireplaces and four-poster beds; some have big, share-able tubs. The most intriguing feature, though, are the more than 100 self-portraits painted by mysterious beauty Beatrice Turner, who lived here for several years.

DINING IN NEWPORT

Asterix & Obelix – *599 Thames St. Dinner only.* ☐ ☎ *401-841-8833.* **$$$ International.** Named for the French comic-book characters, this popular bar/restaurant has a lot going for it: a French-bistro atmosphere, a colorful mural behind the bar, and outdoor tables in season. The menu covers the waterfront and circles the globe, from crab cakes remoulade to crispy salmon with mushroom-asparagus-orzo risotto to steak au poivre with *pommes frites.* Big appetites will enjoy *le obelisk grand* (1 lobster, 16 oysters, 6 shrimp, 12 clams—sharing advised). Desserts are likewise multilingual—Pavlova (with mango ice cream and passion fruit curd), iced tiramisu parfait, and brioche Napoleon (with cinnamon and peaches).

Scales and Shells – *527 Thames St. Dinner only.* ☐ ☎ *401-846-3474. www. scalesandshells.com.* **$$$ Seafood.** The atmosphere is boisterous and casual at this popular restaurant, located on bustling Thames Street. Diners can watch their meal being prepared in the open kitchen, where a vast, ever-changing menu of fish and shellfish specials—red snapper, halibut, coho salmon, striped bass, lobster, to name a few—are grilled over fragrant wood. Start your meal with a selection of oysters, cherrystones or littlenecks from the raw bar.

Black Pearl – *Bannister's Wharf. Closed Jan 1–mid-Feb.* ☎ *401-846-5264. www.blackpearlnewport.com* **$$ Seafood.** A classic New England seafood house perched on Bannister's Wharf, the Black Pearl serves surf—and turf—specialties in its dark-paneled tavern or in the more formal (and pricier) Commodore Room *(jacket required)* overlooking the marina. The seafood menu changes daily to feature such fresh catches as lobster, sweet Nantucket Cape scallops and grey sole. Local clams fill the restaurant's creamy chowder.

Brick Alley Pub & Restaurant – *140 Thames St.* ☎ *401-849-6334. www. brickalley.com.* **$$ American.** Visitors and savvy locals alike give a thumbs-up to the Brick Alley. With its lively décor—a fire truck on the roof, a 1937 truck as a room divider, sports paraphernalia—as well as an affordable menu, this pub/restaurant offers the proverbial "something for everyone." Feast on nachos, wings, "stuffies" (stuffed clams), burgers, steaks and fries and, to round things out, crab cakes, homemade pasta, ahi tuna and Kentucky Derby pie. Choose a table on the tree-shaded patio in summertime.

The Mansions★★★ *Map below.*

🕭 *The nine mansions operated by the Preservation Society of Newport County (The Breakers, Marble House, Château-sur-Mer, Rosecliff, The Elms, Hunter House, Isaac Bell House, Kingscote and Chepstow) can be visited by guided tour (1hr for each mansion) only. Houses are generally open mid-Apr–Nov daily 10am–5pm (last tour at 4pm). Schedules vary the rest of the year. Call for information about opening times & fees:*
☎ *401-847-1000 or www.newportmansions.org.*
Tickets are available at the mansions, at the Newport County Convention and Visitors Bureau (23 America's Cup Ave.), and online (Web site above). Combination tickets are available at a savings and include Green Animals Topiary Garden in nearby Portsmouth, another Preservation Society property.
Newport's other mansions are The Astor's Beechwood, Belcourt Castle and Rough Point.
♿ *See entries for details.*

World-famous for their mammoth size, décor and ostentation, Newport's "cottages" were built in the late 1800s and early 1900s by some of America's richest families. The evolution in the style of these estates begins with the eclecticism of the mid-19C Victorian period, as illustrated by Kingscote (1839) and Château-sur-Mer (1852). Displaying a splendor and magnificence never before expressed in American architecture, Marble House (1892), The Breakers (1895), The Elms (1901) and Rosecliff (1902) represent elaborate imitations of the châteaux of France and the palaces of Italy. Taken together they provide a fascinating picture of the excesses of the gilded age.

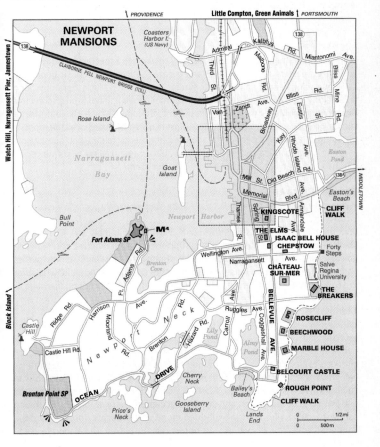

The majority of the mansions may be seen by driving along **Bellevue Avenue**★★★, which runs south from Memorial Boulevard to Land's End where it intersects with **Ocean Drive**★★. From that point, Ocean Drive follows the coast for 10mi to the southern end of the island. Be sure to catch the breathtaking sunset **views** along Ocean Drive, especially from **Brenton Point State Park**.

Straddling the rocky shoreline that separates The Breakers, Rosecliff, Marble House and Salve Regina University *(Ochre Point Ave.)* from the sea, **Cliff Walk**★★ winds for 3.5mi along the bluffs overlooking the sea. In the 19C, when fishermen protested against estate owners who attempted to close off the path, the state ruled in favor of the "toilers of the sea," and the walk has remained a public way ever since. Cliff Walk extends from Memorial Boulevard *(near Easton's Beach)* to Bailey's Beach *(private)*, with an additional access point at the Forty Steps *(at the end of Narragansett Ave.)*.

The Breakers★★★

Ochre Point Ave. ◐ *Open mid-Apr–Dec daily 9am–5pm. Rest of the year call for schedule.* ▭ *$15.* ♿▭.

In 1885 **Cornelius Vanderbilt II**, the grandson of the "Commodore," who had made his fortune in steamships and railroads, purchased the Ochre Point property with its modest wood and brick summer house. After the original structure burned in 1892, Vanderbilt hired architect **Richard Morris Hunt** to design another summer residence on the site. Selecting a High Renaissance Italian palace as his model, Hunt created this opulent 70-room mansion, which was completed in 1895. The exterior, heavily ornamented with arcades, columns and cornices, reveals the Italian influence. Within, The Breakers blends rich marbles and wooden trim with 22-carat gilded plaster, mosaics and ceiling painting.

Interior

The **Great Hall**, more than two stories high, showcases a spectacular array of columns and pilasters, marble plaques and ornate cornices. In the Music Room, the coffered ceiling bears a painting with figures representing Music, Harmony, Song and Melody. The **Morning Room** contains corner panels painted in oil on silver leaf representing the Muses; the room looks out onto the loggia, where a beautiful hand-laid Italian mosaic decorates the ceiling. Most richly embellished of all the rooms is the 2,400sq ft **Dining Room** where the Vanderbilts entertained their guests amid a setting of warm rose alabaster columns, a vaulted carved ceiling, oil paintings and gilt. Two 12ft-high Baccarat chandeliers light this room.

Marble House★★★

Bellevue Ave. ◐ *Open mid-Apr–Dec daily 10am–5pm. Rest of the year, call for schedule.* ▭ *$10.* ▭.

Built for millionaire yachtsman **William K. Vanderbilt** and his wife Alva in 1892, Marble House, with its classical portico supported by four marble Corinthian columns, recalls the Petit Trianon at Versailles. Among the most lavish dinner parties and balls held at Marble House was the debut of Consuelo Vanderbilt, who, after the celebration, locked herself in her room to protest her upcoming marriage to the ninth Duke of Marlborough. The marriage nevertheless took place a short time later, in 1895.

Interior

Containing some 500,000 cubic feet of American, African and Italian marble, the interior is as elegant as the exterior suggests. Tapestries decorate the huge entrance hall, which is faced with yellow Siena marble. In the **Gold Ballroom**, the most ornate ballroom in Newport, gilt panels, pilasters, arches and doorways are reflected in the glittering crystal chandeliers and mirrors that capture every ray of light. In striking contrast to the ballroom is the subdued mood of the **Gothic Room**, where the Vanderbilt collection of medieval art objects was displayed. The elaborate use of pink Numidian marble creates the luxuriant atmosphere of the **Dining Room**. The bronze Louis XIV chairs, weighing about 70 pounds each, made it necessary for the host to provide each guest with a footman, who would move the chair when the guest wished to sit or leave the table. The tour includes a visit to the spacious basement **kitchen**, boasting an elegance all its own with its 25ft-long stove, built-in iceboxes, and shiny monogrammed cookware.

The Elms★★

Bellevue Ave. ⏰ *Open mid-Apr–Dec daily 10am–5pm. Rest of the year, call for schedule.* 🎟 *$10.* 🅿.

Inspired by the 18C Château d'Asnières near Paris, architect Horace Trumbauer designed this dignified country estate for **Edward Julius Berwind**. The son of German immigrants, Berwind rose to prominence in the second half of the 19C as the "king" of America's coal industry. In 1899, he commissioned Trumbauer to build a residence to rival the cottages of Newport's established millionaires, who regarded him as a nouveau-riche outsider.

The housewarming given by the Berwinds in August 1901 was the social highlight of the season; countless varieties of exotic plants were used to adorn the house, and monkeys scampered about the grounds.

Interior

The large-scale proportions of the rooms, especially of the entrance hall and **ballroom**, are impressive. In the ballroom, smoothly curved corners, restrained decoration, and an abundance of natural light create an inviting and pleasant atmosphere, despite the size of the room. The French Classical style predominates: The **Conservatory** was intended to house tropical flora, the **Drawing Room** reflects the Louis XVI style, the stucco reliefs and fine woodwork of the ballroom suggest the earlier style of Louis XV. Three of the four black and gold lacquer panels ornamenting the **Breakfast Room** date from China's K'ang-hsi period (17C); the fourth is a reproduction.

Rosecliff★★

Bellevue Ave. ⏰ *Open mid-Apr–Dec daily 10am–5pm. Rest of the year, call for schedule* 🎟 *$10.* ♿🅿.

In 1891 **Theresa Oelrichs**, the daughter of a wealthy Irish immigrant who had discovered the Comstock Silver Lode in Nevada, purchased the Rosecliff estate—named for its many rose beds. Finding the house on the property too modest for her taste,

Rosecliff Ballroom

she engaged **Stanford White** to design a more elaborate residence. The result was a graceful imitation of the Grand Trianon at Versailles.

Mrs. Oelrichs was one of Newport's most celebrated hostesses. At one of her noteworthy galas, the "Mother Goose" Ball, guests dressed as fairy-tale characters. Designed primarily for entertaining, Rosecliff boasts the largest **ballroom** (80ft by 40ft) in Newport. Windows open onto the terraces, allowing the outdoors to become an extension of the ballroom. Scenes from *The Great Gatsby* (1974) were filmed here.

Château-sur-Mer★

Bellevue Ave. ⏰ *Open mid-Apr–mid-Nov daily 10am–5pm.* 👓 *$10. Rest of the year, call for schedule.* 📷.

Constructed in the Second Empire style, this "Castle by the Sea," with its massive asymmetrical silhouette, was built in 1852 for **William S. Wetmore**, who earned his wealth in the China trade. Extremely spacious and luxurious for its day, Château-sur-Mer was enlarged in 1872 by Richard Morris Hunt. After Hunt's substantial alterations were completed, Château-sur-Mer was considered the most "substantial and expensive residence in Newport."

Interior

Inside, light streams into the three-story entrance hall through a colored-glass ceiling panel 45ft above its floor; the hall, the Morning Room and the grand staircase are all paneled with white oak wainscoting hand-carved in the Eastlake style. Illuminated by stained-glass windows, the stairwell is lined with canvas painted to resemble tapestries.

Kingscote★

Bellevue Ave. ⏰ *Open late Jun–late Sept daily 10am–5pm.* 👓 *$10.* 📷.

Designed in 1839, this house is an early example of the Gothic Revival motif. Kingscote's irregular shape, expressed in wood rather than stone, and emphasized by gables, arches, eaves and varied rooflines, form a striking contrast to the symmetrical, solid shape of earlier dwellings.

This mansion was built for southern planter **George Noble Jones**, then sold in the 1860s to **William H. King** after whom it (King's Cottage) was named.

The Victorian interior contains Tiffany windows, heavy furniture and somber rooms. Among the furnishings is a prized collection of Oriental paintings, rugs and porcelain.

Isaac Bell House★

Corner of Bellevue Ave. and Perry St. ⏰ *Open late Jun–late Sept daily 10am–5pm.* 👓 *$10.*

When wealthy New York cotton trader Isaac Bell retired to Newport at age 31, he chose the newly formed firm of McKim, Mead and White to design his retreat on Bellevue Avenue. The shingle and brick house, completed in 1883, is a superb example of the American Shingle style with its gabled roof and rounded, tower-shaped, two-story porch. Arranged in an open floor plan, the interior features handsome oak paneling in the living room, rattan wall coverings in the dining room, and large sash windows in the drawing room that allow guests to walk out onto the porch.

Chepstow★

Narragansett Ave. at Clay St. Visit by appointment only late Jun–late Sept daily 10am–5pm. 👓 *$10.*

Built for Dutch bachelor W.C. Schermerhorn by Newport architect George C. Mason, Chepstow was completed in 1860. The white Italianate villa-style mansion later came to be owned by the Gallatin family, who named the house after a Welsh castle. Today the rooms reflect the "Victorian clutter" favored by Chepstow's most recent owner, along with a fine collection of 17C and 18C antiques and paintings by Fitz Henry Lane and members of the Hudson River school.

Hunter House★★

54 Washington St., in Newport's historic Point section. ♿ *See Additional Sights.*

More Mansions

The mansions listed below are privately owned and do not operate under the auspices of the Preservation Society of Newport County.

Belcourt Castle★

Bellevue Ave. 🚶 *Visit by guided tour (1hr) only, Memorial Day–Labor Day daily 9am–5pm. Rest of the year daily 10am–4pm.* 🕐 *Closed Jan, Thanksgiving Day & Dec 25.* 💰 *$12.* 🅿 ☎ *401-846-0669. www.belcourtcastle.com.*

A hunting lodge owned by Louis XIII was the model for this castle (1896) designed for the 35-year-old bachelor **Oliver Hazard Perry Belmont**. In 1898 Belmont married Alva Smith Vanderbilt, after her divorce from William K. Vanderbilt. After she moved in, Alva had the house redecorated. The castle, owned since 1959 by the Tinney family, contains an outstanding **collection** of European furnishings and decorative arts.

The interior is inspired by different periods of French, Italian and English design. Adorned with plush red upholstery and stained-glass windows, the vast **Banquet Hall** can comfortably accommodate 250 dinner guests. A huge, tiered crystal chandelier, which formerly graced a palace in St. Petersburg, Russia, dominates the room. From the oval Family Dining Room on the second floor there is a view out to the ocean. The spacious **French Gothic Ballroom** contains 13C French stained-glass windows, Oriental carpets, tapestries, distended vaults and an enormous fireplace surmounted by a 32ft-high plaster castle. The ballroom's 70ft-high ceiling creates excellent acoustics; in the castle's heyday, a 60-piece orchestra played from the upper-level gallery.

The Astors' Beechwood Mansion★★

580 Bellevue Ave. 🚶 *Visit by guided tour (45min) only May–Dec daily 10am–5pm. Feb–Apr Fri–Sun 10am–4pm.* 💰 *$18.* 🅿 ☎ *401-846-3772. www.astors-beechwood.com.*

A tour of this Mediterranean-style villa, acquired in 1880 by **William** and **Caroline Astor**, is unlike that offered by its palatial neighbors. From the moment visitors are greeted at the door by the "butler," they are transported back to the 1890s by "servants" and "house guests" (portrayed by members of a theater group) who accompany callers throughout the house.

Beechwood is famous as the home of Caroline Astor—*the* Mrs. Astor as she insisted upon being called—whose husband was the grandson of John Jacob Astor. Mrs. Astor, the grand dame of New York as well as Newport society, is known for compiling the list of society's elite "400"—the number of persons her New York ballroom could accommodate.

A copy of Duran's portrait of Caroline Astor hangs in the entrance hall. Among the public rooms on the main floor is the light-filled **ballroom**, ornamented with gesso relief, and containing more than 800 mirrors.

Rough Point★★

At the south end of Bellevue Ave. 🕐 *Open mid-Apr to mid-May, Thu–Sat 10am–2pm; mid-May to early Nov Tue–Sat 9:30am–4pm.* 🚶 *Visit by guided tour (1hr) only May–Oct. Call for hours. Advance reservations recommended* 🚶 *$25.* ♿. ☎ *401-849-7300. www.newportrestoration.org.*

Named for the rocky spit of land on which it sits, Rough Point was built in 1891 for Frederick W. Vanderbilt (grandson of the Commodore) on a ten-acre oceanfront site landscaped by Frederick Law Olmsted. The Gothic-style manse was purchased in 1922 by James B. Duke, North Carolina tobacco magnate and founder of Duke

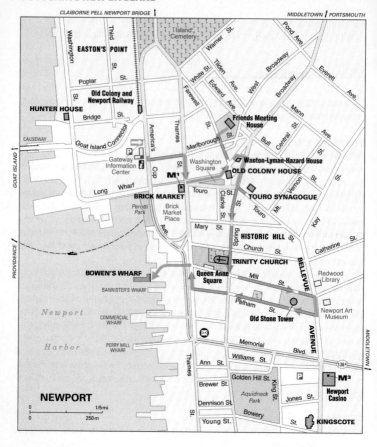

NEWPORT

Power. James Duke died in 1925, and his only child, Doris, inherited the house and its collection of art and antiques. In the 68 years that Doris owned Rough Point, she added significantly to that collection, purchasing a wealth of fine European furnishings and portraits dating from the 16C to the 18C.

Interior

Today the 40,000sq ft "cottage" is a monument to Duke's discerning taste, left virtually unchanged since her death in 1993 when she bequeathed it to the Newport Restoration Foundation—an organization she founded. The monumental **Great Hall** remains a gallery for art and tapestries, including a set of c.1510 Brussels tapestries, 17C portraits by Anthony Van Dyck and Ferdinand Bol (a student of Rembrandt), and a group of Ming Dynasty garden seats and wine jars. Used as a drawing room, the graceful **Yellow Room** is outfitted with Louis XVI furniture, some boasting its original embroidered fabric. The **Music Room**, with its rock-crystal chandeliers and hand-painted 18C Chinese wallpaper, was a favorite of Duke, who spent several hours a day here playing the Steinway piano. Upstairs, Duke's **bedroom** contains striking French mother-of-pearl pieces: an oval side table, two delicate chairs and a settee.

Colonial Newport Walking Tour★★ *Map opposite.*

Newport's extraordinarily large group of colonial structures constitutes one of the nation's great architectural treasures. The itinerary below represents a selection of these dwellings and public buildings.

▶ *From the Gateway Information Center, head south on America's Cup Ave. and turn left on Marlborough St. Turn right on Thames St. and walk one block south to the Brick Market.*

Brick Market★
127 Thames St.
This handsome three-story building with its arcaded base and massive pilasters above provides a fine example of the Palladian style's influence on Georgian architecture. The market was the commercial center of Newport; open market stalls were located on the ground floor, while the upper floors were reserved for offices and storage. Today two floors are occupied by the **Museum of Newport History** (**M¹**), which includes displays on Newport's early colonial life, maritime commerce and naval history (🕐 *open Apr–Oct Wed–Mon 10am–5pm; rest of the year Fri–Sat 11am–4pm, Sun 1pm–4pm;* 👓 *$5;* 🅿 ☎ *401-846-0813; www.newporthistorical.org).*

Old Colony House★
Washington Square. ☎ *401-846-0813.*
This building, designed by **Richard Munday**, was the seat of Rhode Island's government from the colonial period through the early 19C. In 1781 General Washington and Count Rochambeau, the leader of the French troops, met here to discuss plans for the battle of Yorktown.
Furniture made by local craftsmen Goddard and Townsend, and one of Gilbert Stuart's full-length portraits of George Washington decorate the interior.

▶ *Turn left on Farewell St. and continue to Marlborough St.*

Friends Meeting House
Marlborough St. 👓 *Visit by guided tour (45min) only, Jun–Sept Thu–Sat 10am–4pm.* 👓 *$4.* ♿ ☎ *401-846-0813.*
By the end of the 17C, Newport supported a large population of Quakers. This meetinghouse, constructed by the Society of Friends in 1699 and enlarged as the society grew, served as the regional center for New England's Quakers. The building is architecturally interesting for its pulley-operated walls, its large stone supports—which prevent the lower floor from resting directly on the ground—and its remarkable vault.

▶ *Walk back to Broadway and turn left.*

Wanton-Lyman-Hazard House
17 Broadway. 👓 *Visit by guided tour (45min) only Jun–Sept Thu–Sat 10am–4pm. Rest of the year by appointment only.* 👓 *$4.* ♿ ☎ *401-846-0813. www.newporthistorical.org.*
Prior to the Revolution, this house (c.1675) was the residence of Martin Howard, a Loyalist and lawyer widely criticized opponents of the Crown. During the Stamp Act riots, while the patriots ransacked his house, Howard fled Newport. Considering himself fortunate to have escaped, he eventually settled in England, never to return. In 1765 Quaker merchant John Wanton purchased the house, which was owned by his relatives until 1911. Rooms in the house, which were restored in 2000, are furnished with period pieces reflecting the late 17C to the early 18C.

▶ *Walk around the house to Spring St. Turn right and follow Spring St. to Touro St. Turn left onto Touro St.*

Touro Synagogue★★

85 Touro St. ⬫ Visit by guided tour (20min) only, Jul–Labor Day Sun–Fri 10am–5pm. Rest of the year Mon–Fri 1pm–3pm, Sun 11am–3pm. ⏰ Closed Jewish holidays. ⬫ $5. ☎ 401-847-4794. www.tourosynagogue.org.

The earliest members of Newport's Jewish community arrived from the Carribean in 1658. However, it was not until a century later, under the guidance of their leader, Isaac de Touro, that a synagogue was dedicated in 1763.

One of the earliest synagogues constructed in the US, the building was designed by architect **Peter Harrison** and successfully adapts the Georgian style to Sephardic Jewish tradition. Situated on a quiet street and set on a diagonal with the east wall facing the direction of Jerusalem, the exterior of the synagogue is almost stark in appearance. The interior is richly adorned with hand-carved paneling, balustrades and columns.

▷ *Return to Spring St. and turn left.*

Trinity Church★

Queen Anne Sq. ⏰ Open Jul–Aug daily 10am–4pm. Jun & Sept–Oct Mon–Fri 10am–1pm. ⬫ $2 contribution suggested. ♿ ☎ 401-846-0660. www.trinitynewport.org.

This white clapboard church (1726) rising above **Queen Anne Square**, features an arcaded belfry with a tall Colonial spire. Inside, the original three-tiered pulpit is the only one of its kind in the country. The left wall of the nave features two Tiffany stained-glass windows, one of which commemorates Cornelius Vanderbilt (the face is said to be that of the Commodore himself).

▷ *Continue south on Spring St. and turn left on Mill St.*

Old Stone Tower

Nicknamed the Mystery Tower because of the various legends surrounding its origin, this stone structure has been attributed to the Vikings, the Portuguese, the Indians and the Irish. Less romantic, but a bit more realistic, is the theory that the tower is the remnant of a 17C windmill.

▷ *Continue on Bellevue Ave. Turn right on Pelham St., which is lined with colonial dwellings. Turn right on Thames St., then left on Mill St. to the waterfront.*

Bowen's Wharf★

Salty old dockside structures have been transformed into indoor and outdoor eateries here. Along with neighboring craft shops and boutiques, they form the heart of this waterfront square.

Additional Sights

Hunter House★★

54 Washington St. ⬫ Visit by guided tour (45min) by appointment only, late Jun–mid-Sept daily 10am–5pm. ⬫ $25. ☎ 401-847-1000. www.newportmansions.org.

This elegant dwelling, built in 1748 by a prosperous merchant, was purchased by ambassador William Hunter and subsequently served as the home of two governors and as the headquarters of Admiral Charles de Ternay, commander of the French fleet during the Revolution.

The house is a beautiful example of the 18C Colonial style. The carved pineapple ornamenting the doorway is a symbol of hospitality that originated during the

Hunter House

Courtesy Preservation Society of Newport County

colonial period when a sea captain, returning home from a voyage, placed a pineapple outside his home to announce his safe arrival and to invite everyone to share the refreshments that were waiting inside.

Old Colony and Newport Railway

Kids *Departs from depot at 19 America's Cup Ave.* ⊙ *Open year-round. Trips Sun 11:45am and 1:45pm.* ⊚ *$7.50.* ☎ *401-624-6951. www.ocnrr.com.*

Chartered in the 19C, the railway experienced its busiest year in 1913 when 24 trains daily, including the Boston "Dandy Express," arrived and departed from Newport. Today the railway offers scenic excursions via a 10mi roundtrip along the eastern shore of Narragansett Bay. You'll travel through the Navy base, between two large naval aircraft carriers, and get a look at the pleasure boats in Newport Harbor.

International Tennis Hall of Fame (M³)

194 Bellevue Ave. ⊙ *Open year-round daily 9:30am–5pm.* ⊚ *$9.* ⊙ *Closed Thanksgiving Day & Dec 25.* ☎ *401-849-3990. www.tennisfame.org.*

Located in the historic **Newport Casino** complex, the Tennis Hall of Fame is home to one of the largest collections of tennis memorabilia in the country. This interactive museum offers the only lawn courts available for public use in the U.S.

Fort Adams State Park

Fort Adams Rd., off Harrison Ave. Park ⊙ *open year-round daily dawn–dusk.* ⌲ *Fort open by guided tour (45min) only, mid-May–mid-Oct 10am–4pm.* ⊚ *$8.* ♿☐ ☎ *401-847-2400. www.fortadams.org.*

With walls constructed of granite hauled from Maine by schooner, Fort Adams was built to guard the entrance to Narragansett Bay. The fort ultimately developed into the command post for the coastal batteries in the Northeast; until 1945 it was the center of a system of defenses used to protect the bay and Long Island Sound. Today the fort is a state park and site of the annual **JVC Jazz Festival**, as well as **Newport Creamery's Newport Folk Festival** *(both in Aug).* From the park's roadway there is a sweeping **view**★★ of the harbor, Newport Bridge and downtown Newport.

Museum of Yachting (M⁴)

⊙ *Open mid-May–Oct daily 10am–5pm. Rest of the year by appointment only.* ⊚ *$5.* ☐ ☎ *401-847-1018. www.moy.org.*

This small, two-story museum houses classic small craft and displays on Newport yachting history. Videos focusing on 12-meter yachts are shown continuously and the two-time America's Cup winner, *Courageous,* is moored offshore *(no boarding permitted).*

Excursions

Jamestown

3mi west of Newport via the Claiborne Pell Newport Bridge (toll), on Conanicut Island in Narragansett Bay.

At the center of this residential island stands the 1787 **Jamestown Windmill** *(380 N. Main Rd.;* ⊙ *open mid-Jun–Labor Day weekends 1pm–4pm;* ⊚ *donation requested;* ☐ ☎ *401-423-1798).* Several sites on the island offer some worthwhile **views**: From **Beaver Tail Lighthouse** *(end of Beaver Tail Rd.)* you can see along the south shore; an expansive vista across the bay to Newport stretches from **Fort Wetherill** *(off Rte. 138 & Walcott Ave.),* whose ramparts are built on granite cliffs that rise up to 100ft. The shores of picturesque **Mackerel Cove** are flecked with summer homes.

Green Animals Topiary Gardens

Green Animals Topiary Gardens★

[Kids] *9mi north of Newport via Rte. 114 in Portsmouth. Turn left off Rte. 114 onto Cory's Lane.* 🕐 *Open late Jun–late Sept daily 10am–5pm.* 🎟 *$10.* 🅿 ☎ *401-847-1000. www.newportmansions.com.*

Textile executive Thomas Brayton began creating this garden when he purchased the seven-acre estate in 1872. Today colorful flower beds, arbors and fruit trees punctuate the 80 boxwood and tree sculptures, which include fanciful representations of a giraffe, a unicorn and an elephant—some of them now 80 years old. The modest wood-frame country house contains a toy museum, a doll collection and dollhouses.

Little Compton

23mi east of Newport via Rte. 138 East and Rte. 77 South. ℹ *Tourist information:* ☎ *401-849-8048. www.gonewport.com.*

Located in the southeastern portion of the state and known for its production of "Rhode Island Red" chickens, Little Compton is one of Rhode Island's prettiest villages. Marshes fringe the narrow tree-lined roads (such as Route 77) that wind through the rural countryside down to the coast.

Narragansett Pier

11mi southwest of Newport. Cross the Jamestown Bridge and take Rte. 1A South. From Narragansett Pier, drive south on Ocean Rd. (Rte. 1A) along the coast to Galilee.

In the 19C heyday of this fashionable seaside resort, all activity centered on the pier (only the name survives), which extended from the southern end of Town Beach into the ocean. Today, the **Towers**, two stone structures joined by an arch extending across Ocean Road, are all that remain of the lavish Narragansett Casino, designed by McKim, Mead and White in 1884. The main section of the casino along with many of Narragansett's grand hotels were destroyed by fire in 1900.

Narragansett Pier and the coastal region extending south to the rocky headland of Point Judith and the fishing villages of Galilee and Jerusalem possess some of the finest beaches in New England. The lively atmosphere of **Scarborough Beach** draws a young crowd, while surfers prefer **East Matunuck State Beach**. Families with young children are drawn to the calm waters at **Galilee Beach**. In September Galilee hosts the annual **Rhode Island Tuna Tournament**, a major sporting event.

Newport Festivals

Visiting Newport is great; visiting Newport during a festival is even better. The city plays host to a lively line-up of special events. Of course you've heard of the JVC Jazz Festival-Newport (Aug)—here are more events to consider when planning your next Newport getaway. For details, visit www.GoNewport.com.

May:	Newport Spring Boat Show
June:	Schweppe's Great Chowder Cook-Off
	Newport International Film Festival
July:	Newport Music Festival
	Black Ships Festival
	Newport International Kite Festival
Aug:	Newport Folk Festival
	Wooden Boat Show
Sept:	Newport Waterfront Irish Festival
	Aquafina Taste of Rhode Island
	Newport Mansions Food & Wine Weekend
Oct:	Bowen's Wharf Seafood Festival
Nov/Dec:	Christmas at the Newport Mansions

Watch Hill

45mi southwest of Newport via Rte. 138 West to US-1 South. At Haversham, pick up Rte. 1A and follow it south to Watch Hill.

Located at the southwesternmost point on the mainland of Rhode Island, Watch Hill was named during King George's War (1740s) when a watchtower was built here to survey Block Island Sound for signs of naval attack. Today this fashionable seaside community boasts elegant summer houses and a host of recreational activities, including golfing, boating, and browsing in the myriad Bay Street boutiques. Kids will enjoy taking a spin on the c.1883 **Flying Horse Carousel** Kids *(Bay St. and Larkin Rd.;* 🕐 *open Memorial Day–Columbus Day;* 💲 *$1; children only)*, whose 20 hand-carved wooden horses feature leather saddles, agate eyes, and manes and tails made of real horsehair. And "fly" they do, since they hang from a central unit that enables them to swing outward as the carousel turns. The child who can grab the traditional brass ring wins a second ride, free.

PROVIDENCE★★

POPULATION 173,618
MICHELIN MAP 581 M 10 AND MAP P 342
TOURIST INFORMATION ☎ 800-233-1636 OR WWW.PWCVB.COM

The capital of Rhode Island, and the third-largest city in New England (after Boston and Worcester, Massachusetts), Providence is the hub of a metropolitan region with more than 900,000 residents.

The city's location on a natural harbor at the head of Narragansett Bay offered special advantages for the shipping and commercial activity that allowed Providence to prosper and expand. One result of this expansion was the development of the College Hill district with its lovely 18C and 19C structures. Today this tree-shaded residential neighborhood is the home of Brown University and the Rhode Island School of Design. Across the city from College Hill, the majestic capitol building rises above the growing business area below.

▶ **Orient Yourself:** Providence is located off I-95, about 90 miles from Boston.

▣ **Parking:** The city has several public parking lots, including a multi-level garage at Providence Place mall.

◉ **Don't Miss:** WaterFire, a public art event, held at night in summer and early fall.

◕ **Organizing Your Time:** A perfect day in Providence: Go sightseeing or shopping, take in a performance of WaterFire, and have dinner at one of the city's best restaurants.

▨ **Especially for Kids:** Roger Williams Park Zoo is a fun excursion for kids.

◔ **Also See:** Slater Mill Historic Site, in Pawtucket (7mi north of Providence) is a five-acre site built around the first water-powered textile mill in the US.

A Bit of History

After **Roger Williams** was banished from his pastorate in Salem, Massachusetts, he traveled south with a group of his followers until they arrived on the banks of the Moshassuck (later the Providence) River in June 1636. Settling here, they bought land from the Narragansett Indians and named it Providence, in honor of the divine Providence they believed had led them to this place. Williams declared that the new colony would be a safe refuge for all people seeking freedom of worship.

Originally a farming settlement, Providence rapidly developed into a commercial center as its inhabitants turned to shipping and trade. Strongly defended as the "backdoor to Boston" during the Revolution, Providence prospered as a privateering and supply depot. Following the war, the city emerged as Rhode Island's leading port. In 1787 Providence resident John Brown sent his first ship to China. Other merchants followed his lead and amassed great fortunes in the China trade.

Providence Today – The city has been recognized for its urban revitalization projects in recent years, notably **Waterplace Park** (near Exchange St.) site of summer concerts and other events. Downtown buildings include the landmark Art Deco **Fleet Building** (Fulton St.) and the 1828 Arcade. Located near the State House, block-long **Providence Place Mall** dominates downtown, housing major retailers like Nordstrom and local specialty stores as well as myriad eateries and entertainment venues, including an IMAX theater. The famed **Trinity Repertory Company** holds performances in Lederer Theater Sept–Jun (201 Washington St.; ☎ 401-351-4242; www.trinityrep.com). **WaterFire** has become a popular rite of summertime. During these public art events, bonfires, accompanied by music, are lit after dark in 100 iron

---

FINE DINING IN FEDERAL HILL

You're in the area known as Federal Hill when you pass under the huge *pigna* (pine cone), the Italian symbol for abundance that graces the arch spanning the eastern end of **Atwells Avenue**, located west of Empire Street. Never mind that some locals claim it's a pineapple or even an artichoke. Atwells is *the* street for Italian food, no matter what your budget. The **Mediterraneo Caffé** (no. 134; ☎ 401-331-7760; www.mediterraneocaffe.com) draws youngish crowds with its artsy décor, alfresco seating and nouvelle cuisine, while the formal **Blue Grotto** (no. 210; ☎ 401-272-9030; www.bluegrottorestaurant.com) is a go-to destination for exquisitely prepared upscale Italian food and impeccable service. (The landmark **L'Epicureo Ristorante** has moved to the Hotel Providence at 311 Westminster St). A nice middle ground is **Camille's Roman Garden** (71 Bradford St.; ☎ 401-751-4812; www.camillesonthehill.com), where the food is always superb, enhanced by the friendly waitstaff. Have your after-dinner espresso and dessert at **Caffé Dolce Vita** (59 DePasquale Plaza; ☎ 401-331-8240; www.caffedolcevita.com).

braziers placed in and along the rivers fronting Waterplace Park and the **Riverwalk** *(for schedule, call ☎ 401-272-3111 or access www.waterfire.org).*

College Hill★★

This area's charming, tree-shaded streets, lined with architecture ranging from Colonial to Italianate, represents one of the most beautifully preserved historic districts in the nation. High on the hill sits **Thayer Street**—the shopping center of the university community—which brims with bookstores, coffee houses, shops and restaurants. Former warehouses below the hill on South Main Street have been converted into boutiques and restaurants, adding to the aura of the past that pervades this section of the city. This district is home to **Brown University**.

Walking Tour

Located downtown, the Providence/Warwick Convention and Visitors Bureau (1 W. Exchange St.; ☎ 401-274-1636; www.providencecvb.com) provides maps and information about the city.

▶ *Begin at the intersection of College and Main St., and walk north on Main.*

First Baptist Church in America★
75 N. Main St. 🕐 *Open Jun–Sept Mon–Fri 10am–noon & 1pm–4pm, Sat 10am–2pm, Sun tour at 11:15pm. Rest of the year Mon–Fri 10am–noon & 1pm–3pm, Sun tour at 11:15pm.* 🕐 *Closed major holidays. Contribution suggested.* ♿ ☎ *401-454-3418. www.fbcia.org.*

Founded by Roger Williams, the Baptist Church dates back to 1638. The first house of worship built by the Baptists in America stood on North Main Street, a short distance from the present site of this wooden clapboard church (1775) designed by Joseph Brown. The handsome steeple rises 185ft. Inside, the paneling, scrolled pediments, lighted urns and arches are painted in soft tones of green and white. Enormous columns support the galleries and roof, leading the eye upward to the carved ceiling.

▶ *Return to Waterman St. and turn left. After one block, turn right on Benefit St.*

Benefit Street
Spend some time strolling Benefit Street to admire the more than 100 homes, ranging from Colonial to Victorian in style, that line the narrow streets and brick walks leading to the Rhode Island School of Design and to Brown University.

Rhode Island School of Design
Bounded by Waterman, Prospect, Benefit and Thomas Sts. ☎ *401-454-6100. www.risd.edu.*

Established in the 19C to train artisans for industry, RISD (RIZ-dee) is renowned as a teaching institution for design, architecture and the visual arts. Facilities available to the school's 2,000 students include sculpture, wood and metal labs; apparel design studios; and textile workshops.

Benefit Street

Courtesy RI Tourism Division/Melissa Devine

Address Book

  For a description of price categories for hotels and restaurants, see the legend on the cover flap.

WHERE TO STAY

The Old Court Bed & Breakfast – *144 Benefit St.* 📶 ☎ *401-751-2002. www.old-court.com. 10 rooms.* **$$$** In the heart of College Hill, this redbrick 1863 Italianate manse features 12ft ceilings, elaborate moldings and rooms decorated in styles ranging from Empire to Eastlake. All have private baths, phone and TV (two also have wet bars, one boasts a marble fireplace and another an antique stove). Breakfast is served in the sunny first-floor dining room. A true benefit is walking the street's "mile of history," lined with houses dating as far back as 1707.

Providence Biltmore – *Kennedy Plaza.* 🍴♿ ☎ *401-421-0700 or 800-294-7709. www.providencebiltmore.com. 298 rooms.* **$$$** A local institution since 1922, the Biltmore is the unquestioned grand dame of Providence hotels. Recently refurbished, it boasts spacious contemporary guest rooms (the state's largest, with the majority of rooms measuring 600sq ft) and modern amenities—voice mail, data ports, and a 24-hour fitness center. But the property's claim to fame continues to be the hotel's original soaring gold-leafed lobby with its centerpiece glass elevator and marble staircase. Between the lavish lobby and the restored rooftop ballroom, you feel you have stepped back into a more gracious era. Even so, most of the revitalized downtown, including the Rhode Island Convention Center and Providence Place Mall, is within easy walking distance.

Westin Providence – *1 W. Exchange St.* 📶 ☎ *401-598-8000 or 800-937-8461; www.westin.com. 364 rooms.* **$$$** Among the chain hotels, the Westin is the most stylish choice. Hard to find, it's not: The red brick, turreted towers of this 25-story hotel rise over downtown. Sleekly spare, Euro-style guest rooms are done up in crisp white linens; many have views of the city. The best reason to stay here is the convenience factor: the hotel is connected by skywalks to the convention center and Provdence Place Mall.

The Cady House – *127 Power St.* 📶 ☎ *401-273-5398. www.cadyhouse.com. 5 units.* **$** Well situated on a quiet residential street in the College Hill neighborhood, this stately Classical Revival house (c.1839) is an eclectic delight inside, with Victorian antiques, Oriental rugs and a fascinating mix of American folk and African art. Three rooms offer queen-size beds, air conditioning and private, often oversized baths; two apartments are also available. Expanded Continental breakfast is served in the dining room and, in season, in the terraced garden out back, the owner's pride and joy. A Portuguese water dog and a cocker spaniel are in residence.

DINING IN PROVIDENCE

Pot au Feu – *44 Custom House St.* 🕐 *Closed Sun.* ☎ *401-273-8953.* **$$$** **French.** Julia Child declared Pot au Feu the kind of place she wished she had access to in Cambridge. Whether she was referring to the upstairs salon's classically inspired Parisian cuisine *(carre d'agneau bordelais, entrecôte de veau Robert, tournedos Diane)* or the downstairs bistro's provincial fare (bouillabaisse, beef bourguignonne and *pot au feu*), one can only guess. But legions of others share her enthusiasm. Owner Robert Burke, a fourth-generation Rhode Islander, prides himself on his fresh seafood *(coquilles St. Jacques Nantucket, homard en crôute)* and prix-fixe option. The bistro is one of the best values in Providence.

CAV – *14 Imperial Place.* ♿ ☎ *401-751-9164.* **$$ Mediterranean.** Like its eclectic décor—a mix of Tabriz tapestries, ships' models, antiques and art objects from around the world—the global menu at this unique restaurant (CAV stands for Coffee, Antiques, Vittles) reflects the owner's desire to bring world cultures together. This is fusion fare at its finest. Try the *poulet aux poires*, a pan-seared chicken breast with pears poached in red wine, ginger pear sauce and Asian chive dumplings. Other delights include lobster chowder, tenderloin with raspberry sauce and coconut-rum-sauced rice, and walnut-crusted salmon with sweet basil-liqueur sauce. For dessert, Milanese *frutti di bosco* is *magnifico*.

Union Station Brewery – *36 Exchange Terrace.* ☎ *401-274-2739. www.unionstationbrewery.com.* **$$ American**. Even first-timers will feel welcomed by the affable staff at Rhode Island's first microbrewery restaurant (est. 1993), located in a former train-station. Regulars often start with fried calamari tossed with scallions and peppers and dipped in pomodoro sauce, then graduate to one of the all-American entrées—grilled meatloaf with garlic mashed spuds, ale-battered fish and chips, chicken potpie—or penne with chicken and Gorgonzola-white-wine sauce (winner of the Providence Pasta Challenge). For dessert, Chocolate Euphoria Cake topped with vanilla ice cream and chocolate ganache is hard to resist.

Café Paragon/Viva – *234 Thayer St.* ☎ *401-331-6200.* **$ American**. College students know the best places to dine well on the cheap, and in Providence, they favor this two-for-one cafe (Paragon is the light, bright nonsmoking side, Viva the darker, more clubby smoking side). The food is hip American, with sandwiches (try the chicken with peppersand mozzarella), pizzas, pastas, the cafe's renowned namesake salads and half-pound gourmet burgers available at lunch and dinner. The dinner menu adds trendy tapas (lamb carpaccio; octopus, crab and lobster cakes Onassis) and value-packed entrées (lobster ravioli with shrimp and swordfish in pinot grigio sauce; chargrilled filet mignon). Tables spill onto the sidewalk in the warmer months.

Museum of Art, Rhode Island School of Design★★

224 Benefit St. 🕐 *Open year-round Tue–Sun 10am–5pm. Third Thurs of month util 9pm.* 🕐 *Closed major holidays.* 👜 *$8.* ♿ ☎ *401-454-6500. www.risd.edu.*

The museum presents, in an engaging manner, collections of art from various periods and civilizations: Egyptian, Greek, Roman, Asian, European, African and American. Many exhibits are arranged in chronological order, but they often cross period boundaries to illustrate common trends in contemporary sculpture, painting and textiles.

The fourth level *(entrance)* is devoted to special exhibitions; third-floor galleries contain 20C art. Medieval carvings, 19C American and French paintings, and Greek bronzes fill the fifth level. On the sixth floor you'll find Oriental, Eastern and Egyptian art. Standing nearly 10ft tall, the **Dainichi Buddha** (10C Japan), a wooden temple figure discovered in 1933 in the attic of a farmhouse, claims a gallery to itself.

Museum, Rhode Island School of Design

Courtesy Rhode Island School of Design/RI Tourism Division

Adjoining the museum is elegant **Pendleton House**, built in 1906 to display the **Charles Pendleton collection** of 18C American furnishings and decorative arts, the highlight of the museum. The group of American and British silver (17C-20C) includes fine examples of work by colonial Rhode Island silversmiths.

Constructed in 1993, the three-level Daphne Farago Wing features changing exhibits of contemporary art in all media.

Modern sculptures decorate the museum garden, including works by George Rickey and Clement Meadmore.

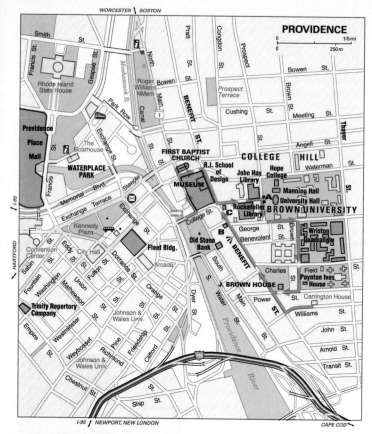

▶ *Turn left on College St.*

Brown University★

Bounded by George, Prospect, Waterman and Thayer Sts. ☎ *401-863-1000. www.brown.edu.*
The seventh college established in the US (1764), this Ivy League school was founded
at Warren as Rhode Island College and renamed in 1804 for its principal benefactor, Nicholas Brown II. The university is known for its liberal education philosophy,
implemented in 1969.

Approximately 5,700 undergraduate and 1,500 graduate students are enrolled at
Brown's 140-acre College Hill campus, which consists of some 245 buildings.

At the main entrance to the university, on Prospect Street, are the **Van Wickle
Gates (A)**, which are opened twice a year: inward on the first day of classes for fresh-
men, and outward on commencement day. From within the gates *(note campus map
table to the left)*, Brown's oldest buildings are visible. The central **University Hall**
(1771), a stately brick building known as the College Edifice, was the sole university
structure until 1822. To the left of University Hall, the building with the four granite
columns is **Manning Hall** (1835), a Greek Revival structure that houses the University
chapel; left of Manning Hall is **Hope College** (1822), which serves as a dormitory.
On the west side of Prospect Street, opposite the gates, stand the Classical Revival
John Hay Library (1910) and the contemporary **Rockefeller Library** (1964). The
"Rock," as it is popularly known, houses the university's general collection in the
humanities and social sciences.

▶ *Continue south one block on Prospect St. and turn left on George St. After one block,
turn right on Brown St.*

The Brown Brothers

At the end of the 18C, the four Brown brothers were prominent among the leaders of Providence. Bold and adventurous, **John**, a leader of the attack on the *Gaspee*, was a prosperous merchant. His was the first ship from Providence to reach China. **Joseph**, an architect, designed the Market House, the First Baptist Church and the John Brown House, among other buildings. **Moses**, a prosperous Quaker who established the Providence Bank, was the first to finance the development of the textile industry in the US at Pawtucket. **Nicholas** was a successful businessman whose mercantile enterprise was internationally known.

On Brown Street you will pass **Wriston Quadrangle** (1952), the campus residence of approximately 1,000 students.

▶ *Continue south on Brown St. to Power St.*

At the corner of Brown and Power Streets stands **Poynton Ives House** *(no. 66)*, a classic example of Federal architecture.

John Brown House★★

52 Power St. 🕭 *Visit by guided tour (45min) only, Mar–Dec Tue–Sat 10am–5pm, Sun noon–4pm. Rest of the year Fri–Sat 10am–5pm, Sun noon–4pm.* 🕭 *$8.* ☎ *401-273-7507. www.rihs.org.*

The three-story brick mansion (1788), designed for John Brown by his brother Joseph, impressed many who came to see it. John Quincy Adams, who visited the house, proclaimed it to be "the most magnificent and elegant private mansion that I have ever seen on this continent."

Inside, the carved doorways, columns, cornices and lavish plaster-ornamented ceilings provide an appropriate setting for the treasured collection of Rhode Island furnishings, most of which are Brown family pieces. The unique **blockfront secretary** boasts nine shells carved into its front (shell secretaries normally have only six carved shells). Attributed to Rhode Island cabinetmaker John Goddard, this piece is one of the finest existing examples of American Colonial furniture.

▶ *Continue west on Power St. and turn left on Benefit St. Continue south on Benefit St. and then turn left on Williams St. At no. 66 stands another Federal-style mansion, the Carrington House. Return to Benefit St. and continue north.*

Just beyond Benevolent Street, there is a good **view** of the gilded ribbed dome of the **Old Stone Bank** on South Main Street. A little farther, on the left, is an 18C red clapboard dwelling, the **Stephen Hopkins House** *(no. 43)* (**B**), formerly the home of Quaker governor Stephen Hopkins, signer of the Declaration of Independence and ten-time governor of Rhode Island. The Greek Revival style is represented by the **Providence Athenaeum** (**C**) (1838, William Strickland) where, after the death of his wife in 1847, Edgar Allen Poe unsuccessfully courted poet Sarah Whitman, a resident of Benefit Street.

FAMILY FUN IN PROVIDENCE

This city gets a lot of press for its great restaurants, but the fact is, Providence wins high marks from small fry. Here are two reasons why: The **Roger Williams Park Zoo** is home to some 1500 animals (156 species) including the tallest (Masai giraffe), heaviest (African elephant), and fastest (cheetah) creatures on the planet. This zoo wins accolades for its conservation and education efforts; don't miss the Marco Polo Trail, which traces three years of Marco Polo's journey through Asia. (☎ *401-785-3510; www.rogerwilliamsparkzoo.org).* And what young baseball fan wouldn't love to take in a PawSox (**Pawtucket Red Sox**) game at McCoy Field in nearby Pawtucket? As the AAA farm team of the Boston Red Sox, the PawSox grows lots of great talent. Nomar Garciaparra and Jon Papelbon are among the players who've gone on to the majors; (☎ *401-724-7300; www.pawsox.com).*

VERMONT

AREA: 9,609SQ MI
POPULATION: 608,827
CAPITAL: MONTPELIER
NICKNAME: THE GREEN MOUNTAIN STATE
STATE FLOWER: RED CLOVER
OFFICIAL WEB SITE: WWW.TRAVEL-VERMONT.COM

In 1609, when French explorer Samuel de Champlain first set eyes on the forested mountains extending southward from the lake that now bears his name, he reportedly exclaimed, *"Les verts monts!"* (**"The green mountains!"**). More than a century later, Champlain's description of these peaks was adopted as the state's official name.

Rural and uncluttered, Vermont has miles of back roads that skirt rocky streams and cross wooden covered bridges scattered throughout the open countryside. Dormant under a heavy cover of glistening white snow in winter, the region becomes a palette of rich greens in summer and blazes with color in autumn.

An Independent State – In 1777 Vermont declared itself independent, and a constitution was drawn up outlawing slavery and eliminating property ownership. Denied admission to the Union because of land claims by New York, Vermont remained independent for 14 years, coining its own money and negotiating with foreign powers. After the dispute with New York was settled, Vermont joined the Union in 1791 as the 14th state.

Economy – Agriculture, primarily dairy farming, fuels the state's economy. Vermont's farms supply milk and dairy products, including the famous **cheddar cheese**, to the Boston region and to southern New England. **Maple syrup** is the state's other important agricultural product. **Granite** quarried near Barre and **marble** from the Green Mountains near Danby are leading state exports. Year-round tourism is the second-largest industry. Outdoor advertising is prohibited by law; a uniform state-wide sign system indicates lodging and services.

Collecting Maple Sugar

Vermont Department of Tourism & Marketing/Peter Miller

BENNINGTON ★

POPULATION 15,737

MICHELIN MAP 581 I 7

TOURIST INFORMATION ☎ 802-447-3311 OR WWW.BENNINGTON.ORG

Surrounded by the Taconic Range and the Green Mountains, this southern Vermont community includes commercial North Bennington; the historic district known as Old Bennington; and the business district of Bennington Center. During the early days of the nation, Bennington was the home of Revolutionary War hero Ethan Allen and his Green Mountain Boys.

▶ **Orient Yourself:** Tucked into the southwestern corner of Vermont, Bennington is bisected by north-south Rte. 7 and east-west Rte. 9. The old First Church and Battle Monument border the historic district.

▣ **Parking:** Metered street parking is available. Also, there are several downtown lots, including one on County St. and two on Pleasant St., within walking distance of the downtown Welcome Center.

◉ **Don't Miss:** A self-guided walking tour of the historic district. Maps are available from the Bennington Convention and Visitors Center (☎ 802-447-3311; www.bennington.com).

◉ **Organizing Your Time:** Most downtown Bennington sights can be seen in a half day or so, but allow a full day to drive the Molly Stark Trail scenic byway, with ample time for browsing, swimming, and picnics along the way.

Kids **Especially for Kids:** Pick up freshly baked goods and fresh apple cider at the Apple Barn and Country Bake Shop (Rte. 7, ☎ 888-827-7537; www.theapplebarn.com). In the fall, it's home to Vermont's oldest cornfield maze.

◉ **Also See:** Bennington Museum; pottery lovers should also consider the Bennington Potters historic pottery sites self-guided walking tour (☎ 800-205-8033; www.benningtonpotters.com).

A Bit of History

The Battle of Bennington – Bennington was an important rallying point and supply depot for colonial troops even before the outbreak of the Revolution. In May 1775, **Ethan Allen** (1738-89) and the Green Mountain Boys gathered here before they marched north to attack Fort Ticonderoga.

Bennington Today – Located as it is near the states of New York and Massachusetts, Bennington is a crossroads community, divided by several US and local routes. Known primarily for its pottery, the town supports gift shops and craft centers that sell a variety of ceramics and glassware made by local artisans. Chief among these is the **Potters Yard**, where Bennington Potters was founded in 1948 (the craft of pottery had its actual beginnings in Bennington in the 1820s). Tourism and **Bennington College**, a liberal-arts school distinguished for its progressive ideas and programs, also draw revenue for the town.

Old Bennington★

Blessed with a rich ensemble of early American architecture, this historic section of Bennington, situated largely between the Old First Church and the Battle Monument, is a peaceful reminder of unhurried times. More than 80 primarily Georgian and Federal houses, the earliest dating from c.1761, have been preserved amid shade trees and expansive grounds. *A walking-tour brochure is available from the Chamber of Commerce at 100 Veterans Memorial Dr. (☎ 802-447-3311; www.bennington.com).*

Old First Church★

Monument Ave. at Church Lane. From the junction of Rtes. 9 and US-7, take Rte. 9 West and turn left onto Monument Ave. ◐ *Open weekends Memorial Day–June daily Jul–Oct Mon–Sat 10am–noon & 1pm-4pm, Sun 1pm–4pm.* ☎ *413-738-5420. www.oldfirstchurchben.com.*

This white clapboard church (1805) was built on the site of the 1763 meeting-house that served as the first Protestant church in Vermont.

The old cemetery behind the church is the resting place of Revolutionary War soldiers and early founders of Vermont. One tombstone marks the grave of poet **Robert Frost** (1874-1963), who penned his own epitaph: "I had a lover's quarrel with the world."

Vermont Department of Tourism and Marketing/ Andre Jenny

Old First Church

Bennington Battle Monument

15 Monument Ave. ◐ *Open mid-Apr–Oct daily 9 am–5pm.* ⊛ *$2.* ♿ ⊞ ☎ *802-447-0550. www.historicvermont.org.*

This 306ft obelisk was erected in 1891 to commemorate the Battle of Bennington. The **view**★★ from the observation deck *(accessible by elevator)* includes the Berkshires, the Green Mountains and New York State.

Bennington Museum★

1mi west of Bennington center on W. Main St. (Rte. 9). ◐ *Open daily 10am–5pm.* ◐ *Closed Wed, Jan 1, Thanksgiving Day & Dec 25.* ⊛ *$8.* ♿ ⊞ ☎ *802-447-1571. www.benningtonmuseum.com.*

RATTLESNAKE CAFE

230 North St. ☎ *802-447-7018.*
Awash in eye-catching colors, this small house in Bennington Center is home to fine and festive Mexican cuisine, popular with the local dinner crowd. For appetizers, try the House Quesadilla (jack cheese, guacamole, sour cream and smoked trout topped with salsa cruda) or the Queso Fundido (a crock of spiced cheese, chorizo sausage, mushrooms, onions and bell peppers). Entrées such as Aztec shrimp or steak *rioja* come with mango salsa and other accompaniments.

Grandma Moses

The story of **Anna Mary Robertson Moses'** career as a painter is as memorable as her paintings. Grandma Moses (1860-1961), as she became known, lacked formal training in art. After years of life as a farm wife, she began to paint at the age of 70. Her simple scenes of the countryside and farm life appealed to the public, and her first show, in 1940, won her immediate fame. Grandma Moses continued to paint until her death at age 101.

Potters Yard

324 County St. ☎ *800-205-8033. www.benningtonpotters.com.* Recognizable by its metal tower, this complex—the site of the Bennington Potters—contains a gallery shop and a factory outlet store, with kitchen accessories, candles, linens, glassware, and Bennington dinnerware—distinguished by its dark, mottled appearance—offered at reduced prices. If you're patient you may find a real bargain in the bins containing "seconds." *Tours of the production facility are held daily at 10am & 2pm.*

The museum's diverse collections are related to Vermont and New England history and life. Highlights include examples of fine 19C and 20C American glassware, 18C and 19C American furniture, 19C **Bennington pottery** and the Bennington Flag, one of the oldest Stars and Stripes in existence. Here you'll also find the largest public collection of paintings by **Grandma Moses**.

Excursions

Molly Stark Trail

This scenic 40mi stretch of Route 9 between Bennington and Brattleboro winds through forested mountains and small towns. About 10mi east of Bennington, you'll come to 400-acre **Woodford State Park** (○ *open mid-May–mid-Oct daily 10am–9pm;* ⊕ *$2.50/day;* ♿ ⛺ 🅿 ☎ *802-447-7169 in season, 800-837-6668 off-season; www.vtstateparks.com).* Midway along Route 9, stop at the roadside village of **Wilmington** to sample its attractive shops and eateries. From the turnout on **Hogback Mountain** (2,410ft), there are views east to Mt. Monadnock (3,165ft) in New Hampshire and south to the Berkshire Hills and the Holyoke Range in Massachusetts.

At the end of the trail, the industrial and commercial center of **Brattleboro** lies beside the Connecticut River. While you're in the area, check out the work of international and local artists at the **Brattleboro Museum and Art Center** *(10 Vernon St., at Main St.;* ○ *open daily 11am-5pm;* ○ *closed Tue;* ⊕ *$4;* ☎ *802-257-0124; www.brattleboromuseum.org).*

RIVERVIEW CAFE

36 Bridge St., Brattleboro. ☎ *802-254-9841.* For a superb view of the wide Connecticut River, have lunch or dinner on the cafe's rear deck, where you'll be perched right over the water. The menu here emphasizes top quality regional and organic ingredients and features vegetarian selections as well as prime rib and lamb shanks. For lunch, order a burger (beef or veggie) topped with Vermont-made Grafton cheddar or maple barbecue sauce. Dinner selections include Vermont free-range chicken, Vermont goat cheese tart, angel hair pasta with littleneck clams, and baked rainbow trout.

BURLINGTON★

POPULATION 38,889

MICHELIN MAP 581 H 2

TOURIST INFORMATION ☎ 802-863-3489 OR WWW.VERMONT.ORG

Located on Lake Champlain, Burlington, the most populous city in the state, reigns as the urban and industrial heart of Vermont. Its successful past as an industrial center and commercial port in the 19C is evidenced in the lovely residences remaining from this period.

A colorful, four-block downtown pedestrian mall, **Church Street Marketplace**★, forms the retail heart of the city with its bustling cafes, boutiques and lively student atmosphere. Enjoy the lake views from **Battery Park** and **Ethan Allen Park** *(North Ave. to Ethan Allen Pkwy.)* or experience Lake Champlain firsthand by taking one of the several cruises offered (☝ *see Lake Champlain)*.

▶ **Orient Yourself:** The lively downtown is anchored on the east by the University of Vermont and on the west by the shoreline of Lake Champlain, with the Adirondack Mountains of New York rising in the distance. It is easily accessed via north-south I-89.

🅿 **Parking:** The Waterfront Lot *(on the right just before the Boathouse Circle)* offers all-day parking.

🚫 **Don't Miss:** A guided boat excursion on Lake Champlain for scenic views, history, and fun anecdotal stories.

🕐 **Organizing Your Time:** Start at the hub of downtown, Church Street Marketplace, to browse shops and take in the lively street scene, then visit one of the waterfront beaches. Allow a full day for scenic drives and excursions in the area and another to tour Shelburne Museum.

🧒 **Especially for Kids:** ECHO Lake Aquarium and Science Center *(on the waterfront;* ☎ *802-864-1848; www.echovermont.org)* has an array of kid-friendly exhibits.

👶 **Also See:** Nearby Shelburne Museum is a must-stop.

Sights

University of Vermont

Main campus bordered by Prospect St., East Ave., Main St. and Colchester Ave. ☎ *802-656-3131. www.uvm.edu.*

As old as the state itself, the university was chartered in 1791 as the fifth college in New England. From the campus green *(between S. Prospect St. and University Pl.),* the grounds rise to a line of buildings that includes the landmark **Ira Allen Chapel** (1925), and the adjacent **Billings Center** (1885).

Burlington Boathouse

Situated at the foot of College Street, the community's sizable boathouse (🕐 *open May–Oct;* ☎ *802-865-3377)* contains public phones and restrooms, a café, a visitor information booth and sailboat rentals *(in season;* ☎ *802-863-5090).* It's also the departure point for some of the scenic cruises on Lake Champlain. Order a morning coffee or afternoon lemonade and take in the lake views, the cool breezes and waterfront activities from the vantage point of this lovable landmark.

Address Book

For price ranges for hotels and restaurants, see the legend on the cover flap.

WHERE TO STAY

Basin Harbor Club – *On Lake Champlain, Vergennes.* ☎ *802-475-2311 or 800-622-4000. www. basinharbor.com. 115 rooms.* **$$$$** This beachside resort on Lake Champlain has been family owned and operated for more than a century. There are 38 rooms in the original historic lodge and 77 more housed in individual one-, two- and three-bedroom cottages. Each room is unique; many overlook the lake and feature fireplaces. With its own golf course, tennis center, and a wealth of water-sports options from kayaking to fishing, you won't be bored here. Four on-site restaurants serve award-winning cuisine (a Modified American Plan is offered in spring and fall; the Full American Plan is the only choice in summer).

Inn at Essex – *70 Essex Way, Essex Junction.* ☎ *802-878-1100 or 800-727-4295. 120 rooms. www. vtculinaryresort.com.* **$$$** Located just a few miles away from Burlington and the airport, this Colonial-style inn offers all the comforts of home with gourmet dining to boot. Accommodations range from standard "Country Inn" rooms, individually appointed in tones of forest green, cranberry and indigo, to mini-suites with kitchenettes and spacious deluxe suites. Many rooms boast gas fireplaces and some have whirlpool tubs. Diners at **Butler's Restaurant** or at the casual **Tavern** feast on American cuisine created by students of the New England Culinary Institute, which is located on site.

Willard Street Inn – *349 S. Willard St.* ☎ *802-651-8710 or 800-577-8712. www.willardstreetinn.com. 14 rooms.* **$$$** Built by Vermont State Senator Charles Woodhouse in the 1880s, this brick Georgian Revival-style home is immaculately preserved today, with intricate moldings, cherry-paneled foyer and original wooden floors. The inn's convenient location lies within walking-distance of Church Street Marketplace and the waterfront. All rooms have private baths and are furnished with a mix of antiques and period reproductions to recall the turn of the 19C. Breakfast and afternoon tea, served in a solarium overlooking Lake Champlain, are included in the rates.

WHERE TO EAT

Five Spice Café – *175 Church St.* ☎ *802-864-4045. www.fivespicecafe.com.* **$$$ Pan-Asian.** Only the dragon wallhanging suggests what is to come at the nondescript storefront that houses this long-running Asian-fusion eatery, specializing in the cuisine of Vietnam, China, Burma, Indonesia and Thailand. The signature five-spice fritters pair pancakes of scallions, onions, leeks and breadcrumbs with delicate spices; the various Indonesian satays are equally tempting. Can't decide? Start with a sampler appetizer platter. For a main course, the standout is Evil Jungle Prince (chicken in a sauce of coconut milk, garlic, lemongrass, lime and hot peppers).

Smokejacks – *156 Church St.* ☎ *802-658-1119. www.smokejacks.com.* **$$$ New American.** A modern, deliberately hip restaurant, with immaculately polished mahogany and funky furniture, overlooks both sides of the city's busiest intersection. The lengthy menu changes weekly and features contemporary cuisine made with regional ingredients and organic produce, such as a spicy sweet potato soup, Maine crab cakes or smoky sugar-cured pork loin.

Red Onion Café – *140 ½ Church St.* ☎ *802-865-2563.* **$ American.** Simplicity has never gone out of style at this small bakery/cafe where the locals go for Burlington's best sandwiches. Six types of bread, from honey-oat to baguettes, baked fresh on the premises each morning, are used to make an array of tempting sandwiches. Try the house specialty, the Red Onion: turkey, bacon, apples, red onion, gruyère and sun-dried tomato mayonnaise served warm on your choice of bread. The rest of the menu is devoted to oversize cookies, each of which is a meal in itself.

Robert Hull Fleming Museum

61 Colchester Ave. on university campus. 🕐 *Open May–Labor Day Tue–Fri noon–4pm, weekends 1pm–5pm. Rest of the year Tue–Fri 9am–4pm, weekends 1pm–5pm.* 🕐 *Closed major holidays.* ⊠ *$5.* ♿🅿 ☎ *802-656-2090. www.uvm.edu/~fleming.*

The museum's collection includes Egyptian, Asian and Native American artifacts and contemporary Vermont art, as well as **American paintings** and **European works** from the 17C to the 19C. On the grounds, note the abstract, five-figure sculpture entitled *Lamentations Group, 1989*, by Vermont resident Judith Brown.

Lake Champlain

🛈 *Tourist information:* ☎ *802-863-3489 or www.vermont.org.*

Cradled in a broad valley between the Adirondacks and the Green Mountains, this 125mi-long lake straddles the Vermont–New York border. Lake Champlain and its surroundings have become a popular recreation and vacation area. At the northern end of the lake, bridges provide access to Isle la Motte, North Hero and Grand Isle.

Cruises★

The stern-wheeler *Spirit of Ethan Allen* offers narrated scenic cruises on Lake Champlain with views of the islands and the Adirondacks. *Departs from Burlington Boathouse (College St.).* ⛴ *Dinner cruises also available. Round-trip 1hr 30min. Commentary.* ⊠ *$9.95.* 🍴♿🅿 *For seasonal schedules, contact Green Mountain Boat Lines Ltd.:* ☎ *802-862-8300 or www.soea.com.*

Ferries

Ferry services operating on Lake Champlain afford lake crossings between Grand Isle, Burlington and Charlotte, Vermont and New York State. Contact Lake Champlain Ferries (☎ 802-864-9804 or www.ferries.com) for fares and schedules. Shorewell Ferries, Inc. (☎ 802-897-7999) offers service from Larrabees Point to Fort Ticonderoga. In winter, ferries operate if weather permits.

Vermont Department of Tourism & Marketing / Andre Jenny

Lake Champlain

Excursions

Shelburne Museum★★★

12mi south on Rte. 7. 🧒 *in Shelburne Village.* 🕐 *Open May–Oct daily 10am–5pm.* 🚌 *$18* ♿ ✕ 🅿 ☎ *802-985-3346. www.shelburnemuseum.org.*

Established by New Yorker **Electra Havemeyer Webb**, this endearing museum preserves many of the home crafts, folk art, fine arts, trade tools, modes of transportation and furnishings that she began collecting in 1907. Now encompassing some 80,000 pieces, the preeminent collection represents 300 years of American life, history and art, and is housed in 37 buildings spread across 45 acres on a magnificent site overlooking the Lake Champlain Valley. The **Horseshoe Barn**★★★, with its 225 sleighs and carriages; the wooden 1901 **Round Barn**★★; the Victorian-style **railroad station**★★; and the side-wheeler steamship **The Ticonderoga**★★ are a few of the many highlights.

> **NE CULINARY INSTITUTE**
>
> *At the Inn at Essex, 70 Essex Way, Essex Junction.* ☎ *802-872-3400. www.neculinary.com.* The Culinary Institute (NECI) opened its second campus at the Inn at Essex in 1989. In addition to the inn's colonial tavern and Butlers restaurant, NECI operates two other eateries in Burlington and three in Montpelier where diners can feast on artfully presented dishes that incorporate the freshest regional ingredients.

Shelburne Farms

1611 Harbor Rd., 1.5mi northeast of Shelburne Village. 🕐 *Open mid-May–Oct daily 9:30am–4pm. Rest of the year daily 10am–4pm, weather permitting.* 🚌 *$6 (activities and tours)* ✕ 🅿 ☎ *802-985-8686. www.shelburnefarms.org.*

This grand 19C agricultural estate and National Historic Landmark on the shore of Lake Champlain was the country home of railroad tycoon **William Seward Webb** and his wife **Lila Vanderbilt Webb**, granddaughter of Cornelius Vanderbilt, who founded the Vanderbilt dynasty.

The 1,400-acre farm now operates as an nonprofit environmental education center, with a working dairy on the premises. **Shelburne House**★, a 110-room 1899 country manor house boasting **views**★★ of Lake Champlain and the Adirondacks, operates as the 24-room **Inn at Shelburne Farms** (🕐 *open mid-May–Mid-Oct;* ☎ *802-985-8498; www.shelburnefarms.org).*

Vermont Wildflower Farm

5mi south of Shelburne on US-7 in Charlotte. 🕐 *Open Apr–Oct daily 10am–5pm.* 🅿 ☎ *802-985-9455. www.vermontwildflowerfarm.com.*

Meadows abloom with Jack-in-the-pulpit, black-eyed Susans, asters and Devil's paintbrush color the farm's six acres from spring through fall. Paths are lined with more than 1,000 species of wildflowers. Also on the premises are a seed store and a gift shop.

Courtesy Vermont Wildflower Farm

A young visitor enjoys Vermont Wildflower Farm

Royal Lipizzan Stallions

North Hero, Vermont, serves as the summer residence of these famed horses, who are presented to the public there yearly in July and August under the direction of Col. Ottomar Herrmann. The stallions take their name from the little village of **Lipizza** (now Lipica), Slovenia (formerly part of Yugoslavia), near Trieste, Italy, where the Archduke Karl of Austria founded a stud farm in 1580. The farm was established to breed and rear stallions for the **Spanish Riding School of Vienna**, one of the few places in the world where *haute école* dressage, a rigorous equestrian ballet dating from the 16C, can still be seen. Horses are taught a repertoire of exacting movements based on Renaissance battle maneuvers, including trots, jumps, and pirouettes (the horse turns on its haunches at the canter). But the show-stopper is the demanding **capriole**, in which the horse jumps up and kicks his hind legs out parallel to the ground.

The present Lipizzaners descend from several great sires, all stemming from an old Spanish strain, famous at the time of Caesar. These magnificent white horses are born grey, bay or chestnut and get their brilliant white coats between 4 and 10 years of age. Characterized by their intelligence, agility and vigor, they are considered the best saddle and parade horses in the world.

Ethan Allen Homestead★

2mi north on Rte. 127. From Burlington, take US-7 North, turn left on Pearl St., then right on N. Champlain St. to road's end. Turn left, then immediate right onto Rte. 127 North and exit at North Ave. Beaches. Take the first right at the sign for the homestead. ◷ *Open May daily 1pm-4pm; Jun-Oct Mon-Sat 10am-4pm, Sun 1pm-4pm.* ↝ *Visit of house by guided tour (30min) only, on the half hour.* ⊜ *$5.* ♿ ☎ *802-865-4556. www.ethanallenhomestead.org.*

Dedicated to the legendary folk hero, this 5-acre site threaded by the Winooski River includes a reconstructed frame house (c.1785) believed to have been the final home of **Ethan Allen**. The modern visitor center houses exhibits on regional history and the escapades of Allen and his Green Mountain Boys. A re-created tavern in the center serves as the setting for a multimedia presentation *(15min)* in which Allen is remembered by friends and associates. Trails lead along the river.

MANCHESTER★

POPULATION 4,180
MICHELIN MAP 581 I 6 AND MAP OPPOSITE
TOURIST INFORMATION ☎ 802-362-2100 OR WWW.MANCHESTERVERMONT.NET

Favored as a summer resort and cultural center for more than a century, Manchester has become popular during the winter as well, with the development of Bromley and Stratton ski areas.

Manchester Center is a busy place year-round, with its restaurants and shops, while farther south off Route 7A, countrified estates nestle among the foothills of the Taconic Range. In **Manchester Village**★, the 19C Equinox Hotel has catered for years to an elite clientele, including presidents Grant, Theodore Roosevelt and Taft.

Manchester is home to the Orvis Company, one of the oldest surviving (1856) fishing tackle manufacturers in the US. Today it is joined by numerous designer and upscale outlet stores along routes 7A and 11.

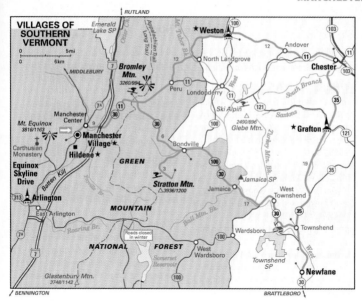

Sights

Hildene★

On Rte. 7A, 2mi south of the junction with Rte. 11/30. ◷ *Open Jun–Oct daily 9:30am–4:30pm; Nov–May Thu–Mon 11am–3pm.* ⊜ *$10 house tours, $5 grounds pass.* 🅿 ☎ *802-362-1788. www.hildene.org.*

This 412-acre estate was the home of **Robert Todd Lincoln** (1843-1926), the eldest of the four children of Abraham and Mary Lincoln. The furnishings are family pieces, and the tour includes a demonstration of the 1,000-pipe Aeolian organ (1908). From the gardens there are sweeping **views**★★ of mountains and valleys below.

American Museum of Fly-Fishing

Seminary Ave., north of the Equinox Hotel at Rte. 7A. ◷ *Open year-round daily 10am–4pm.* ◷ *Closed major holidays.* ⊜ *$5.* ♿ ☎ *802-362-3300. www.amff.com.*

Anglers will be interested in this museum devoted to the history and lore of fly-fishing. Early books on the subject, an array of multicolored artificial flies, and fly-fishing tackle belonging to Daniel Webster, Andrew Carnegie, Ernest Hemingway and other well-known Americans are among the artifacts in the collection.

Southern Vermont Arts Center★

West Rd. From the village green, take West Rd. 1mi north. Follow winding drive to the mansion. ◷ *Open daily Tue–Sat 10am–5pm.* ⊜ *$8.* ♿ ☎ *802-362-1405. www.svac.org.*

Founded in the 1930s to support Vermont artists, the permanent collection of more than 700 paintings, sculptures and works on paper is now housed in the spacious **Elizabeth de C. Wilson Museum**.

Equinox Skyline Drive

5mi south of Manchester by Rte. 7A. ◷ *Open May–Oct daily 9am–dusk.* ⊜ *$7/car.* ☎ *802-362-1114. www.equinoxmountain.com/skylinedrive.*

The 5.5mi drive leads to the crest of Mt. Equinox (3,816ft), the highest point in the Taconic Range. The **view**★ reaches from the Hudson River Valley deep into the Green Mountains.

Address Book

For price ranges for hotels and restaurants, see the legend on the cover flap.

WHERE TO STAY

Inn at Sawmill Farm – *Crosstown Rd. & Rte 100, West Dover.* ◷ *Closed Apr & May.* ✕ ♿ 🄿 🛉 ☎ *802-464-8131. www. theinnatsawmillfarm.com. 21 rooms.* **$$$$$** Set on a pastoral hillside in a quiet corner of southern Vermont, the Inn at Sawmill Farm is operated by chef/owner Brill Williams, whose architect father restored the farmhouse to create this Relais & Châteaux property—incorporating the barn's hand-hewn beams and weathered boards. Rooms, whether in the main building or cottage suites, are individually decorated in English chintzes and antiques; many feature fireplaces. The inn's acclaimed **restaurant** *(open to the public; dinner only)* has won numerous industry awards—for its Continental fare, as well as for its 30,000-bottle wine cellar. Rates include breakfast and a gourmet dinner.

The Equinox – *Rte. 7A, Manchester Center.* ✕ ♿ 🄿 🛉 ☎ *802-362-4700 or 800-362-4747. www.equinoxresort.com. 183 rooms.* **$$$$** The largest full-service resort in Vermont, the Equinox was renovated by its previous owner, Guinness Brewing Co., as the sister resort to Scotland's fabled Gleneagles. As such, the resort claims some unusual activities—a falconry program, the Land Rover off-road driving school, shooting and fly-fishing instruction. Guinness and Harp are still on tap in the hotel's tavern, while the main dining room is strictly New England (lobster and prime rib). Rooms in the white-columned main building are all differently shaped and laid out along labyrinthine corridors. Next door, the separate Charles Orvis Inn boasts 11 deluxe suites (**$$$$$**) set in the original home of America's first mail-order retailer.

1811 House – *3654 Main St., Manchester Center.* ✕ 🄿 ☎ *802-362-1811 or 800-432-1811. www.1811house.com. 14 rooms.* **$$$** Guests at this historic B&B are encouraged to help themselves to coffee and homemade cookies from the kitchen. Lace-canopy beds, chintz curtains and Oriental rugs belie the informal attitude here. Rooms have air conditioning and private baths; some have mountain views. In your leisure time, you can play chess in front of the fireplace in one of the common rooms, enjoy a game of pool in the basement, or sample the adjoining pub's extensive list of single-malt whiskies.

WHERE TO EAT

Zoey's Deli & Bakery – *Rte. 11/30, Manchester. Lunch only.* ◷ *Closed Tue.* ☎ *803-362-0005 or 800-564-3354. www. zoeys.com.* **$ Deli.** The best sandwiches in Vermont can be found at this innocuous bakery, whose owners adhere to a simple logic: Make everything, from breads to cookies to honey mustard, on the premises from the freshest possible ingredients. Zoey's stunning sandwiches—worth a trip in themselves—are paired with unparalleled homemade chips made from Vermont potatoes. After building a loyal and devoted lunch following, Zoey's recently opened a full-service restaurant, the **Double Hex**, just up the road *(Rte. 11/30;* ☎ *802-362-4600)*, which is open for lunch and dinner.

The Perfect Wife – *2594 Depot St. (Rte. 11/30), Manchester. Dinner only.* ☎ *802-362-2817. www.perfectwife. com.* **$$ New American.** Chef-owner Amy Chamberlain has become a minor culinary celebrity in Vermont, and her intriguing restaurant explains why. She utilizes fresh local produce and offers a menu emphasizing mainstream entrées (Peking duck, turkey schnitzel, sesame-crusted yellowfin tuna), but she also features pure vegan selections. Start with the acclaimed crab cake appetizer. The farmhouse setting offers diners the choice of a unique cobblestone-walled dining room with piano accompaniment, or a greenhouse garden room. In the separate tavern you can play darts, enjoy live music, and sample a broad selection of single-malt whiskies and eight local beers on tap. Here chicken wings and nachos share billing with hot curry-and-goat-cheese dip with eggplant fries.

Curtis' Barbecue – Rte. 5 *at Exit 4 off I-91, Putney. Open Wed–Sun, Apr–mid-Oct.* ☎ *802-387-5474. www.curtisbbqvt.com.* **$ Barbecue**. More of a roadside stand than a restaurant, Curtis' occupies a compound consisting of two old school buses—one converted into a large smoker—and several picnic tables. For more than 25 years, Curtis has been serving up some of the finest BBQ in Vermont. Orders are placed and picked up at the bus windows, and the menu is simple: ribs, pulled pork and brisket, as plates or sandwiches, with standard sides of cole slaw, beans and the like.

Arlington
8mi south of Manchester by Rte. 7A.
This tranquil village and its residents served as models for illustrator **Norman Rockwell**, who lived here at one time. The **Batten Kill River** provides Arlington with some of the best trout fishing in New England.

Villages of Southern Vermont★★ *Map p 353.*

Driving Tour

▷ *Leave Manchester Village by Rte. 7A. At Manchester Center take Rte. 30 East and continue on Rte. 11.*

Bromley Mountain
The Bromley ski area has become popular during the summer season because of its **alpine slide** 🖼️ (🕐 *open mid-Jun–Labor Day daily 9:30am–5pm; Sept–mid-Oct & late-May-mid-Jun weekends only 10am–5pm;* ⚬ *$8;* 🍴⚬ ☎ *802-824-5522; www.bromley.com)*. Bromley's summit (3,260ft) can be reached by hiking trails and offers **views** of the Green Mountains.

Appalachian Trail
🚶 The longest continuous marked footpath in the US, the 2,167mi **Appalachian National Scenic Trail** begins at Springer Mountain in north Georgia and traverses 14 states, 2 national parks, and 8 national forests before ending on the rocky summit of Mt. Katahdin in Maine. Tracing part of an ancient Native American route, the well-maintained but often rugged path crosses some 250,000 acres of mostly mountainous terrain along the Appalachian chain. The nation's first official scenic trail is protected by the National Trails System Act of 1968, which includes the preservation of natural habitats bordering the trail and the hundreds of species inhabiting them.

The trail's 3 million annual users, on average, are mostly weekend hikers, but the number of "through hikers," who begin in Georgia in early spring and walk northward for three to five months, is growing. Those not inclined to walk the entire "A.T." can start on any of 500 access points located at roughly 5–10mi intervals along the trail's length. Permits are not required for hiking, but they are mandatory for overnight camping in Shenandoah National Park, the Great Smoky Mountains National Park and Baxter State Park. More than 250 shelters are situated roughly a day's hike apart and campsites are numerous; lodges are located in New Hampshire's White Mountains. No bicycles, motorized vehicles or even pack animals are allowed on the trail; dogs must be kept on a leash.

Long Trail to Bromley Summit

From the Bromley ski area, follow Rte. 11 approximately 2mi east. A small sign indicates the Long Trail. Parking is on the right.

From the parking lot, a dirt road leads to the trail (*5.6mi round-trip*), which is a segment of both the Long Trail and the Appalachian Trail. After gently ascending through forest for 2mi, the trail climbs steeply, then crosses open meadowland. A **panorama**★★ of Stratton Mountain (to the south) and the surrounding Green Mountains is afforded from an observation tower.

▶ *Two miles after Bromley, take the road on the left through Peru. At the fork bear left and continue through North Landgrove, turning left in front of the town hall. After passing the Village Inn, bear right at the fork and continue to Weston.*

Weston★

With its attractive village green, craft shops and general stores, Weston is a popular tourist stop on Route 100. Looking out on the green is the **Farrar-Mansur House**, a late-18C tavern that serves as the local history museum (*open late Jul–Labor Day Wed 1pm–5pm & weekends 1pm–5pm; Sept–Oct weekends only 2pm–5pm; $2; 802-824-8190*).

▶ *From Weston follow Rte. 100 past the green, then bear right at the sign for Chester. Continue through Andover, then east on Rte. 11.*

Chester

The wide main street of this community is lined with lodgings and shops, several of which are housed in historic buildings (*a walking-tour brochure is available from the information booth on the village green Jun–Oct*).

▶ *From Chester take Rte. 35 to Grafton.*

VERMONT COUNTRY STORE

Main St./Rte. 100, Weston Village. 802-824-3184. www.vermontcountrystore.com. Founded in 1946, this popular general merchandiser has expanded over the years from its original home to four buildings (and there's a second store in Rockingham, VT). The growth has resulted largely from the firm's mail-order catalog business and its penchant for selling what "must work, be useful, and make sense." The store itself (*open year-round Mon–Sat*) enjoys a statewide reputation for its varied merchandise, from local cheeses to long underwear.

Grafton★

Check out the **Grafton Village Cheese Company** (*800-472-3866; www.graftonvillagecheese.com*) and the 1801 **Old Tavern**. Once frequented by such luminaries as Ulysses S. Grant, Oliver Wendell Holmes and Rudyard Kipling, the three-story brick tavern has been restored to its innkeeping tradition.

▶ *In Grafton turn right, cross the bridge and turn left before the tavern. Follow this road to Rte. 35, which leads to Townshend, then take Rte. 30 South to Newfane.*

Newfane

Situated deep in the Green Mountains, this town has grown little since the 18C, when it was selected as the Windham county seat. Newfane's village **green**★, with its white Congregational church, **Windham County Courthouse** and two old inns, is pretty at any time of year, but it becomes a spectacular sight in the fall.

▶ *Take Rte. 30 back through Townshend. Between Townshend and West Townshend you will pass a covered bridge on the left. Continue through Jamaica into Bondville, where Stratton Mountain Rd. to the left leads to the Stratton Mountain Ski Area.*

Vermont Pasture

Vermont Department of Tourism & Marketing/ Dennis Curran

Stratton Mountain

Off Rte. 30; from Bondville, follow Stratton Mountain Rd. 4mi to resort. ☎ 802-297-4000 or 800-STRATTON. www.stratton.com.

With 92 trails accessible by a gondola and 14 chairlifts, this mountain (3,936ft) is one of the major ski areas in Vermont.

▶ *Return to Manchester via Rte. 30.*

MIDDLEBURY★

POPULATION 8,183
MICHELIN MAP 581 H 4 AND MAP P 359
TOURIST INFORMATION ☎ 802-388-7951 OR WWW.MIDVERMONT.COM

Set amid gently sloping hills and rolling countryside, Middlebury is a typical Vermont village with its central green, pristine Congregational church, and Victorian-style buildings converted into stores and restaurants. The town was founded in 1761 and is known today as the site of Middlebury College.

Overlooking the village green, the stately **Middlebury Inn** still welcomes visitors as it has since 1827 (👓 *see Address Book*). The inn serves afternoon tea and a nightly candlelight buffet dinner. Middlebury is also the starting point for scenic excursions through Brandon and Middlebury gaps, which cut through the hills and dales of Green Mountain National Forest southeast of town.

CREEKSIDE CUISINE

A great little place for lunch, the **Storm Cafe** *(3 Mill St.; open for lunch & dinner;* ☎ *802-388-1063)* occupies the top floor of Frog Hollow Mill. An outdoor patio overlooking Otter Creek invites alfresco dining and there's indoor seating in the small, attractive dining room. A variety of soups and salads, sandwiches, burgers and light-lunch combos are creatively presented.

Sights

Middlebury College

Campus bounded by S. Main St. and College St. (Rte. 125). ☎ *802-443-5000. www. middlebury.edu.*

The main campus covers some 500 acres and features impressive stone and marble buildings of eclectic architectural styles. Highlights are **Painter Hall** (1815), the oldest surviving college building in the state, and **Le Château** (1925), modeled after a pavilion of the French Château de Fontainebleau.

Center for the Arts
On Rte. 30, .5mi from US-7.
This center houses a dance and studio theater, a concert hall and the **Middlebury College Museum of Art** (⊙ *open year-round Tue–Fri 10am–5pm, weekends noon–5pm;* ⊙ *closed holidays and during college breaks;* ✗♿▣ ☎ 802-443-5007; www. middlebury.edu/arts/museum). The museum's permanent collection includes works by such notables as Vermont native Hiram Powers, Gilbert Stuart, Alexander Calder and John Frederick Kensett.

Frog Hollow
Mill and Main Sts.
This pretty area, perched above the cascading waters of Otter Creek, contains a number of small boutiques. Located in a renovated mill, the **Vermont State Craft Center** displays and sells fine blown glass, metalwork, jewelry, wooden ware and hand-woven fabrics made by leading Vermont craftspeople *(1 Mill St.;* ⊙ *open year-round Mon-Sat 10am–5:30pm, Sun noon-5pm.* ♿ ☎ 802-388-3177; www.froghollow.org).

Excursions

UVM Morgan Horse Farm
▣ *2.5mi northwest of Middlebury, in Weybridge. From the center of Middlebury bear right onto College St. (Rte. 125), then turn right onto Rte. 23 (Weybridge St.). Follow the signs to the farm, bearing left at the fork with the covered bridge.* ⊙ *Open May–Oct daily 9am–4:30pm.* ⊛ *$5.* ♿▣ ☎ 802-656-3131. www.uvm. edu/morgan.
Owned by the University of Vermont, the farm operates as a breeding, training and instructional facility. Visitors may tour the 19C barn, where descendants of the original Morgan are housed *(20min slide presentation shown hourly).*

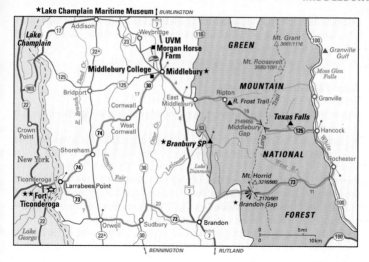

Branbury State Park★

10mi southeast of Middlebury. Take US-7 South, then Rte. 53. 3570 Lake Dunmore Rd.
🕐 *Open mid-May–mid-Oct daily 10am–dusk.* 🚸 *$2.50/day.* ♿ ⛺ 🅿 ☎ *802-247-5925 (in season); 800-837-6668 (off season). www.vtstateparks.com.*

This popular warm-weather destination has a large sandy beach on Lake Dunmore *(boat rentals available)* and hiking trails to the **Falls of Llana** *(1.1mi round-trip)* and to **Silver Lake** *(3mi round-trip)*.

Lake Champlain Maritime Museum★

👶 *21mi northwest of Middlebury in Basin Harbor. Take US-7 North to Vergennes, then West Main St. to Panton Rd. Turn right onto Basin Harbor Rd.* 🕐 *Open mid-Jun–mid-Oct Wed–Sun 10am–6pm.* 🚸 *$9* 🍴 🅿 ☎ *802-475-2022. www.lcmm. org.*

Ten exhibit buildings, including a stone schoolhouse (c.1818), trace the history of the lake and its maritime traditions. The grounds showcase a variety of small vessels that have plied the waters of Lake Champlain.

WHITFORD HOUSE INN

12 Grandey Rd., Vergennes (13mi northwest of Middlebury via US-7). ☎ *802-758-2704. www.whitfordhouseinn.com.* **$$$** Set on 37 acres surrounded by the verdant farmlands of peaceful Champlain Valley, this inviting inn is located in Vergennes, which, at 1.8sq mi, is hailed as the smallest incorporated city in the US. The inn boasts exquisite views of the Adirondacks. Three rooms house guests in the late-18C country house and a guest cottage nearby features its own brick patio for taking in the views.

Brandon and Middlebury Gaps

ℹ️ *Tourist Information:* ☎ *802-247-6401 or www.brandon.org.*

This itinerary leads through the Green Mountain National Forest and into the Lake Champlain Valley. Along the way you'll traverse wooded mountain gaps and cross open farmlands. Outdoor enthusiasts will find many reasons to linger in this area.

Driving Tour *81mi.*

▶ *This tour begins and ends in Middlebury. Take Rte. 125 East, named Robert Frost Memorial Dr. for the well-known New England poet.*

On Route 125, 2mi beyond Ripton, the ⬛ **Robert Frost Interpretive Trail** offers a 1mi loop through scenic marshland and forest, punctuated by markers inscribed with poems by the renowned poet.

▶ *Continue east on Rte. 125 through Middlebury Gap (2,149ft).*

Texas Falls Recreation Area
Left from Rte. 125.
A short trail leads to a series of falls that tumble over rocks and giant holes formed by glaciers.

▶ *Continue east to the tiny crossroads community of Hancock. From Hancock, take Rte. 100 South to Rochester and follow Rte. 73 West through Brandon Gap.*

Route 73 passes tidy houses and tranquil meadows along the White River Valley as it enters the Green Mountain National Forest and skirts the base of rocky **Mt. Horrid** (3,216ft) before reaching **Brandon Gap**⋆ (2,170ft). From this point there is a **view**⋆ of the Lake Champlain Valley, with the Adirondacks as a backdrop.

Descending west through the gap, the road continues to the village of **Brandon**, chartered in 1761 and now anchored by its historic inn. Begun as a one-room tavern in 1786, the current stone and wood hostelry features a late-19C Dutch Colonial interior. After Brandon Route 73 continues west to Lake Champlain, yielding vistas of rock-studded pasturelands, dairy farms and the Adirondack Mountains to the west.

At **Larrabees Point** the ferry *(for schedules, see Lake Champlain, under entry heading Burlington)* crosses Lake Champlain, and provides access to Fort Ticonderoga in New York.

Fort Ticonderoga★★
🧒 *Rte. 74 in Ticonderoga, New York.* 🕐 *Open early May–late Oct daily 9am–5pm.* 💲 *$12. Fife & drum corps performances & artillery drills Jul & Aug daily.* 🍴 🅿 ☎ *518-585-2821. www.fort-ticonderoga.org.*
Built in 1755 by the French, Fort Ticonderoga was captured by the British in 1759. The fort is famous for the surprise attack launched here against the British on May 10, 1775 by **Ethan Allen** and the Green Mountain Boys along with **Benedict Arnold** and his men. The supplies captured here were used the following spring by General Washington to drive the British out of Boston.

▶ *Take the ferry back to Vermont and follow Rte. 74 East through Shoreham and West Cornwall to Cornwall. Then take Rte. 30 North back to Middlebury.*

MONTPELIER

POPULATION 8,035
MICHELIN MAP 581 J 3
TOURIST INFORMATION ☎ 802-229-5711 OR WWW.CENTRAL-VT.COM

This small city, the capital of Vermont since 1805, sits among the wooded hill-sides that rise above the Winooski River. The golden dome of the State House, ablaze in the afternoon sun, dominates the city and makes a magnificent sight when the trees change color in autumn. The granite industry, which enabled the city to develop and prosper, has been supplanted in importance by state government and the insurance industry.

▶ **Orient Yourself:** North-south I-89 provides easy access to the city. The Winooski River runs parallel to State St., while North Branch River bisects downtown near Capitol Plaza.

- **Parking:** There are several parking lots in the downtown area including two on State St. near Capitol Plaza. The city is compact and pedestrian friendly; you can walk to major sights, parks and attractions.
- **Don't Miss:** A tour of the historic State House.
- **Organizing Your Time:** Pick up maps and brochures for three self-guided walking tours (State St. tour, Main St. tour and College St. tour) at the information booth on State Street or in City Hall. The tours, about an hour each, will give you a good feel for the city. Allow an hour for the State House visit.
- **Especially for Kids:** North Branch Nature Center (*2mi from downtown;* ☎ *802-229-6206; www.vinsweb.org/montpelier*) is a hit with young and old alike, with riverside trails, butterfly garden, critter room and special events and activities.
- **Also See:** The villages and farmlands of the Mad River Valley (*see driving tour below*).

Sights

State House

State St. ◷ *Open year-round Mon–Fri 8am–4pm.* ⬤ *Free 30min guided tours Jul–Oct Mon–Fri 10am–3:30pm Sat 11am–2:30pm. Closed major holidays.* ✗ & ☎ *802-828-2228. www.vtstatehouse.org.*

This elegant Classical Revival edifice, built in 1859, is the third state house erected on this site. The first state house (demolished) dated from 1808. The second (1838) was destroyed by fire. The present structure incorporates the Doric columns and portico of the second state house, which was modeled after the Temple of Theseus in Greece. A 14ft statue of Ceres, the Roman goddess of agriculture, rises from the pinnacle of the golden dome.

Vermont Museum★

109 State St., in the Pavilion Office Building. ◷ *Open May-Oct Tue-Sat 10am-4pm Sun noon-4pm.* ⬤ *$12 (family rate)* & ☎ *802-828-2291. www.vermonthistory.org.*

The Victorian facade of this building was modeled after the Pavilion Hotel, which stood on the site between 1876 and 1965. Inside, the 19C lobby has been reconstructed. Beyond it are the rooms occupied by the Vermont Historical Society. Photographs, documents and artifacts relate the history, economy and traditions of Vermont.

Mad River Valley★

Remote, rural, and set in the midst of broad expanses of rolling, mountainous terrain, the Mad River Valley is a premier four-season resort famed for its ski areas, **Sugarbush** and **Mad River Glen**. The lovely setting, abundant accommodations and superb downhill and cross-country skiing facilities have contributed to its great success.

Driving Tour *8mi from Waitsfield to Warren.*

Warren

23mi southwest of Montpelier via I-89 West to Rte. 100 South.

This small village contains craft shops and a country store frequented for its freshly baked goods and salads. The Warren covered bridge is reflected in the Mad River, which flows underneath it.

If time permits, continue south from Warren on Route 100 to **Granville** and enjoy spectacular **views**★★ of the Green Mountains.

▶ *To reach Waitsfield from Warren, take E. Warren Rd./Rte. 100 North.*

Address Book

⚖ *For price ranges for hotels and restaurants, see the legend on the cover flap.*

WHERE TO STAY

The Pitcher Inn – *275 Main St., Warren.* ✕ ⚖ 🅿 ☎ 802-496-6350 or 888-867-4824. www.pitcherinn.com. *11 rooms.* **$$$$$** This tiny gem (the second of Vermont's two Relais & Châteaux properties) is one of the top inns in the country. Each of its 11 exquisite guest rooms is decorated with original art and antiques representing some facet of Vermont: The Trout Room turns the interior into an actual log cabin, while in the School Room, a huge slate blackboard serves as a mantelpiece. One room celebrates the life of Calvin Coolidge, the only Vermont-born president. More than half the rooms are outfitted with fireplaces and Jacuzzi tubs; others boast wet bars and steam rooms.

WHERE TO EAT

Chef's Table – *118 Main St., Montpelier.* ☎ 802-229-9202. www.necidining.com. **$$$ American**. The flagship of the seven eateries operated by the students and staff of the Montpelier-based New England Culinary Institute, this fine-dining restaurant features American fare with a New England regional focus. Starters include roasted red beet soup and sweetbread ragout; main courses such as pecan-crusted salmon and seared venison loin allow chefs-in-training to get creative.

The Common Man – *At Sugarbush Ski Resort, German Flats Rd., Warren. Dinner only.* ☎ 802-583-2800. www.commonmanrestaurant.com. **$$$ Continental**. For 30 years this restaurant has been the standout among the many dining choices along the access road to the Sugarbush ski area. Set in a dramatic 19C barn, with exposed wood and rafters in every direction, and anchored by a huge fireplace at one end, The Common Man fully captures the feel of a country ski town, while serving up fine European cuisine. Appetizers include escargot, and in-house cured gravlax, while an ever-changing menu might offer duck, steak and shellfish entrées.

American Flatbread – *At The Lareau Farm Inn, 46 Lareau Rd., Waitsfield. Dinner only, 5:30pm–9:30pm Fri & Sat.* ☎ 802-496-8856. www.americanflatbread.com. **$$ Pizza**. Considered by connoisseurs to be the best frozen pizzas available, these Vermont-made flatbreads are sold at gourmet shops and supermarkets in 20 states. Every weekend, the actual factory itself becomes a restaurant, allowing patrons to sample the wares straight from the wood-fired ovens. This is as rustic an experience as can be found, with a handful of tables arranged amidst the ovens in one building of the working farm that yields many of the organic ingredients. Flatbreads themselves are made from organic wheat custom-milled for the purpose, unfiltered well water and fresh yeast.

Main Street Grill – *118 Main St., Montpelier.* ☎ 802-223-3188. www.necidining.com. **$$ New American**. This casual venue is also run by the New England Culinary Institute, and is open for lunch and dinner (breakfast also on Sat-Sun). Choose among the floor-level main room and a pub or wine room downstairs. An observation window allows diners to watch their food being prepared upstairs. The innovative menu includes dishes like Vermont cheddar ale soup, crispy calamari and portabella eggplant cannelloni.

The drive along East Warren Road parallels the Mad River and the Green Mountains to the west. After 5mi, you will pass the **Round Barn** (1909), one of several built in the valley, now part of an inn.

▸ *The road continues straight ahead over the Waitsfield covered bridge (1833) and crosses the Mad River before reaching Waitsfield.*

Waitsfield

This town has been a commercial center since the 19C, when the daily stagecoach from Waitsfield linked the valley with the railroad in nearby Middlesex. Two shopping centers today provide the inhabitants and visitors in the area with a variety of stores and services. Farming continues to be a principal activity in Waitsfield, despite the influx of professionals and artists in recent years.

At Waitsfield, consider a detour west along Route 17 through the **Appalachian Gap** (2,356ft), where **views**★★ of the region's unspoiled beauty unfold.

RUTLAND

POPULATION 17,292
MICHELIN MAP 581 I 5
TOURIST INFORMATION ☎ 802-773-2747 OR WWW.RUTLANDVERMONT.COM

Situated at the junction of Otter and East creeks, Rutland is Vermont's second-largest city. The surrounding mountains and lakes make the region a year-round playground for those who love the outdoors. Killington, one of the largest ski resorts in the East, lies nearby to the east.

Settled in the 1770s, the town developed into a railroad center in the 19C and marble quarrying flourished, giving Rutland the nickname "the marble city."

Sights

Norman Rockwell Museum

2mi east of Rutland near the corners of Rte. 4 and Rte. 7. 🕐 *Open year-round daily 9am–5pm.* 🕐 *Closed major holidays.* 🔊 *$4.* ♿🅿 ☎ *802-773-6095 or 877-773-6095. www.normanrockwell.vt.com.*

The museum contains over 2,500 examples of the work of **Norman Rockwell** (1894-1978), illustrator, humorist and chronicler of more than half a century of American life. The series of more than 300 magazine covers that Rockwell created for the *Saturday*

Vermont Snowboarding

Vermont Department of Tourism and Marketing/ Dennis Curran

Address Book

WHERE TO STAY

Cortina Inn – *103 Rte. 4, Killington.* ☎ 802-773-3333 or 800-451-6108. www.cortinainn.com. 96 rooms. **$$$** Just outside downtown Rutland, halfway between the city and the nearby ski resorts of Killington and Pico, sits one of the area's best hotels. Although modern, the inn features distinctive New England architecture, with dormers and peaked roofs, and the common areas are log-cabin cozy. On-site facilities include both a full-service restaurant and tavern, a fly-fishing school, tennis courts and snowmobiling equipment. For romantic winter getaways, larger rooms feature fireplaces and whirlpool baths or hot tubs, and the inn offers horse-drawn sleigh rides around the grounds.

WHERE TO EAT

Casey's Caboose – *Killington Access Rd., at Killington Ski Resort. Dinner only.* ☎ 802-422-3795.www.killingtonsbest.com. **$$ American**. The railroad-themed dining room is located in an observation cupola overlooking a 35-ton railroad car. Casey's famous daily happy hour offers free chicken wings from 3pm–6pm, and the menu features grilled meats and fresh lobster, pulled from a tank in the lobby. The barbecue ribs would pass muster in Memphis.

Little Harry's – *121 West St., Rutland. Dinner only.* ☎ 802-747-4848. **$$ International**. One of Vermont's most eclectic restaurants, Harry's successfully dispenses both New England regional specialties and Pacific Rim cuisine, with a touch of Italian thrown in. The décor is local tavern, and the dishes range from tasty peanut-infused pad Thai noodles to rack of local lamb. Appetizers are equally thought-provoking, and choices include corn chowder, steamed chicken wontons with peanut sauce, and red-chili shrimp.

Three Tomatoes Trattoria – *88 Merchants Row, Rutland.* ☎ 802-747-7747. **$$ Italian**. The prominent wood-fired oven is the major feature of this casual, airy trattoria. Crispy thin-crust pizzas topped with choices such as soprasetta, artichoke hearts and smoked salmon are just a small part of the extensive menu. Main courses put the hardwood-charcoal-burning oven to good use as well, producing meat with a smoky, roasted flavor. Traditionally prepared pasta dishes emphasizing garlic and olive oil are also available, along with an impressive selection of Italian wines.

Inn At Long Trail – *Sherburne Pass, Rte. 4, Killington.* ☎ 802-775-7181. *www.innatlongtrail.com.* **$ Pub Fare**. Living up to its name, the inn sits at the intersection of the state's longest hiking trail and the even longer Appalachian Trail. The availability of limited lodging, mail and package handling, and Guinness stout on tap have made the inn an extremely popular way station for through-hikers on both routes. A trailhead in the inn's parking lot leads day hikers to the summit of Pico Mountain, burning calories to justify the shepherd's pie, corn beef and red-cabbage reuben, or the house specialty—Guinness stew. A hungry crowd of hikers or skiers can be found here anytime of year.

Evening Post, and for which he is best remembered, is displayed here together with other magazine covers, movie and war posters, advertising work, calendars and greeting cards—which also brought him fame.

Excursions

Vermont Marble Exhibit★

52 Main St., Proctor. 6mi north of Rutland via West St. and Rte. 3 North. ○ *Open mid-May–Oct daily 9am–5:30pm.* ∞ *$7.* ♿ ▣ ☎ *802-459-2300 or 800-427-1396. www.vermont-marble.com.*

Visitors explore the origin, quarrying and finishing of marble. Polished marble slabs from Vermont and around the world illustrate the rich diversity of colors and graining characteristic of this stone. Visitors can view a video about marble *(13min)* and observe a sculptor at work.

Wilson Castle

W. Proctor Rd., 4mi south of Proctor. 🐾 *Visit by guided tour (45min) only. Open late May–late Oct daily 9am–6pm. Last tour 5:30pm. $8.40* ▣ ☎ *802-773-3284. www.wilsoncastle.com.*

This massive brick mansion (1867), built by a Vermont doctor, offers a glimpse of the opulence that characterized the private homes of 19C America's upper classes. Luxurious furnishings and art pieces are complemented by the surrounding heavily carved woodwork, stained-glass windows and hand-painted and polychromed ceilings. Note the Louis XVI crown-jewel case.

New England Maple Museum

On Rte. 7, in Pittsford. 9mi north of Rutland via Rte. 7. ○ *Open mid-May–Oct daily 8:30am–5:30pm; Nov–mid-Dec & Mid-Mar–mid-May daily 10am–4pm.* ∞ *$2.50.* ♿ ☎ *802-483-9414. www.maplemuseum.com.*

Located in the rear of a large retail store, this small museum features homespun exhibits on the history of maple sugaring. The self-guided tour ends with a 10min slide show illustrating the entire process, plus a display relating to syrup grades.

Killington

10mi east of Rutland on Rte. 4.

With over 200 trails cut on six interconnecting mountains and on Pico Mountain, Killington is one of New England's most popular ski resorts. The **Killington gondola** is reputedly the longest *(2.5mi)* ski lift of its kind in the US *(station located 15mi east of Rutland on Rte. 4;* ∞ *$14 round-trip;* ○ *open Jul–mid-Oct daily 10am–5pm;* ♿ ▣ ☎ *802-422-6200 or 877-458-4637; www.killington.com).* A ride on the gondola affords great **views**★★ of the Green Mountains.

Lake St. Catherine State Park

20mi southwest of Rutland on Rte. 30; 3mi south of Poultney. Take Rte. 4 to Exit 4, then Rte. 30 South. ○ *Open mid-May–mid-Oct daily 8am–dusk.* ∞ *$2.50/day.* ⛺ ▣ ☎ *802-287-9158 (in season) or 802-483-2001 (off season). www.vtstateparks.com.*

Cool breezes sweep the calm surface of Lake St. Catherine, making this a popular spot for windsurfing, sailing and fishing for trout and northern pike.

ST. JOHNSBURY

POPULATION 7,571
MICHELIN MAP 581 K 2
TOURIST INFORMATION ☎ 802-748-3678, 800-639-6379 OR WWW.NEKCHAMBER.COM

Manufacturing and maple syrup production are major occupations in this small, blue-collar city, gateway to the vast, rural Northeast Kingdom. St. Johnsbury began to prosper in the 1830s when a grocer named Thaddeus Fairbanks invented and began to manufacture the platform scale here; Fairbanks scales have been produced and shipped around the world ever since.

The St. Johnsbury Athenaeum and the Fairbanks Museum and Planetarium, both in the downtown area, were established by members of the wealthy Fairbanks family, devoted patrons of their hometown.

Sights

St. Johnsbury Athenaeum★
1171 Main St. 🕐 *Open year-round Mon–Fri 10am–5:30pm (Mon & Wed til 8pm), Sat 9:30am–4pm.* 🕐 *Closed Sun and major holidays.* ♿🅿 ☎ *802-748-8291. www.stjathenaeum.org.*
Horace Fairbanks built this brick Second Empire building as a public library in 1871, adding an **art gallery** in 1873. With paintings still hung in the style of a Victorian salon, the gallery is dominated by Albert Bierstadt's monumental painting *Domes of Yosemite*. Also represented are Asher B. Durand and other painters of the Hudson River school as well as Vermont natives Hiram Powers and Thomas Waterman Wood. The handsome building, with its ornate woodwork and spiral staircases, is a National Historic Landmark.

Address Book

🍴 *For price ranges for hotels and restaurants, see the legend on the cover flap.*

WHERE TO STAY
Rabbit Hill Inn – *48 Lower Waterford Rd., Lower Waterford.* ✗♿🅿 ☎ *802-748-5168 or 800-762-8669. www.rabbithillinn.com. 21 rooms.* **$$$$** Decorated in lace, this romantic getaway caters to couples. More than half the rooms have oversized tubs or two-person Jacuzzi baths, and many have fireplaces, dressing areas and other special touches. In summer, wander the paths along the banks of the Connecticut River; in winter, hone your cross-country skiing or snowshoeing skills. friendly innkeepers are the best you'll find and the gourmet dining is top-notch.

WHERE TO EAT
P&H Truck Stop – *2886 Rte. 302, Wells River.* ☎ *802-429-2141.* **$ Diner**. Vermont's largest truck stop is also its best, serving hearty diner-style food 24 hours a day. A wide variety of breakfast dishes are available, accompanied by homemade cinnamon bread, which also forms the basis of a notable French toast. Burgers, sandwiches and platters of meatloaf, ham steaks and the like are also available, as is fresh-made fried chicken, a house specialty. Most people come for P&H's famous homemade pies, especially the berry varieties. At least a dozen, and sometimes two dozen, are available daily; sample a slice or get a whole pie to go.

Maple Sugaring

Vermont is the leading producer of maple syrup in the US. From early March to mid-April, when night temperatures drop below freezing but the days get steadily warmer, more than 1,000,000 hard rock or sugar maple trees are tapped with small metal spouts. Under these spouts buckets are hung to collect the 10 to 15 gallons of sap each tree is liable to produce. The sap is then taken to a ventilated sugarhouse to be boiled down, filtered through layers of cloth, and jarred. Each gallon of syrup is the product of about 40 gallons of sap. Some 60 sugaring enterprises throughout the state invite visitors to witness the process during the season, or sample their wares off-season at roadside gift shops. Syrup comes in three grades: delicate light amber, all-purpose medium amber and robust dark amber. Try all three, and be sure to sample the sweet maple-sugar candy.

Fairbanks Museum and Planetarium★

Kids *1302 Main St.* ○ *Open year-round Mon–Sat 9am–5pm, Sun 1pm–5pm.* ○ *Closed Jan 1, Easter Sunday, Thanksgiving Day & Dec 25.* ⌗ *$5 museum, $3 planetarium.* ♿ ☎ *802-748-2372. www.fairbanksmuseum.org.*

This institution was founded in 1891 by industrialist Franklin Fairbanks, who donated his collection of taxidermied wildlife to the museum. Today the museum houses 4,500 mounted birds and mammals and a large collection of antique dolls. The ornate Romanesque Revival **building**★, designed by Vermont architect Lambert Packard, is carved of red sandstone, and the interior features a magnificent barrel-vaulted ceiling.

Maple Grove Farms

Kids *On Rte. 2 east of the city center.* ○ *Open year-round Mon–Fri 8am–4:15pm. Sugarhouse tours mid-May–mid-Dec Mon-Fri 8am–2pm.* ○ *Closed major holidays.* ☎ *802-748-5141. www.maplegrove.com.*

Exhibits and brief films illustrate how maple syrup is harvested and produced. The factory tour *(20min; $1)* introduces visitors to the step-by-step procedures involved in transforming maple syrup into Maple Grove candies.

Northeast Kingdom★★

🛈 *Tourist Information:* ☎ *802-525-4386 or www.travelthekingdom.com.*
This region of forests, lakes, wide-open valleys and back roads that girdle tiny villages includes the three northeastern counties (Caledonia, Essex and Orleans) that surround St. Johnsbury and extend to the Canadian and New Hampshire borders. The region is busiest in the fall, when the countryside is a symphony of color: copper, gold, and the blazing reds of the maple trees.

Seven villages in the region—Barnet, Cabot, Groton, Marshfield, Peacham, Plainfield and Walden—participate in the week-long **Northeast Kingdom Foliage Festival** *(late Sept–early Oct;* ☎ *802-626-8511 or 800-884-8001)* during which a different village, each day, hosts activities ranging from church breakfasts to house tours and craft shows.

Two other interesting towns in the area are **Craftsbury Common**, with its immense hilltop village green that appears to meet the sky at the horizon; and Danville, home of the American Society of Dowsers.

Lake Willoughby and Brownington★

Circle tour north of St. Johnsbury. 87mi.

▶ *From St. Johnsbury, take Rte. 5 North through Lyndonville to Rte. 114 and continue north on Rte. 114 to East Burke. From there, follow an unmarked road north to Burke Hollow and West Burke.*

The Burkes

East Burke, Burke Hollow and West Burke are tiny hamlets at the base of the Burke Mountain ski area. The gentle mountain landscape is especially scenic when viewed from the road that leads to the summit of **Burke Mountain** (3,262ft). In the distance, you can see Lake Willoughby to the northwest through the gap. *Access to the Burke Mountain Auto Road (toll) is from Rte. 114 in East Burke.*

▶ *From West Burke take Rte. 5A North to Lake Willoughby.*

Lake Willoughby★

Two mountains rising abruptly opposite each other in a formation resembling the entrance to a mountain pass signal the location of Lake Willoughby *(swimming in season)*. The taller mountain, towering above the southeastern end of the lake, is **Mt. Pisgah** (2,751ft).

▶ *Follow Rte. 5A North along the lake shoreline to Rte. 58 west. Continue approximately 4mi on Rte. 58 to Evansville. Turn right on the road marked Brownington Center, which becomes a dirt road. Take the second left and continue to Brownington Center. There, bear right up the hill 1.5mi to Brownington Village Historic District.*

Brownington Village Historic District★

This charming hamlet has changed little since the early 19C, A four-story granite dormitory building called the **Old Stone House** (1836) now functions as a museum, with period rooms and exhibits about the school (🕐 *open May–mid-Oct Wed–Sun 11am–5pm;* 🎫 *$5;* 🅿 ☎ *802-754-2022; www.oldstonemuseum.org).*

At the north edge of the village, an observatory platform on Prospect Hill affords a **panorama**★★ of Willoughby Gap *(southeast)*, Mt. Mansfield *(southwest)*, Jay Peak *(west)* and Lake Memphremagog *(north)*.

▶ *From Prospect Hill, turn right, continue past the Congregational church and follow the unmarked road 2mi west to the junction with Rte. 58. Turn right and continue through the town of Orleans (1mi). Take Rte. 5 South for 5mi to Rte. 16 South. Take Rte. 16 through the town of Glover, then turn left onto Rte. 122 South and continue for about 1mi.*

Bread and Puppet Museum

Rte. 122. 🕐 *Open Jun–Oct daily 10am–6pm. Rest of the year by appointment only.* ☎ *802-525-3031. www.vmga.org.*

In a cavernous barn built in 1863, the socially committed Bread and Puppet Theater Company dramatically displays its larger-than-life puppets. These head masks and mannequin-like creations have been used in pageants and shows in Europe, Latin America and the US.

▶ *Return to St. Johnsbury via Rte. 5 South. From St. Johnsbury take Rte. 2 West to Danville.*

Peacham and Barnet Center

Circle tour south of St. Johnsbury 65mi.

▶ *From St. Johnsbury, take Rte. 2 West to Danville.*

Danville

Because of its high elevation, this rural agricultural community enjoys refreshing breezes and clear air even on hot summer days.

▶ *Continue south on Rte. 2 to Marshfield. Turn right onto Rte. 215 to Cabot.*

Jay Peak

Located only 8mi from the border crossing into southern Quebec at North Troy, Jay Peak (3,861ft) attracts both Americans and Canadians during the winter. An **aerial tram** lifts passengers to the peak's summit (🕐 *open Jul–Labor Day & mid-Sep-Columbus Day, daily 10am–4pm; commentary;* 🎫 *$10;* ♿ ☎ *802-988-2611 or 800-451-4449; www.jaypeakresort.com).* From the top, there are sweeping **views**★★ of Lake Champlain, the Adirondacks, the White Mountains and, to the north, Canada. Several drives in the area are especially picturesque during Indian summer; in particular, **Route 242** from Montgomery Center to Route 101, and **Route 58** from Lowell to Irasburg, offer views of northern Vermont against the backdrop of the surrounding mountain ranges.

Cabot

This small community is associated with the production of cheese. The **Cabot Creamery**, in business since 1919, is perhaps the best-known purveyor of Vermont dairy products. A tour (🚶 *30min;* 🎫 *$2)* of the plant operations, opening with a 15min video presentation, explains in detail how cheese, yogurt and butter are made *(on Main St.;* 🕐 *open Jun–Oct daily 9am–5pm; rest of the year Mon–Sat 9am–4pm;* 🕐 *closed Jan & major holidays;* ♿🅿 ☎ *802-563-3393 or 800-837-4261; www.cabotcheese.com).*

▶ *Return to Danville via Rte. 215 and Rte. 2. Take the unmarked road south through Harvey and Ewell Mills to Peacham.*

Peacham★

Surrounded by a breathtaking hill-and-dale setting, Peacham may be the most photographed of all Vermont's villages during the fall.

▶ *Continue to Barnet Center through South Peacham, turning left to West Barnet. At Barnet Center, turn left before the church and continue up the hill.*

Barnet Center

From a vantage point past the church near the top of the hill, you can look down on a beautiful pastoral scene of a large barn with its silo. Beyond the barn stretches a spectacular **view**★★ of the countryside.

▶ *Return to the foot of the hill and turn left in the direction of Barnet. From there, take Rte. 5 North to St. Johnsbury.*

STOWE★

POPULATION 4,339
MICHELIN MAP 581 I 2
TOURIST INFORMATION ☎ 802-253-7321 OR WWW.GOSTOWE.COM

As Route 108 winds through this small village, situated at the foot of Stowe's distinctive landmark, Mt. Mansfield, the slender white spire of Christ Community Church comes into view. The valley's exceptionally long snow season and abundance of Swiss-style chalets, lodgings and restaurants account for Stowe's sobriquet, "the ski capital of the east."

During the winter up to 8,000 skiers use the trail systems on the slopes of Stowe's two interconnected mountains, **Mt. Mansfield** (4,393ft), Vermont's highest peak, and **Spruce Peak** (3,320ft). Colorful shops, galleries and restaurants line Stowe's Main Street. Serving the townspeople since 1895, **Shaw's General Store** is a local institution, offering a wide variety of outdoor clothing, sporting goods, footwear and

©Dennis Curran/ Courtesy Stowe Area Association, Inc.

Sleigh Ride at Trapp Family Lodge

household supplies. Ski buffs will enjoy a visit to the **Vermont Ski Museum** located in the Old Town Hall, where displays of skiing memorabilia chronicle the 100-year history of skiing in Vermont *(1 S. Main St.;* ◷ *open year round Wed–Mon 10am–5pm; Apr–May call for hours;* ♿🅿 ☎ *802-253-9911; www.vermontskimuseum.org).*

▶ **Orient Yourself:** The mountain village of Stowe sits in north-central Vermont at the junction of Rtes. 108 and 100 (10 miles north on Rte. 100 from I-89). Most of the activities are centered on the historic village and along Mountain Road leading from the village to the ski area.

🅿 **Parking:** There's free parking in the village, on the street and in small lots off Main St.

😎 **Don't Miss:** A bike ride along the award-winning Recreation Path. Several shops on or near the 5.3mi paved trail offer bike rentals.

◷ **Organizing Your Time:** Start with a meander through the historic village. Allow a couple hours to ride the Recreation Path and save a half-day or more for a hike (try the Pinnacle Trail, a 1.4mi hike to the summit of 2,740-foot Pinnacle peak).

Kids **Especially for Kids:** The fast-moving alpine slide and the summit-climbing gondola ride at Stowe Mountain Resort are sure to be hits.

♿ **Also See:** Smugglers Notch, by way of a scenic drive.

Sights

Mount Mansfield★★

From the summit there is a sweeping **view**★★ of the entire region, including Jay Peak to the northeast, Lake Champlain and the Adirondacks of New York to the west and the White Mountains of New Hampshire to the east. On a clear day, you can see Montreal to the north.

There are several ways to access the summit: via the 4.5mi **Mt. Mansfield Auto Road** *(Rte. 108, 7mi north of Stowe;* ◷ *open mid-May–mid-Oct daily 9am–5pm;* 🚗 *$16/car;* ☎ *802-253-3500 or 800-*

Stowe Recreation Path

Traversing farmlands, wildflower meadows and wooden bridges on the West Branch River, this 5mi paved trail through the Green Mountains has is a delight for cyclists and walkers. The path begins in back of the village's Community Church and ends on Brook Road. Views from the trail are particularly beautiful in spring and fall. *For specifics, contact the Stowe Area Association:* ☎ *877-467-8693 or 802-253-7321; www.gostowe.com.*

Address Book

For price ranges for hotels and restaurants, see the legend on the cover flap.

WHERE TO STAY

Trapp Family Lodge – *700 Trapp Hill Rd., off Rte. 108.* ✕ & P ☑ ☎ *802-253-8511 or 800-826-7000. www.trappfamily. com. 93 rooms.* **$$$$$** After the famous singing Von Trapp family fled the Nazis and inspired the movie *The Sound of Music*, they ended up here in Stowe, where they opened this rustic Tyrolean chalet-style lodge. Expanded repeatedly over the years, the lodge now sits on 2,700 acres and comprises a main building, numerous outlying chalets, an Austrian tea house, and a wide range of sporting facilities including clay tennis courts and over 70mi of cross-country skiing trails. And yes, the descendants of the Von Trapps still don their costumes and perform regularly for guests.

Green Mountain Inn – *18 Main St.* ✕ & P ☑ ☎ *802-253-7301 or 800-253-7302. www.greenmountaininn.com 100 rooms.* **$$$** The largest hotel in the pedestrian-friendly Main Street area, the Green Mountain Inn has been in continuous operation since 1833. Guest rooms are spread between the main inn and adjacent town houses, and all feature handmade quilts and period furnishings. The modern Mansfield House offers 22 deluxe rooms with Jacuzzi tubs and other modern amenities. The inn maintains 120 private acres of hiking, cross-country skiing and snowshoeing trails for guests. A freestanding three-bedroom carriage house is available at the ski center.

WHERE TO EAT

Gracie's – *1652 Mountain Rd.* ☎ *802-253-6888. www.gracies.com* **$$ American**. A canine theme pervades this casual all-day eatery. Pictures of dogs adorn the walls, and menu items are all named for different breeds. Enjoy chicken wings from mild to Dalmatian, followed by a choice of more than a dozen specialty burgers (the Chihuahua, for example, comes with lettuce, tomato and guacamole). Salads and Mexican specialties are also available.

Mr. Pickwick's – *433 Mountain Rd. in Ye Olde England Inne.* ☎ *802-253-7558. www.englandinn.com.* **$$ Pub Fare**. Vermont's most authentic English pub boasts more than a dozen imported beers and even cider on tap, plus over 150 specialty whiskies. Traditional English fare includes bangers and mash, steak and kidney pie, along with other specialties, like beef Wellington, Vermont pheasant, and ostrich filet.

Restaurant Swisspot – *128 Main St. Dinner only.* ☎ *802-253-4622. www. gostowe.com.* **$$ Swiss**. Specializing in fondues, this longtime local favorite brings a touch of traditional Alpine flavor to downtown with specialties of Switzerland's Zermatt region. Fondue choices include traditional cheese, rouge (with tomato sauce) and heartier meat-based offerings such as beef fondue oriental and beef *bourguignonne*.

The Shed – *1859 Mountain Rd.* ☎ *802-253-4364. www.gostowe.com.* **$$ American**. At any time, a half-dozen fresh-brewed lagers, stouts and ales accompany a menu featuring comfort foods such as fried chicken, burgers and BBQ ribs, along with pasta, chicken and seafood entrées. The trademark Ski of Beer—served on an actual ski—lets you sample tastes of all the brews, and growlers, refillable half-gallon jugs of beer, are available to go.

253-4754; www.stowe.com); or aboard the eight-passenger **Mt. Mansfield Gondola** *(Rte. 108, 8mi north of Stowe; operates Jul–mid-Oct daily 10am–5pm;* ☞ *$18;* & *www. stowe.com),* which lifts visitors to Cliff House.

Smugglers Notch★★

Rte. 108, 7mi north of Stowe; ◷ *closed in winter.* ☺ *Exercise caution when proceeding between the large roadside boulders that have split from the walls of the notch.*
The road linking Stowe and Jeffersonville to the northwest is extremely narrow and climbs rapidly as it twists through the rugged scenic notch (2,162ft) between

Mt. Mansfield and Spruce Peak. The forest admits little light, even on a bright day. Smugglers Notch earned its name because of the slaves and contraband items that were smuggled from the US into Canada through this pass during the War of 1812.

Ben & Jerry's Ice Cream Factory★

Kids *Rte. 100, 9mi south of Stowe in Waterbury.* ○ *Open Jul–late-Aug daily 9am–9pm. Jun daily 9am–6pm. Late-Aug–Oct daily 9am–7pm. Rest of the year daily 10am–5pm.* ○ *Closed Jan 1, Thanksgiving Day & Dec 25.* ☙ *$3 (tour)* ✗ & ☎ *802-882-1260. www. benjerry.com.*

Now a Vermont landmark and headquarters for the nationally recognized gourmet ice cream company, this playful building, with its Holstein polka dots, offers tours (◔ *30min;* ☙ *$3),* including a 10min movie on the history of the company, a look at the production process and samples of the flavors of the day.

Moss Glen Falls

Rte. 100, 3mi north of Stowe. From Rte. 100, take Randolph Rd., then the first right to the small parking area.

A short trail leads to the falls and continues somewhat steeply *(not well marked)* upstream to a brook where you can take a dip in the cool water.

Alpine Slide

Kids *Spruce Peak. Rte. 108, 8.5mi north of Stowe.* ○ *Open mid-Jun–Labor Day daily 10am–5pm. Labor Day-Columbus Day weekends 10am-5pm.* ☙ *$15.* ☎ *802-253-3500. www.stowe.com.*

Stowe is one of several ski areas in New England where an alpine slide operates on the mountain slopes during the mild seasons.

COLD HOLLOW CIDER MILL

On Rte. 100, in Waterbury Center. ☎ *802-244-8771 or 800-327-7537. www.coldhollow.com.* You can't miss this en route to Stowe. The retail shop is stocked with apple-derived products, Vermont cheeses, jams, condiments, and all kinds of maple syrup concoctions. A cider jelly manufacturing facility and a bakery are on the premises. You'll find free samples of cider, cheeses and jellies in almost every corner.

WOODSTOCK★★

POPULATION 3,232
MICHELIN MAP 581 J 5
TOURIST INFORMATION ☎ 802-457-3555 OR WWW.WOODSTOCKVT.COM

A touch of urban elegance has characterized this pretty village since the 18C, when it was selected as the Windsor County seat. Businessmen, lawyers, doctors and teachers settled here during the next 200 years, building frame, brick and stone dwellings and shops that reflected the wealth of the community. A lack of industrial development in the 19C and the devotion of the town's residents to Woodstock's architectural heritage★ have ensured the preservation of the gracious 18C and 19C structures bordering the village green and lining Elm, Pleasant and Central Streets.

▶ **Orient Yourself:** The quintessential Vermont village is accessed off north-south I-89 and bisected by east-west Rte. 4. The village green sits in the center of town, surrounded by shops, galleries, and restaurants. The Ottauquechee River flows through the center of town.

P **Parking:** Street parking is available around the village green.

- ⊘ **Don't Miss:** Billings Farm and Museum; also cross-country skiing or hiking on area trails.
- ⏱ **Organizing Your Time:** Plan two hours at the Billings Farm and Museum and reserve a day to enjoy outdoor activities.
- **Kids Especially for Kids:** The nearby Vermont Institute of Natural Science (1/4mi west of Quechee Gorge on Rte. 4; ☎ 802-359-5000; www.vinsweb.org) has a cool raptor center and hands-on exhibits.
- �“ **Also See:** Marsh-Billings-Rockefeller National Historic Park, with pretty woodland trails.

A Bit of History

Established in 1761 by settlers from Massachusetts, Woodstock developed quickly after it was selected as the county seat. During the 19C, the prosperous, self-sufficient village became a fashionable vacation spot.

The lovely Woodstock Inn, facing the village green, was opened in 1969. The hotel's lodging and conference facilities attract business travelers as well as tourists. **F.H. Gillingham & Sons** has been the town's general store since 1886 and stocks hand-made Vermont products as well as hardware, housewares, gourmet foods, pet supplies and fresh produce.

Sights

To enjoy Woodstock, stroll along **Elm** and **Pleasant Streets**, browse in the emporiums and galleries on **Central Street** and walk across the covered bridge (in the middle of town) that spans the Ottauquechee River. The oval **village green** is fringed with buildings of different styles: Federal mansions, the Greek Revival **Windsor County Courthouse** and the Romanesque-style **Norman Williams Library**. Located near the corner of Elm and Central Streets, the Town Crier bulletin board posts notices of auctions, flea markets and other community events.

PANE E SALUTE

61 Central St., second floor. ⏱ Closed Tue & Wed. ☎ 802-457-4882. www.osteriapaneesalute.com. The delights of Italy land in Woodstock at this tiny osteria. In its 22-seat green-walled dining room, diners will be treated to a taste of la dolce vita. Seasonal fare here spotlights local produce, cheeses and meats raised in Vermont, as well as traditional products imported from Italy. If you're not up for a multicourse meal, try one of the thin-crust Tuscan pizzas, or take a seat in the cozy wine bar to sample hard-to-find Italian wines and nosh on tasting plates

Billings Farm and Museum★★

Kids River Rd. at Rte. 12 North. Follow Elm St., cross the bridge, turn right, then .2mi on River Rd. ⏱ Open May–Oct daily 10am–5pm, Dec weekends 10am–4pm. ⏱ Closed Thanksgiving Day & Dec 25. ⊜ $10. ♿ P ☎ 802-457-2355. www.billingsfarm.org.

The Billings complex is both an operating modern-day dairy farm and an interpretive museum depicting life on a Vermont farm in 1890. The restored 1890 **farmhouse**, appointed with period furniture and tiled fireplaces, features a basement creamery with daily demonstrations of butter making. Life-size displays in several restored barns illustrate the daily activities performed by a 19C Vermont farm family. Visitors can view the Academy Award-nominated film (1999), A Place in the Land (30min), which examines the property's role in the history of conservation in the US.

Address Book

For price ranges for hotels and restaurants, see the legend on the cover flap.

WHERE TO STAY

Woodstock Inn – *14 The Green, Woodstock.* ☎ *802-457-1100 or 800-448-7900. www.woodstockinn.com. 144 rooms.* **$$$$** Laurance S. Rockefeller purchased, renovated and expanded the inn in 1969, and kept it as a prized family possession when he later sold the rest of his acclaimed Rockresorts chain. Today the property still overlooks one of New England's most beautiful village greens, a short walk to shops, galleries and restaurants. Woodstock Inn is a full-service resort with a spa facility, indoor and outdoor tennis centers, golf course and cross-country centers. Rooms vary in size and shape, but all accommodate guests lavishly with such amenities as handmade quilts, glassed-in sun porches and wood-burning fireplaces.

Juniper Hill Inn – *153 Pembroke Rd., Windsor.* ☎ *802-674-5273 or 800-359-2541. www.juniperhillinn.com. 16 rooms.* **$$** This lovely country inn offers an impressive value. All 16 rooms have private baths, many with antique claw-foot tubs. More than half have fireplaces, and all are individually decorated with four-poster beds and period antiques. Bedside chocolates and sherry decanters in each room add a homey touch. If you're a history buff, book the grand suite with private balcony, which once hosted President Teddy Roosevelt.

WHERE TO EAT

The Parker House Inn – *16 Main St., Quechee. Dinner only.* ☎ *802-295-6077. www.theparkerhouseinn.com.* **$$$ Continental**. For cozy, relaxed dining and gourmet food, head to this country inn in downtown Quechee. The menu changes frequently but always features homemade soup along with a chicken, veal, beef, seafood, shellfish and pasta dish, typically prepared in French style. Tables are spread throughout two country-style dining rooms, and there is also a small bar area, where guests may eat or sample the extensive wine list. In summer, a wraparound patio offers outdoor dining overlooking the Ottauquechee River.

Corners Inn Restaurant – *Bridgewater Corners, Rte. 4, Bridgewater. Dinner only.* ☎ *802-672-9968 or 877-672-9968.* **$$ Italian**. Just outside Woodstock, hidden behind an unimpressive facade, lies one of the region's best-kept culinary secrets. Chef/owner Brad Pirkey turns out tasty traditional pasta dishes with carbonara, bolognese and tomato-vodka cream sauces, his popular lobster ravioli, as well as veal parmigiana and other entrées. A sure bet is the huge cioppino, an Italian fish and shellfish stew served over pasta, and nightly specials such as nut-crusted salmon or veal with wild mushrooms.

The Skunk Hollow Tavern – *10 Brownsville Rd., Hartland Four Corners. Dinner only. Closed Mon & Tue.* ☎ *802-436-2139.* **$$ American**. Locals flock from throughout the region to enjoy this quintessential New England tavern. The two-part menu includes tavern favorites such as burgers, enchiladas and the house specialty, Chicken Carlos—a spicy half-fried, half-baked chicken with hand-cut fries. The other section features fine-dining entrées (filet mignon, chicken, fish and lamb, each with a different preparation weekly) along with exquisite homemade soups. A full-time baker turns out fresh popovers and an extensive slate of desserts, including the signature Heathbar cake.

The Prince & the Pauper – *24 Elm St. Dinner only;* ☎ *802-457-1818; www. princeandpauper.com.* **$$ French**. Tucked away off a charming alley, The Prince & the Pauper serves formal food in an informal atmosphere. In the simply decorated main dining room, choose from French-inspired starters such as seafood-packed crepes, followed by boneless rack of lamb in puff pastry or roast duckling. A prix-fixe dinner option is also available, along with a wine list that is short but includes some outstanding selections.

Marsh-Billings-Rockefeller National Historical Park★★

Across the street from the Billings Farm and Museum. 🕐 *Open late May–Oct daily 10am–5pm.* 🎫 *$6 (mansion and garden tour).* ♿ 🅿 ☎ *802-457-3368. www.nps.gov/mabi.*

Opened in June 1998, Vermont's first national historic site centers on a meticulously preserved, art-filled Queen Anne mansion and the conservation efforts of three of its residents: prescient environmentalist George Perkins Marsh, author of *Man and Nature* (1865); Frederick Billings, founder of the Billings Farm; and Billings' granddaughter Mary French Rockefeller, who, with her husband, Laurance, sustained the farm and property from the mid- to late 20C. American landscape paintings by such renowned artists as Thomas Cole, Albert Bierstadt and Asher B. Durand deck the house's sumptuous interior.

SIMON PEARCE RESTAURANT

In The Mill in Quechee. ☎ *802-295-1470. www.simonpearce.com.* After ogling handmade pottery and glassware in the Simon Pearce glass-blowing store, have lunch or dinner in the airy, country-style dining room with its expansive arched windows, or on the outdoor terrace overlooking the falls of the Ottauquechee River. Homemade soups, salads and breads as well as seafood, beef, veal and duck are presented on lovely pottery, and beverages are served in hand-blown glassware—all made on the premises.

Excursions

Quechee Gorge★

6mi east of Woodstock via US-4.

Formed over thousands of years by the erosive action of the Ottauquechee River, Quechee Gorge is spanned by the Route 4 highway bridge—which provides the best view. Sheer walls of the gorge rise approximately 165ft from the river below. A trail, steep in sections *(round-trip 1.5mi)*, leads to the bottom of the gorge, a popular swimming area in season. *Hikers can park at the gift shop on the east side of the bridge.*

Silver Lake State Park

10mi north of Woodstock via Rte. 12 in Barnard. 🕐 *Open mid-May–mid-Oct daily 10am–9pm.* 🎫 *$2.50.* ⛺ 🅿 ☎ *802-234-9451. www.vtstateparks.com.*

Located within walking distance of Barnard village, the park contains a small lakefront beach, picnic area, country store and campsites set in a fragrant pine grove.

Windsor

25mi southeast of Woodstock via US-4 East and I-91 South.

The State of Vermont was born in this historic town on the banks of the Connecticut River in 1777 when representatives met in an old tavern here. That tavern is now the **Constitution House** (*16 N. Main St.;* 🔍 *visit by 1hr guided tour only, late May–mid-Oct, Wed–Sun 11am–5pm;* 🎫 *$2.50;* 🅿 ☎ *802-828-3051; www.historicvermont.org*), where exhibits describe the development of the state's constitution and include examples of early Vermont crafts.

Spanning the Connecticut River between New Hampshire and Vermont, the **Windsor-Cornish Covered Bridge** (*south of Constitution House; after two sets of lights, turn left*) ranks as the longest covered bridge (460ft) in New England.

INDEX

INDEX

INDEX

INDEX

Hotels

INDEX

Restaurants

Legend

★★★ **Highly recommended**
★★ **Recommended**
★ **Interesting**

Sight symbols

Recommended itineraries with departure point

✝ ⚱ Church, chapel	▨ Building described
○ Town described	▢ Other building
B Letter locating a sight	▪ Small building, statue
▪ ▲ Other points of interest	○ ⚘ Fountain – Ruins
⚒ ◠ Mine – Cave	🚩 Visitor information
⚑ ⚓ Windmill – Lighthouse	⛴ ☀ Ship – Shipwreck
☆ ⛪ Fort – Mission	☀ ⋎ Panorama – View

Other symbols

🛡 Interstate highway	🛡 US highway	⑱⑧⓪ Other route
═══ Highway, bridge		═══ Major city thoroughfare
═══ Toll highway, interchange		═══ City street with median
═══ Divided highway		◄── One-way street
─── Major, minor route		⇢┤⇐ Tunnel – Pedestrian street
╲ 18 Distance in miles		┅┅ Steps – Gate
⤳ 2149 ↗ Pass *(elevation in feet)*		🅿 ✉ Parking – Main post office
△ 6288 Mtn. peak *(elevation in feet)*		�++ 🚌 Train station – Bus station
✈ ✚ Airport – Airfield		🪦 Cemetery
⛴ Ferry: Cars and passengers		Swamp
⛴ Ferry: Passengers only		━━ International boundary
⟨ ‹ ⊢ Waterfall – Lock – Dam		━━ State boundary
⚱ Winery		● Subway station

Recreation

▪-○-○-○-▪ Gondola, chairlift		▨ ▨ Park, garden – Wooded area
⛴ ◊ Harbor, lake cruise – Marina		🌐 Wildlife reserve
⛷ ⛳ Ski area – Golf Course		🦁 Zoo
⬭ Stadium		───── Walking path, trail

Abbreviations

NP National Park	NMem National Memorial	SF State Forest
NM National Monument	NHS National Historic Site	SP State Park
NWR National Wildlife Refuge	NHP National Historical Park	SR State Reserve

Symbols specific to this guide

⛪ Picturesque village		⛴ Seasonal ferry: Cars and passengers
🚌 Covered bridge		⛴ Seasonal ferry: Passengers only

FZ Map grid reference

All maps are oriented north, unless otherwise indicated by a directional arrow.

MAPS AND PLANS

COMPANION
PUBLICATIONS

NORTH AMERICA ROAD ATLAS

A geographically organized atlas with extensive detailed coverage of the USA, Canada and Mexico. Includes 246 city maps, distance chart, state and provincial driving requirements and a climate chart.

- Comprehensive city and town index
- Easy to follow "Go-to" pointers

MAP 581 NEW ENGLAND/ HUDSON VALLEY

Large-format, large-scale map providing comprehensive road network information with distances and interchanges. The map features places of interest including state and national parks, wineries, ski areas and amusement parks.

- Comprehensive index of more than 6,500 cities, towns and villages.
- Scale 1:500,000 (1 inch = approx. 8 miles)

MAP 583 NORTHEASTERN USA/ EASTERN CANADA

Large-format map providing detailed road systems and including driving distances, interstate rest stops, border crossings and interchanges.

- Comprehensive city and town index
- Scale 1:2,400,000 (1 inch = approx. 38 miles)

MAP 761 USA ROAD MAP

Covers the principal US road network and presents shaded relief detail of the overall physiography of the land.

- Features state flags with statistical data and state tourism office telephone numbers.
- Scale 1:3,450,000 (1 inch = 55 miles)

REGIONAL ROAD ATLAS

Measuring a slim 4.5" x 10", and only fractions of an inch thick, Michelin's regional road atlases can actually fit in your glove box, your purse, or anywhere you need. They are a convenient alternative to large, cumbersome road maps and you'll never have to worry about folding them up.

- Clear, colorful and easy to read cartography
- Detailed city maps are indexed alphabetically in the back of the book.

New England is included in the following Regional Road Atlases

- New England Regional Road Atlas
- Northeast Corridor Road Atlas

REGIONAL ROAD ATLAS + TRAVEL GUIDE

For the traveler who wants to know more of what to do along the way, without sacrificing portability, Michelin's Road Atlas + Travel Guide series is the perfect solution. You get the same great Michelin mapping from the road atlases, paired with charming hotel & restaurant selections, scenic tours, fabulous color photos and much, much more!

New England is included in the following Regional Road Atlas + Travel Guide titles:

- New England Regional Road Atlas + Travel Guide
- Northeast Corridor Road Atlas + Travel Guide

Michelin North America
One Parkway South – Greenville, SC 29615 USA
☏ 800-423-0485
www.MichelinTravel.com
michelin.guides@us.michelin.com

Manufacture française des pneumatiques Michelin

Société en commandite par actions au capital de 304 000 000 EUR
Place des Carmes-Déchaux – 63000 Clermont-Ferrand (France)
R.C.S. Clermont-Fd B 855 200 507

No part of this publication may be reproduced in any form
without the prior permission of the publisher.

© Michelin et Cie, Propriétaires-éditeurs
Dépot légal novembre 2006 – ISSN: 0763-1383
Printed in France: octobre 2006
Printing and Binding: IME
Made in: France